THE Java™ Tutorial

Second Edition

Object-Oriented Programming for the Internet

The Java™ Series

Lisa Friendly, Series Editor
Tim Lindholm, Technical Editor
Please see our web site (http://www.awl.com /cseng/javaseries) for more information on these titles.

Ken Arnold and James Gosling, *The Java™ Programming Language, Second Edition*
ISBN 0-201-31006-6

Mary Campione and Kathy Walrath, *The Java™ Tutorial, Second Edition: Object-Oriented Programming for the Internet* (Book/CD)
ISBN 0-201-31007-4

Mary Campione, Kathy Walrath, Alison Huml, and the Tutorial Team, *The Java™ Tutorial Continued: The Rest of the JDK™* (Book/CD)
ISBN 0-201-48558-3

Patrick Chan, *The Java™ Developers Almanac 1999*
ISBN 0-201-43298-6

Patrick Chan and Rosanna Lee, *The Java™ Class Libraries, Second Edition, Volume 2: java.applet, java.awt, java.beans*
ISBN 0-201-31003-1

Patrick Chan, Rosanna Lee, and Doug Kramer, *The Java™ Class Libraries, Second Edition, Volume 1: java.io, java.lang, java.math, java.net, java.text, java.util*
ISBN 0-201-31002-3

Patrick Chan, Rosanna Lee, and Doug Kramer, *The Java™ Class Libraries, Second Edition, Volume 1: Supplement for the Java™ 2 Platform, Standard Edition, v1.2*
ISBN 0-201-48552-4

Li Gong, *Inside the Java™ 2 Platform Security Architecture: Cryptography, APIs, and Implementation*
ISBN 0-201-31000-7

James Gosling, Bill Joy, and Guy Steele, *The Java™ Language Specification*
ISBN 0-201-63451-1

James Gosling, Frank Yellin, and The Java Team, *The Java™ Application Programming Interface, Volume 1: Core Packages*
ISBN 0-201-63453-8

James Gosling, Frank Yellin, and The Java Team, *The Java™ Application Programming Interface, Volume 2: Window Toolkit and Applets*
ISBN 0-201-63459-7

Jonni Kanerva, *The Java™ FAQ*
ISBN 0-201-63456-2

Doug Lea, *Concurrent Programming in Java™: Design Principles and Patterns*
ISBN 0-201-69581-2

Sheng Liang, *The Java™ Native Interface: Programmer's Guide and Specification*
ISBN 0-201-32577-2

Tim Lindholm and Frank Yellin, *The Java™ Virtual Machine Specification, Second Edition*
ISBN 0-201-43294-3

Henry Sowizral, Kevin Rushforth, and Michael Deering, *The Java™ 3D API Specification*
ISBN 0-201-32576-4

Kathy Walrath and Mary Campione, *The JFC Swing Tutorial: A Guide to Constructing GUIs*
ISBN 0-201-43321-4

Seth White, Maydene Fisher, Rick Cattell, Graham Hamilton, and Mark Hapner, *JDBC™ API Tutorial and Reference, Second Edition: Universal Data Access for the Java™ 2 Platform*
ISBN 0-201-43328-1

THE Java™ Tutorial

Second Edition

Object-Oriented Programming for the Internet

Mary Campione
and
Kathy Walrath

ADDISON-WESLEY

An imprint of Addison Wesley Longman, Inc.

Reading, Massachusetts • Harlow, England • Menlo Park, California
Berkeley, California • Don Mills, Ontario • Sydney
Bonn • Amsterdam • Tokyo • Mexico City

Library of Congress Cataloging-in-Publication Data

Campione, Mary.

The Java tutorial : object-oriented programming for the Internet / Mary Campione, Kathy Walrath. — 2nd ed.

p. cm. -- (The Java series)

ISBN 0-201-31007-4

1. Object-oriented programming (Computer science) 2. Java (Computer program language) 3. Internet (Computer network) I. Walrath, Kathy. II. Title. III. Series.

QA76.64.C35 1998

005.13'3--dc21 97-43574

CIP

The publisher offers discounts on this book when ordered in quantity for special sales.
For more information, please contact: Corporate, Government and Special Sales; Addison Wesley Longman, Inc.; One Jacob Way; Reading, Massachusetts 01867.

Text printed on recycled and acid-free paper.

ISBN 0201310074

4 5 6 7 8 9 CRS 02 01 00 99

4th Printing July 1999

To Richard and Sophia

—Mary

To Nathan, Laine, and Cosmo

—Kathy

Contents

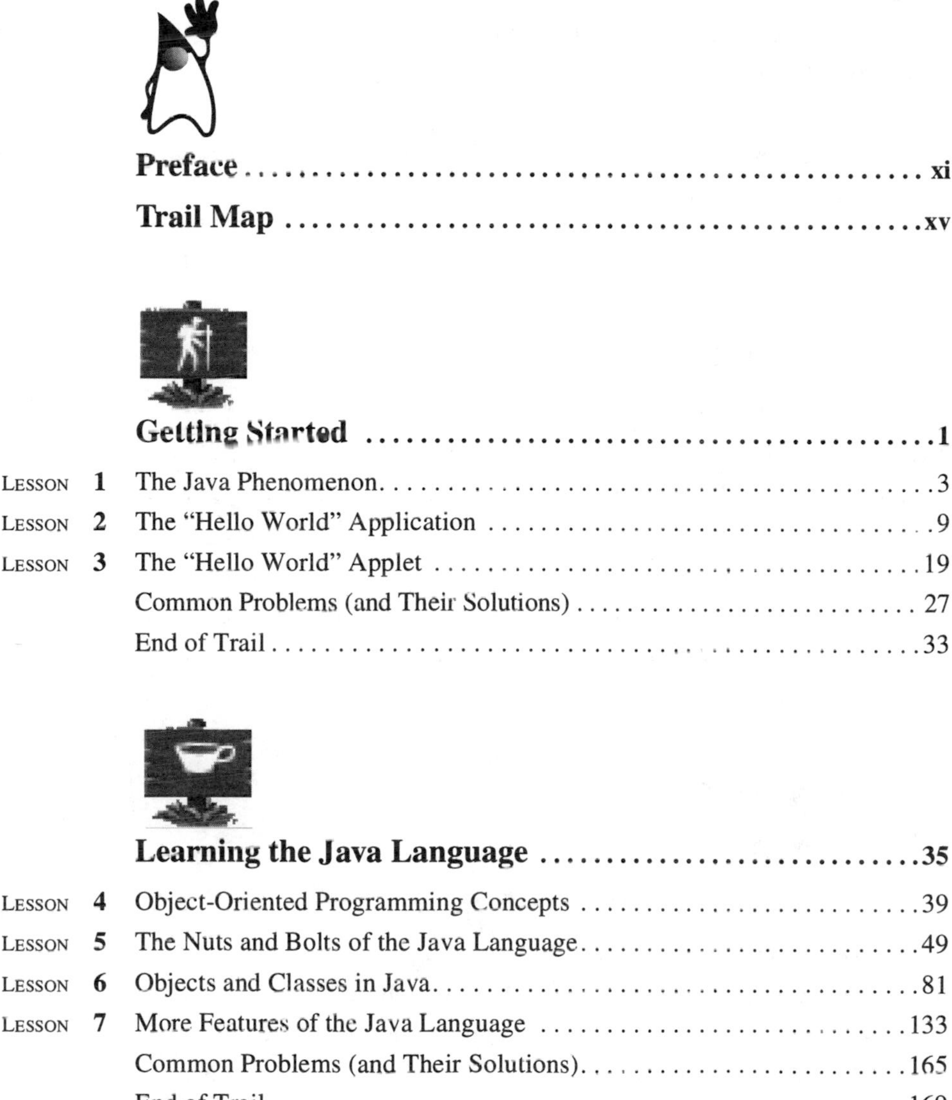

Preface

SINCE the release of the JDK 1.0.2 in May of 1996, the Java engineering team has been hard at work improving and enhancing the Java platform. We have been similarly laboring to update *The Java Tutorial* to reflect the work of the engineers. From the first page to the last, this edition now documents the APIs in JDK 1.1. We have fully integrated JDK 1.1 updates into the text, plus we've added coverage of some of the new features of 1.1 such as the new AWT event model, object serialization, and inner classes. We also added a new trail to the end of the book that provides a summary of what changed for 1.1, information to help you decide when to convert 1.0 programs to 1.1, and instructions about how to perform the conversion. And finally we've included a preview of what's likely to come in the next major release of the JDK.

Yet, this edition of *The Java Tutorial* is more than just an update of the previous edition. It's more polished and mature. We have rewritten, clarified, and reorganized many areas of the book based on feedback from readers and reviewers.

Like the first edition, this book is based on the online tutorial hosted at the Java Web site.

```
http://java.sun.com/docs/books/tutorial/index.html
```

The first draft of the online tutorial was made available in May 1995. At that time, it contained a few basic lessons on writing applets, the fundamentals of the language itself, and some key classes. Since then, the tutorial has grown to over 10MB of HMTL files, images, and running programs. It contains dozens of lessons covering topics ranging from applet communication to security, from internationalization to JavaBeans™. We are constantly updating the online version of the tutorial to cover new APIs developed by the engineering team.

Like the online version, this book reflects the latest Java advances. However, unlike the online version, page count limits what this book can cover. Hence, it focuses on the Java APIs needed by most beginning to intermediate Java programmers. If you don't find information in this book about part of the Java platform, check our Web site for it.

From the online tutorial to the first edition, and from the first edition to the second, our intent has always been to create a fun, easy-to-read, task-oriented programmer's guide with lots of practical examples to help people learn to program in Java.

Who Should Read This Book?

This tutorial assumes that you have some programming experience, whether it be traditional procedural programming or object-oriented programming, and are familiar with programming tenets and terminology and at least one high-level language.

All Java programmers—novice and experienced alike—can benefit from this book. The first section begins with an overview of the Java platform and what it can help you do. It then presents two Java programs—one application and one applet—and shows you how to compile and run both. Finally, it describes how they work.

From this hands-on beginning, you can follow your own course of learning:

- *New programmers* can benefit most by reading the book from beginning to end, including the beginning material on object-oriented concepts, the standard features of the Java language, and the object-oriented features of the Java language.
- *Programmers experienced with procedural languages* such as C may wish to skip the section that describes the standard features of Java and start with the material on object-oriented concepts and the object-oriented features of Java.
- *Experienced object programmers* may want to jump feet first into more advanced trails, such as those on applets, essential classes, or UIs.

No matter what type of programmer you are, you can find a path through this book that fits your learning requirements.

What You Need

This book documents the JDK 1.1 release of the Java platform. To compile and run the examples in this book you need a development environment that is compatible with JDK 1.1. You can use a commercially-available Java development environment or you can use the JDK itself.

You can use the version of JDK 1.1 that's on the CD-ROM accompanying this book. Or you might want to visit the Java Web side to download the latest version of the JDK:

```
http://java.sun.com/products/jdk/1.1/
```

If you are using the JDK provided by Sun Microsystems you will need one of the following systems:

- Microsoft Windows 95/NT 4.0 running on Intel (or compatible) x86
- Solaris 2.4, or 2.5 running on SPARC
- Solaris 2.5 running on x86

If you are developing applets, you will need a browser that supports the 1.1 API. For testing applets, you can use a special limited browser called the Applet Viewer that ships with the JDK. For information about the browsers that are currently available and support 1.1, see the Web page for this book:

```
http://java.sun.com/docs/books/tutorial/2e/book.html
```

Finally, you need an editor that can save files in ASCII format with a `.java` extension. Also, the editor must allow you to specify both uppercase and lowercase letters in the filename.

Acknowledgments

For the Second Edition of the Tutorial

Many Internet readers have helped us maintain and improve the quality of the tutorial by sending us e-mail and cheerfully pointing out our numerous typos, broken links, and more importantly, areas of the tutorial that caused confusion or could benefit from rewriting.

Many members of the Java engineering and documentation team have given us counsel, answered our many questions, reviewed our material, and even made contributions to it. They also make JavaSoft a fun place to work. The list is long but we'd particularly like to note the contributions of Brian Beck, Joshua Bloch, David Connelly, Chris Darke, Bill Foote, Carol Hayes, Herb Jellinek, Doug Kramer, Marianne Mueller, Marla Parker, Mark Reinhold, John Rose, John Wegis, and Beth Whitman. Kathy would like to thank all the members of the Swing engineering team for being such a great group to work with. And, notably, Ron Mandel, who kept our Macs and PCs operating in a mostly Sun environment.

We are grateful for the other writers at Sun who have contributed to the online tutorial as guest authors. So far this list of professional and talented writers includes Mary Dageforde, Andy Quinn, Beth Stearns, and Greg Voss.

The Java language wouldn't exist without its creator, James Gosling. We'd like to thank James, not only for creating the language but also for staying involved as the Java platform develops. On a personal note, we'd like to thank him for accepting an award for us from JavaWorld (who named the tutorial as one of three finalists in the Best Training Aid category).

Our team managers, Lisa Friendly, Rick Levenson, and Stans Kleijnen, create a work environment that lets us get our job done. We especially appreciate their support of flexible, if a bit unusual, work arrangements.

Mike Hendrickson, our editorial advisor at Addison-Wesley, is always a calming influence and keeps us on schedule. Sarah Weaver was the production manager on the book and Laura Michaels was our copy editor and grammar queen. The whole team at Addison-Wesley have been a pleasure to work with and continually strive for excellence on this and the other books in the series.

Our heartfelt appreciation goes to the newest member of the tutorial team, Alison Huml, who calmly and professionally managed this edition of the book. She managed our schedule, handled the relationship with the copy editor, incorporated copy edits, drew or fixed many diagrams and images in the book, and handled all of the PC and Mac file conversions—all within the first month of working with us. Alison provides us with a fresh perspective and renewed energy. We look forward to her contributions to future book projects and to the online version of the tutorial.

For the First Edition of the Tutorial

Of course, the Java team made everything possible by creating Java in the first place. But many individuals contributed to getting this book out the door.

A million thanks go to the Java team members who answered questions, reviewed material, and in some cases, contributed examples—all of this in the face of tight deadlines: Thomas Ball, Brenda Bowden, David Brown, Patrick Chan, Tom Chavez, David Connelly, Pavani Diwanji, Amy Fowler, Jim Graham, Herb Jellinek, Jonni Kanerva, Doug Kramer, Eugene Kuerner, Tim Lindholm, Ron Mandel, Henry McGilton, Marianne Mueller, Scott Rautmann, Benjamin Renaud, Hassan Schroeder, Richard Scorer, Sami Shaio, Arthur van Hoff, Frank Yellin, and Steve Zellers.

Painful though they may have been, the feedback our reviewers provided us was invaluable. These reviewers were Mike Ballantyne, Richard Campione, Lee Collins, Greg Crisp, Matt Fahrner, Murali Ghanta, Bill Harts, Eileen Head, Murali Murugan, Roberto Quijalvo, Philip Resnik, Roger Riggs, Roman Rorat, Neil Sundaresan, Michael Weiss, the ones who preferred to remain anonymous, and all of the Internet readers who were kind enough to take the time to send us e-mail to let us know of problem areas.

Chris Warth spent several weeks writing scripts and filters to convert our complex web of HTML pages into MIF format. He was most patient with us despite our demands and changes. Marsh Chamberlain designed and created our trail icons, and Jan Kärrman provided us with the `html2ps` script, which we used to create PostScript files from HTML and print our first review copy of the manuscript. Nathan Walrath created the figure in the Trail Map section. When we both went on maternity leave after giving the book to Addison-Wesley, Randy Nelson served as our backup, taking care of the CD-ROM and the Web site for the tutorial.

The staff at Addison-Wesley—Mike Hendrickson, Katie Duffy, Pamela Yee, and Marty Rabinowitz—were professional, competent, and courteous throughout the development of this book and provided us with guidance, encouragement, and instruction. They also managed the practical things like copy editing, page design, graphics, and reviewers so that all we had to do was worry about content.

Lisa Friendly, the Java Series editor, our manager, and our friend, made this book possible by suggesting that we turn the online tutorial into a book. She kept us calm, reassured us often, and managed everything, from our relationship with Addison-Wesley to consistency with other books in the series. Without her encouragement and hard work, this tutorial would not exist.

About the Dedication

Mary: This book is dedicated to my husband, Richard Campione, for being my greatest friend. It's also dedicated to Sophia, a delightful child and a constant reminder of what's truly important.

Kathy: This book is dedicated to my husband, Nathan Walrath, and to our children, Laine and Cosmo. Nathan has done whatever it takes to help me write this book, from distracting kids to dispensing advice and art criticism. Laine and Cosmo are not old enough to help—quite the opposite—but like their dad, they sure are fun.

The Tutorial Babies

Cosmo Walrath (born June 1996)
Sophia Campione (born May 1996)
The Java Tutorial (first printed August 1996)

Trail Map

WELCOME to *The Java Tutorial!* This book is adapted from the online Java tutorial, drafts of which have been available on the JavaSoft Web site since May 1995. We're dedicated to keeping this book up-to-date with the most current information. To learn what's new since this book went to press, use any Web browser to visit the following URL:

```
http://java.sun.com/docs/books/tutorial/2e/book.html
```

How to Use this Book

True to its hypertext roots, this book is designed so that you can either read it straight through or skip around from topic to topic. Whenever a topic is discussed in another place, you'll see a link to that place in the tutorial. Links are underlined and are followed by page numbers, like this: The "Hello World" Applet (page 19).

Where to Start

We recommend that you start with the trail Getting Started (page 1). This trail lets you dive in quickly—writing, compiling, and running a simple application and a simple applet.

Terminology Note: *Applications* are stand-alone Java programs, such as the HotJava browser. *Applets* are similar to applications, but they don't run standalone. Instead, applets adhere to a set of conventions that let them run within a Java-compatible browser.

What Next?

This table might help you decide where to go after you've finished the Getting Started (page 1).

Trail	Program Types	Notes
Getting Started (page 1) The Java Phenomenon (page 3) The "Hello World" Application (page 9) The "Hello World" Applet (page 19)	All	Quick, easy introduction to writing Java programs. Goes on to discuss the anatomy of an application and of an applet. Introduces some basic Java concepts along the way.
Learning the Java Language (page 35) Object-Oriented Programming Concepts (page 39) The Nuts and Bolts of the Java Language (page 49) Objects and Classes in Java (page 81) More Features of the Java Language (page 133)	All	Introduces object-oriented concepts and Java's implementation of them. Experienced object-oriented programmers might want to skip this trail.
Writing Applets (page 171) Overview of Applets (page 175) Taking Advantage of the Applet API (page 189) Practical Considerations of Writing Applets (page 211) Finishing an Applet (page 231)	Applets only	Has (or points to) everything you need to know to write applets.
Essential Java Classes (page 241) Using String and StringBuffer (page 247) Setting Program Attributes (page 259) Accessing System Resources (page 267) Handling Errors with Exceptions (page 293) Doing Two or More Tasks at Once: Threads (page 327) Reading and Writing (but No 'rithmetic) (page 365)	All	Background information needed for most nontrivial programs.
Creating a User Interface (page 403) Overview of the Java UI (page 407) Using Components, the GUI Building Blocks (page 425) Laying Out Components Within a Container (page 503) Working with Graphics (page 525)	All	Lists all programs' UI options, and then gives in-depth descriptions of how to construct a graphical UI using the AWT (Abstract Window Toolkit).
Custom Networking (page 581) Overview of Networking (page 585) Working with URLs (page 591) All About Sockets (page 605) All About Datagrams (page 619)	All	Tells you how to use the standard Java networking and security classes.
To 1.1— and Beyond! (page 631) What's New in 1.1 (page 635) Migrating to 1.1 (page 643) A Preview of Things to Come (page 679)	All	Summarizes the changes in 1.1. Includes information on converting 1.0 programs to 1.1, and a preview of the next major release of the JDK.

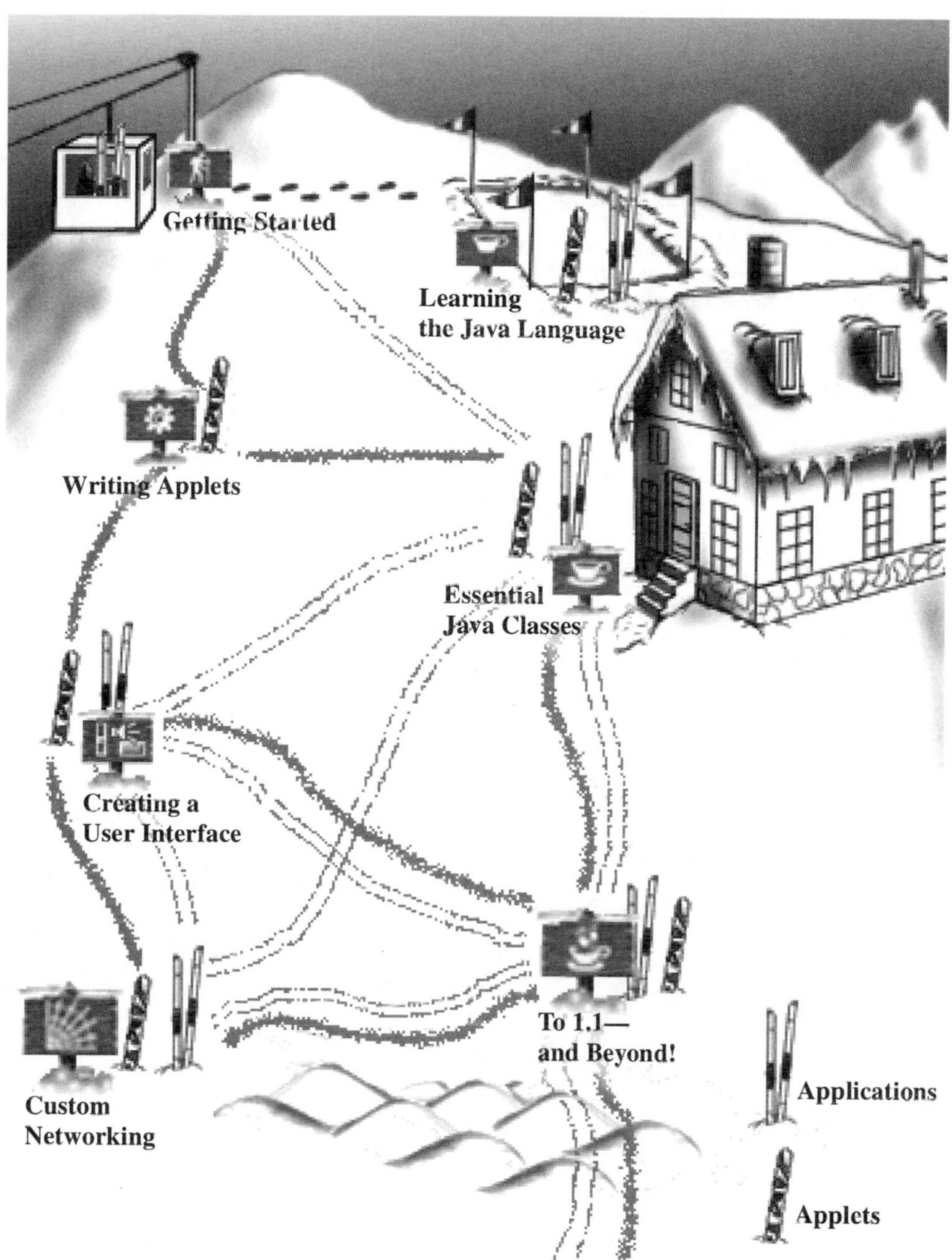

Some Possible Paths Through the Tutorial

Getting Started

THE lessons in this trail give a quick introduction to Java programming. They tell you what Java is and provide you with an opportunity to compile and run some simple Java programs. Finally, they give you the background knowledge you need to understand how the programs work.

The Java Phenomenon (page 3) talks a bit about the Java language and platform. Its aim is to give you an idea of what Java can do for you. It also covers some basic Java concepts that will help you understand the process of writing a Java program.

If you can't wait to write your first program, skip ahead to one of the following two lessons.

The "Hello World" Application (page 9) leads you through compiling and running a standalone *application*—a Java program that executes independently of a browser. The lesson also introduces some general Java techniques: how to define a class and how to use supporting classes and objects.

The "Hello World" Applet (page 19) tells you how to compile and run an *applet*—a Java program to be included in HTML pages and executed in Java-enabled browsers. The lesson also introduces some general Java concepts and techniques: how to create a subclass, what packages are, and how to import classes and packages into a program.

If you have trouble compiling or running the programs in this trail, see **Common Problems (and Their Solutions)** (page 27).

http://java.sun.com/docs/books/tutorial/getStarted/intro/index.html

1 The Java Phenomenon

JAVA seems to be everywhere—even in TV commercials. Despite Java's ubiquity, finding out what Java really is and what it can do can be difficult. Programmers who are new to Java often have three questions:

What Is Java?

Java is two things: a programming language and a platform.

The Java Programming Language

Java is a high-level programming language that is all of the following:

- Simple
- Object-oriented
- Distributed
- Interpreted
- Robust
- Secure
- Architecture-neutral
- Portable
- High-performance
- Multithreaded
- Dynamic

Each of the preceding buzzwords is explained in *The Java Language Environment* white paper, by James Gosling and Henry McGilton. You can find this white paper on the Java Web site.[1]

[1] http://java.sun.com/docs/books/tutorial/2e/book.html

Java is also unusual in that each Java program is both compiled and interpreted. With a compiler, you translate a Java program into an intermediate language called *Java bytecodes*—the platform-independent codes interpreted by the Java interpreter. With an interpreter, each Java bytecode instruction is parsed and run on the computer. Compilation happens just once; interpretation occurs each time the program is executed. Figure 1 illustrates how this works.

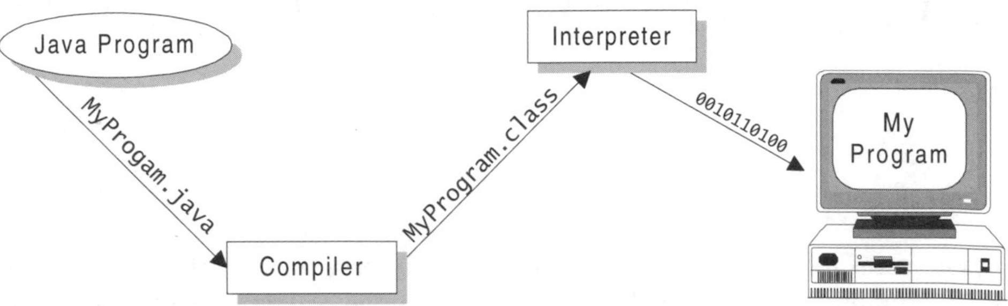

Figure 1: Java programs are both compiled and interpreted.

You can think of Java bytecodes as the machine code instructions for the *Java Virtual Machine* (Java VM). Every Java interpreter, whether it's a Java development tool or a Web browser that can run Java applets, is an implementation of the Java VM. The Java VM can also be implemented in hardware.

Java bytecodes help make "write once, run anywhere" possible. You can compile your Java program into bytecodes on any platform that has a Java compiler. The bytecodes can then be run on any implementation of the Java VM. For example, the same Java program can run on Windows NT, Solaris, and Macintosh. See Figure 2.

The Java Platform

A platform is the hardware or software environment in which a program runs. The Java platform differs from most other platforms in that it's a software-only platform that runs on top of other, hardware-based platforms. Most other platforms are described as a combination of hardware and operating system.

The Java platform has two components:

- The *Java Virtual Machine* (Java VM)
- The *Java Application Programming Interface* (Java API)

You've already been introduced to the Java VM. It's the base for the Java platform and is ported onto various hardware-based platforms.

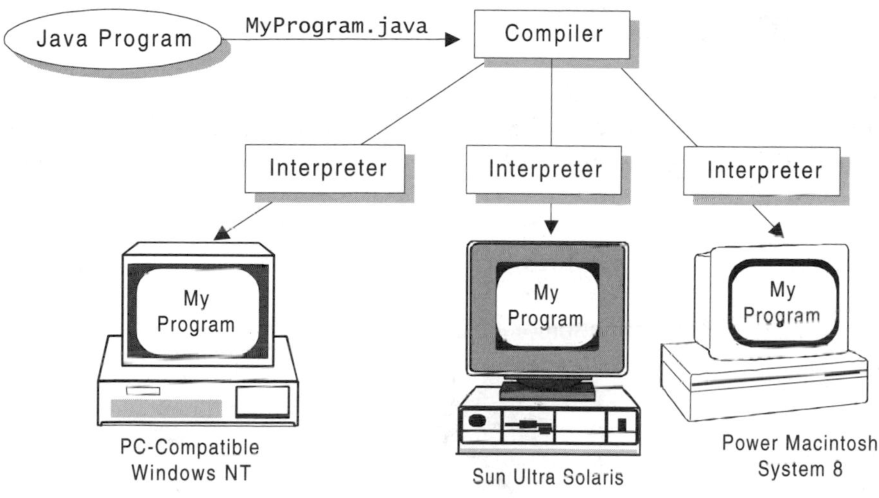

Figure 2: Java programs can be written once, and run on almost any platform.

The Java API is a large collection of ready-made software components that provide many useful capabilities, such as graphical user interface (GUI) widgets. The Java API is grouped into libraries (*packages*) of related components. The next section, What Can Java Do? (page 6), highlights each area of functionality provided by the packages in the Java API.

Figure 3 depicts a Java program, such as an application or applet, that's running on the Java platform. As the figure shows, the Java API and Virtual Machine insulate the Java program from hardware dependencies.

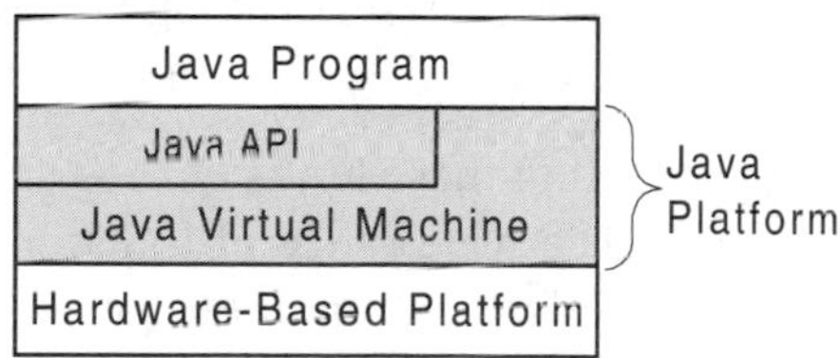

Figure 3: The API and VM insulate the Java program from hardware dependencies.

As a platform-independent environment, Java can be a bit slower than native code. However, smart compilers, well-tuned interpreters, and just-in-time bytecode compilers can bring Java's performance close to that of native code without threatening portability.

What Can Java Do?

Probably the most well-known Java programs are *Java applets*. An applet is a Java program that adheres to certain conventions that allow it to run within a Java-enabled browser. To see a running applet, go to this page in the online version of this tutorial:

```
http://java.sun.com/docs/books/tutorial/getStarted/index.html
```

There you can see an animation of Java's mascot, Duke, waving at you:

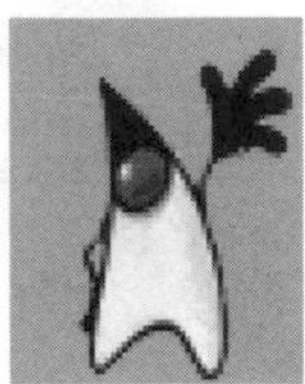

However, Java is not just for writing cute, entertaining applets for the World Wide Web ("Web"). Java is a general-purpose, high-level programming language and a powerful software platform. Using the generous Java API, you can write many types of programs.

The most common types of programs are probably applets and applications, where a Java application is a standalone program that runs directly on the Java platform. A special kind of application known as a *server* serves and supports clients on a network. Examples of servers include Web servers, proxy servers, mail servers, print servers, and boot servers. Another specialized program is a *servlet*. Servlets are similar to applets in that they are runtime extensions of applications. Instead of working in browsers, though, servlets run within Java servers, configuring or tailoring the server.

How does the Java API support all of these kinds of programs? With packages of software components that provide a wide range of functionality. The *core API* is the API included in every full implementation of the Java platform. The core API gives you the following features:

- **The Essentials:** Objects, strings, threads, numbers, input and output, data structures, system properties, date and time, and so on.
- **Applets:** The set of conventions used by Java applets.
- **Networking:** URLs, TCP and UDP sockets, and IP addresses.
- **Internationalization:** Help for writing programs that can be localized for users worldwide. Programs can automatically adapt to specific locales and be displayed in the appropriate language.

- **Security:** Both low-level and high-level, including electronic signatures, public/private key management, access control, and certificates.
- **Software components:** Known as JavaBeans, can plug into existing component architectures such as Microsoft's OLE/COM/Active-X architecture, OpenDoc, and Netscape's Live Connect.
- **Object serialization:** Allows lightweight persistence and communication via Remote Method Invocation (RMI).
- **Java Database Connectivity (JDBC):** Provides uniform access to a wide range of relational databases.

Java not only has a core API, but also standard extensions. The standard extensions define APIs for 3D, servers, collaboration, telephony, speech, animation, and more.

This book covers the Java language and parts of the core API that we expect beginning to intermediate Java programmers to use most frequently. If you need additional information not found in this book, you can explore the online tutorial for additional coverage, located at this URL:

```
http://java.sun.com/docs/books/tutorial/index.html
```

How Will Java Change My Life?

We can't promise you fame, fortune, or even a job if you learn Java. Still, Java is likely to make your programs better and requires less effort than other languages. We believe that Java will help you do the following:

- **Get started quickly:** Although Java is a powerful object-oriented language, it's easy to learn, especially for programmers already familiar with C or C++.
- **Write less code:** Comparisons of program metrics (class counts, method counts, and so on) suggest that a program written in Java can be four times smaller than the same program in C++.
- **Write better code:** The Java language encourages good coding practices, and its garbage collection helps you avoid memory leaks. Java's object orientation, its JavaBeans component architecture, and its wide-ranging, easily extendible API let you reuse other people's tested code and introduce fewer bugs.
- **Develop programs faster:** Your development time may be as much as twice as fast versus writing the same program in C++. Why? You write

fewer lines of code with Java and Java is a simpler programming language than C++.

- **Avoid platform dependencies with 100% Pure Java:** You can keep your program portable by following the purity tips mentioned throughout this book and avoiding the use of libraries written in other languages.
- **Write once, run anywhere:** Because 100% Pure Java programs are compiled into machine-independent bytecodes, they run consistently on any Java platform.
- **Distribute software more easily:** You can upgrade applets easily from a central server. Applets take advantage of the Java feature of allowing new classes to be loaded "on the fly," without recompiling the entire program.

The programs in the following two lessons demonstrate only a few of these features. Still, you need to start somewhere, so why not with "Hello World."

What Next?

From here, you can do the following:

- Go to the next lesson, The "Hello World" Application (page 9), which steps you through writing and running an application.
- Go to the lesson after that, The "Hello World" Applet (page 19), if you prefer to start with applets.
- Learn more about the Java language by going to Learning the Java Language (page 35).

2 The "Hello World" Application

BY following the steps outlined in this lesson, you can create and use a standalone Java *application*—a Java program that executes independently of any browser. If you're interested only in applets—Java programs that run within browsers—feel free to skip ahead to The "Hello World" Applet (page 19).

To compile and run an application, you can use tools from the Java Development Kit (JDK), which is included on the CD-ROM that accompanies this book. The JDK compiler lets you compile any kind of Java program. The JDK interpreter lets you run standalone applications.

Note: Although the example in this chapter shows the JDK compiler and interpreter, you can use any 1.1 Java platform to compile and run the Java programs in this book. If you use the JDK, you might want to occasionally check the JDK home page[1] to make sure you have the latest, greatest version of the JDK.

Create a Java Source File

Using a text editor, create a file named `HelloWorldApp.java` (page 695) with the following Java code:

---

[1] http://java.sun.com/products/jdk/index.html

```
/**
 * The HelloWorldApp class implements an application that
 * simply displays "Hello World!" to the standard output.
 */
class HelloWorldApp {
    public static void main(String[] args) {
        System.out.println("Hello World!"); //Display the string.
    }
}
```

Note: Don't worry about getting the text between the `/**` and the `*/` exactly right. This text is a comment and is ignored by the compiler.

Compile the Source File

Compile the source file using the Java compiler.

Platform-specific Details: Compiling a Java Source File Using the JDK

UNIX:

```
javac HelloWorldApp.java
```

DOS shell (Windows 95/NT):

```
javac HelloWorldApp.java
```

If the compilation succeeds, the compiler creates a file named `HelloWorldApp.class` in the same directory as the Java source file (`HelloWorldApp.java`). This class file contains Java bytecodes—platform-independent codes interpreted by the Java interpreter.

If the compilation fails, make sure you typed in and named the program exactly as displayed, making sure you include the capitalization as shown. If you can't find the problem, Compiler Problems (page 28) might help you.

Run the Application

Run the program using the Java interpreter.

Platform-specific Details: Interpreting a Java Application Using the JDK

UNIX:

```
java HelloWorldApp
```

DOS shell (Windows 95/NT):

```
java HelloWorldApp
```

Note: The argument to the Java interpreter is the name of the class to run, not the name of a file. Be sure to capitalize the class name exactly as shown here.

You should see "Hello World!" displayed in the window where you invoked the interpreter. If you have any trouble running the "Hello World" application, see Interpreter Problems (page 30).

What Next?

Next, you can do this:

- Continue on in this lesson to learn more about the anatomy of applications, how the "Hello World" application works, and how the Java language implements object-oriented concepts.
- Go to the next lesson, The "Hello World" Applet (page 19), which steps you through writing and running an applet and introduces you to a few more Java features.
- Learn more about the Java language by going to Learning the Java Language (page 35).

Warning: The rest of this lesson assumes that you're familiar with object-oriented concepts. If you start feeling overwhelmed, just skip ahead to Learning the Java Language (page 35). You can always return here later.

The Anatomy of a Java Application

Now that you've seen a Java application, and perhaps even compiled and run it, you may be wondering how it works and how similar it is to other applications. This section dissects the "Hello World" application. Here, again, is its code:

```
/**
 * The HelloWorldApp class implements an application that
 * simply displays "Hello World!" to the standard output.
 */
class HelloWorldApp {
    public static void main(String[] args) {
        System.out.println("Hello World!"); //Display the string.
    }
}
```

The "Hello World" application has two blocks of comments. The first block, at the top of the program, uses the `/**` and `*/` delimiters. Later, a line of code is explained with a comment marked by `//` characters. The Java language supports a third kind of comment—the familiar C-style comment, which is delimited with `/*` and `*/`. Comments in Java Code (page 12) further explains the three forms of comments that the Java language supports.

In the Java language, each *method* (a function-like block of code) and variable exists within a *class*, which is defined in the next section, Defining a Class (page 13). The Java language does not support global functions or variables. Thus, the skeleton of any Java program is a *class definition*.

The entry point of every Java application is its `main` method. When you run an application with the Java interpreter, you specify the name of the class that you want to run. The interpreter invokes the `main` method defined in that class. The `main` method controls the flow of the program, allocates whatever resources are needed, and runs any other methods that provide the functionality for the application. The main Method (page 14) tells you more about this.

The other components of a Java application are the supporting objects, classes, methods, and Java language statements that you write to implement the application. Using Classes and Objects (page 15) introduces these components.

Comments in Java Code

The Java language supports three kinds of comments:

`/* text */`

The compiler ignores everything from the `/*` to the `*/`.

`/** documentation */`

This indicates a documentation comment (*doc comment*, for short). The compiler ignores this kind of comment, just like it ignores comments that use `/*` and `*/`. The JDK `javadoc` tool uses doc comments when preparing automatically generated documentation. For more information on javadoc, see the Java tool documentation.[1]

// text The compiler ignores everything from the // to the end of the line.

For example, the bold parts in the following listing are comments:

```
/**
 * The HelloWorldApp class implements an application that
 * simply displays "Hello World!" to the standard output.
 */
class HelloWorldApp {
    public static void main(String[] args) {
        System.out.println("Hello World!"); //Display the string.
    }
}
```

Defining a Class

The first bold line in the following listing begins a *class definition block*:

```
/**
 * The HelloWorldApp class implements an application that
 * simply displays "Hello World!" to the standard output.
 */
class HelloWorldApp {
    public static void main(String[] args) {
        System.out.println("Hello World!"); //Display the string.
    }
}
```

A *class* is the basic building block of an object-oriented language such as Java. It is a blueprint that describes the state and behavior associated with *instances* of that class. When you *instantiate* a class, you create an *object* that has the same states and behaviors as other instances of the same class. The state associated with a class or object is stored in *member variables*. The behavior associated with a class or object is implemented with *methods*, which are similar to the functions or procedures in procedural languages such as C.

A recipe—say, Julia Child's recipe for rack of lamb—is like a class. It's a blueprint for making a specific instance of the recipe. Her rendition of the rack of lamb is one instance of the recipe, and mine is (quite) another.

---

[1] http://java.sun.com/products/jdk/1.1/docs/index.html#tools

A more traditional example from the world of programming is a class that represents a rectangle. The class defines variables for the origin, width, and height of the rectangle. It might also define a method that calculates the area of the rectangle. An instance of the rectangle class, a rectangle object, contains the information for a specific rectangle, such as the dimensions of the floor of your office or the dimensions of this page.

In the Java language, this is simplest form of a class definition:

```
class RackOfLamb {
    . . .
}
```

The keyword `class` begins the class definition for a class named `RackOfLamb`. The variables and methods of the class are embraced by the curly brackets that begin and end the class definition block. The `Hello WorldApp` class has no variables and has a single method named `main`.

The main Method

The bold lines in the following listing begin and end the definition of the `main` method:

```
/**
 * The HelloWorldApp class implements an application that
 * simply displays "Hello World!" to the standard output.
 */
class HelloWorldApp {
    public static void main(String[] args) {
        System.out.println("Hello World!"); //Display the string.
    }
}
```

Every Java application must contain a `main` method declared like this:

```
public static void main(String[] args)
```

The `main` method declaration starts with three modifiers:

- **`public`**: Allows any class to call the `main` method.
- **`static`**: Means the `main` method is a class method.
- **`void`**: Indicates that the `main` method does not return a value.

How the main Method Gets Called

The `main` method in the Java language is similar to the `main` function in C and C++. When you invoke the Java interpreter, you give it the name of the class that you want to run. This class is the application's controlling class and must contain a `main` method. When invoked, the interpreter starts by calling the class's `main` method, which then calls all of the other methods required to run the application.

If you try to invoke the Java interpreter on a class that does not have a `main` method, the interpreter can't run your program. It displays an error message similar to this:

```
In class NoMain: void main(String argv[]) is not defined
```

Arguments to the main Method

As you can see from the declaration of the `main` method, it accepts a single argument: an array of elements of type `String`, like this:

```
public static void main(String[] args)
```

This array is the mechanism through which the Java VM passes information to your application. Each `String` in the array is called a *command-line argument*. Command-line arguments let users affect the operation of the application without recompiling it.

The "Hello World" application ignores its command-line arguments, so there isn't much more to discuss here. However, you can get more information about command-line arguments in Command-Line Arguments (page 264).

Note to C and C++ Programmers: The number and type of arguments passed to the `main` method in the Java runtime environment differ from the number and type of arguments passed to the C and C++ `main` function. For further information, refer to Command-Line Arguments (page 264).

Using Classes and Objects

The "Hello World" application is about the simplest Java program you can write that actually does something. Because it is such a simple program, it doesn't need to define any classes except `HelloWorldApp`.

However, the "Hello World" application does *use* another class, `System`, that is part of the Java API. The `System` class provides system-independent access to system-dependent functionality. For information about the `System` class, see Accessing System Resources (page 267).

One feature provided by the `System` class is the *standard output stream*—a place to send text that usually refers to the terminal window in which you invoked the Java interpreter.

Impurity Alert! Using the standard output stream isn't recommended in 100% Pure Java programs. However, it's fine to use during the development cycle. We use it in many of our example programs because otherwise our code would be longer and harder to read.

The following bold line shows `HelloWorldApp`'s use of the standard output stream to display the string "Hello World":

```
/**
 * The HelloWorldApp class implements an application that
 * simply displays "Hello World!" to the standard output.
 */
class HelloWorldApp {
    public static void main(String[] args) {
        System.out.println("Hello World!"); //Display the string.
    }
}
```

This one line of code uses both a *class variable* and an *instance method.* Class variables and instance methods are defined in the next section).

Using a Class Variable

Let's take a look at the first segment of the statement:

```
System.out.println("Hello World!");
```

The construct `System.out` is the full name of the `out` variable in the `System` class. The application never instantiates the `System` class. Instead, it refers to `out` directly through the class. This is because `out` is a *class variable*—a variable associated with a class rather than with an object. The Java VM allocates a class variable once per class, no matter how many instances of that class exist.

Java also has the notion of *class methods* used to implement class-specific behaviors.

Using an Instance Method

While System's `out` variable *is* a class variable, it *refers* to an instance of the `PrintStream` class (another class provided in the Java API that implements an easy-to-use output stream). When the `System` class is loaded into the application, it instantiates `PrintStream` and assigns the new `PrintStream` object to the `out` class variable. Now that you have an instance of a class, you can call one of its *instance methods*:

```
System.out.println("Hello World!");
```

An instance method implements behavior specific to instances of a class.

Java also has *instance variables*. An instance variable is a member variable associated with an object rather than with a class. Each time you instantiate a class, the new object gets its own copy of all of the instance variables defined in its class.

If this discussion of member variables, methods, instances, and classes has left you with nothing but questions, Object-Oriented Programming Concepts (page 39) and Objects and Classes in Java (page 81) can help.

Or, if you're anxious to write an applet, go to the next lesson, The "Hello World" Applet (page 19).

The "Hello World" Applet

BY following the steps outlined in this lesson, you can create and use an applet—a Java program to be included in HTML pages and executed in Java-enabled browsers. If you aren't interested in applets, feel free to skip ahead to the trail Learning the Java Language (page 33).

To compile and run the applet, you can use tools from the JDK, which is included on the CD-ROM that accompanies this book. The JDK compiler lets you compile any kind of Java program. The JDK Applet Viewer lets you run Java applets. After you know that the applet works, you might want to view it in a full Web browser that is compatible with JDK 1.1. See the Web site for this book to see which browsers currently support 1.1:

```
http://java.sun.com/docs/books/tutorial/2e/book.html
```

Create a Java Source File

Using a text editor, create a file named HelloWorld.java (page 696) with the Java code shown here:

```
import java.applet.Applet;
import java.awt.Graphics;

public class HelloWorld extends Applet {
    public void paint(Graphics g) {
        g.drawString("Hello world!", 50, 25);
    }
}
```

Compile the Source File

Compile the source file using the Java compiler.

Platform-specific Details: Compiling a Java Source File Using the JDK

UNIX:
```
javac HelloWorld.java
```

DOS shell (Windows 95/NT):
```
javac HelloWorld.java
```

If the compilation succeeds, the compiler creates a file named `HelloWorld.class` in the same directory as the Java source file (`HelloWorld.java`). This class file contains Java bytecodes.

If the compilation fails, make sure you typed in and named the program exactly as shown here. If you can't find the problem for the failure, reviewing Compiler Problems (page 28) might help.

Create an HTML File That Includes the Applet

Using a text editor, create a file named `Hello.html` (page 696) in the same directory as `HelloWorld.class`. Your HTML file should contain the following text:

```
<HTML>
<HEAD>
<TITLE> A Simple Program </TITLE>
</HEAD>
<BODY>
Here is the output of my program:
<APPLET CODE="HelloWorld.class" WIDTH=150 HEIGHT=25>
</APPLET>
</BODY>
</HTML>
```

Run the Applet

To run the applet, you need to load the HTML file into a browser that supports JDK 1.1. (You can also use the Applet Viewer provided in the JDK instead of a full Web browser.) To load the HTML file, you usually need to tell the browser the URL of the HTML file you created. For example, you might enter something like the following into a browser's Location or Address field:

```
file:/home/kwalrath/java/Hello.html
```

On most browsers, you can also open a local file from the File menu of your browser.

Platform-specific Details: Viewing an Applet Using the Applet Viewer

UNIX:

```
appletviewer file:/home/kwalrath/java/Hello.html
```

DOS shell (Windows 95/NT):

```
appletviewer file:/home/kwalrath/java/Hello.html
```

Once you've successfully completed these steps, you should see something like this in the browser window:

Here is the output of my program: `Hello world!`

What Next?

Next, you can do the following:

- Continue in this lesson to learn about the anatomy of applets and about importing classes.
- Go back to The Anatomy of a Java Application (page 11), if you haven't already read it and you're interested in a quick introduction to key Java concepts.
- Learn more about writing applets by going to Writing Applets (page 171).
- Return to the Trail Map (page xvii) for an overview of the trails to follow.

Warning: The rest of this lesson assumes that you're familiar with object-oriented concepts. If you start getting overwhelmed, just skip ahead to Learning the Java Language (page 35). You can always return here later.

The Anatomy of a Java Applet

Now that you've seen a Java applet, you're probably wondering how it works. Remember that a *Java applet* is a program that adheres to a set of conventions that allows it to run within a Java-enabled browser.

Here again is the code for the "Hello World" applet:

```
import java.applet.Applet;
import java.awt.Graphics;

public class HelloWorld extends Applet {
    public void paint(Graphics g) {
        g.drawString("Hello world!", 50, 25);
    }
}
```

This code begins with two `import` statements. By importing classes or packages, a class can easily refer to classes in other packages. In the Java language, packages are used to group classes, similar to the way libraries group C functions. Importing Classes and Packages (page 23) gives you more information about packages and the `import` statement.

Every applet must define a subclass of the `Applet` class. In the "Hello World" applet, this subclass is called `HelloWorld`. Applets inherit a great deal of functionality from the `Applet` class, ranging from the ability to communicate with the browser to the ability to present a Graphical User Interface (GUI). Defining an Applet Subclass (page 24) tells you more.

The "Hello World" applet implements just one method: `paint`. Every applet must implement at least one of the following methods: `init`, `start`, or `paint`. Unlike Java applications, applets do *not* need to implement a `main` method. Implementing Applet Methods (page 24) talks about the `paint` method, how the "Hello World" applet implements it, and the other methods that applets commonly implement.

Applets are designed to be included in HTML pages. Using the `<APPLET>` HTML tag, you specify (at a minimum) the location of the `Applet` subclass and the dimensions of the applet's on-screen display area. When a Java-enabled browser encounters an `<APPLET>` tag, it reserves on-screen space for the applet, loads the `Applet` subclass onto the computer on which it is executing, and creates an instance of the `Applet` subclass. Running an Applet (page 25) gives more details.

Importing Classes and Packages

The first two lines of the following listing import two classes used in the applet: `Applet` and `Graphics`:

```
import java.applet.Applet;
import java.awt.Graphics;

public class HelloWorld extends Applet {
    public void paint(Graphics g) {
        g.drawString("Hello world!", 50, 25);
    }
}
```

If you removed the first two lines, you could still compile and run the program, but only if you changed the rest of the code like this (as shown in bold):

```
public class HelloWorld extends java.applet.Applet {
    public void paint(java.awt.Graphics g) {
        g.drawString("Hello world!", 50, 25);
    }
}
```

As you can see, importing the `Applet` and `Graphics` classes lets the program refer to them later without any prefixes. The `java.applet.` and `java.awt.` prefixes tell the compiler which packages it should search for the `Applet` and `Graphics` classes. The `java.applet` package contains classes that are essential to Java applets. The `java.awt` package contains classes used by all Java programs with a GUI.

You might have noticed that The "Hello World" Application (page 9) uses the `System` class without any prefix, yet it does not import the `System` class. This is because the `System` class is part of the `java.lang` package and everything in the `java.lang` package is automatically imported into every Java program.

You can not only import individual classes, but also import entire packages. Here's an example:

```
import java.applet.*;
import java.awt.*;

public class HelloWorld extends Applet {
    public void paint(Graphics g) {
        g.drawString("Hello world!", 50, 25);
    }
}
```

In the Java language, every class is in a package. If the source code for a class doesn't have a `package` statement at the top declaring in which package the class is, then the class is in the *default package*. Almost all of the example classes in this tutorial are in the default package. See Creating and Using Packages (page 156) for information on using the `package` statement.

Within a package, all classes can refer to each other without prefixes. For example, the `java.awt Component` class refers to the `java.awt Graphics` class without any prefixes and without importing the `Graphics` class.

Defining an Applet Subclass

The first bold line of the following listing begins a block that defines the `HelloWorld` class:

```
import java.applet.Applet;
import java.awt.Graphics;

public class HelloWorld extends Applet {
    public void paint(Graphics g) {
        g.drawString("Hello world!", 50, 25);
    }
}
```

The `extends` keyword indicates that `HelloWorld` is a subclass of the class whose name follows: `Applet`. If the term "subclass" is new to you, you can learn about it in the lesson Object-Oriented Programming Concepts (page 39).

From the `Applet` class, applets inherit a great deal of functionality. Perhaps most important is the ability to respond to browser requests. For example, when a Java-enabled browser loads a page containing an applet, the browser sends a request to the applet, telling the applet to initialize itself and start executing. You can learn more about what the `Applet` class provides by going to the Overview of Applets (page 175).

An applet is not restricted to defining just one class. In addition to the necessary `Applet` subclass, an applet can define additional custom classes. When the applet attempts to use a class, the application that is executing the applet first looks on the local host for the class. If the class is not available locally, it is loaded from the location from which the `Applet` subclass originated.

Implementing Applet Methods

The bold lines of the following listing implement the `paint` method:

```
import java.applet.Applet;
import java.awt.Graphics;

public class HelloWorld extends Applet {
    public void paint(Graphics g) {
        g.drawString("Hello world!", 50, 25);
    }
}
```

Every applet must implement one or more of the `init`, `start`, and `paint` methods. You can learn about these methods in the Overview of Applets (page 175).

In the previous code snippet, the `Graphics` object passed into the `paint` method represents the applet's on-screen drawing context. The first argument to the `Graphics drawString` method is the string to draw on-screen. The second and third arguments are the *(x,y)* position of the lower-left corner of the text on-screen. This applet draws the string "Hello world!" starting at location (50,25). The applet's coordinate system starts at (0,0), which is at the upper-left corner of the applet's display area. You can learn about drawing to the screen in Creating a User Interface (page 403).

Running an Applet

The bold lines of the following listing comprise the `<APPLET>` tag that includes the "Hello World" applet in an HTML page:

```
<HTML>
<HEAD>
<TITLE> A Simple Program </TITLE>
</HEAD>
<BODY>
Here is the output of my program:
<APPLET CODE="HelloWorld.class" WIDTH=150 HEIGHT=25>
</APPLET>
</BODY>
</HTML>
```

The `<APPLET>` tag specifies that the browser should load the class whose compiled code (bytecodes) is in the file named `HelloWorld.class`. The browser looks for this file in the same directory as the HTML document that contains the tag.

When the browser finds the class file, it loads it over the network, if necessary, onto the computer on which the browser is running. The browser then creates an

instance of the class. If you include an applet twice in one HTML page, the browser loads the class file once and creates two instances of the class.

The `WIDTH` and `HEIGHT` attributes are like the attributes of the same name in an `<IMG>` tag: They specify the size in pixels of the applet's display area. Most browsers do not let the applet resize itself to be larger or smaller than this display area. For example, all of the drawing that the "Hello World" applet does in its `paint` method occurs within the 150x25-pixel display area reserved by the `<APPLET>` tag.

For more information on the `<APPLET>` tag, see Using the <APPLET> Tag (page 206).

Common Problems (and Their Solutions)

IF you're having trouble compiling your Java source code or running your application or applet, this section might help you find and fix your problem. If nothing in this section helps, refer to the documentation for the compiler or interpreter you're using.

Some of the problems that first-time Java programmers experience are the result of incorrectly installed development environments. If you can't compile even a single program, double-check that you installed your development environment correctly and that your path has been updated so that the operating system can find your development environment.

You can find installation instructions for the JDK in the `README.txt` file at the top of the JDK release. You can also find these instructions on the JDK Web site.[1]

Another common problem results from using a text editor that saves files in 8.3 format or with a TXT suffix. Most Java development tools are picky about filenames. Save yourself some trouble: Avoid editors that don't give you full control over filenames.

One problem that vexes beginners and experts alike results from incorrectly setting the `CLASSPATH` environment variable. Do *not* set `CLASSPATH` unless you are sure of what you're doing.

1 http://java.sun.com/products/jdk/index.html

Compiler Problems

Can't Run the Compiler

If you can't get the compiler to run at all, it's because the operating system can't find it. You probably need to either specify the full path to the compiler or set your path environment variable so that it contains the JDK's `bin` directory.

Platform-specific Details: Setting the Path

UNIX:

If you use the C shell (`csh`), you can set the path by adding the following line to your startup file (`~/.cshrc`):

```
set path=($path /usr/local/jdk1.1/bin)
```

Then load the startup file and use the `which` command to verify that the path is set correctly:

```
% source ~/.cshrc
% which javac
```

DOS shell (Windows 95/NT):

Open the `C:\AUTOEXEC.BAT` file and edit the `PATH` statement. Ensure that no other versions of the JDK are in the path and then add the JDK to the end of the path. Here's an example of a `PATH` statement:

```
PATH C:\WINDOWS;C:\WINDOWS\COMMAND;C:\DOS;C:\JDK1.1\BIN
```

Can't Find the File

If the compiler can't find the file you're trying to compile, try these solutions:

- Make sure the file is named exactly *`Class`*`.java`, where *`Class`* is the name of the class in the file you're trying to compile.
- Make sure you're invoking the compiler from the directory in which the `.java` file is located.
- Make sure you invoked the compiler, rather than the interpreter. The compiler is named `javac`; the interpreter is named `java`.

Note: A source file's name must exactly match the name of the class that the file contains, including the same capitalization. Be sure the full `.java` suffix is after the class name.

Changes Didn't Take Effect

If you changed your program and recompiled it, but the changes didn't take effect, try these solutions:

- Make sure that the program compiled cleanly. If the program couldn't compile, the old class files might still exist.
- If your program compiled successfully, make sure you're specifying the new class files and not a back-up copy of the old files. Delete the old class files, if necessary, to avoid confusion.
- Make sure that the tool you're using hasn't cached the old class files. Usually you can empty a cache by quitting the tool and then restarting it. If you are trying to view changes made to an applet in a browser, try pressing *Shift* + the *Reload* button. If this doesn't work, try explicitly clearing the cache on your browser.

Syntax Errors

If you mistype part of a program, the compiler may issue a *syntax error*. The message usually displays the name of the file in which the error occurred, the line number where the error was detected, a description of the error (to the best abilities of the compiler), the code on that line, and the position of the error within the code. Here's an error caused by the omission of a semicolon (;) at the end of a statement:

```
testing.java:14: ';' expected.
System.out.println("Counted " + count + " chars.")
                                                  ^
1 error
```

Sometimes the compiler can't guess your intent, so it prints one or more confusing error messages for one mistake. For example, the following code snippet omits a semicolon (;) from the boldfaced line:

```
while (in.read() != -1)
    count++
System.out.println("Counted " + count + " chars.");
```

When processing this code, the compiler issues two error messages:

```
testing.java:13: Invalid type expression.
        count++
                ^
```

```
testing.java:14: Invalid declaration.
    System.out.println("Counted " + count + "chars.");
                      ^
2 errors
```

The compiler issues two error messages because after it processes `count++`, the compiler's state indicates that it's in the middle of an expression. Without the semicolon, the compiler has no way of knowing that the statement is complete.

If you see any compiler errors, your program did not successfully compile and the compiler did not create or update your `.class` file. Carefully verify the program, fix the errors, and try again.

Semantic Errors

In addition to verifying that your program is syntactically correct, the compiler checks for basic correctness. For example, it warns you each time you use a variable that has not been initialized:

```
testing.java:13: Variable count may not have been initialized.
        count++
^
testing.java:14: Variable count may not have been initialized.
System.out.println("Counted " + count + " chars.");
                                       ^
2 errors
```

Again, your program did not successfully compile, and the compiler did not create a `.class` file. Fix the error and try again.

Interpreter Problems

Can't Find Class

If the interpreter says that it can't find the class you just compiled, try these solutions:

- Make sure you specified the *class* name—not the class *file* name—to the interpreter. For example, the following command doesn't work: `java HelloWorldApp.class`. Instead, use `java HelloWorldApp`. (Notice that you shouldn't add `.class`!)
- Unset the `CLASSPATH` environment variable if it's set. See Setting the Class Path (page 164) for information about `CLASSPATH`.

- Make sure you're invoking the interpreter from the directory in which the `.class` file is located.
- Make sure you invoked the interpreter, rather than the compiler. The compiler is named `javac`; the interpreter is named `java`.

The main Method Is Not Defined

If the interpreter tells you that the `main` method is not defined, try these solutions:

- Make sure the program you tried to execute is really an application and not just an applet. Most applets don't have `main` methods, since applets are designed to be executed in browsers.
- If the program really should be an application, make sure it has a `main` method.
- Make sure the program's `main` method is defined exactly as described in The main Method (page 14). For example, make sure that you specify the `main` method as `public`.

Applet Problems

See Common Problems (and Their Solutions) (page 235) if you have trouble getting an applet to run.

End of Trail

YOU'VE reached the end of the **Getting Started** trail. Take a break—have a cup of steaming hot java.

What Next?

Once you've caught your breath, you have several choices of where to go next. You can go back to the Trail Map (page xvii) to see all of your choices, or you can go directly to one of the following popular trails:

Learning the Java Language (page 35): This trail is a gentle introduction to object-oriented concepts and how the Java language implements them.

Writing Applets (page 171): This is the starting point for learning everything about writing applets.

Essential Java Classes (page 241): This trail discusses strings, exceptions, threads, and other Java features that are used in all kinds of Java programs.

http://java.sun.com/docs/books/tutorial/java/index.html

Learning the Java Language

THIS trail covers the fundamentals of programming in the Java language.

Object-Oriented Programming Concepts (page 39) cuts through the hype surrounding object-oriented technology and teaches you its core concepts: objects, messages, classes, and inheritance. You need to understand these concepts before learning how they are applied in the Java language. This lesson contains a bibliography for further reading on the subject. Feel free to skip this lesson if you are already familiar with object-oriented programming.

The Nuts and Bolts of the Java Language (page 49) explains a simple Java program line by line. Following this example, you will read about the syntax and semantics of the Java language.

Because Java's syntax is similar to that of other programming languages, particularly C and C++, much of this material will be familiar to seasoned programmers. You may wish to skim this lesson for its main points and use it as a reference.

Objects and Classes in Java (page 81) shows you how Java implements the concepts described in the first lesson of this trail. You will learn how to create, use, and destroy objects and how to write the classes from which objects are created. The last section introduces you to the `Spot` applet and uses it to discuss the practicalities of subclassing another class, implementing an interface, and using an inner class to implement an adapter class. Every Java programmer needs to be facile with the technology presented by this lesson.

More Features of the Java Language (page 133) is a lesson about family planning. The topics discussed here—inheritance, interfaces, nested classes, and packages—are all features of the Java language that help you to organize and structure your classes and their relationships to one another. This lesson not only shows you how to use these features of Java, but also talks about when and why you would use them.

If you don't need this information right away and want to get on with the business of writing some applets, feel free to leave this lesson for later and go straight to the next trail, Writing Applets (page 171).

http://java.sun.com/docs/books/tutorial/java/concepts/index.html

4 Object-Oriented Programming Concepts

YOU'VE heard it a lot in the past several years. Everybody is saying it.

What is all the fuss about objects and object-oriented technology? Is it real? Or is it hype? Well, the truth is—it's a little bit of both. Object-oriented technology, does, in fact, provide many benefits to software developers and their products. However, historically a lot of hype has surrounded this technology, causing confusion in both managers and programmers alike. Many companies fell victim to this hardship (or took advantage of it) and claimed that their software products were object-oriented when, in fact, they weren't. These false claims confused consumers and resulted in widespread misinformation and mistrust of object-oriented technology.

Despite the overuse and misuse of the term "object-oriented," the computer industry is now beginning to overcome the hype. More people are gaining a better understanding of object-oriented technology and its benefits.

This lesson slashes through the hype and explains the four key concepts behind object-oriented programming, design, and development by answering these four questions:

If you already know the answers to these questions, consider skipping this lesson and moving on to the next: The Nuts and Bolts of the Java Language (page 49).

What Is an Object?

As the term "object-oriented" implies, objects are key to understanding object-oriented technology. You can look around you now and see many examples of real-world objects: your dog, your desk, your television set, your bicycle.

These real-world objects share two characteristics: They all have *state*, and they all have *behavior*. For example, dogs have state (name, color, breed, the condition of being hungry) and dogs have behavior (barking, fetching, slobbering on your newly cleaned slacks). Bicycles have state (current gear, current pedal cadence, two wheels, number of gears) and behavior (braking, accelerating, slowing down, changing gears).

Software objects are modeled after real-world objects in that they, too, have state and behavior. A software object maintains its state in *variables* and implements its behavior with *methods*.

Definition: An *object* is a software bundle of variables and related methods.

You can represent real-world objects using software objects. For example, you might want to represent dogs as software objects in an animation program or a bicycle as a software object within an electronic exercise bike. However, you can also use software objects to model abstract concepts. For example, an event is a common object used in GUI window systems to represent the action of a user pressing a mouse button or a key on the keyboard.

Figure 4 shows a common visual representation of a software object.

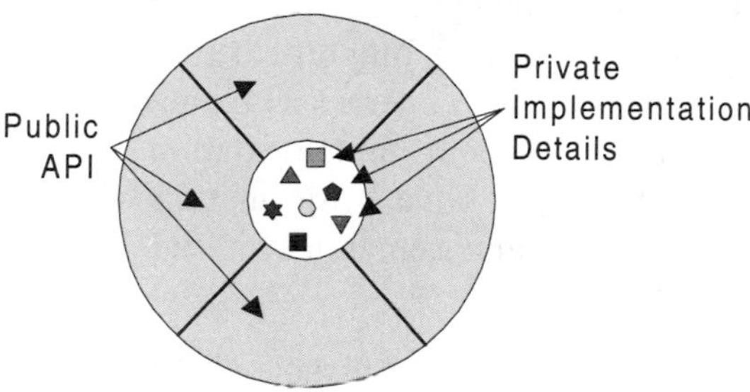

Figure 4: A software object.

Everything that the software object knows (its state) and can do (its behavior) is expressed by the variables and methods within that object. A software object that models your bicycle has variables that indicate the bicycle's current state: Its speed is 10 mph, its pedal cadence is 90 rpm, and its current gear is fifth. Variables and methods associated with a specific object, such as your bicycle, are called *instance variables* and *instance methods* to distinguish them from *class variables* and *class methods*, which are described later in What Is a Class? (page 44). Figure 5 illustrates your bicycle modeled as a software object.

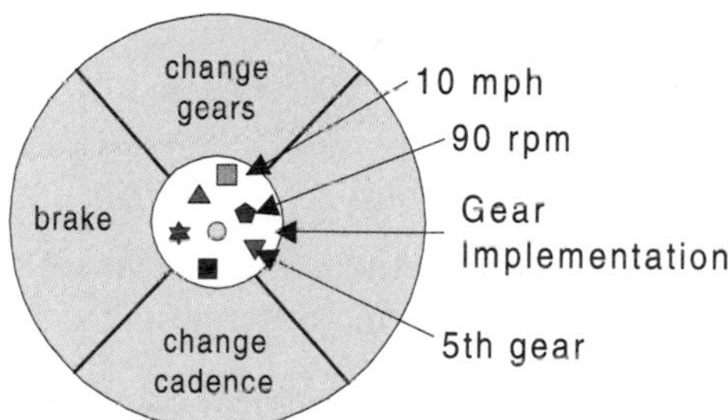

Figure 5: A bicycle modeled as a software object.

The software bicycle also has methods to brake, change the pedal cadence, and change gears. (The bike does not have a method for changing the speed of the bicycle, as the bike's speed is really just a side effect of what gear it's in, how fast the rider is pedaling, whether the brakes are on, and how steep the terrain is.) Anything that an object does not know or cannot do is excluded from the object. For example, your bicycle (probably) doesn't have a name and it can't run, bark, or fetch. Thus there are no variables or methods for those states and behaviors in the bicycle object.

As Figures 4 and 5 show, the *nucleus* of the object is comprised of private variables and private methods. The *membrane* of the object surrounds and hides its

nucleus. The membrane is the object's public interface that other objects use to interact with it. The public interface may affect the hidden components of an object, but it doesn't matter. Objects interact with one another through their public interfaces without worrying about implementation details. This is important because an object can change its private information without affecting another object as long as the syntax and semantics of the object's public interface remains the same.

When you want to change gears on your bicycle you don't need to know how the gear mechanism works; you just need to know which lever to move. Similarly in software programs, you don't need to know how an object is implemented; you just need to know how to use its public interface. Thus the implementation details can change at any time without affecting other parts of the program.

Hiding information within an object's nucleus and then providing a public interface for interacting with it is called *encapsulation* and is a critical benefit to object-oriented programming.

In many languages, including Java, objects have complete control over whether other objects can access its variables and methods. In fact, Java objects can specify exactly which other objects have access based on inheritance and package relationships. Variable and method access in Java is covered in Controlling Access to Members of a Class (page 113).

The Benefits of Objects

Encapsulating related variables and methods into a neat software bundle is a simple yet powerful idea that provides two major benefits to software developers:

- **Modularity:** The source code for an object can be written and maintained independently from the source code for other objects. Also, an object can be easily passed around in the system. You can give your bicycle to someone else, and it will still work.
- **Information hiding:** An object has a public interface that other objects can use to communicate with it. However, the object can maintain private information and methods that can be changed at any time without affecting the other objects that depend on it. You don't need to understand the gear mechanism on your bike in order to use it.

What Is a Message?

A single object alone is generally not very useful and usually appears as a component of a larger program or application that contains many other objects. Through the interaction of these objects, programmers achieve higher-order functionality and more complex behavior. Your bicycle hanging from a hook in the garage is just a bunch of titanium alloy and rubber; by itself, it is incapable of any activity. It is useful only when another object (you) interacts with it (starts pedaling).

Software objects interact and communicate with each other by sending *messages* to each other. When object A wants object B to perform one of B's methods, object A sends a message to object B. Figure 6 illustrates this concept.

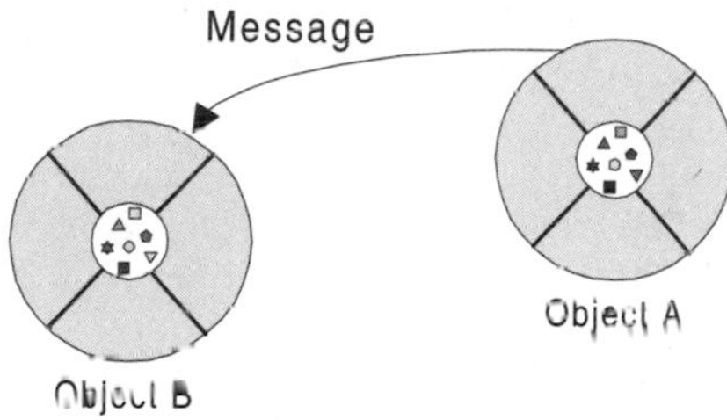

Figure 6: Objects interact by sending each other *messages*.

Sometimes the receiving object needs more information so that it knows exactly what to do. For example, when you want to change gears on your bicycle, you have to indicate which gear you want. This information is passed along with the message as a *parameter* to a method, as illustrated in Figure 7.

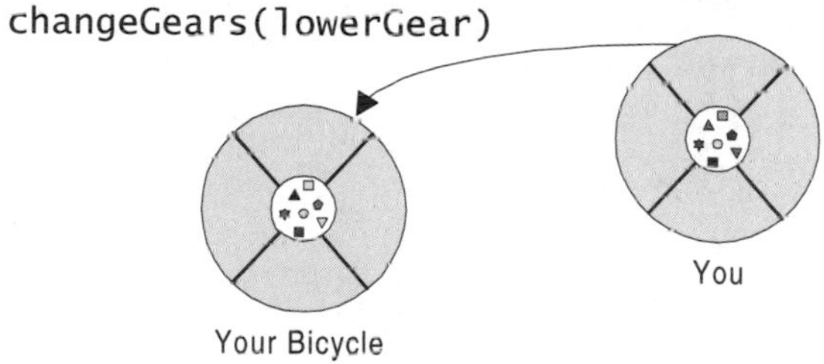

Figure 7: Messages use parameters to pass along extra information that the object needs, in this case, which gear the bicycle should be in (`lowerGear`).

Three components comprise a message:

1. The object to whom the message is addressed (Your Bicycle)
2. The name of the method to perform (`changeGears`)
3. Any parameters needed (e.g., `lowerGear`)

These three components are enough information for the receiving object to perform the desired method. No other information or context is required.

The Benefits of Messages

- An object's behavior is expressed through its methods, so, aside from direct variable access, message passing supports all possible interactions between objects.
- Objects don't need to be in the same process or even on the same machine to send and receive messages back and forth to each other.

What Is a Class?

In the real world, you often have many objects of the same kind. For example, your bicycle is just one of many bicycles in the world. Using object-oriented terminology, we say that your bicycle object is an *instance* of the class of objects known as bicycles. Bicycles have in common some state (e.g., current gear, current cadence, and two wheels) and behavior (e.g., they change gears and brake). However, each bicycle's state is independent of and can be different from that of other bicycles.

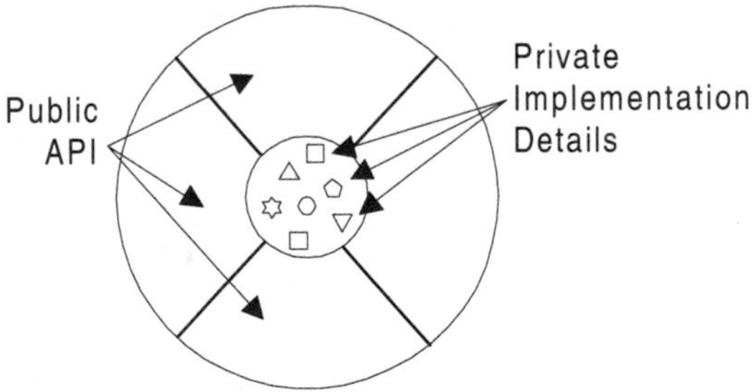

Figure 8: A visual representation of a class.

When building bicycles, manufacturers take advantage of the fact that bicycles share characteristics by using the same blueprint to build many bicycles. It would be very inefficient to produce a new blueprint for every individual bicycle they manufactured. In object-oriented software, it's also possible to have many objects of the same kind that share characteristics; examples of these objects include rectangles, employee records, and video clips. Like the bicycle manufacturers, you can take advantage of the fact that objects of the same kind are similar, and you can create a blueprint for those objects. Software blueprints for objects are called *classes*.

Definition: A *class* is a blueprint or prototype that defines the variables and methods common to all objects of a certain kind.

To continue with our bicycle example, you can create a bicycle class that declares, for each bicycle object, several instance variables to contain the current gear, the current cadence, and other characteristics. This class also declares and provides implementations for the instance methods that allow the rider to change gears, brake, and change the pedaling cadence.

The values for instance variables are provided by each instance of the class. So, after you've created the bicycle class, you must *instantiate* it—that is, create an instance of it—before you can use it. When you create an instance of a class, you create an object of that type and the system allocates memory for the instance variables declared by the class. Then you can invoke the object's instance methods to make it do something. Instances of the same class share the same instance method implementations, which reside in the class itself. (Method implementations are not duplicated on a per object basis.)

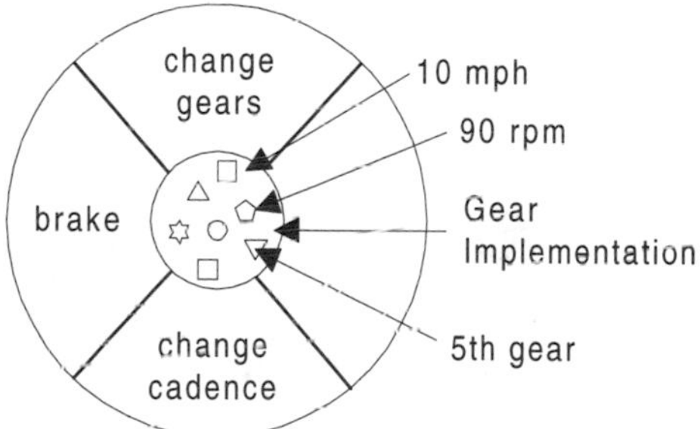

Figure 9: The bicycle class.

Classes can define not only instance variables and instance methods, but also *class variables* and *class methods*. You can access class variables and methods from an instance of the class or directly from a class; you don't have to instanti-

ate a class to use its class variables and methods. Class methods can operate only on class variables. They cannot access instance variables or instance methods.

The system creates a single copy of all class variables for a class the first time it encounters the class in a program; all instances of that class share its class variables. For example, suppose all bicycles have the same number of gears. In this case, defining an instance variable for number of gears is inefficient. Each instance would have its own copy of the variable, but the value would be the same for every instance. In such cases, you can define a class variable that contains the number of gears. All instances share this variable. A class variable changed by one object changes for all other objects of that type.

Understanding Instance and Class Members (page 118) discusses instance variables and methods and class variables and methods in detail.

Objects versus Classes

You probably noticed that the illustrations of objects and classes resemble each other. And indeed, the difference between classes and objects is often the source of some confusion. In the real world, it's obvious that classes are not themselves the objects that they describe—a blueprint of a bicycle is not a bicycle. However, it's a little more difficult to differentiate classes and objects in software. This is partly because software objects are abstract concepts in the first place. But it's also because many people use the term "object" inconsistently and use it to refer to both classes and instances.

In the figures, the class is not shaded because it represents a blueprint of an object rather than an object itself. In comparison, an object is shaded. This indicates that the object actually exists and that you can use it.

The Benefit of Classes

Objects provide the benefit of modularity and information hiding. Classes provide the benefit of reusability. Bicycle manufacturers reuse the same blueprint over and over again to build many bicycles. Software programmers use the same class, and thus the same code, over and over again to create many objects.

What Is Inheritance?

Generally speaking, objects are defined in terms of classes. You know a lot about an object by knowing its class. Even if you don't know what a penny-farthing is, if I told you it was a bicycle, you would know that it had two wheels, handle bars, and pedals, and what it was for.

Object-oriented systems take this a step further and allow classes to be defined in terms of other classes. For example, mountain bikes, racing bikes, and tandems are all different kinds of bicycles. In object-oriented terminology, mountain bikes, racing bikes, and tandems are all *subclasses* of the bicycle class, while the bicycle class is the *superclass* of mountain bikes, racing bikes, and tandems. Figure 10 shows the hierarchy of the bicycle class.

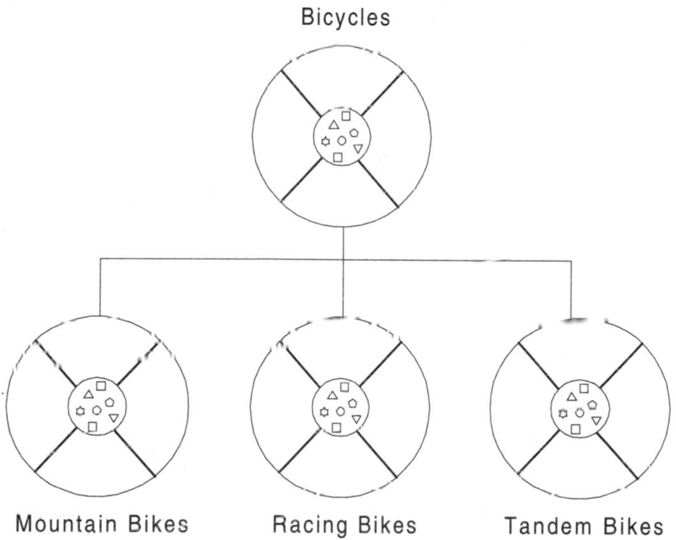

Figure 10: The hierarchy of the bicycle class.

Each subclass *inherits* state (in the form of variable declarations) from the superclass. Mountain bikes, racing bikes, and tandems share some states: cadence, speed, and the like. Also, each subclass inherits methods from the superclass. Mountain bikes, racing bikes, and tandems also share some behaviors; for example, braking and changing pedaling speed.

However, subclasses are not limited to the state and behaviors provided to them by their superclass; they can add other variables and methods. Tandem bicycles have two seats and two sets of handlebars, and some mountain bikes have an extra set of gears that have a lower gear ratio.

Subclasses can also *override* inherited methods and provide specialized implementations for those methods. For example, if you have a mountain bike with an

extra set of gears, you can override the `changeGears` method so that the rider can use those new gears.

You are not limited to just one layer of inheritance. The inheritance tree, or *class hierarchy*, can be as deep as needed. Methods and variables are inherited down through the levels. In general, the further down in the hierarchy a class appears, the more specialized its behavior.

The Benefits of Inheritance

- Subclasses provide specialized behaviors from the basis of common elements provided by the superclass. Using inheritance, programmers can reuse the code in the superclass many times.
- Programmers can implement superclasses called *abstract classes*. An abstract class defines "generic" behaviors. The abstract superclass defines and may partially implement the behavior but much of the class is undefined and unimplemented. Other programmers fill in the details with specialized subclasses.

Where Can I Get More Information?

This lesson gave you a glimpse into the world of object-oriented design and development and may have whetted your appetite for more. Check out the following object-oriented books to get more information about this exciting technology:

An Introduction to Object-Oriented Programming, Second Edition, Timothy Budd. Addison-Wesley Publishing Company, Reading, Massachusetts, 1997. This book examines the ideas of object-oriented design and software construction, presenting concepts of object-oriented analysis and programming in a language independent fashion. The book includes sections on inheritance, static and dynamic binding, and the development of exciting new object-oriented languages such as the Java programming language, Beta, and CLOS.

Object Technology: A Manager's Guide, Second Edition, David A. Taylor, Ph.D. Addison-Wesley Publishing Company, Reading, Mass., 1998. An excellent discussion of object-oriented technology for the nontechnical reader. Includes an assessment of the advantages and disadvantages of this technology.

http://java.sun.com/docs/books/tutorial/java/nutsandbolts/index.html

5 The Nuts and Bolts of the Java Language

THE Count class shown below contains a method named countChars that reads and counts characters from a Reader (an object that implements an input stream of characters) and then displays the number of characters read. Even a small method such as this uses many of the traditional language features of Java and classes from the Java API.

```
import java.io.*;
public class Count {
    public static void countChars(Reader in) throws IOException
    {
        int count = 0;

        while (in.read() != -1)
            count++;
        System.out.println("Counted " + count + " chars.");
    }
    // ... main method omitted ...
}
```

Through a line-by-line investigation of this simple method, this lesson describes Java's traditional language features such as variables and data types, operators, expressions, control flow statements, and so on.

Impurity Alert! Using System.out is not 100% Pure Java because some systems don't have the notion of standard output.

Running the countChars Method

The following `main` method for the `Count` class opens a `Reader` on a file named on the command line and then calls `countChars` with that `Reader`. You can use this application to run `countChars`.

```
import java.io.*;
public class Count {
    // ... countChars method omitted ...
    public static void main(String[] args) throws Exception
    {
        if (args.length >= 1)
            countChars(new FileReader(args[0]));
        else
            System.err.println("Usage: Count filename");
    }
}
```

The output of this program depends on what's in the file named on the command line. The following instructions show you how to run the application on a file named `testing` that contains the following ASCII text and displays the results:

```
Ich bin ein Berliner.
I am a jelly doughnut.
```

Platform-specific Details: Run the Character-Counting Program

UNIX:

```
% java Count testing
Counted 44 chars.
```

DOS shell (Win32):

```
C:\> java Count testing
Counted 45 chars.
```

Note: The program gives different results for different platforms because the program counts new line characters. On UNIX, a new line is a single character: `\n`. In Win32, it's two: `\r\n`.

Now that you've seen the `countChars` method in action, the remainder of this lesson looks at the various components that make up the method and how they fit into the Java language.

Variables and Data Types

Variables are the nouns of a programming language—that is, they are the entities (values and data) that act or are acted upon. The `countChars` method defines two variables—`count` and `in`. The program increments `count` each time it reads a character from the other variable `in`. The declarations for both variables appear in bold in the following listing:

```
import java.io.*;
public class Count {
    public static void countChars(Reader in) throws IOException
    {
        int count = 0;

        while (in.read() != -1)
            count++;
        System.out.println("Counted " + count + " chars.");
    }
    // ... main method omitted ...
}
```

A variable declaration always contains two components: the type of the variable and its name. The location of the variable declaration, that is, where the declaration appears in relation to other code elements, determines its scope.

Data Types

All variables in the Java language must have a data type. A variable's data type determines the values that the variable can contain and the operations that can be performed on it. For example, the declaration `int count` declares that `count` is an integer (`int`). Integers can contain only whole number values (both positive and negative), and you can use the standard arithmetic operators (+, -, *, and /) on integers to perform the standard arithmetic operations (addition, subtraction, multiplication, and division, respectively).

There are two major categories of data types in the Java language: *primitive* and *reference*. Table 1 lists, by keyword, all of the primitive data types supported by Java, their sizes and formats, and a brief description of each.

Purity Tip: In other languages, the format and size of primitive data types may depend on the platform on which a program is running. In contrast, the Java language specifies the size and format of its primitive data types. Hence, you don't have to worry about system dependencies.

Table 1: Java's primitive data types.

Type	Size/Format	Description
Integers		
`byte`	8-bit two's complement	Byte-length integer
`short`	16-bit two's complement	Short integer
`int`	32-bit two's complement	Integer
`long`	64-bit two's complement	Long integer
Real Numbers		
`float`	32-bit IEEE 754	Single-precision floating-point
`double`	64-bit IEEE 754	Double-precision floating-point
Other Types		
`char`	16-bit Unicode character	A single character
`boolean`	`true` or `false`	A boolean value (`true` or `false`)

A variable of primitive type contains a single value of the appropriate size and format for its type: a number, character, or boolean value. For example, the value of an `int` is an integer, the value of a `char` is a 16-bit Unicode character, and so on. The value of the `count` variable in `countChars` ranges from its initial value of zero to a number that represents the number of characters in the input.

Arrays, classes, and interfaces are reference types. The value of a reference type variable, in contrast to that of a primitive type, is a *reference* to the actual value or set of values represented by the variable. A reference is like your friend's address: The address is not your friend, but it's a way to reach your friend. A reference type variable is not the array or object itself but rather a way to reach it.

The `countChars` method uses one variable of reference type `in`, which is a `Reader` object. When used in a statement or expression, the name `in` evaluates to a reference to the object. So you can use the object's name to access its member variables or call its methods (just as `countChars` does to call `read`).

Note to C and C++ Programmers:

Three data types supported by C and C++ are not supported by the Java language: pointers, structures, and unions. In Java, you use classes and interfaces instead.

Pointers

Some data types in Java, such as objects and arrays, are reference data types. Variables of this type evaluate to a reference. References are similar to pointers used in other languages such as C and C++. However, Java does not have an explicit pointer type. You cannot construct a reference to anonymous memory. This makes programming easier, as well as prevents common errors due to pointer mismanagement.

Structures and Unions

The Java language does not support either structures or unions. Instead, you use classes or interfaces to build composite types. Classes and interfaces allow you to bundle together data and methods and to control who has access to those class members. This makes them much more powerful mechanisms than structures or unions.

Variable Names

A program refers to a variable's value by its name. For example, when the `countChars` method wants to refer to the value of the `count` variable, it simply uses the name `count`.

In Java, the following must hold true for a variable name:

1. It must be a legal Java identifier comprised of a series of Unicode characters. Unicode is a character-coding system designed to support text written in diverse human languages. It allows for the codification of up to 65,536 characters; currently, 34,168 have been assigned. This allows you to use characters in your Java programs from various alphabets, such as Japanese, Greek, Russian, and Hebrew. This is important so that programmers can write code that is meaningful in their native languages.
2. It must not be a keyword (page 931) or a boolean literal (`true` or `false`).
3. It must not have the same name as another variable whose declaration appears in the same scope.

By Convention: Variable names begin with a lowercase letter and class names begin with an uppercase letter. If a variable name consists of more than one word, such as `isVisible`, the words are joined together and each word after the first begins with an uppercase letter.

Rule #3 implies that variables may have the same name as another variable whose declaration appears in a different scope. This is true. In addition, in some

situations, a variable may share names with another variable that is declared in a nested scope. Scope is covered in the next section.

Scope

A variable's *scope* is the block of code within which the variable is accessible and determines when the variable is created and destroyed. The location of the variable declaration within your program establishes its scope and places it into one of these four categories:

1. Member variable
2. Local variable
3. Method parameter
4. Exception-handler parameter

Figure 11 shows you the scope of each kind of variable (on the left) and where it's declared within a class (in italics in the code snippet).

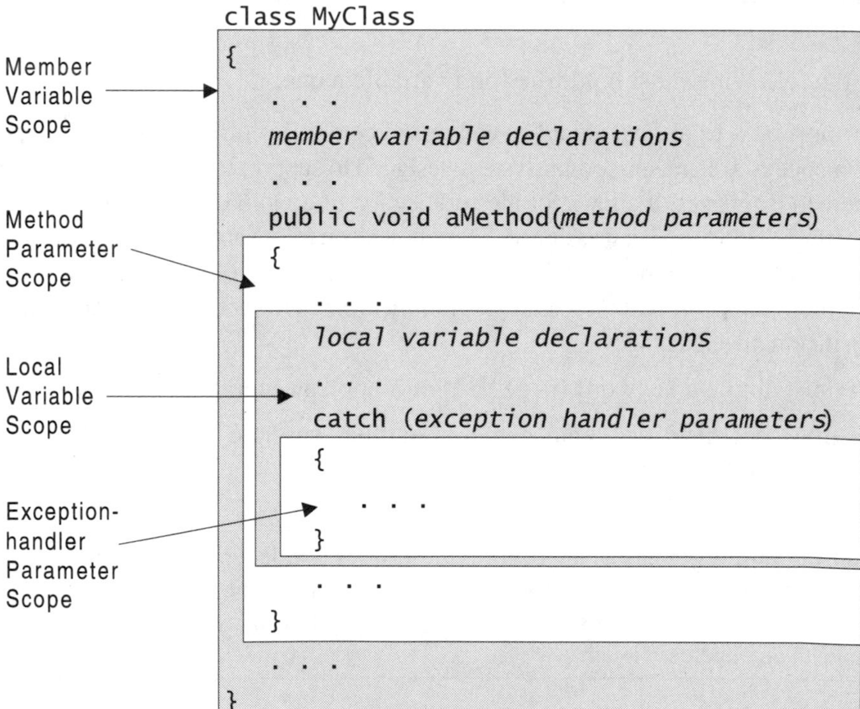

Figure 11: The scope of the four categories of variables.

A member variable is a member of a class or an object. It can be declared anywhere in a class but not in a method. The member is available to all code in the class. The `Count` class that contains the `countChars` method doesn't declare any member variables. For information about declaring member variables, refer to Declaring Member Variables (page 99) in the next lesson.

You can declare local variables anywhere in a method or within a block of code in a method. In `countChars`, `count` is a local variable. The scope of `count`, that is, the code that can access `count`, extends from the declaration of `count` to the end of the `countChars` method (indicated by the first right curly bracket} that appears in the program code). In general, a local variable is accessible from its declaration to the end of the code block in which it was declared.

Method parameters are formal arguments to methods and are used to pass values into methods. The discussion about writing methods in the next lesson, Implementing Methods (page 101), talks about passing values into methods through parameters. You can also pass values into constructors in the same manner, so the discussion regarding method parameters applies equally well to parameters to constructors. In `countChars`, `in` is a parameter to the `countChars` method. The scope of a method parameter is the entire method for which it is a parameter. So, in `countChars`, the scope of `in` is the entire `countChars` method.

Exception-handler parameters are similar to method parameters but are arguments to an exception handler rather than to a method or a constructor. The `countChars` method does not have any exception handlers, so it doesn't have any exception-handler parameters. Catching and Handling Exceptions (page 306) talks about using Java exceptions to handle errors and shows you how to write an exception handler that has a parameter.

Variable Initialization

Local variables and member variables can be initialized with an assignment statement when they're declared. The data type of both sides of the assignment statement must match. The `countChars` method provides an initial value of zero for `count` when declaring it:

```
int count = 0;
```

Method parameters and exception-handler parameters cannot be initialized in this way; the value for a parameter is set by the caller.

Final Variables

You can declare a variable in any scope to be final, including parameters to methods and constructors. The value of a final variable cannot change after it has been initialized.

To declare a final variable, use the `final` keyword in the variable declaration before the type:

```
final int aFinalVar = 0;
```

The previous statement declares a final variable and initializes it, all at once. Subsequent attempts to assign a value to `aFinalVar` result in a compiler error.

You may, if necessary, defer initialization of a final variable. Simply declare the variable and initialize it later, like this:

```
final int blankfinal;
. . .
blankfinal = 0;
```

A final variable that has been declared but not yet initialized is called a *blank final*. Again, once a final variable has been initialized it cannot be set and any later attempts to assign a value to `blankfinal` result in a compile-time error.

Operators

The `countChars` method uses several operators, including =, !=, ++, and +, which are circled in this listing:

```
import java.io.*;
public class Count {
    public static void countChars(Reader in) throws IOException
    {
        int count = 0;

        while (in.read() != -1)
            count++;
        System.out.println("Counted " + count + " chars.");
    }
    // ... main method omitted ...
}
```

Operators perform some function on either one or two or three operands. Operators that require one operand are called *unary operators*. For example, ++ is a

unary operator that increments the value of its operand by 1. Operators that require two operands are *binary operators*. For example, = is a binary operator that assigns the value from its right-hand operand to its left-hand operand. And finally *tertiary operators* are those that require three operands. The Java language has one tertiary operator, `?:` , which is a short-hand `if-else` statement.

Java's unary operators can use either prefix or postfix notation. Prefix notation means that the operator appears *before* its operand:

```
operator op
```

Postfix notation means that the operator appears *after* its operand:

```
op operator
```

All of Java's binary operators use infix notation, which means that the operator appears *between* its operands:

```
op1 operator op2
```

Java's only tertiary operator is also infix, each component of the operator appears between its operands:

```
expr ? op1 : op2
```

In addition to performing the operation, an operator also returns a value. The value and its type depend on the operator and the type of its operands. For example, the arithmetic operators, which perform basic arithmetic operations such as addition and subtraction, return numbers—the result of the arithmetic operation. The data type returned by the arithmetic operators depends on the type of its operands: If you add two integers, you get an integer back. An operation is said to *evaluate to* its result.

It's useful to divide Java's operators into these categories: arithmetic, relational and conditional, bitwise and logical, and assignment. These are discussed in the following sections.

Arithmetic Operators

The Java language supports various arithmetic operators for all floating-point and integer numbers. These include + (addition), - (subtraction), * (multiplication), / (division), and % (modulo). For example, you can use this code to add two numbers:

```
addThis + toThis
```

Or you can use the following Java code to compute the remainder that results from dividing divideThis by byThis:

```
divideThis % byThis
```

Table 2 summarizes Java's binary arithmetic operators.

Table 2: Java's binary arithmetic operators.

Operator	Use	Description
+	op1 + op2	Adds op1 and op2.
-	op1 - op2	Subtracts op2 from op1.
*	op1 * op2	Multiplies op1 and op2.
/	op1 / op2	Divides op1 by op2.
%	op1 % op2	Computes the remainder of dividing op1 by op2.

Note: The Java language extends the definition of the + operator to include string concatenation. The countChars method uses + to concatenate "Counted ", the value of count, and " chars.", as shown here:

```
System.out.println("Counted " + count + " chars.");
```

This operation automatically coerces the value count to a String. You'll see more about this in Arrays and Strings (page 76).

The + and - operators have unary versions that perform the operations described in Table 3.

Table 3: The unary versions of the + and - operators.

Operator	Use	Description
+	+ op	Promotes op to int if it's a byte, short, or char.
-	- op	Arithmetically negates op.

There also are two shortcut arithmetic operators: ++, which increments its operand by 1, and --, which decrements its operand by 1. The countChars method

uses ++ to increment the `count` variable each time it reads a character from the input source with this statement:

```
count++;
```

Note that the ++ operator appears after its operand in this example. This is the *postfix version* of the operator. ++ also has a *prefix version* in which ++ appears before its operand. Both the prefix and postfix versions of this operator increment the operand by 1. So why are there two different versions? Each version evaluates to a different value: `op++` evaluates to the value of the operand *before* the increment operation, and `++op` evaluates to the value of the operand *after* the increment operation.

In the `countChars` method, suppose that `count` is 5 before the following statement is executed:

```
count++;
```

After the statement is executed, the value of `count` is 6. No surprises there. However, the statement `count++` evaluates to 5. In the same scenario, the prefix version of ++ would also set `count` to 6. However, the statement `++count` does not evaluate to 5 like the postfix version of ++ does; rather, it evaluates to 6:

```
++count;
```

This difference is unimportant in `countChars`, but it is critical when the value of the statement is used in the middle of a more complex computation, for flow control, or for something else. For example, the following loop will execute one less time if you change `count++` to `++count`:

```
do {
    . . .
} while (count++ < 6);
```

Similarly, -- also has prefix and postfix versions, which function in the same way as ++. The operations of these operators are summarized in Table 4.

Relational and Conditional Operators

A *relational operator* compares two values and determines the relationship between them. For example, `!=` returns `true` if the two operands are unequal. The `countChars` method uses `!=` to determine whether the value returned by `in.read` is not equal to `-1`. Table 5 summarizes Java's relational operators.

Table 4: Operation of ++ and -- .

Operator	Use	Description
++	op++	Increments op by 1; evaluates to value before incrementing.
++	++op	Increments op by 1; evaluates to value after incrementing.
--	op--	Decrements op by 1; evaluates to value before decrementing.
--	--op	Decrements op by 1; evaluates to value after decrementing.

Table 5: Java's relational operators.

Operator	Use	Returns **true** If . . .
>	op1 > op2	op1 is greater than op2.
>=	op1 >= op2	op1 is greater than or equal to op2.
<	op1 < op2	op1 is less than to op2.
<=	op1 <= op2	op1 is less than or equal to op2.
==	op1 == op2	op1 and op2 are equal.
!=	op1 != op2	op1 and op2 are not equal.
instanceof	op1 instanceof op2	op1 and op2 are assignment compatible.

Relational operators often are used with the conditional operators to construct more complex decision-making expressions. One such operator is &&, which performs the *boolean and* operation. For example, you can use two different relational operators along with && to determine if both relationships are true. The following line of code uses this technique to determine if an array index is between two boundaries. It determines if the index is both greater than 0 and less than NUM_ENTRIES (which is a previously defined constant value).

```
0 < index && index < NUM_ENTRIES
```

Note that in some instances, the second operand to a conditional operator may not be evaluated. Consider this expression:

```
((count > NUM_ENTRIES) && (in.read() != -1))
```

If count is less than NUM_ENTRIES, the left-hand operand for && evaluates to false. The && operator returns true only if *both* operands are true. So in this situation, the return value of && can be determined without evaluating the right-

hand operand. In such a case, Java does not evaluate the right-hand operand. Thus `in.read` won't get called and a character will not be read from the stream.

The operator & is similar to && if both of its operands are of boolean type. However, & always evaluates both its operands and returns `true` if both are `true`. Likewise, | is a similar to || if both of its operands are boolean. This operator always evaluates both of its operands and returns `false` if they are both `false`.

Java supports five binary conditional operators, shown in Table 6.

Table 6: Java's binary conditional operators.

Operator	Use	Returns true If . . .
&&	`op1 && op2`	`op1` and `op2` are both true; conditionally evaluates `op2`.
||	`op1 || op2`	either `op1` or `op2` is true; conditionally evaluates `op2`.
!	`! op`	`op` is false.
&	`op1 & op2`	`op1` and `op2` are both true; always evaluates `op1` and `op2`.
|	`op1 | op2`	either `op1` or `op2` is true; always evaluates `op1` and `op2`.

In addition, Java supports one other conditional operator—the `?:` operator. This operator is a ternary operator and is basically shorthand for an `if-else` statement:

```
expression ? op1 : op2
```

The `?:` operator evaluates `expression` and returns `op1` if it's true and `op2` if it's false.

Bitwise and Logical Operators

A *bitwise operator* allows you to perform bit manipulation on data. Table 7 summarizes the bitwise and logical operators available in the Java language.

Table 7: Java's bitwise and logical operators.

Operator	Use	Operation
>>	`op1 >> op2`	Shifts bits of `op1` right by distance `op2`.
<<	`op1 << op2`	Shifts bits of `op1` left by distance `op2`.
>>>	`op1 >>> op2`	Shifts bits of `op1` right by distance `op2` (unsigned).
&	`op1 & op2`	Performs the bitwise and.
|	`op1 | op2`	Performs the bitwise or.
^	`op1 ^ op2`	Performs the bitwise xor.
~	`~ op`	Performs the bitwise complement.

The three shift operators simply shift the bits of the left-hand operand over by the number of positions indicated by the right-hand operand. The shift occurs in the direction indicated by the operator itself. For example, the following statement shifts the bits of the integer 13 to the right by one position:

```
13 >> 1;
```

The binary representation of the number 13 is 1101. The result of the shift operation is 1101 shifted to the right by one position—110, or 6 in decimal notation. Note that the bit farthest to the right falls off the end into the bit bucket. See Table 8.

Table 8: The results of bitwise and operations.

op1	op2	Result
0	0	0
0	1	0
1	0	0
1	1	1

The bitwise and operation performs the "and" function on each parallel pair of bits in each operand; seeTable 8. The "and" function sets the resulting bit to 1 if both operands are 1.

Suppose you were to "and" the values 12 and 13 as in the following statement:

```
12 & 13
```

The result of this operation is 12. Why? Well, the binary representation of 12 is 1100, and the binary representation of 13 is 1101. The "and" function sets the resulting bit to 1 if both operand bits are 1; otherwise, the resulting bit is 0. So, if you line up the two operands and perform the "and" function, you can see that the two high-order bits (the two bits farthest to the left of each number) of each operand are 1. Thus the resulting bit in the result is also 1. The low-order bits evaluate to 0 because either one or both bits in the operands are 0:

```
  1101
& 1100
------
  1100
```

The | operator performs the inclusive or operation and ^ performs the exclusive or operation. *Inclusive or* means that if either of the 2 bits are 1, then the result is 1 as shown in Table 9.

Table 9: The results of inclusive or operations.

op1	op2	Result
0	0	0
0	1	1
1	0	1
1	1	1

Exclusive or means that if the two operand bits are different, the result is 1; otherwise, the result is 0. This is shown in Table 10.

Finally, the complement operator, ~, inverts the value of each bit of the operand. If the operand bit is 1, the result is 0 and if the operand bit is 0, the result is 1.

Among other things, bitwise manipulations are useful for managing sets of boolean flags. Suppose, for example, that you have several boolean flags in your program that indicate the state of various components in your program—is it visible, is it draggable, and so on. Rather than defining a separate boolean variable to hold each flag, you can define a single variable, `flags`, for all of them. Each bit within `flags` represents the current state of one of the flags. You then use bit manipulations to set and get each flag.

Table 10: The results of exclusive or operations.

op1	op2	Result
0	0	0
0	1	1
1	0	1
1	1	0

First, set up constants that indicate the various flags for your program. These flags should each be a different power of 2 to ensure that the "on" bit doesn't overlap with another flag. Then define a variable, `flags`, whose bits are set according to the current state of each flag. The following code sample initializes `flags` to 0, thereby indicating that all flags are `false` (that is, no bits are set):

```
final int VISIBLE = 1;
final int DRAGGABLE = 2;
final int SELECTABLE = 4;
final int EDITABLE = 8;

int flags = 0;
```

To set the visible flag when something became visible, use this statement:

```
flags = flags | VISIBLE;
```

To test for visibility, you then write:

```
if (flags & VISIBLE)
    . . .
```

Assignment Operators

You use the basic *assignment operator*, =, to assign one value to another. The `countChars` method uses = to initialize `count` with this statement:

```
int count = 0;
```

Java also provides several shortcut assignment operators that allow you to perform an arithmetic, logical, or bitwise operation and an assignment operation, all with one operator. Suppose you want to add a number to a variable and assign the result back into the variable, like this:

```
i = i + 2;
```

You can shorten this statement using the shortcut operator +=:

```
i += 2;
```

The two previous lines of code are equivalent. Table 11 lists the shortcut assignment operators and their lengthy equivalents.

Table 11: Java's shortcut assignment operators and their equivalents.

Operator	Use	Equivalent To
+=	`op1 += op2`	`op1 = op1 + op2`
-=	`op1 -= op2`	`op1 = op1 - op2`
*=	`op1 *= op2`	`op1 = op1 * op2`
/=	`op1 /= op2`	`op1 = op1 / op2`
%=	`op1 %= op2`	`op1 = op1 % op2`
&=	`op1 &= op2`	`op1 = op1 & op2`
|=	`op1 |= op2`	`op1 = op1 | op2`
^=	`op1 ^= op2`	`op1 = op1 ^ op2`
<<=	`op1 <<= op2`	`op1 = op1 << op2`
>>=	`op1 >>= op2`	`op1 = op1 >> op2`
>>>=	`op1 >>>= op2`	`op1 = op1 >>> op2`

Expressions

Expressions perform the work of a Java program. Among other things, expressions are used to compute and assign values to variables and to help control the execution flow of a program. The job of an expression is twofold: perform the computation indicated by the elements of the expression and return some value that is the result of the computation.

Definition: An *expression* is a series of variables, operators, and method calls (constructed according to the syntax of the language) that evaluates to a single value.

As discussed in the previous section, operators return a value, so the use of an operator is an expression. For example, the statement from the `countChars` method is an expression:

```
count++;
```

This particular expression evaluates to the value of count before the increment of count occurs.

The data type of the value returned by an expression depends on the elements used in the expression. The expression count++ returns an integer because ++ returns a value of the same data type as its operand and count is an integer. Other expressions return strings, boolean values, and so on.

The countChars method contains, in addition to the count++ expression, a few other expressions, including this one:

```
in.read() != -1
```

This expression is interesting because it actually consists of two expressions. The first expression is a method call:

```
in.read()
```

A method call expression evaluates to the return value of the method. Therefore, the data type of a method call expression is the same as the data type of its return value. The in.read method is declared to return an integer, so the expression in.read() evaluates to an integer.

The second expression contained in the statement in.read() != -1 uses the != operator. Recall that != compares two operands for inequality. In this, in.read() and -1 are the operands. in.read() is a valid operand for != because it is an expression and evaluates to an integer. So in.read() != -1 compares two integers: the value returned by in.read() and -1. The value returned by != is either true or false depending on the outcome of the comparison.

As you can see, Java allows you to construct compound expressions and statements from various smaller expressions as long as the data types required by both parts of the expression match.

Also, as you may have concluded from the previous example, the order in which a compound expression is evaluated matters! Take for example this compound expression:

```
x * y * z
```

Here, the order in which the expression is evaluated is unimportant because the results of the multiplication operations are independent of order. That is, the outcome is always the same regardless of the order in which you apply the multiplications. However, this is not true of all expressions. For example, the following expression gives different results depending on whether you perform the addition operation or the division operation first:

```
x + y / 100
```

You can direct the Java compiler to evaluate an expression in a specified order by using balanced parentheses `(` and `)`. For example, to make the previous statement unambiguous, you could write `(x + y)/ 100`.

If you don't explicitly tell the compiler the order in which you want operations to be performed, it decides based on the *precedence* assigned to the operators and other elements in use within the expression. Operators with a higher precedence get evaluated first. For example, the division operator has a higher precedence than the addition operator. Therefore, in the compound expression shown previously, `x + y / 100`, the compiler evaluates `y / 100` first. Thus the following two statements are equivalent:

```
x + y / 100
x + (y / 100)
```

By Convention: Use parentheses sparingly in your Java code, either to direct the compiler to evaluate an expression in nonprecedence order or to clarify your code. Precedence is part of the Java language and should be well understood.

The table Operator Precedence in Java (page 930) shows the precedence assigned to Java's operators. The operators in the table are listed in order of precedence: the higher in the table, the greater the operator's precedence. Operators with higher precedence are evaluated before operators with a lower precedence. Operators on the same line have equal precedence. When operators of equal precedence appear in the same expression, some rule must govern which is evaluated first. In Java, all binary operators except for the assignment operators are evaluated from left to right. Assignment operators are evaluated right to left.

Control Flow Statements

The `countChars` method uses a `while` statement to loop through all of the characters of the input source and count them:

```
import java.io.*;
public class Count {
    public static void countChars(Reader in) throws IOException
    {
        int count = 0;

        while (in.read() != -1)
            count++;
        System.out.println("Counted " + count + " chars.");
    }
    // ... main method omitted ...
}
```

Generally speaking, a `while` statement performs some action *while* a certain condition remains `true`. The general syntax of the `while` statement is

```
while (expression)
    statement
```

That is, while *`expression`* is `true`, do *`statement`*. In `countChars`, while the `read` method returns a value that is *not* `-1`, the program increments `count`.

By Convention: The opening curly bracket { is at the end of the same line as the `while` statement, and the closing curly bracket } begins a new line aligned with the `while`, as shown.

`statement` can be one statement, as shown in `countChars`, or it can be a *statement block*. A statement block is a series of legal Java statements contained within curly brackets { and }. For example, suppose that in addition to incrementing `count` within the `while` loop, you also wanted to print the count each time a character was read. You could write the following `while` loop instead:

```
while (in.read() != -1) {
    count++;
    System.out.println("Read a character. Count = " + count);
}
```

Note: Although `goto` is a reserved word, currently the Java language does not support the `goto` statement. Use Branching Statements (page 74) instead.

A statement such as the `while` statement is a *control flow statement*, that is, it determines the order in which other statements are executed. Besides `while`, the

Java language supports several other control flow statements, including those shown in Table 12.

Table 12: Java's control flow statements.

Type of Statement	Keyword
Decision-making	`if-else, switch-case`
Loop	`for, while, do-while`
Exception	`try-catch-finally, throw`
Branching	`break, continue, label:, return`

The if-else Statement

Java's `if-else` statement enables your programs to selectively execute other statements based on some criteria. For example, suppose your program prints debugging information based on the value of some boolean variable named `DEBUG`. If `DEBUG` is set to `true`, then your program prints debugging information such as the value of a variable `x`. Otherwise, your program proceeds normally. A segment of code to implement this might look like this:

```
if (DEBUG)
    System.out.println("DEBUG: x = " + x);
```

This is the simplest version of the `if` statement: The statement governed by the `if` statement is executed if some condition is `true`. Generally, the simple form of `if` can be written like this:

```
if (expression)
    statement
```

Suppose you want to execute a different set of statements if *`expression`* is `false`. You can use the `else` statement for that. Consider another example. Suppose your program needs to perform different actions depending on whether the user clicks OK or Cancel in an alert window. Your program could do this using an `if` statement and an `else` statement:

```
// response is either OK or CANCEL depending
// on the button that the user pressed

if (response == OK) {
```

```
        // code to perform OK action
    } else {
        // code to perform Cancel action
    }
```

This particular use of the `else` statement is the catch-all form. The `else` block is executed if the `if` part is `false`.

Another form of the `else` statement, `else if`, executes a statement based on another expression. For example, suppose you write a program that assigns grades based on the value of a test score: an A for a score of 90% or above, a B for a score of 80% or above, and so on. You can use an `if` statement with a series of companion `else if` statements and an `else`:

```
int testscore;
char grade;

if (testscore >= 90) {
    grade = 'A';
} else if (testscore >= 80) {
    grade = 'B';
} else if (testscore >= 70) {
    grade = 'C';
} else if (testscore >= 60) {
    grade = 'D';
} else {
    grade = 'F';
}
```

An `if` statement can have any number of companion `else if` statements, but only one `else`. You may have noticed that some values of `testscore` could satisfy more than one of the expressions in the compound `if` statement. For example, a score of 76 evaluates to `true` for two of the expressions in the `if` statement: `testscore >= 70` and `testscore >= 60`. However, as the runtime system processes a compound `if` statement such as this one, as soon as one of the conditions is satisfied (76 >= 70), the appropriate statements are executed (`grade = 'C'`), and control passes out of the `if` statement without evaluating the remaining conditions.

The switch Statement

A `switch` statement lets you conditionally perform statements based on some value. For example, suppose your program contains an integer named `month` whose value indicates the month in some date. Suppose also that you want to display the name of the month based on its integer equivalent. You can use Java's `switch` statement to perform this feat:

```
int month;
. . .
switch (month) {
    case 1:  System.out.println("January"); break;
    case 2:  System.out.println("February"); break;
    case 3:  System.out.println("March"); break;
    case 4:  System.out.println("April"); break;
    case 5:  System.out.println("May"); break;
    case 6:  System.out.println("June"); break;
    case 7:  System.out.println("July"); break;
    case 8:  System.out.println("August"); break;
    case 9:  System.out.println("September"); break;
    case 10: System.out.println("October"); break;
    case 11: System.out.println("November"); break;
    case 12: System.out.println("December"); break;
}
```

The `switch` statement uses a value, in this case the value of `month`, to choose the appropriate `case` statement to execute. Of course, you could implement this as an `if` statement.

```
int month;
. . .
if (month == 1) {
    System.out.println("January");
} else if (month == 2) {
    System.out.println("February");
. . .
// you get the idea
. . .
```

Deciding whether to use an `if` statement or a `switch` statement is a judgment call. You can decide which to use based on readability and other factors. An `if` statement can be used to make decisions based on ranges of values or conditions, whereas a `switch` statement is appropriate for making decisions based on a single value. Each `case` statement must be unique, and the value provided to each must be of the same data type as the data type returned by the expression provided to the `switch` statement.

Also of interest in the `switch` statement are the `break` statements after each `case`. The `break` statements cause control to break out of the `switch` and continue with the first statement following the `switch` statement. They are necessary because case statements fall through; that is, without an explicit break statement, control will flow sequentially through subsequent case statements. In the previous example, you don't want control to flow from one case to the next, so you have to put in break statements.

However, there are certain scenarios in which you do want control to proceed sequentially through case statements. An example is the following Java code that computes the number of days in a month according to the old rhyme that starts "Thirty days hath September . . .":

```
int month;
int numDays;
. . .
switch (month) {
  case 1:
  case 3:
  case 5:
  case 7:
  case 8:
  case 10:
  case 12:
    numDays = 31;
    break;
  case 4:
  case 6:
  case 9:
  case 11:
    numDays = 30;
    break;
  case 2:
    if ( ((year % 4 == 0) && (year % 100 != 0)) ||
                             (year % 400 == 0) )
        numDays = 29;
    else
        numDays = 28;
    break;
}
```

You can use a default statement at the end of the switch to handle all values that aren't explicitly handled by one of the case statements. This is shown in bold in the following code:

```
int month;
. . .
switch (month) {
  case 1:  System.out.println("January"); break;
```

```
    case 2:  System.out.println("February"); break;
    case 3:  System.out.println("March"); break;
    case 4:  System.out.println("April"); break;
    case 5:  System.out.println("May"); break;
    case 6:  System.out.println("June"); break;
    case 7:  System.out.println("July"); break;
    case 8:  System.out.println("August"); break;
    case 9:  System.out.println("September"); break;
    case 10: System.out.println("October"); break;
    case 11: System.out.println("November"); break;
    case 12: System.out.println("December"); break;
    default: System.out.println("Hey, that's not a valid month!");
      break;
}
```

Loop Statements

You were introduced to Java's while statement earlier in this lesson (page 67). Java has two other looping constructs that you can use in your programs: the `for` loop and the `do-while` loop.

Use the `for` loop when you know the constraints of the loop: its initialization instruction, termination criteria, and increment instruction. For example, `for` loops are often used to iterate over the elements in an array or the characters in a string.

```
// a is an array of some kind
. . .
int length = a.length;
for (int i = 0; i < length; i++) {
    . . .
    // do something to the ith element of a
    . . .
}
```

You know when writing the program that you want to start at the beginning of the array, stop at the end, and hit every element. Thus the `for` statement is a good choice. The general form of the `for` statement can be expressed like this:

```
for (initialization; termination; increment)
    statements
```

initialization is a statement that initializes the loop—it is executed once at the beginning of the loop. *termination* is an expression that determines when to terminate the loop. This expression is evaluated at the top of each iteration of the loop. When the expression evaluates to `false`, the `for` loop terminates. Finally, *increment* is an expression that gets invoked for each iteration through the loop. Any (or all) of these components can be empty statements.

The do-while loop is similar to the while loop you met earlier, except that the expression is evaluated at the bottom of the loop:

```
do {
    statements
} while (booleanExpression);
```

The do-while statement is a less common loop construct in programming, but it does have its uses. It is convenient when the statements within the loop must be executed at least once. For example, when reading information from a file, you always have to read at least one character if only to find out if the character is the end-of-file character, so you may wish to use a do-while loop:

```
int c;
Reader in;
. . .
do {
    c = in.read();
    . . .
} while (c != -1);
```

Exception-Handling Statements

When an error occurs within a Java method, the method can use the throw statement to throw an exception indicating to its caller that an error occurred and the type of error that occurred. The calling method can use the try, catch, and finally statements to catch and handle the exception. See Essential Java Classes (page 241) for information about throwing and handling exceptions.

Branching Statements

You saw the break statement used in the switch statement earlier in this lesson. As noted there, break causes the flow of control to jump to the statement immediately following the current statement.

Another form of the break statement causes flow of control to break out of a labeled statement. You label a statement by placing a legal Java identifier (the label) followed by a colon : before the statement:

```
statementName: someJavaStatement
```

To break out of the statement labeled `statementName`, use the following form of the `break` statement:

```
break statementName;
```

Labeled breaks are a more controlled alternative to the `goto` statement, which is not supported by the Java language.

Use the `continue` statement within loops to jump to another statement. The `continue` statement has two forms: unlabeled and labeled. If you use the unlabeled form, control transfers to and reevaluates the termination condition of the loop. In `for` and `while` loops, this means that control returns to the top of the loop. In `do-while` loops, this means that control returns to the bottom of the loop.

Note: The `continue` statement can be called only from within a loop.

The labeled form of `continue` statement continues at the next iteration of the labeled loop. Consider this implementation of the `String` class's `indexOf` method, which uses the labeled form of `continue`:

```
public int indexOf(String str, int fromIndex) {
    char[] v1 = value;
    char[] v2 = str.value;
    int max = offset + (count - str.count);

  test:
    for (int i = offset + ((fromIndex < 0) ? 0 : fromIndex);
          i <= max ; i++) {
        int n = str.count;
        int j = i;
        int k = str.offset;
        while (n-- != 0) {
            if (v1[j++] != v2[k++]) {
                continue test;
            }
        }
        return i - offset;
    }
    return -1;
}
```

The last of Java's branching statements is the *return statement*. Use a `return` statement to exit from the current method and proceed with the statement that follows the original method call. There are two forms of `return`: one returns a value and one doesn't. To return a value, put the value, or an expression that calculates the value, after the `return` keyword:

```
return ++count;
```

The data type of the value returned by `return` must match the type of the method's declared return value.

When a method is declared `void`, use the form of `return` that doesn't return a value:

```
return;
```

Arrays and Strings

Like other programming languages, Java allows you to collect and manage multiple values through an array object. You manage data comprised of multiple characters through a `String` object.

Arrays

The `countChars` method doesn't use an array, but the `Count` class's `main` method declares an array as a parameter to `main`. This section shows you how to create and use arrays in your Java programs.

As for other variables, before you can use an array you must first declare it. Again, as for other variables, a declaration of an array has two primary components: the array type and the array name. The array type includes the data type of the elements contained within the array. You cannot have a generic array; the data type of an array's elements must be identified when the array is declared. Here's a declaration for an array of integers:

```
int[] arrayOfInts;
```

The `int[]` part of the declaration indicates that `arrayOfInts` is an array of integers. The declaration does not allocate any memory to contain the array elements. If your program attempts to assign or access any values to any elements of `arrayOfInts` before memory for it has been allocated, the compiler prints an error message similar to the following and refuses to compile your program:

```
testing.java:64: Variable arrayOfInts may not have been
initialized.
```

To allocate memory for the elements of the array, you must instantiate the array. You use Java's `new` operator to instantiate arrays. Actually, the steps you take to create an array are similar to the steps you take to create an object from a class: declaration, instantiation, and initialization. You can learn more about creating objects in the Creating Objects section (page 86) of the next lesson.

The following statement allocates enough memory for `arrayOfInts` to contain ten integers:

```
int[] arrayOfInts = new int[10];
```

In general, when creating an array, use the `new` operator, the data type of the array elements, and the number of elements desired, enclosed within square brackets `[` and `]`:

```
elementType[] arrayName = new elementType[arraySize];
```

Now that some memory has been allocated for your array, you can assign values to its elements and retrieve those values:

```
for (int j = 0; j < arrayOfInts.length; j++) {
    arrayOfInts[j] = j;
    System.out.println("[j] = " + arrayOfInts[j]);
}
```

This example shows that to reference an array element, you append square brackets to the array name. Between the square brackets indicate (either with a variable or some other expression) the index of the element you want to access. Note that in Java, array indices begin at 0 and end at the array length minus 1.

There's another interesting element (so to speak) in this code sample. The `for` loop iterates through each element of `arrayOfInts`, assigning values to its elements and printing out those values. Note the use of `arrayOfInts.length` to retrieve the current length of the array. `length` is a property provided for all Java arrays.

Let's look again at the `main` method that calls `countChars`. In particular note the use of the `args` array:

```
import java.io.*;
public class Count {
    // ... countChars method omitted ...
```

```
        public static void main(String[] args) throws Exception {
            if (args.length >= 1)
                countChars(new FileReader(args[0]));
            else
                System.err.println("Usage: Count filename");
        }
    }
```

The Java runtime allocates the space for the args array, so main doesn't have to bother with it. The main method ensures that there's at least one element in the args array, and if there is, it uses the first element in the array (presumably the name of a file) to open a FileReader.

Arrays can contain any legal Java data type, including reference types such as objects or other arrays. For example, the following declares and allocates memory for an array of ten String objects:

```
String[] arrayOfStrings = new String[10];
```

The elements in this array are reference types, that is, each element contains a reference to a String object. At this point, enough memory has been allocated to contain the String references, but no memory has been allocated for the String objects themselves. If you attempt to access one of the arrayOfStrings elements at this point, you will get a NullPointerException because the array is empty and contains no String objects. This is often a source of some confusion for programmers new to the Java language. You have to allocate the actual String objects separately, like this:

```
for (int i = 0; i < arrayOfStrings.length; i++)
    arrayOfStrings[i] = new String("String # " + i);
```

You use arrays when you know in advance the required size of the array. If you don't know the size of array that you need, consider using the java.util.Vector[1] class which implements a growable array.

Strings

A sequence of character data is called a *string*. A string is implemented in the Java platform by the String[2] class (a member of the java.lang package). Count's main method uses String in its declaration of the args array:

---

1 http://java.sun.com/products/jdk/1.1/docs/api/java.util.Vector.html

2 http://java.sun.com/products/jdk/1.1/docs/api/java.lang.String.html

```
String[] args
```

This statement explicitly declares an array named `args` that contains `String` objects. The empty brackets indicate that the length of the array is unknown at compilation time because the array is passed in at runtime. The `countChars` method also uses two `Strings` both in the form of a *literal string* (a series of characters between double quotation marks):

```
"Counted "
    . . .
" chars."
```

The program implicitly allocates two `String` objects, one for each of the two literal strings shown previously.

`String` objects are *immutable*—that is, they cannot be changed once they've been created. The `java.lang` package provides a different class, `StringBuffer`, which you can use to create and manipulate character data on the fly. Using String and StringBuffer (page 247) covers thoroughly the use of both the `String` and `StringBuffer` classes.

String Concatenation

Java lets you concatenate strings together easily using the + operator. The `countChars` method uses this feature of the Java language to print its output. The following code snippet concatenates three strings together to produce its output:

```
"Counted " + count + " chars."
```

Two of the strings concatenated together are literal strings: `"Counted "` and `" chars."`. The third string—the one in the middle—is actually an integer that first gets converted to a `String` and then is concatenated to the others.

6

Objects and Classes in Java

IN the lesson entitled Object-Oriented Programming Concepts (page 39) you read about the concepts behind object-oriented programming. Now it's time to get to work and put those concepts to practical use in Java.

To understand objects, you must understand classes. To understand classes, you need to understand objects. It's a circular process of learning. But you've got to begin somewhere. So, let's begin with two classes—`Point` and `Rectangle`—that are small and easy to understand. After a brief discussion of these classes and the introduction of some important concepts and terminology, The Life Cycle of an Object (page 86) shows you how to create a Rectangle object from the `Rectangle` class, use it, and eventually get rid of it.

Following that, Creating Classes (page 93) provides a complete description of a larger class, `Stack`, and describes all of the components in a class that provide for the life cycle of an object created from it. It talks first about constructors, then about member variables and methods, and finally about the `finalize` method.

The last section of this chapter, Reality Break! The Spot Applet (page 125), contains the code for a fun little applet. Through that applet, you will learn how to subclass another class, how to implement an interface, and how to use an inner class to implement an adapter.

A Brief Introduction to Classes

Following is the code for a class called `Point` that represents a point in 2D space:

```
public class Point {
    public int x = 0;
    public int y = 0;
}
```

This segment of code declares a class—a new data type really—called `Point`. The `Point` class contains two integer *member variables*, `x` and `y`. The public keyword preceding the declaration for `x` and `y` means that any other class can freely access these two members.

You create an object from a class such as `Point` by instantiating the class. When you create a new `Point` object (we show you how shortly), space is allocated for the object and its members `x` and `y`. In addition, the `x` and `y` members inside the object are initialized to `0` because of the assignment statements in the declarations of these two members. See Figure 12.

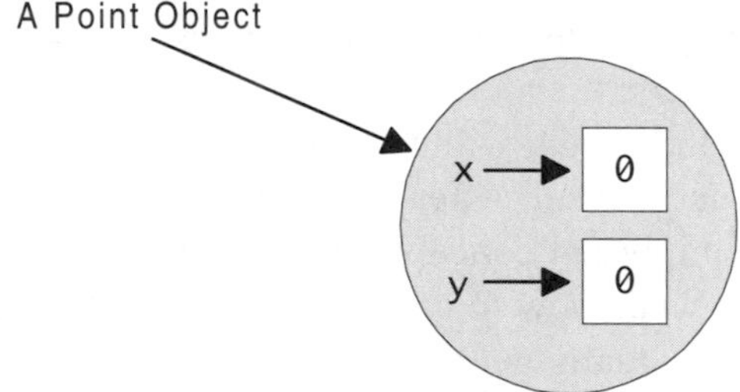

Figure 12: When you create a new `Point` object, space is allocated for the object and its members `x` and `y;` `x` and `y` are also initialized to `0`.

Now, here's a class, `Rectangle`, that represents a rectangle in 2D space:

```
public class Rectangle {
    public int width = 0;
    public int height = 0;
    public Point origin = new Point();
}
```

This segment of code declares a class (another data type)—`Rectangle`—that contains two integer members, `width` and `height`. `Rectangle` also contains a third member, `origin`, whose data type is `Point`. Notice that the class name

`Point` is used in a variable declaration as the variable's type. You can use the name of a class anywhere you can use the name of a primitive type.

Just as `width` "is an" integer and `height` "is an" integer, `origin` "is a" `Point`. On the other hand, a `Rectangle` object "has a" `Point`. The distinction between "is a" and "has a" is critical because only an object that "is a" `Point` can be used where a `Point` is called for.

As with `Point`, when you create a new `Rectangle` object, space is allocated for the object and its members, and the members are initialized according to their declarations. Interestingly, the initialization for the `origin` member creates a `Point` object with this code: `new Point()`. Figure 13 illustrates this.

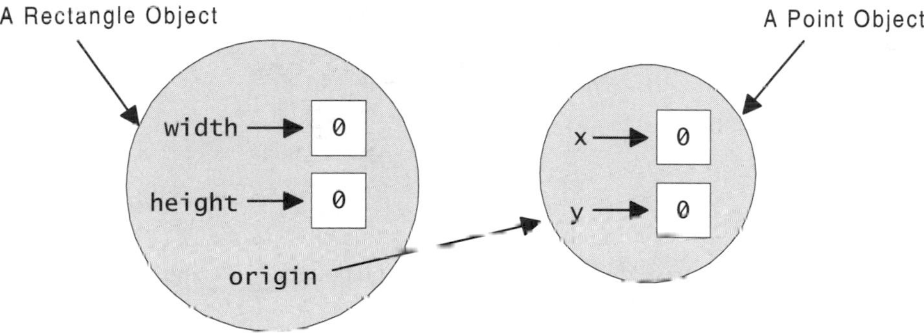

Figure 13: A new `Rectangle` object.

This diagram shows the difference between primitive types and reference types. Both `width` and `height` are integers and are fully contained within `Rectangle`. On the other hand, `origin` simply references a `Point` object somewhere else.

The `Point` and `Rectangle` classes as shown are simplistic implementations for these classes. Both should provide a mechanism for initializing their members to values other than `0`. Additionally, `Rectangle` could provide a method for computing its area, and because `Rectangle` creates a `Point` when it's created, the class should provide for the clean up of the `Point` when `Rectangle` gets cleaned up. So, here's a new version of `Point` that contains a constructor which you can use to initialize a new `Point` to a value other than (0,0):

```
public class Point {
    public int x = 0;
    public int y = 0;
    // a constructor!
    public Point(int x, int y) {
```

```
            this.x = x;
            this.y = y;
        }
    }
```

Now, when you create a `Point`, you can provide initial values for it like this:

```
new Point(44, 78)
```

The values `44` and `78` are passed into the constructor and subsequently assigned to the `x` and `y` members of the new `Point` object. Figure 14 illustrates this.

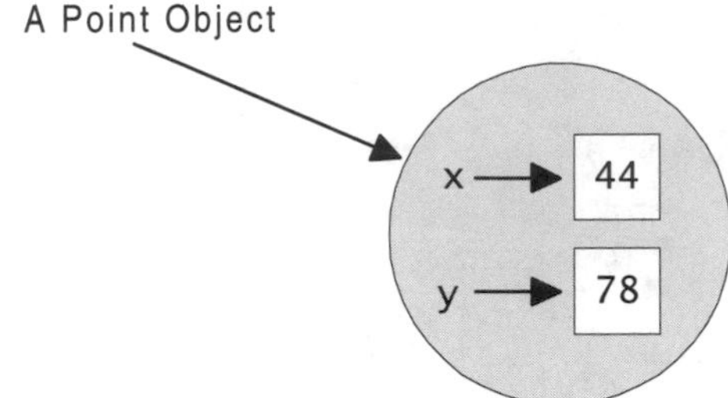

Figure 14: Values are passed into the constructor and assigned to `x` and `y`.

Now, let's beef up the `Rectangle` class. Here's a new version of `Rectangle` that contains four constructors, a method to "move" the rectangle, a method to compute the area of the rectangle, and a `finalize` method to provide for clean up:

```
public class Rectangle {
    public int width = 0;
    public int height = 0;
    public Point origin;
    // four constructors
    public Rectangle() {
        origin = new Point(0, 0);
    }
    public Rectangle(Point p) {
        origin = p;
    }
    public Rectangle(int w, int h) {
        this(new Point(0, 0), w, h);
    }
    public Rectangle(Point p, int w, int h) {
        origin = p;
        width = w;
        height = h;
```

```
    }
    // a method for moving the rectangle
    public void move(int x, int y) {
        origin.x = x;
        origin.y = y;
    }
    // a method for computing the area of the rectangle
    public int area {
        return width * height;
    }
    // clean up!
    protected void finalize() throws Throwable {
        origin = null;
        super.finalize();
    }
}
```

The four constructors allow for different types of initialization. You can create a new `Rectangle` and let it provide default values for everything, or you can specify initial values for the origin, the width and the height, or for all three when you create the object. You'll see more of this version of the `Rectangle` class in the next section.

This section glossed over some details and left some things unexplained, but it provides the basis you need to understand the rest of this lesson. After reading this section, you should know

- Objects are created from classes
- An object's class is its type
- How "is a" differs from "has a"
- The difference between reference and primitive types

You also should have a general understanding or a feeling for the following:

- How to create an object from a class
- What constructors are
- What the code for a class looks like
- What member variables are
- How to initialize objects
- What methods look like

Now, let's look in detail at the life cycle of an object, specifically how to create, use, and destroy an object.

The Life Cycle of an Object

Typically, a Java program creates many objects from a variety of classes. These objects interact with one another by sending each other messages. Through these object interactions, a Java program can implement a GUI, run an animation, or send and receive information over a network. Once an object has completed the work for which it was created, it is garbage-collected and its resources are recycled for use by other objects. The following three sections, describe the typical life cycle of an object:

1. Creation
2. Use
3. Destruction

Creating Objects

In Java, you create an object by creating an *instance* of a class or, in other words, *instantiating* a class. Often, you will see a Java object created with a statement like the following, which creates a new `Rectangle` object from the `Rectangle` class given in the previous section:

```
Rectangle rect = new Rectangle();
```

This single statement performs three actions:

1. **Declaration:** `Rectangle rect` is a variable declaration that declares to the compiler that the name `rect` will be used to refer to a `Rectangle` object. Notice that a class name is used as the variable's type.
2. **Instantiation:** `new` is a Java operator that creates the new object (allocates space for it).
3. **Initialization:** `Rectangle()` is a call to `Rectangle`'s constructor, which initializes the object.

Declaring an Object

The declaration of an object is not a necessary part of object creation, although it often appears on the same line. Like other variable declarations, object declarations can also appear alone, like this:

```
Rectangle rect;
```

Variables and Data Types (page 51) in the previous lesson discussed variable declarations in detail. To declare an object, you just follow the same rules and declare a variable to refer to that object by declaring its type and name:

```
type name
```

In Java, classes and interfaces can be used as data types. So *type* can be the name of a class such as the `Rectangle` class or the name of an interface. Classes and interfaces are both reference types (the variable's actual value is a reference to the value or set of values represented by the variable). In this tutorial, a reference may also be called an *object reference* or an *array reference*, depending on the data to which the reference refers.

Declarations notify the compiler that you will use *name* to refer to a variable whose type is *type*. *Declarations do not create new objects.* `Rectangle rect` does not create a new `Rectangle` object, just a variable named `rect` to hold a `Rectangle` object. To create a `Rectangle` object or any other object, use the `new` operator.

Instantiating an Object

The `new` operator instantiates a class by allocating memory for a new object of that type. `new` requires a single, postfix argument: a call to a constructor. Each Java class provides a set of constructors used to initialize new objects of that type. The `new` operator creates the object, and the constructor initializes it. Here's an example of using the `new` operator to create a `Rectangle` object:

```
new Rectangle(100, 200)
```

Here, `Rectangle(100, 200)` is the argument to `new`. The `new` operator returns a reference to the newly created object. This reference can be assigned to a variable of the appropriate type, as shown here:

```
Rectangle rect = new Rectangle(100, 200);
```

After this statement, `rect` refers to a `Rectangle` object whose origin is at (0, 0), width is 100, and height is 200.

Initializing an Object

As shown in the code for the `Rectangle` class on page 84, classes can provide one or more constructors to initialize a new object of that type. You can recognize a class's constructors because they have the same name as the class and have no return type. Here are the declarations for `Rectangle`'s constructors:

```
public Rectangle(Point p)
public Rectangle(int w, int h)
public Rectangle(Point p, int w, int h)
public Rectangle()
```

Each of these constructors lets you provide initial values for different aspects of the rectangle: the origin, the width and height, all three, or none. If a class has multiple constructors, they all have the same name but a different number of arguments or different typed arguments. The compiler differentiates the constructors, and knows which one to call, depending on the arguments. So when the compiler encounters the following code, it knows to call the constructor that requires two integer arguments (which initializes the width and height of the new rectangle to the values provided by the arguments):

```
Rectangle rect = new Rectangle(100, 200);
```

And when the compiler encounters the next line of code, it knows to call the constructor that requires a `Point` (which provides the initial values for the origin of the new `Rectangle`):

```
Rectangle rect = new Rectangle(new Point(44,78));
```

The `Rectangle` constructor used below doesn't take any arguments:

```
Rectangle rect = new Rectangle();
```

A constructor that takes no arguments, such as the one shown, is called a no-argument constructor. If a class (like the very first versions of the `Point` and `Rectangle` classes) does not explicitly define any constructors at all, Java automatically provides a no-argument constructor, called the *default constructor*, that does nothing. Thus all classes have at least one constructor.

This section talked about how to use a constructor. Providing Constructors for Your Classes (page 96) later in this lesson explains how to write constructors for your classes.

Using Objects

Once you've created an object, you probably want to use it for something. You may need information from it, want to change its state, or have it perform some action.

Objects give you two ways to do these things:

1. Manipulate or inspect its variables.
2. Call its methods.

Ideal object-oriented programming discourages the direct manipulation of an object's variables; you could potentially put the object into an inconsistent state. Instead, an ideal object provides methods through which you can inspect or change its state. These methods ensure that the object never gets into an inconsistent state. However, in practical situations, it sometimes makes sense to use an object's variables directly.

Both the `Point` class and the `Rectangle` class allow free access to their member variables. You cannot put a `Point` object in an inconsistent state by setting `x` or `y` directly, and you cannot put a `Rectangle` object in an inconsistent state by setting `width`, `height`, or `origin`.

Java provides an access control mechanism whereby classes can restrict or allow access to its variables and methods. A class should protect variables against direct manipulation by other objects if those manipulations could endanger the object's state. State changes should then be affected and therefore controlled by method calls. If an object grants access to its variables, you can assume that you can inspect and change them without adverse effects. To learn more about Java's access control mechanism, refer to Controlling Access to Members of a Class (page 113).

So, back to the `Rectangle` object. Suppose a `Rectangle` object represents a rectangular object in a drawing program and the user just dragged it to a new location. You need to update the `Rectangle` object's point of origin. The `Rectangle` class provides two equivalent ways of doing this:

1. Manipulate the object's `origin` variable directly.
2. Call the `move` method.

`Rectangle`'s `origin` member is accessible to other classes (it's declared public), so you can assume that manipulating a `Rectangle`'s `origin` member directly is safe.

Referencing an Object's Variables

This section focuses on how to move the `Rectangle` by modifying its `origin` variable directly. The next section shows you how to move the rectangle by calling the `move` method.

Assume you created a rectangle named `rect` as described in the previous section. To move `rect` to a new location, you would write:

```
rect.origin = new Point(15, 37);
```

This statement moves the rectangle by setting its point of origin to a new position. `rect.origin` is the name of `rect`'s `origin` variable. You can use these kinds of object variable names in the same manner as you use other variables names. Thus, as in the previous example code, you can use the = operator to assign a value to `rect.origin`.

The `Rectangle` class has two other variables—`width` and `height`—that are accessible to objects outside of the class. You can use the same notation to access them and calculate the rectangle's area using this statement (or you could just call the `area` method):

```
area = rect.height * rect.width;
```

In general, to refer to an object's variables, append the name of the variable to an *object reference* with an intervening period (`.`):

```
objectReference.variable
```

The first part of the variable's name, *`objectReference`*, must be a reference to an object. You can use an object name here just as was done in the previous examples with `rect`. You also can use any expression that returns an object reference. Recall that the `new` operator returns a reference to an object. So you could use the value returned from `new` to access a new object's variables:

```
height = new Rectangle().height;
```

This statement creates a new `Rectangle` object and immediately gets its height. Effectively, the statement calculates the default height of a `Rectangle`. Note that after this statement has been executed, the program no longer has a reference to the `Rectangle` that was created because the program never stored the reference in a variable. Thus the object becomes eligible for garbage collection.

Here's a final word about accessing an object's variables to clear up a point of some confusion that beginning Java programmers often have. All objects of the same type have the same variables. All `Rectangle` objects have `origin`, `width`, and `height` variables that they got from the `Rectangle` class. When you access a variable through an object reference, you reference that particular object's variables. Suppose that `bob` is also a rectangle in your drawing program and it has a different height and width than `rect`. The following instruction calculates the area of the rectangle named `bob`, which differs from the previous instruction that calculated the area of `rect`:

```
area = bob.height * bob.width;
```

Calling an Object's Methods

To move `rect` to a new location using its `move` method, you write this:

```
rect.move(15, 37);
```

This Java statement calls `rect`'s `move` method with two integer parameters, 15 and 37. It moves the `rect` object because the `move` method assigns new values to `origin.x` and `origin.y` and is equivalent to the assignment statements used previously:

```
rect.origin = new Point(15, 37);
```

The notation used to call an object's method is similar to that used when referring to its variables: You append the method name to an object reference with an intervening period (.). Also, you provide any arguments to the method within enclosing parentheses. If the method does not require any arguments, use empty parentheses.

```
objectReference.methodName(argumentList);
   or
objectReference.methodName();
```

As stated previously in this lesson, *`objectReference`* must be a reference to an object. You can use a variable name here, but you also can use any expression that returns an object reference. The `new` operator returns an object reference, so you can use the value returned from `new` to call a new object's methods:

```
new Rectangle(100, 50).area()
```

The expression `new Rectangle(100, 50)` returns an object reference that refers to a `Rectangle` object. As shown, you can use the dot notation to call the new `Rectangle`'s `area` method to compute the area of the new rectangle.

Some methods, like `area`, return a value. For methods that return a value, you can use the method call in expressions. You can assign the return value to a variable, use it to make decisions, or control a loop. This code assigns the value returned by `area` to a variable:

```
int areaOfRectangle = new Rectangle(100, 50).area();
```

Remember, invoking a method on a particular object is the same as sending a message to that object. In this case, the object is the rectangle called `rect`. You will probably get a different response if you send the same message to `bob`.

Cleaning Up Unused Objects

Many other object-oriented languages require that you keep track of all of the objects you create and that you explicitly destroy them when they are no longer needed. This technique of managing memory is tedious and often error-prone. Java allows you to create as many objects as you want (limited, of course, by what your system can handle), and you never have to worry about destroying them. The Java runtime environment deletes objects when it determines that they are no longer being used. This process is called *garbage collection*. The next section discusses this in more detail.

An object is eligible for garbage collection when there are no more references to that object. References that are held in a variable are naturally dropped when the variable goes out of scope. Or you can explicitly drop an object reference by setting the variable to `null`.

The Garbage Collector

The Java platform has a garbage collector that periodically frees the memory used by objects that are no longer needed. The Java garbage collector is a *mark-sweep* garbage collector. A mark-sweep garbage collector scans dynamic memory areas for objects and marks those that are referenced. After all possible paths to objects are investigated, unmarked objects (unreferenced objects) are known to be garbage and are collected. (A more complete description of Java's garbage collection algorithm might be "a compacting, mark-sweep collector with some conservative scanning.")

The garbage collector runs in a low-priority thread and runs either *synchronously* or *asynchronously* depending on the situation and the system on which Java is running. It runs synchronously when the system runs out of memory or in response to a request from a Java program.

The Java garbage collector runs *asynchronously* when the system is idle, but it does so only on systems, such as Win32, that allow the Java runtime environment to note when a thread has begun and to interrupt another thread. As soon as another thread becomes active, the garbage collector is asked to get to a consistent state and terminate.

Finalization

Before an object gets garbage-collected, the garbage collector gives the object an opportunity to clean up after itself through a call to the object's `finalize` method. This process is known as *finalization*.

During finalization, an object may wish to free system resources such as files and sockets or to drop references to other objects so that they in turn become eligible for garbage collection. The `finalize` method for the `Rectangle` class releases the `Point` object by setting its reference to `origin` to `null`:

```
protected void finalize() throws Throwable {
    origin = null;
    super.finalize();
}
```

The `finalize` method is a member of the `Object` class. The `Object` class is the top of Java's class hierarchy and the parent of everything. A class should override the `finalize` method to perform any finalization necessary for objects of that type. Note that `Rectangle`'s `finalize` method calls `super.finalize` to give the parent class a chance for final cleanup as well. Generally speaking, a `finalize` method should call `super.finalize` as the last thing it does. You can read more in Writing a finalize Method (page 125).

Creating Classes

Now that we've covered how to create, use, and destroy objects, it's time to show you how to write the classes from which objects are created. This section shows you the main components of a class through a small example that implements a last-in-first-out (LIFO) stack. The diagram in Figure 15 lists the class and identifies the structure of the code.

This implementation of a stack uses another object, a `Vector`[1], to store its elements. `Vector` is a growable array of objects and does a nice job of allocating space for new objects as space is required. The `Stack` class makes use of this code by using a `Vector` to store its elements. However, it imposes LIFO restrictions on the `Vector`—that is, you can only add elements to and remove elements from the top of the stack.

Figure 15 shows that two primary components make up the implementation of a class: the *class declaration* and the *class body*. The class declaration declares the

---

1 http://java.sun.com/products/jdk/1.1/docs/api/java.util.Vector.html

name of the class along with other attributes. The class declaration for the `Stack` class is fairly simple and indicates that the class is `public` and that its name is `Stack`. Often, a minimal class declaration such as this one is all you'll need.

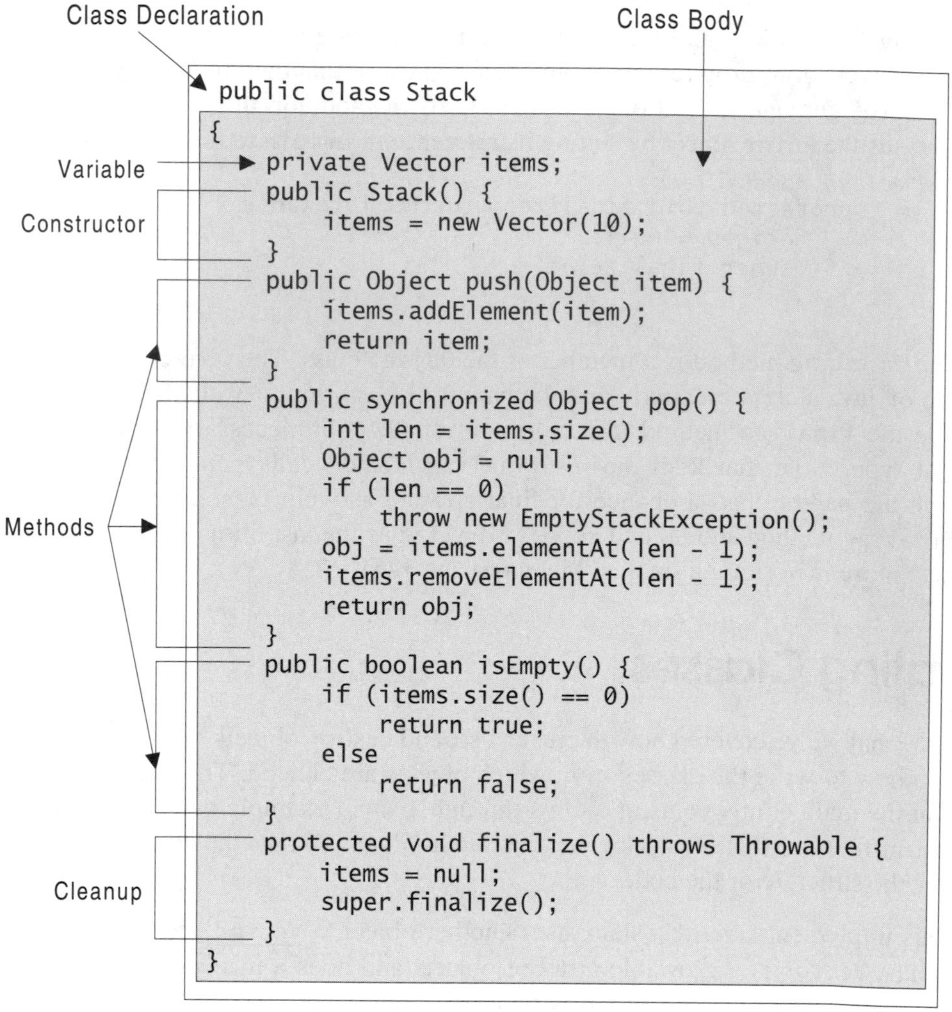
Class Declaration
Class Body
Variable
Constructor
Methods
Cleanup
public class Stack
{
private Vector items;
public Stack() {
items = new Vector(10);
}
public Object push(Object item) {
items.addElement(item);
return item;
}
public synchronized Object pop() {
int len = items.size();
Object obj = null;
if (len == 0)
throw new EmptyStackException();
obj = items.elementAt(len - 1);
items.removeElementAt(len - 1);
return obj;
}
public boolean isEmpty() {
if (items.size() == 0)
return true;
else
return false;
}
protected void finalize() throws Throwable {
items = null;
super.finalize();
}
}

Figure 15: The class and structure of the code implementing a LIFO stack.

However, the class declaration can say more about the class, such as the name of the superclass and if it can be subclassed. The left side of Figure 16 shows the possible components of a class declaration in the order they should or must appear in your class declaration. The right side describes their purposes. The required components are the `class` keyword and the class name and are shown in bold. All the other components are optional, and each appears on a line by itself (thus "extends *Super*" is a single component). Italics indicates an identifier such as the name of a class or interface. If you do not explicitly declare the optional items, the Java compiler assumes certain defaults: a nonpublic, nonabstract, nonfinal subclass of `Object` that implements no interfaces.

`public`	Class is publicly accessible.
`abstract`	Class cannot be instantiated.
`final`	Class cannot be subclassed.
`class` *NameOfClass*	***Name of the Class.***
`extends` *Super*	Superclass of the class.
`implements` *Interfaces*	Interfaces implemented by the class.
`{` *ClassBody* `}`	

Figure 16: The possible components of a class declaration and their purposes.

The following list provides a few more details about each class declaration component. It also provides references to sections later in this trail that talk about what each component means, how to use each, and how it affects your class, other classes, and your Java program.

`public` By default, a class can be used only by other classes in the same package. The `public` modifier declares that the class can be used by any class regardless of its package. Look in Creating and Using Packages (page 156) for information about how to use `public` to limit access to your classes and how it affects your access to other classes.

`abstract` Declares that the class cannot be instantiated. For a discussion about when abstract classes are appropriate and how to write them, see Writing Abstract Classes and Methods (page 142).

`final` Declares that the class cannot be subclassed. Writing Final Classes and Methods (page 141) shows you how to use `final` and discusses the reasons for using it.

`class` *NameOfClass*

The `class` keyword indicates to the compiler that this is a class declaration and that the name of the class is ***NameOfClass***.

`extends` *`Super`*

The `extends` clause identifies `Super` as the superclass of the class, thereby inserting the class within the class hierarchy. Reality Break! The Spot Applet (page 125) in this lesson shows you a subclass of `Applet` and talks briefly about the responsibilities and benefits of subclasses. Managing Inheritance (page 134) in the next lesson goes into further detail on this subject.

`implements` *`Interfaces`*

To declare that your class implements one or more interfaces, use the keyword `implements` followed by a comma-delimited list of the names of the interfaces implemented by the class. Implementing an Interface (page 127) explains how the `Spot` applet implements an interface. Details about writing your own interfaces can be found in Creating Interfaces (page 145).

The class body contains all of the code that provides for the life cycle of the objects created from it: constructors for initializing new objects, declarations for the variables that provide the state of the class and its objects, methods to implement the behavior of the class and its objects, and when necessary, a `finalize` method to provide for cleaning up an object after it has done its job.

Variables and methods collectively are called *members*.

Note: Constructors are not methods. Nor are they members.

The `Stack` class defines one member variable in its body to contain its elements—the `items Vector`. It also defines one constructor—a no-argument constructor—and four methods: `push`, `pop`, `isEmpty`, and `finalize`. Recall that `finalize` is a special method that provides for the clean up of `Stack` objects.

Providing Constructors for Your Classes

All Java classes have constructors that are used to initialize a new object of that type. A constructor has the same name as the class. For example, the name of the `Stack` class's constructor is `Stack`, the name of the `Rectangle` class's constructor is `Rectangle`, and the name of the `Thread` class's constructor is `Thread`. `Stack` defines a single constructor:

```
public Stack() {
    items = new Vector(10);
}
```

Java supports name overloading for constructors so that a class can have any number of constructors, all of which have the same name. Following is another constructor that could be defined by `Stack`. This particular constructor sets the initial size of the stack according to its parameter:

```
public Stack(int initialSize) {
    items = new Vector(initialSize);
}
```

Both constructors share the same name, `Stack`, but they have different parameter lists. The compiler differentiates these constructors based on the number of parameters in the list and their types.

Typically, a constructor uses its arguments to initialize the new object's state. When creating an object, choose the constructor whose arguments best reflect how you want to initialize the new object.

Based on the number and type of the arguments that you pass into the constructor, the compiler can determine which constructor to use. The compiler knows that when you write the following code, it should use the constructor that requires a single integer argument:

```
new Stack(10)
```

Similarly, when you write the following code, the compiler chooses the no-argument constructor or the default constructor:

```
new Stack()
```

When writing your own class, you don't have to provide constructors for it. The default constructor is automatically provided by the runtime system for any class that contains no constructors. The default provided by the runtime system doesn't do anything. So, if you want to perform some initialization, you will have to write some constructors for your class.

The constructor for the following subclass of `Thread` performs animation, sets up some default values, such as the frame speed and the number of images, and then loads the images:

```
class AnimationThread extends Thread {
    int framesPerSecond;
    int numImages;
    Image[] images;

    AnimationThread(int fps, int num) {

        super("AnimationThread");
        this.framesPerSecond = fps;
        this.numImages = num;

        this.images = new Image[numImages];
        for (int i = 0; i <= numImages; i++) {
            . . .
            // Load all the images.
            . . .
        }
    }
    . . .
}
```

Note how the body of a constructor is like the body of a method; that is, it contains local variable declarations, loops, and other statements. However, one line in the `AnimationThread` constructor that you wouldn't see in a method is the second line:

```
super("AnimationThread");
```

This line invokes a constructor provided by the superclass of `AnimationThread`, namely, `Thread`. This particular `Thread` constructor takes a `String` that sets the name of `Thread`. Often a constructor wants to take advantage of initialization code written in a class's superclass. Indeed, some classes *must* call their superclass constructor in order for the object to work properly. If present, the superclass constructor must be the first statement in the subclass's constructor: An object should perform the higher-level initialization first.

When declaring constructors for your class, use the following access specifiers in the constructor declaration to specify what other objects can create instances of your class:

`private` No other class can instantiate your class. Your class may contain public class methods (sometimes called *factory methods*), and those methods can construct an object and return it, but no other classes can.

`protected` Only subclasses of your class can create instances of it.

`public` Any class can create an instance of your class.

`package` Only classes within the same package as your class can construct an instance of it.

Constructors provide a way to initialize a new object. Initializing Instance and Class Members (page 122) describes other ways you can provide for the initialization of your class and a new object created from the class. This section also discusses when and why you would use each technique.

Declaring Member Variables

`Stack` uses the following line of code to define its single member variable:

```
private Vector items;
```

This declares a member variable and not some other type of variable (like a local variable) because the declaration appears within the class body but outside of any methods or constructors. The member variable declared is named `items`, and its data type is `Vector`. Also, the `private` keyword identifies `items` as a private member. This means that only code within the `Stack` class can access it.

`accessLevel`	Indicates the access level for this member.
`static`	Declares a class member.
`final`	Indicates that it is constant.
`transient`	This variable is transient.
`volatile`	This variable is volatile.
`type name`	The type and name of the variable.

Figure 17: Member Variable Declarations. Only the type and name are required components of a member variable declaration. The rest are optional.

This is a relatively simple member variable declaration, but declarations can be more complex. You can specify not only type, name, and access level, but also other attributes, including whether the variable is a class or instance variable and whether it's a constant. Each component of a member variable declaration is further defined below:

`accessLevel`

Lets you control which other classes have access to a member variable by using one of four access levels: public, protected, package, and private. You control access to methods in the same way. Controlling Access to Members of a Class (page 113) covers access levels in detail.

`static` Declares this is a class variable rather than an instance variable. You also use `static` to declare class methods. Understanding Instance and Class Members (page 118) later in this lesson talks about declaring instance and class variables.

`final` Indicates that the value of this member cannot change. The following variable declaration defines a constant named `AVOGADRO`, whose value is Avogadro's number (6.023×10^{23}) and cannot be changed:

```
final double AVOGADRO = 6.023e23;
```

It's a compile-time error if your program ever tries to change a final variable. By convention, the name of constant values are spelled in uppercase letters.

`transient` The `transient` marker is not fully specified by *The Java Language Specification* but is used in object serialization, which is covered in Object Serialization (page 388), to mark member variables that should *not* be serialized.

`volatile` The `volatile` keyword is used to prevent the compiler from performing certain optimizations on a member. This is an advanced Java feature, used by only a few Java programmers, and is outside the scope of this tutorial.

type Like other variables, a member variable must have a type. You can use primitive type names such as `int`, `float`, or `boolean`. Or you can use reference types, such as array, object, or interface names.

name A member variable's name can be any legal Java identifier and, by convention, begins with a lowercase letter. You cannot declare more than one member variable with the same name in the same class, but a subclass can hide a member variable of the same name in its superclass. Additionally, a member variable and a method can have the same name. For example, the following code is legal:

```
public class Stack {
    private Vector items;
    // a method with same name as a member variable
    public Vector items() {
        . . .
    }
}
```

Implementing Methods

Figure 18 shows the code for Stack's push method. This method pushes an object, the one passed in as an argument, onto the top of the stack, and returns it.

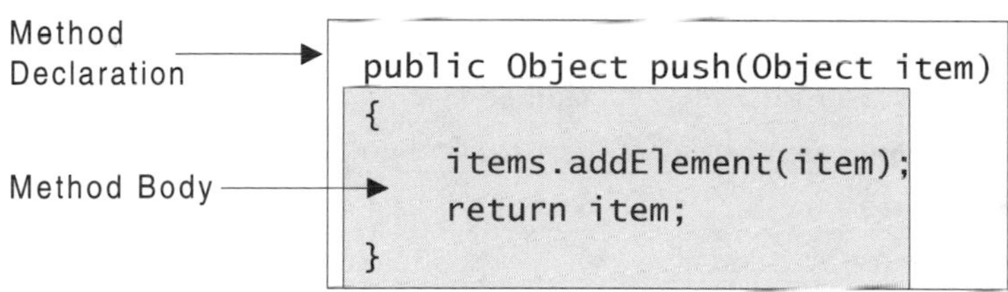

Figure 18: The code for Stack's push method.

Like a class, a method has two major parts: *method declaration* and *method body.* The method declaration defines all of the method's attributes, such as access level, return type, name, and arguments, as illustrated in Figure 19.

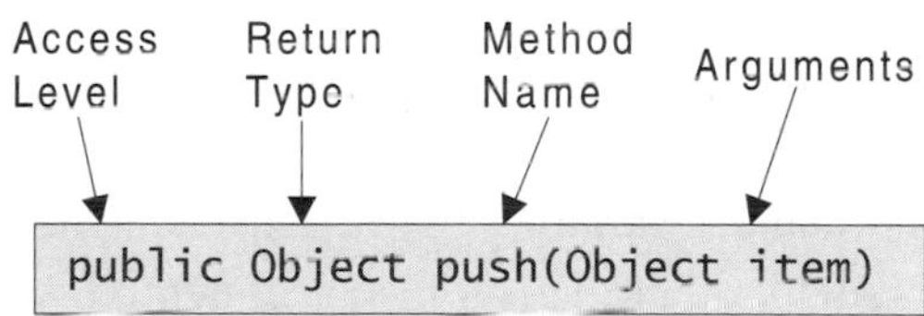

Figure 19: The parts of the method declaration.

The method body is where all the action takes place. It contains the Java instructions that implement the method.

Details of a Method Declaration

A method's declaration provides a lot of information about the method to the compiler, to the runtime system, and to other classes and objects. Included is not only the name of the method, but also such information as the return type of the method, the number and type of the arguments required by the method, and which other classes and objects can call the method.

While this may sound like writing a novel rather than simply declaring a method, most method attributes can be declared implicitly. The only required elements of a method declaration are the method's name, its return type, and a pair of parentheses ( ). Figure 20 shows the elements of a method declaration.

accessLevel	Access level for this method.
static	This is a class method.
abstract	This method is not implemented.
final	Method cannot be overridden.
native	Method implemented in another language.
synchronized	Method requires a monitor to run.
returnType methodName	The return type and method name.
(*paramlist*)	The list of arguments.
throws *exceptions*	The exceptions thrown by this method.

Figure 20: Elements of a method declaration.

Each element of a method declaration is further defined below:

accessLevel

As with member variables, you control which other classes have access to a method using one of four access levels: public, protected, package, and private. Controlling Access to Members of a Class (page 113) covers access levels in detail.

`static` As with member variables, `static` declares this method as a class method rather than an instance method. Understanding Instance and Class Members (page 118) talks about declaring instance and class methods.

`abstract` An abstract method has no implementation and must be a member of an abstract class. Refer to Writing Abstract Classes and Methods (page 142) for information about why you might want to write an abstract method and how such methods affect subclasses.

`final` A final method cannot be overridden by subclasses. Writing Final Classes and Methods (page 141) discusses why you might want to write `final` methods, how they affect subclasses, and whether you might want to write a `final` class instead.

`native` If you have a significant library of functions written in another language such as C, you may wish to preserve that investment and use those functions from Java. Methods implemented in a language other than Java are called *native methods* and are declared as such using the `native` keyword. Check our Web site for information about writing native methods.[1]

`synchronized`

Concurrently running threads often invoke methods that operate on the same data. These methods may be declared `synchronized` to ensure that the threads access information in a thread-safe manner. Synchronizing method calls is covered in Doing Two or More Tasks at Once: Threads (page 327). Take particular note of the section entitled Synchronizing Threads (page 346).

`returnType` Java requires that a method declare the data type of the value that it returns. If your method does not return a value, use the keyword `void` for the return type. Returning a Value from a Method (page 104) talks about the issues related to returning values from a method.

`methodName` A method name can be any legal Java identifier. You need to consider several issues in regards to Java method names. These are covered in Method Names (page 105).

`(` *`paramlist`* `)`

You pass information into a method through its arguments. See the next section, Passing Information into a Method (page 106).

`throws` ***`exceptions`***

If your method throws any checked exceptions, your method declaration must indicate the type of those exceptions. See

---

[1] http://java.sun.com/docs/books/tutorial/native1.1/index.html

Handling Errors with Exceptions (page 293) for information. In particular, refer to Specifying the Exceptions Thrown by a Method (page 316).

Returning a Value from a Method

You declare a method's return type in its method declaration. Within the body of the method, you use the `return` operator to return the value. Any method that is *not* declared `void` must contain a `return` statement. The `Stack` class declares the `isEmpty` method, which returns a `boolean`:

```
public boolean isEmpty() {
    if (items.size() == 0)
        return true;
    else
        return false;
}
```

The data type of the return value must match the method's return type; you can't return an `Object` type from a method declared to return an integer. The `isEmpty` method returns either the `boolean` value `true` or `false`, depending on the outcome of a test. A compiler error results if you try to write a method in which the return value doesn't match the return type.

The `isEmpty` method returns a primitive type. Methods also can return a reference type. For example, `Stack` declares the `pop` method that returns the `Object` reference type:

```
public synchronized Object pop() {
    int len = items.size();
    Object obj = null;
    if (len == 0)
        throw new EmptyStackException();
    obj = items.elementAt(len - 1);
    items.removeElementAt(len - 1);
    return obj;
}
```

When a method returns an object such as `pop` does, the class of the returned object must be either a subclass of or the exact class of the return type. This can be a source of confusion, so let's look at this more closely. Suppose you have a class hierarchy where `ImaginaryNumber` is a subclass of `java.lang.Number`, which is, in turn, a subclass of `Object`, as illustrated in Figure 21.

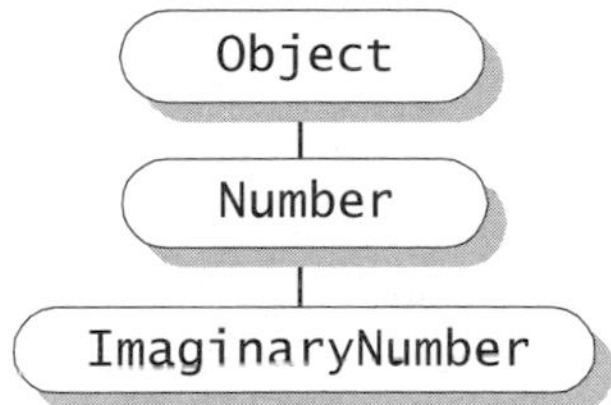

Figure 21: `ImaginaryNumber` is a subclass of `java.lang.Number`, which is a subclass of `Object`.

Now suppose you have a method declared to return a `Number`:

```
public Number returnANumber() {
    . . .
}
```

The `returnANumber` method can return an `ImaginaryNumber` but not an `Object`. `ImaginaryNumber` "is a" `Number` because it's a subclass of `Number`. However, an `Object` is not necessarily a `Number`—it could be a `String` or some other type.

You also can use interface names as return types. In this case, the object returned must implement the specified interface.

Method Names

Java supports method name overloading so that multiple methods can share the same name. For example, suppose you are writing a class that can render various types of data (strings, integers, and so on) to its drawing area. You need to write a method that knows how to render each data type. In other languages, you have to think of a new name for each method, for example, `drawString`, `drawInteger`, `drawFloat`, and so on. In Java, you can use the same name for all of the drawing methods but pass a different type of parameter to each method. So, in your data rendering class, you can declare three methods named `draw`, each of which takes a different type of parameter:

```
class DataRenderer {
    void draw(String s) {
        . . .
    }
```

```
        void draw(int i) {
            . . .
        }
        void draw(float f) {
            . . .
        }
    }
```

Overloaded methods are differentiated by the number and type of the arguments passed into the method. In the code sample, `draw(String s)` and `draw(int i)` are distinct and unique methods because they require different argument types. You cannot declare more than one method with the same name and the same number and type of arguments because the compiler cannot differentiate them. So, `draw(String s)` and `draw(String t)` are identical and result in a compiler error.

A class may override a method in its superclass. The overriding method must have the same name, return type, and parameter list as the method it overrides. Overriding Methods (page 136) shows you how to override methods.

Passing Information into a Method

When you write a method, you declare the number and type of the arguments required by that method. You must declare the type and name for each argument in the method signature. For example, the following code is a method that computes the monthly payments for a home loan. The payment is based on the amount of the loan, the interest rate, the length of the loan (the number of periods), and the future value of the loan (presumably the future value of the loan is zero because at the end of the loan, the loan will have been paid off).

```
double computePayment(double loanAmt, double rate,
                      double futureValue, int numPeriods) {
    double I, partial1, denominator, answer;

    I = rate / 100.0;
    partial1 = Math.pow((1 + I), (0.0 - numPeriods));
    denominator = (1 - partial1) / I;
    answer = ((-1 * loanAmt) / denominator) - ((futureValue *
             partial1) / denominator);
    return answer;
}
```

This method takes four arguments: the loan amount, the interest rate, the future value, and the number of periods. The first three are double-precision floating-point numbers, and the fourth is an integer.

As with this method, the set of arguments to any method is a comma-delimited list of variable declarations in which each variable declaration is a type/name pair:

```
type name
```

As you can see from the body of the `computePayment` method, you simply use the argument name to refer to the argument's value.

Argument Types. In Java, you can pass an argument of any valid Java data type into a method. This includes primitive data types such as `double`, `float`, and `integer`, as shown in the `computePayment` method, and reference data types such as classes and arrays. Here's an example of a factory method that accepts an array as an argument. In this example, the method creates a new `Polygon` object from a list of `Points`. (`Point` is a class that represents an *x, y* coordinate).

```
static Polygon polygonFrom(Point[] listOfPoints) {
    . . .
}
```

Unlike with other languages, you cannot pass methods into Java methods. But you can pass an object into a method and then invoke the object's methods.

Argument Names. When you declare an argument to a Java method, you provide a name for that argument. This name is used within the method body to refer to the item.

A method argument can have the same name as one of the class's member variables. In this case, the argument *hides* the member variable. Arguments that hide member variables are often used in "setter methods" to change the value of a member variable. For example, take the following `Circle` class and its `setRadius` method:

```
public class Circle {
    int x, y, radius;
    public void setRadius(int radius) {
        . . .
    }
}
```

The `Circle` class has three member variables: `x`, `y`, and `radius`. In addition, the `setRadius` method for the `Circle` class accepts one integer argument which shares its name with the member variable to be set.

The argument name hides the member variable. So `radius` within the body of the `setRadius` refers to the argument, *not* to the member variable. To access the member variable, you must reference it through `this`, the current object:

```
public class Circle {
    int x, y, radius;
    public void setRadius(int radius) {
        this.radius = radius;
    }
}
```

Names of method arguments cannot be the same as another argument name for the same method, the name of any variable local to the method, or the name of any parameter to a `catch` clause within the same method.

Pass-by-Value. In Java methods, arguments are *passed by value*. When the method is invoked, it receives the value of the variable passed in. When the argument is a primitive type, pass-by-value means the method cannot change its value. When the argument is a reference type, pass-by-value means the method cannot change the object reference, but the method can invoke the object's methods and modify the accessible variables within the object.

This is often a source of confusion—you write a method that attempts to modify the value of one of its arguments, and the method doesn't work as expected. Let's look at such method and then investigate how to change it so that it does what you originally intended.

Consider this series of Java statements, which attempts to retrieve the current color of a `Pen` object in a graphics application:

```
. . .
int r = -1, g = -1, b = -1;
pen.getRGBColor(r, g, b);
System.out.println("red = " + r + ", green = " + g +
                   ", blue = " + b);
. . .
```

When the `getRGBColor` method is called, the variables `r`, `g`, and `b` all have the value `-1`. The caller is expecting the `getRGBColor` method to set the values of `r`, `g`, and `b` to the current red, green, and blue color settings of the pen, thereby returning all three values.

However, the Java runtime system passes the values (`-1`) of the variables into the `getRGBColor` method, *not* a reference to the `r`, `g`, and `b` variables. Visualize the call to `getRGBColor` like this: `getRGBColor(-1, -1, -1)`.

When control passes into the getRGBColor method, the arguments come into scope (get allocated) and are initialized to the value passed into the method:

```
public class Pen {
    int redValue, greenValue, blueValue;
    public void getRGBColor(int red, int green, int blue) {
        // red, green, and blue have been created and
        // their values are -1
        . . .
    }
}
```

So getRGBColor gets access to the *values* (not the actual variables) of r, g, and b in the caller through its arguments red, green, and blue, respectively. The method gets its own copy of the values to use within the scope of the method. Any changes made to these local copies are not reflected in the original variables from the caller.

Now, look at the full implementation of getRGBColor that goes with the previous method declaration:

```
public class Pen {
    int redValue, greenValue, blueValue;
    . . .
        // this method does not work as intended
    public void getRGBColor(int red, int green, int blue) {
        red = redValue;
        green = greenValue;
        blue = blueValue;
    }
}
```

The getRGBColor method will not work as intended. When control gets to the println statement in the following code, which was shown previously, getRGBColor's arguments, red, green, and blue, no longer exist. Therefore the assignments made to them within the method had no effect; r, g, and b are all still equal to -1:

```
. . .
int r = -1, g = -1, b = -1;
pen.getRGBColor(r, g, b);
System.out.println("red = " + r + ", green = " + g +
                   ", blue = " + b);
. . .
```

Passing variables by value affords the programmer some safety; that is, methods cannot unintentionally modify a variable that is outside of its scope. However, you often want a method to be able to modify one or more of its arguments. The `getRGBColor` method is a case in point. The caller wants the method to return three values through its arguments. However, the method cannot modify its arguments, and, furthermore, a method can return only one value through its return value. So how can a method return more than one value or modify some value outside of its scope?

For a method to modify an argument, it must be of a reference type such as a class or an array. Objects and arrays are also passed by value, but the value of an object is a reference. The effect is that arguments of reference types are passed in by reference. Hence the name. A reference to an object is the address of the object in memory. Now, the argument in the method is referring to the same memory location as the caller.

Here's a rewrite of the `getRGBColor` method so that it actually does what you want. First, introduce a new object, `RGBColor`, that can hold the `red`, `green`, and `blue` values of a color in RGB space:

```
public class RGBColor {
    public int red, green, blue;
}
```

Next, rewrite `getRGBColor` so that it accepts an `RGBColor` object as an argument. The `getRGBColor` method returns the current color of the pen by setting the `red`, `green`, and `blue` member variables of its `RGBColor` argument:

```
public class Pen {
    int redValue, greenValue, blueValue;
    public void getRGBColor(RGBColor aColor) {
        aColor.red = redValue;
        aColor.green = greenValue;
        aColor.blue = blueValue;
    }
}
```

And finally, rewrite the calling sequence:

```
. . .
RGBColor penColor = new RGBColor();
pen.getRGBColor(penColor);
System.out.println("red = " + penColor.red + ", green = " +
                   penColor.green + ", blue = " + penColor.blue);
. . .
```

The modifications made to the `RGBColor` object within the `getRGBColor` method affect the object created in the calling sequence because the names `penColor` (in the calling sequence) and `aColor` (in the `getRGBColor` method) refer to the same object.

this

Within a method body, you can use `this` to refer to the current object. Why would you want to do this?

Typically, within an object's method body you can just refer directly to the object's member variables by name. However, sometimes a member variable is hidden by a method parameter that has the same name. In this case, you need to explicitly refer to a member variable through an object reference.

For example, the following method for the `HSBColor` class sets the object's member variables according to the arguments passed into the method. Each argument to the method has the same name as one of the object's member variables:

```
public class HSBColor {
    int hue, saturation, brightness;
    public void setColor (int hue,
                          int saturation, int brightness) {
        this.hue = hue;
        this.saturation = saturation;
        this.brightness = brightness;
    }
}
```

You must use `this` to refer to the member variable `hue` because it's hidden by the argument `hue`. And so on with the other member variables.

Some programmers always use `this` when referring to a member variable of the current object. Doing so makes the intent of the code explicit and reduces the frequency of errors that can result from name sharing.

You also can use `this` to call one of the current object's methods. This, too, is necessary only if there is some ambiguity in the method name and `this` is often used to make the intent of the code clearer.

super

If your method hides a member variable of a superclass, your method can refer to the hidden variable through the use of `super`. Similarly, if your method overrides one of its superclass's methods, your method can invoke the overridden method through the use of `super`. For example, consider this class:

```
class ASillyClass {
    boolean aVariable;
    void aMethod() {
        aVariable = true;
    }
}
```

Now, look at its subclass, which hides `aVariable` and overrides `aMethod()`:

```
class ASillierClass extends ASillyClass {
    boolean aVariable;
    void aMethod() {
        aVariable = false;
        super.aMethod();
        System.out.println(aVariable);
        System.out.println(super.aVariable);
    }
}
```

First, `aMethod` sets `aVariable` (the one declared in `ASillierClass` that hides the one declared in `ASillyClass`) to `false`. Next, `aMethod` invokes its overridden method with this statement:

```
super.aMethod();
```

This sets the hidden version of `aVariable` (the one declared in `ASillyClass`) to `true`. Then `aMethod` displays both versions of `aVariable`, which have different values:

```
false
true
```

Local Variables

Within the body of the method, you can declare more variables for use within that method. These variables are called *local variables*. A local variable lives only while control remains within the method. The following method declares a local variable `i` that it uses to iterate over the elements of its array argument. After this method returns, `i` no longer exists.

```
Object findObjectInArray(Object o, Object[] arrayOfObjects) {
    int i;      // local variable
    for (i = 0; i < arrayOfObjects.length; i++) {
        if (arrayOfObjects[i] == o)
```

```
            return o;
        }
        return null;
    }
```

Controlling Access to Members of a Class

One benefit of classes is that they can protect their member variables and methods from access by other objects. Why is this important? Well, consider the `Stack` class. It stores its elements in a `Vector` but keeps the `Vector` private to itself. This has two advantages:

1. Other objects can't jeopardize the integrity of the stack by modifying the `Vector` in a way inconsistent with the `Stack`'s intent. All interactions with `Vector` are controlled indirectly through `Stack`'s methods.
2. If a new `Vector` class, `NewAndImprovedVector`, became available, `Stack` could switch to it without affecting code in other objects.

In Java, you can use access specifiers to protect both a class's variables and its methods when you declare them. The Java language supports four distinct access levels for member variables and methods: `private`, `protected`, `public`, and, if left unspecified, `package`.

Table 13: Java's access levels.

Specifier	**Class**	**Subclass**	**Package**	**World**
`private`	✔			
`protected`	✔	✔	✔	
`public`	✔	✔	✔	✔
`package`	✔		✔	

The following sections examine each access level in more detail.

Private

The most restrictive access level is `private`. A private member is accessible only to the class in which it is defined. Use this access level to declare members that should be used only by the class. This includes variables that contain information that, if accessed by an outsider, could put the object in an inconsistent state, or methods that, if invoked by an outsider, could jeopardize the state of the object or

the program in which it is running. Private members are like secrets you never tell anybody.

To declare a private member, use the `private` keyword in its declaration. The following class contains one private member variable and one private method:

```
class Alpha {
    private int iamprivate;
    private void privateMethod() {
        System.out.println("privateMethod");
    }
}
```

Code within the `Alpha` class can inspect or modify the `iamprivate` variable and can invoke `privateMethod`, but code in any other class cannot. For example, the `Beta` class defined next cannot access the `iamprivate` variable or invoke `privateMethod` on an object of type `Alpha`:

```
class Beta {
    void accessMethod() {
        Alpha a = new Alpha();
        a.iamprivate = 10;      // illegal
        a.privateMethod();      // illegal
    }
}
```

When one of your classes is attempting to access a member variable to which it does not have access, the compiler prints an error message similar to the following and refuses to compile your program:

```
Beta.java:9: Variable iamprivate in class Alpha not accessible
from class Beta.
        a.iamprivate = 10;     // illegal
         ^
1 error
```

Also, if your program is attempting to access a method to which it does not have access, you will see a compiler error like this:

```
Beta.java:12: No method matching privateMethod() found in class
Alpha.
        a.privateMethod();          // illegal
1 error
```

New object-oriented programmers might ask if one `Alpha` object can access the private members of another `Alpha` object. The answer is yes. This is illustrated by the following example. Suppose the `Alpha` class contains an instance method that compares the current `Alpha` object (`this`) to another object based on their `iamprivate` variables:

```
class Alpha {
    private int iamprivate;
    boolean isEqualTo(Alpha anotherAlpha) {
        if (this.iamprivate == anotherAlpha.iamprivate)
            return true;
        else
            return false;
    }
}
```

This is perfectly legal. Objects of the same type have access to one another's private members. This is because access restrictions apply to classes (all instances of a class) rather than to instances (this particular instance of a class).

Protected

The next access level specifier is `protected`, which allows the class itself, subclasses, and classes in the same package to access the members. Protected members are like family secrets—you don't mind if the whole family knows, and even a few trusted friends, but you don't want any outsiders to know.

To declare a protected member, you use the keyword `protected`. First, we show you how the protected specifier affects access for classes in the same package. Then we show you how it affects access for subclasses.

Consider the following version of the `Alpha` class. It is declared to be within a package named `Greek`, and it has one protected member variable and one protected method declared:

```
package Greek;

class Alpha {
    protected int iamprotected;
    protected void protectedMethod() {
        System.out.println("protectedMethod");
    }
}
```

Now, suppose that the class `Gamma` is in the `Greek` package, but it is not a subclass of `Alpha`. The `Gamma` class can legally access an `Alpha` object's `iamprotected` member variable and can legally invoke its `protectedMethod`:

```
package Greek;

class Gamma {
    void accessMethod() {
        Alpha a = new Alpha();
        a.iamprotected = 10;     // legal
        a.protectedMethod();     // legal
    }
}
```

If Gamma *were* a subclass of Alpha, this code would still be legal because the class is in the same package as Alpha and is covered by package access. Subclasses outside of the superclass's package also have access to iamprotected and protectedMethod, but with an interesting twist. These subclasses must reference protected members through an object reference that is "at least" the type of the subclass. What does this mean?

To show you, we introduce a new class, Delta, a subclass of Alpha but in a different package—Latin. The Delta class can access both iamprotected and protectedMethod, but only through references to objects of type Delta or its subclasses. The Delta class cannot access iamprotected or protectedMethod on objects of type Alpha. accessMethod in the following code sample attempts to access the iamprotected member variable on an object of type Alpha, which is illegal, and on an object of type Delta, which is legal. Similarly, accessMethod attempts to invoke an Alpha object's protectedMethod, which is illegal:

```
package Latin;

import Greek.*;

class Delta extends Alpha {
    void accessMethod(Alpha a, Delta d) {
        a.iamprotected = 10;     // illegal
        d.iamprotected = 10;     // legal
        a.protectedMethod();     // illegal
        d.protectedMethod();     // legal
    }
}
```

Public

The easiest access specifier is public. Any class of any parentage in any package has access to a class's public members. Declare members to be public only if such access cannot produce undesirable results if an outsider uses them. There are no personal or family secrets here. This is for stuff you don't mind anybody else knowing.

To declare a public member, use the keyword `public`. For example:

```
package Greek;

public class Alpha {
    public int iampublic;
    public void publicMethod() {
        System.out.println("publicMethod");
    }
}
```

We'll rewrite the `Beta` class one more time, put it in a different package than `Alpha`, and make sure that it is completely unrelated to (not a subclass of) `Alpha`:

```
package Roman;

import Greek.*;

class Beta {
    void accessMethod() {
        Alpha a = new Alpha();
        a.iampublic = 10;         // legal
        a.publicMethod();         // legal
    }
}
```

As this code snippet shows, `Beta` can legally inspect and modify the `iampublic` variable in the `Alpha` class and can legally invoke `publicMethod`.

Package

The package access level is default if you don't explicitly set a member's access to one of the other levels. This access level allows classes in the same package as your class to access the members regardless of their parentage. This level of access assumes that classes in the same package are trusted friends. It is like that which you extend to your closest friends but wouldn't trust even to your family.

For example, the following version of the `Alpha` class declares a single member variable and a single method, both with default (package) access. `Alpha` lives in the `Greek` package:

```
package Greek;

class Alpha {
    int iampackage;
    void packageMethod() {
        System.out.println("packageMethod");
    }
}
```

The `Alpha` class has access both to `iampackage` and `packageMethod`. In addition, all of the classes declared within the same package as `Alpha` also have access to `iampackage` and `packageMethod`. Suppose that both `Alpha` and `Beta` are declared as part of the `Greek` package:

```
package Greek;

class Beta {
    void accessMethod() {
        Alpha a = new Alpha();
        a.iampackage = 10;      // legal
        a.packageMethod();      // legal
    }
}
```

`Beta` can legally access `iampackage` and `packageMethod` as shown because it's in the same package as `Alpha`. A subclass of `Alpha` in a different package *cannot* access `iampackage` or `packageMethod`.

Understanding Instance and Class Members

Unless otherwise specified, a member declared within a class is an instance member. The `AnIntegerNamedX` class has one instance variable, an integer named `x`, and two instance methods, `x` and `setX`, that let other objects set and query the value of `x`:

```
class AnIntegerNamedX {
    int x;
    public int x() {
        return x;
    }
    public void setX(int newX) {
        x = newX;
    }
}
```

Every time you instantiate a new object from a class, you get a new copy of each of the class's instance variables. These copies are associated with the new object. In the previous code, every time you instantiate a new `AnIntegerNamedX` object, you get a new copy of `x` that is associated with the new `AnIntegerNamedX` object.

All instances of a class share the same implementation of an instance method; so all instances of `AnIntegerNamedX` share the same implementation of the `x` and `setX` methods. Note that both methods, `x` and `setX`, refer to the object's instance variable `x` by name. Within an instance method, the name of an instance variable refers to the copy of that variable in the current object (assuming that the instance variable isn't hidden by a method parameter). So, within `x` and `setX`, `x` is equivalent to `this.x`.

Objects outside of `AnIntegerNamedX` that wish to access `x` must do so through a particular instance of `AnIntegerNamedX`. Suppose this code snippet is in another object's method. It creates two different objects of type `AnIntegerNamedX`, sets their `x` values to different values, and then displays them:

```
. . .
AnIntegerNamedX myX = new AnIntegerNamedX();
AnIntegerNamedX anotherX = new AnIntegerNamedX();
myX.setX(1);
anotherX.x = 2;
System.out.println("myX.x = " + myX.x());
System.out.println("anotherX.x = " + anotherX.x());
. . .
```

Note that the code uses `setX` to set the `x` value for `myX` but just assigns a value to `anotherX.x` directly. Either way, the code is manipulating two different copies of `x`: the one contained in the `myX` object and the one contained in the `anotherX` object. The output produced by this code snippet is

```
myX.x = 1
anotherX.x = 2
```

This shows that each instance of the class `AnIntegerNamedX` has its own copy of the instance variable `x` and each `x` has a different value.

When declaring a member, either a method or a variable, you can specify that the member be associated with the class rather than with an instance of it. A member associated with a class is called a *class member* (or more specifically, a *class variable* or a *class method*). The system creates a single copy of a class variable the first time it encounters the class in which the variable is defined. All instances of that class share the same copy of the class variable. Class methods can operate only on class variables; they cannot access the instance variables defined in the class.

To specify that a member variable is a class variable, use the `static` keyword. For example, change the `AnIntegerNamedX` class such that its `x` variable is now a class variable:

```
class AnIntegerNamedX {
    static int x;
    public int x() {
        return x;
    }
    public void setX(int newX) {
        x = newX;
    }
}
```

Now the code snippet at the bottom of page 119 produces this different output:

```
myX.x = 2
anotherX.x = 2
```

The output is different because `x` is now a class variable. Hence, there is only one copy of that variable, and it is shared by all instances of `AnIntegerNamedX`, including `myX` and `anotherX`. When you invoke `setX` on either instance, you change the value of `x` for all instances of `AnIntegerNamedX`.

You use class variables for items that you need only one copy of and that must be accessible by all objects inheriting from the class in which the variable is declared. For example, class variables are often declared `final` to define constants. This is more memory efficient than using final instance variables because constants can't change. So you really need only one copy.

Similarly, when declaring a method, you can specify that method to be a class method rather than an instance method. Class methods can operate only on class variables; they cannot access the instance variables defined in the class. To specify that a method is a class method, use the `static` keyword in the method declaration. In the previous example, change the `AnIntegerNamedX` class such that its member variable `x` is once again an instance variable and its two methods are now class methods:

```
class AnIntegerNamedX {
    int x;
    static public int x() {
        return x; //won't work
```

```
    }
    static public void setX(int newX) {
        x = newX; //won't work
    }
}
```

When you try to compile this version of `AnIntegerNamedX`, you will get the following compiler errors:

```
AnIntegerNamedX.java:4: Can't make a static reference to
    nonstatic variable x in class AnIntegerNamedX.
        return x;
               ^
AnIntegerNamedX.java:7: Can't make a static reference to
     nonstatic variable x in class AnIntegerNamedX.
        x = newX;
        ^
2 errors
```

The errors occur because class methods cannot access instance variables unless the method created an instance of `AnIntegerNamedX` first and accessed the variable through it.

You can fix `AnIntegerNamedX` by making its `x` variable a class variable:

```
class AnIntegerNamedX {
    static int x;
    static public int x() {
        return x;
    }
    static public void setX(int newX) {
        x = newX;
    }
}
```

Now the class will compile and the previous code snippet (on page 119) produces this output:

```
myX.x = 2
anotherX.x = 2
```

Again, changing `x` through `myX` also changes it for other instances of `AnIntegerNamedX`.

Another difference between instance members and class members is that class members are accessible from the class itself. You don't need to instantiate a class

to access its class members. You can rewrite the code so that it accesses `x` and `setX` directly from the `AnIntegerNamedX` class:

```
. . .
AnIntegerNamedX.setX(1);
System.out.println("AnIntegerNamedX.x = " +
   AnIntegerNamedX.x());
. . .
```

Note that you no longer have to create `myX` and `anotherX`. You can set and retrieve `x` directly using the `AnIntegerNamedX` class. You cannot do this with instance members; instead, you must invoke instance methods through an object reference and must access instance variables through an object reference. You can access class variables and methods using either an instance of the class or the class itself.

Initializing Instance and Class Members

You can use *static initializers* and *instance initializers* to provide initial values for class and instance members when you declare them in a class:

```
class BedAndBreakfast {
    static final int MAX_CAPACITY = 10;  // static initializer
    boolean full = false;  // instance initializer
}
```

This works well for members of primitive data type. Sometimes, it even works when creating arrays and objects. But this form of initialization has limitations, as follows:

1. Initializers can perform only initializations that can be expressed in an assignment statement.
2. Initializers cannot call any method that can throw a checked exception.
3. If the initializer calls a method that throws a runtime exception, then it cannot do error recovery.

If you have some initialization to perform that cannot be done in an initializer because of one of these limitations, you have to put the initialization code elsewhere. To initialize class members, put the initialization code in a *static initialization block*. To initialize instance members, put the initialization code in a constructor.

Using Static Initialization Blocks. Here's an example of a static initialization block:

```
import java.util.ResourceBundle;
class Errors {
    static ResourceBundle errorStrings;
    static {
        try {
            errorStrings = ResourceBundle.
                                getBundle("ErrorStrings");
        } catch (java.util.MissingResourceException e) {
            // error recovery code here
        }
    }
}
```

The errorStrings resource bundle must be initialized in a static initialization block. This is because error recovery must be performed if the bundle cannot be found. Also, errorStrings is a class member and it doesn't make sense for it to be initialized in a constructor. As the previous example shows, a static initialization block begins with the static keyword and is a normal block of Java code enclosed in curly braces {}.

A class can have any number of static initialization blocks that appear anywhere in the class body. The runtime system guarantees that static initialization blocks and static initializers are called in the order (left-to-right, top-to-bottom) that they appear in the source code.

Initializing Instance Members. If you want to initialize an instance variable and cannot do it in the variable declaration for the reasons cited previously, then put the initialization in the constructor(s) for the class. Suppose the errorStrings bundle in the previous example is an instance variable rather than a class variable. Then you'd use the following code to initialize it:

```
import java.util.ResourceBundle;
class Errors {
    ResourceBundle errorStrings;
    Errors() {
        try {
            errorStrings = ResourceBundle.
                                getBundle("ErrorStrings");
        } catch (java.util.MissingResourceException e) {
```

```
                // error recovery code here
            }
        }
    }
```

The code that initializes `errorStrings` is now in a constructor for the class.

Sometimes a class contains many constructors and each constructor allows the caller to provide initial values for different instance variables of the new object. For example, `java.awt.Rectangle` has these three constructors:

```
Rectangle();
Rectangle(int width, int height);
Rectangle(int x, int y, int width, int height);
```

The no-argument constructor doesn't let the caller provide initial values for anything, and the other two constructors let the caller set initial values either for the size or for the origin and size. Yet, all of the instance variables, the origin and the size, for `Rectangle` must be initialized. In this case, classes often have one constructor that does all of the work. The other constructors call this constructor and provide it either with the values from its parameters or with default values. For example, here are the possible implementations of the three `Rectangle` constructors shown previously (assume `x`, `y`, `width`, and `height` are the names of the instance variables to be initialized):

```
Rectangle() {
    this(0,0,0,0);
}
Rectangle(int width, int height) {
    this(0,0,width,height);
}
Rectangle(int x, int y, int width, int height) {
    this.x = x;
    this.y = y;
    this.width = width;
    this.height = height;
}
```

The Java language supports instance initialization blocks, which you could use instead. However, these are intended to be used with anonymous classes, which cannot declare constructors.

The approach described here that uses constructors is better for these reasons:

- All of the initialization code is in one place, thus making the code easier to maintain and read.

- Defaults are handled explicitly.
- Constructors are widely understood by the Java community, including relatively new Java programmers, while instance initializers are not and may cause confusion to other reading your code.

Writing a finalize Method

When all references to an object are dropped, the object is no longer required and becomes eligible for garbage collection. Before an object is garbage collected, the runtime system calls its `finalize` method to release system resources such as open files or open sockets before the object is collected.

Your class can provide for its finalization simply by defining and implementing a `finalize` method in your class. This method must be declared as follows:

```
protected void finalize() throws Throwable
```

The `Stack` class creates a `Vector` when it's created. To be complete and well-behaved, the `Stack` class should release its reference to the `Vector`. Here's the `finalize` method for the `Stack` class:

```
protected void finalize() throws Throwable {
    items = null;
    super.finalize();
}
```

The `finalize` method is declared in the `Object` class. As a result, when you write a `finalize` method for your class, you are overriding the one in your superclass. Overriding Methods (page 136) talks more about how to override methods.

The last line of `Stack`'s `finalize` method calls the superclass's `finalize` method. Doing this cleans up any resources that the object may have unknowingly obtained through methods inherited from the superclass.

Reality Break! The Spot Applet

Let's do something a bit more fun and look at an applet, `Spot`. With this applet, we show you how to subclass another class and implement an interface. The last section of this lesson, Using an Inner Class to Implement an Adapter (page 129), shows you two alternative implementations of this class, both of which use inner classes.

The following is a snapshot of Spot, an applet that displays a small spot when you click over the applet with the mouse:

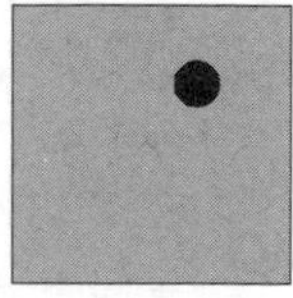

http://java.sun.com/docs/books/tutorial/java/javaOO/spot.html

And here's the source code for the applet:

```
import java.applet.Applet;
import java.awt.*;
import java.awt.event.*;

public class Spot extends Applet implements MouseListener{
    private Point clickPoint = null;
    private static final int RADIUS = 7;

    public void init() {
        addMouseListener(this);
    }
    public void paint(Graphics g) {
        g.drawRect(0, 0, getSize().width - 1,
                         getSize().height - 1);
        if (clickPoint != null)
            g.fillOval(clickPoint.x - RADIUS,
                       clickPoint.y - RADIUS,
                       RADIUS * 2, RADIUS * 2);
    }
    public void mousePressed(MouseEvent event) {
        clickPoint = event.getPoint();
        repaint();
    }
    public void mouseClicked(MouseEvent event) {}
    public void mouseReleased(MouseEvent event) {}
    public void mouseEntered(MouseEvent event) {}
    public void mouseExited(MouseEvent event) {}
}
```

The `extends` clause indicates that the `Spot` class is a subclass of `Applet`. The next section talks about this aspect of `Spot`. The `implements` clause shows that `Spot` implements one interface named `MouseListener`. Read about this aspect of the `Spot` class in Implementing an Interface (page 127) later in this lesson.

Extending a Class

If you look at the online javadoc for Applet[1], you can see a long list of methods implemented by that class. All of these methods are inherited by Spot. Also, if you look at Applet's ascendants, you will notice that Applet descends from a long line of auspicious classes: Panel, Container, Component, and finally, Object. Hence, Applet, and consequently, Spot, inherit a large number of variables and methods from these classes that, among other things, manage the space in which the applet runs.

Inheritance provides one of the premier benefits of object-oriented programming: code reuse. This is shown here. With a tiny amount of code, Spot actually implements a fairly complex program (Spot reserves space in an HTML page, is started and stopped as the browser instructs, handles mouse click events, and draws in its area).

Being a subclass comes with responsibilities as well. Depending on the superclass, a subclass may be required to implement certain methods or be expected to override some. One responsibility that comes with subclassing Applet is that the subclass must implement at least one of these methods: init, start, or paint. Spot implements both init and paint but does not implement start. You should fully understand the parent class when creating a subclass of it. To find out what a subclass inherits from its parents, what it must override, what it cannot override, and so on, go to Understanding Inheritance (page 135). To find out more about the benefits and responsibilities of subclassing Applet, go to the next trail, Writing Applets (page 171).

Implementing an Interface

An interface defines a protocol of behavior. A class that implements an interface adheres to the protocol defined by that interface. Let's look at the Spot class to get a better idea of what this means.

To get mouse events from the AWT, the AWT requires a class to adhere to a certain protocol. For example, for a class to be notified by the AWT when the user presses a mouse button, the class must have a mousePressed method, for a class to be notified when the user releases the mouse button it must have a mouseReleased method, and so on. This protocol is codified in the MouseListener[2] interface, which declares these five methods, one for each type of mouse event:

---

1 http://java.sun.com/products/jdk/1.1/docs/api/java.applet.Applet.html
2 http://java.sun.com/products/jdk/1.1/docs/api/java.awt.event.MouseListener.html

```
mouseClicked(MouseEvent)
mouseEntered(MouseEvent)
mouseExited(MouseEvent)
mousePressed(MouseEvent)
mouseReleased(MouseEvent)
```

Any class interested in getting mouse events must adhere to the protocol. It does this by implementing the `MouseListener` interface.

To declare a class that implements an interface, include an `implements` clause in the class declaration. Your class can implement more than one interface (Java supports multiple interface inheritance), so the `implements` keyword is followed by a comma-delimited list of the interfaces implemented by the class.

`Spot`, which displays a spot where the user presses the mouse button, needs to know about mouse pressed events (the event when the mouse button is initially pressed down) in order to function. Therefore, `Spot` must implement the `MouseListener` interface:

```
public class Spot extends Applet implements MouseListener {
    . . .
}
```

By Convention: The `implements` clause follows the `extends` clause, if it exists.

When a class declares that it implements an interface, it's basically signing a contract to the effect that it will provide implementations for all of the methods in the interface. So `Spot` must implement all five of `MouseListener`'s methods:

```
public void mousePressed(MouseEvent event) {
    clickPoint = event.getPoint();
    repaint();
}
public void mouseClicked(MouseEvent event) {}
public void mouseReleased(MouseEvent event) {}
public void mouseEntered(MouseEvent event) {}
public void mouseExited(MouseEvent event) {}
```

Note that the last four methods have empty implementations. This is because `Spot` is interested only in "mouse pressed" events. When the user presses the mouse button, `Spot` displays a spot where the click occurred. However, because `Spot` is declared to implement the `MouseListener` interface and `MouseListener` declares five methods, `Spot` must implement them all. You can use inner classes in conjunction with several `java.awt.event` "adapter classes" to avoid writing empty methods. The next section shows you how.

For a complete discussion about interfaces, what they're for, and how to write them, go to Creating Interfaces (page 145) in the next lesson.

Using an Inner Class to Implement an Adapter

In the previous section, `Spot` contains empty implementations because it isn't interested in all of the kinds of mouse events. In this section, we rewrite `Spot` so that those empty methods aren't necessary. This can be done using an *inner class* to implement an adapter. An inner class is one kind of *nested class* (a class that is defined within another class). To find out more about nested classes, read Implementing Nested Classes (page 152).

The bold text in this new version of the applet shows how this version of the class differs from that in the previous section:

```
import java.applet.Applet;
import java.awt.*;
import java.awt.event.*;

public class AdapterSpot extends Applet //no implements clause
{
    private Point clickPoint = null;
    private static final int RADIUS = 7;

    public void init() {
        addMouseListener(new MyMouseAdapter());
    }
    public void paint(Graphics g) {
        g.drawRect(0, 0, getSize().width - 1,
                         getSize().height - 1);
        if (clickPoint != null)
            g.fillOval(clickPoint.x-RADIUS,
                       clickPoint.y-RADIUS,
                       RADIUS*2, RADIUS*2);
    }
    class MyMouseAdapter extends MouseAdapter {
        public void mousePressed(MouseEvent event) {
            clickPoint = event.getPoint();
            repaint();
        }
    }
    /* no empty methods! */
}
```

Now, instead of implementing the interface itself, `AdapterSpot` declares an inner class, `MyMouseAdapter`. `MyMouseAdapter` is a subclass of `MouseAdapter`, which implements the `MouseListener` interface. `MouseAdapter` provides empty implementations for all of the methods declared in `MouseListener`. Through the use of this inner class, the `AdapterSpot` class can write only the method for the one type of event it is interested in: `mousePressed`.

You will see a lot of inner classes, and even implement some, if you plan to handle events from the AWT.

Anonymous Classes

In the previous example, the name of the inner class adds nothing to the meaning of the program. You can forego naming an inner class and just define it where it's used. This is called an *anonymous class.*

Definition: A class without a name is called an *anonymous class.*

Here's yet another version of the applet, rewritten to use an anonymous class (changes are in bold):

```
import java.applet.Applet;
import java.awt.*;
import java.awt.event.*;

public class AnonymousSpot extends Applet {
    private Point clickPoint = null;
    private static final int RADIUS = 7;
    public void init() {
        addMouseListener(
            new MouseAdapter() {
                public void mousePressed(MouseEvent event) {
                    clickPoint = event.getPoint();
                    repaint();
                }
            }
        );
    }
    /* paint method not shown */
}
```

You should restrict your use of anonymous classes to those classes that are for a single use and very small (no more than a method or two). Otherwise, you may jeopardize the readability of your code.

Summary

The section Creating Classes (page 93) focused on the pedantic details of writing the classes from which objects are created. The `Spot` applet described at the end of this lesson is a typical (if somewhat simplistic) applet that bridged the gap between the academics and the reality of writing a class. The next lesson takes you back to school and talks about all of the features of Java that help you define and enforce relationships between classes.

7 More Features of the Java Language

THE previous lesson, Objects and Classes in Java (page 81), described features of the Java language that every Java programmer needs to know to use objects and write classes in Java. This lesson builds on that, discussing more features of the Java language that help you to organize and design your code.

Managing Inheritance (page 134) tells you what you need to know to manage inheritance up and down from your classes. First, it describes generally what a subclass gets from its ancestors and specifically what every class gets from the `Object` class. Second, it discusses how to control whether your class can be subclassed and whether its subclasses can override its methods.

You saw an example of implementing an interface in the previous chapter. You can read more about interfaces—what they are for, why you might need to write an interface, and all about how to write one—in Creating Interfaces (page 145).

You learned how to use inner classes to implement an adapter in Using an Inner Class to Implement an Adapter (page 129) in the previous lesson. Inner classes are one type of *nested classes* that you will learn about in Implementing Nested Classes (page 152).

And finally, Creating and Using Packages (page 156) describes how to bundle your classes into packages and how to use classes that are in packages.

Managing Inheritance

Recall from the previous lesson that the `extends` clause declares that your class is a subclass of another. You can specify only one superclass for your class (Java does not support multiple class inheritance), and even though you can omit the `extends` clause from your class declaration, your class has a superclass. So, every class in Java has one and only one immediate superclass. This statement leads to the question, "Where does it all begin?"

As depicted in Figure 22, the top-most class, the class from which all other classes are derived, is the `Object`[1] class defined in `java.lang`.

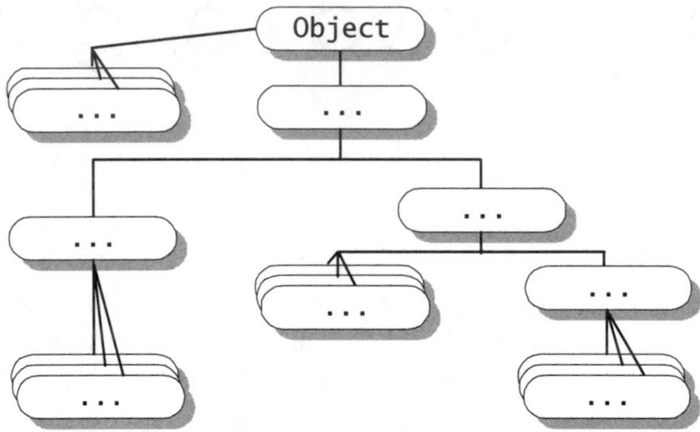

Figure 22: All classes are ancestors of the `Object` class.

The `Object` class defines and implements behavior that every class in the Java system needs. It is the most general of all classes. Its immediate subclasses, and other classes near top of the hierarchy, implement general behavior; classes near the bottom of the hierarchy provide for more specialized behavior.

Definition: A *subclass* is a class that extends another class. A subclass inherits state and behavior from all of its ancestors. The term "superclass" refers to a class's direct ancestor as well as to all of its ascendant classes.

The next section talks about the various issues involved in extending any class, such as which members it inherits, which members it can override or hide, and which it cannot. The section that follows, Being a Descendent of Object (page

---

1 http://java.sun.com/products/jdk/1.1/docs/api/java.lang.Object.html

138), describes what all classes inherit from the `Object` class and how these classes implement their inherited functionality.

Understanding Inheritance

A subclass inherits variables and methods from its superclass and all of its ancestors. The subclass can use these members as is, or it can hide the member variables or override the methods.

What Members Does a Subclass Inherit?

Rule: A subclass inherits all of the members in its superclass that are accessible to that subclass unless the subclass explicitly hides a member variable or overrides a method. Note that constructors are not members and are not inherited by subclasses.

The following list itemizes the members that are inherited by a subclass:

- Subclasses inherit those superclass members declared as `public` or `protected`.
- Subclasses inherit those superclass members declared with no access specifier as long as the subclass is in the same package as the superclass.
- Subclasses don't inherit a superclass's member if the subclass declares a member with the same name. In the case of member variables, the member variable in the subclass hides the one in the superclass. In the case of methods, the method in the subclass overrides the one in the superclass.
- Subclasses don't inherit the superclass's `private` members.

Creating a subclass can be as simple as including the `extends` clause in your class declaration. However, you usually have to make other provisions in your code when subclassing a class, such as overriding methods or providing implementations for abstract methods.

Hiding Member Variables

As mentioned in the previous section, member variables defined in the subclass hide member variables that have the same name in the superclass.

While this feature of the Java language is powerful and convenient, it can be a fruitful source of errors. When naming your member variables, be careful to hide only those member variables that you actually wish to hide.

One interesting feature of Java member variables is that a class can access a hidden member variable through its superclass. Consider the following superclass and subclass pair:

```
class Super {
    Number aNumber;
}
class Subbie extends Super {
    Float aNumber;
}
```

The `aNumber` variable in `Subbie` hides `aNumber` in `Super`. But you can access `Super`'s `aNumber` from `Subbie` with

```
super.aNumber
```

`super` is a Java language keyword that allows a method to refer to hidden variables and overridden methods of the superclass.

Overriding Methods

The ability of a subclass to override a method in its superclass allows a class to inherit from a superclass whose behavior is "close enough" and then override methods as needed.

For example, all classes are descendents of the `Object` class. `Object` contains the `toString` method, which returns a `String` object containing the name of the object's class and its hash code. Most, if not all, classes will want to override this method and print out something meaningful for that class.

Let's resurrect the `Stack` class example and override the `toString` method. The output of `toString` should be a textual representation of the object. For the `Stack` class, a list of the items in the stack would be appropriate.

```
public class Stack
{
    private Vector items;

    // code for Stack's methods and constructor not shown

    // overrides Object's toString method
    public String toString() {
        int n = items.size();
        StringBuffer result = new StringBuffer();
        result.append("[");
        for (int i = 0; i < n; i++) {
            result.append(items.elementAt(i).toString());
```

```
            if (i < n-1) result.append(",");
        }
        result.append("]");
        return result.toString();
    }
}
```

The return type, method name, and number and type of the parameters for the overriding method must match those in the overridden method. The overriding method can have a different `throws` clause as long as it doesn't declare any types not declared by the `throws` clause in the overridden method. Also, the access specifier for the overriding method can allow more access than the overridden method, but not less. For example, a `protected` method in the superclass can be made `public` but not `private`.

Calling the Overridden Method. Sometimes, you don't want to completely override a method. Rather, you want to add more functionality to it. To do this, simply call the overridden method using the `super` keyword. For example, `Stack`'s implementation of `finalize` (which overrides `Object`'s `finalize` method) should include any finalization done by the `Object` class:

```
protected void finalize() throws Throwable {
    items = null;
    super.finalize();
}
```

Methods a Subclass Cannot Override. A subclass cannot override methods that are declared final in the superclass (by definition, final methods cannot be overridden). If you attempt to override a final method, the compiler displays an error message similar to the following and refuses to compile the program:

```
FinalTest.java:7: Final methods can't be overridden. Method
void iamfinal() is final in class ClassWithFinalMethod.
    void iamfinal() {
         ^
1 error
```

Also, a subclass cannot override methods that are declared `static` in the superclass. In other words, a subclass cannot override a class method.

Methods a Subclass Must Override. A subclass must override methods that are declared `abstract` in the superclass, *or* the subclass itself must be

abstract. The upcoming section Writing Abstract Classes and Methods (page 142) discusses abstract classes and methods in detail.

Being a Descendent of Object

The `Object` class sits at the top of the class hierarchy tree in the Java platform. Every class in the Java system is a descendent, direct or indirect, of the `Object` class. This class defines the basic state and behavior that all objects must have, such as the ability to compare oneself to another object, to convert to a string, to wait on a condition variable, to notify other objects that a condition variable has changed, and to return the class of the object.

Your classes may want to override the following `Object` methods:

- `clone`
- `equals`
- `finalize`
- `toString`

Your class cannot override these `Object` methods (they are final):

- `getClass`
- `notify`
- `notifyAll`
- `wait`
- `hashCode`

The clone Method

You use the `clone` method to create objects from other objects of the same type. By default, objects are not cloneable, so `Object`'s implementation of this method throws a `CloneNotSupportedException`. If you want your class to be cloneable, you must implement the `Cloneable` interface and override this method.

Your version of the `clone` method must provide for a field-by-field copy of the object being cloned. Here's a partial listing of a new version of the `Stack` class that implements the `Cloneable` interface and overrides the `clone` method (changes are shown in bold):

```
public class Stack implements Cloneable
{
    private Vector items;

    // code for Stack's methods and constructor not shown
```

```
            Stack s = (Stack)super.clone();
            s.items = (Vector)items.clone();
            return s;
        } catch (CloneNotSupportedException e) {
            // this shouldn't happen because Stack is Cloneable
            throw new InternalError();
        }
    }
}
```

The implementation for Stack's clone method is relatively simple: It calls super.clone (Object's implementation of the clone method) to create an instance of the correct type. The only member of Stack, a Vector, is also cloneable. Be careful: clone should not use new to create the clone and should not call constructors. Instead, the method should call super.clone, which creates an object of the correct type and allows the hierarchy of superclasses to perform the copying necessary to get a proper clone.

The equals Method

You use the equals method to compare two objects for equality. This method returns true if the objects are equal, false otherwise. Note that equality does not necessarily mean that the objects are the same object. Consider this code that tests two Integers, one and anotherOne, for equality:

```
Integer one = new Integer(1), anotherOne = new Integer(1);

if (one.equals(anotherOne))
    System.out.println("objects are equal");
```

This program displays objects are equal even though one and anotherOne reference two distinct objects. They are considered equal because they contain the same integer value.

Your classes should override the equals method to provide an appropriate equality test. Your equals method should compare the contents of the objects to see if they are functionally equivalent and return true if they are.

The finalize Method

The Object class provides a method, finalize, that cleans up an object before it is garbage collected. This method's role during garbage collection was discussed previously in Cleaning Up Unused Objects (page 92). Also, Writing a finalize Method (page 125) showed you how to override the finalize method to handle the finalization needs for your classes.

The toString Method

Object's toString method returns a String representation of the object. You can use toString along with System.out.println to display a text representation of an object, such as the current thread:

```
System.out.println(Thread.currentThread().toString());
```

The String representation for an object depends entirely on the object. The String representation of an Integer object is the integer value displayed as text. The String representation of a Thread object contains various attributes about the thread, such as its name and priority. For example, the previous line of code displays the following output:

```
Thread[main,5,main]
```

The toString method is very useful for debugging. It behooves you to override this method in all your classes.

The getClass Method

The getClass method is a final method that returns a runtime representation of the class of this object. This method returns a Class object. You can query the Class object for various information about the class, such as its name, its superclass, and the names of the interfaces that it implements. This following method gets and displays the class name of an object:

```
void PrintClassName(Object obj) {
    System.out.println("The Object's class is " +
                       obj.getClass().getName());
}
```

One handy use of the getClass method is to create a new instance of a class without knowing what the class is at compile time. The following sample method creates a new instance of the same class as obj, which can be any class that inherits from Object (which means that it could be any class):

```
Object createNewInstanceOf(Object obj) {
    return obj.getClass().newInstance();
}
```

Note: You also can get a Class object from a class name using a class literal. For example, to get the Class object for the String class use String.class. This is equivalent to, but more efficient than, calling Class.forName(String).

The notify, notifyAll, and wait Methods

You cannot override `Object`'s `notify` and `notifyAll` methods and its three versions of `wait`. This is because they are critical for ensuring that threads are synchronized. The use of these methods is covered in Doing Two or More Tasks at Once: Threads (page 327). Take particular note of the section titled Synchronizing Threads (page 346).

Writing Final Classes and Methods

You can declare that your class is final, that is, that your class cannot be subclassed. There are (at least) two reasons why you might want to do this: to increase system security by preventing system subversion, and for reasons of good object-oriented design.

Security One mechanism that hackers use to subvert systems is to create a subclass of a class and then substitute their class for the original. The subclass looks and feels like the original class but does vastly different things, possibly causing damage or getting into private information. To prevent this kind of subversion, you can declare your class to be final and thereby prevent any subclasses from being created. The `String` class in the `java.lang` package is a final class for just this reason. This class is so vital to the operation of the compiler and the interpreter that the Java system must guarantee that whenever a method or object uses a `String` it gets exactly a `java.lang.String` and not some other string. This ensures that all strings have no strange, inconsistent, undesirable, or unpredictable properties.

If you try to compile a subclass of a final class, the compiler prints an error message and refuses to compile your program. In addition, the bytecode verifier ensures that the subversion is not taking place at the bytecode level. It does this by checking to make sure that a class is not a subclass of a final class.

Design You may also wish to declare a class as final for object-oriented design reasons. You may think that your class is "perfect" or that, conceptually, your class should have no subclasses.

To specify that your class is final, use the keyword `final` before the `class` keyword in your class declaration.

For example, if you want to declare your (perfect) `ChessAlgorithm` class as final, its declaration should look like this:

```
final class ChessAlgorithm {
    . . .
}
```

Any subsequent attempts to subclass `ChessAlgorithm` will result in a compiler error such as the following:

```
Chess.java:6: Can't subclass final classes: class
ChessAlgorithm
class BetterChessAlgorithm extends ChessAlgorithm {
      ^
1 error
```

Final Methods

Does creating a final class seem heavy-handed for your needs? Do you really just want to protect some of your class's methods from being overridden? You can use the `final` keyword in a method declaration to indicate to the compiler that the method cannot be overridden by subclasses. As just shown, the `Object` class does this; some of its methods are final and some are not.

You might wish to make a method final if it has an implementation that should not be changed and it is critical to the consistent state of the object. For example, instead of making your `ChessAlgorithm` class final, you might want instead to make the `nextMove` method final:

```
class ChessAlgorithm {
    . . .
    final void nextMove(ChessPiece pieceMoved,
                        BoardLocation newLocation) {
        . . .
    }
    . . .
}
```

Writing Abstract Classes and Methods

Sometimes, a class that you define represents an abstract concept and, as such, should not be instantiated. Take, for example, food in the real world. Have you ever seen an instance of food? No. What you see instead are instances of carrot, apple, and (our favorite) chocolate. Food represents the abstract concept of things that we all can eat. It doesn't make sense for an instance of food to exist.

Similarly in object-oriented programming, you may want to model an abstract concept without being able to create an instance of it. For example, the `Number` class in the `java.lang` package represents the abstract concept of numbers. It makes sense to model numbers in a program, but it doesn't make sense to create a generic number object. Instead, the `Number` class makes sense only as a superclass to classes like `Integer` and `Float`, both of which implement specific kinds of numbers. A class such as `Number`, which represents an abstract concept and should not be instantiated, is called an *abstract class*. An abstract class is a class that can only be subclassed—it cannot be instantiated.

To declare that your class is an abstract class, use the keyword `abstract` before the `class` keyword in your class declaration:

```
abstract class Number {
    . . .
}
```

If you attempt to instantiate an abstract class, the compiler displays an error similar to the following and refuses to compile your program:

```
AbstractTest.java:6: class AbstractTest is an abstract class.
It can't be instantiated.
        new AbstractTest();
        ^
1 error
```

Abstract Methods

An abstract class may contain *abstract methods* (methods with no implementation). In this way, an abstract class can define a complete programming interface, thereby providing its subclasses with the method declarations for all of the methods necessary to implement that programming interface. However, the abstract class can leave some or all of the implementation details of those methods up to its subclasses.

Here's an example of when you might want to create an abstract class with an abstract method in it. In an object-oriented drawing application, you can draw circles, rectangles, lines, Bezier curves, and so on. All of these graphics objects use certain states (e.g., position and bounding box) and behavior (e.g., move, resize, and draw). You can take advantage of these similarities and declare them all to inherit from the same parent object—`GraphicObject`. See Figure 23.

However, the graphic objects also substantially differ from each other in many ways; for example, drawing a circle is quite different from drawing a rectangle.

The graphic objects cannot share these types of states or behavior. On the other hand, all GraphicObjects must know how to draw themselves; they just differ in how they are drawn. Also, it does not make sense for a program to instantiate a GraphicObject. This situation is perfect for an abstract superclass.

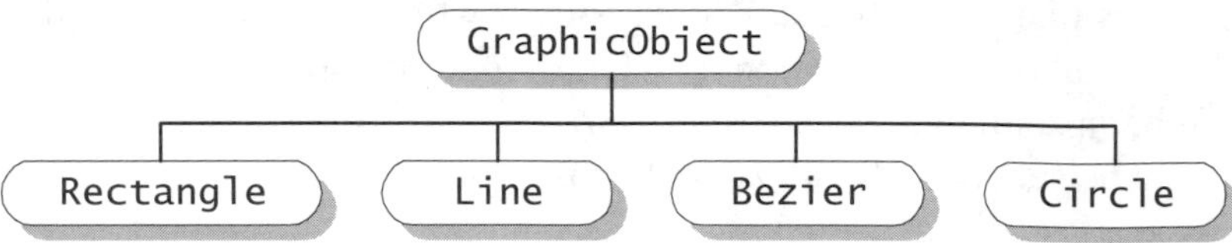

Figure 23: Classes Rectangle, Line, Bezier, and Circle inherit certain states and behavior from its common parent, GraphicObject.

First, you declare an abstract class, GraphicObject, to provide member variables and methods that are needed by all subclasses, such as the current position and the moveTo method. GraphicObject also declares abstract methods for methods, such as draw, that need to be implemented by all subclasses but that are implemented in entirely different ways (no default implementation in the superclass makes sense). The GraphicObject class looks something like this:

```
abstract class GraphicObject {
    int x, y;
    . . .
    void moveTo(int newX, int newY) {
        . . .
    }
    abstract void draw();
}
```

Each nonabstract subclass of GraphicObject, such as Circle and Rectangle, inherits the moveTo method and its implementation but must provide an implementation for the draw method:

```
class Circle extends GraphicObject {
    void draw() {
        . . .
    }
}
class Rectangle extends GraphicObject {
    void draw() {
        . . .
    }
}
```

An abstract class is not required to contain an abstract method. But any class that does or that does not provide an implementation for any abstract methods declared in its superclasses *must* be declared as an abstract class.

Creating Interfaces

The Java language supports interfaces that you use to define a protocol of behavior that can be implemented by any class anywhere in the class hierarchy. This section defines the term "interface," shows you an example of an interface and how to use it, and talks about why you may need interfaces in your programs.

What Is an Interface?

In English, an *interface* is a device or system that unrelated entities use to interact. According to this definition, a remote control is an interface between you and a television set, the English language is an interface between two people, and the protocol of behavior enforced in the military is the interface between people of different ranks. Similarly, a Java interface is a device that unrelated objects use to interact with one another. Java interfaces are probably most analogous to protocols (an agreed-upon behavior). In fact, other object-oriented languages have the functionality of Java's interfaces, but they call their interfaces *protocols*.

A Java interface defines a set of methods but does not implement them. A class that implements the interface agrees to implement all of the methods defined in the interface, thereby agreeing to certain behavior.

Definition: An *interface* is a named collection of method definitions (without implementations). An interface can also include constant declarations.

Interfaces are best understood through examples, so let's look at a concrete example of an interface and two classes that use it to interact. Then we'll talk more about interfaces in the abstract and clear up some common confusion.

Example: AlarmClock and Sleeper

This example is fairly simple, but it shows you how to create and use an interface. It also gives you some insight as to why you need them and how to decide when to use an interface versus when to use a class or an abstract class.

The `AlarmClock` class, shown in full on page 704 of Appendix A, is a service provider—it notifies objects after a certain amount of time has elapsed.

To get on AlarmClock's list of "sleepers," an object must do two things:

1. Ask the alarm clock to wake it up.
2. Implement the wakeUp method.

To satisfy the first requirement, an object calls AlarmClock's letMeSleepFor method, which is implemented like this:

```
public synchronized boolean letMeSleepFor(Sleeper s,
                                          long time) {
    int index = findNextSlot();
    if (index == NOROOM) {
        return false;
    } else {
        sleepers[index] = s;
        sleepFor[index] = time;
        new AlarmThread(index).start();
        return true;
    }
}
```

If AlarmClock has space, then it registers the sleeper, starts a new AlarmThread for it, and returns true. After the specified a mount of time has elapsed the AlarmClock will call s's wakeUp method.

This leads to the second requirement. An object that wants to use AlarmClock must implement the wakeUp method (so that AlarmClock can call it to notify the object after the time has elapsed). But how is this enforced? It's enforced through the data type of the object being registered.

The first argument to the letMeSleepFor method is the object that wants to get woken up. The data type of this argument is Sleeper, which is the name of this interface:

```
public interface Sleeper {
    public void wakeUp();

    public long ONE_SECOND = 1000;// in milliseconds
    public long ONE_MINUTE = 60000;// in milliseconds
}
```

The Sleeper interface defines the wakeUp method but does not implement it. It also defines two useful constants. Classes that implement this interface "inherit" the constants and must implement wakeUp.

Any object that is a Sleeper (and can therefore be passed into letMeSleepFor) implements this interface. This means it implements all of the methods defined by the interface. Thus a Sleeper object implements the wakeUp method, thereby satisfying AlarmClock's second requirement.

For example, check out the following small class that implements the Sleeper interface. The GUIClock class (page 706) is an applet that displays the current time and uses an AlarmClock object to wake it up every minute so that it can update its display:

```
public class GUIClock extends Applet implements Sleeper {
    . . .
    public void wakeUp() {
        repaint();
        clock.letMeSleepFor(this, ONE_MINUTE);
    }
}
```

Now that you've seen an interface in action, we'll answer some of the inevitable questions.

Why Can't I Just Use an Abstract Class?

At this point, many programmers wonder how an interface differs from an abstract class. An interface is simply a list of unimplemented, and therefore abstract, methods. Wouldn't the following Sleeper class do the same thing as the Sleeper interface?

```
public abstract class Sleeper {
    public abstract void wakeUp();
}
```

No. The two are not equivalent. If Sleeper is an abstract class, then all objects that wish to use AlarmClock must be instances of a class inherited from Sleeper. However, many objects that wish to use AlarmClock already have a superclass. For example, the GUIClock is an Applet; it must be an applet to run inside a browser. But Java doesn't support multiple inheritance. So GUIClock can't be both a Sleeper and an Applet. Hence, you use an interface instead.

This is the practical explanation of the problem. The conceptual explanation is this: AlarmClock should not force a class relationship on its users. It doesn't matter what their class is. It simply matters that they implement a specific method.

Oh! So Interfaces Provide for Multiple Inheritance?

Often interfaces are touted as an alternative to multiple *class* inheritance. While interfaces may solve similar problems, interface and multiple class inheritance are quite different animals, in particular:

- A class inherits only constants from an interface.
- A class cannot inherit method implementations from an interface.
- The interface hierarchy is independent of the class hierarchy. Classes that implement the same interface may or may not be related through the class hierarchy. This is not true for multiple inheritance.

Yet, Java does allow multiple interface inheritance. That is, an interface can have multiple *superinterfaces*.

So Tell Me, What Can I Use Interfaces For?

You use an interface to define a protocol of behavior that can be implemented by any class anywhere in the class hierarchy. Interfaces are useful for the following:

- Capturing similarities between unrelated classes without artificially forcing a class relationship
- Declaring methods that one or more classes are expected to implement
- Revealing an object's programming interface without revealing its class. (Objects such as these are called *anonymous objects* and can be useful when shipping a package of classes to other developers.)

Defining an Interface

Figure 24 shows that an interface definition has two components: the *interface declaration* and the *interface body*. The interface declaration declares various attributes about the interface such as its name and whether it extends another interface. The interface body contains the constant and method declarations within that interface.

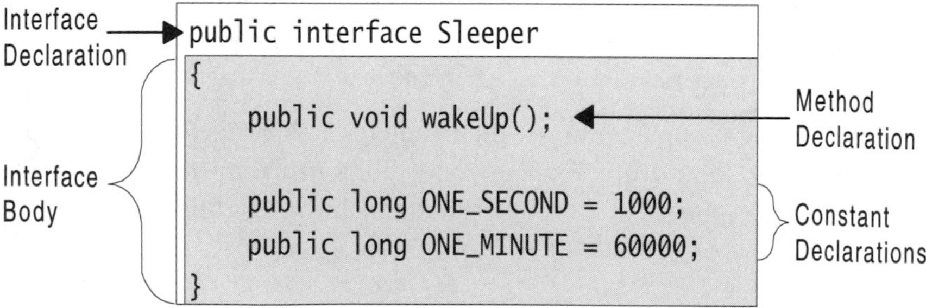

Figure 24: `Sleeper` interface definition.

The Interface Declaration

The declaration for the `Sleeper` interface uses the required elements of an interface declaration—the `interface` keyword and the name of the interface—plus the `public` access specifier:

```
public interface Sleeper {
    . . .
}
```

An interface declaration can have one other component: a list of *superinterfaces*. The full interface declaration looks like Figure 25.

`public`	Makes this interface public.
`interface` *`InterfaceName`*	Class cannot be instantiated.
`extends` *`SuperInterfaces`*	This interface's superinterfaces.

`{`
    `InterfaceBody`
`}`	

Figure 25: The full interface declaration.

The `public` access specifier indicates that the interface can be used by any class in any package. If you do not specify that your interface is public, then your interface will be accessible only to classes that are defined in the same package as the interface.

An interface can extend other interfaces just as a class can extend or subclass another class. However, while a class can extend only one other class, an interface can extend any number of interfaces. The list of superinterfaces is a comma-delimited list of all of the interfaces extended by the new interface. An interface inherits all constants and methods from its superinterfaces, unless the interface hides a constant with another of the same name or redeclares a method with a new method declaration.

The Interface Body

The interface body contains method declarations for all of the methods included in the interface. Here's the body of the `Sleeper` interface:

```
public interface Sleeper {
    public void wakeUp();
```

```
        public long ONE_SECOND = 1000;
        public long ONE_MINUTE = 60000;
    }
```

The method declaration for `wakeUp` is followed by a semicolon (`;`) because an interface does not provide implementations for the methods declared within it. All methods declared in an interface are implicitly `public` and `abstract`. The use of these modifiers on a method declaration in an interface is discouraged as a matter of style.

An interface can contain constant declarations in addition to method declarations. The `Sleeper` interface declares two constants that are useful arguments to `letMeSleepFor`. All constant values defined in an interface are implicitly `public`, `static`, and `final`. The use of these modifiers on a constant declaration in an interface is discouraged as a matter of style.

Any class can use an interface's constants from the name of the interface, like this:

```
Sleeper.ONE_SECOND
```

Classes that implement an interface can treat the constants as though they were inherited. This is why `GUIClock` can use `ONE_MINUTE` directly when calling `letMeSleepFor`:

```
public class GUIClock extends Applet implements Sleeper {
    . . .
    public void wakeUp() {
        repaint();
        clock.letMeSleepFor(this, ONE_MINUTE);
    }
}
```

Member declarations in an interface disallow the use of some declaration modifiers; you may not use `transient`, `volatile`, or `synchronized` in a member declaration in an interface. Also, you may not use the `private` and `protected` specifiers when declaring members of an interface.

Note: Previous releases of the Java platform allowed you to use the `abstract` modifier on interface declarations and on method declarations within interfaces. However this is unnecessary, since interfaces and their methods are implicitly abstract. You should no longer be using `abstract` in your interface declarations or in your method declarations within interfaces.

Implementing the Sleeper Interface

Implementing an Interface (page 127) in the previous lesson already showed you how to implement an interface. Here, the `GUIClock` class implements one interface—`Sleeper`:

```
public class GUIClock extends Applet implements Sleeper {
    . . .
    public void wakeUp() {
        // update the display
    }
}
```

Remember that when a class implements an interface, it is essentially signing a contract. The class must provide method implementations for all of the methods declared in the interface and its superinterfaces. Or, the class must be declared `abstract`. The method signature (the name and the number and type of arguments) for the method in the class must match the method signature as it appears in the interface.

Using an Interface as a Type

When you define a new interface, you are in essence defining a new reference data type. You can use interface names anywhere you can use any other data type name.

For example, the `AlarmClock` class uses the `Sleeper` type in two places:

- To declare an array of `Sleepers` (shown in bold):

```
private Sleeper[] sleepers = new Sleeper[MAX_CAPACITY];
```

- As an argument to `letMeSleepFor` (shown in bold):

```
public synchronized boolean letMeSleepFor(Sleeper s,
                                          long time)
{
    . . .
}
```

Warning! Interfaces Cannot Grow

If you ship public interfaces to other programmers, here's a limitation of interfaces that you should be aware of: *Interfaces cannot grow.* Let's look at why this is the case.

Suppose you want to add some functionality to `AlarmClock` for its 2.0 release. For example, `GUIClock` needs to update its display every minute so that it makes continual requests to be woken up. Really, `GUIClock` just wants `AlarmClock` to beep at it every minute. It would be preferable to register a single request with `AlarmClock`, for two reasons:

- It's more efficient because it involves fewer method calls.
- `GUIClock` wouldn't have to maintain its own `AlarmClock` because it wouldn't risk losing its bed.

`AlarmClock` needs to differentiate such "beeps" from an actual wake up call. So now the `Sleeper` interface must include a `beep` method:

```
public interface Sleeper {
    public void wakeUp();
    public void beep();

    public long ONE_SECOND = 1000;
    public long ONE_MINUTE = 60000;
}
```

However, if you make this change to `Sleeper`, all classes that implement the old `Sleeper` will break because they don't implement the interface anymore! Programmers relying on this interface will protest loudly.

Try to anticipate all uses for your interface up front and specify it completely from the beginning. Given that this is often impossible, you may need either to create more interfaces later or to break your customer's code.

Implementing Nested Classes

As you learned in Using an Inner Class to Implement an Adapter (page 129), Java lets you define a class as a member of another class. Such a class is called a *nested class* and is illustrated here:

```
class EnclosingClass {
    . . .
    class ANestedClass {
        . . .
    }
}
```

Definition: A *nested class* is a class that is a member of another class.

You use nested classes to reflect and enforce the relationship between two classes. You should define a class within another class when the nested class makes sense only in the context of its enclosing class or when it relies on the enclosing class for its function. For example, a text cursor makes sense only in the context of a particular text component.

As a member of its enclosing class, a nested class has a special privilege: It has unlimited access to its enclosing class's members, even if they are declared private.[1] However, this special privilege isn't really special at all. It is fully consistent with the meaning of `private` and the other access specifiers. The access specifiers restrict access to members for classes *outside* of the enclosing class. The nested class is *inside* of its enclosing class so that it has access to its enclosing class's members.

Like other members, a nested class can be declared static (or not). A static nested class is called just that: a *static nested class*. A nonstatic nested class is called an *inner class*. These are illustrated in the following code:

```
class EnclosingClass {
    . . .
    static class AStaticNestedClass {
        . . .
    }
    class InnerClass {
        . . .
    }
}
```

As with static methods and variables (normally called class methods and variables), a static nested class is associated with its enclosing class. And like class methods, a static nested class cannot refer directly to instance variables or methods defined in its enclosing class—it can use them only via an object reference.

As with instance methods and variables, an inner class is associated with an instance of its enclosing class and has direct access to that object's instance variables and methods. Also, because an inner class is associated with an instance, it cannot define any static members itself.

To further help differentiate the terms nested class and inner class, you could think about them in the following way. The term "nested class" reflects the *syntactic relationship between two classes*; that is, syntactically, the code for one class appears within the code of another. The term "inner class" reflects the *relationship between instances of the two classes*. Consider the following classes:

---

[1] Due to a bug in the JDK 1.1 compiler, an inner class should not attempt to call a private method in its enclosing class. Use the default access instead of `private` for that method.

```
class EnclosingClass {
    . . .
    class InnerClass {
        . . .
    }
}
```

The interesting feature about the relationship between these two classes is *not* that `InnerClass` is syntactically defined within `EnclosingClass`. Rather, it's that an instance of `InnerClass` can exist only within an instance of `EnclosingClass` and that it has direct access to instance variables and methods of its enclosing instance. Figure 26 illustrates this idea.

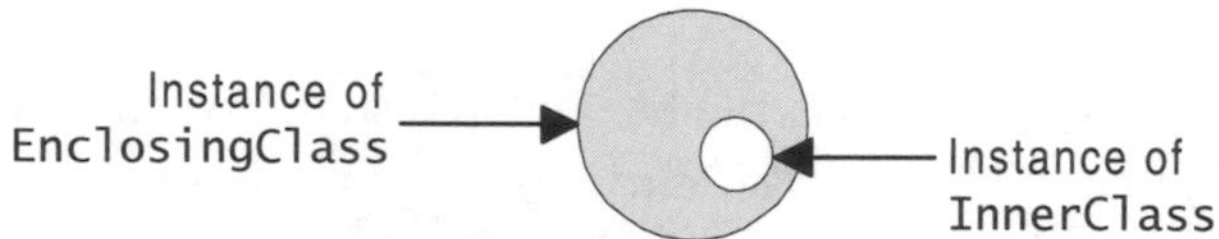

Figure 26: An instance of `InnerClass` can only exist within an instance of `EnclosingClass`.

You may encounter nested classes of both kinds in the Java API and be required to use them. However, most nested classes that you write will be inner classes.

Definition: An *inner class* is a nested class whose instance exists within an instance of its enclosing class and has direct access to the instance members of its enclosing instance.

Inner Classes

To help you get a handle on inner classes and what they are good for, let's revisit the `Stack` class. Suppose you want to add a feature to this class that lets another class enumerate over the elements in the stack using the interface defined in `java.util.Enumeration`. This interface contains two method declarations:

```
public boolean hasMoreElements();
pubilc Object nextElement();
```

The `Enumeration` interface defines the interface for a single loop over the elements:

```
while (hasMoreElements())
    nextElement()
```

If `Stack` implemented the `Enumeration` interface itself, you could not restart the loop and you could not enumerate the contents more than once. Also, you couldn't allow two enumerations to happen simultaneously. So `Stack` shouldn't implement `Enumeration`. Rather, a helper class should do the work for `Stack`.

The helper class must have access to the `Stack`'s elements. It also must be able to access them directly because the `Stack`'s public interface supports only LIFO access. This is where inner classes come in. The following code is an implementation of `Stack` that defines a helper class (called an *adapter class*) for enumerating over its elements. Note that the `StackEnum` class refers directly to `Stack`'s `items` instance variable:

```
public class Stack
{
    private Vector items;

    // code for Stack's methods and constructors not shown

    public Enumeration enumerator() {
        return new StackEnum();
    }
    class StackEnum implements Enumeration {
        int currentItem = items.size() - 1;
        public boolean hasMoreElements() {
            return (currentItem > 0);
        }
        public Object nextElement() {
            if (currentItem == 0)
                throw new NoSuchElementException();
            else
                return items.elementAt[--currentItem];
        }
    }
}
```

Inner classes are used primarily to implement adapter classes like the one shown in this example. If you plan on handling events from the AWT, then you'll want to know about using adapter classes because the event-handling mechanism in the AWT makes extensive use of them.

Anonymous Classes

As shown in Using an Inner Class to Implement an Adapter (page 129), you can declare a class without a name. Here's yet another version of the now-tired `Stack` class, in this case using an anonymous class for its enumerator:

```
public class Stack
{
    private Vector items;

    // code for Stack's methods and constructors not shown

    public Enumeration enumerator() {
        return new Enumeration () {
            int currentItem = items.size() - 1;
            public boolean hasMoreElements() {
                return (currentItem > 0);
            }
            public Object nextElement() {
                if (currentItem == 0)
                    throw new NoSuchElementException();
                else
                    return items.elementAt[--currentItem];
            }
        }
    }
}
```

Anonymous classes can make code difficult to read.You should limit their use to those classes that are very small (no more than a method or two) and whose use is well-understood (like the AWT event-handling adapter classes).

Other Facts about Nested Classes

Like other classes, nested classes can be declared `abstract` or `final`. The meaning of these two modifiers for nested classes is the same as for other classes. Also, the access specifiers—`private`, `public`, `protected`, and `package`—may be used to restrict access to nested classes just as they do to other class members.

Any nested class, not just anonymous ones, can be declared in any block of code. A nested class declared within a method or other smaller block of code has access to any final, local variables in scope.

Creating and Using Packages

To make classes easier to find and use, to avoid naming conflicts, and to control access, programmers bundle groups of related classes into *packages*.

Definition: A *package* is a collection of related classes and interfaces that provides access protection and namespace management.

The classes and interfaces that are part of the JDK are members of various packages that bundle classes by function: applet classes are in `java.applet`, I/O classes are in `java.io`, and the GUI widget classes are in `java.awt`. You can put your classes and interfaces in packages, too.

Let's look at a set of classes and examine why you might want to put them in a package. Suppose you write a group of classes that represent a collection of graphics objects such as circles, rectangles, lines, and points. You also write an interface `Draggable` that classes implement if they can be dragged with the mouse by the user.

```
abstract class Graphic {
    . . .
}
class Circle extends Graphic implements Draggable {
    . . .
}
class Rectangle extends Graphic implements Draggable {
    . . .
}
interface Draggable {
    . . .
}
```

You should bundle these classes and the interface together in a package, for several reasons:

- You and other programmers can easily determine that these classes and interfaces are related.
- You and other programmers know where to find classes and interfaces that provide graphics-related functions.
- The names of your classes won't conflict with class names in other packages because the package creates a new namespace.
- You can allow classes within the package to have unrestricted access to each other, yet still restrict access for classes outside the package.

Creating a Package

To create a package, you simply put a class or interface in it. To do this, you put a `package` statement at the top of the source file in which the class or interface is defined. For example, the following code appears in the source file `Circle.java` and puts the `Circle` class in the `graphics` package:

```
package graphics;
class Circle extends Graphic implements Draggable {
    . . .
}
```

The `Circle` class is a *member* of the `graphics` package.

You must include a `package` statement at the top of every source file that defines a class or interface that is to be a member of the `graphics` package. So you would also include the statement in `Rectangle.java` and so on:

```
package graphics;
class Rectangle extends Graphic implements Draggable {
    . . .
}
```

The scope of the `package` statement is the entire source file, so all classes and interfaces defined in `Circle.java` and `Rectangle.java` are also members of the `graphics` package.

If you do not use a `package` statement, your class or interface ends up in the *default package*, which is a package that has no name. Generally speaking, the default package is only for small or temporary applications or when you are just beginning development. Otherwise, classes and interfaces belong in named packages.

Naming a Package

With programmers all over the world writing Java classes and interfaces, it is conceivable and even likely that two programmers will use the same name for two different classes. In fact, the previous example does just that: It defines a `Rectangle` class when there is already a `Rectangle` class in the `java.awt` package. Yet, the compiler allows both classes to have the same name. Why? Because they are in different packages and the actual name of each class includes the package name. That is, the name of the `Rectangle` class in the `graphics` package is really `graphics.Rectangle`, and the name of the `Rectangle` class in the `java.awt` package is really `java.awt.Rectangle`.

This works just fine unless two independent programmers use the same name for their packages. What prevents this? Convention.

By Convention: Companies use their reversed Internet domain name in their package names, like this: `com.company.package`. Name collisions that occur within a single company need to be handled by convention within that company, perhaps by including the region or project name after the company name, for example, `com.company.region.package`.

Using Package Members

Only public package members are accessible outside the package in which they are defined. To use a public package member from outside its package, you must either

1. refer to the member by its long (disambiguated) name,
2. import the package member, or
3. import the member's entire package.

Each is appropriate for different situations, as explained in the following sections.

Referring to a Package Member by Name

So far, the examples in this book have referred to classes and interfaces by the name specified in their declaration (such as `Rectangle`, `AlarmClock`, and `Sleeper`). Such names are called *short names*. You can use a package member's short name if the code you are writing is in the same package as that member or if the member's package has been imported.

However, if you are trying to use a member from a different package and that package has not been imported, then you must use the member's *long name,* which includes the package name. This is the long name for the `Rectangle` class declared in the `graphics` package in the previous example:

```
graphics.Rectangle
```

You could use this long name to create an instance of `graphics.Rectangle`:

```
graphics.Rectangle myRect = new graphics.Rectangle();
```

You'll find that using long names is okay for one-shot uses. But you'd likely get annoyed if you had to write `graphics.Rectangle` again and again. Also, your code would get very messy and difficult to read. In such cases, you can just import the member instead.

Importing a Package Member

To import a specific member into the current file, put an `import` statement at the beginning of your file before any class or interface definitions (but after the

package statement, if there is one). Here's how you would import the Circle class from the graphics package created in the previous section:

```
import graphics.Circle;
```

Now you can refer to the Circle class by its short name:

```
Circle myCircle = new Circle();
```

This approach works just fine if you use just a few members from the graphics package. But if you use many classes and interfaces from a package, you really just want to import the whole package and forget about it.

Importing an Entire Package

To import all of the classes and interfaces contained in a particular package, use the import statement with the asterisk * wildcard character:

```
import graphics.*;
```

Now you can refer to any class or interface in the graphics package by its short name:

```
Circle myCircle = new Circle();
Rectangle myRectangle = new Rectangle();
```

The asterisk in the import statement can be used only to specify all of the classes within a package, as shown here. It cannot be used to match a subset of the classes in a package. For example, the following does not match all of the classes in the graphics package that begin with "A":

```
import graphics.A*;// does not work
```

Instead, it generates a compiler error. With the import statement, you can import only a single package member or an entire package.

For your convenience, the Java runtime system automatically imports three packages for you:

- The default package (the package with no name)
- The java.lang package
- The current package

Disambiguating a Name

If by some chance a member in one package shares the same name with a member in another package and both packages are imported, you must refer to the member by its long name. For example, the previous example defined a class named `Rectangle` in the `graphics` package. The `java.awt` package also contains a `Rectangle` class. If both `graphics` and `java.awt` have been imported, then the following is ambiguous:

```
Rectangle rect;
```

In such a situation, you have to be more specific and indicate exactly which `Rectangle` class you want by using the member's long name:

```
graphics.Rectangle rect;
```

Managing Source and Class Files

The JDK relies on hierarchical file systems to manage source and class files for Java programs, although *The Java Language Specification* does not require this. The strategy is as follows.

You put the source code for a class or interface in a text file whose name is the short name of the class or interface and whose extension is `.java` (the JDK requires this extension for public classes and it's a good idea for other classes). Then, you put the source file in a directory whose name reflects the name of the package to which the class or interface belongs. For example, the source code for the `Rectangle` class would be in a file named `Rectangle.java`. and the file would be in a directory named `graphics`. The `graphics` directory may be anywhere on the file system. Figure 27 shows how this works.

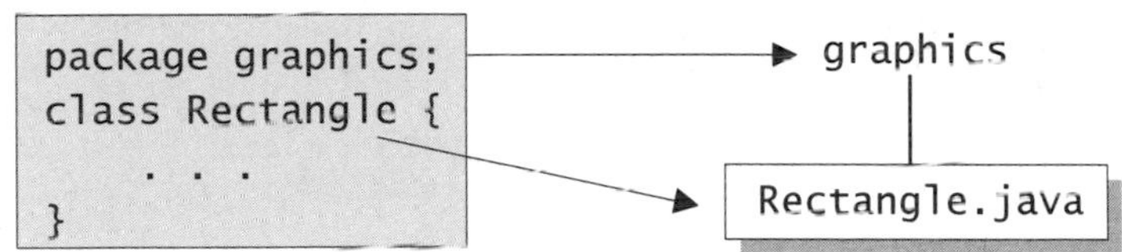

Figure 27: The source code for the `Rectangle` class is in the file `Rectangle.java`, which is located in a folder named `graphics`.

The long name of the package member and the pathname to the file are parallel (assuming the UNIX filename separator slash /):

```
graphics.Rectangle             class name
graphics/Rectangle.java        pathname to file
```

Furthermore, by convention, each company uses its reversed Internet domain name in its package names. (However, some companies now choose to drop "com" from their package names.) The fictional company called Taranis Interactive whose Internet domain name is `taranis.com` would precede all of its package names with `com.taranis`. Each component of the package name corresponds to a subdirectory. So, if Taranis had a graphics package that contained a `Rectangle.java` source file, it would be contained in a series of subdirectories, as shown in Figure 28.

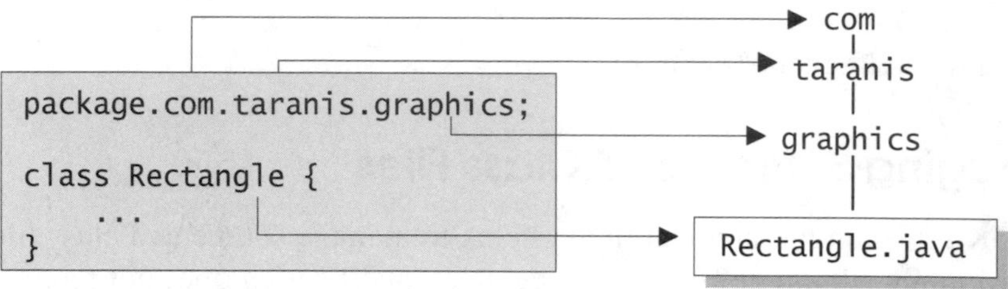

Figure 28: By convention, in their package names companies use their Internet domain name in reverse.

When you compile a source file, the compiler creates a different output file for each class and interface defined in it. The basename of the output file is the name of the class or interface, and its extension is `.class`; see Figure 29.

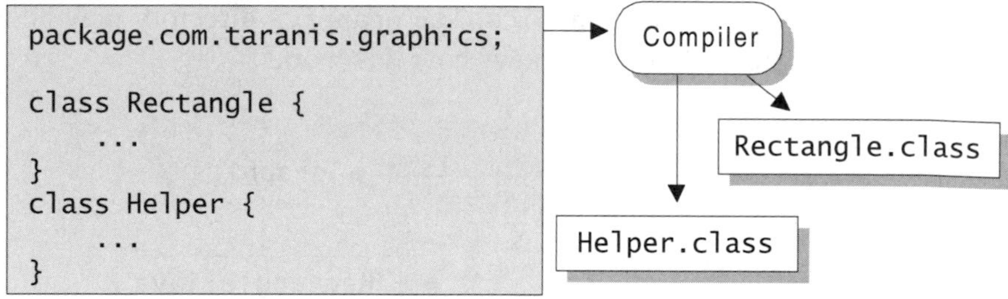

Figure 29: The compiler creates a separate `.class` file for every class.

Like a `.java` file, a `.class` file should also be in a series of directories that reflect the package name. However, it does not have to be in the same directory as its source. You could arrange your source and class directories separately, as shown in Figure 30.

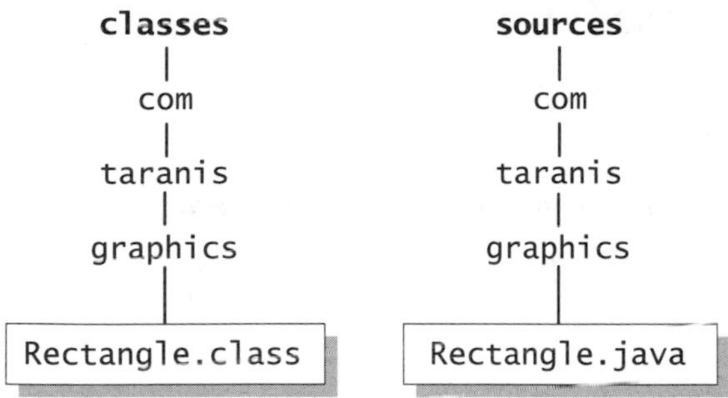

Figure 30: An example of how to arrange your source and class directories separately.

By doing this, you can give the classes directory to other programmers without revealing your sources.

Why all the bother about directories and filenames? You need to manage your source and class files in this manner so that the compiler and the interpreter can find all of the classes and interfaces used by your program. When the compiler encounters a new class as it's compiling your program, it must be able to find the class so as to resolve names, do type checking, and so on. Similarly, when the interpreter encounters a new class as it's running your program, it must be able to find the class to invoke its methods, and so on. Both the compiler and the interpreter search for classes in each directory or zip file listed in your *class path*.

Definition: A *class path* is a list of directories or zip files to search for class files.

Each directory listed in the class path is a top-level directory in which package directories appear. From the top-level directory, the compiler and the interpreter can construct the rest of the path based on the package and class name for the class. For example, the class path entry for the directory structure shown in the diagram on the previous page would include `classes`, but not `com` or any of the directories below `com`. Both the compiler and the interpreter construct the path name to a `.class` file with its full package name.

By default, the compiler and the interpreter search the current directory and the zip file containing the JDK class files. In other words, the current directory and the JDK class files are automatically in your class path. Most, if not all, classes can be found in these two locations. So it's likely that you don't have to worry about your class path. In some cases, however, you may have to set your class path.

Setting the Class Path

If you must, you can change your class path. This can be done in either of two ways:

1. Set the `CLASSPATH` environment variable (*not recommended*).
2. Use the `-classpath` runtime option when you invoke the compiler or the interpreter.

We don't recommend setting the `CLASSPATH` environment variable because it can be long-lived (particularly if you set it in a login or startup script). It's also easy to forget about, and then one day, your programs won't work because the compiler or interpreter loads a crusty old class file instead of the one you want. An old, out-of-date `CLASSPATH` variable is a fruitful source of confusing problems.

The second option, setting the class path with the runtime option, is preferable because it sets the class path only for the current invocation of the compiler or the interpreter. Here's how to use the runtime option `-classpath` to set your class path.

Platform-specific Details: Using the `-classpath` Runtime Option

UNIX:

```
javac -classpath .:~/classes:/JDK/lib/classes.zip
```

DOS shell (Win32):

```
javac -classpath .;C:\classes;C:\JDK\lib\classes.zip
```

When you specify a class path in this manner, you completely override the current class path. Thus you must include the `classes.zip` file from the JDK in the class path. It's a good idea to include the current directory as well.

The order of the entries in the class path is important. When the Java interpreter is looking for a class, it searches the entries in your class path, in order, until it finds a class with the correct name. The Java interpreter runs the first class with the correct name that it encounters and does not search the remaining entries.

Note: If you load an applet into a Java application such as HotJava or the Applet Viewer and the loaded class is in the class path, the applet doesn't have the restrictions that applets loaded over the network do, so it can never be reloaded. We recommend never starting an application such as HotJava in the same directory as an `Applet` class because the current directory "`.`" is usually part of the class path.

Common Problems (and Their Solutions)

THIS section covers some common problems that you might encounter when learning the Java language. After each problem is a list of possible solutions.

Problem: The compiler complains that it can't find a class.

- Make sure you've imported the class or its package.
- Unset the `CLASSPATH` environment variable, if it's set.
- Make sure you're spelling the class name exactly the same way as it is declared. Case matters!
- If your classes are in packages, make sure that they appear in the correct subdirectory as outlined in Managing Source and Class Files (page 161).
- Also, some programmers use different names for the class name from the `.java` filename. Make sure you're using the class name and not the filename. In fact, make the names the same and you won't run into this problem for this reason.

Problem: The interpreter says it can't find one of my classes.

- Make sure you specified the *class* name—not the class *file* name—to the interpreter.
- Unset the `CLASSPATH` environment variable, if it's set.

- If your classes are in packages, make sure that they appear in the correct subdirectory as outlined in Managing Source and Class Files (page 161).
- Make sure you're invoking the interpreter from the directory in which the `.class` file is located.

Problem: My program doesn't work! What's wrong with it?

The following is a list of common programming mistakes by novice Java programmers. Make sure one of these isn't what's holding you back.

- Did you forget to use `break` after each `case` statement in a `switch` statement?
- Did you use the assignment operator = when you really wanted to use the comparison operator ==?
- Are the termination conditions on your loops correct? Make sure you're not terminating loops one iteration too early or too late. That is, make sure you are using < or <= and > or >= as appropriate for your situation.
- Remember that array indices begin at 0, so iterating over an array looks like this:

```
for (int i = 0; i < array.length; i++)
    . . .
```

- Are you comparing floating-point numbers using ==? Remember that floats are approximations of the real thing. The greater than and less than (> and <) operators are more appropriate when conditional logic is performed on floating-point numbers.
- Are you having trouble with encapsulation, inheritance, or other object-oriented programming and design concepts? Review the information in Object-Oriented Programming Concepts (page 39).
- Make sure that blocks of statements are enclosed in curly brackets `{}`. The following code looks right because of indentation, but it doesn't do what the indents imply because the brackets are missing:

```
for (int i = 0; i < arrayOfInts.length; i++)
    arrayOfInts[i] = i;
    System.out.println("[i] = " + arrayOfInts[i]);
```

- Are you using the correct conditional operator? Make sure you understand && and `||` and are using them appropriately.

- Do you use the negation operator `!` a lot? Try to express conditions without it. Doing so is less confusing and error-prone.
- Are you using a `do-while`? If so, do you know that the loop executes one more time than a similar `while` loop?
- Are you trying to change the value of an argument from a method? Arguments in Java are passed by value and can't be changed in a method.
- Did you inadvertently add an extra semicolon (;), thereby terminating a statement prematurely? Notice the extra semicolon at the end of this `for` statement:

```
for (int i = 0; i < arrayOfInts.length; i++) ;
    arrayOfInts[i] = i;
```

End of Trail

YOU'VE reached the end of the **Learning the Java Language** trail. Take a break—have a cup of steaming hot java.

What Next?

Once you've caught your breath, you have several choices of where to go next. You can go back to the Trail Map (page xvii) to see all of your choices, or you can go directly to one of the following popular trails:

Writing Applets (page 171): The next trail in the tutorial. This is the starting point for learning everything about writing applets.

Essential Java Classes (page 241): This trail covers the classes that you are likely to use frequently: `Strings`, `System`, `Threads`, and the I/O classes. This trail also includes lessons on exception handling and setting program attributes.

Writing Applets

DIRECTLY or indirectly, this trail covers everything you need to know to write a Java applet. Because applets can use almost all of the Java API, this trail mentions many features that are explained elsewhere. Feel free to cross over to other trails to learn about the features that interest you. Once you're ready to write an applet, you can return to this trail to find out how the applet environment affects the features you want to use.

Overview of Applets (page 175) tells you how applets work. You should thoroughly understand this lesson before going further in this trail.

Taking Advantage of the Applet API (page 189) talks about how to use the API to which only applets have access. It covers sound, applet parameters, the `<APPLET>` tag, interapplet communication, and making requests to the browser.

Practical Considerations of Writing Applets (page 211) discusses topics that are covered elsewhere in this tutorial but that are affected by the applet environment. For example, it mentions some factors you should consider when writing the graphical user interface (GUI) for your applet. It also talks about security restrictions on applets and how a server-side application can help you get around those restrictions.

Finishing an Applet (page 231) describes the characteristics of a high-quality applet. It includes Before You Ship That Applet (page 231), a checklist of some annoying behaviors you should avoid in your applet.

For the latest tips on writing and delivering applets, see the online Web page for this book:

```
http://java.sun.com/docs/books/tutorial/2e/book.html
```

8 Overview of Applets

THIS lesson discusses the parts of an applet. If you haven't yet compiled an applet and included it in an HTML page, you might want to do so now. Step-by-step instructions are in The "Hello World" Applet (page 19) in the Getting Started trail.

Every applet is implemented by creating a subclass of the Applet class. Figure 31 shows the inheritance hierarchy of the Applet class. This hierarchy determines much of what an applet can do and how it does it, as you'll see on the next few pages.

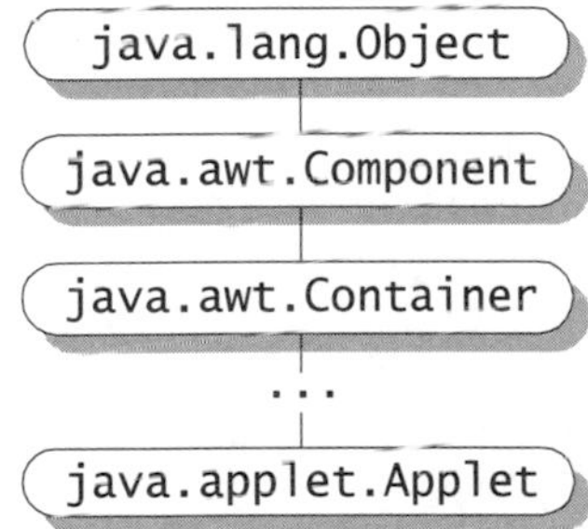

Figure 31: The Applet class inherits much of its functionality from its superclasses.

A Simple Applet

Following is the source code for an applet called Simple. The Simple applet displays a descriptive string whenever it encounters a *milestone*—a major event in an applet's life cycle, such as when the user first visits the page that contains the applet. The following pages build upon the Simple applet to illustrate concepts

that are common to many applets. If you find yourself baffled by the Java source code, you might want to go to the trail Learning the Java Language (page 35) to learn more about the Java language.

```
import java.applet.Applet;
import java.awt.Graphics;

public class Simple extends Applet {

    StringBuffer buffer;

    public void init() {
        buffer = new StringBuffer();
        addItem("initializing... ");
    }

    public void start() {
        addItem("starting... ");
    }

    public void stop() {
        addItem("stopping... ");
    }

    public void destroy() {
        addItem("preparing for unloading...");
    }

    void addItem(String newWord) {
        System.out.println(newWord);
        buffer.append(newWord);
        repaint();
    }

    public void paint(Graphics g) {
        //Draw a Rectangle around the applet's display area.
        g.drawRect(0, 0,
                   getSize().width - 1,
                   getSize().height - 1);

        //Draw the current string inside the rectangle.
        g.drawString(buffer.toString(), 5, 15);
    }
}
```

The Life Cycle of an Applet (page 177) uses the `Simple` applet to teach you about the milestones in every applet's life.

The `Applet` class provides a framework for applet execution, defining methods that the system calls when milestones occur. Methods for Milestones (page 179) tells you how most applets override some or all of these methods to respond appropriately to milestones.

Applets inherit the drawing and event-handling methods of the AWT `Component` class. (AWT stands for Abstract Window Toolkit; Java programs use the AWT to produce user interfaces.) *Drawing* refers to anything related to representing an applet on-screen—drawing images, presenting user interface components such as buttons, or using graphics primitives. *Event handling* is the detection and processing of user input such as mouse clicks and key presses, as well as more abstract events, such as value and appearance changes. Methods for Drawing and Event Handling (page 181) gives an overview of how applets can use the methods they inherit from the `Component` class.

Methods for Adding UI Components (page 183) discusses the methods that applets inherit from the AWT `Container` class. As a `Container`, an applet is designed to hold `Components`. Components are user interface objects such as buttons, labels, pop-up lists, and scroll panes. Like other containers, applets use layout managers to control the positioning of components.

Although applets can in theory invoke any API in the Java platform, in practice they're limited in doing this because of security considerations. What Applets Can and Cannot Do (page 184) gives an overview of applet capabilities and limitations.

Once you've written an applet, you'll need to add it to an HTML page so that you can try it out. Test Driving an Applet (page 185) describes how to use the `<APPLET>` HTML tag to add an applet to an HTML page.

After you've read every page in this lesson, you'll have seen almost everything you need to be able to write applets. For a review, see the Summary (page 186).

The Life Cycle of an Applet

Here is a picture of the `Simple` applet. You can find its source code on page 708.

initializing... starting...

http://java.sun.com/docs/books/tutorial/applet/overview/lifeCycle.html

Loading the Applet

The "initializing... starting..." text you see in the previous applet is the result of the applet's being loaded. When an applet is loaded, here's what happens:

- An instance of the applet's controlling class (an `Applet` subclass) is created.
- The applet *initializes* itself.
- The applet *starts* running.

Note: Some browsers let you load *serialized applets*—applets that have been saved while running. When a serialized applet is loaded, it doesn't initialize itself; it simply starts running.

Leaving and Returning to the Applet's Page

When the user leaves the page—for example, to go to another page—the applet has the option of *stopping* itself. When the user returns to the page, the applet can *start* itself again. The same sequence occurs when the user iconifies and then deiconifies the window that contains the applet. (Other terms used instead of iconify are *miniaturize*, *minimize*, and *close*.)

Try This: Go to the online version of this section in a Java-enabled browser, like Netscape Navigator, HotJava, Internet Explorer, or the JDK Applet Viewer. The URL to visit is `http://java.sun.com/docs/books/tutorial/applet/overview/lifeCycle.html`. Leave and then return to the page. You'll see "stopping..." added to the applet output, as the applet is given the chance to stop itself. You'll also see "starting..." when the applet is told to start itself again. Next, iconify the window that contains the online version of this section, and then open it again. Many window systems provide a button in the title bar that lets you iconify the window. You should see "stopping..." and then "starting..." added to the applet output.

Reloading the Applet

Some browsers let the user reload applets, a process that consists of unloading the applet and then loading it again. Before an applet is unloaded, it's given the chance to *stop* itself and then to perform a *final cleanup* so that the applet can release any resources it holds. After that, the applet is unloaded and then loaded again, as described in Loading the Applet (page 178).

Try This: If your browser lets you easily reload applets, reload the applet. (In Netscape Navigator, Shift-Reload tells the browser to reload the applet.) Look at the standard output to see what happens when you reload the applet. (See Displaying Diagnostics to the Standard Output and Standard Error Streams (page 216) for information about the standard output.) You should see "stopping..." and "preparing for unloading..." when the applet is unloaded. You can't see this in the applet GUI because the applet is unloaded before the text can be displayed. When the applet is reloaded, you should see "initializing..." and "starting...", just like when you loaded the applet for the first time.

Quitting the Browser

When the user quits the browser, the applet has the chance to *stop* itself and do *final cleanup* before the browser exits.

Summary

An applet can react to milestones in the following ways:

- It can *initialize* itself.
- It can *start* running.
- It can *stop* running.
- It can perform a *final cleanup*, in preparation for being unloaded.

The next section describes the four applet methods that correspond to these four reactions.

Methods for Milestones

The `Simple` applet, like every other applet, contains a subclass of the `Applet` class. The `Simple` class overrides four `Applet` methods so that it can respond to major events:

```
public class Simple extends Applet {
    . . .
    public void init() { . . . }
    public void start() { . . . }
    public void stop() { . . . }
    public void destroy() { . . . }
    . . .
}
```

`init`
: To *initialize* the applet each time it is loaded or reloaded

`start`
: To *start* the applet's execution, such as when the applet is loaded or when the user revisits a page that contains the applet

`stop`
: To *stop* the applet's execution, for example, when the user leaves the applet's page or quits the browser

`destroy`
: To perform a *final cleanup* in preparation for unloading

Not every applet needs to override every one of these methods. Some simple applets override none of them. For example, the The "Hello World" Applet (page 19) doesn't override any of these methods, since it doesn't do anything except draw itself. It just displays a string once using its `paint` method. (The `paint` method is described in the next section.) Most applets, however, do more.

The `init` method is useful for one-time initialization that doesn't take very long. In general, it should contain the code that you would normally put into a constructor. Applets usually shouldn't have constructors. This is because an applet isn't guaranteed to have a full environment until its `init` method is called. For example, the `Applet` image-loading methods simply don't work inside of a constructor. The `init` method, on the other hand, is a great place to call the image-loading methods, since the methods return quickly.

Note: When a browser loads a serialized applet, it does not invoke the applet's `init` method. The reason: The `init` method was presumably executed before the applet was serialized. See Object Serialization (page 388) for more information.

Every applet that does something after initialization (except in direct response to user actions) must override the `start` method. The `start` method either performs the applet's work or (more likely) starts up one or more threads to perform the work. You can read more about threads later in this trail, in Threads in Applets (page 219). The next section talks more about handling the events that represent user actions.

Most applets that override `start` should also override the `stop` method. `stop` should suspend the applet's execution so that it doesn't take up system resources when the user isn't viewing the applet's page. For example, an applet that displays animation should stop drawing the animation when the user isn't viewing it in the current browser window.

Many applets don't need to override the `destroy` method, since their `stop` methods (called before `destroy`) do everything necessary to shut down the applet's execution. However, `destroy` is available for applets that need to release additional resources.

The `init`, `start`, `stop`, and `destroy` methods are discussed and used throughout this tutorial. For more information, you can also refer to the Applet API documentation.[1]

Methods for Drawing and Event Handling

The `Simple` applet defines its on-screen appearance by overriding the `paint` method:

```
class Simple extends Applet {
    . . .
    public void paint(Graphics g) { . . . }
    . . .
}
```

The `paint` method is one of two display methods that applets can override:

`paint`
: The basic display method. Many applets implement the `paint` method to draw the applet's representation within a browser window.

`update`
: A method that you can use with `paint` to improve drawing performance

Applets inherit their `paint` and `update` methods from the `Applet` class, which inherits them from the AWT `Component` class. For an overview of the `Component` class and the AWT in general, see the Overview of the Java UI (page 407). Within that overview, the architecture of the AWT drawing system is discussed in the Drawing section (page 418).

Applets inherit event-related functionality and methods from the `Component` class. [The architecture of the AWT event system is discussed in the Event Handling section (page 420).] The `Component` class defines several methods, such as `addMouseListener` and `addKeyListener`, that register objects to be automati-

---

1 http://java.sun.com/products/jdk/1.1/api/java.applet.Applet.html

cally notified about various kinds of events. To be registered, an object must implement the appropriate interface.

For example, for an object to be registered as a mouse listener on an applet, that object must implement the MouseListener interface. Once registered, that listener object will be notified every time the user clicks in the applet's drawing area. This notification comes in the form of calling the listener's mouseClicked method. The listener can be the Applet object itself, or any other object. The only requirement is that the object implement the correct listener interface.

Adding the following bold code to the Simple applet registers it as a mouse listener and makes it respond to mouse clicks.

```
import java.awt.event.MouseListener;
import java.awt.event.MouseEvent;
. . .
public class Simple extends Applet
                     implements MouseListener {
    . . .
    public void init() {
        addMouseListener(this);
        . . .
    }
    . . .
    public void mouseClicked(MouseEvent event) {
        addItem("click!... ");
    }
. . .
}
```

Note: To keep the example simple, we've left out a few empty method definitions. For a discussion of ways of avoiding empty methods, see Reality Break! The Spot Applet (page 125).

Following is the resulting output from the applet. (You can find the revised source code on page 709.) When you click within its rectangle, it displays the word "click!...".

initializing... starting... click!... click!...

http://java.sun.com/docs/books/tutorial/applet/overview/componentMethods.html

Methods for Adding UI Components

The `Simple` applet's display code (implemented in its `paint` method) is flawed: It doesn't support scrolling. Once the text it displays reaches the end of the display rectangle, you can't see any new text.

Here's an example of the problem:

```
initializing... starting... stopping... starting... stopping... starting... stopp
```

The simplest cure for this problem is to use a premade user interface (UI) component that has the right behavior. The Java platform supplies many UI components, including buttons, text fields, and menus.

Note: This section glosses over many details. To learn more about using UI components, go to the trail Creating a User Interface (page 403).

Methods for Using UI Components in Applets

Because the `Applet` class inherits from the AWT `Container` class, it's easy to add components to applets. Here are some of the `Container` methods an applet can use:

`add`
: Adds the specified `Component` to the applet.

`remove`
: Removes the specified `Component` from the applet.

`setLayout`
: Sets the applet's layout manager, which controls the positions and sizes of the components in the applet.

Adding an Uneditable Text Field to the Simple Applet

Using the `TextField` class, you can add a scrolling, uneditable text field to the `Simple` applet. You can find the revised source code on page 711. The changes are in bold font in the following code:

```
//Importing java.awt.Graphics is no longer necessary
//since this applet no longer implements the paint method.
. . .
import java.awt.TextField;
```

```
public class Simple extends Applet {

    //Instead of using a StringBuffer, use a TextField:
    TextField field;

    public void init() {
        //Create the text field and make it uneditable.
        field = new TextField();
        field.setEditable(false);

        //Set the layout manager so that the text field will
        //be as wide as possible.
        setLayout(new java.awt.GridLayout(1,0));
        //Add the text field to the applet.
        add(field);

        addItem("initializing... ");
    }
    . . .
    void addItem(String newWord) {
        //This used to append the string to the StringBuffer;
        //now it appends it to the TextField.
        String t = field.getText();
        System.out.println(newWord);
        field.setText(t + newWord);
    }

    //The paint method is no longer necessary,
    //since the TextField paints itself automatically.
```

The revised `init` method creates an uneditable text field, a `TextField` instance. It sets the applet's layout manager to one that makes the text field as wide as possible and then adds the text field to the applet. You can read about layout managers in Laying Out Components Within a Container (page 503).

Following is the output of the resulting applet. By dragging the mouse, you can scroll backward or forward to see all of the messages that have been displayed.

initializing... starting...

http://java.sun.com/docs/books/tutorial/applet/overview/containerMethods.html

What Applets Can and Cannot Do

In theory, when you write an applet you can use any of the API in the Java platform. In practice, however, applets are limited in a couple of ways:

- An applet can use only the API supported by the browser in which it runs. For example, unless a browser supports the API defined in JDK 1.1, no applet that uses 1.1 API can run in that browser. For this reason, the online version of this book contains 1.0 applets in its pages, except for the applets that demonstrate 1.1 features. See What's New in 1.1 (page 635) for more information.
- An untrusted applet can't perform operations that might pose a security threat. For example, an untrusted applet cannot read or write files on the computer on which it is executing. See Security Restrictions (page 212) for more information.

Despite these restrictions, applets have access to a wide range of functionality. For example, applets can communicate with certain other applets running in the same browser. Applets can also request that the browser display a particular URL. See Taking Advantage of the Applet API (page 189) for information about the API that's reserved just for applets. See Practical Considerations of Writing Applets (page 211) for information about the other API applets commonly use.

Test Driving an Applet

Once you've written some code for your applet, you'll want to run your applet to test it. To run an applet, you first need to add the applet to an HTML page, using the `<APPLET>` tag. You then specify the URL of the HTML page to your Java-enabled browser.

Note: Because you can't always rely on browsers to reload your applet's classes, you might want to use a quick-starting tool like the JDK Applet Viewer for most of your applet testing. Every time you change your applet, you can restart the Applet Viewer to make sure it loads all of the latest classes.

Here's the simplest form of the `<APPLET>` tag:

```
<APPLET CODE="AppletSubclass.class" WIDTH=anInt HEIGHT=anInt>
</APPLET>
```

This tag tells the browser to load the applet whose `Applet` subclass is named *AppletSubclass*. Figure 32 shows where the applet class file must be, relative to the HTML document that contains the `<APPLET>` tag. As the figure shows, unless the applet is declared to be in a package, its class file should be in the same directory as the HTML file that has the `<APPLET>` tag.

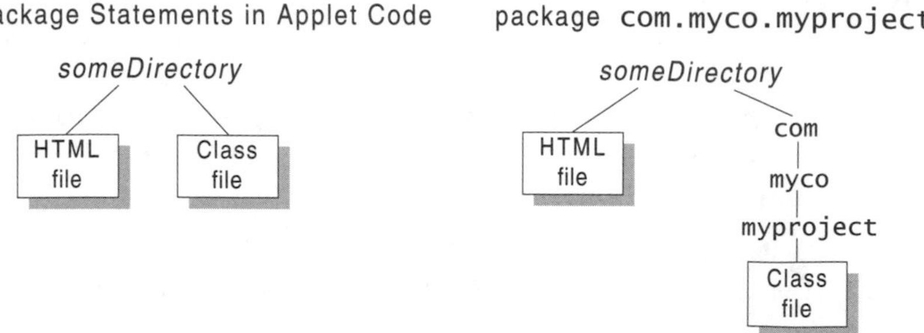

Figure 32: An applet's class files live under the same directory as the HTML file that includes the applet.

When a Java-enabled browser encounters an <APPLET> tag, it reserves a display area of the specified width and height for the applet, loads the bytecodes for the specified `Applet` subclass, creates an instance of the subclass, and then calls the instance's `init` and `start` methods.

The <APPLET> tag has many options that you can use to customize your applet's execution. For example, you can put your applet's files into an archive.

You can also specify parameters to be passed to the applet. These options are described in Using the <APPLET> Tag (page 206).

Summary

This lesson gave you lots of information—almost everything you need to know to start writing a Java applet. In this section, we summarize the lesson, adding bits of information to help you understand the whole picture.

To write an applet you must create a subclass of the `java.applet Applet` class. In your `Applet` subclass, you must implement at least one of the following methods: `init`, `start`, and `paint`. The `init` and `start` methods, along with `stop` and `destroy`, are called when major events (milestones) occur in the applet's life cycle. The `paint` method is called when the applet needs to draw itself to the screen.

The `Applet` class extends the `Panel` class, which extends the `Container` class, which extends the `Component` class. From `Component`, an applet inherits the ability to draw and handle events. From `Container`, an applet inherits the ability to include other components and to have a layout manager control the size and position of those components. From `Applet`, an applet inherits several capabilities, including the ability to respond to milestones. The next lesson tells you more about what the `Applet` class provides.

You include applets in HTML pages using the `<APPLET>` tag. When a browser user visits a page that contains an applet, here's what happens:

1. The browser finds the class file (which contains Java bytecodes) for the applet's `Applet` subclass.
2. The browser brings the `Applet` subclass bytecodes over the network to the user's computer.
3. The browser creates an instance of the `Applet` subclass. When we refer to an *applet*, we're generally referring to this instance.
4. The browser calls the applet's `init` method. This method performs any initialization that is required.
5. The browser calls the applet's `start` method. This method often starts a thread to perform the applet's duties.

An applet's `Applet` subclass is its main, controlling class, but applets can use other classes, as well. These other classes can be either local to the browser (provided as part of the Java platform) or custom classes that you supply. When the applet tries to use a class for the first time, the browser tries to find the class on the host that is running the browser and applet. If the browser cannot find the class there, it looks for the class in the same place from which the applet's `Applet` subclass came. When the browser finds the class, it loads the bytecodes for the class (over the network, if necessary) and continues executing the applet.

Loading executable code over the network is a classic security risk. For Java applets, some of this risk is reduced because the Java language is designed to be safe—for example, it doesn't allow pointers to random memory. In addition, browsers enforce security by imposing restrictions on untrusted applets.

Taking Advantage of the Applet API

THE applet API lets you take advantage of the close relationship that applets have with Web browsers. The API is provided by the `java.applet` package—mainly by the `Applet`[1] class and the `AppletContext`[2] interface. Thanks to the applet API, applets can do the following:

- Be notified by the browser of milestones.
- Load data files specified relative to the URL of the applet or the page in which it is running.
- Display short status strings.
- Make the browser display a document.
- Find other applets running in the same page.
- Play sounds.
- Get parameters specified by the user in the `<APPLET>` tag.

This lesson discusses each of these topics in turn, except for the milestone methods (`init`, `start`, and so on), which are explained in Methods for Milestones (page 179). For information about how to use non-applet-specific API in an applet, see Practical Considerations of Writing Applets (page 211).

The `Applet` `getCodeBase` and `getDocumentBase` methods get information from the browser about where the applet and its HTML page came from. Finding and

---

1 http://java.sun.com/products/jdk/1.1/api/java.applet.Applet.html

2 http://java.sun.com/products/jdk/1.1/api/java.applet.AppletContext.html

Loading Data Files (page 190) describes how to use these methods to help you load your applet's data files, such as images.

Displaying Short Status Strings (page 191) describes how to make an applet display a string on the status line of the application in which it is running.

Displaying Documents in the Browser (page 192) tells you how to use the two `showDocument` methods to request that the browser visit a particular URL.

Using the `AppletContext getApplet` and `getApplets` methods, an applet can get the `Applet` objects for other applets running on the same page. Once an applet has another's `Applet` object, the applet can send messages to it. Sending Messages to Other Applets (page 194) provides details and example applets that communicate with each other.

The `Applet` class and `AudioClip` interface provide support for playing sounds. Playing Sounds (page 198) tells you about this support and includes an example of using sound in an applet.

You can improve the versatility of your applet by providing parameters. Defining and Using Applet Parameters (page 200) describes how to decide which parameters to provide, how to implement them, and how to inform the user about them.

Finally, Using the <APPLET> Tag (page 206) tells you how to customize an applet by editing its HTML tag.

Finding and Loading Data Files

Whenever an applet needs to load some data from a file that's specified with a *relative URL* (a URL that doesn't completely specify the file's location), the applet usually uses either the code base or the document base to form the complete URL. The *code base*, returned by the `Applet getCodeBase` method, is a URL that specifies the directory from which the applet's classes were loaded. The *document base*, returned by the `Applet getDocumentBase` method, specifies the directory of the HTML page that contains the applet.

Unless the `<APPLET>` tag specifies a code base, both the code base and document base refer to the same directory on the same server. For example, in Figure 33 (page 191), the code and document bases would both specify the `someDirectory` directory.

Data that the applet always needs, or needs to rely on as a backup, is usually specified relative to the code base. Data that the applet user specifies, often by using parameters, is usually specified relative to the document base.

Note: For security reasons, browsers limit the URLs from which untrusted applets can read. For example, most browsers don't allow untrusted applets to use ".." to get to directories above the code base or document base. Also, since untrusted applets can't read files except those on the applet's originating host, the document base isn't generally useful if the document and the untrusted applet are on different servers.

The `Applet` class defines convenient forms of image-loading and sound-loading methods that let you specify images and sounds relative to a base URL. For example, assume an applet is set up with one of the directory structures shown in Figure 33.

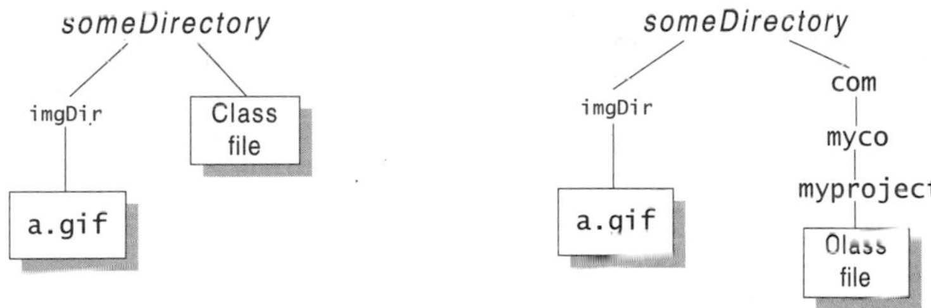

Figure 33: This applet's image file is in the `imgDir` directory, relative to the code base.

To create an `Image` object using the `a.gif` image file under `imgDir`, the applet can use the following code:

```
Image image = getImage(getCodeBase(), "imgDir/a.gif");
```

Displaying Short Status Strings

Most browsers allow applets to display a short status string. This string typically appears on the status line of the window containing the applet. In full-fledged Web browsers, all applets on the page, as well as the browser itself, generally share the same status line.

You should never put crucial information in the status line. If many users might need the information, it should instead be displayed within the applet area. If only a few, sophisticated users might need the information, consider displaying it on the standard output. See Displaying Diagnostics to the Standard Output and Standard Error Streams (page 216) for more details.

The status line is not usually very prominent, and it can be overwritten by other applets or by the browser. For these reasons, use it only for incidental, transitory information. For example, an applet that loads several image files might display the name of the image file it is currently loading.

Applets display status lines with the `showStatus` method. Here's an example of its use:

```
showStatus("MyApplet: Loading image file " + filename);
```

Note: Please don't put scrolling text in the status line. Browser users find such status line abuse highly annoying!

Displaying Documents in the Browser

Have you ever wanted an applet to display formatted HTML text? Here's the easy way to do it: Ask the browser to display the text for you.

With the `AppletContext` `showDocument` methods, an applet can tell the browser which URL to show and in which browser window. (By the way, the JDK Applet Viewer ignores these methods, since it can't display documents.) Here are the two forms of `showDocument`:

```
showDocument(java.net.URL url)
showDocument(java.net.URL url, String targetWindow)
```

The one-argument form of `showDocument` simply tells the browser to display the document at the specified URL, without specifying the window in which to display the document.

Terminology Note: In this discussion, *frame* refers not to a `Frame` object, but to an HTML frame within a browser window.

The two-argument form of `showDocument` lets you specify the window or HTML frame in which to display the document. The second argument can have any one of the following values:

`"_blank"`
Displays the document in a new, nameless window.

`"windowName"`
: Displays the document in a window named *`windowName`*. This window is created if necessary.

`"_self"`
: Displays the document in the window and frame that contain the applet.

`"_parent"`
: Displays the document in the applet's window but in the parent frame of the applet's frame. If the applet frame has no parent frame, this acts the same as `"_self"`.

`"_top"`
: Displays the document in the applet's window but in the top-level frame. If the applet's frame is the top-level frame, this acts the same as `"_self"`.

The following applet lets you try every option of both forms of `showDocument`. The applet brings up a window that lets you type in a URL and choose any of the `showDocument` options. When you press Return or click the Show document button, the applet calls `showDocument`.

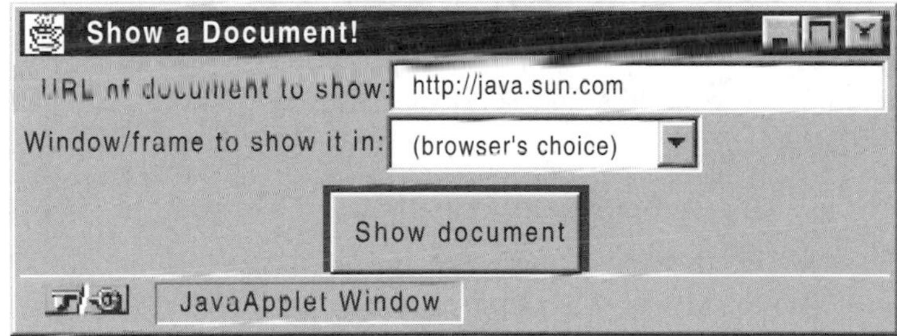

http://java.sun.com/docs/books/tutorial/applet/appletsonly/browser.html

Following is the applet code that calls `showDocument`. You can find the whole program on page 712.

```
    ...//In an Applet subclass:
    urlWindow = new URLWindow(getAppletContext());
    . . .

class URLWindow extends Frame {
    . . .
    public URLWindow(AppletContext appletContext) {
        . . .
        this.appletContext = appletContext;
        . . .
    }
```

```
    public void actionPerformed(ActionEvent event) {
        String urlString = /* user-entered string */;
        URL url = null;
        try {
            url = new URL(urlString);
        } catch (MalformedURLException e) {
            ...//Inform the user and return...
        }

        if (url != null) {
            if (/* user doesn't want to specify window */) {
                appletContext.showDocument(url);
            } else {
                appletContext.showDocument(url,
                /* user-specified window */);
            }
        }
    }
}
```

Sending Messages to Other Applets

Applets can find other applets and send messages to them, with the following security restrictions:

- Many browsers require that the applets originate from the same server.
- Many browsers further require that the applets originate from the same directory on the server (the same code base).
- The Java API requires that the applets be running on the same page, in the same browser window.

Note: Some browsers let applets invoke methods on other applets—even applets on different pages in the same browser—as long as all of the applets come from the same code base. This method of interapplet communication isn't supported by the Java API, so it's possible that it will not be supported by all browsers.

An applet can find another applet either by looking it up by name (using the `AppletContext getApplet` method) or by finding all of the applets on the page (using the `AppletContext getApplets` method). Both methods, if successful, give the caller one or more `Applet` objects. Once the caller finds an `Applet` object, the caller can invoke methods on the object.

Finding an Applet by Name: the getApplet Method

The `getApplet` method looks through all the applets on the current page to see if one has the specified name. If so, `getApplet` returns the applet's `Applet` object.

By default, an applet has no name. For an applet to have a name, you must specify one in the HTML code that adds the applet to a page. You can do this in one of two ways:

- By specifying a `NAME` attribute within the applet's `<APPLET>` tag; for example:

```
<APPLET CODEBASE="example/" CODE="Sender.class"
        WIDTH=450 HEIGHT=200
        NAME="buddy">
. . .
</APPLET>
```

- By specifying a `NAME` parameter with a `<PARAM>` tag; for example:

```
<APPLET CODEBASE="example/" CODE="Receiver.class"
        WIDTH=450 HEIGHT=35>
<PARAM NAME="name" VALUE="old pal">
. . .
</APPLET>
```

Browser Note: Although at least one Java-enabled browser conducts a case-sensitive search, the expected behavior is for the `getApplet` method to perform a case-*in*sensitive search. For example, `getApplet("old pal")` and `getApplet("OLD PAL")` should both find an applet named `"Old Pal"`.

Following are two applets that illustrate lookup by name. The first, the Sender, looks up the second, the Receiver. When the Sender finds the Receiver, it sends a message to the Receiver by invoking one of the Receiver's methods (passing the Sender's name as an argument). The Receiver reacts to this method call by changing its leftmost text string to "Received message from *sender-name*!"

http://java.sun.com/docs/books/tutorial/applet/appletsonly/iac.html

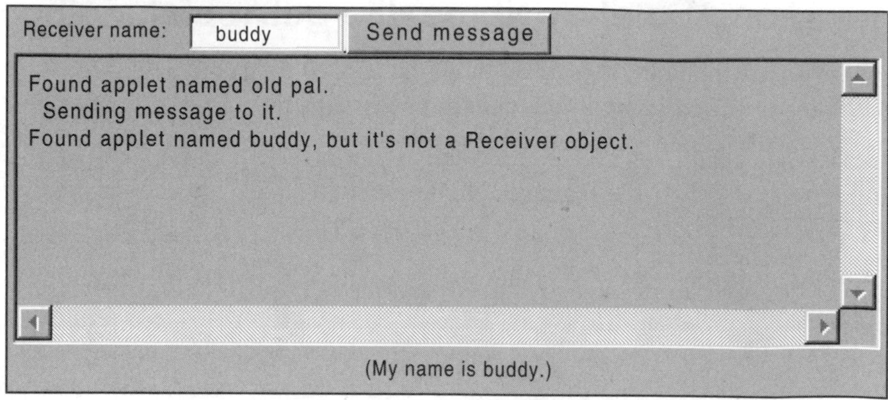

http://java.sun.com/docs/books/tutorial/applet/appletsonly/iac.html

---

Try This: Visit the page that contains these applets: `http://java.sun.com/docs/books/tutorial/applet/appletsonly/iac.html`.
Click the Send message button of the top applet (the Sender). Some status information will appear in the Sender's window, and the Receiver will confirm, with its own status string, that it received a message. After you've read the Receiver's status string, press its Clear button to reset it. In the Sender's text field labeled "Receiver name:", type `buddy` and press Return. Since `"buddy"` is the Sender's own name, it will find an applet named `"buddy"`, but it won't send it a message, since it isn't a `Receiver` instance.

You can find the whole Sender program on page 715 and the Receiver program on page 717. The code the Sender uses to look up and communicate with the Receiver is listed next. Code that you can use in your own applet is in bold.

```
Applet receiver = null;
String receiverName = nameField.getText(); //Name to search for
receiver = getAppletContext().getApplet(receiverName);
```

The Sender goes on to make sure that the Receiver was found and that it's an instance of the correct class (`Receiver`). If all goes well, the Sender sends a message to the Receiver.

```
if (receiver != null) {
    //Use the instanceof operator to make sure the applet
    //we found is a Receiver object.
    if (!(receiver instanceof Receiver)) {
        status.append("Found applet named "
                      + receiverName + ", "
```

```
                    + "but it's not a Receiver object."
                    + newline);
        } else {
            status.append("Found applet named "
                    + receiverName + newline
                    + "  Sending message to it.);
                    + newline);
            //Cast the receiver to be a Receiver object
            //(instead of just an Applet object) so that the
            //compiler will let us call a Receiver method.
            ((Receiver)receiver).processRequestFrom(myName);
        }
    }
```

From an applet's point of view, its name is stored in a parameter called `NAME`. It can get the value of the parameter using the `Applet getParameter` method. For example, `Sender` gets its own name with the following code:

```
myName = getParameter("NAME");
```

For more information on using `getParameter`, see Writing the Code to Support Parameters (page 203).

The example applets in this section perform one-way communication—from the Sender to the Receiver. If you want your receiver to be able to send messages to the sender, just have the sender give a reference to itself (`this`) to the receiver. For example:

```
((Receiver)receiver).startCommunicating(this);
```

Finding All of the Applets on a Page: the getApplets Method

The `getApplets` method returns a list (an `Enumeration`[1] to be precise) of all of the applets on the page. For security reasons, `getApplets` returns only those applets that originated from the same host as the applet that is calling `getApplets`. Following is an applet that simply lists all of the applets it can find on its page:

The following code contains the relevant parts of the method that calls `getApplets`. You can find the entire program on page 718.

---

1 http://java.sun.com/products/jdk/1.1/api/java.util.Enumeration.html

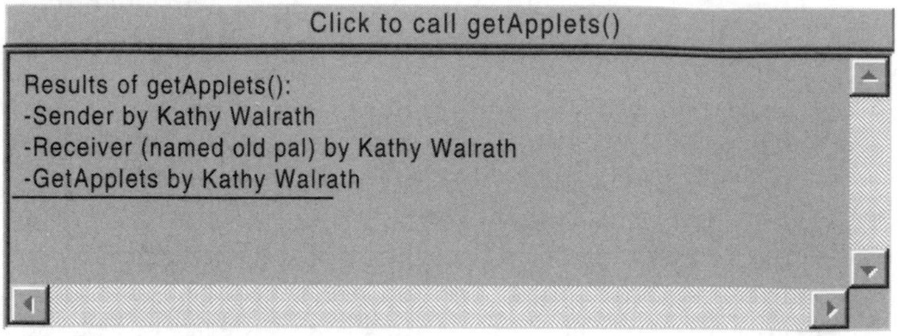

Click to call getApplets()

Results of getApplets():
-Sender by Kathy Walrath
-Receiver (named old pal) by Kathy Walrath
-GetApplets by Kathy Walrath

http://java.sun.com/docs/books/tutorial/applet/appletsonly/iac.html

```
public void printApplets() {
    //Enumeration will contain all applets on this page
    //(including this one) that we can send messages to.
    Enumeration e = getAppletContext().getApplets();
    . . .
    while (e.hasMoreElements()) {
        Applet applet = (Applet)e.nextElement();
        String info = applet.getAppletInfo();
        if (info != null) {
            textArea.append("- " + info + newline);
        } else {
            textArea.append("- "
                                + applet.getClass().getName()
                                + newline);
        }
    }
    . . .
}
```

Playing Sounds

In the Java applet package (`java.applet`), the `Applet`[1] class and `AudioClip`[2] interface provide basic support for playing sounds. Currently, the Java API supports only one sound format: 8-bit, μ law, 8000 Hz, one-channel, Sun ".au" files. You can create these on a Sun workstation using the `audiotool` application. You can convert files from other sound formats using an audio format conversion program.

1 http://java.sun.com/products/jdk/1.1/api/java.applet.Applet.html
2 http://java.sun.com/products/jdk/1.1/api/java.applet.AudioClip.html

Sound-Related Methods

Following are the sound-related `Applet` methods:

`AudioClip getAudioClip(URL)`
`AudioClip getAudioClip(URL, String)`
Return an object that implements the `AudioClip` interface.

`void play(URL)`
`void play(URL, String)`
Play the `AudioClip` corresponding to the specified URL.

The two-argument form of each method takes a base URL, which is usually returned by either `getCodeBase` or `getDocumentBase`, and the location of the sound file relative to the base URL. You should use the code base for sounds that are integral to the applet. The document base is for sounds specified by the applet user, such as through applet parameters.

The `AudioClip` interface defines the following methods:

`void loop()`
Starts playing the clip repeatedly.

`void play()`
Plays the clip once.

`void stop()`
Stops the clip. Works with both looping and one-time sounds.

An Example: SoundExample

Here is an applet called `SoundExample` that illustrates a few things about sound:

http://java.sun.com/docs/books/tutorial/applet/appletsonly/sound.html

The `SoundExample` applet provides an architecture for loading and playing multiple sounds in an applet. For this reason, it is more complex than necessary. Essentially, the sound loading and playing code boils down to this:

```
AudioClip onceClip, loopClip;
onceClip = applet.getAudioClip(getCodeBase(), "bark.au");
loopClip = applet.getAudioClip(getCodeBase(), "train.au");
onceClip.play();//Play it once.
onceClip.stop();//Cut off the sound.
loopClip.loop();//Start the sound loop.
loopClip.stop();//Stop the sound loop.
```

Since there's nothing more annoying than an applet that continues to make noise after you've left its page, the SoundExample applet stops playing the continuously looping sound when the user leaves the page and resumes playing it when the user comes back. It does this by implementing its stop and start methods as follows:

```
public void stop() {
    onceClip.stop();         //Cut short the one-time sound.
    if (looping) {
        loopClip.stop();    //Stop the sound loop.
    }
}

public void start() {
    if (looping) {
        loopClip.loop();    //Restart the sound loop.
    }
}
```

This example is discussed in more detail in Using a Thread to Perform a One-Time Task (page 223).

Defining and Using Applet Parameters

Parameters are to applets what command-line arguments are to UNIX applications. They allow the user to customize the program's operation. By defining parameters, you can increase your applet's flexibility, making your applet work in multiple situations without your having to recode and recompile it.

The next few pages discuss parameters from the applet programmer's point of view. To learn about the user's view of parameters, see Specifying Parameters (page 206).

Deciding Which Parameters to Support (page 201) discusses how to design parameters.

Applets get the user-defined values of parameters by calling the Applet getParameter method. Writing the Code to Support Parameters (page 203) tells you how to use getParameter.

By implementing the getParameterInfo method, applets provide information that browsers can use to help the user set parameter values. Giving Information about Parameters (page 205) tells you how to implement getParameterInfo.

Deciding Which Parameters to Support

This section guides you through the four questions you should ask as you implement parameters:

- What should the applet allow the user to configure?
- What should the parameters be named?
- What kind of value should each parameter take?
- What should the default value of each parameter be?

This section ends with a discussion of the parameters defined by a class named `AppletButton`.

What Should the Applet Allow the User to Configure?

Which parameters your applet should support depends on what your applet does and on how flexible you want it to be. Applets that display images might have parameters to specify the image locations. Similarly, applets that play sounds might have parameters to specify the sounds.

Besides parameters that specify resource locations (such as image and sound files), applets sometimes provide parameters for specifying details of the applet's appearance or operation. For example, an animation applet might let the user specify the number of images shown per second. Or an applet might let the user change the strings that the applet displays. Anything is possible.

What Should the Parameters Be Named?

Once you decide what parameters your applet will support, you need to determine their names. Here are some typical parameter names:

`SOURCE` or `SRC`
: For a data file such as an image file.

***`XXX`*`SOURCE` (for example, `IMAGESOURCE`)**
: Used in applets that let the user specify more than one type of data file.

***`XXX`*`S`**
: For a parameter that takes a list of *`XXX`*`s` (where *`XXX`* might be `IMAGE`, again).

`NAME`
: Used *only* for an applet's name. Applet names are used for interapplet communication, as described in Sending Messages to Other Applets (page 194).

Clarity of names is more important than keeping the name length short. Do *not* use names of `<APPLET>` tag attributes, which are documented in The `<APPLET>` Tag (page 801).

Note: Although this tutorial usually refers to parameter names using all uppercase letters, parameter names actually are case insensitive. For example, `IMAGESOURCE` and `imageSource` both refer to the same parameter. Parameter *values*, on the other hand, are case sensitive unless you take steps to interpret them otherwise, such as by using the `String toLowerCase` method before interpreting the parameter's value.

What Kind of Value Should Each Parameter Take?

Parameter values are all strings. Whether or not the user puts quotation marks around a parameter value, that value is passed to your applet as a string. However, your applet can interpret the string in many ways, typically as one of the following types:

- A URL
- An integer
- A floating-point number
- A boolean value—typically `"true"`/`"false"` or `"yes"`/`"no"`
- A string—for example, the string to use as a window title
- A list of any of the above

What Should the Default Value of Each Parameter Be?

Applets should attempt to provide useful default values for each parameter so that the applet will execute even if the user doesn't specify a parameter or specifies it incorrectly. For example, an animation applet should provide a reasonable setting for the number of images it displays per second. In this way, if the user doesn't specify the relevant parameter, the applet will still work well.

An Example: AppletButton

Throughout this tutorial, applets that need to bring up windows use the highly configurable class `AppletButton.java` (page 796). One online tutorial page alone[1] uses `AppletButton` five times for five different examples, one per layout manager the AWT provides. `AppletButton`'s GUI is simple; it consists of a button and a label that displays status. When the user clicks the button, the applet brings up a window.

The `AppletButton` class is flexible because it defines parameters that let the user specify any or all of the following:

---

1 http://java.sun.com/docs/books/tutorial/ui/layout/using.html

- The type of window to bring up
- The window's title
- The window's height
- The window's width
- The label of the button that brings up the window

Here's what a typical <APPLET> tag for AppletButton looks like:

```
<APPLET CODE="AppletButton.class" WIDTH=350 HEIGHT=60>
<PARAM NAME="windowClass" VALUE="BorderWindow">
<PARAM NAME="windowTitle" VALUE="BorderLayout">
<PARAM NAME="buttonText"
       VALUE="Click here to see a BorderLayout in action">
</APPLET>
```

You can see this applet running at the URL

```
http://java.sun.com/docs/books/tutorial/ui/layout/border.html
```

When the user doesn't specify a value for a parameter, AppletButton uses a reasonable default value. For example, if the user doesn't specify the window's title, AppletButton uses the window's type as the title.

The next section shows you the code that AppletButton uses to get its parameter values from the user.

Writing the Code to Support Parameters

Applets use the Applet getParameter method to get user-specified values for applet parameters. The getParameter method is declared as follows:

```
String getParameter(String name)
```

Your applet might need to convert the string that getParameter returns into another form, such as an integer. The java.lang package provides classes such as Integer that help convert strings to primitive types. Here's an example from the AppletButton class of converting a parameter's value into an integer:

```
int requestedWidth = 0;
. . .
String windowWidthString = getParameter("WINDOWWIDTH");
if (windowWidthString != null) {
    try {
        requestedWidth = Integer.parseInt(windowWidthString);
```

```
        } catch (NumberFormatException e) {
            //Use default width.
        }
    }
```

Note that if the user doesn't specify a value for the `WINDOWWIDTH` parameter, this code uses a default value of `0`, which the applet interprets as "use the window's natural size." It's important to supply default values wherever possible.

Besides using the `getParameter` method to get values of applet-specific parameters, you also can use `getParameter` to get the values of attributes of the applet's `<APPLET>` tag. For example, by specifying `"HEIGHT"` to the `getParameter` method, an applet could read the height that the user specified in the `<APPLET>` tag. See The <APPLET> Tag (page 933) for a complete list of `<APPLET>` tag attributes.

An Example: AppletButton

Following is the `AppletButton` code that gets the applet's parameters. For more information, see Defining and Using Applet Parameters (page 200).

```
    String windowClass;
    String buttonText;
    String windowTitle;
    int requestedWidth = 0;
    int requestedHeight = 0;
    . . .
    public void init() {
        windowClass = getParameter("WINDOWCLASS");
        if (windowClass == null) {
            windowClass = "TestWindow";
        }

        buttonText = getParameter("BUTTONTEXT");
        if (buttonText == null) {
            buttonText = "Click here to bring up a " + windowClass;
        }

        windowTitle = getParameter("WINDOWTITLE");
        if (windowTitle == null) {
            windowTitle = windowClass;
        }

        String windowWidthString = getParameter("WINDOWWIDTH");
        if (windowWidthString != null) {
            try {
                requestedWidth = Integer.parseInt(windowWidthString);
            } catch (NumberFormatException e) {
```

```
            //Use default width.
        }
    }

    String windowHeightString = getParameter("WINDOWHEIGHT");
    if (windowHeightString != null) {
        try {
            requestedHeight =
                Integer.parseInt(windowHeightString);
        } catch (NumberFormatException e) {
            //Use default height.
        }
    }
```

Giving Information about Parameters

Now that you've provided all of those nice parameters to the user, you need to help the user set the parameter values correctly. Of course, your applet's documentation should describe each parameter and give the user examples and hints for setting them. Your job doesn't stop there, though. You also should implement the `getParameterInfo` method so that it returns information about your applet's parameters. Browsers can use this information to help the user set your applet's parameter values.

The following code is an example of implementing the `getParameterInfo` method. This example is from the `Animator`[1] applet, a wonderfully flexible applet that provides 13 parameters for users to customize their animation.

```
public String[][] getParameterInfo() {
    String[][] info = {
      // Parameter Name  Kind of Value Description
        {"imagesource", "URL",         "a directory"},
        {"startup",     "URL",         "displayed at startup"},
        {"background",  "URL",         "displayed as background"},
        {"startimage",  "int",         "start index"},
        {"endimage",    "int",         "end index"},
        {"namepattern", "URL",         "used to generate " +
                                           "indexed names"},
        {"pause",       "int",         "milliseconds"},
        {"pauses",      "ints",        "milliseconds"},
        {"repeat",      "boolean",     "repeat or not"},
        {"positions",   "coordinates", "path"},
        {"soundsource", "URL",         "audio directory"},
        {"soundtrack",  "URL",         "background music"},
```

1 To find the Animator applet, see the Web page for this book: http://java.sun.com/docs/books/tutorial/2e/book.html

```
        {"sounds",     "URLs",       "audio samples"},
    };
    return info;
}
```

As you can see, the getParameterInfo method must return an array of three-String arrays. In each three-String array, the first string is the parameter name. The second string hints as to what general kind of value the applet needs for the parameter. The third string describes the meaning of the parameter.

Using the <APPLET> Tag

This section tells you most of what you need to know to use the <APPLET> tag. It starts by showing you the tag's simplest form. It then discusses some of the most common additions to that simple form: the <PARAM> tag, alternate HTML code and text, the CODEBASE attribute, and the ARCHIVE attribute. For a detailed description of the <APPLET> tag, refer to The <APPLET> Tag (page 933).

You should already have seen the simplest form of the <APPLET> tag:

```
<APPLET CODE="AppletSubclass.class" WIDTH=numPixels
HEIGHT=numPixels>
</APPLET>
```

This tag tells the browser to load the applet whose Applet subclass is named *AppletSubclass*, displaying it in an area of the specified width and height.

Specifying Parameters

Some applets let the user customize the applet's configuration with parameters, as described in Defining and Using Applet Parameters (page 200). For example, AppletButton (an applet used throughout this tutorial to provide a button that brings up a window) allows the user to set the button's text by specifying the value of a parameter named BUTTONTEXT.

The user specifies the value of a parameter using a <PARAM> tag. The <PARAM> tags should appear just after the <APPLET> tag for the applet they affect:

```
<APPLET CODE="AppletSubclass.class" WIDTH=numPixels
HEIGHT=numPixels>
<PARAM NAME=parameter1Name VALUE=aValue>
<PARAM NAME=parameter2Name VALUE=anotherValue>
</APPLET>
```

Here's an example of the <PARAM> tag in use:

```
<APPLET CODE="Animator.class" WIDTH=460 HEIGHT=160>
<PARAM NAME="imageSource" VALUE="images/Beans">
<PARAM NAME="backgroundColor" VALUE="0xc0c0c0">
<PARAM NAME="endImage" VALUE=10>
<PARAM NAME="soundSource" VALUE="audio">
<PARAM NAME="soundtrack" VALUE="spacemusic.au">
<PARAM NAME="sounds"
    VALUE="1.au|2.au|3.au|4.au|5.au|6.au|7.au|8au|9.au|0.au">
<PARAM NAME="pause" VALUE=200>
. . .
</APPLET>
```

Specifying Alternate HTML Code and Text

Note the ellipsis points (. . .) in the previous HTML example. What did the example leave out? It omitted *alternate HTML code*—HTML code interpreted only by browsers that don't understand the <APPLET> tag. Alternate HTML code is any text that appears between the <APPLET> and </APPLET> tags, after any <PARAM> tags. Java-enabled browsers ignore alternate HTML code.

To specify alternate text to Java-enabled browsers and other browsers that understand the <APPLET> tag, use the ALT attribute. If the browser can't display an applet for some reason, it can display the applet's ALT text.

We use alternate HTML code throughout the online version of this tutorial to tell readers about the applets they're missing. Often, the alternate HTML code includes one or more pictures of the applet. Here's the complete HTML code for the Animator example shown previously:

```
<APPLET CODE="Animator.class" WIDTH=460 HEIGHT=160
 ALT="If you could run this applet, you'd see some animation">
<PARAM NAME="imageSource" VALUE="images/Beans">
<PARAM NAME="backgroundColor" VALUE="0xc0c0c0">
<PARAM NAME="endImage" VALUE=10>
<PARAM NAME="soundSource" VALUE="audio">
<PARAM NAME="soundtrack" VALUE="spacemusic.au">
<PARAM NAME="sounds"
    VALUE="1.au|2.au|3.au|4.au|5.au|6.au|7.au|8au|9.au|0.au">
<PARAM NAME="pause" VALUE=200>
Your browser is completely ignoring the &lt;APPLET&gt; tag!
</APPLET>
```

A browser that doesn't understand the <APPLET> tag ignores everything in the previous HTML code except the line that starts with "Your." A browser that *does*

understand the <APPLET> tag ignores everything on that line. If the applet-savvy browser can't run the applet, it might display the text listed after the ALT tag.

Specifying the Applet Directory

By default, a browser looks for an applet's class and archive files in the same directory as the HTML file that has the <APPLET> tag. (If the applet's class is in a package, then the browser uses the package name to construct a directory path underneath the HTML file's directory.) Sometimes, however, it's useful to put the applet's files somewhere else. You can use the CODEBASE attribute to tell the browser in which directory the applet's files are located:

```
<APPLET CODE="AppletSubclass.class" CODEBASE="aURL"
        WIDTH=anInt HEIGHT=anInt>
</APPLET>
```

If *aURL* is a relative URL, then it's interpreted relative to the HTML document's location. By making *aURL* an absolute URL, you can load an applet from just about anywhere—even from another HTTP server.

This tutorial uses CODEBASE="someDirectory/" frequently, since we group the examples for each lesson in subdirectories. For example, here's the <APPLET> tag that includes the Simple applet in The Life Cycle of an Applet (page 177):

```
<APPLET CODE="Simple.class" CODEBASE="example/"
        WIDTH=500 HEIGHT=20>
</APPLET>
```

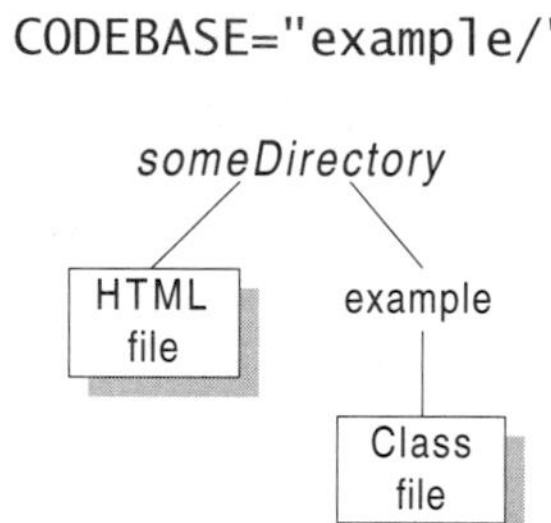

Figure 34: The location of an applet's class file when CODEBASE = "example/".

Figure 34 shows the location of the class file, relative to the HTML file, when CODEBASE is set to "example/". Figure 35 shows where the applet class can be if you specify an absolute URL for the value of CODEBASE.

```
CODEBASE="http:// someServer/.../someOtherDirectory/"
```


Figure 35: The directory hierarchy when CODEBASE is set to an absolute URL.

Combining an Applet's Files into a Single File

If your applet has more than one file, you should consider providing an archive file that bundles the applet's files into a single file. Whether archive files make sense for your applet depends on several factors, including your applet's size, performance considerations, and the environment you expect your users to have.

Archive files reduce your applet's total download time. Much of the time saved comes from reducing the number of HTTP connections that the browser must make. Each HTTP connection can take several seconds to start. This means that for a multifile applet, connection time can dwarf transfer time. You can further reduce transfer time by compressing the files in your archive file.

If you specify one or more archive files, then the browser looks for the archive files in the same directory that it would search for the applet class file. The browser then looks for the applet's class files in the archive files. If a file isn't in the archive, then the browser generally tries to load it just as it would if the archive file weren't present.

The standard Java archive format, called JAR, was introduced in JDK 1.1 and is based on the ZIP file format. You specify JAR files using the ARCHIVE attribute of the <APPLET> tag. You can specify multiple archive files by separating them with commas:

```
<APPLET CODE="AppletSubclass.class" ARCHIVE="file1, file2"
        WIDTH=anInt HEIGHT=anInt>
</APPLET>
```

Platform-specific Details: Creating a JAR File

You can create JAR files using the JDK `jar` tool. Some examples of creating JAR files follow.

To create a JAR file named `file.jar` that includes compressed versions of all of the class and GIF files in the current directory:

```
jar cvf file.zip *.class *.gif
```

To create a JAR file for an applet whose classes are in a package named `com.mycompany.myproject`:

```
jar cvf file.zip com/mycompany/myproject/*.class *.gif
```
(Solaris)

```
jar cvf file.zip com\mycompany\myproject\*.class *.gif
```
(Windows 95/NT)

Unfortunately, not all browsers understand the same archive format or use the same HTML code to specify the applet archive. See the Web page for this book for the latest information about browser support for archives.[1]

Other <APPLET> Tag Attributes

This section didn't discuss every attribute of the `<APPLET>` tag. Other attributes—which might seem familiar, since the `<IMG>` tag uses them—include `ALIGN`, `VSPACE`, and `HSPACE`. The `<APPLET>` tag also allows you load a *serialized* (saved) applet by specifying the `OBJECT` attribute instead of specifying a class file with `CODE`. Finally, you can name an applet using the `NAME` attribute. For a detailed description of the `<APPLET>` tag, see The <APPLET> Tag (page 933).

---

1 http://java.sun.com/docs/books/tutorial/2e/book.html

http://java.sun.com/docs/books/tutorial/applet/finishing/index.html

11 Finishing an Applet

WHEN is your applet finished? When it works and meets at least the minimum standards described in the following section, Before You Ship That Applet. Some higher standards we'd like you to meet are described in The Perfectly Finished Applet (page 232).

Before You Ship That Applet

Stop! Before you let the whole world know about your applet, make sure the answer to all of the following questions is **yes**.

1. Have you removed or disabled debugging output?
Debugging output (generally created with `System.out.println`), while useful to you, is generally confusing or annoying to users. It also can slow down your applet. If you need to give textual feedback to the user, try to do it inside the applet's display area or in the status area at the bottom of the window. Information on using the status area is in Displaying Short Status Strings (page 191).

2. Does the applet stop running when it's off-screen?
Most applets should not use CPU resources when the browser is iconified or is displaying a page that doesn't contain the applet. If your applet code doesn't launch any threads explicitly, then you're probably OK.

If your applet code launches any threads, then unless you have a *really good* excuse not to, you should implement the `stop` method so that it notifies the threads that they should stop. For an example of implementing the `stop` method, see Using a Thread to Perform Repeated Tasks (page 221).

3. If the applet does something that might get annoying—play sounds or animation, for example—does it give the user a way to stop the annoying behavior?

Be kind to your users. Give them a way to stop the applet in its tracks, without leaving the page. In an applet that otherwise doesn't respond to mouse clicks, you can do this by implementing the `mouseClicked` method so that a mouse press suspends or resumes the annoying thread. For example:

```
boolean frozen = false; //an instance variable

public void mouseClicked(MouseEvent e) {
    if (frozen) {
        frozen = false;
        start();
    } else {
        frozen = true;
        stop();
    }
}
```

The Perfectly Finished Applet

The previous section listed some rules you should follow to avoid making your applet's users want to throttle you. This section offers tips that can make dealing with your applet as pleasant as possible. Some of the tips here aren't easy to implement. Still, you should be aware of them and implement what makes sense for your applet.

1. Test your applet well.

Before you unleash your applet on the world, test it thoroughly. Once it works well in your normal browser/platform combination, run it in as many browser/platform combinations as you can find. Ask people whose computers are behind firewalls to test it. Take advantage of the Web; you can usually get other people to perform much of the testing for you.

2. Make sure your applet follows the 100% Pure Java guidelines.

Throughout this tutorial, you can find tips on how to make programs work well on any Java platform.

3. Use parameters to make your applet as flexible as possible.

You often can define parameters that let your applet be used in a variety of situations without any rewriting. See Defining and Using Applet Parameters (page 200) for information.

4. **If your applet has more than one file, consider providing an archive.**
   See Combining an Applet's Files into a Single File (page 209) for information.
5. **Make your applet appear as soon as possible.**
   Applets can do several things to decrease their perceived startup time. The `Applet` subclass can be a small one that immediately displays a status message. Some or all of the applet's files can be compressed into an archive file to decrease total download time. If some of the applet's classes or data aren't used right away, the applet can either delay loading them until they're needed or use a background thread to load them. If you can't avoid a lengthy delay in your applet's startup, consider using a small helper applet nearby to give status.
6. **Make your applet adjust well to different sizes, different available fonts, and different platforms.**
   Applets don't always get all of the screen real estate they want. Also, the amount of space required to display your applet's UI can be affected by platform/machine variances in font availability, drawing techniques, resolution, and so on.

   By using layout managers wisely, you can make your applet adjust well. If your applet has a minimum required size, you can use the `getSize` method to check whether your applet is big enough. If your applet or custom components in it draw text using graphics primitives, you should check and adjust font sizes as described in Working with Text (page 534).
7. **If your applet can't do its job, make it fail gracefully.**
   Sometimes your applet doesn't get the resources it needs. It might get so little space that it can't present a meaningful user interface. Or it might not be able to connect to a server. Even if your applet can't adjust successfully to the lack of resources, you should at least attempt to make your applet fail gracefully. For example, you might display a visible message—either in the applet's drawing area or in a helper applet near it—that explains what happened and gives hints on how to fix the problem.
8. **Be wary of using text in images.**
   Although using images to draw text can result in good-looking, predictably sized text, on some low-resolution displays the result may be illegible.
9. **Use windows wisely.**
   Windows have good points and bad points. Some platforms, such as TV-based browsers, might not allow top-level windows. Also, since applet-created windows can take a while to appear, they can be disconcerting to the user. However, putting some or all of an applet's UI in a window makes sense when your applet needs more space than it can get in the browser. Using a window might also

make sense in the rare case when your applet needs to remain visible even when the user changes pages.

10. Supply alternate text for your applet.

By using alternate text to explain what your users are missing, you can be kind to users who can't run your applet. You can supply alternate text as described in Specifying Alternate HTML Code and Text (page 207).

11. Implement the `getParameterInfo` method.

Implementing the `getParameterInfo` method now might make your applet easier to customize in the future. Browsers can use this method to help generate a GUI that allows the user to interactively set parameter values. See Giving Information about Parameters (page 205) for information on implementing `getParameterInfo`.

12. Implement the `getAppletInfo` method.

The `getAppletInfo` method returns a short, informative string describing an applet. Browsers and other applets can use this to give information about your applet. Here's an example of implementing `getAppletInfo`:

```
public String getAppletInfo() {
    return "GetApplets by Kathy Walrath";
}
```

Common Problems (and Their Solutions)

THIS section covers some common problems that you might encounter when writing Java applets. After each problem is a list of possible solutions.

Problem: Applet Viewer says there's no <APPLET> tag on my HTML page, but it really is there.

- Check whether you have a closing applet tag: </APPLET>.
- Check whether you entered the correct URL for the page.

Problem: I recompiled my applet, but my browser won't show the new version, even though I told it to reload it.

- In many browsers, reloading isn't reliable. This is why we recommend that you use the JDK Applet Viewer, invoking it anew each time you change the applet.
- In some browsers, using Shift-Reload might reload the applet.
- If the applet has an archive file, make sure you updated the archive.
- If you get an old version of the applet no matter what you do, then make sure that you don't have an old copy of the applet in a directory in your CLASSPATH. See Setting the Class Path (page 164) for information.

Problem: The light gray background of my applet causes the applet to flicker when it is drawn on a page of a different color.

- You need to set the background color of the applet so that it works well with the page color. See Creating a User Interface (page 214) for details.
- You might need to implement double buffering. See Eliminating Flashing (page 561).

Problem: The applet `getImage` method doesn't work.

- Make sure you're calling `getImage` from the `init` method or a method that's called after `init`. The `getImage` method does not work when it's called from a constructor.

Problem: I've copied my applet's class file onto my HTTP server, but the applet doesn't work.

- Does your applet define more than one class? If so, make sure that the class file (*ClassName*`.class`) for each class is on the HTTP server. Even if all of the classes are defined in one source file, the compiler produces one class file per class or interface. If you use inner classes, be sure to copy their class files as well.
- Did you copy all of the data files for your applet—image and sound files, for example—to the server?
- Make sure all of the applet's class and data files can be read by everyone and that the directories they're in can be read and searched by everyone.
- Make sure the class and data files are in the right directory, relative to the document. If you specify a code base, make sure the class and data files are under the code base directory and that the directory name has the proper capitalization. Similarly, if your applet's classes are in a package, make sure the class files are in the right directory under the code base. See Figure 34 (page 208) and Figure 35 (page 209) for examples of directory structures.
- Make sure the applet's class and data files weren't garbled during the transfer. One common source of trouble is using the ASCII mode of FTP (rather than the BINARY mode) to transfer files.

Problem: When I restart my applet, it seems to show up twice—or at least the components it contains show up twice.

- Your applet's `init` method is being called twice. This isn't supposed to happen, although the Applet Viewer lets you do it. One solution is to

implement the applet's `destroy` method so that it calls `removeAll`, which `Applet` inherits from `Container`.

Problem: I want to use the latest API, but I also want to be able to provide something reasonable for people using older browsers.

- See Version Compatibility (page 644) for more information.

Other problems that affect applets are discussed in the Creating a User Interface trail's Common Problems (and Their Solutions) (page 573). If you still haven't found the solution, check the Web version of this section:

`http://java.sun.com/docs/books/tutorial/applet/problem/index.html`

End of Trail

YOU'VE reached the end of the **Writing Applets** trail. Take a break—have a cup of steaming hot java.

What Next?

Once you've caught your breath, you have several choices of where to go next. You can go back to the Trail Map (page xvii) to see all of your choices, or you can go directly to one of the following popular trails:

Learning the Java Language (page 35): If you aren't completely comfortable yet with the Java language, take this trail.

Essential Java Classes (page 241): By taking this trail, you can find out about strings, exceptions, threads, and other Java features that are used in all kinds of Java programs, including applets.

Creating a User Interface (page 403): This trail teaches you how to produce GUIs. It includes information on using the AWT components, drawing custom graphics and images to the screen, and performing animation.

To 1.1— and Beyond! (page 631): This trail tells you how to upgrade your 1.0 program to use the JDK 1.1 API.

http://java.sun.com/docs/books/tutorial/essential/index.html

Essential Java Classes

THIS trail discusses classes from the Java platform that are essential to most programmers. In particular, it focuses on classes from the `java.lang` and `java.io` packages, including these:

- `String` and `StringBuffer`
- `Properties`
- `System`
- `SecurityManager`
- `Thread` and its related classes
- `Throwable` and `Exception`, and their friends
- The `Reader`, `Writer`, `InputStream`, and `OutputStream` classes from `java.io` and their descendants

Like the rest of the tutorial, this trail is designed so that you can skip around. Feel free to read only the lessons for the classes that interest you.

Using String and StringBuffer (page 247) illustrates how to manipulate character data using the `String` and `StringBuffer` classes. It also teaches you about accessor methods and how the compiler uses `Strings` and `StringBuffers` behind the scenes.

Setting Program Attributes (page 259) describes how you can set attributes for your Java programs through the use of properties and command-line arguments. Use properties to change attributes for every invocation of your program; use command-line arguments to change attributes for only the current invocation of your program.

Accessing System Resources (page 267) shows you how, through the `System` class, your Java programs can manage properties, set up a security manager, and access system resources such as the standard input and output streams. The `System` class provides a system-independent programming interface to system resources, thus allowing your programs to use them without compromising portability. This lesson also contains a brief discussion of the `Runtime` class and why most programmers should avoid using it.

Handling Errors with Exceptions (page 293) explains how you can use Java's exception mechanism to handle errors in your programs. This lesson describes what an exception is, how to throw and catch exceptions, what to do with an exception once you've caught it, and how to best use the exception class hierarchy provided by the Java platform.

Doing Two or More Tasks at Once: Threads (page 327) discusses in detail the use of threads that enable your Java applications or applets to perform multiple tasks simultaneously. This lesson describes when and why you might want to use threads, how to create and manage threads and thread groups in your Java program, and how to avoid common pitfalls such as deadlock, starvation, and race conditions.

Reading and Writing (but No 'rithmetic) (page 365) describes the process of getting information into your program and sending it out again through the use of the stream classes in `java.io`. Reading and writing information provides the basis for all kinds of interesting behaviors, such as serializing objects, invoking methods on objects in another VM, communicating over a network, or just accessing the file system.

12

Using String and StringBuffer

THE java.lang package contains two string classes: String[1] and StringBuffer.[2] You've already seen the String class on several occasions in this tutorial. You use it when you work with strings that cannot change. You use StringBuffer to manipulate the contents of the string on the fly.

The following reverseIt method uses both the String and StringBuffer classes to reverse the characters of a string. If you have a list of words, you can use this method in conjunction with a sort program to create a list of rhyming words (a list of words sorted by last syllable). Just reverse all of the strings in the list, sort the list, and then reverse the strings again. You can see the reverseIt method produce rhyming words in the piped streams example in Reading and Writing (but No 'rithmetic) (page 365).

```
public class ReverseString {
    public static String reverseIt(String source) {
        int i, len = source.length();
        StringBuffer dest = new StringBuffer(len);

        for (i = (len - 1); i >= 0; i--)
            dest.append(source.charAt(i));
        return dest.toString();
    }
}
```

1 http://java.sun.com/products/jdk/1.1/docs/api/java.lang.String.html
2 http://java.sun.com/products/jdk/1.1/docs/api/java.lang.StringBuffer.html

The `reverseIt` method accepts an argument of type `String` called `source` that contains the string data to be reversed. The method creates a `StringBuffer`, `dest`, the same size as `source`. It then loops backwards over all the characters in `source` and appends them to `dest`, thereby reversing the string. Finally, the method converts `dest`, a `StringBuffer`, to a `String` and returns it.

This lesson not only highlights the differences between `Strings` and `StringBuffers`, it also illustrates several features of the `String` and `StringBuffer` classes, including:

- Creating `Strings` and `StringBuffers`
- Using accessor methods to get information about a `String` or `StringBuffer`
- Modifying a `StringBuffer`
- Converting one type of string to the other

Note to C and C++ Programmers: Java strings are first-class objects, unlike C and C++ strings, which are simply null-terminated arrays of 8-bit characters. Strings as objects provide several advantages to the programmer:

- The manner in which you obtain strings and elements of strings is consistent across all strings and all systems.
- Since the programming interface for the `String` and `StringBuffer` classes is well-defined, Java strings function predictably every time.
- The strings provide functionality necessary for writing global programs such as character conversion.
- The `String` and `StringBuffer` classes do extensive runtime checking for boundary conditions and catch errors for you.

Why Two String Classes?

The Java platform provides two classes that store and manipulate character data: `String`, for constant strings, and `StringBuffer`, for strings that can change.

Use the `String` class when you don't want the value of the string to change. For example, if you write a method that requires string data and the method is not going to modify the string in any way, use a `String` object. Typically, you'll want to use `Strings` to pass character data into and out of methods. The `reverseIt` method takes a `String` argument and returns a `String` value:

```
public class ReverseString {
    public static String reverseIt(String source) {
        int i, len = source.length();
        StringBuffer dest = new StringBuffer(len);

        for (i = (len - 1); i >= 0; i--)
            dest.append(source.charAt(i));
        return dest.toString();
    }
}
```

The `StringBuffer` class provides for strings that will be modified; use `StringBuffers` when you know that the value of the character data will change. In general, use `StringBuffers` for constructing character data on the fly, as in the `reverseIt` method.

`Strings` typically use less memory and are faster to allocate and use than `StringBuffers`. This is because `Strings` are constants and their size never changes after creation. `Strings` also can be shared. So use `Strings` whenever you can.

Creating Strings and StringBuffers

The bold line in this listing of the `reverseIt` method creates a `StringBuffer` named `dest` whose initial length is the same as `source`:

```
public class ReverseString {
    public static String reverseIt(String source) {
        int i, len = source.length();
        StringBuffer dest = new StringBuffer(len);

        for (i = (len - 1); i >= 0; i--)
            dest.append(source.charAt(i));
        return dest.toString();
    }
}
```

The code `StringBuffer dest` declares to the compiler that `dest` will refer to an object whose type is `StringBuffer`. The `new` operator allocates memory for a new object, and `StringBuffer(len)` initializes the object. These three steps—declaration, instantiation, and initialization—were described in Creating Objects (page 86).

Creating a String

Many Strings are created from *string literals*—a series of characters enclosed within double quotation marks—such as this one:

```
"Gobbledy gook"
```

When the compiler encounters a string literal, it creates a String object whose value is the text that appears between the quotes. So when the compiler encounters the previous string literal, it creates a String object whose value is Gobbledy gook.

You can also create String objects as you would any other Java object: by using the new keyword and a String constructor. The following Java statement is equivalent to (but less efficient than) using the string literal itself:

```
new String("Gobbledy gook");
```

Creating a StringBuffer

To create a StringBuffer, you use the new operator and a constructor. The constructor used by reverseIt to initialize dest requires an integer argument indicating the initial size of the new StringBuffer:

```
StringBuffer(int length)
```

reverseIt could have used StringBuffer's default constructor that leaves the buffer's length undetermined until later. However, it's more efficient to specify the length of the buffer if it's known, instead of allocating more memory on an as-needed basis.

Accessor Methods

Methods used to obtain the value of an object's variables are called *accessor methods*. The reverseIt method uses two of String's accessor methods (shown here in bold) to obtain information about the source string:

```
public class ReverseString {
    public static String reverseIt(String source) {
        int i, len = source.length();
        StringBuffer dest = new StringBuffer(len);
        for (i = (len - 1); i >= 0; i--)
```

```
            dest.append(source.charAt(i));
        return dest.toString();
    }
}
```

First, reverseIt uses String's length accessor method to obtain the length of the String source:

```
int len = source.length();
```

Second, reverseIt uses the charAt accessor, which returns the character at the position specified in the parameter:

```
source.charAt(i)
```

The character returned by charAt is then appended to the StringBuffer dest. Since the loop variable i begins at the end of source and proceeds backwards over the string, the characters are appended in reverse order to the String-Buffer, thereby reversing the string.

More Accessor Methods

String supports a number of other accessor methods that provide access to substrings and the indices of specific characters in the String. StringBuffer has its own set of similar accessor methods.

For the String Class

In addition to the length and charAt accessors described in the previous section, the String class provides two accessors that return the position within the string of a specific character or string: indexOf and lastIndexOf. The indexOf method searches forward from the beginning of the string, and the lastIndexOf method searches backward from the end of the string.

The indexOf and lastIndexOf methods are often used with substring, which returns a substring of the string. The following class illustrates the use of lastIndexOf and substring to isolate different parts of a filename:

```
// This class assumes that the string used to initialize
// fullPath has a directory path, filename, and extension.
// The methods won't work if it doesn't.

public class Filename {
```

```
    private String fullPath;
    private char fileSeparator, extensionSeparator;

    public Filename(String str, char sep, char ext) {
        fullPath = str;
        pathSeparator = sep;
        extensionSeparator = ext;
    }

    public String extension() {
        int dot = fullPath.lastIndexOf(extensionSeparator);
        return fullPath.substring(dot + 1);
    }

    public String filename() {
        int dot = fullPath.lastIndexOf(extensionSeparator);
        int sep = fullPath.lastIndexOf(pathSeparator);
        return fullPath.substring(sep + 1, dot);
    }

    public String path() {
        int sep = fullPath.lastIndexOf(pathSeparator);
        return fullPath.substring(0, sep);
    }
}
```

Impurity Alert! Even though `Filename` does a good job of avoiding system dependencies related to file and extension separators, the class does assume that a filename has a directory path, basename, and extension. This may not be true of filenames on all systems.

Here's a small program that constructs a `Filename` object with a UNIX pathname and calls all of its methods:

```
public class FilenameTest {
    public static void main(String[] args) {
        Filename myHomePage = new
                Filename("/home/mem/index.html", '/', '.');
        System.out.println("Extension = " +
                            myHomePage.extension());
        System.out.println("Filename = " +
                            myHomePage.filename());
        System.out.println("Path = " + myHomePage.path());
    }
}
```

And here's the output from the program:

```
Extension = html
Filename = index
Path = /home/mem/
```

The `extension` method uses `lastIndexOf` to locate the last occurrence of the extension separator (a period (`.`) in the example) in the filename. Then `substring` uses the return value of `lastIndexOf` to extract the filename extension—that is, the substring from the period to the end of the string. This code assumes that the filename actually has a period in it; if the filename does not have a period, then `lastIndexOf` returns `-1` and the `substring` method throws a `StringIndexOutOfBoundsException`.

Notice that `extension` uses `dot +1` as the argument to `substring`. If the period is the last character of the string, then `dot +1` is equal to the length of the string, which is one larger than the largest index into the string (because indices start at 0). This doesn't cause a problem because `substring` accepts an index equal to the length of the string and interprets it to mean "the end of the string."

Try This: Inspect the other methods in the `Filename` class and determine how the `lastIndexOf` and `substring` methods work together to isolate different parts of a filename.

While the methods in the `Filename` example use only one version of the `lastIndexOf` method, the `String` class actually supports four different versions of both the `indexOf` and `lastIndexOf` methods. The declarations for all four versions of both methods follow, along with a description of each:

`indexOf(int` *character*`)`
`lastIndexOf(int` *character*`)`
Returns the index of the first (last) occurrence of the specified character.

`indexOf(int` *character*`, int` *from*`)`
`lastIndexOf(int` *character*`, int` *from*`)`
Returns the index of the first (last) occurrence of the specified character, searching forward (backward) from the specified index.

`indexOf(String` *string*`)`
`lastIndexOf(String` *string*`)`
Returns the index of the first (last) occurrence of the specified `String`.

`indexOf(String` ***string*****`, int`** ***from*****`)`**
`lastIndexOf(String` ***string*****`, int`** ***from*****`)`**
Returns the index of the first (last) occurrence of the specified `String`, searching forward (backward) from the specified index.

For the StringBuffer Class

Like `String`, `StringBuffer` provides `length` and `charAt` accessor methods. It also has a method called `capacity`. The `capacity` method differs from `length` in that it returns the amount of space currently allocated for the `StringBuffer`, rather than the amount of space used. For example, the capacity of the `StringBuffer` in the `reverseIt` method shown here never changes, while the length of the `StringBuffer` increases by one for each iteration of the loop:

```
public class ReverseString {
    public static String reverseIt(String source) {
        int i, len = source.length();
        StringBuffer dest = new StringBuffer(len);

        for (i = (len - 1); i >= 0; i--)
            dest.append(source.charAt(i));
        return dest.toString();
    }
}
```

Modifying StringBuffers

The `reverseIt` method uses `StringBuffer`'s `append` method to add a character to the end of the destination string, `dest`:

```
public class ReverseString {
    public static String reverseIt(String source) {
        int i, len = source.length();
        StringBuffer dest = new StringBuffer(len);

        for (i = (len - 1); i >= 0; i--)
            dest.append(source.charAt(i));
        return dest.toString();
    }
}
```

If the appended character causes the size of the `StringBuffer` to grow beyond its current capacity, the `StringBuffer` allocates more memory. Because memory allocation is a relatively expensive operation, you can make your code more efficient by initializing a StringBuffer's capacity to a reasonable first guess, thereby minimizing the number of times memory must be allocated for it. For example, the reverseIt method constructs the StringBuffer with an initial capacity equal to the length of the source string, thus ensuring only one memory allocation for dest.

The version of the append method used in reverseIt is only one of the StringBuffer methods that appends data to the end of a StringBuffer. Others append data of various types to the end of the StringBuffer, such as float, int, boolean, and even Object. The data is converted to a String before the append operation takes place.

Inserting Characters

At times, you may want to insert data into the middle of a StringBuffer. You do this with one of StringBuffer's insert methods. The following example illustrates how to insert a string into a StringBuffer:

```
StringBuffer sb = new StringBuffer("Drink Java!");
sb.insert(6, "Hot ");
System.out.println(sb.toString());
```

This code snippet prints this:

```
Drink Hot Java!
```

With StringBuffer's many insert methods, you specify the index *before the position* where you want the data inserted. In the example, "Hot " must be inserted before the 'J' in "Java". Indices begin at 0, so the index for 'J' is 6. To insert data at the beginning of a StringBuffer, use an index of 0. To add data at the end of a StringBuffer, use an index equal to the current length of the StringBuffer or use one of the append methods.

Setting Characters

Another useful StringBuffer modifier is setCharAt. setCharAt replaces the character at a specific location in the StringBuffer with the character specified in the argument list. It is useful when you want to reuse a StringBuffer.

Converting Objects to Strings

Often a program must convert an object to a `String` because it needs to pass it to a method that accepts only `String` values or return it from a method whose return type is a `String`. For example, `System.out.println` does not accept `StringBuffers`, so you need to convert a `StringBuffer` to a `String` before you can print it. The bold line in this listing of the `reverseIt` method uses `StringBuffer`'s `toString` method to convert the `StringBuffer` to a `String` object before returning it:

```
public class ReverseString {
    public static String reverseIt(String source) {
        int i, len = source.length();
        StringBuffer dest = new StringBuffer(len);

        for (i = (len - 1); i >= 0; i--)
            dest.append(source.charAt(i));
        return dest.toString();
    }
}
```

All classes inherit the `toString` method from the `Object` class. Also, many classes in the `java.lang` package override this method to provide an implementation that is meaningful to that class. For example, the "type wrapper" classes—`Character`, `Integer`, `Boolean`, and the others—all override `toString` to provide a `String` representation of the object.

Converting Primitive Data Types to Strings

As a convenience, the `String` class provides the class method `valueOf`. You can use `valueOf` to convert variables of different types to `Strings`. For example, to print the value of π:

```
System.out.println(String.valueOf(Math.PI));
```

Converting Strings to Numbers

The `String` class itself does not provide any methods for converting a `String` to a floating-point number, integer, or other numerical type. However, the "type wrapper" classes (`Integer`, `Double`, `Float`, `Long`, and so on) provide a class method named `valueOf` that converts a `String` to an object of that type. Here's a small, contrived example of using the `Float` class's `valueOf` method:

```
String piStr = "3.14159";
Float pi = Float.valueOf(piStr);
```

Strings and the Java Compiler

Before moving on to another lesson, you need to understand one final, important peculiarity about `Strings` and `StringBuffers`. The Java compiler uses the `String` and `StringBuffer` classes behind the scenes to handle literal strings and concatenation.

Literal Strings

In Java, you specify literal strings between double quotation marks:

```
"Hello World!"
```

You can use literal strings anywhere you would use a `String` object. For example, `System.out.println` accepts a `String` argument, so you could use a literal string in place of a `String` there, as in this example:

```
System.out.println(
    "And might I add that you look lovely today.");
```

You also can use `String` methods directly from a literal string:

```
int len = "Goodbye Cruel World".length();
```

Since the compiler creates a new `String` object for every literal string it encounters automatically, you can use a literal string to initialize a `String`, as done here:

```
String s = "Hola Mundo";
```

This construct is equivalent to, but more efficient than, the following construct, which ends up creating two `Strings` instead of one:

```
String s = new String("Hola Mundo");
```

The compiler creates the first string when it encounters the literal string `"Hola Mundo!"` and the second one when it encounters `new String()`.

Concatenation and the + Operator

In Java, you can use the + operator to concatenate `Strings` together:

```
String cat = "cat";
System.out.println("con" + cat + "enation");
```

This is a little deceptive because, as you know, `String`s can't be changed. However, behind the scenes the compiler uses `StringBuffer`s to implement concatenation. This example compiles to this:

```
String cat = "cat";
System.out.println(new StringBuffer().append("con")
                    .append(cat).append("enation").toString());
```

You also can use the + operator to append values to a `String` that are not themselves `String`s:

```
System.out.println("Java's Number " + 1);
```

The compiler converts the non-`String` value (the integer `1` in the example) to a `String` object before performing the concatenation operation.

Other Interesting Features

This lesson covers the most commonly used methods in the `String` and `StringBuffer` classes. But `String` and `StringBuffer` provide several other useful ways to manipulate string data, including comparison, substitution, and conversion between uppercase and lowercase. The API documentation for the `String`[1] and `StringBuffer`[2] classes summarizes and lists all of the methods and variables supported by these two classes.

---

1 http://java.sun.com/products/jdk/1.1/docs/api/java.lang.String.html
2 http://java.sun.com/products/jdk/1.1/docs/api/java.lang.StringBuffer.html

http://java.sun.com/docs/books/tutorial/essential/attributes/index.html

13

Setting Program Attributes

JAVA programs run within an environment that contains *system attributes:* a host machine, a user, a current directory, and an operating system. A Java program also can set up its own configurable attributes, called *program attributes*. Program attributes allow the user to configure various startup options, preferred window size, and so on for the program. Sometimes the term *preferences* is used instead of program attributes.

System attributes are maintained by the `System` class and are covered later in System Properties (page 273). Java programs can set their own set of program attributes through three mechanisms: properties, command-line arguments, and applet parameters.

A *property* defines attributes on a persistent basis. That is, you use properties when attribute values need to persist between invocations of a program. Using Properties to Manage Program Attributes (page 260) shows you how to do this in your programs.

A *command-line argument* defines attributes for Java applications on a nonpersistent basis. You use command-line arguments to set one or more attributes for a single invocation of an application. Command-Line Arguments (page 264) shows how to accept and process command-line arguments in a Java program.

An *applet parameter* is similar to a command-line argument, except that it is used with applets, not applications. Use applet parameters to set one or more attributes for a single invocation of an applet. For information about applet parameters, see Defining and Using Applet Parameters (page 200).

Using Properties to Manage Program Attributes

An attribute has two parts: a name and a value. For example, "`os.name`" is the name for one of the Java platform's system attributes; its value contains the name of the current operating system, such as "`Solaris`".

The `Properties`[1] class in the `java.util` package manages a set of *key/value pairs*. A key/value pair is like a dictionary entry: The key is the word, and the value is the definition. This is a perfect match for managing the names and values of attributes. Each `Properties` key contains the name of a system attribute, and its corresponding `Properties` value is the current value of that attribute.

The `System` class uses a `Properties` object for managing system properties. Any Java program can use a `Properties` object to manage its program attributes. The `Properties` class itself provides methods for the following:

- Loading key/value pairs into a `Properties` object from a stream
- Retrieving a value from its key
- Listing the keys and their values
- Enumerating over the keys
- Saving the properties to a stream

`Properties` extends the `Hashtable`[2] class and inherits methods from it for doing the following:

- Testing to see if a particular key or value is in the `Properties` object
- Getting the current number of key/value pairs
- Removing a key and its value
- Adding a key/value pair to the `Properties` list
- Enumerating over the values or the keys
- Retrieving a value by its key
- Finding out if the `Properties` object is empty

Security Considerations: Access to properties is subject to approval by the current security manager. The example code segments in this section are assumed to be in standalone applications, which, by default, have no security manager. If you attempt

---

1 http://java.sun.com/products/jdk/1.1/docs/api/java.util.Properties.html
2 http://java.sun.com/products/jdk/1.1/docs/api/java.util.Hashtable.html

to use this code in an applet, it may not work, depending on the browser or viewer in which it is running. See Security Restrictions (page 212) for information about security restrictions on applets.

The Life Cycle of a Program's Properties

Figure 38 illustrates how a typical program might manage its attributes with a `Properties` object over the course of its execution.

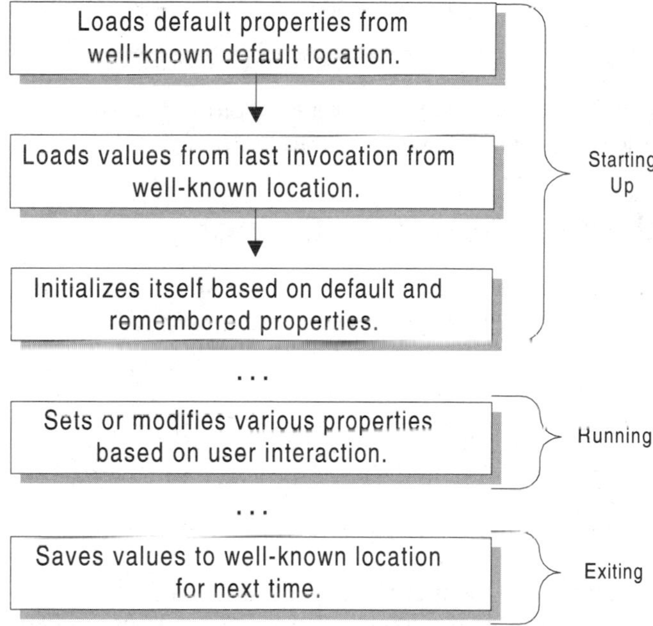

Figure 38: A program loads, modifies, and stores properties during execution.

Starting Up

The actions given in the first three boxes occur when the program is starting up. First, the program loads the default properties from a well-known location into a `Properties` object. Normally, the default properties are stored in a file on disk along with the `.class` and other resource files for the program.

Next, the program creates another `Properties` object and loads the properties that were saved from the last time the program was run. Many applications store properties on a per-user basis, so the properties loaded in this step are usually in a specific file in a particular directory maintained by this application in the user's home directory. Finally, the program uses the default and remembered properties to initialize itself.

The key here is consistency. The application must always load and save properties to the same location so that it can find them the next time it's executed.

Running

During the execution of the program, the user may change some settings, perhaps in a Preferences window, and the `Properties` object is updated to reflect these changes. For them to have a permanent effect, they must be saved.

Exiting

Upon exiting, the program saves the properties to its well-known location, to be loaded again when the program is next started up.

Setting Up Your Properties Object

The following Java code performs the first two steps described in the previous section: loading the default properties and loading the remembered properties:

```
. . .
// create and load default properties
Properties defaultProps = new Properties();
FileInputStream in = new FileInputStream("defaultProperties");
defaultProps.load(in);
in.close();

// create program properties with default
Properties applicationProps = new Properties(defaultProps);

// now load properties from last invocation
in = new FileInputStream("appProperties");
applicationProps.load(in);
in.close();
. . .
```

First, the application sets up a default `Properties` object. This object contains the set of properties to use if values are not explicitly set elsewhere. Then the `load` method reads the default values from a file on disk named `defaultProperties`.

Next, the application uses a different constructor to create a second `Properties` object, `applicationProps`, whose default values are contained in `default-`

Props. The defaults come into play when a property is being retrieved. If the property can't be found in `applicationProps`, then its default list is searched.

Finally, the code loads a set of properties into `applicationProps` from a file named `appProperties`. The properties in this file are those that were saved from the program the last time it was invoked (the next section shows you how this was done).

Saving Properties

The following example writes out the application properties from the previous example using `Properties`'s `save` method. The default properties don't need to be saved each time because they never change.

```
FileOutputStream out = new FileOutputStream("appProperties");
applicationProps.save(out, "---No Comment---");
out.close();
```

The `save` method needs a stream to write to, as well as a string that it uses as a comment at the top of the output.

Getting Property Information

Once you've set up your `Properties` object, you can query it for information about various keys/values that it contains. An application gets information from a `Properties` object after start up so that it can initialize itself based on choices made by the user. The `Properties` class has several methods for getting property information:

`contains(Object` ***value*****`)`**
`containsKey(Object` ***key*****`)`**
: Returns `true` if the value or the key is in the `Properties` object. `Properties` inherits these methods from `Hashtable`. Thus they accept `Object` arguments. You should pass in `String`s.

`getProperty(String` ***key*****`)`**
`getProperty(String` ***key*****`, String`** ***default*****`)`**
: Returns the value for the specified property. The second version allows you to provide a default value. If the key is not found, the default is returned.

`list(PrintStream` ***s*****`)`**
`list(PrintWriter` ***w*****`)`**
: Writes all of the properties to the specified stream or writer. This is useful for debugging.

`elements()`
`keys()`
`propertyNames()`
Returns an `Enumeration` containing the keys or values (as indicated by the method name) contained in the `Properties` object.

`size()`
Returns the current number of key/value pairs.

Setting Properties

A user's interaction with a program during its execution may impact property settings. These changes should be reflected in the `Properties` object so that they are saved when the program exits (and calls the `save` method). You can use the following methods to change the properties in a `Properties` object:

`put(Object` ***key*****`, Object`** ***value*****`)`**
Puts the key/value pair in the `Properties` object.

`remove(Object` ***key*****`)`**
Removes the key/value pair associated with *key*.

Both `put` and `remove` come from `Hashtable` and thus take `Objects`. You should pass in `Strings`.

A Real-Life Example

One of the trails in the online tutorial, Putting It All Together[1], shows and documents a complete client/server application that implements the game of BINGO. Both the client and the server application in that example use `Properties` to maintain program attributes.

Command-Line Arguments

A Java application can accept any number of arguments from the command line. Command-line arguments allow the user to affect the operation of an application for one invocation. For example, an application might allow the user to specify *verbose mode*—that is, specify that the application display a lot of trace information. This is done using the command-line argument `-verbose`.

---

1 http://java.sun.com/docs/books/tutorial/together/index.html

---

Purity Tip: Programs that use command-line arguments are not 100% Pure Java because some systems, like the Mac OS, don't normally have a command line or command-line arguments. Consider using properties instead so that your programs fit more naturally into the environment. If you really must use command-line arguments, have them comply with the POSIX conventions summarized in the Appendix on page 935.

The user enters command-line arguments when invoking the application and specifies them after the name of the class to run. For example, suppose you have a Java application, called `Sort`, that sorts lines in a file. To sort the data in a file named `friends.txt`, you would run it like this:

```
java Sort friends.txt
```

In the Java language, when you invoke an application, the runtime system passes the command-line arguments to the application's `main` method via an array of `Strings`. Each `String` in the array contains one of the command-line arguments. In the previous example, the command-line arguments passed to the `Sort` application is an array that contains a single `String`: "`friends.txt`".

Note to C and C++ Programmers:

The command-line arguments passed to a Java application differ in number and in type than those passed to a C or C++ program. When you invoke a Java application, the system passes only one parameter to it:

args: An array of strings that contains the arguments

You can derive the number of command-line arguments with the array's length attribute:

```
numberOfArgs = args.length;
```

In Java, you always know the name of the application because it's the name of the class in which the `main` method is defined. So the Java runtime system does not pass the class name you invoke to the `main` method. Rather, it passes only the items on the command line that appear after the class name. For example, consider the following statement, which is used to invoke a Java application:

```
java diff file1 file2
```

The command-line arguments are in bold.

Echoing Command-Line Arguments

The following simple application displays each of its command-line arguments on a line by itself:

```
public class Echo {
    public static void main (String[] args) {
        for (int i = 0; i < args.length; i++)
            System.out.println(args[i]);
    }
}
```

Here's an example of how to invoke the application using Windows 95/NT. You enter the words that are shown here in bold:

```
java Echo Drink Hot Java
Drink
Hot
Java
```

Note that the application displays each word—`Drink`, `Hot`, and `Java`—on a line by itself. This is because the space character separates command-line arguments. If you want `Drink`, `Hot`, and `Java` to be interpreted as a single argument, you would join them by enclosing them within double quotation marks. On Windows 95/NT, you run it like this:

```
java Echo "Drink Hot Java"
Drink Hot Java
```

Parsing Numeric Command-Line Arguments

If your program needs to support a numeric command-line argument, it must convert a `String` argument that represents a number, such as `"34"`, to a number. Here's a code snippet that converts a command-line argument to an `int`:

```
int firstArg;
if (args.length > 0)
    firstArg = Integer.parseInt(args[0]);
```

`parseInt` throws a `NumberFormatException` if the format of `args[0]` isn't valid. All of the `Number` classes—`Integer`, `Float`, `Double`, and so on—have `parse`*`XXX`* methods that convert a `String` representing a number to an object of their type.

http://java.sun.com/docs/books/tutorial/essential/system/index.html

14 Accessing System Resources

SOMETIMES, a program requires access to system resources such as system properties, standard input and output, or the current time. Your program could make system calls directly to the window or operating system, but then your program would be able to run only in that particular environment. Each time you want to run the program in a new environment, you'd have to port your program by rewriting the system-dependent sections of code.

The Java platform lets your program access system resources through a (relatively) system-independent API implemented by the `System`[1] class and through a system-dependent API implemented by the `Runtime`[2] class.

Purity Tip: Some of the system resources available through the `System` and `Runtime` classes cannot be used in 100% Pure Java programs. These resources are noted throughout this lesson.

Most system programming needs are met through the `System` class. However, in rare cases, a program might have to access the system through the `Runtime` object that represents the current runtime environment. The last section of this lesson, The Runtime Object (page 291), explains how to do this and talks about the trade-offs of accessing the system directly via the `Runtime` object.

1 http://java.sun.com/products/jdk/1.1/docs/api/java.lang.System.html
2 http://java.sun.com/products/jdk/1.1/docs/api/java.lang.Runtime.html

Figure 39 shows that the System class allows your Java programs to use system resources but insulates them from system-specific details.

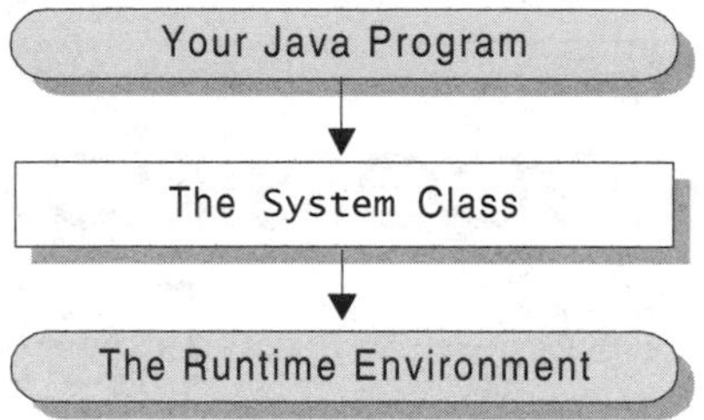

Figure 39: The System class allows your Java programs to use system resources, while insulating them from system-specific details.

If you've experimented with other lessons in this tutorial, you've no doubt already seen the System class's standard output stream used in several examples to display text. This and other resources available through System are briefly described here and covered in the sections indicated.

The Standard I/O Streams (page 270)
: Probably the most frequently used items from the System class are the streams used for reading and writing text. The System class provides one stream for reading text—the standard input stream—and two streams for writing text—the standard output and standard error streams.

System Properties (page 273)
: Properties are key/value pairs that your Java programs can use to set up various attributes or parameters between invocations. The Java platform itself maintains a set of system properties that contain information about the current platform. You can access the system properties through the System class.

Forcing Finalization and Garbage Collection (page 277)
: In Java, you don't have to free an object when you're done with it—the garbage collector runs periodically in the background and cleans up unreferenced objects. Or you can force the garbage collector to run using System's gc method. Also, you can request that the runtime system perform object finalization using System's runFinalization method.

Providing Your Own Security Manager (page 279)
: The security manager is an application-wide object that determines whether potentially threatening operations should be allowed. You use the System class to set and get the security manager for an application. Subclasses of java.lang.SecurityManager implement a specific management policy.

Miscellaneous System Methods (page 288)
The System class includes several miscellaneous methods that let you get the current time in milliseconds, exit the interpreter, and copy arrays.

Using the System Class

The following small Java program uses the System class twice, first to retrieve the current user's name and then to display it:

```
public class UserNameTest {
    public static void main(String[] args) {
        String name = System.getProperty("user.name");
        System.out.println(name);
    }
}
```

Notice that this program never instantiates a System object. It just references the getProperty method and the out variable directly from the class. This is because all of the members of System are class members. In addition, you *cannot* instantiate the System class—all of its constructors are private.

As covered in Understanding Instance and Class Members (page 118), to use a class variable, you use it directly from the name of the class using Java's dot (.) notation. For example, to reference the System's class variable out, append the variable name to the class name, separated by a period, like this:

```
System.out
```

You call class methods in a similar fashion. So to call System's getProperty method, append the method name to the end of the class name, separated by a period:

```
System.getProperty("user.name");
```

The code in UserNameTest uses System's getProperty method to search the properties database for the property called "user.name". System Properties (page 273) later in this lesson talks more about system properties and the getProperty method.

UserNameTest also uses System.out, a PrintStream that implements the standard output stream. The println method prints its argument to the standard output stream. The next section discusses the standard output stream and the other two standard I/O streams provided by the System class.

The Standard I/O Streams

The concept of standard input and output streams is a C library concept that has been assimilated into the Java platform. There are three standard streams, all of which are managed by the `java.lang.System` class:

Standard input: referenced by `System.in`
: Used for program input. Typically reads input the user enters at a keyboard.

Standard output: referenced by `System.out`
: Used for program output. Typically displays information to the user in a terminal window or browser console window.

Standard error: referenced by `System.err`
: Used to display error messages to the user in a terminal window or browser console window.

Purity Tip: Avoid using the standard I/O streams in your programs—they are not 100% Pure Java. Some systems, such as the Mac OS, do not normally have standard I/O. Even though the Java platform may provide some sort of implementation for them on such systems, they are not a normal part of the platform. Also, the standard I/O streams are implemented with byte streams that are not portable to platforms that have non-ASCII file systems. Instead of using the standard I/O streams, provide a GUI interface for getting text from and displaying text to the user.

The standard I/O streams are implemented by classes in the `java.io` package. To learn about the classes that implement the standard I/O streams and all of the other I/O streams in the Java platform, see Reading and Writing (but No 'rithmetic) (page 365).

Standard Input Stream

The `System` class provides a stream for reading text: the standard input stream. A Java program can read text typed in by the user at the keyboard by invoking the `System.in.read` method. Instead, however, you should write your programs to use a GUI to get input from a user. Use of standard input is recommended only for prototyping and debugging.

Purity Tip: Not recommended for 100% Pure Java programs, although we document standard input, output, and error streams here since they are commonly used for debugging.

Standard Output and Standard Error Streams

Probably the most frequently used items from the `System` class are the standard output and standard error streams, which display text to the user. The standard output stream is typically used for command output to display the results of a command to the user. Standard error stream typically displays any errors that occur when a program is running.

The print, println, and write Methods

Both standard output and standard error are `PrintStream`[1] objects. You use one of `PrintStream`'s three methods to print text to the stream: `print`, `println`, or `write`.

The `print` and `println` methods are essentially the same; they both write their `String` argument to the stream. They differ only in that `println` appends a newline to the end of its output, while `print` does not. In other words, the following two statements are equivalent:

```
System.out.print("Duke is not a penguin!" +
                     System.getProperty("line.separator"));

System.out.println("Duke is not a penguin!");
```

Note the extra code in the first statement: `+ System.getProperty("line.separator")`. This appends the system's line separator (a new line) to the output. The `println` method automatically does this.

The `write` method is used less frequently than either of the `print` methods. The `write` method writes bytes to the stream. Use `write` to write non-ASCII data.

Arguments to print and println

The `print` and `println` methods both take a single argument. The argument may be one of any of the following data types: `Object`, `String`, `char[]`, `int`, `long`, `float`, `double`, or `boolean`. In addition, there's an extra version of `println` that takes no arguments and just prints a newline.

Printing Objects of Different Data Types

The following program uses `System.out.println` to output data of various types to the standard output stream:

---

1 http://java.sun.com/products/jdk/1.1/docs/api/java.io.PrintStream.html

```
public class DataTypePrintTest {
    public static void main(String[] args) {

        Thread objectData = new Thread();
        String stringData = "Java Mania";
        char[] charArrayData = { 'a', 'b', 'c' };
        int integerData = 4;
        long longData = Long.MIN_VALUE;
        float floatData = Float.MAX_VALUE;
        double doubleData = Math.PI;
        boolean booleanData = true;

        System.out.println(objectData);
        System.out.println(stringData);
        System.out.println(charArrayData);
        System.out.println(integerData);
        System.out.println(longData);
        System.out.println(floatData);
        System.out.println(doubleData);
        System.out.println(booleanData);
    }
}
```

This program produces this output:

```
Thread[Thread-4,5,main]
Java Mania
abc
4
-9223372036854775808
3.40282e+38
3.14159
true
```

Note that you can print an object—the first `println` method call prints a `Thread` object and the second prints a `String` object. When you use `print` or `println` to print an object, the data printed depends on the type of the object. In the example program, printing a `String` object yields the contents of the `String`. However, printing a `Thread` yields a string of this format:

`ThreadClass[name,priority,group]`

Changing the Standard I/O Streams

You can set the standard I/O streams to a stream that you create with one of these methods:

```
setIn(InputStream in)
setErr(PrintStream err)
setOut(PrintStream out)
```

Use these with caution, as the standard input and output streams are well-known and well-understood and should work as expected.

System Properties

The `System` class maintains a set of properties—key/value pairs—that define traits or attributes of the current working environment. When the Java platform first starts, the system properties are initialized to contain information about the runtime environment, including information about the current user, the current version of the Java platform, and even the character used to separate components of a filename.

Try This: Compile and run the following program on your system. Look at the program output to see which system properties are set automatically for you.

```
public class DisplaySystemProps {
    public static void main(String[] args) {
        System.getProperties().list(System.out);
    }
}
```

Table 16 lists the system properties guaranteed to be set when the Java platform starts up, regardless of the system you are running.

Your Java programs can get or modify system properties through several methods in the `System` class. You can use a key to look up one property in the properties list, or you can get the whole set of properties all at once. You can also change the set of system properties completely.

Security Consideration: Applets can read *some, but not all,* system properties. For a complete list of the system properties that can and cannot be used by applets, refer to Getting System Properties (page 217).

Table 16: System properties set when the Java platform starts.

Key	Meaning	Examples (on UNIX)
`file.separator`	File separator	Slash /
`line.separator`	Line separator	Newline `\n`
`path.separator`	Path separator	Colon `:`
`java.class.path`	Java classpath	`.:/home/classes:...`
`java.class.version`	Java class version number	`45.3`
`java.home`	Java installation directory	`/java/solaris`
`java.vendor`	Java vendor-specific string	Sun Microsystems, Inc.
`java.vendor.url`	Java vendor URL	`http://www.sun.com/`
`java.version`	Java version number	`1.1`
`os.arch`	Operating system architecture	sparc
`os.name`	Operating system name	Solaris
`"user.dir"`	User's current working directory	`/home/mystuff`
`"user.home"`	User's home directory	`/home`
`"user.name"`	User's account name	`mem`

Getting System Properties

Your program might want to look at a system property so as to do something in a system-independent fashion. For example, if your program manipulates pathnames or filenames, it can retrieve the file separator from the system properties and use it to find the various components of a pathname.

Impurity Alert! You also can use system properties to do something that is not 100% Pure Java. For example, avoid writing code like this:

```
// IMPURE CODE!
if (System.getProperty("os.name") == "Solaris")
    doSomething();
else if (System.getProperty("os.name") == "Windows 95")
    doSomethingElse();
```

The `System` class has two methods that you can use to get the system properties: `getProperty`, which searches for a specific property by key, and `getProperties`, which returns the whole properties list.

The class has two different versions of `getProperty`. Both retrieve the value of the property whose key was provided as an argument to the method. The simpler of the two takes a single argument: the key for the property you want to search for. For example, to get the value of `"path.separator"`, use the following statement:

```
System.getProperty("path.separator");
```

The `getProperty` method returns a string containing the value of the property. If the property does not exist, this version of `getProperty` returns `null`.

The second version of `getProperty` requires two `String` arguments: The first is the key to look up and the second is a default value to return if the key cannot be found or if it has no value. For example, the following call to `getProperty` looks up the `System` property called `"subliminal.message"`. This is not a valid system property, so instead of returning `null`, this method returns the default value provided as a second argument: `"Buy Java Now!"`:

```
System.getProperty("subliminal.message", "Buy Java Now!");
```

You should use this version of `getProperty` if you don't want to risk a `NullPointerException` or if you really want to provide a default value for a property that doesn't have a value or that cannot be found.

The last method provided by the `System` class to access properties values is the `getProperties` method. This method returns a `Properties`[1] object that contains the complete set of system property key/value pairs. You can use the various `Properties` class methods to query the `Properties` objects for specific values or to list the entire set of properties. For information about the `Properties` class, see Using Properties to Manage Program Attributes (page 260).

Setting System Properties

You can modify the existing set of system properties using `System`'s `setProperties` method. This method takes a `Properties` object that has been initialized to contain the key/value pairs for the properties that you want to set. It replaces the

1 http://java.sun.com/products/jdk/1.1/docs/api/java.util.Properties.html

entire set of system properties with the new set represented by the `Properties` object.

Impurity Alert! Modifying system properties is not 100% Pure Java and may provide for unpredictable results.

The next example is a Java program that creates a `Properties` object and initializes it from the file called `myProperties.txt`, which contains this text:

```
subliminal.message=Buy Java Now!
```

This example program then uses `System.setProperties` to install the new `Properties` object as the current set of system properties:

```
import java.io.FileInputStream;
import java.util.Properties;

public class PropertiesTest {
    public static void main(String[] args) throws Exception {
        // set up new properties object from
        // file "myProperties.txt"
        FileInputStream propFile = new FileInputStream(
                                         "myProperties.txt");
        Properties p = new Properties(System.getProperties());
        p.load(propFile);

        // set the system properties
        System.setProperties(p);
        // display the system properties
        System.getProperties().list(System.out);
    }
}
```

The example program creates the `Properties` object that is used as the argument to `setProperties` like this:

```
Properties p = new Properties(System.getProperties());
```

This statement initializes the new properties object, `p`, with the current set of system properties. In this case, this is the set of properties initialized by the runtime system. Then the program loads additional properties into `p` from the file `myProperties.txt` and sets the system properties to `p`. This has the effect of adding the properties listed in `myProperties.txt` to the set of properties created

by the runtime system at startup. Note that you can create `p` without any default `Properties` object, like this:

```
Properties p = new Properties();
```

If you do this, your application won't have access to the system properties.

Note that the value of system properties can be overwritten! For example, if `myProperties.txt` contains the following line, the `"java.vendor"` system property will be overwritten:

```
java.vendor=Acme Software Company
```

In general, you should not overwrite system properties. You may end up doing something that is not 100% Pure Java.

The `setProperties` method changes the set of system properties for the currently running application. These changes are not persistent. That is, changing the system properties within an application will not affect future invocations of the Java interpreter for this or any other application. The runtime system reinitializes the system properties each time it starts up. If you want your changes to the system properties to be persistent, then your application must write the values to some file before exiting and read them in again upon startup.

Note: Previous versions of the `System` class supported a method called `getenv` that retrieved the value of an environment variable. This method was UNIX-specific and has been deprecated. The properties mechanism is more versatile and portable, so your Java programs should use properties instead of `getenv`.

Forcing Finalization and Garbage Collection

The Java platform performs memory management tasks for you. When your program has finished using an object—that is, when there are no more references to an object—the object is *finalized* and then garbage collected. These tasks happen asynchronously in the background. However, you can force object finalization and garbage collection using the appropriate methods in the `System` class.

Finalizing Objects

Before an object is garbage-collected, the Java platform gives the object a chance to clean up after itself. This step is called *finalization* and is achieved through a call to the object's `finalize` method. The object should override the `finalize` method to perform any final cleanup tasks, such as freeing system resources like files and sockets. For information about the `finalize` method, see Writing a finalize Method (page 125).

You can force object finalization to occur by calling `System`'s `runFinalization` method:

```
System.runFinalization();
```

This method calls the `finalize` methods on all objects that are waiting to be garbage-collected.

You also can specify, using the following method, that finalizers should be run before the Java runtime exits:

```
System.runFinalizersOnExit(true);
```

By default, this is disabled and the runtime does not run finalizers when exiting. Calling this method is subject to approval by the security manager.

Running the Garbage Collector

You can suggest that the Java Virtual Machine run the garbage collector by calling `System`'s `gc` method:

```
System.gc();
```

When `System.gc` returns, the VM has made a best effort to reclaim space from all used objects.

You might want to run the garbage collector to ensure that it runs at the best time for your program rather than when it's most convenient for the Java platform to run it. For example, your program may wish to run the garbage collector right before it enters a compute- or memory-intensive section of code or when it knows there will be some idle time.

The garbage collector requires time to complete its task. The amount of time varies depending on certain factors; for example, how big your heap is and how fast your processor is. Your program should run the garbage collector only when doing so will have no performance impact on your program.

For more information about Java's garbage collection scheme, see Cleaning Up Unused Objects (page 92).

Providing Your Own Security Manager

Security becomes a major concern when writing and using programs that interact with the Internet. Will you download something that corrupts your file system? Will you be open for a virus attack? It's unlikely that computers on the Internet will ever be completely safe from attack from the few evildoers out there. However, you can take steps to provide a significant level of protection for your computers and data. One way that Java provides protection from attack is through the use of a *security manager.*

The security manager is an application-wide object that acts as a full-time security guard for an application. An application's security manager determines whether potentially threatening operations should be allowed and it implements and imposes the application's security policy. By default, an application does not have a security manager. So, by default, an application allows all operations that might be subject to security restrictions.

To change this lenient behavior, an application must create and install its own security manager. The `SecurityManager`[1] class in the `java.lang` package is an abstract class that provides the programming interface and partial implementation for all Java security managers. To create a security manager for your application, you must create a subclass of `SecurityManager` and install an instance of it as your application's security manager.

Note: Most, if not all, of the existing browsers and applet viewers *do* create their own security manager when starting up. Consequently, an applet is subject to whatever access restrictions are imposed on it by the security manager for the particular application in which the applet is running.

The `SecurityManager` class defines many methods that can be used to verify many kinds of operations. For example, `SecurityManager`'s `checkAccess` method verifies thread accesses and `checkPropertyAccess` verifies access to the

---

1 http://java.sun.com/products/jdk/1.1/docs/api/java.lang.SecurityManager.html

specified property. Each operation or group of operations has its own `checkXXX` methods.

The set of `checkXXX` methods defined in `SecurityManager` represents the set of operations in the Java platform that are already subject to the protection of the security manager. Normally, your code does not have to invoke any of `SecurityManager`'s `checkXXX` methods. The Java platform does this for you so that any operation represented by a `checkXXX` method is already verified by the security manager. However, your code may invoke those methods if you choose.

When writing your own security manager, you must subclass `SecurityManager` and override its `checkXXX` methods to implement the security policy for specific operations. Alternatively, you may have to add a few of your own to put other kinds of operations under the scrutiny of the security manager. Deciding Which SecurityManager Methods to Override (page 286) explains which operation or group of operations each `checkXXX` method in the `SecurityManager` class is designed to protect.

Getting the Current Security Manager

You can get the current security manager for an application using the `System` class's `getSecurityManager` method:

```
SecurityManager appsm = System.getSecurityManager();
```

This method returns `null` if there is no current security manager for the application. You should make sure that you have a valid `SecurityManager` object before calling any of its methods.

Getting Permission to Perform a Potentially Risky Task

Once you have the security manager, you can request permission to allow or disallow certain operations. For example, the `System.exit` method, which terminates the Java interpreter, uses the security manager's `checkExit` method to approve the exit operation:

```
SecurityManager security = System.getSecurityManager();
if (security != null) {
    security.checkExit(status);
}
. . .
// code continues here if checkExit() returns
```

If the security manager approves the exit operation, `checkExit` returns normally and the operation is allowed. If the security manager disallows the operation, the `checkExit` method throws a `SecurityException`. In this manner, the security manager allows or disallows a potentially threatening operation before it is attempted.

Your application can catch the `SecurityException` thrown and display an error message or do some other sort of recovery. Even if your application doesn't handle the exception, the operation was prevented.

Writing a Security Manager

To provide a custom security manager for your application, you must create a subclass of the `SecurityManager` class. This subclass will override methods from the `SecurityManager` class to customize the verifications and approvals needed in your Java application.

This section walks you through an example security manager that restricts reading and writing to the file system. The policy implemented by the example security manager prompts the user for a password when the application attempts to open a file for reading or for writing. If the password is correct, then the access is allowed. You can see the complete code for this example in Appendix A, Co[illegible] Examples (page 757).

Let's begin at the top of the class. Like all security managers, th[illegible] rity manager, PasswordSecurityManager (page 756), ex[illegible] ager:

```
public class PasswordSecurityManager
    . . .
}
```

Next, `PasswordSecurityManager` declar[illegible] word to contain the password that the u[illegible] system accesses, and `buffy`, an object [illegible] two member variables are set in the c[illegible]

```
private String password;
private BufferedReader bu
public PasswordSecurityMa
    super();
    this.password = p;
    this.buffy = b;
}
```

The next method in the PasswordSecurityManager class is a private helper method named accessOK:

```
private boolean accessOK() {
    int c;
    String response;

    System.out.println("What's the secret password?");
    try {
        response = buffy.readLine();
        if (response.equals(password))
            return true;
        else
            return false;
    } catch (IOException e) {
        return false;
    }
}
```

This method prompts the user for a password and then verifies the password the user enters. If the user enters a valid password, the method returns true; otherwise, it returns false.

The SecurityManager superclass provides five methods that verify file system
...s: three versions of checkRead and two versions of checkWrite. These
...are called by the I/O classes in the Java platform before certain file
...ttempted. To impose a custom policy on file system accesses, the
...nager subclass overrides all five of these methods. Also,
...ger provides empty implementations for checkProper-
...cess. This is because these methods are called by
... get the system property that indicates the current
...se PasswordSecurityManager needs to allow

```
...Descriptor filedescriptor) {
...ception("Not a Chance!");
...filename) {
...tion("No Way!");
...name, Object executionContext)
```

Table 17: Objects you can perform operations on and `SecurityManager` methods that approve them.

Operations On	Approved By
	`checkLink(String` *`library`*`)`
	`checkRead(FileDescriptor` *`filedescriptor`*`)`
	`checkRead(String` *`filename`*`)`
	`checkRead(String` *`filename`*`,` `Object` *`executionContext`*`)`
	`checkWrite(FileDescriptor` *`filedescriptor`*`)`
	`checkWrite(String` *`filename`*`)`
Runtime Commands	`checkExec(String` *`command`*`)`
System Commands	`checkExit(int` *`status`*`)`
Packages	`checkPackageAccess(String` *`packageName`*`)`
	`checkPackageDefinition(String` *`packageName`*`)`
Properties	`checkPropertiesAccess()`
	`checkPropertyAccess(String` *`key`*`)`
Window System	`checkTopLevelWindow(Object` *`window`*`)`
	`checkAWTEventQueueAccess()`
Any Object	`checkMemberAccess(Class` *`class`*`, int` *`which`*`)`
System Clipboard	`checkSystemClipboardAccess()`
PrintJobs	`checkPrintJobAccess()`
Security	`checkSecurityAccess(String` *`action`*`)`

Many of the `check`*`XXX`* methods are called in multiple situations. For example, the `checkAccess(ThreadGroup` *`g`*`)` method is invoked when you create a `ThreadGroup`, set its daemon status, stop it, and so on. When overriding a `check`*`XXX`* method, ensure you understand all of the situations in which it can be invoked.

If you wish to put other types of operations under the scrutiny of the security manager, then your `SecurityManager` subclass must implement other `check`*`XXX`* methods and call them at the appropriate time.

Miscellaneous System Methods

The `System` class provides several more methods that provide miscellaneous functionality, including copying arrays and getting the current time.

Copying Arrays

Use `System`'s `arraycopy` method to efficiently copy data from one array into another. The `arraycopy` method requires five arguments:

```
public static void arraycopy(Object source,
                             int srcIndex,
                             Object dest,
                             int destIndex,
                             int length)
```

The two `Object` arguments indicate from which array to copy and to which array to copy. The three integer arguments indicate the starting location in both the source and the destination arrays and the number of elements to copy. Figure 40 illustrates how the copy takes place.

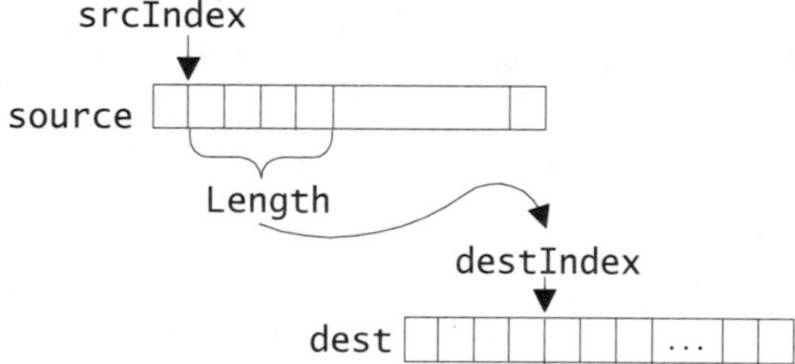

Figure 40: Copying from one array to another.

The following Java program uses `arraycopy` to copy some elements from the `copyFrom` array to the `copyTo` array:

```
public class ArrayCopyTest {
    public static void main(String[] args) {
        char[] copyFrom = { 'd', 'e', 'c', 'a', 'f', 'f', 'e',
                            'i', 'n', 'a', 't', 'e', 'd' };
        char[] copyTo = new char[7];

        System.arraycopy(copyFrom, 2, copyTo, 0, 7);
        System.out.println(new String(copyTo));
    }
}
```

The `arraycopy` method call in this program begins the copy at element number 2 in the source array. Recall that array indices start at 0, so the copy begins at the array element `'c'`. The `arraycopy` method call puts the copied elements into the destination array beginning at the first element (element 0) in the destination array `copyTo`. The copy copies seven elements: `'c'`, `'a'`, `'f'`, `'f'`, `'e'`, `'i'`, and `'n'`. Effectively, the `arraycopy` method takes the `"caffein"` out of `"decaffeinated"`, as shown in Figure 41.

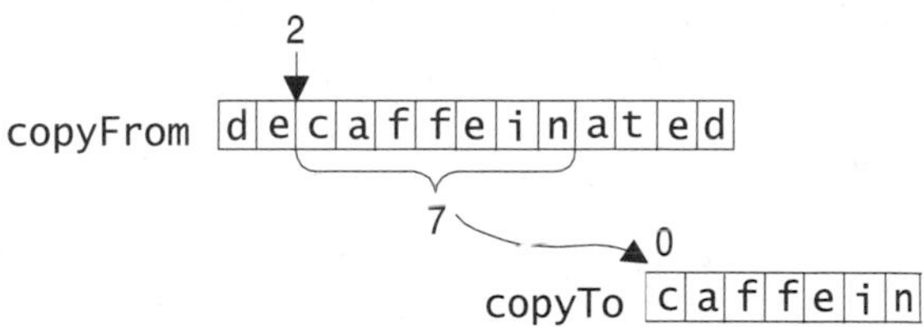

Figure 41: Copying `"caffein"` from `"decaffeinated"` into another array.

Note that the destination array must be allocated before you call `arraycopy` and must be large enough to contain the data being copied.

Getting the Current Time

The `currentTimeMillis` method returns the current time in milliseconds since 00:00:00, January 1, 1970. The `currentTimeMillis` method is commonly used during performance tests; a program would get the current time, perform the operation, and then get the current time again. The difference between the two time samples is roughly the length of time that the operation took to execute.

Often in GUIs, the time difference between mouse clicks is used to determine whether a user double-clicked. The `TimingIsEverything` applet (page 758) uses `currentTimeMillis` to compute the number of milliseconds between two mouse clicks. If the time period between the clicks is less than 200 milliseconds, the two mouse clicks are interpreted as a double mouse click.

Here's what the applet looks like after you've double-clicked it:

Double Click!! (Interval = 110)

http://java.sun.com/docs/books/tutorial/essential/system/misc.html

And here's the source code for the `TimingIsEverything` applet:

```
import java.awt.*;
import java.awt.event.*;

public class TimingIsEverything extends java.applet.Applet {

    public long firstClickTime = 0;
    public String displayStr;

    public void init() {
        displayStr = "Double Click Me";
        addMouseListener(new MyAdapter());
    }
    public void paint(Graphics g) {
       g.drawRect(0, 0, getSize().width-1, getSize().height-1);
        g.drawString(displayStr, 40, 30);
    }
    class MyAdapter extends MouseAdapter {
        public void mouseClicked(Event evt) {
            long clickTime = System.currentTimeMillis();
            long clickInterval = clickTime - firstClickTime;
            if (clickInterval < 200) {
                displayStr = "Double Click!! (Interval = " +
                                clickInterval + ")";
                firstClickTime = 0;
            } else {
                displayStr = "Single Click!!";
                firstClickTime = clickTime;
            }
            repaint();
        }
    }
}
```

You could use the return value from the `CurrentTimeMillis` method to compute the current date and time. However, you'll probably find that it's more convenient to get the current date and time from the `Calendar`[1] class.

Exiting the Runtime Environment

To exit the Java interpreter, call the `System.exit` method. The interpreter exits with the integer exit code that you specify to the `exit` method:

```
System.exit(-1);
```

1 http://java.sun.com/products/jdk/1.1/docs/api/java.util.Calendar.html

Note: The `exit` method is a drastic way of terminating all threads and the interpreter. A gentler way to exit the runtime environment is to let the `main` method exit normally or to ask the interpreter's daemon threads to exit.

Security Consideration: Invocation of the `exit` method is subject to security restrictions. A call to `exit` from within an applet will likely result in a `SecurityException`; whether it does is browser-dependent. See Security Restrictions (page 212) for information about the security restrictions placed on applets.

The Runtime Object

At the core of the Java platform are the Java virtual machine, the Java interpreter, and the host operating system.

In Figure 42, the oval labeled *Runtime* represents the current runtime environment. It is an instance of the `Runtime`[1] class. The current runtime environment can be anything from Sun's implementation of the Java virtual machine and interpreter running on Solaris to ACME Company's implementation of the virtual machine and interpreter running on the ACME toaster.

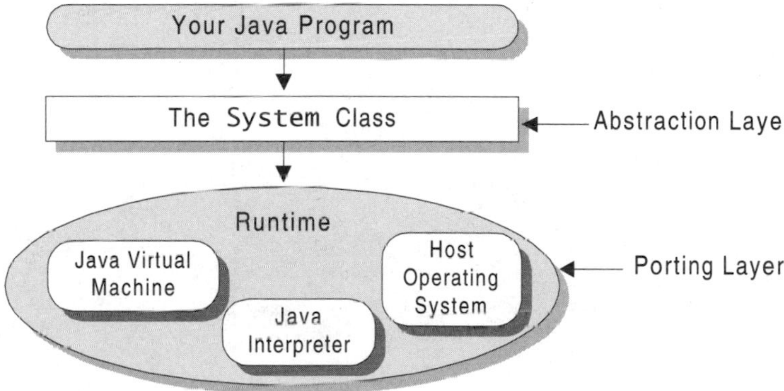

Figure 42: The `Runtime` class interacts directly with the runtime system and is system-dependent.

1 http://java.sun.com/products/jdk/1.1/docs/api/java.lang.Runtime.html

The `Runtime` object provides two services. First, it communicates with the components of the runtime environment—getting information and invoking functions. Second, it is the interface to system-dependent capabilities. For example, a UNIX `Runtime` object might support the `getenv` and `setenv` functions. Another `Runtime` object, such as a Mac's, might not support `getenv` and `setenv` because the host operating system doesn't support these functions; however, it might support others.

Purity Tip: The `Runtime` class is system-dependent because it is tightly integrated with the implementation of the Java interpreter, the Java virtual machine, and the host operating system. If objects in your program send messages to the `Runtime` object directly, you sacrifice the system-independent nature of your Java program. In general, this is not a good idea (particularly for applets). In particular, if a program calls `Runtime`'s `exec` method, then it is not 100% Pure Java.

---

http://java.sun.com/docs/books/tuturial/essential/exceptions/index.html

15

Handling Errors with Exceptions

IF there's a golden rule of programming it's this: Errors occur in software programs. This we know. But what really matters is what happens *after* the error occurs. How is the error handled? Who handles it? Can the program recover, or should it just die?

The Java language uses *exceptions* to provide error-handling capabilities for its programs. An exception is an event that occurs during the execution of a program that disrupts the normal flow of instructions. You can learn more about this in What's an Exception, and Why Should I Care? (page 294).

If you have done any amount of Java programming at all, you have undoubtedly already encountered exceptions. Your First Encounter with Java Exceptions (page 301) was probably in the form of an error message from the compiler like this one:

```
InputFile.java:11: Exception java.io.FileNotFoundException
must be caught, or it must be declared in the throws clause of
this method.
        in = new FileReader(filename);
             ^
```

This message indicates that the compiler found an exception that is not being handled. The Java language requires that a method either catch all "checked" exceptions (those that are checked by the runtime system) or specify that it can throw that type of exception. Java's Catch or Specify Requirement (page 303) discusses the reasoning behind this requirement and what it means to you and your Java programs. Dealing with Exceptions (page 305) features an example program that can throw two different kinds of exceptions. Using this program, you can learn how to catch an exception and handle it and, alternatively, how to specify that your method can throw it.

The Java runtime system and many classes from Java packages throw exceptions under some circumstances by using the `throw` statement. You can use the same mechanism to throw exceptions in your Java programs. How to Throw Exceptions (page 318) shows you how to throw exceptions from your Java code.

Although Java requires that methods catch or specify checked exceptions, they do not have to catch or specify *runtime exceptions*, that is, exceptions that occur within the Java runtime system. Because catching or specifying an exception is extra work, programmers may be tempted to write code that throws only runtime exceptions and therefore doesn't have to catch or specify them. This is "exception abuse" and is not recommended. Runtime Exceptions—The Controversy (page 324), the last section in this lesson, explains why.

Note to C++ Programmers: Java exception handlers can have a `finally` block, which allows programs to clean up after the `try` block. See The finally Block (page 310) for information about how to use `finally`.

What's an Exception, and Why Should I Care?

The term *exception* is shorthand for the phrase "exceptional event."

Definition: An *exception* is an event that occurs during the execution of a program that disrupts the normal flow of instructions.

Many kinds of errors can cause exceptions. They range from serious hardware errors, such as a hard disk crash, to simple programming errors, such as trying to access an out-of-bounds array element. When such an error occurs within a Java method, the method creates an exception object and hands it off to the runtime system. The exception object contains information about the error, including its type and the state of the program when the error occurred. The runtime system is then responsible for finding some code to handle the error. In Java terminology, creating an exception object and handing it to the runtime system is called *throwing an exception*.

After a method throws an exception, the runtime system leaps into action to find something to handle it. The set of possible "somethings" to handle the exception is the set of methods in the call stack of the method where the error occurred. The runtime system searches backwards through the call stack, beginning with the method in which the error occurred, until it finds a method that contains an appropriate *exception handler*. An exception handler is considered appropriate if the type of the exception thrown is the same as the type of exception handled by the handler. The exception bubbles up through the call stack until an appropriate handler is found and one of the calling methods handles the exception. The exception handler chosen is said to *catch the exception*. If the runtime system exhaustively searches all of the methods on the call stack without finding an appropriate exception handler, the runtime system (and consequently, the Java program) terminates.

By using exceptions to manage errors, Java programs have the following advantages over traditional error management techniques:

Advantage 1: Separating Error-Handling Code from "Regular" Code

In traditional programming, error detection, reporting, and handling often lead to confusing spaghetti code. For example, consider the following pseudocode method that reads an entire file into memory.

```
readFile {
    open the file;
    determine its size;
    allocate that much memory;
    read the file into memory;
    close the file;
}
```

At first glance, this function seems simple enough, but it ignores all of these potential errors:

- What happens if the file can't be opened?
- What happens if the length of the file can't be determined?

- What happens if enough memory can't be allocated?
- What happens if the read fails?
- What happens if the file can't be closed?

To handle these cases, the `readFile` function must have more code to do error detection, reporting, and handling. The function might look like this:

```
errorCodeType readFile {
    initialize errorCode = 0;
    open the file;
    if (theFileIsOpen) {
        determine the length of the file;
        if (gotTheFileLength) {
            allocate that much memory;
            if (gotEnoughMemory) {
                read the file into memory;
                if (readFailed) {
                    errorCode = -1;
                }
            } else {
                errorCode = -2;
            }
        } else {
            errorCode = -3;
        }
        close the file;
        if (theFileDidntClose && errorCode == 0) {
            errorCode = -4;
        } else {
            errorCode = errorCode and -4;
        }
    } else {
        errorCode = -5;
    }
    return errorCode;
}
```

There's so much error detection, reporting, and returning here that the original seven lines of code are lost in the clutter. And worse yet, the logical flow of the code also has been lost, thus making it difficult to tell if the code is doing the right thing: Is the file *really* being closed if the function fails to allocate enough memory? It's even more difficult to ensure that the code continues to do the right thing after you modify the function three months after writing it. Many programmers "solve" this problem by simply ignoring it—errors are "reported" when their programs crash.

Java provides an elegant solution to the problem of error management: exceptions. Exceptions enable you to write the main flow of your code and deal with the exceptional cases elsewhere. If the `readFile` function used exceptions instead of traditional error management techniques, it would look more like this:

```
readFile {
    try {
        open the file;
        determine its size;
        allocate that much memory;
        read the file into memory;
        close the file;
    } catch (fileOpenFailed) {
        doSomething;
    } catch (sizeDeterminationFailed) {
        doSomething;
    } catch (memoryAllocationFailed) {
        doSomething;
    } catch (readFailed) {
        doSomething;
    } catch (fileCloseFailed) {
        doSomething;
    }
}
```

Note that exceptions don't spare you the effort of doing the work of detecting, reporting, and handling errors. What they do provide is the means to separate from the main logic of a program the grungy details of what to do when something out-of-the-ordinary happens.

Advantage 2: Propagating Errors Up the Call Stack

A second advantage of exceptions is the ability to propagate error reporting up the call stack of methods. Suppose that the `readFile` method is the fourth method in a series of nested method calls made by the main program: `method1` calls `method2`, which calls `method3`, which finally calls `readFile`:

```
method1 {
    call method2;
}
method2 {
    call method3;
```

```
}
method3 {
    call readFile;
}
```

Suppose also that `method1` is the only method interested in the errors that might occur within `readFile`. Traditional error notification techniques force `method2` and `method3` to propagate the error codes returned by `readFile` up the call stack until the error codes finally reach `method1`—the only method that is interested in them:

```
method1 {
    errorCodeType error;
    error = call method2;
    if (error)
        doErrorProcessing;
    else
        proceed;
}
errorCodeType method2 {
    errorCodeType error;
    error = call method3;
    if (error)
        return error;
    else
        proceed;
}
errorCodeType method3 {
    errorCodeType error;
    error = call readFile;
    if (error)
        return error;
    else
        proceed;
}
```

Recall that the Java runtime system searches backwards through the call stack to find any methods that are interested in handling a particular exception. A Java method can "duck" any exceptions thrown within it, thereby allowing a method further up the call stack to catch it. Hence, only the methods that care about errors have to worry about detecting errors.

```
method1 {
    try {
        call method2;
    } catch (exception) {
```

```
        doErrorProcessing;
    }
}
method2 throws exception {
    call method3;
}
method3 throws exception {
    call readFile;
}
```

However, as the pseudocode shows, ducking an exception requires some effort on the part of the "middleman" methods. Any checked exceptions that can be thrown within a method must be specified in the `throws` clause of the method.

Note: The code that uses exceptions is more compact and easier to understand.

Advantage 3: Grouping and Differentiating Error Types

Often exceptions fall into categories or groups. For example, imagine a group of exceptions, each of which represents a specific type of error that can occur when manipulating an array, such as the index is out of range for the size of the array, the element being inserted into the array is of the wrong type, or the element being sought is not in the array. Furthermore, you might want some methods to handle all exceptions that fall within a category (all array exceptions) and other methods to handle specific exceptions (just the invalid index exceptions, please).

Because all exceptions thrown within a Java program are objects, grouping or categorizing of exceptions is a natural outcome of the class hierarchy. Java exceptions must be instances of `Throwable` or any `Throwable` descendant. As for other Java classes, you can create subclasses of the `Throwable` class and subclasses of your subclasses. Each leaf class (a class with no subclasses) represents a specific type of exception and each node class (a class with one or more subclasses) represents a group of related exceptions.

For example, in Figure 43 `ArrayException` is a subclass of `Exception` (a subclass of `Throwable`) and `ArrayException` has three subclasses—`InvalidIndexException`, `ElementTypeException`, and `NoSuchElementException`—which are all leaf classes.

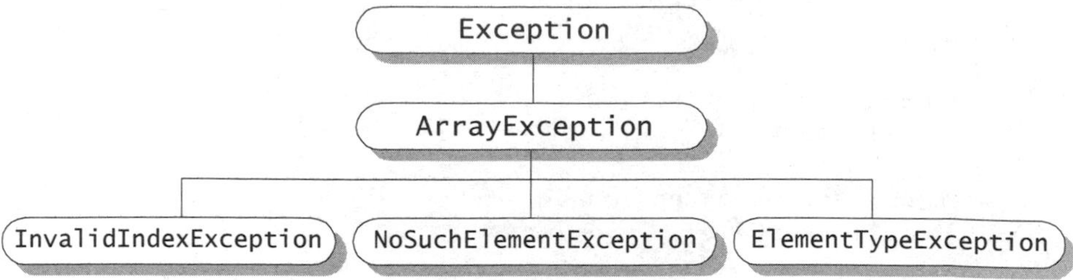

Figure 43: A hypothetical hierarchy of array exception classes.

Each class represents a specific type of error that can occur when an array is being manipulated. One way a method can catch exceptions is to catch only those that are instances of a leaf class. For example, an exception handler that handles only invalid index exceptions has a `catch` statement like this:

```
catch (InvalidIndexException e) {
    . . .
}
```

`ArrayException` is a node class and represents any error that can occur when manipulating an array object, including those errors specifically represented by one of its subclasses. A method can catch an exception based on its group or general type by specifying any of the exception's superclasses in the `catch` statement. For example, to catch all array exceptions regardless of their specific type, an exception handler specifies an `ArrayException` argument:

```
catch (ArrayException e) {
    . . .
}
```

This handler will catch all array exceptions, including `InvalidIndexException`, `ElementTypeException`, and `NoSuchElementException`. You can find out precisely which type of exception occurred by querying the exception-handler parameter `e`.

You could even set up an exception handler that handles any `Exception` with this handler:

```
catch (Exception e) {    // a (too) general exception handler
    . . .
}
```

Exception handlers that are too general, such as the one shown here, can make your code more error-prone by catching and handling exceptions that you didn't anticipate and therefore don't handle correctly. As a rule, we don't recommend that you write general exception handlers.

As we've shown, you can create groups of exceptions and handle exceptions in a general fashion or you can use the specific exception type to differentiate exceptions and handle exceptions in an exact fashion.

What's Next?

Now that you've read about what exceptions are and the advantages of using them in your Java programs, it's time to learn how to use them.

Your First Encounter with Java Exceptions

The Java language requires that methods either *catch* or *specify* all checked exceptions that can be thrown within the scope of that method. (Details about what this actually means are covered in the next section, Java's Catch or Specify Requirement (page 303).) The following error message is one of two similar error messages you will see if you try to compile the InputFile class (page 759). (You may have seen similar messages when attempting to compile your own programs.)

```
InputFile.java:11: Warning: Exception
java.io.FileNotFoundException must be caught, or it must be
declared in throws clause of this method.
        in = new FileReader(filename);
             ^
```

If the compiler detects a method, such as the ones in `InputFile`, that doesn't catch or specify all checked exceptions as required, it issues an error message like the one shown here and refuses to compile the program.

Let's look at `InputFile` in more detail and see what's going on. The `InputFile` class "has a" `FileReader` and provides a method, `getWord`, for reading a word from the current position in the reader:

```
// Note: This class won't compile by design!
import java.io.*;

public class InputFile {
```

```
    private FileReader in;

    public InputFile(String filename) {
        in = new FileReader(filename);
    }

    public String getWord() {
        int c;
        StringBuffer buf = new StringBuffer();

        do {
            c = in.read();
            if (Character.isWhitespace((char)c))
                return buf.toString();
            else
                buf.append((char)c);
        } while (c != -1);
        return buf.toString();
    }
}
```

The compiler prints the first error message because of the bold line in the code listing. That bold line creates a new `FileReader` object and uses it to open a file whose name is passed into the `FileReader` constructor.

So what should the `FileReader` do if the named file does not exist on the file system? Well, that depends on what the program using the `FileReader` wants to do. The implementers of `FileReader` have no idea what the `InputFile` class wants to do if the file does not exist. Should the `FileReader` kill the program? Should it try an alternative filename? Should it just create a file of the indicated name? There's no possible way the `FileReader` implementers could choose a solution that would suit every user of `FileReader`. So, they punted, or rather, threw, an exception. If the file named in the argument to the `FileReader` constructor does not exist on the file system, the constructor throws a `java.io.FileNotFoundException`. By throwing an exception, `FileReader` allows the calling method to handle the error in whatever way is most appropriate for it.

As the code shows, the `InputFile` class completely ignores the fact that the `FileReader` constructor can throw an exception. However, the Java language has its catch or specify requirement. The `InputFile` class does neither, so the compiler refuses to compile the program and prints an error message.

In addition to the first error message shown previously, you also see this error message when you attempt to compile the `InputFile` class:

```
InputFile.java:19: Warning: Exception java.io.IOException must
be caught, or it must be declared in throws clause of this
method.
        c = in.read();
                 ^
```

The InputFile class's getWord method reads from the FileReader that was opened in InputFile's constructor. The FileReader read method throws a java.io.IOException if for some reason it can't read from the file. Again, the InputFile class makes no attempt to catch or specify this exception. As a result, you see the second error message.

At this point, you have two options. Either the methods in the InputFile class can arrange to catch the exceptions or they can "duck" and allow other methods further up the call stack to catch the exceptions. Either way, the InputFile methods must do something, either catch or specify the exceptions, before the InputFile class can be compiled. For the diligent, the Code Examples in Appendix A provide a class, InputFileDeclared (page 760), that fixes the bugs in InputFile by specifying the exceptions.

The next section describes in further detail Java's catch or specify requirement. The subsequent sections show you how to comply with it.

Java's Catch or Specify Requirement

As stated previously, Java requires that a method either catch or specify all checked exceptions that can be thrown within the scope of the method. This requirement has several components that need further description: "catch," "specify," "checked exceptions," and "exceptions that can be thrown within the scope of the method."

Catch

A method can catch an exception by providing an exception handler for that type of exception. The next section, Dealing with Exceptions (page 305), introduces an example program, talks about catching exceptions, and shows you how to write an exception handler for it.

Specify

If a method chooses not to catch an exception, the method must specify that it can throw it. Why did the Java designers make this requirement? Because any exception that can be thrown by a method is really part of the method's public programming interface. Callers of a method must know about the exceptions that a method can throw so that they can decide what to do about them.

The next section, Dealing with Exceptions (page 305), talks about specifying exceptions that a method throws and shows you how to do it.

Checked Exceptions

Java has different types of exceptions, including I/O exceptions, runtime exceptions, and exceptions of your own creation, to name a few. Runtime exceptions are those exceptions that occur within the Java runtime system. This includes arithmetic exceptions (such as dividing by zero), pointer exceptions (such as trying to access an object through a `null` reference), and indexing exceptions (such as trying to access an array element with an index that is too large or too small).

Definition: *Checked exceptions* are exceptions that are not runtime exceptions and are checked by the compiler. The compiler checks that these exceptions are caught or specified.

Some consider the fact that you do not have to catch or specify runtime exceptions a loophole in Java's exception-handling mechanism. Many programmers are tempted to throw only runtime exceptions and to make all of their exception classes runtime exceptions so that they don't have to catch or specify them. In general, this is not recommended. Runtime Exceptions—The Controversy (page 324) talks about when it's appropriate to use runtime exceptions.

Exceptions That Can Be Thrown within the Scope of the Method

The statement "exceptions that can be thrown within the scope of the method" may seem obvious at first: Just look for the code that says `throw`. However, that's not the whole story. The key is in the phrase "within the scope of." This phrase includes any exception that can be thrown while the flow of control remains within the method. This statement includes both

- exceptions that are thrown directly by the method with Java's `throw` statement and
- exceptions that are thrown indirectly by the method through calls to other methods.

Next, we discuss how you can catch or specify exceptions in your programs.

Dealing with Exceptions

Your First Encounter with Java Exceptions (page 301) briefly described how you were (probably) first introduced to Java exceptions: a compiler error complaining that you must either catch or specify exceptions. Then, Java's Catch or Specify Requirement (page 303) discussed what exactly the error message means. Before we discuss how to catch an exception and how to specify one, we look at the example that will be used.

The ListOfNumbers Example

The following example defines and implements a class named `ListOfNumbers` (page 761). This class calls two methods from classes in the Java packages that can throw exceptions. These method calls are shown in bold in the following code:

```
// Note: This class won't compile by design!
import java.io.*;
import java.util.Vector;

public class ListOfNumbers {
    private Vector victor;
    private static final int size = 10;

    public ListOfNumbers () {
        victor = new Vector(size);
        for (int i = 0; i < size; i++)
            victor.addElement(new Integer(i));
    }
    public void writeList() {
        PrintWriter out = new PrintWriter(
                                     new FileWriter("OutFile.txt"));

        for (int i = 0; i < size; i++)
            out.println("Value at: " + i + " = " +
                                victor.elementAt(i));

        out.close();
    }
}
```

Upon construction, `ListOfNumbers` creates a `Vector` that contains ten `Integer` elements with sequential values 0 through 9. The `ListOfNumbers` class also

defines a method named writeList that writes the list of numbers into a text file called OutFile.txt.

The writeList method calls two methods that can throw exceptions. First, this line invokes the constructor for FileWriter:

```
out = new PrintWriter(new FileWriter("OutFile.txt"));
```

This constructor throws an IOException if the file cannot be opened.

Second, the Vector class's elementAt method throws an ArrayIndexOutOfBoundsException if you pass in an index whose value is too small (a negative number) or too large (larger than the number of elements currently contained by the Vector). Here's how ListOfNumbers invokes elementAt:

```
out.println("Value at: " + i + " = " + victor.elementAt(i));
```

If you try to compile the ListOfNumbers class, the compiler prints an error message about the exception thrown by the FileWriter constructor. However, it does *not* display an error message about the exception thrown by elementAt. This is because IOException (thrown by the FileWriter constructor) is a checked exception and ArrayIndexOutOfBoundsException (thrown by the elementAt method) is a runtime exception. Java requires only that a program deal with checked exceptions, so you get only one error message.

The next section, Catching and Handling Exceptions (page 306), shows you how to write an exception handler for the writeList method of ListOfNumbers. Then, Specifying the Exceptions Thrown by a Method (page 316) shows you how to specify that the writeList method throw the exceptions instead of catch them.

Catching and Handling Exceptions

Now that you're familiar with the ListOfNumbers class and where the exceptions can be thrown within it, you're ready to read about how to write exception handlers to catch and handle those exceptions.

This section shows you how to use the three components of an exception handler—the try, catch, and finally blocks—to write an exception handler for the writeList method of ListOfNumbers. It also contains a walk-through of the writeList method and analyzes what occurs within the method during various scenarios.

The try Block

The first step in constructing an exception handler is to enclose the statements that might throw an exception within a `try` block. In general, a `try` block looks like this:

```
try {
    Java statements
}
```

The segment of code labeled *`Java statements`* contains one or more legal Java statements that might throw an exception.

To construct an exception handler for the `writeList` method from the `ListOfNumbers` class, you need to enclose the exception-throwing statements of the `writeList` method within a `try` block. There is more than one way to do this. You can put each statement that might potentially throw an exception within its own `try` block and provide separate exception handlers for each. Or you can put all of the `writeList` statements within a single `try` block and associate multiple handlers with it. The following listing uses one `try` block for the entire method because the code in question is very short:

```
PrintWriter out = null;

try {
    System.out.println("Entering try statement");
    out = new PrintWriter(new FileWriter("OutFile.txt"));

    for (int i = 0; i < size; i++)
        out.println("Value at: " + i + " = " +
                    victor.elementAt(i));
}
```

A `try` block defines the scope of any exception handlers associated with it. In other words, if an exception occurs within the `try` block, that exception is handled by the exception handler associated with it. To associate an exception handler with a `try` block, put a `catch` statement after it. The next section shows you how.

The catch Block(s)

You associate exception handlers with a `try` block by providing one or more `catch` blocks directly after the `try` (there can be no code between the end of the `try` and the beginning of the first `catch` statement):

```
try {
    . . .
} catch (ExceptionType name) {
    . . .
} catch (ExceptionType name) {
    . . .
} . . .
```

Each `catch` block is an exception handler and handles the type of exception indicated by its argument. The argument to the `catch` statement looks like an argument declaration for a method. The argument type, *`ExceptionType`*, declares the type of exception that the handler can handle and must be the name of a class that inherits from the `Throwable`[1] class. The handler can refer to the exception with *`name`* .

The `catch` block contains a series of legal Java statements. These statements are executed if and when the exception handler is invoked. The runtime system invokes the exception handler when the handler is the first one in the call stack whose *`ExceptionType`* matches the type of the exception thrown. The system considers it a match if the thrown object can legally be assigned to the exception handler's argument.

Here are two exception handlers for `writeList` method—one for each of the two types of exceptions that can be thrown within the `try` block:

```
try {
    . . .
} catch (ArrayIndexOutOfBoundsException e) {
    System.err.println(
       "Caught ArrayIndexOutOfBoundsException: " +
       e.getMessage());
} catch (IOException e) {
    System.err.println(
       "Caught IOException: " + e.getMessage());
}
```

Catching Multiple Exception Types with One Handler. The two exception handlers used by the `writeList` method are very specialized. Each handles only one type of exception. You can write general exception handlers that handle multiple types of exceptions. Here's how.

All Java exceptions are `Throwable` objects; they are instances of `Throwable` or a subclass of `Throwable`. The Java packages contain numerous classes that derive

---

1 http://java.sun.com/products/jdk/1.1/docs/api/java.lang.Throwable.html

from `Throwable` and thus build a hierarchy of `Throwable` classes as shown in Figure 44.

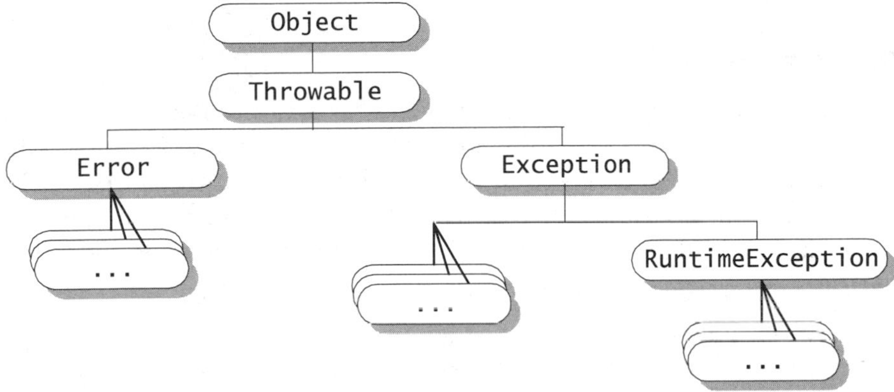

Figure 44: The `Throwable` hierarchy of classes.

Your exception handler can be written to handle any class that inherits from `Throwable`. If you write a handler for a leaf class, you've written a specialized handler: It will handle only exceptions of that specific type. If you write a handler for a node class, you've written a general handler: It will handle any exception whose type is the node class or any of its subclasses.

Let's modify the `writeList` method once again. Only this time, let's write it so that it handles both `IOExceptions` and `ArrayIndexOutOfBoundsExceptions`. The closest common ancestor of `IOException` and `ArrayIndexOutOfBoundsException` is the `Exception` class. An exception handler that handles both types of exceptions looks like this:

```
try {
    . . .
} catch (Exception e) {    // very general handler
    System.err.println("Exception caught: " + e.getMessage());
}
```

The `Exception` class is pretty high in the `Throwable` class hierarchy. So it will catch numerous other types in addition to the `IOException` and `ArrayIndexOutOfBoundsException` types that this exception handler is intended to catch. Generally speaking, your exception handlers should be more specialized. Handlers that can catch most or all exceptions are typically useless for error recovery. This is because the handler has to determine what type of exception occurred anyway in order to determine the best recovery strategy. Also, exception han-

dlers that are too general can make code *more* error-prone by catching and handling exceptions that weren't anticipated by the programmer and for which the handler was not intended.

The finally Block

The final step in setting up an exception handler is to clean up before (possibly) allowing control to be passed to a different part of the program. You do this by enclosing the cleanup code within a `finally` block. Java's `finally` block provides a mechanism that allows your method to clean up after itself regardless of what happens within the `try` block. Use the `finally` block to close files or release other system resources.

The `try` block of the `writeList` method that you've been working with here opens a `PrintWriter`. The program should close that stream before exiting the `writeList` method. This poses a somewhat complicated problem because `writeList`'s `try` block can exit in one of three ways:

1. The `new FileWriter` statement fails and throws an `IOException`.
2. The `victor.elementAt(i)` statement fails and throws an `ArrayIndexOutOfBoundsException`.
3. Everything succeeds and the `try` block exits normally.

The runtime system always executes the statements within the `finally` block regardless of what happens within the `try` block. So it's the perfect place to perform clean up.

Here's a `finally` block for the `writeList` method that cleans up and closes the `PrintWriter`:

```
finally {
    if (out != null) {
        System.out.println("Closing PrintWriter");
        out.close();
    } else {
        System.out.println("PrintWriter not open");
    }
}
```

Is the finally Statement Really Necessary? At first, the need for a `finally` statement may not be immediately apparent. Programmers often ask, "Is the `finally` statement really necessary, or is it just sugar for my Java?" In

particular, C++ programmers doubt the need for a `finally` statement because C++ doesn't have one.

The need for a `finally` statement is not apparent until you consider the following scenario: How does the `PrintWriter` in the `writeList` method get closed if you don't provide an exception handler for the `ArrayIndexOutOfBoundsException` and consequently an `ArrayIndexOutOfBoundsException` occurs? (It is easy and legal to omit an exception handler for `ArrayIndexOutOfBoundsException` because it is a runtime exception and the compiler won't alert you that the `writeList` contains a method call that might throw one.) The answer is that the `PrintWriter` does not get closed if an `ArrayIndexOutOfBoundsException` occurs and `writeList` does not provide a handler for it—unless the `writeList` provides a `finally` statement.

There are other benefits to using the `finally` statement. One is that in the `writeList` example, you can provide for cleanup without the intervention of a `finally` statement. For example, you could put the code to close the `PrintWriter` at the end of the `try` block and again within the exception handler for `ArrayIndexOutOfBoundsException`, as shown here:

```
try {
    . . .
    out.close();        // don't do this; it duplicates code
} catch (ArrayIndexOutOfBoundsException e) {
    out.close();        // don't do this; it duplicates code
    System.err.println(
         "Caught ArrayIndexOutOfBoundsException: "
         + e.getMessage());
} catch (IOException e) {
    System.err.println(
         "Caught IOException: " + e.getMessage());
}
```

However, this duplicates code, thus making the code hard to read and error-prone if you later modify the code. For example, if you add code to the `try` block that may throw a new type of exception, you have to remember to close the `PrintWriter` within the new exception handler (which, if you're anything like us, you are bound to forget).

Putting It All Together

The previous sections describe how to construct the `try`, `catch`, and `finally` code blocks for the `writeList` example. Next, we walk you through the code and investigate what happens during three scenarios.

When all of the components are put together, the `writeList` method looks like this:

```
public void writeList() {
    PrintWriter out = null;

    try {
        System.out.println("Entering try statement");
        out = new PrintWriter(new FileWriter("OutFile.txt"));

        for (int i = 0; i < size; i++)
            out.println("Value at: " + i + " = " +
                        victor.elementAt(i));
    } catch (ArrayIndexOutOfBoundsException e) {
        System.err.println(
            "Caught ArrayIndexOutOfBoundsException: " +
            e.getMessage());
    } catch (IOException e) {
        System.err.println("Caught IOException: " +
                           e.getMessage());
    } finally {
        if (out != null) {
            System.out.println("Closing PrintWriter");
            out.close();
        } else {
            System.out.println("PrintWriter not open");
        }
    }
}
```

The `try` block in this method has three different exit possibilities:

1. The `new FileWriter` statement fails and throws an `IOException`.
2. The `victor.elementAt(i)` statement fails and throws an `ArrayIndexOutOfBoundsException`.
3. Everything succeeds and the `try` statement exits normally.

Let's look at what happens in the `writeList` method during each of these exit possibilities.

Scenario 1: An IOException Occurs. The statement that creates a `FileWriter` can fail for any number of reasons. For example, the user doesn't have write permission on the file or directory, or the file system is full, or the directory for the file doesn't exist. If any of these situations exists, then the constructor for `FileWriter` throws an `IOException`.

When the `IOException` is thrown, the runtime system immediately stops executing the `try` block. Then the runtime system attempts to locate an exception handler appropriate for handling an `IOException`.

The runtime system begins its search at the top of the method call stack. When the exception occurred, the `FileWriter` constructor was at the top of the call stack. However, the `FileWriter` constructor doesn't have an appropriate exception handler, so the runtime system checks the next method in the method call stack—the `writeList` method. The `writeList` method has two exception handlers: one for `ArrayIndexOutOfBoundsException` and one for `IOException`.

The runtime system checks `writeList`'s handlers in the order in which they appear after the `try` statement. The argument to the first exception handler is `ArrayIndexOutOfBoundsException`, but the exception that was thrown is an `IOException`. An `IOException` cannot legally be assigned to an `ArrayIndexOutOfBoundsException`, so the runtime system continues its search for an appropriate exception handler.

The argument to `writeList`'s second exception handler is an `IOException`. The exception thrown by the `FileWriter` constructor is also an `IOException` and can be legally assigned to this exception handler's `IOException` argument. Thus this handler is deemed appropriate and the runtime system executes this handler, which prints this statement:

```
Caught IOException: OutFile.txt
```

After the exception handler has executed, the runtime system passes control to the `finally` block. In this particular scenario, the `PrintWriter` was never opened and doesn't need to be closed. After the `finally` block has completed executing, the program continues with the first statement after the `finally` block.

Here's the complete output that you see from the `ListOfNumbers` program when an `IOException` is thrown:

```
Entering try statement
Caught IOException: OutFile.txt
PrintWriter not open
```

The bold code in the following listing shows the statements that get executed during this scenario:

```
public void writeList() {
    PrintWriter out = null;

    try {
        System.out.println("Entering try statement");
        out = new PrintWriter(new FileWriter("OutFile.txt"));

        for (int i = 0; i < size; i++)
            out.println("Value at: " + i + " = " +
                        victor.elementAt(i));
    } catch (ArrayIndexOutOfBoundsException e) {
        System.err.println(
            "Caught ArrayIndexOutOfBoundsException: " +
            e.getMessage());
    } catch (IOException e) {
        System.err.println("Caught IOException: " +
                           e.getMessage());
    } finally {
        if (out != null) {
            System.out.println("Closing PrintWriter");
            out.close();
        } else {
            System.out.println("PrintWriter not open");
        }
    }
}
```

Scenario 2: An ArrayIndexOutOfBoundsException Occurs. This scenario is the same as the first except that a different error occurs during the `try` block. In this scenario, the argument passed to the `Vector`'s `elementAt` method is out of bounds. The argument is either less than 0 or is larger than the size of the array. (Because of how the code is written, this is actually impossible, but suppose a bug is introduced into the code when someone modifies it.)

As in scenario 1, when the exception occurs the runtime system stops executing the `try` block and attempts to locate an exception handler suitable for an `ArrayIndexOutOfBoundsException`. The runtime system searches for an appropriate exception handler as it did before. It comes upon the `catch` statement in the `writeList` method that handles exceptions of the type `ArrayIndexOutOfBoundsException`. Since the type of the thrown exception matches the type of the exception handler, the runtime system executes this exception handler.

After the exception handler has run, the runtime system passes control to the `finally` block. In this particular scenario, the `PrintWriter` was open, so the `finally` statement closes it. After the `finally` block has completed executing, the program continues with the first statement after the `finally` block.

The complete output that you see from the ListOfNumbers program when an ArrayIndexOutOfBoundsException is thrown is this:

```
Entering try statement
Caught ArrayIndexOutOfBoundsException: 10 >= 10
Closing PrintWriter
```

The bold code in the following listing shows the statements that get executed during this scenario:

```
public void writeList() {
    PrintWriter out = null;

    try {
        System.out.println("Entering try statement");
        out = new PrintWriter(new FileWriter("OutFile.txt"));

        for (int i = 0; i < size; i++)
            out.println("Value at: " + i + " = " +
                        victor.elementAt(i));
    } catch (ArrayIndexOutOfBoundsException e) {
        System.err.println(
          "Caught ArrayIndexOutOfBoundsException: " +
          e.getMessage());
    } catch (IOException e) {
        System.err.println("Caught IOException: " +
                            e.getMessage());
    } finally {
        if (out != null) {
            System.out.println("Closing PrintWriter");
            out.close();
        } else {
            System.out.println("PrintWriter not open");
        }
    }
}
```

Scenario 3: The try Block Exits Normally. In this scenario, all of the statements within the scope of the try block execute successfully and throw no exceptions. Execution falls off the end of the try block, and the runtime system passes control to the finally block. Since everything was successful, the PrintWriter is open when control reaches the finally block, which closes the PrintWriter. Again, after the finally block has completed executing, the program continues with the first statement after the finally block.

Here is the output from the `ListOfNumbers` program when no exceptions are thrown:

```
Entering try statement
Closing PrintWriter
```

The bold code in the following listing shows the statements that get executed during this scenario:

```
public void writeList() {
    PrintWriter out = null;

    try {
        System.out.println("Entering try statement");
        out = new PrintWriter(new FileWriter("OutFile.txt"));

        for (int i = 0; i < size; i++)
            out.println("Value at: " + i + " = " +
                        victor.elementAt(i));
    } catch (ArrayIndexOutOfBoundsException e) {
        System.err.println(
            "Caught ArrayIndexOutOfBoundsException: " +
            e.getMessage());
    } catch (IOException e) {
        System.err.println("Caught IOException: " +
                           e.getMessage());
    } finally {
        if (out != null) {
            System.out.println("Closing PrintWriter");
            out.close();
        } else {
            System.out.println("PrintWriter not open");
        }
    }
}
```

Specifying the Exceptions Thrown by a Method

If it is not appropriate for a method to catch and handle an exception thrown by a method that it calls, you must specify in the method declaration that the method throws the exception. The same applies if your method itself throws its own exception. This section uses the `ListOfNumbers` class to demonstrate how to specify exceptions that a method throws.

The previous section showed you how to write an exception handler for the `writeList` method in the `ListOfNumbers` class. Sometimes, it's appropriate for your code to catch exceptions that can occur within it. In other cases, however, it's better to let a method further up the call stack handle the exception. For example, if you were providing the `ListOfNumbers` class as part of a package of classes, you probably couldn't anticipate the needs of all of the users of your package. In this case, it's better to *not* catch the exception and to allow a method further up the call stack to handle it.

If the `writeList` method doesn't catch the exceptions that can occur within it, then the `writeList` method must specify that it can throw them. Let's modify the `writeList` method to specify the methods that it can throw instead of catching them. To remind you, here's the original version of the `writeList` method that won't compile:

```
// Note: This method won't compile by design!
public void writeList() {
    PrintWriter out = new PrintWriter(
                          new FileWriter("OutFile.txt"));

    for (int i = 0; i < size; i++)
        out.println("Value at: " + i + " = " +
                    victor.elementAt(i));

    out.close();
}
```

Recall that the `new FileWriter("OutFile.txt")` statement might throw an `IOException`, which is a checked exception. The `victor.element-At(i)` statement can throw an `ArrayIndexOutOfBoundsException`, which, as a subclass of `RuntimeException`, is a runtime exception.

To specify that `writeList` should throw these two exceptions, you add a `throws` clause to the method declaration for the `writeList` method. The `throws` clause is composed of the `throws` keyword followed by a comma-separated list of all of the exceptions thrown by that method. The clause goes after the method name and argument list and before the curly bracket that defines the scope of the method. Here's an example:

```
public void writeList() throws IOException,
                               ArrayIndexOutOfBoundsException{
```

Remember that `ArrayIndexOutOfBoundsException` is a runtime exception, so you don't have to specify it in the `throws` clause, although you can. You could just write this:

```
public void writeList() throws IOException {
```

How to Throw Exceptions

Before you can catch an exception, some Java code somewhere must throw one. Any Java code can throw an exception: your code, code from a package written by someone else (such as the packages that come with the Java platform), or the Java runtime system. Regardless of what throws the exception, it's always thrown with the Java `throw` statement.

As you have undoubtedly noticed in your travels (travails?) through the Java language, the packages that ship with the Java platform provide numerous exception classes. All of these classes are descendants of the `Throwable` class. And all allow programs to differentiate between the various types of exceptions that can occur during the execution of a Java program.

You also can create your own exception classes to represent problems that can occur within the classes that you write. Indeed, if you are a package developer, you will find that you must create your own set of exception classes so as to allow your users to differentiate an error that can occur in your package from errors that occur in the Java platform or other packages.

The throw Statement

All Java methods use the `throw` statement to throw an exception. The `throw` statement requires a single argument: a *throwable* object. In the Java system, throwable objects are instances of any subclass of the `Throwable`[1] class. Here's an example of a `throw` statement:

```
throw someThrowableObject;
```

If you attempt to throw an object that is not throwable, the compiler refuses to compile your program and displays an error message similar to the following:

```
testing.java:10: Cannot throw class java.lang.Integer; it must
be a subclass of class java.lang.Throwable.
            throw new Integer(4);
            ^
```

Let's look at the `throw` statement in context. The following `pop` method is taken from a class that implements a common stack object. It removes the top element from the stack and returns it:

---

[1] http://java.sun.com/products/jdk/1.1/docs/api/java.lang.Throwable.html

```
public Object pop() throws EmptyStackException {
    Object obj;

    if (size == 0)
        throw new EmptyStackException();

    obj = objectAt(size - 1);
    setObjectAt(size - 1, null);
    size--;
    return obj;
}
```

The `pop` method checks to see if there are any elements on the stack. If the stack is empty (its size is equal to 0), then `pop` instantiates a new `EmptyStackException` object (a member of `java.util`) and throws it. Later sections in this lesson describe how you can create your own exception classes. For now, all you really need to remember is that you can throw only objects that inherit from the `java.lang.Throwable` class.

The throws Clause

Note that the declaration of the `pop` method contains this clause:

```
throws EmptyStackException
```

`EmptyStackException` is a checked exception, and the `pop` method makes no effort to catch it. Hence, the method must use the `throws` clause to declare that it can throw that type of exception.

The Throwable Class and Its Subclasses

The objects that inherit from the `Throwable` class include direct descendants (objects that inherit directly from the `Throwable` class) as well as indirect descendants (objects that inherit from children or grandchildren of the `Throwable` class). Figure 45 illustrates the class hierarchy of the `Throwable` class and its most significant subclasses. As you can see, `Throwable` has two direct descendants: `Error` and `Exception`.

Errors

When a dynamic linking failure or some other "hard" failure in the virtual machine occurs, the virtual machine throws an `Error`. Typical Java programs should not catch `Errors`. Also, it's unlikely that typical Java programs will ever throw `Errors`.

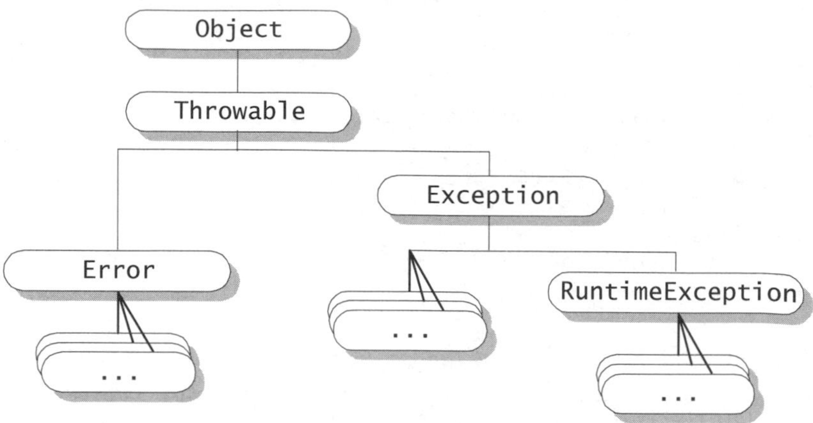

Figure 45: The Throwable class and its most significant subclasses.

Exceptions

Most programs throw and catch objects that derive from the Exception class. An Exception indicates that a problem occurred, but it is not a serious system problem. Most programs you write will throw and catch Exceptions (as opposed to Errors).

The Exception class has many descendants defined in the Java packages. These descendants indicate various types of exceptions that can occur. For example, IllegalAccessException signals that a particular method could not be found, and NegativeArraySizeException indicates that a program attempted to create an array with a negative size.

One Exception subclass has special meaning in the Java language: RuntimeException.

Runtime Exceptions

The RuntimeException class represents exceptions that occur within the Java virtual machine during runtime. An example of a runtime exception is NullPointerException. A NullPointerException occurs when a method tries to access a member of an object through a null reference. One can occur anywhere a program tries to dereference a reference to an object. The cost of checking for the exception often outweighs the benefit of catching it.

You can catch runtime exceptions just like other exceptions but you don't have to. The compiler allows runtime exceptions to go uncaught and unspecified. This is because runtime exceptions are ubiquitous and attempting to catch or specify

all of them all of the time would be fruitless (but a fruitful source of unreadable and unmaintainable code).

Runtime Exceptions—The Controversy (page 324) discusses when it is appropriate for you to subclass `RuntimeException` and when it is appropriate for your programs to throw them.

Creating Your Own Exception Classes

When you design a package of Java classes that collaborate to provide some useful function to your users, you work hard to ensure that your classes interact well together and that their interfaces are easy to understand and use. You should spend just as much time designing the exceptions that your classes throw.

Suppose you are writing a linked list class that you're planning to distribute as freeware. Your linked list class supports these methods, among others:

`objectAt(int n)`
: Returns the object in the *n*th position in the list.

`firstObject()`
: Returns the first object in the list.

`indexOf(Object o)`
: Searches the list for the specified `Object` and returns its position in the list.

What Can Go Wrong?

Because many programmers will be using your linked list class, you can be assured that many will misuse or abuse your class and its methods. Also, some legitimate calls to your linked list's methods may result in undefined results. Regardless, you want your linked list class to be as robust as possible, to do something reasonable about errors, and to communicate errors to the calling program. However, you can't anticipate how each user of your linked list class will want the object to behave under adversity. Often, the best thing to do when an error occurs is to throw an exception.

Each method supported by your linked list might throw an exception under certain conditions, and each might throw a different type of exception than the others. For example:

`objectAt`
: Throws an exception if the integer passed into the method is less than 0 or larger than the number of objects currently in the list.

`firstObject`
: Throws an exception if the list contains no objects.

`indexOf`
Throws an exception if the object passed into the method is not in the list.

But what type of exception should each method throw? Should it be an exception provided with the Java platform? Or should you roll your own?

Choosing the Exception Type to Throw

When faced with choosing the type of exception to throw, you have two choices:

1. Use one written by someone else. The Java platform provides a lot of exception classes that you can use.
2. Write one of your own.

You should write your own exception classes if you answer "yes" to any of the following questions. Otherwise, you can probably get away with using someone else's.

- Do you need an exception type that isn't represented by those in the Java platform?
- Would it help your users if they could differentiate your exceptions from those thrown by classes written by other vendors?
- Does your code throw more than one related exception?
- If you use someone else's exceptions, will your users have access to those exceptions? A similar question is, should your package be independent and self-contained?

The linked list class can throw multiple exceptions, and it would be convenient to be able to catch all exceptions thrown by the linked list with one exception handler. Also, if you plan to distribute your linked list in a package, all related code should be packaged together. Thus the linked list should provide its own set of exception classes.

Figure 46 illustrates one possible class hierarchy for the exceptions thrown by the linked list.

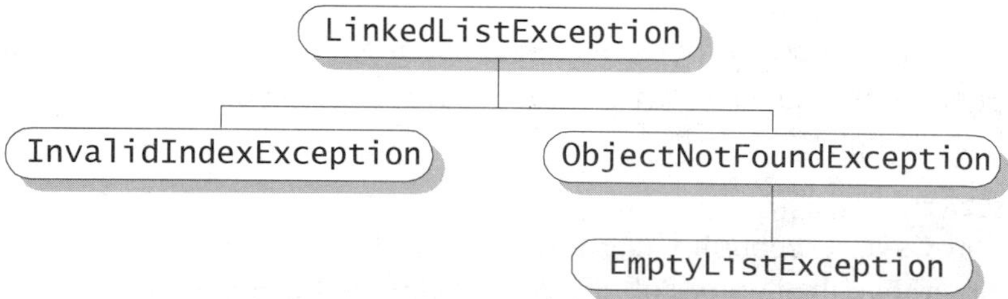

Figure 46: A possible class hierarchy for the exceptions thrown by a linked list.

LinkedListException is the parent class of all of the possible exceptions that can be thrown by the linked list class. Users of the linked list class can write a single exception handler to handle all linked list exceptions with a catch statement like this:

```
catch (LinkedListException) {
    . . .
}
```

Alternatively, users could write more specialized handlers for each subclass of LinkedListException.

Choosing a Superclass

Figure 46 does not indicate the superclass of the LinkedListException class. Recall that Java exceptions must be throwable objects; that is, they must be instances of Throwable or a subclass of Throwable. So, you might be tempted to make LinkedListException a subclass of Throwable. However, the java.lang package provides two Throwable subclasses that further divide the type of problems that can occur within a Java program: Errors and Exceptions. Most applets and applications that you write will throw objects that are Exceptions. (Errors are reserved for serious, hard errors that occur deep in the system.)

Theoretically, any Exception subclass can be used as the parent class of LinkedListException. However, a quick perusal of those classes shows that they are inappropriate because they are either too specialized or completely unrelated to LinkedListException. Therefore the parent class of LinkedListException should be Exception.

Because runtime exceptions don't have to be specified in the throws clause of a method, many package developers ask: "Isn't it easier if I just make all of my exceptions inherit from RuntimeException?" The answer to this question is covered in detail in Runtime Exceptions—The Controversy (page 324). However, the bottom line is that you shouldn't subclass RuntimeException unless your class really is a runtime exception! For most programmers, this means the short answer is, "No, your exceptions shouldn't inherit from RuntimeException."

Naming Conventions

It's good practice to append the string "Exception" to the names of all classes that inherit (directly or indirectly) from the Exception class. Similarly, names of classes that inherit from the Error class should end with the string "Error."

Runtime Exceptions—The Controversy

Because the Java language does not require methods to catch or specify runtime exceptions, programmers can be tempted to write code that throws only runtime exceptions or to make all of their exception subclasses inherit from `RuntimeException`. Both of these shortcuts allow programmers to write Java code without bothering with all of the nagging errors from the compiler and without bothering to specify or catch any exceptions. While this may seem convenient to the programmer, it sidesteps the intent of Java's catch or specify requirement and can cause problems for programmers using your classes.

Why did the Java designers decide to force a method to specify all uncaught checked exceptions that can be thrown within its scope? Because any exception that can be thrown by a method is really part of the method's public programming interface. Callers of a method must know about the exceptions that a method can throw in order to intelligently and consciously decide what to do about them. These exceptions are as much a part of that method's programming interface as its parameters and return value.

Your next question might be, "Well, then, if it's so good to document a method's API, including the exceptions it can throw, why not specify runtime exceptions, too?" Runtime exceptions represent problems that are detected by the runtime system. This includes arithmetic exceptions (such as dividing by zero), pointer exceptions (such as trying to access an object through a null reference), and indexing exceptions (such as attempting to access an array element through an index that is too large or too small). Runtime exceptions can occur anywhere in a program and in a typical program can be very numerous. Typically, the cost of checking for runtime exceptions exceeds the benefit of catching or specifying them. Thus the compiler does not require that you catch or specify runtime exceptions, although you can.

Checked exceptions represent useful information about the operation of a legally specified request that the caller may have had no control over and about which the caller needs to be informed. Examples include the file system is now full, or the remote end has closed the connection, or the access privileges don't allow this action.

What does it buy you if you throw a `RuntimeException` or create a subclass of `RuntimeException` just because you don't want to deal with specifying it? Simply, you get the ability to throw an exception without specifying that you do so. In other words, it is a way to avoid documenting the exceptions that a method can throw. When is this good? Well, when is it ever good to avoid documenting a method's behavior? The answer is, hardly ever.

Rules of Thumb: When to Throw a `RuntimeException`

- A method can detect and throw a `RuntimeException` when it encounters an error in the virtual machine runtime. However, it's typically easier to just let the virtual machine detect and throw it. Normally, the methods you write should throw `Exceptions`, not `RuntimeExceptions`.
- Similarly, you create a subclass of `RuntimeExceptions` when you are creating an error in the virtual machine runtime (which you probably aren't). Otherwise, you should subclass `Exception`.
- Do not throw a `RuntimeException` or create a subclass of `RuntimeException` simply because you don't want to be bothered with specifying the exceptions that your methods can throw.

http://java.sun.com/docs/books/tutorial/essential/threads/index.html

16 Doing Two or More Tasks at Once: Threads

FOLLOWING is a snapshot of three copies of an applet that animates different sorting algorithms. No, this lesson is not about sorting algorithms. But these applets do provide a visual aid to understanding a powerful capability of the Java language—threads.

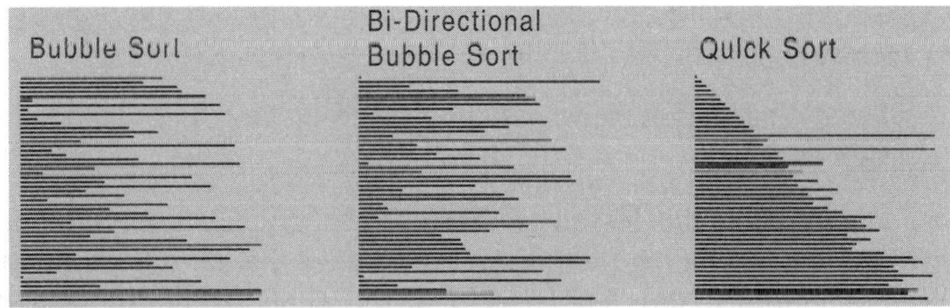

http://java.sun.com/docs/books/tutorial/essential/threads/index.html

---

Try This: Bring up the online version of this lesson[1] and start each applet, one by one, by clicking it with the mouse. Try scrolling the page or bringing up one of your browser's panels.

These three applets run side by side at the same time. If you look at these applets in a browser, you can see each applet working its way through the data, sorting it,

1 http://java.sun.com/docs/books/tutorial/essential/threads/index.html

with shorter lines on top and longer lines on bottom. While the applets are sorting, also notice that you can scroll the page or bring up one of your browser's panels. All of this is due to *threads*.

What Is a Thread? (page 328) talks about threads. A *thread*—sometimes called an *execution context* or a *lightweight process*—is a single sequential flow of control within a program. You use threads to isolate tasks. When you run one of these sorting applets, it creates a thread that performs the sort operation. Each thread is a sequential flow of control within the same program (the browser). Each sort operation runs independently from the others, but at the same time.

First, you need to get a thread to do something by providing the `run` method for a thread. Customizing a Thread's run Method (page 330) shows you two different ways to do this. Once you know how to get a thread to do something, you need to understand The Life Cycle of a Thread (page 335). Also, a thread's priority affects when it runs in relation to other threads. Understanding Thread Priority (page 340) talks about how this affects your programs.

The first sample programs in this lesson use either one thread or multiple threads that run asynchronously. However, it is often useful to use multiple threads that share data and therefore must synchronize their activities. Synchronizing Threads (page 346) teaches you how to synchronize threads and how to avoid problems such as starvation and deadlock.

Grouping Threads (page 356) shows you how to group threads and what you can do with a group of threads.

When you've completed this lesson on threads, you will have toured the intricacies of Java threads, including the life cycle of a Java thread, scheduling, thread groups, and synchronization. The Java platform supports multithreaded programs through the language, the libraries, and the runtime system. The final section in this lesson, Summarizing Threads in Java (page 362), highlights the features in the Java platform that support threads and shows you where to find further documentation about those features.

What Is a Thread?

All programmers are familiar with writing sequential programs. You've probably written a program that displays "Hello World!", or sorts a list of names, or computes a list of prime numbers. These are sequential programs. That is, each has a beginning, an execution sequence, and an end. At any given time during the runtime of the program, there is a single point of execution.

A thread is similar to the sequential programs described previously. A single thread also has a beginning, a sequence, and an end and at any given time during the runtime of the thread, there is a single point of execution. However, a thread itself is not a program; it cannot run on its own. Rather, it runs within a program. Figure 47 shows this relationship.

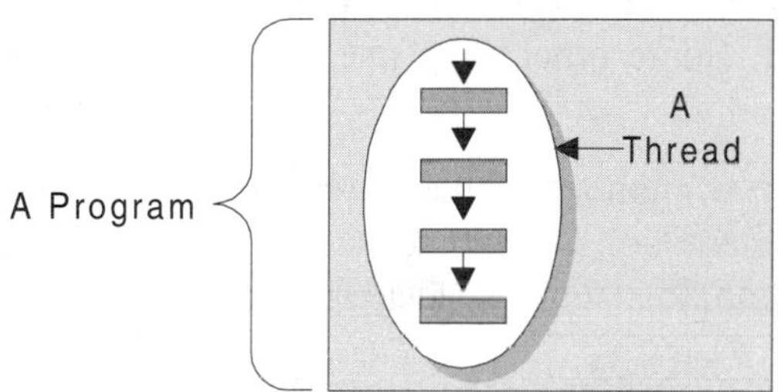

Figure 47: A thread is not a program; it runs *within* a program.

Definition: A *thread* is a single sequential flow of control within a program.

There is nothing new in the concept of a single thread. The real hoopla surrounding threads is not about a single sequential thread. Rather, it's about the use of multiple threads in a single program, running at the same time and performing different tasks. This is illustrated in Figure 48.

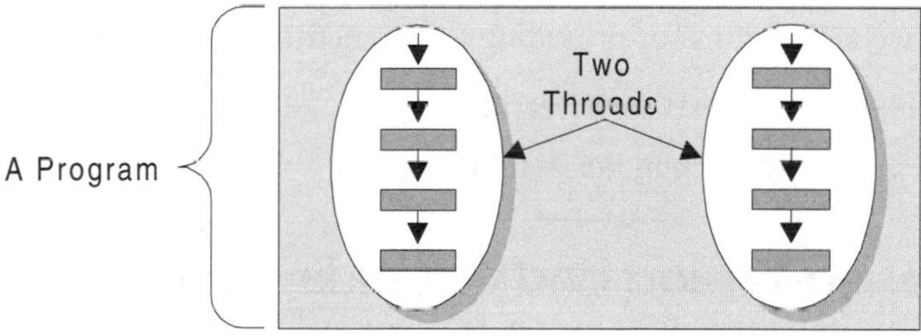

Figure 48: Two threads running concurrently in a single program.

The HotJava Web browser is an example of a multithreaded application. Within that browser, you can scroll a page while it's downloading an applet or image, play animation and sound concurrently, print a page in the background while you download a new page, or watch three sorting algorithms race to the finish.

Some texts call a thread a *lightweight process*. A thread is similar to a real process in that a thread and a running program are both a single sequential flow of control. However, a thread is considered lightweight because it runs within the context of a full-blown program and takes advantage of the resources allocated for that program and the program's environment.

As a sequential flow of control, a thread must carve out some of its own resources within a running program. For example, it must have its own execution stack and program counter. The code running within the thread works only within that context. Some other texts use *execution context* as a synonym for thread.

The `Thread`[1] class, a member of the `java.lang` package, provides a system-independent implementation of a thread[2] and provides all of the generic behavior for Java threads, including starting, sleeping, running, yielding, and having a priority.

Customizing a Thread's run Method

The `run` method gives a thread something to do. Its code implements the thread's running behavior. It can do anything that can be encoded in Java statements: compute a list of prime's, sort some data, perform some animation.

The `Thread` class implements a generic thread that, by default, does nothing. That is, the implementation of its `run` method is empty. This is not particularly useful, so the `Thread` class defines API that lets a `Runnable`[3] object provide a more interesting `run` method for a thread.

There are two techniques for providing a `run` method for a thread:

- Subclassing `Thread` and overriding `run`
- Implementing the `Runnable` interface

Subclassing Thread and Overriding run

The first way to customize what a thread does when it is running is to subclass `Thread` (itself a `Runnable` object) and override its empty `run` method so that it does something. Let's look at the `SimpleThread` class, the first of two classes in this example, which does just that:

---

1 http://java.sun.com/products/jdk/1.1/docs/api/java.lang.Thread.html

2 The actual implementation of concurrent operation is provided by a system-specific implementation. For most programming needs, the underlying implementation doesn't matter.

3 http://java.sun.com/products/jdk/1.1/docs/api/java.lang.Runnable.html

```
public class SimpleThread extends Thread {
    public SimpleThread(String str) {
        super(str);
    }
    public void run() {
        for (int i = 0; i < 10; i++) {
            System.out.println(i + " " + getName());
            try {
                sleep((long)(Math.random() * 1000));
            } catch (InterruptedException e) {}
        }
        System.out.println("DONE! " + getName());
    }
}
```

The first method in the `SimpleThread` class is a constructor that takes a `String` as its only argument. This constructor is implemented by calling a superclass constructor. It is interesting only because it sets the `Thread`'s name, which is used later in the program.

The next method in the `SimpleThread` class is the `run` method. This method is the heart of any `Thread`. It defines what the `Thread` does when it's running. The `run` method of the `SimpleThread` class overrides the empty method implementation in the `Thread` class and contains a `for` loop that iterates ten times. In each iteration, the method displays the iteration number and the name of the `Thread`. Then it sleeps for a random interval of up to 1 second. After the loop has finished, the `run` method prints "`DONE!`", along with the name of the thread. That's it for the `SimpleThread` class. Let's put it to use in `TwoThreadsTest`.

The `TwoThreadsTest` class contains a `main` method that creates two `SimpleThread` threads: `Jamaica` and `Fiji`. (If you can't decide where to go on vacation, use this program to help you.)

```
public class TwoThreadsTest {
    public static void main (String[] args) {
        new SimpleThread("Jamaica").start();
        new SimpleThread("Fiji").start();
    }
}
```

The `main` method also starts each thread immediately following its construction by calling the `start` method which in turn calls the `run` method. Compile and run the program and watch your vacation fate unfold. You should see output similar to this:

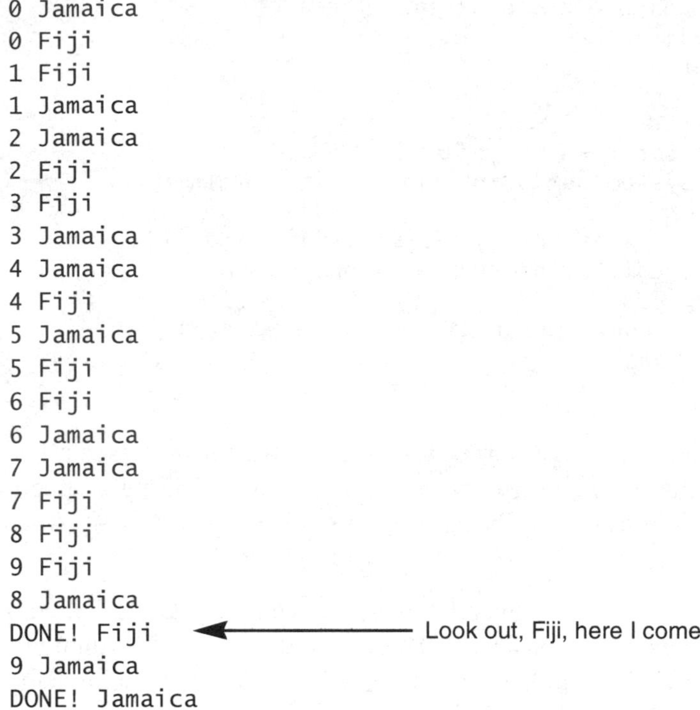

```
0 Jamaica
0 Fiji
1 Fiji
1 Jamaica
2 Jamaica
2 Fiji
3 Fiji
3 Jamaica
4 Jamaica
4 Fiji
5 Jamaica
5 Fiji
6 Fiji
6 Jamaica
7 Jamaica
7 Fiji
8 Fiji
9 Fiji
8 Jamaica
DONE! Fiji
9 Jamaica
DONE! Jamaica
```

Look out, Fiji, here I come!

Note how the output from each thread is intermingled with the output from the other. This is because both `SimpleThread` threads are running concurrently. So both `run` methods are running and both threads are displaying their output at the same time. When the loop completes, the thread stops running and dies.

Try This: Change the `main` program so that it creates a third thread with the name `Bora Bora`. Compile and run the program again. Does this change your vacation destiny? The source for the new `main` program, which is now named `ThreeThreadsTest` (page 764), is in Appendix A.

Now, let's look at another example, the `Clock` applet, that uses the other technique for providing a `run` method to a `Thread`.

Implementing the Runnable Interface

The following `Clock` applet displays the current time and updates its display every second. If you bring up the online version of this section in an HTML browser, you can scroll the page and perform other tasks while the clock updates.

This is because the code that updates the clock's display runs within its own thread.

11:21:16 AM

http://java.sun.com/docs/books/tutorial/essential/threads/clock.html

The `Clock` applet uses a different technique than `SimpleThread` for providing the `run` method for its thread. Instead of subclassing `Thread`, `Clock` implements the `Runnable` interface (and therefore implements the `run` method defined in it). `Clock` then creates a thread with itself as the `Thread`'s target. When created in this way, the `Thread` gets its `run` method from its target. The code that accomplishes this is shown in bold here:

```
import java.awt.Graphics;
import java.util.*;
import java.text.DateFormat;
import java.applet.Applet;

public class Clock extends Applet implements Runnable {
    private Thread clockThread = null;
    public void start() {
        if (clockThread == null) {
            clockThread = new Thread(this, "Clock");
            clockThread.start();
        }
    }
    public void run() {
        Thread myThread = Thread.currentThread()
        while (clockThread == myThread) {
            repaint();
            try {
                Thread.sleep(1000);
            } catch (InterruptedException e) {
                // the VM doesn't want us to sleep anymore,
                // so get back to work
            }
        }
    }
    public void paint(Graphics g) {
        // get the time and convert it to a date
        Calendar cal = Calendar.getInstance();
        Date date = cal.getTime();
        // format it and display it
       DateFormat dateFormatter = DateFormat.getTimeInstance();
        g.drawString(dateFormatter.format(date), 5, 10);
```

```
        }
        // overrides Applet's stop method, not Thread's
        public void stop() {
            clockThread = null;
        }
    }
```

The `Clock` applet's `run` method loops until the browser asks it to stop. During each iteration of the loop, the clock repaints its display. The `paint` method figures out what time it is, formats it in a localized way, and displays it. You'll see more of the `Clock` applet in The Life Cycle of a Thread (page 335), which uses it to teach you about the life of a thread.

Deciding to Use the Runnable Interface

You have now seen two ways to provide the `run` method for a Java thread:

1. Subclass the `Thread` class defined in the `java.lang` package and override the `run` method.

Example: See the `SimpleThread` class described in Subclassing Thread and Overriding run (page 330).

---

2. Provide a class that implements the `Runnable` interface (also defined in the `java.lang` package) and therefore implements the `run` method. In this case, a `Runnable` object provides the `run` method to the thread.

Example: See the `Clock` applet just shown.

There are good reasons for choosing either of these options over the other. However, for most cases, including that of the `Clock` applet, the following rule of thumb will guide you to the best option.

Rule of Thumb: If your class *must* subclass some other class (the most common example being `Applet`), you should use `Runnable` as described in option #2.

To run in a Java-enabled browser, the `Clock` class has to be a subclass of the `Applet` class. Also, the `Clock` applet needs a thread so that it can continuously update its display without taking over the process in which it is running. (Some browsers might create a new thread for each applet so as to prevent a misbehaved applet from taking over the main browser thread. However, you should not count on this when writing your applets; your applets should create their own threads when doing computer-intensive work.) But since the Java language does not support multiple class inheritance, the `Clock` class cannot be a subclass of both `Thread` and `Applet`. Thus the `Clock` class must use the `Runnable` interface to provide its threaded behavior.

The Life Cycle of a Thread

Now that you've seen how to give a thread something to do, we'll review some details that were glossed over in the previous section. In particular, we look at the life cycle of a thread: how to create and start a thread, some of the special things it can do while it's running, and how to stop it.

Figure 49 shows the states that a Java thread can be in during its life. It also illustrates which method calls cause a transition to another state. This figure is not a complete finite state diagram, but rather an overview of the more interesting and common facets of a thread's life. The remainder of this section uses the `Clock` applet previously introduced to discuss a thread's life cycle in terms of its state.

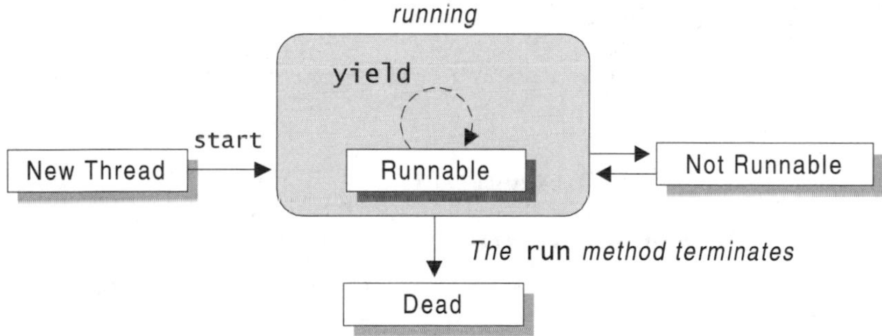

Figure 49: Possible states of a Java thread.

Creating a Thread

The application in which an applet is running calls the applet's `start` method when the user visits the applet's page. The `Clock` applet creates a `Thread`, `clockThread`, in its `start` method with the bold code shown here:

```
public void start() {
    if (clockThread == null) {
        clockThread = new Thread(this, "Clock");
        clockThread.start();
    }
}
```

After the bold statement has been executed, `clockThread` is in the New Thread state. When a thread is a New Thread, it is merely an empty `Thread` object; no system resources have been allocated for it yet. When a thread is in this state, you can only start the thread. Calling any method besides `start` when a thread is in this state makes no sense and causes an `IllegalThreadStateException`. (In fact, the runtime system throws an `IllegalThreadStateException` any time a method is called on a thread and that thread's state does not allow for that method call.)

Notice that `this`—the `Clock` instance—is the first argument to the thread constructor. The first argument to this thread constructor must implement the `Runnable` interface and becomes the thread's target. The clock thread gets its `run` method from its target `Runnable` object—in this case, the `Clock` instance.

The second argument is just a name for the thread.

Starting a Thread

Now consider the next line of code in `Clock`'s `start` method shown here in bold:

```
public void start() {
    if (clockThread == null) {
        clockThread = new Thread(this, "Clock");
        clockThread.start();
    }
}
```

The `start` method creates the system resources necessary to run the thread, schedules the thread to run, and calls the thread's `run` method. `ClockThread`'s `run` method is the one defined in the `Clock` class.

After the `start` method has returned, the thread is "running." Yet, it's somewhat more complex than that. As Figure 49 shows, a thread that has been started is actually in the Runnable state. Many computers have a single processor, thus making it impossible to run all "running" threads at the same time. The Java runtime system must implement a scheduling scheme that shares the processor between all "running" threads. (See Understanding Thread Priority (page 340)

for more information about scheduling.) So at any given time, a "running" thread actually may be waiting for its turn in the CPU.

Here's another look at `Clock`'s `run` method:

```
public void run() {
   Thread myThread = Thread.currentThread();
   while (clockThread == myThread) {
         repaint();
         try {
             Thread.sleep(1000);
         } catch (InterruptedException e) {
             // the VM doesn't want us to sleep anymore,
             // so get back to work
         }
    }
}
```

`Clock`'s `run` method loops while the condition `clockThread == myThread` is `true`. This exit condition is explained in more detail in Stopping a Thread (page 338). However, for now, know that it allows the thread, and thus the applet, to exit gracefully.

Within the loop, the applet repaints itself and then tells the thread to sleep for one second (1000 milliseconds). An applet's `repaint` method ultimately calls the applet's `paint` method, which does the actual update of the applet's display area. The `Clock` `paint` method gets the current time, formats, and displays it:

```
public void paint(Graphics g) {
    // get the time and convert it to a date
    Calendar cal = Calendar.getInstance();
    Date date = cal.getTime();
    // format it and display it
    DateFormat dateFormatter = DateFormat.getTimeInstance();
    g.drawString(dateFormatter.format(date), 5, 10);
}
```

Making a Thread Not Runnable

A thread becomes Not Runnable when one of these events occurs:

- Its `sleep` method is invoked.
- The thread calls the `wait` method to wait for a specific condition to be satisifed.
- The thread is blocking on I/O.

The `clockThread` in the `Clock` applet becomes Not Runnable when the `run` method calls `sleep` on the current thread:

```
public void run() {
    Thread myThread = Thread.currentThread();
    while (clockThread == myThread) {
        repaint();
        try {
            Thread.sleep(1000);
        } catch (InterruptedException e) {
            // the VM doesn't want us to sleep anymore,
            // so get back to work
        }
    }
}
```

During the second that the `clockThread` is asleep, the thread does not run, even if the processor becomes available. After the second has elapsed, the thread becomes Runnable again and, if the processor becomes available, the thread begins running again.

For each entrance into the Not Runnable state, there is a specific and distinct escape route that returns the thread to the Runnable state. An escape route works only for its corresponding entrance. For example, if a thread has been put to sleep, then the specified number of milliseconds must elapse before the thread becomes Runnable again. The following list describes the escape route for every entrance into the Not Runnable state:

- If a thread has been put to sleep, then the specified number of milliseconds must elapse.
- If a thread is waiting for a condition, then another object must notify the waiting thread of a change in condition by calling `notify` or `notifyAll`. More information is available in Synchronizing Threads (page 346).
- If a thread is blocked on I/O, then the I/O must complete.

Stopping a Thread

A program doesn't stop a thread like it stops an applet (by calling a method). Rather, a thread arranges for its own death by having a `run` method that terminates naturally. For example, the `while` loop in this `run` method is a finite loop—it will iterate 100 times and then exit:

```
public void run() {
    int i = 0;
    while (i < 100) {
        i++;
        System.out.println("i = " + i);
    }
}
```

A thread with this `run` method dies naturally when the loop completes and the `run` method exits.

Let's look at how the `Clock` applet thread arranges for its own death. You might want to use this technique with your applets. Recall `Clock`'s `run` method:

```
public void run() {
    Thread myThread = Thread.currentThread();
    while (clockThread == myThread) {
        repaint();
        try {
            Thread.sleep(1000);
        } catch (InterruptedException e) {
            // the VM doesn't want us to sleep anymore,
            // so get back to work
        }
    }
}
```

The exit condition for this `run` method is the exit condition for the `while` loop because there is no code after the `while` loop:

```
while (clockThread == myThread) {
```

This condition indicates that the loop will exit when the currently exiting thread is not equal to `clockThread`. When would this ever be the case?

When you leave the page, the application in which the applet is running calls the applet's `stop` method. This method then sets the `clockThread` to `null`, thereby telling the main loop in the `run` method to terminate:

```
public void stop() {    // applets' stop method
    clockThread = null;
}
```

If you revisit the page, the `start` method is called again and the clock starts up again with a new thread. Even if you stop and start the applet faster than one iteration of the loop, clockThread will be a different thread than myThread and the loop will still terminate.

The isAlive Method

A final word about thread state: The API for the Thread class includes a method called isAlive. The isAlive method returns true if the thread has been started and not stopped. If the isAlive method returns false, you know that the thread either is a New Thread or is Dead. If the isAlive method returns true, you know that the thread is either Runnable or Not Runnable. You cannot differentiate between a New Thread or a Dead thread. Nor can you differentiate between a Runnable thread and a Not Runnable thread.

Understanding Thread Priority

As mentioned briefly in the previous section, most computer configurations have a single CPU. Hence, threads actually run one at a time in such a way as to provide an illusion of concurrency. Execution of multiple threads on a single CPU in some order is called *scheduling*. The Java runtime supports a very simple, deterministic scheduling algorithm called *fixed priority scheduling*. This algorithm schedules threads based on their *priority* relative to other Runnable threads.

When a Java thread is created, it inherits its priority from the thread that created it. You also can modify a thread's priority at any time after its creation by using the setPriority method. Thread priorities are integers ranging between MIN_PRIORITY and MAX_PRIORITY (constants defined in the Thread class). The higher the integer, the higher the priority. At any given time, when multiple threads are ready to be executed, the runtime system chooses for execution the Runnable thread that has the highest priority. Only when that thread either stops, yields, or becomes Not Runnable for some reason will a lower-priority thread start executing. If two threads of the same priority are waiting for the CPU, the scheduler chooses one of them to run in a round-robin fashion. The chosen thread runs until one of the following conditions is true:

- A higher-priority thread becomes Runnable.
- It yields, or its run method exits.
- On systems that support time-slicing, its time allotment has expired.

Then the second thread is given a chance to run, and so on, until the interpreter exits.

The Java runtime system's thread scheduling algorithm is also *preemptive*. If at any time a thread with a higher priority than all other Runnable threads becomes Runnable, the runtime system chooses the new higher-priority thread for execution. This new thread is said to *preempt* the other threads.

Rule of Thumb: At any given time, the highest-priority thread is running. However, this is not guaranteed. The thread scheduler may choose to run a lower-priority thread to avoid starvation. For this reason, use thread priority only to affect scheduling policy for efficiency purposes. Do not rely on it for algorithm correctness.

The 400,000 Micron Thread Race

RaceApplet (page 765) is an applet that animates a race between two "runner" threads that have different priorities. When you click the mouse on the applet, it starts the two runners. Runner 2 has a priority of 2; runner 3 has a priority of 3.

Try This: Go to the online version of this section and run the applet. Note that this applet may not work as intended in browsers that have security restrictions regarding setting a thread's priority. If this is true for your browser, try running this applet in an applet viewer instead.

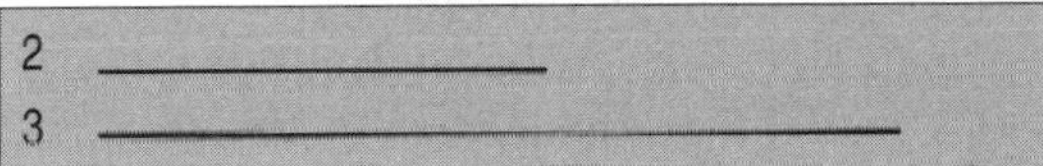

http://java.sun.com/docs/books/tutorial/essential/threads/priority.html

This is the run method for both runners (page 767):

```
public int tick = 1;
public void run() {
    while (tick < 400000)
        tick++;
}
```

This run method simply counts from 1 to 400,000.

This applet has a third thread that handles the drawing. The drawing thread's `run` method loops until the applet stops. During each iteration of the loop, it draws a line for each runner, whose length is computed from the runner's `tick` variable; it then sleeps for 10 milliseconds. The drawing thread has a thread priority of

4—higher than either runner. So, whenever the drawing thread wakes up after 10 milliseconds, it becomes the highest-priority thread, preempting whichever runner is currently running, and draws the lines. You can see the lines inch their way across the page.

This is not a fair race because one runner has a higher priority than the other. Each time the drawing thread yields the CPU by going to sleep for 10 milliseconds, the scheduler chooses the highest-priority Runnable thread to run; in this case, it's always runner 3.

Here is another version of the applet, one that implements a fair race, where, both runners have the same priority and an equal chance of being chosen to run.

Try This: Go to the online version of this section and run the applet.

http://java.sun.com/docs/books/tutorial/essential/threads/priority.html

In this race, each time the drawing thread yields the CPU by going to sleep, there are two Runnable threads of equal priority—the runners—waiting for the CPU. The scheduler must choose one of the threads to run. In this case, the scheduler chooses the next thread to run in a round-robin fashion.

Selfish Threads

The `Runner` class used in the previous races actually implements "socially impaired" thread behavior. Recall the `run` method from the `Runner` class used in the races:

```
public int tick = 1;
public void run() {
    while (tick < 400000)
        tick++;
}
```

The `while` loop in the `run` method is in a tight loop. Once the scheduler chooses a thread with this thread body for execution, the thread never voluntarily relinquishes control of the CPU; it just continues to run until the `while` loop terminates naturally or until the thread is preempted by a higher-priority thread. This thread is called a *selfish thread.*

In some cases, having selfish threads doesn't cause any problems because a higher-priority thread preempts the selfish one, just as the drawing thread in `RaceApplet` preempts the selfish runners. However, in other cases, threads with CPU-greedy `run` methods can take over the CPU and cause other threads to wait for a long time, even forever, before getting a chance to run.

Time-Slicing

Some systems, such as Windows 95/NT, fight selfish thread behavior with a strategy known as *time-slicing*. Time-slicing comes into play when there are multiple Runnable threads of equal priority and those threads are the highest-priority threads competing for the CPU. For example, a stand-alone Java program (page 767) based on `RaceApplet` creates two equal-priority selfish threads that have this `run` method:

```
public void run() {
    while (tick < 400000) {
        tick++;
        if ((tick % 50000) == 0)
            System.out.println("Thread #" + num + ", tick = " +
                               tick);
    }
}
```

This `run` method contains a tight loop that increments the integer `tick`. Every 50,000 ticks prints out the thread's identifier and its `tick` count.

When running this program on a time-sliced system, you will see messages from both threads intermingled with one another, like this:

```
Thread #1, tick = 50000
Thread #0, tick = 50000
Thread #0, tick = 100000
Thread #1, tick = 100000
Thread #1, tick = 150000
Thread #1, tick = 200000
Thread #0, tick = 150000
Thread #0, tick = 200000
Thread #1, tick = 250000
Thread #0, tick = 250000
Thread #0, tick = 300000
Thread #1, tick = 300000
Thread #1, tick = 350000
Thread #0, tick = 350000
Thread #0, tick = 400000
Thread #1, tick = 400000
```

This output is produced because a time-sliced system divides the CPU into time slots and iteratively gives each equal-and-highest priority thread a time slot in which to run. The time-sliced system iterates through the equal-and-highest priority threads, allowing each one a bit of time to run, until one or more finishes or until a higher-priority thread preempts them. Note that time-slicing makes no guarantees as to how often or in what order threads are scheduled to run.

When running this program on a system that is not time-sliced, you will see messages from one thread finish printing before the other thread ever gets a chance to print one message. The output will look like this:

```
Thread #0, tick = 50000
Thread #0, tick = 100000
Thread #0, tick = 150000
Thread #0, tick = 200000
Thread #0, tick = 250000
Thread #0, tick = 300000
Thread #0, tick = 350000
Thread #0, tick = 400000
Thread #1, tick = 50000
Thread #1, tick = 100000
Thread #1, tick = 150000
Thread #1, tick = 200000
Thread #1, tick = 250000
Thread #1, tick = 300000
Thread #1, tick = 350000
Thread #1, tick = 400000
```

This is because a system that is not time-sliced chooses one of the equal-and-highest priority threads to run and allows that thread to run until it relinquishes the CPU (by either sleeping, yielding, or finishing its job) or until a higher-priority preempts it.

Purity Tip: The Java platform does not implement (and therefore does not guarantee) time-slicing. However, some platforms do support time-slicing. Your Java programs should not rely on time-slicing, as it may produce different results on different systems.

Try This: Compile and run the RaceTest (page 767) and SelfishRunner (page 767) classes on your computer. Can you tell if you have a time-sliced system?

As you can imagine, writing CPU-intensive code can have negative repercussions on other threads running in the same process. In general, try to write well-

behaved threads that voluntarily relinquish the CPU periodically and give other threads an opportunity to run.

A thread can voluntarily yield the CPU by calling the `yield` method. The `yield` method gives other threads of the same priority a chance to run. If no equal priority threads are Runnable, then the `yield` is ignored.

Try This: Rewrite the `SelfishRunner` class to be a `PoliteRunner` (page 768) by calling the yield method from the run method. Be sure to modify the main program (page 768) to create `PoliteRunners` instead of `SelfishRunners`. Compile and run the new classes on your computer. Now isn't that better?

Summarizing Thread Priority

- Most computers have only one CPU, so threads must share the CPU with other threads. The execution of multiple threads on a single CPU, in some order, is called *scheduling*. The Java platform supports a simple, deterministic scheduling algorithm called fixed-priority scheduling.
- Each Java thread is given a numeric priority between `MIN_PRIORITY` and `MAX_PRIORITY` (constants defined in the `Thread` class). At any given time, when multiple threads are ready to be executed, the highest-priority thread is chosen for execution. Only when that thread stops or is suspended for some reason, will a lower-priority thread start executing.
- Scheduling of the CPU is fully preemptive. If a thread with a higher priority than the currently executing thread needs to execute, the higher-priority thread is immediately scheduled.
- The Java platform will not preempt the currently running thread for another thread of the same priority. In other words, the Java platform does not time-slice. However, the system implementation of threads underlying the Java `Thread` class may support time-slicing. Do not write code that relies on time-slicing.
- A given thread may, at any time, give up its right to execute by calling the `yield` method. Threads can yield the CPU only to other threads of the same priority. Attempts to yield to a lower-priority thread are ignored.
- When all of the Runnable threads in the system have the same priority, the scheduler chooses the next thread to run in a simple, nonpreemptive, round-robin scheduling order.

Synchronizing Threads

The examples in this lesson so far have contained independent, asynchronous threads. Each thread contained all of the data and methods required for its execution and didn't require any outside resources or methods. Also, the threads in those examples ran at their own pace without concern for the state or activities of any other concurrently running threads.

However, there are many interesting situations in which separate, concurrently running threads do share data and must consider the state and activities of other threads. In one such set of programming situations, called producer/consumer scenarios, the producer generates a stream of data that then is consumed by a consumer.

For example, imagine a Java application in which one thread (the producer) writes data to a file while a second thread (the consumer) reads data from the same file. Or, as you type characters on the keyboard, the producer thread places mouse events in an event queue and the consumer thread reads the events from the same queue. Both of these examples use concurrent threads that share a common resource: The first shares a file, and the second shares an event queue. Because the threads share a common resource, they must be synchronized in some way.

This lesson teaches you about Java thread synchronization through a simple producer/consumer example.

Producer/Consumer Example

The `Producer` (page 769) generates an integer between 0 and 9 (inclusive), stores it in a `CubbyHole` object, and prints the generated number. To make the synchronization problem more interesting, the `Producer` sleeps for a random amount of time between 0 and 100 milliseconds before repeating the number-generating cycle:

```
public class Producer extends Thread {
    private CubbyHole cubbyhole;
    private int number;

    public Producer(CubbyHole c, int number) {
        cubbyhole = c;
        this.number = number;
    }

    public void run() {
```

```
            for (int i = 0; i < 10; i++) {
                cubbyhole.put(i);
                System.out.println("Producer #" + this.number +
                                   " put: " + i);
                try {
                   sleep((int)(Math.random() * 100));
                } catch (InterruptedException e) { }
            }
        }
    }
```

The Consumer (page 770), being ravenous, consumes all integers from the CubbyHole (the exact same object into which the Producer put the integers in the first place) as quickly as they become available:

```
    public class Consumer extends Thread {
        private CubbyHole cubbyhole;
        private int number;

        public Consumer(CubbyHole c, int number) {
            cubbyhole = c;
            this.number = number;
        }

        public void run() {
            int value = 0;
            for (int i = 0; i < 10; i++) {
                value = cubbyhole.get();
                System.out.println("Consumer #" + this.number +
                                   " got: " + value);
            }
        }
    }
```

The Producer and Consumer in this example share data through a common CubbyHole object. Also, although the Consumer ideally will get each value produced once and only once, neither the Producer nor the Consumer makes any effort whatsoever to ensure that happens. The synchronization between these two threads occurs at a lower level, within the get and put methods of the CubbyHole object. However, assume for a moment that these two threads make no arrangements for synchronization, and let's discuss the potential problems that might arise from this.

One problem arises when the Producer is quicker than the Consumer and generates two numbers before the Consumer has a chance to consume the first one. In this situation, the Consumer misses a number. Part of the output might look like this:

```
    . . .

Consumer #1 got: 3
Producer #1 put: 4     <----------  Consumer missed 4
Producer #1 put: 5
Consumer #1 got: 5

    . . .
```

Another problem might arise when the Consumer is quicker than the Producer and consumes the same value twice. In this situation, the Consumer might produce output that looks like this:

```
    . . .

Producer #1 put: 4
Consumer #1 got: 4     <----------  Consumer got 4 twice
Consumer #1 got: 4
Producer #1 put: 5

    . . .
```

Either way, the result is wrong because the Consumer should get each integer produced by the Producer exactly once. A problem such as this is called a *race condition*. Race conditions arise from multiple, asynchronously executing threads trying to access a single object at the same time and getting the wrong result.

Race conditions in the producer/consumer example are prevented by having the storage of a new integer into the CubbyHole by the Producer be synchronized with the retrieval of an integer from the CubbyHole by the Consumer. The Consumer must consume each integer exactly once.

The activities of the Producer and Consumer must be synchronized in two ways. First, the two threads must not simultaneously access the CubbyHole. A Java thread can prevent this from happening by locking an object. When an object is locked by one thread and another thread tries to call a synchronized method on the same object, the second thread will block until the object is unlocked.

And second, the two threads must do some simple coordination. That is, the Producer must have some way to indicate to the Consumer that the value is ready and the Consumer must have some way to indicate that the value has been retrieved. The Thread class provides a collection of methods—wait, notify, and notifyAll—to help threads wait for a condition and notify other threads of when that condition changes.

Locking an Object

The code segments within a program that access the same object from separate, concurrent threads are called *critical sections*. In the Java language, a critical section can be a block or a method and is identified with the `synchronized` keyword. The Java platform then associates a lock with every object that has synchronized code.

In the producer/consumer example, the `put` and `get` methods of the `CubbyHole.java` (page 770) are the critical sections. The `Consumer` should not access the `CubbyHole` when the `Producer` is changing it, and the `Producer` should not modify it when the `Consumer` is getting the value. So `put` and `get` in the `CubbyHole` class should be marked with the `synchronized` keyword.

Here's a code skeleton for the `CubbyHole` class:

```
public class CubbyHole {
    private int contents;
    private boolean available = false;

    public synchronized int get() {
        ...
    }

    public synchronized void put(int value) {
        ...
    }
}
```

Note that the method declarations for both `put` and `get` contain the `synchronized` keyword. Hence, the system associates a unique lock with every instance of `CubbyHole` (including the one shared by the `Producer` and the `Consumer`). Whenever control enters a synchronized method, the thread that called the method locks the object whose method has been called. Other threads cannot call a synchronized method on the same object until the object is unlocked.

So, when the `Producer` calls `CubbyHole`'s `put` method, it locks the `CubbyHole`, thereby preventing the `Consumer` from calling the `CubbyHole`'s `get` method:

```
public synchronized void put(int value) {
    // CubbyHole locked by the Producer
    ..
    // CubbyHole unlocked by the Producer
}
```

When the put method returns, the Producer unlocks the CubbyHole.

Similarly, when the Consumer calls CubbyHole's get method, it locks the CubbyHole, thereby preventing the Producer from calling put:

```
public synchronized int get() {
    // CubbyHole locked by the Consumer
    ...
    // CubbyHole unlocked by the Consumer
}
```

The acquisition and release of a lock is done automatically and atomically by the Java runtime system. This ensures that race conditions cannot occur in the underlying implementation of the threads, thus ensuring data integrity.

Synchronization isn't the whole story. The two threads must also be able to notify one another when they've done their job. Learn more about that after a brief foray into reentrant locks.

Reaquiring a Lock

The same thread can call a synchronized method on an object for which it already holds the lock, thereby reacquiring the lock.

The Java runtime system allows a thread to reacquire a lock because Java locks are *reentrant*. Reentrant locks are important because they eliminate the possibility of a single thread's deadlocking itself on a lock that it already holds.

Consider this class:

```
public class Reentrant {
    public synchronized void a() {
        b();
        System.out.println("here I am, in a()");
    }
    public synchronized void b() {
        System.out.println("here I am, in b()");
    }
}
```

Reentrant contains two synchronized methods: a and b. The first, a, calls the other, b. When control enters method a, the current thread acquires the lock for the Reentrant object. Now, a calls b, and because b is also synchronized, the thread attempts to acquire the same lock again. Because Java supports reentrant locks, this works. The current thread can acquire the Reentrant object's lock again, and both a and b execute to conclusion, as is evidenced by the output:

```
here I am, in b()
here I am, in a()
```

In systems that don't support reentrant locks, this sequence of method calls causes deadlock.

Using the notifyAll and wait Methods

Let's investigate the code in CubbyHole's put and get methods that helps the Producer and Consumer coordinate their activities.

The CubbyHole stores its value in a private member variable called contents. CubbyHole has another private member variable, available, that is a boolean. available is true when the value has just been put but not yet gotten and is false when the value has been gotten but not yet put. So, here's one possible implementation for the put and get methods:

```
public synchronized int get() {     // won't work!
    if (available == true) {
        available = false;
        return contents;
    }
}
public synchronized int put(int value) {     // won't work!
    if (available == false) {
        available = true;
        contents = value;
    }
}
```

As implemented, these two methods won't work. Look at the get method. What happens if the Producer hasn't put anything in the CubbyHole and available isn't true? get does nothing. Similarly, if the Producer calls put before the Consumer got the value, put doesn't do anything.

You really want the Consumer to *wait* until the Producer puts something in the CubbyHole and the Producer must *notify* the Consumer when it's done so. Similarly, the Producer must *wait* until the Consumer takes a value (and notifies the Producer of its activities) before replacing it with a new value. The two threads must coordinate more fully and can use Object's wait and notifyAll methods to do so.

Here are the new implementations of get and put that wait on and notify each other of their activities:

```
public synchronized int get() {
    while (available == false) {
        try {
            // wait for Producer to put value
            wait();
        } catch (InterruptedException e) { }
    }
    available = false;
    // notify Producer that value has been retrieved
    notifyAll();
    return contents;
}
public synchronized void put(int value) {
    while (available == true) {
        try {
            // wait for Consumer to get value
            wait();
        } catch (InterruptedException e) { }
    }
    contents = value;
    available = true;
    // notify Consumer that value has been set
    notifyAll();
}
```

The code in the `get` method loops until the `Producer` has produced a new value. Each time through the loop, `get` calls the `wait` method. The `wait` method relinquishes the lock held by the `Consumer` on the `CubbyHole` (thereby allowing the `Producer` to get the lock and update the `CubbyHole`) and then waits for notification from the `Producer`. When the `Producer` puts something in the `CubbyHole`, it notifies the `Consumer` by calling `notifyAll`. The `Consumer` then comes out of the wait state, `available` is now `true`, the loop exits, and the `get` method returns the value in the `CubbyHole`.

The `put` method works in a similar fashion, waiting for the `Consumer` thread to consume the current value before allowing the `Producer` to produce a new one.

The `notifyAll` method wakes up all threads waiting on the object in question (in this case, the `CubbyHole`). The awakened threads compete for the lock. One thread gets it, and the others go back to waiting. The `Object` class also defines the `notify` method, which arbitrarily wakes up one of the threads waiting on this object.

The Object class contains not only the version of wait that is used in the producer/consumer example and which waits indefinitely for notification, but also two other versions of the wait method:

wait(long *timeout*)
: Waits for notification or until the timeout period has elapsed. *timeout* is measured in milliseconds.

wait(long *timeout*, int *nanos*)
: Waits for notification or until *timeout* milliseconds plus *nanos* nanoseconds have elapsed.

Note: Besides using these timed wait methods to synchronize threads, you also can use them in place of sleep. Both wait and sleep delay for the requested amount of time. You can easily wake up wait with a notify, but a sleeping thread cannot be awoken prematurely. This doesn't matter too much for threads that don't sleep for long, but it could be important for threads that sleep for minutes at a time.

Running the Producer/Consumer Example

Here's a small standalone Java application (page 771) that creates a CubbyHole object, a Producer, and a Consumer and then starts both the Producer and the Consumer:

```
public class ProducerConsumerTest {
    public static void main(String[] args) {
        CubbyHole c = new CubbyHole();
        Producer p1 = new Producer(c, 1);
        Consumer c1 = new Consumer(c, 1);

        p1.start();
        c1.start();
    }
}
```

Here's the output of ProducerConsumerTest:

```
Producer #1 put: 0
Consumer #1 got: 0
Producer #1 put: 1
Consumer #1 got: 1
Producer #1 put: 2
Consumer #1 got: 2
Producer #1 put: 3
```

```
Consumer #1 got: 3
Producer #1 put: 4
Consumer #1 got: 4
Producer #1 put: 5
Consumer #1 got: 5
Producer #1 put: 6
Consumer #1 got: 6
Producer #1 put: 7
Consumer #1 got: 7
Producer #1 put: 8
Consumer #1 got: 8
Producer #1 put: 9
Consumer #1 got: 9
```

Avoiding Starvation and Deadlock

If you write a program in which several concurrent threads are competing for resources, you must take precautions to ensure fairness. A system is fair when each thread gets enough access to limited resource to make reasonable progress. A fair system prevents *starvation* and *deadlock*. Starvation occurs when one or more threads in your program is blocked from gaining access to a resource and, as a result, cannot make progress. Deadlock is the ultimate form of starvation. It occurs when two or more threads are waiting on a condition that cannot be satisfied. Deadlock most often occurs when two (or more) threads are each waiting for the other(s) to do something.

The story of the dining philosophers is often used to illustrate various problems that can occur when many synchronized threads are competing for limited resources. The story goes like this. Five philosophers are sitting at a round table. In front of each philosopher is a bowl of rice. Between each pair of philosophers is one chopstick. Before an individual philosopher can take a bite of rice, he must have two chopsticks: one taken from the left and one taken from the right. The philosophers must find some way to share chopsticks so that they all get to eat.

This particular algorithm works as follows. Duke always reaches for the chopstick on his right first. If the chopstick is there, Duke takes it and raises his right hand. Next, Duke tries for the left chopstick. If the chopstick is available, Duke picks it up and raises his other hand. Now that Duke has both chopsticks, he takes a bite of rice and says "Mmm!" He then puts both chopsticks down, thereby allowing either of his two neighbors to get the chopsticks. Duke then starts all over again by trying for the right chopstick. Between each attempt to grab a chopstick, Duke pauses for a random period of time.

The following applet is a rough animation using an image of Duke for each philosopher:

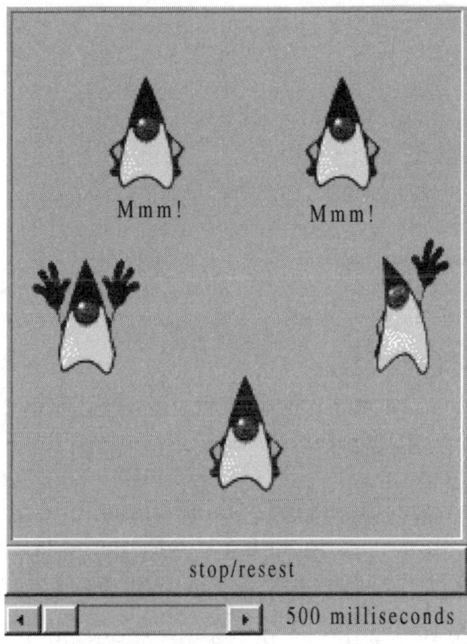

http://java.sun.com/docs/books/tutorial/essential/threads/deadlock.html

The slider controls the amount of time that each philosopher waits before attempting to pick up a chopstick. When the slider is set to 0, the philosophers don't wait—they just grab—and the applet ends up in deadlock—that is, all of the philosophers are frozen with their right hand in the air. Why? Because each immediately has one chopstick and is waiting on a condition that cannot be satisfied. That is, they are all waiting for the left chopstick, which is held by the philosopher to their left.

When you move the slider so that the waiting period is longer, the applet may proceed for a while without deadlocking. However, deadlock is always possible with this particular implementation of the dining philosophers problem because it is possible for all five philosophers to be holding their right chopsticks. Rather than rely on luck to prevent deadlock, you must either explicitly prevent it or detect it.

For most Java programmers, the best choice is to prevent deadlock rather than to try to detect it. The simplest approach to preventing deadlock is to impose ordering on the condition variables. In the dining philosopher applet, there is no ordering imposed on the condition variables because the philosophers and the chopsticks are arranged in a circle. All chopsticks are equal.

However, you can change the rules in the applet by numbering the chopsticks 1 through 5 and insisting that the philosophers pick up first the chopstick that has the lower number. The philosopher who is sitting between chopsticks 1 and 2 and the philosopher who is sitting between chopsticks 1 and 5 must now reach for the same chopstick first (chopstick 1) rather than picking up the one on the right. Whoever gets chopstick 1 first is then free to take another chopstick. Whoever doesn't get chopstick 1 must now wait for the first philosopher to release it. Deadlock is not possible.

Grouping Threads

Every Java thread is a member of a *thread group*. A thread group provides a mechanism for collecting multiple threads into a single object and manipulating those threads all at once, rather than individually. For example, you can interrupt all of the threads within a group with a single method call. Java thread groups are implemented by the `ThreadGroup`[1] class in the `java.lang` package.

The runtime system puts a thread into a thread group during thread construction. When you create a thread, you can either allow the runtime system to put the new thread in some default group or explicitly set the new thread's group. The thread is a permanent member of whatever thread group it joins on its creation. You cannot move a thread to a new group after the thread has been created.

The Default Thread Group

If you create a new thread without specifying its group in the constructor, the runtime system automatically places the new thread in the same group as the thread that created it (called the *current thread group* and the *current thread*, respectively). When a Java application first starts up, the Java runtime system creates a `ThreadGroup` named `main`. Thus all new threads that a program creates become members of the `main` thread group, unless it explicitly creates other groups and puts threads in them.

Note: If you create a thread within an applet, the new thread's group may be something other than `main`, depending on the browser or viewer in which the applet is running. Refer to Threads in Applets (page 219) for information.

---

1 http://java.sun.com/products/jdk/1.1/docs/api/java.lang.ThreadGroup.html

Many Java programmers ignore thread groups altogether and allow the runtime system to handle all of the details regarding thread groups. However, if your program creates a lot of threads that should be manipulated as a group or if you are implementing a custom security manager, you will likely want more control over thread groups. Continue reading for more details.

Creating a Thread Explicitly in a Group

Recall that a thread is a permanent member of whatever thread group it joins when it is created and that you cannot move a thread to a different group. To put a new thread in a thread group other than the default, you must specify the thread group explicitly when you create it. The `Thread` class has three constructors that set a new thread's group:

```
public Thread(ThreadGroup group, Runnable target)
public Thread(ThreadGroup group, String name)
public Thread(ThreadGroup group, Runnable target, String name)
```

Each constructor creates a new thread, initializes it based on the `Runnable` and `String` parameters, and makes the new thread a member of the specified group. For example, the following code sample creates a thread group (`myThreadGroup`) and then creates a thread (`myThread`) in that group:

```
ThreadGroup myThreadGroup =
    new ThreadGroup("My Group of Threads");
Thread myThread =
     new Thread(myThreadGroup, "a thread for my group");
```

The `ThreadGroup` passed into a `Thread` constructor can be any group: one created by your program, by the Java runtime system, or by the browser in which an applet is running.

Getting a Thread's Group

To find out what group a thread is in, call its `getThreadGroup` method:

```
theGroup = myThread.getThreadGroup();
```

Once you've obtained a thread's `ThreadGroup`, you can query the group for information, such as what other threads are in the group. You also can modify the threads in that group, such as suspending, resuming, or stopping them, by using a single method invocation.

Using the ThreadGroup Class

The `ThreadGroup` class manages groups of threads for Java applications. A `ThreadGroup` can contain any number of threads and can contain other `ThreadGroups`, as well. The threads in a group are generally related in some way, such as by who created them, what function they perform, or when they should be started and stopped.

The top-most thread group in a Java application is the thread group named `main`. A program can create threads and groups in the `main` group or in its subgroups. The result is a hierarchy of threads and groups, as shown in Figure 50.

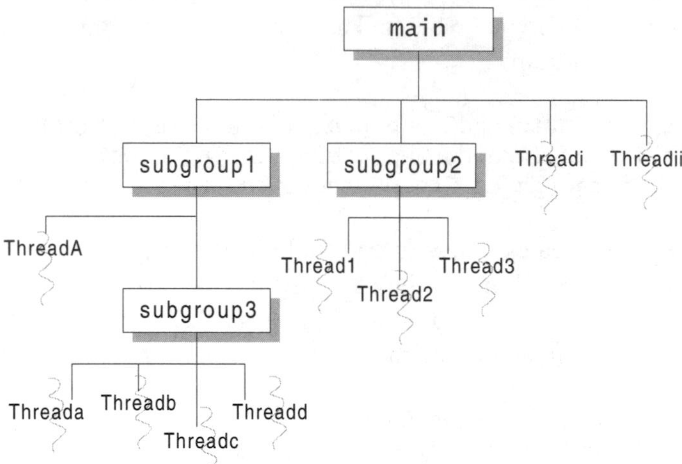

Figure 50: Thread groups can be nested, thereby creating a hierarchy of groups and threads.

The `ThreadGroup` class has methods that can be categorized as follows:

- Collection Management Methods (page 359): Methods that manage the collection of threads and subgroups contained in the thread group
- Methods That Operate on the Group (page 359): Methods that set or get attributes of the `ThreadGroup` object
- Methods That Operate on All Threads within a Group (page 361): A set of methods that perform some operation on all of the threads and subgroups within the group
- Access Restriction Methods (page 361): Methods that allow the security manager to restrict access to threads based on group membership; allowed by `ThreadGroup` and `Thread`

Collection Management Methods

The ThreadGroup provides a set of methods that manage the threads and subgroups within the group and allow other objects to query the ThreadGroup for information about its contents. For example, you can call ThreadGroup's activeCount method to learn the number of active threads currently in the group. This method is often used with the enumerate method to get an array filled with references to all of the active threads in a ThreadGroup. For example, the listCurrentThreads method in the following example fills an array with all of the active threads in the current thread group and prints their names:

```
public class EnumerateTest {
    public void listCurrentThreads() {
        ThreadGroup currentGroup =
            Thread.currentThread().getThreadGroup();
        int numThreads = currentGroup.activeCount();
        Thread[] listOfThreads = new Thread[numThreads];

        currentGroup.enumerate(listOfThreads);
        for (int i = 0; i < numThreads; i++)
            System.out.println("Thread #" + i + " = " +
                listOfThreads[i].getName());
    }
}
```

Other collection management methods provided by the ThreadGroup class include activeGroupCount and list.

Methods That Operate on the Group

The ThreadGroup class supports several attributes that are set and retrieved from the group as a whole. These attributes include the maximum priority that any thread within the group can have, whether the group is a daemon group, the name of the group, and the parent of the group.

The methods that get and set ThreadGroup attributes operate at the group level. They inspect or change the attribute on the ThreadGroup object, but they do not affect any of the threads within the group. Following are the ThreadGroup methods that operate at the group level:

- getMaxPriority and setMaxPriority
- getDaemon and setDaemon
- getName
- getParent and parentOf
- toString

For example, when you use setMaxPriority to change a group's maximum priority, you are changing only the attribute on the group object; you are not changing the priority of any of the threads within it. Consider the following program that creates a group and a thread within that group:

```
public class MaxPriorityTest {
    public static void main(String[] args) {

        ThreadGroup groupNORM = new ThreadGroup(
                                "A group with normal priority");
        Thread priorityMAX = new Thread(groupNORM,
                                "A thread with maximum priority");

        // set Thread's priority to max (10)
        priorityMAX.setPriority(Thread.MAX_PRIORITY);

        // set ThreadGroup's max priority to normal (5)
        groupNORM.setMaxPriority(Thread.NORM_PRIORITY);

        System.out.println("Group's maximum priority = " +
                groupNORM.getMaxPriority());
        System.out.println("Thread's priority = " +
                priorityMAX.getPriority());
    }
}
```

When the ThreadGroup groupNORM is created, it inherits its maximum priority attribute from its parent thread group. In this case, the parent group priority is the maximum (MAX_PRIORITY) allowed by the Java runtime system. Next, the program sets the priority of the priorityMAX thread to the maximum allowed by the Java runtime system. Then the program lowers the group's maximum to the normal priority (NORM_PRIORITY). The setMaxPriority method does not affect the priority of the priorityMAX thread, so at this point, the priorityMAX thread has a priority of MAX_PRIORITY which is greater than the maximum priority of its group. Here is the output from the program:

```
Group's maximum priority = 5
Thread's priority = 10
```

As you can see, a thread can have a higher priority than the maximum allowed by its group as long as the thread's priority is set before the group's maximum priority is lowered. A thread group's maximum priority is used to limit a thread's priority when the thread is first created within a group or when you use setPriority to change the thread's priority. Note that the setMaxPriority method *does* change the maximum priority of all its descendant-thread groups.

Similarly, a group's daemon status applies only to the group. Changing a group's daemon status does not affect the daemon status of any thread in the group. Furthermore, a group's daemon status does not in any way determine the daemon status of its threads—you can put any thread within a daemon thread group. The daemon status of a thread group simply indicates that the group will be destroyed when all of its threads have been terminated.

Methods That Operate on All Threads within a Group

The `ThreadGroup` class has a method for interrupting all of the threads within it: `interrupt`. The `ThreadGroup`'s `interrupt` method calls the `interrupt` method on every thread in the group and its subgroups.

Access Restriction Methods

The `ThreadGroup` class itself does not impose any access restrictions, such as allowing threads from one group to inspect or modify threads in a different group. Rather, the `Thread` and `ThreadGroup` classes cooperate with security managers (subclasses of the `java.lang.SecurityManager` class), which can impose access restrictions based on thread group membership.

The `Thread` and `ThreadGroup` classes both have a method, `checkAccess`, that calls the current security manager's `checkAccess` method. The security manager decides whether to allow the access based on the group membership of the threads involved. If access is not allowed, the `checkAccess` method throws a `SecurityException`. Otherwise, `checkAccess` simply returns.

Following is a list of `ThreadGroup` methods that call `ThreadGroup`'s `checkAccess` method before performing the action of the method. These are called *regulated accesses.* A regulated access is an access that must be approved by the security manager before it can be completed.

- `ThreadGroup(ThreadGroup` *`parent`*`, String` *`name`*`)`
- `setDaemon(boolean` *`isDaemon`*`)`
- `setMaxPriority(int` *`maxPriority`*`)`
- `destroy()`

Here are the methods in the `Thread` class that call `checkAccess` before proceeding:

- Constructors that specify a thread group
- `setPriority(int` *`priority`*`)`
- `setName(String` *`name`*`)`
- `setDaemon(boolean` *`isDaemon`*`)`

A standalone Java application does not have a security manager by default. No restrictions are imposed, and any thread can inspect or modify any other thread, regardless of the group in which they are located. You can define and implement your own access restrictions for thread groups by subclassing `SecurityManager`, overriding the appropriate methods, and installing the `SecurityManager` as the current security manager in your application. For information about implementing a security manager, see Providing Your Own Security Manager (page 279).

The HotJava Web browser is an example of an application that implements its own security manager. HotJava needs to ensure that applets are well-behaved and don't do nasty things to other applets that are running at the same time (such as lowering the priority of another applet's threads). HotJava's security manager does not allow threads in different groups to modify one another. Note that access restrictions based on thread groups may vary among browsers and thus applets may behave differently in different browsers.

Summarizing Threads in Java

This lesson provided a great deal of information about using threads in the Java platform. Threads are supported by various components of the Java platform, and it can be hard to find the features that you need. This section summarizes where you can find various classes, methods, and language features that participate in the Java threads story.

Package Support of Threads

`java.lang.Thread`[1]

In the Java platform, threads are objects that derive from `java.lang`'s `Thread` class. The `Thread` class defines and implements Java threads. You can subclass the `Thread` class to provide your own thread implementations.

`java.lang.Runnable`[2]

The Java language package also defines the `Runnable` interface, which allows any class to provide the body (the `run` method) for a thread.

`java.lang.Object`[3]

The root class, `Object`, defines three methods you can use to synchronize methods around a condition variable: `wait`, `notify`, and `notifyAll`.

---

1 http://java.sun.com/products/jdk/1.1/docs/api/java.lang.Thread.html
2 http://java.sun.com/products/jdk/1.1/docs/api/java.lang.Runnable.html
3 http://java.sun.com/products/jdk/1.1/docs/api/java.lang.Object.html

`java.lang.ThreadGroup`[1]
: All threads belong to a thread group, which typically contains related threads. The `ThreadGroup` class in the `java.lang` package implements groups of threads.

Language Support of Threads

The Java language has two keywords related to the synchronization of threads: `volatile` and `synchronized`. Both of these language features help ensure the integrity of data that is shared between two concurrently running threads. Synchronizing Threads (page 346) discusses thread synchronization issues.

Runtime Support of Threads

The Java runtime system contains the scheduler, which is responsible for running all of the existing threads. The Java scheduler uses a fixed priority scheduling algorithm, which boils down to the following simple rule of thumb.

Rule of Thumb: At any given time, the highest-priority thread is running. However, this is not guaranteed. The thread scheduler may choose to run a lower-priority thread to avoid starvation. For this reason, use priority only to affect scheduling policy for efficiency purposes. Do not rely on thread priority for algorithm correctness.

Other Thread Information

Threads in Applets (page 219)
: When you write applets that use threads, you may have to make special provisions, such as ensuring that your applet is well-behaved. Also, some browsers impose security restrictions for applets on the basis of in which thread group a thread is located.

Concurrent Programming in Java
: In spite of its length, this lesson is really just an introduction to concurrent programming with threads. There are many issues to consider when writing complex multithreaded programs. In fact, there are enough issues to fill a book. *Concurrent Programming in Java*, written by Doug Lea, is another member of the Java Series that can help you with the advanced issues related to concurrent programming in Java.

---

[1] http://java.sun.com/products/jdk/1.1/docs/api/java.lang.ThreadGroup.html

17 Reading and Writing (but No 'rithmetic)

OFTEN programs need to bring in information from an external source or send out information to an external destination. The information can be anywhere: in a file, on disk, somewhere on the network, in memory, or in another program. Also, it can be of any type: objects, characters, images, or sounds.

To bring in information, a program opens a *stream* on an information source (a file, memory, a socket) and reads the information serially, as shown in Figure 51.

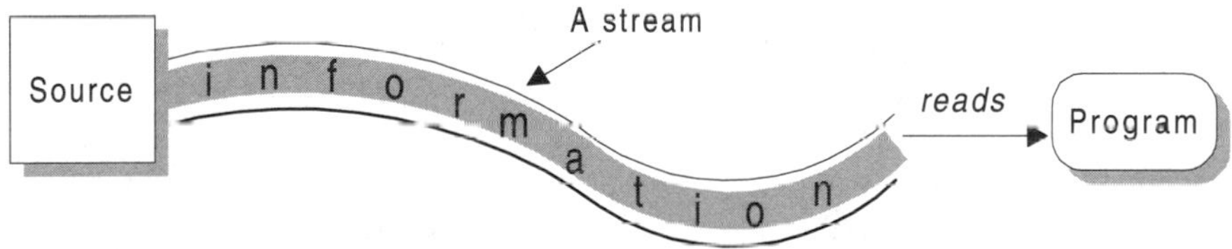

Figure 51: Reading information into a program.

Similarly, a program can send information to an external destination by opening a stream to a destination and writing the information out serially, as in Figure 52.

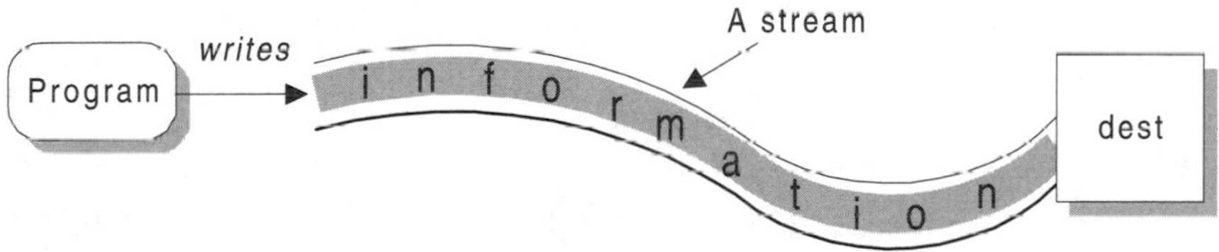

Figure 52: Writing information out of a program.

No matter where the information is coming from or going to and no matter what type of data is being read or written, the algorithms for reading and writing data is pretty much always the same.

Reading	Writing

open a stream
while more information
    read information
close the stream
	open a stream
	while more information
	    write information
	close the stream

The `java.io` package contains a collection of stream classes that support these algorithms for reading and writing. These classes are divided into two class hierarchies based on the data type (either characters or bytes) on which they operate.

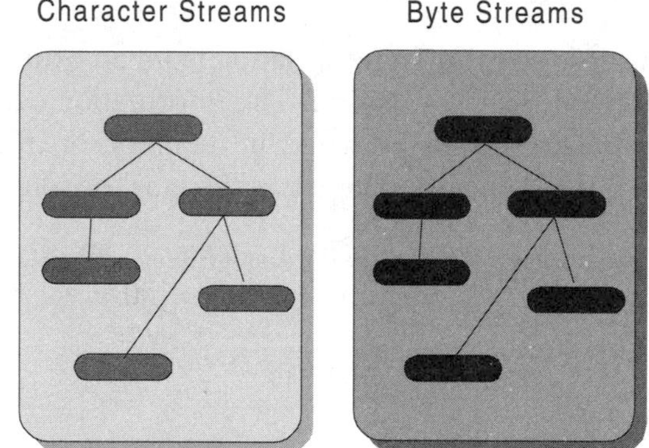

Figure 53: `java.io` contains two independent hierarchies of classes: one for reading and writing bytes, the other for reading and writing characters.

However, it's often more convenient to group the classes based on their purpose rather than on the data type they read and write. Thus, we can cross-group the streams by whether they read from and write to data "sinks" or process the information as its being read or written. See Figure 54.

The next section, Overview of I/O Streams (page 367), describes each type of stream and shows the classes in `java.io` that implement them according to the division in the class hierarchy. Then, because most people think in terms of what they want to do rather than what they are doing it to, we provide two sections, Using the Data Sink Streams (page 371) and Using the Processing Streams (page 376), which show you how to use selected streams based on their purpose.

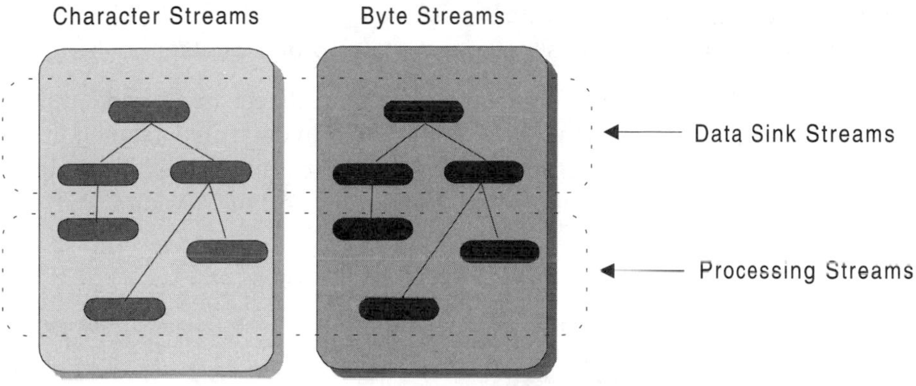

Figure 54: Grouping streams based on purpose rather than data type.

Two of the byte streams, `ObjectInputStream` and `ObjectOutputStream`, are specialized streams that let you read and write objects. Reading and writing objects is a process known as *object serialization*. Object serialization has many uses, including remote method invocation (RMI). In addition to the object streams, `java.io` has other classes and interfaces that define the API to help classes perform serialization for its instances. Read all about this in Object Serialization (page 388).

The character and byte streams are all sequential access streams. In contrast, `RandomAccessFile` lets you randomly access the contents of a file. Working with Random Access Files (page 394) talks about how to use random access files. It also provides a special section that shows you how to write filters for objects that implement the `DataInput` and `DataOutput` interfaces. Filters implemented in this fashion are more flexible than regular filter streams because they can be used on random access files and on some sequential files. And finally, And the Rest . . . (page 399) briefly introduces a few other classes in `java.io`.

Overview of I/O Streams

Character Streams

`Reader`[1] and `Writer`[2] are the abstract superclasses for character streams in `java.io`. `Reader` provides the API and partial implementation for *readers*—

---

1 http://java.sun.com/products/jdk/1.1/docs/api/java.io.Reader.html
2 http://java.sun.com/products/jdk/1.1/docs/api/java.io.Writer.html

streams that read 16-bit characters—and `Writer` provides the API and partial implementation for *writers*—streams that write 16-bit characters.

Subclasses of `Reader` and `Writer` implement specialized streams and are divided into two categories: those that read from or write to data sinks (shown in gray in Figure 55) and those that perform some sort of processing (shown in white in the figure). The figure shows the class hierarchies for the `Reader` and `Writer` classes.

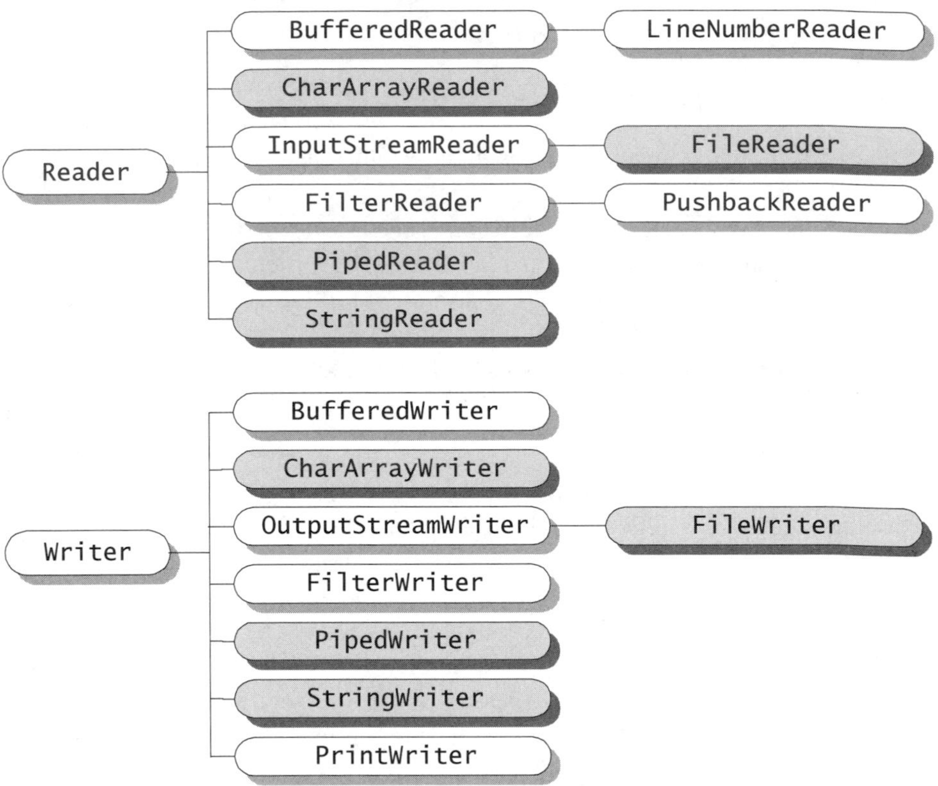

Figure 55: The class hierarchies for readers and writers in `java.io`.

Most programs should use readers and writers to read and write information. This is because they both can handle any character in the Unicode character set (while the byte streams are limited to ISO-Latin-1 8-bit bytes).

Byte Streams

Programs should use the byte streams, descendants of `InputStream`[1] and `OutputStream`[2], to read and write 8-bit bytes. `InputStream` and `OutputStream` pro-

vide the API and some implementation for *input streams* (streams that read 8-bit bytes) and *output streams* (streams that write 8-bit bytes). These streams are typically used to read and write binary data such as images and sounds.

As with `Reader` and `Writer`, subclasses of `InputStream` and `OutputStream` provide specialized I/O that falls into two categories: data sink streams and processing streams. Figure 56 shows the class hierarchies for the byte streams.

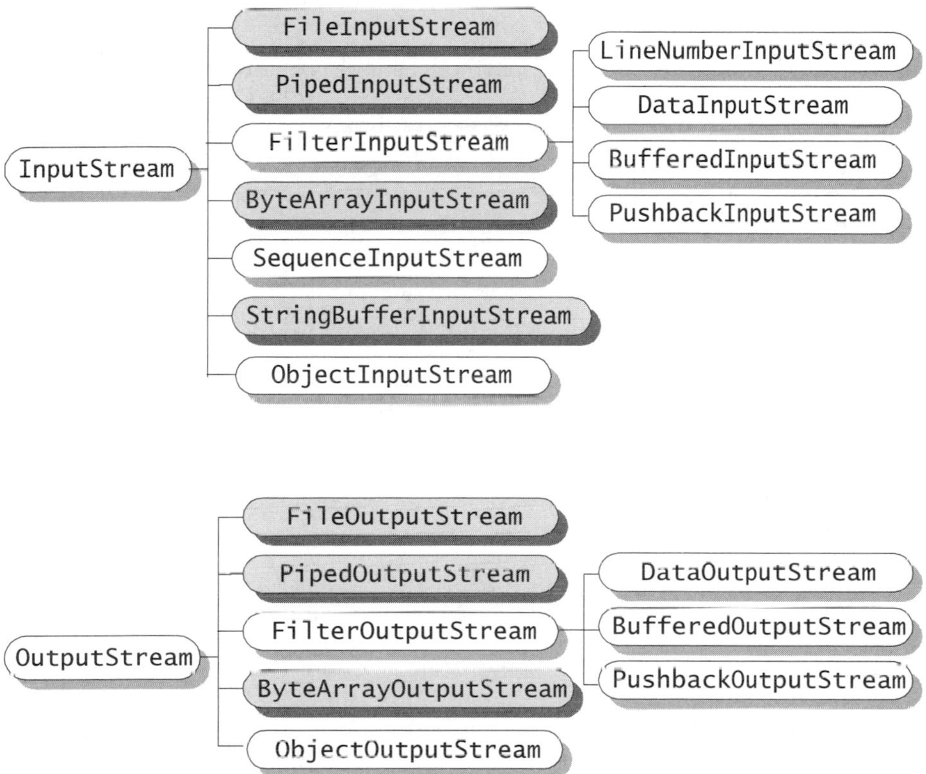

Figure 56: The class hierarchies for input and output streams in `java.io`.

As mentioned, two of the byte stream classes, `ObjectInputStream` and `ObjectOutputStream`, are used for object serialization. These classes are fully covered in Object Serialization (page 388).

1 http://java.sun.com/products/jdk/1.1/docs/api/java.io.InputStream.html
2 http://java.sun.com/products/jdk/1.1/docs/api/java.io.OutputStream.html

Understanding the I/O Superclasses

`Reader` and `InputStream` define similar APIs but for different data types. For example, `Reader` contains these methods for reading characters and arrays of characters:

```
int read()
int read(char cbuf[])
int read(char cbuf[], int offset, int length)
```

`InputStream` defines the same methods but for reading bytes and arrays of bytes:

```
int read()
int read(byte cbuf[])
int read(byte cbuf[], int offset, int length)
```

Also, both `Reader` and `InputStream` provide methods for marking a location in the stream, skipping input, and resetting the current position.

`Writer` and `OutputStream` are similarly parallel. `Writer` defines these methods for writing characters and arrays of characters:

```
int write(int c)
int write(char cbuf[])
int write(char cbuf[], int offset, int length)
```

And `OutputStream` defines the same methods but for bytes:

```
int write(int c)
int write(byte cbuf[])
int write(byte cbuf[], int offset, int length)
```

All of the streams—readers, writers, input streams, and output streams—are automatically opened when created. You can close any stream explicitly by calling its `close` method. Or the garbage collector can implicitly close it, which occurs when the object is no longer referenced.

Learn how to use a selected assortment of these two types of streams in the next two sections: Using the Data Sink Streams (page 371) and Using the Processing Streams (page 376).

Security Consideration: Some I/O operations are subject to approval by the current security manager. The example programs contained in these lessons are standalone applications, which by default have no security manager. This code might not work in an applet depending on the in which browser or viewer it is running. See Security Restrictions (page 212) for information about the security restrictions placed on applets.

Using the Data Sink Streams

Data sink streams read from or write to specialized data sinks such as strings, files, or pipes. Typically, for each reader or input stream intended to read from a specific kind of input source, `java.io` contains a parallel writer or output stream that can create it. Table 18 gives `java.io`'s data sink streams.

Table 18: Java's data sink streams.

Sink Type	Character Streams	Byte Streams
Memory	`CharArrayReader`, `CharArrayWriter`	`ByteArrayInputStream`, `ByteArrayOutputStream`
	`StringReader`, `StringWriter`	`StringBufferInputStream`
Pipe	`PipedReader`, `PipedWriter`	`PipedInputStream`, `PipedOutputStream`
File	`FileReader`, `FileWriter`	`FileInputStream`, `FileOutputStream`

Note that both the character stream group and the byte stream group contain parallel pairs of classes that operate on the same data sinks. These are described next:

`CharArrayReader` and `CharArrayWriter`
`ByteArrayInputStream` and `ByteArrayOutputStream`

Use these streams to read from and write to memory. You create these streams on an existing array and then use the `read` and `write` methods to read from or write to the array.

`FileReader` and `FileWriter`
`FileInputStream` and `FileOutputStream`

Collectively called *file streams*, these streams are used to read from or write to a file on the native file system. How to Use File Streams (page 372) has an example that uses `FileReader` and `FileWriter` to copy the contents of one file into another.

PipedReader and PipedWriter
PipedInputStream and PipedOutputStream

Implement the input and output components of a pipe. Pipes are used to channel the output from one program (or thread) into the input of another. See PipedReader and PipedWriter in action in How to Use Pipe Streams (page 374).

StringReader and StringWriter
StringBufferInputStream

Use StringReader to read characters from a String as it lives in memory. Use StringWriter to write to a String. StringWriter collects the characters written to it in a StringBuffer, which can then be converted to a String. StringBufferInputStream is similar to StringReader, except that it reads bytes from a StringBuffer.

How to Use File Streams

File streams are perhaps the easiest streams to understand. Simply put, the file streams—FileReader[1], FileWriter[2], FileInputStream[3], and FileOutputStream[4]—each read or write from a file on the native file system. You can create a file stream from a filename, a File[5] object, or a FileDescriptor[6] object.

The following Copy program uses FileReader and FileWriter to copy the contents of a file named farrago.txt (page 774) into a file called outagain.txt:

```
import java.io.*;

public class Copy {
    public static void main(String[] args) throws IOException {
        File inputFile = new File("farrago.txt");
        File outputFile = new File("outagain.txt");

        FileReader in = new FileReader(inputFile);
        FileWriter out = new FileWriter(outputFile);
        int c;

        while ((c = in.read()) != -1)
            out.write(c);
```

1 http://java.sun.com/products/jdk/1.1/docs/api/java.io.FileReader.html
2 http://java.sun.com/products/jdk/1.1/docs/api/java.io.FileWriter.html
3 http://java.sun.com/products/jdk/1.1/docs/api/java.io.FileInputStream.html
4 http://java.sun.com/products/jdk/1.1/docs/api/java.io.FileOutputStream.html
5 http://java.sun.com/products/jdk/1.1/docs/api/java.io.File.html
6 http://java.sun.com/products/jdk/1.1/docs/api/java.io.FileDescriptor.html

```
            in.close();
            out.close();
        }
    }
```

This program is very simple. It opens a `FileReader` on `farrago.txt` and opens a `FileWriter` on `outagain.txt`. The program reads characters from the reader as long as there's more input in the input file. When the input runs out, the program closes both the reader and the writer.

Note the code that the `Copy` program uses to create a `FileReader`:

```
File inputFile = new File("farrago.txt");
FileReader in = new FileReader(inputFile);
```

This code creates a `File` object that represents the named file on the native file system. `File` is a utility class provided by `java.io`. This program uses this object only to construct a `FileReader` on `farrago.txt`. However, it could use `inputFile` to get information about `farrago.txt`, such as its full pathname.

After you've run the program, you should find an exact copy of `farrago.txt` in a file named `outagain.txt` in the same directory. Here is the content of the file:

```
So she went into the garden to cut a cabbage-leaf, to
make an apple-pie; and at the same time a great
she-bear, coming up the street, pops its head into the
shop. 'What! no soap?' So he died, and she very
imprudently married the barber; and there were
present the Picninnies, and the Joblillies, and the
Garyalies, and the grand Panjandrum himself, with the
little round button at top, and they all fell to playing
the game of catch as catch can, till the gun powder ran
out at the heels of their boots.
                                  - Samuel Foote 1720-1777
```

Remember that `FileReader` and `FileWriter` read and write 16-bit characters. However, most native file systems are based on 8-bit bytes. These streams encode the characters as they operate according to the default character-encoding scheme. You can find out the default character-encoding by using `System.getProperty("file.encoding")`. To specify an encoding other than the default, you should construct an `OutputStreamWriter` on a `FileOutputStream` and specify it. For information about encoding characters, see the Writing Global Programs[1] trail in the online version of this tutorial.

---

1 http://java.sun.com/docs/books/tutorial/intl/index.html

In the appendix is another version of this program, `CopyBytes` (page 774), which uses `FileInputStream` and `FileOutputStream` in place of `FileReader` and `FileWriter`.

How to Use Pipe Streams

`PipedReader`[1] and `PipedWriter`[2] (and their input and output stream counterparts `PipedInputStream`[3] and `PipedOutputStream`[4]) implement the input and output components of a pipe. Pipes are used to channel the output from one program (or thread) into the input of another. Why is this useful?

Consider a class that implements various string manipulation utilities such as sorting and reversing text. It would be nice if the output of one of these methods could be used as the input for another so that you could string a series of method calls together to perform some higher-order function. For example, you could reverse each word in a list, sort the words, and then reverse each word again to create a list of rhyming words.

Without pipe streams, the program would have to store the results somewhere (such as in a file or in memory) between each step, as shown in Figure 57.

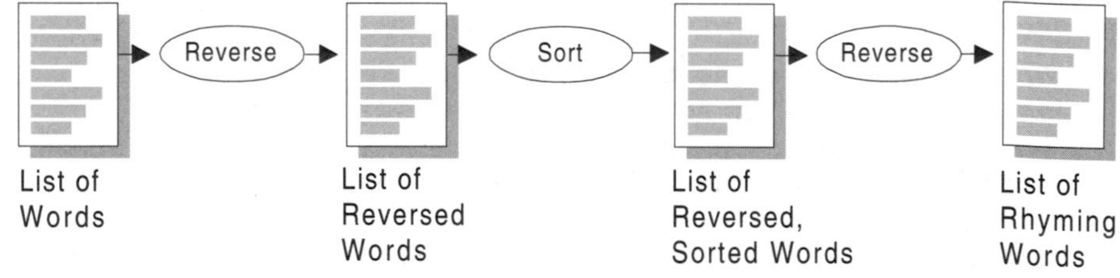

Figure 57: Without a pipe, a program must store intermediate results.

With pipe streams, the output from one method could be piped into the next, as shown in Figure 58.

Next, we investigate a program that implements what's represented by the diagram in Figure 58. This program uses `PipedReader` and `PipedWriter` to connect the input and output of its `reverse` and `sort` methods in order to create a list of rhyming words. Several classes make up this program. This section shows and discusses only the elements of the program that read from and write to the

---

1 http://java.sun.com/products/jdk/1.1/docs/api/java.io.PipedReader.html
2 http://java.sun.com/products/jdk/1.1/docs/api/java.io.PipedWriter.html
3 http://java.sun.com/products/jdk/1.1/docs/api/java.io.PipedInputStream.html
4 http://java.sun.com/products/jdk/1.1/docs/api/java.io.PipedOutputStream.html

pipes. Look in the appendix, Creating a List of Rhyming Words (page 775), for the whole program.

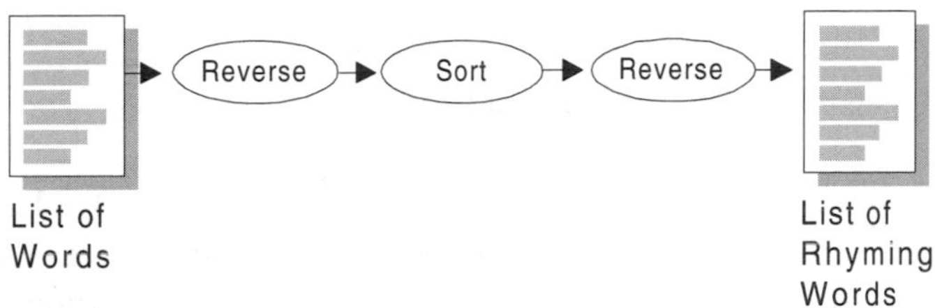

Figure 58: With a pipe, a program can pipe information directly from one method to another.

First, let's look at the calling sequence of the `reverse` and `sort` methods from the `main` method:

```
FileReader words = new FileReader("words.txt");
Reader rhymingWords = reverse(sort(reverse(words)));
```

The innermost call to `reverse` takes a `FileReader` opened on the file `words.txt` (page 779) that contains a list of words. The return value of `reverse` is passed to `sort`, whose return value is then passed to another call to `reverse`.

Let's look at the `reverse` method; the `sort` method is similar and you will understand it once you understand `reverse`.

```
public static Reader reverse(Reader src) throws IOException {
    BufferedReader in = new BufferedReader(src);

    PipedWriter pipeOut = new PipedWriter();
    PipedReader pipeIn = new PipedReader(pipeOut);
    PrintWriter out = new PrintWriter(pipeOut);

    new ReverseThread(out, in).start();

    return pipeIn;
}
```

The bold statements in `reverse` create both ends of a pipe—a `PipedWriter` and a `PipedReader`—and connects them by constructing the `PipedReader` "on" the `PipedWriter`. Whatever's written to the `PipedWriter` can be read from the `PipedReader`. The connection forms a pipe, as illustrated in Figure 59.

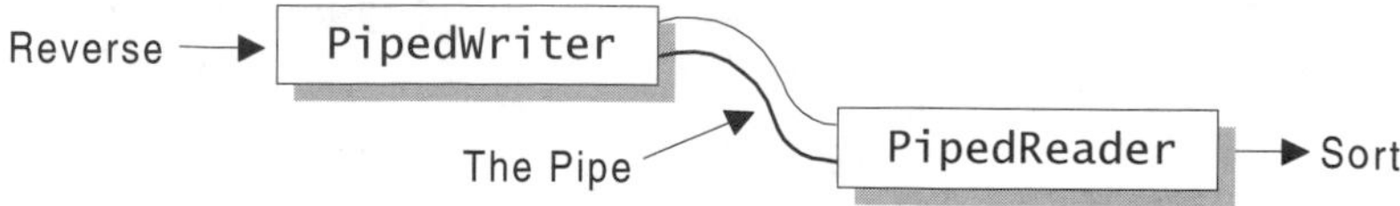

Figure 59: Using `PipedWriter` and `PipedReader` to form a pipe.

`reverse` starts a `WriteReversedThread` (page 776) that writes its output to the `PipedWriter` and then returns the `PipedReader` to the caller. The caller then arranges for a sorting thread to read from it. The `sort` method is exactly the same, except that it creates and starts a `SortThread` (page 777).

Using Streams to Wrap Other Streams

The `reverse` method contains some other interesting code; in particular, these two statements:

```
BufferedReader in = new BufferedReader(source);
...
PrintWriter out = new PrintWriter(pipeOut);
```

The first line opens a `BufferedReader` on `source`, the argument to `reverse` (a `Reader`). This essentially "wraps" `source` in a `BufferedReader`. The program reads from the `BufferedReader`, which in turn reads from `source`. The program does this so that it can use `BufferedReader`'s convenient `readLine` method. Similarly, the `PipedWriter` is wrapped in a `PrintWriter` so that the program can use `PrintWriter`'s convenient `println` method. You will often see streams wrapped in this way so as to combine the various features of the many streams.

Try this: Write another version of this program that uses input streams and output streams in place of readers and writers. See our online tutorial[1] for the solution.

Using the Processing Streams

Processing streams perform some sort of operation, such as buffering or character encoding, as they read and write. Like the data sink streams, `java.io` often contains pairs of streams: one that performs a particular operation during reading

[1] http://java.sun.com/docs/books/tutorial/essential/io/example/RhymingWords.java

and another that performs the same operation (or reverses it) during writing. Table 19 gives `java.io`'s processing streams.

Table 19: Java's processing streams.

Process	Character Streams	Byte Streams
Buffering	`BufferedReader`, `BufferedWriter`	`BufferedInputStream`, `BufferedOutputStream`
Filtering	`FilterReader`, `FilterWriter`	`FilterInputStream`, `FilterOutputStream`
Converting between Bytes and Characters	`InputStreamReader`, `OutputStreamWriter`	
Concatenation		`SequenceInputStream`
Object Serialization		`ObjectInputStream`, `ObjectOutputStream`
Data Conversion		`DataInputStream`, `DataOutputStream`
Counting	`LineNumberReader`	`LineNumberInputStream`
Peeking Ahead	`PushbackReader`	`PushbackInputStream`
Printing	`PrintWriter`	`PrintStream`

Notice that many times, `java.io` contains character streams and byte streams that perform the same processing but for the different data type. The processing streams are briefly described here:

`BufferedReader` and `BufferedWriter`
`BufferedInputStream` and `BufferedOutputStream`
Buffer data while reading or writing, thereby reducing the number of accesses required on the original data source. Buffered streams are typically more efficient than similar nonbuffered streams.

`FilterReader` and `FilterWriter`
`FilterInputStream` and `FilterOutputStream`
Abstract classes, like their parents. They define the interface for filter streams, which filter data as it's being read or written. Working with Filter Streams (page 380) later in this lesson shows you how to use filter streams and how to implement your own.

`InputStreamReader` and `OutputStreamWriter`
A reader and writer pair that forms the bridge between byte streams and character streams. An `InputStreamReader` reads bytes from an `Input-`

Stream and converts them to characters using either the default character-encoding or a character-encoding specified by name. Similarly, an OutputStreamWriter converts characters to bytes using either the default character-encoding or a character-encoding specified by name and then writes those bytes to an OutputStream. You can learn the name of the default character-encoding by calling System.getProperty("file.encoding"). Find out more about character-encoding in the Writing Global Programs[1] trail in the online version of this tutorial.

SequenceInputStream
Concatenates multiple input streams into one input stream. How to Concatenate Files (page 378) has a short example of this class.

ObjectInputStream and ObjectOutputStream
Used to serialize objects. See Object Serialization (page 388).

DataInputStream and DataOutputStream
Read or write primitive Java data types in a machine-independent format. How to Use DataInputStream and DataOutputStream (page 382) shows you an example of using these two streams.

LineNumberReader
LineNumberInputStream
Keeps track of line numbers while reading.

PushbackReader
PushbackInputStream
Two input streams each with a 1-character (or byte) pushback buffer. Sometimes, when reading data from a stream, you will find it useful to peek at the next item in the stream in order to decide what to do next. However, if you do peek ahead, you'll need to put the item back so that it can be read again and processed normally.

PrintWriter
PrintStream
Contain convenient printing methods. These are the easiest streams to write to, so you will often see other writable streams wrapped in one of these.

How to Concatenate Files

SequenceInputStream[2] creates a single input stream from multiple input sources. This example program, Concatenate (page 780), uses SequenceInput-

1 http://java.sun.com/docs/books/tutorial/intl/index.html
2 http://java.sun.com/products/jdk/1.1/docs/api/java.io.SequenceInputStream.html

Stream to implement a concatenation utility that sequentially concatenates files together in the order in which they are listed on the command line.

The following is the controlling class of the Concatenate utility:

```
import java.io.*;

public class Concatenate {
    public static void main(String[] args) throws IOException {
        ListOfFiles mylist = new ListOfFiles(args);

        SequenceInputStream s = new SequenceInputStream(
                                            mylist);
        int c;

        while ((c = s.read()) != -1)
           System.out.write(c);
        s.close();
    }
}
```

First, the Concatenate utility creates a ListOfFiles object named mylist, which is initialized from the command-line arguments entered by the user. The command-line arguments list the files to be concatenated together. mylist is used to initialize the SequenceInputStream. SequenceInputStream then uses mylist to get a new InputStream for every filename listed by the user.

```
import java.util.*;
import java.io.*;

public class ListOfFiles implements Enumeration {

    private String[] listOfFiles;
    private int current = 0;

    public ListOfFiles(String[] listOfFiles) {
        this.listOfFiles = listOfFiles;
    }

    public boolean hasMoreElements() {
        if (current < listOfFiles.length)
            return true;
        else
            return false;
    }

    public Object nextElement() {
```

```
            InputStream in = null;

            if (!hasMoreElements())
                throw new NoSuchElementException("No more files.");
            else {
                String nextElement = listOfFiles[current];
                current++;
                try {
                    in = new FileInputStream(nextElement);
                } catch (FileNotFoundException e) {
                    System.out.println("ListOfFiles: Can't open" +
                                       nextElement);
                }
            }
            return in;
        }
    }
```

`ListOfFiles` implements the `Enumeration`[1] interface. You'll see how this comes into play as you walk through the rest of the program.

After the `main` method creates the `SequenceInputStream`, it reads from that stream one byte at a time. When the `SequenceInputStream` needs an `InputStream` from a new source, such as for the first byte read, or when it runs off the end of the current input stream, it calls `nextElement` on the `Enumeration` object to get the next `InputStream`. `ListOfFiles` creates `FileInputStream` objects lazily. This means that whenever `SequenceInputStream` calls `nextElement`, `ListOfFiles` opens a `FileInputStream` on the next filename in the list and returns the stream. When the `ListOfFiles` object runs out of files to read (it has no more elements), `nextElement` returns `null` and the call to `SequenceInputStream`'s `read` method returns `-1` to indicate the end of input.

`Concatenate` simply echoes all of the data read from the `SequenceInputStream` to the standard output.

Try This: Run `Concatenate` on the `farrago.txt` (page 774) and `words.txt` (page 779) files, both of which are used as input to other examples in this lesson.

Working with Filter Streams

The `java.io` package provides a set of abstract classes that define and partially implement *filter streams*. A filter stream is a stream that filters data as it's being

---

[1] http://java.sun.com/products/jdk/1.1/docs/api/java.util.Enumeration.html

read from or written to the stream. These filter streams are `FilterReader`, `FilterWriter`, `FilterInputStream`, and `FilterOutputStream`.

Filter streams are constructed on another stream (the *underlying* stream). The `read` method in readable filter streams reads input from the underlying stream, filters it, and passes on the filtered data to the caller. The `write` method in writable filter streams filters the data and then writes it to the underlying stream. The filtering done by the streams depends on the stream. Some streams buffer the data, some count data as it goes by, and others convert data to another form.

Most filter streams provided by the `java.io` package are subclasses of `FilterInputStream` and `FilterOutputStream` and are listed here:

- `DataInputStream` and `DataOutputStream`
- `BufferedInputStream` and `BufferedOutputStream`
- `LineNumberInputStream`
- `PushbackInputStream`
- `PrintStream` (This is an output stream.)

The `java.io` package contains only one subclass of `FilterReader`: `PushbackReader`. So this section focuses on filter byte streams.

This section shows you how to use filter streams by presenting an example that uses a `DataInputStream` and a `DataOutputStream`. It also covers how to subclass `FilterInputStream` and `FilterOutputStream` to create your own filter streams.

Using Filter Streams

To use a filter input or output stream, attach the filter stream to another input or output stream. You attach a filter stream to another stream when you create it. For example, you can attach a `DataInputStream` to the standard input stream as in the following code:

```
DataInputStream in = new DataInputStream(System.in);
String input;

while ((input = in.readLine()) != null) {
    . . . // do something interesting here
}
```

You might do this so that you can use the more convenient `read`*`XXX`* methods, such as `readChar`, implemented by `DataInputStream`.

How to Use DataInputStream and DataOutputStream

This section features an example, DataIOTest (page 781), that reads and writes tabular data (invoices for Java merchandise). The tabular data is formatted in columns and each column is separated from the next by tabs. The columns contain the sales price, the number of units ordered, and a description of the item. Conceptually, the data looks like this, although it is read and written in binary form and is non-ASCII:

```
19.99   12      Java T-shirt
9.99    8       Java Mug
```

DataOutputStream, like other filter output streams, must be attached to some other OutputStream. In this case, it's attached to a FileOutputStream that is set up to write to a file named invoice1.txt:

```
DataOutputStream out = new DataOutputStream(new
                                  FileOutputStream("invoice1.txt"));
```

Next, DataIOTest uses DataOutputStream's specialized write*XXX* methods to write the invoice data contained within arrays in the program according to the type of data being written:

```
for (int i = 0; i < prices.length; i ++) {
    out.writeDouble(prices[i]);
    out.writeChar('\t');
    out.writeInt(units[i]);
    out.writeChar('\t');
    out.writeChars(descs[i]);
    out.writeChar('\n');
}
out.close();
```

Note that this code snippet closes the output stream when it's finished.

Next, DataIOTest opens a DataInputStream on the file just written:

```
DataInputStream in = new DataInputStream(new
                                  FileInputStream("invoice1.txt"));
```

DataInputStream also must be attached to some other InputStream, in this case, a FileInputStream set up to read the file just written, invoice1. DataIOTest then just reads the data back in using DataInputStream's specialized read*XXX* methods:

```
try {
    while (true) {
        price = in.readDouble();
        in.readChar();       // throws out the tab
        unit = in.readInt();
        in.readChar();       // throws out the tab
        char chr;
        desc = new StringBuffer(20);
        char lineSep = System.getProperty(
                                "line.separator").charAt(0);
        while ((chr = in.readChar() != lineSep)
            desc.append(chr);
        System.out.println("You've ordered " + unit +
            " units of " + desc + " at $" + price);
        total = total + unit * price;
    }
} catch (EOFException e) {
}
System.out.println("For a TOTAL of: $" + total);
in.close();
```

When all of the data has been read, `DataIOTest` displays a statement summarizing the order and the total amount owed and then closes the stream.

Note the loop that `DataIOTest` uses to read the data from the `DataInputStream`. Normally, when data is read, you see loops like this:

```
while ((input = in.read()) != null) {
    . . .
}
```

The `read` method returns a value, `null`, which indicates the end of the file has been reached. Many of the `DataInputStream` `read`*`XXX`* methods can't do this because any value that could be returned to indicate end-of-file may also be a legitimate value read from the stream. For example, suppose you want to use `-1` to indicate end-of-file. Well, you can't. This is because `-1` is a legitimate value that can be read from the input stream using `readDouble`, `readInt`, or one of the other methods that reads numbers. So `DataInputStream`'s `read`*`XXX`* methods throw an `EOFException` instead. When the `EOFException` occurs, the `while (true)` terminates.

When you run the `DataIOTest` program, you should see the following output:

```
You've ordered 12 units of Java T-shirt at $19.99
You've ordered 8 units of Java Mug at $9.99
You've ordered 13 units of Duke Juggling Dolls at $15.99
You've ordered 29 units of Java Pin at $3.99
You've ordered 50 units of Java Key Chain at $4.99
For a TOTAL of: $892.88
```

How to Write Your Own Filter Streams

Following are the steps to take when you are writing your own filtered input and output streams:

1. Create a subclass of `FilterInputStream` and `FilterOutputStream`. Input and output streams often come in pairs, so it's likely that you will need to create both input and output versions of your filter stream.
2. Override the `read` and `write` methods, and any others, if you need to.
3. Provide any new methods.
4. Make sure the input and output streams work together.

This section shows you how to implement your own filter streams by presenting an example that implements a matched pair of filter input and output streams.

Both the input and the output stream use a checksum class to compute a checksum on the data written to or read from the stream. The checksum is used to determine whether the data read by the input stream matches that written by the output stream.

Four classes and one interface make up this example program:

- The filtered input and output stream subclasses: `CheckedOutputStream` and `CheckedInputStream`
- The `Checksum` interface and the `Adler32` class, which compute a checksum for the streams
- The `CheckedIOTest` class to define the `main` method for the program

Except for `CheckedIOTest`, the classes in this example are based on classes written by David Connelly and are now members of the `java.util.zip` package.

The CheckedOutputStream Class. The `CheckedOutputStream` (page 783) class is a subclass of `FilterOutputStream` that computes a checksum on data as it is being written to the stream. When creating a `CheckedOutputStream`, you must use its only constructor:

```
public CheckedOutputStream(OutputStream out, Checksum cksum) {
    super(out);
    this.cksum = cksum;
}
```

This constructor takes an `OutputStream` argument and a `Checksum` argument. The `OutputStream` argument is the output stream that this `CheckedOutputStream` should filter. The `Checksum` argument is an object that can compute a checksum. `CheckedOutputStream` initializes itself by calling its superclass constructor and initializing a private variable, `cksum`, with the `Checksum` object. The `CheckedOutputStream` uses `cksum` to update the checksum each time data is written to the stream.

`CheckedOutputStream` needs to override `FilterOutputStream`'s `write` methods so that each time the `write` method is called, the checksum is updated. `FilterOutputStream` defines three versions of the `write` method:

1. `write(int` *`i`*`)`
2. `write(byte[]` *`b`*`)`
3. `write(byte[]` *`b`*`, int` *`offset`*`, int` *`length`*`)`

`CheckedOutputStream` overrides all three of these methods by using the following code:

```
public void write(int b) throws IOException {
    out.write(b);
    cksum.update(b);
}

public void write(byte[] b) throws IOException {
    out.write(b, 0, b.length);
    cksum.update(b, 0, b.length);
}

public void write(byte[] b, int off, int len) throws IOException {
    out.write(b, off, len);
    cksum.update(b, off, len);
}
```

The implementations of these three `write` methods are straightforward: Write the data to the output stream that this filter stream is attached to and then update the checksum.

The CheckedInputStream Class. The class CheckedInputStream.java (page 783) is similar to the `CheckedOutputStream` class. A subclass of `Filter-`

`InputStream`, it computes a checksum on data as it is read from the stream. When creating a `CheckedInputStream`, you must use its only constructor:

```
public CheckedInputStream(InputStream in, Checksum cksum) {
    super(in);
    this.cksum = cksum;
}
```

This constructor is similar to `CheckedOutputStream`'s.

Just as `CheckedOutputStream` needed to override `FilterOutputStream`'s `write` methods, `CheckedInputStream` must override `FilterInputStream`'s `read` methods. This is to ensure that each time the `read` method is called, the checksum is updated. As with `FilterOutputStream`, `FilterInputStream` defines three versions of the `read` method. `CheckedInputStream` overrides all of them by using the following code:

```
public int read() throws IOException {
    int b = in.read();
    if (b != -1)
        cksum.update(b);
    return b;
}

public int read(byte[] b) throws IOException {
    int len;
    len = in.read(b, 0, b.length);
    if (len != -1)
        cksum.update(b, 0, b.length);
    return len;
}

public int read(byte[] b, int off, int len) throws IOException {
    len = in.read(b, off, len);
    if (len != -1)
        cksum.update(b, off, len);
    return len;
}
```

The implementations of these three `read` methods are straightforward: Read the data from the input stream to which this filter stream is attached. If any data was actually read, update the checksum.

The Checksum Interface and the Adler32 Class. The interface Checksum.java (page 784) defines four methods for checksum objects to implement. These methods reset, update, and return the checksum value. You could write a Checksum class that computes a specific type of checksum, such as the CRC-32 checksum. Note that inherent in the checksum is the notion of state. The checksum object doesn't just compute a checksum in one pass. Rather, the checksum is updated each time information is read from or written to the stream for which this object computes a checksum. If you want to reuse a checksum object, you must reset it.

For this example, we implemented the checksum Adler32 (page 785), which is almost as reliable as a CRC-32 checksum, but it can be computed much faster.

A Program for Testing. The last class in the example, CheckedIOTest (page 786), contains the main method for the program:

```
import java.io.*;

public class CheckedIOTest {
    public static void main(String[] args) throws IOException {

       Adler32 inChecker = new Adler32();
       Adler32 outChecker = new Adler32();
       CheckedInputStream in = null;
       CheckedOutputStream out = null;

       try {
           in = new CheckedInputStream(
                    new FileInputStream("farrago.txt"),
                    inChecker);
           out = new CheckedOutputStream(
                      new FileOutputStream("outagain.txt"),
                      outChecker);
       } catch (FileNotFoundException e) {
           System.err.println("CheckedIOTest: " + e);
           System.exit(-1);
       } catch (IOException e) {
           System.err.println("CheckedIOTest: " + e);
           System.exit(-1);
       }

       int c;

       while ((c = in.read()) != -1)
          out.write(c);
```

```
            System.out.println("Input stream check sum: " +
                               inChecker.getValue());
            System.out.println("Output stream check sum: " +
                               outChecker.getValue());

            in.close();
            out.close();
        }
    }
```

The main method creates two Adler32 checksum objects, one each for CheckedOutputStream and CheckedInputStream. This example requires two checksum objects. This is because the checksum objects are updated during calls to read and write and those calls occur concurrently.

Next, main opens a CheckedInputStream on a small text file, farrago.txt (page 774). It opens a CheckedOutputStream on an output file named outagain.txt, which doesn't exist until you run the program for the first time.

The main method reads the text from the CheckedInputStream and simply copies it to the CheckedOutputStream. The read and write methods use the Adler32 checksum objects to compute a checksum during reading and writing. After the input file has been completely read and the output file has been completely written, the program prints out the checksum for both the input and output streams (which should match) and then closes them both.

When you run CheckedIOTest, you should see this (or similar) output:

```
Input stream check sum: 736868089
Output stream check sum: 736868089
```

Object Serialization

Two streams in java.io—ObjectInputStream and ObjectOutputStream—are run-of-the-mill byte streams and work like the other input and output streams. However, they are special in that they can read and write objects.

The key to writing an object is to represent its state in a serialized form sufficient to reconstruct the object as it is read. Thus, reading and writing objects is a process called *object serialization*. Object serialization is essential to building all but the most transient applications. You can use object serialization in the following ways:

- Remote Method Invocation (RMI)—communication between objects via sockets.

Note: The client and server programs in one of the online trails, Putting It All Together[1], use RMI to communicate. You can see object serialization used in that example to pass various objects back and forth between the client and server. Refer to the online version of this tutorial for a description of the user of RMI and object serialization in that example.

- Lightweight persistence—the archival of an object for use in a later invocation of the same program.

As a Java programmer, you need to know about object serialization from two points of view. First, you need to know how to serialize objects by writing them to an `ObjectOutputStream` and reading them in again using an `ObjectInputStream`. The next section, Serializing Objects (page 389), shows you how. Second, you will want to know how to write a class so that its instances can be serialized. You can read how to do this in the section after that, Providing Object Serialization for Your Classes (page 391).

Serializing Objects

Reconstructing an object from a stream requires that the object first be written to a stream. So let's start there.

How to Write to an ObjectOutputStream

Writing objects to a stream is a straight-forward process. For example, the following gets the current time in milliseconds by constructing a `Date` object and then serializes that object:

```
FileOutputStream out = new FileOutputStream("theTime");
ObjectOutputStream s = new ObjectOutputStream(out);
s.writeObject("Today");
s.writeObject(new Date());
s.flush();
```

`ObjectOutputStream` is a processing stream, so it must be constructed on another stream. This code constructs an `ObjectOutputStream` on a `FileOutputStream`, thereby serializing the object to a file named `theTime`. Next, the

---

1 http://java.sun.com/docs/books/tutorial/together/index.html

string `Today` and a `Date` object are written to the stream with the `writeObject` method of `ObjectOutputStream`.

If an object refers to other objects, then all of the objects that are reachable from the first must be written at the same time so as to maintain the relationships between them. Thus the `writeObject` method serializes the specified object, traverses its references to other objects recursively, and writes them all.

`ObjectOutputStream` stream implements the `DataOutput` interface that defines many methods for writing primitive data types, such as `writeInt`, `writeFloat`, or `writeUTF`. You can use these methods to write primitive data types to an `ObjectOutputStream`.

The `writeObject` method throws a `NotSerializableException` if it's given an object that is not serializable. An object is serializable only if its class implements the `Serializable` interface.

How to Read from an ObjectOutputStream

Once you've written objects and primitive data types to a stream, you'll likely want to read them out again and reconstruct the objects. This is also straightforward. Here's code that reads in the `String` and the `Date` object that was written to the file named `theTime` in the last example:

```
FileInputStream in = new FileInputStream("theTime");
ObjectInputStream s = new ObjectInputStream(in);
String today = (String)s.readObject();
Date date = (Date)s.readObject();
```

Like `ObjectOutputStream`, `ObjectInputStream` must be constructed on another stream. In this example, the objects were archived in a file, so the code constructs an `ObjectInputStream` on a `FileInputStream`. Next, the code uses `ObjectInputStream`'s `readObject` method to read the `String` and the `Date` objects from the file. The objects must be read from the stream in the same order in which they were written. Note that the return value from `readObject` is an object that is cast to and assigned to a specific type.

The `readObject` method deserializes the next object in the stream and traverses its references to other objects recursively to deserialize all objects that are reachable from it. In this way, it maintains the relationships between the objects.

`ObjectInputStream` stream implements the `DataInput` interface that defines methods for reading primitive data types. The methods in `DataInput` parallel those defined in `DataOutput` for writing primitive data types. They include methods such as `readInt`, `readFloat`, and `readUTF`. Use these methods to read primitive data types from an `ObjectInputStream`.

Providing Object Serialization for Your Classes

An object is serializable only if its class implements the `Serializable` interface. Thus, if you want to serialize the instances of one of your classes, the class must implement the `Serializable` interface. The good news is that `Serializable` is an empty interface. That is, it doesn't contain any method declarations; it's purpose is simply to identify classes whose objects are serializable.

Implementing the Serializable Interface

Here's the complete definition of the `Serializable` interface:

```
package java.io;
public interface Serializable {
    // there's nothing in here!
};
```

Making instances of your classes serializable is easy. You just add the `implements Serializable` clause to your class declaration like this:

```
public class MySerializableClass implements Serializable {
    ...
}
```

You don't have to write any methods. The serialization of instances of this class are handled by the `defaultWriteObject` method of `ObjectOutputStream`. This method automatically writes out everything required to reconstruct an instance of the class, including the following:

- Class of the object
- Class signature
- Values of all non-`transient` and non-`static` members, including members that refer to other objects

For many classes, this default behavior is good enough. However, default serialization can be slow, and a class might want more explicit control over the serialization.

Customizing Serialization

You can customize serialization for your classes by providing two methods for it: `writeObject` and `readObject`. The `writeObject` method controls what information is saved. It is typically used to append additional information to the stream. The `readObject` method either reads the information written by the corresponding `writeObject` method or can be used to update the state of the object after it has been restored

The `writeObject` method must be declared exactly as shown in the following example. Also, it should call the stream's `defaultWriteObject` as the first thing it does to perform default serialization. Any special arrangements can be handled afterwards:

```
private void writeObject(ObjectOutputStream s)
                            throws IOException {
    s.defaultWriteObject();
    // customized serialization code
}
```

The `readObject` method must read in everything written by `writeObject` in the same order in which it was written. Also, the `readObject` method can perform calculations or update the state of the object in some way. Here's the `readObject` method that corresponds to the `writeObject` method just shown:

```
private void readObject(ObjectInputStream s)
                            throws IOException {
    s.defaultReadObject();
    // customized deserialization code
    ...
    // followed by code to update the object, if necessary
}
```

The `readObject` method must be declared exactly as shown.

The `writeObject` and `readObject` methods are responsible for serializing only the immediate class. Any `Serialization` required by the superclasses is handled automatically. However, a class that needs to explicitly coordinate with its superclasses to serialize itself can do so by implementing the `Externalizable` interface.

Implementing the Externalizable Interface

For complete, explicit control of the serialization process, a class must implement the `Externalizable` interface. For `Externalizable` objects, only the identity of the object's class is automatically saved by the stream. The class is responsible for writing and reading its contents, and it must coordinate with its superclasses to do so.

Here's the complete definition of the `Externalizable` interface that extends `Serializable`:

```
package java.io;
public interface Externalizable extends Serializable
{
    public void writeExternal(ObjectOutput out)
                                 throws IOException;
    public void readExternal(ObjectInput in)
                               throws IOException,
                               java.lang.ClassNotFoundException;
}
```

The following holds for an `Externalizable` class:

- It must implement the `java.io.Externalizable` interface.
- It must implement a `writeExternal` method to save the state of the object. Also, it must explicitly coordinate with its supertype to save its state.
- It must implement a `readExternal` method to read the data written by the `writeExternal` method from the stream and restore the state of the object. It must explicitly coordinate with the supertype to restore its state.
- If externally defined format is being written, the `writeExternal` and `readExternal` methods are solely responsible for that format.

The `writeExternal` and `readExternal` methods are public and carry the risk that a client may be able to write or read information in the object other than by using its methods and fields. These methods must be used only when the information held by the object is not sensitive or when exposing that information would not present a security risk.

Protecting Sensitive Information

When developing a class that provides controlled access to resources, you must take care to protect sensitive information and functions. During deserialization, the private state of the object is restored. For example, a file descriptor contains a handle that provides access to an operating system resource. Being able to forge a file descriptor would allow some forms of illegal access, since restoring state is done from a stream. Therefore the serializing runtime must take the conservative approach and not trust the stream to contain only valid representations of objects. To avoid compromising a class, you must provide either that the sensitive state of an object must not be restored from the stream or that it must be reverified by the class.

Several techniques are available to protect sensitive data in classes. The easiest is to mark fields that contain sensitive data as `private transient`. Transient and static fields are not serialized or deserialized. Marking the field will prevent the state from appearing in the stream and from being restored during deserialization. Since writing and reading (of private fields) cannot be superseded outside of the class, the class's transient fields are safe.

Particularly sensitive classes should not be serialized. To accomplish this, the object should not implement either the `Serializable` or `Externalizable` interface.

Some classes may find it beneficial to allow writing and reading but to specifically handle and revalidate the state as it is deserialized. The class should implement `writeObject` and `readObject` methods to save and restore only the appropriate state. If access should be denied, throwing a `NotSerializableException` will prevent further access.

Working with Random Access Files

The input and output streams in this lesson so far have been *sequential access streams*—streams whose contents must be read or written sequentially. While such streams are still incredibly useful, they are a consequence of sequential media such as paper and magnetic tape. A *random access file*, on the other hand, permits nonsequential, or random, access to a file's contents.

So why might you need random access files? Consider the archive format called "ZIP." A ZIP archive contains files and is typically compressed to save space. It also contains a dir-entry at the end that indicates where the various files contained within the ZIP archive begin. This is shown in Figure 60.

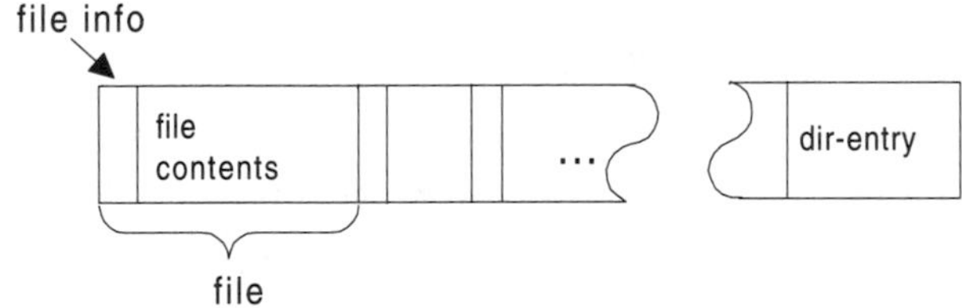

Figure 60: A ZIP archive.

Suppose you want to extract a specific file from a zip archive. If you use a sequential access stream, you have to do the following:

1. Open the ZIP archive.

2. Search through the ZIP archive until you locate the file you want to extract.
3. Extract the file.
4. Close the ZIP archive.

Using this algorithm, you will have to read, on average, half of the ZIP archive before finding the file that you want to extract. You can extract the same file from the ZIP archive more efficiently by using the seek feature of a random access file and following these steps:

1. Open the ZIP archive.
2. Seek to the dir-entry and locate the entry for the file you want to extract from the ZIP archive.
3. Seek (backwards) within the ZIP archive to the position of the file to extract.
4. Extract the file.
5. Close the ZIP archive.

This algorithm is more efficient because you read only the dir-entry and the file that you want to extract.

The `RandomAccessFile`[1] class in the `java.io` package implements a random access file. Unlike the input and output stream classes in `java.io`, `RandomAccessFile` is used for both reading and writing files. You create a `RandomAccessFile` object with different arguments, depending on whether you intend to read or write.

`RandomAccessFile` is somewhat disconnected from the input and output streams in `java.io`, that is, it doesn't inherit from `InputStream` or `OutputStream`. This has some disadvantages in that you can't apply the same filters to `RandomAccessFiles` that you can to streams. However, `RandomAccessFile` does implement the `DataInput` and `DataOutput` interfaces, so if you design a filter that works for either `DataInput` or `DataOutput`, it will work on some sequential access files (the ones that implement `DataInput` or `DataOutput`) as well as on any `RandomAccessFile`.

Using Random Access Files

The `RandomAccessFile` class implements both the `DataInput` and `DataOutput` interfaces and therefore can be used for both reading and writing. `RandomAccessFile` is similar to `FileInputStream` and `FileOutputStream` in that you

---

1 http://java.sun.com/products/jdk/1.1/docs/api/java.io.RandomAccessFile.html

specify a file on the native file system to open when you create it. You can do this with a filename or a `File`[1] object. When you create a `RandomAccessFile`, you must indicate whether you will be just reading the file or also writing to it. (You have to be able to read a file in order to write to it.) The following line of Java code creates a `RandomAccessFile` to read the file named `farrago.txt`:

```
new RandomAccessFile("farrago.txt", "r");
```

This Java statement opens the same file for both reading and writing:

```
new RandomAccessFile("farrago.txt", "rw");
```

After the file has been opened, you can use the common `readXXX` or `writeXXX` methods to perform I/O on the file.

`RandomAccessFile` supports the notion of a *file pointer.* The file pointer indicates the current location in the file as illustrated in Figure 61. When the file is first created, the file pointer is set to 0, indicating the beginning of the file. Calls to the `readXXX` or `writeXXX` methods adjust the file pointer by the number of bytes read or written.

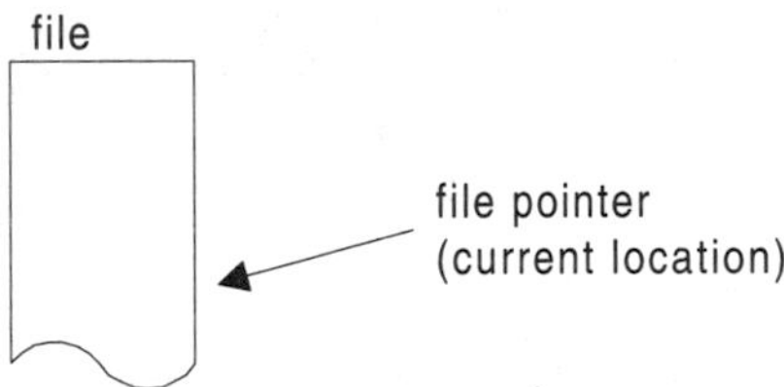

Figure 61: A ZIP file has the notion of a current file pointer.

In addition to the normal file I/O methods for reading and writing that implicitly move the file pointer when the operation occurs, `RandomAccessFile` contains three methods for explicitly manipulating the file pointer:

`skipBytes`
Moves the file pointer forward the specified number of bytes.

`seek`
Positions the file pointer just before the specified byte.

`getFilePointer`
Returns the current byte location of the file pointer.

---

1 http://java.sun.com/products/jdk/1.1/docs/api/java.io.File.html

Writing Filters for Random Access Files

Let's rewrite the example from How to Write Your Own Filter Streams (page 384) so that it works on RandomAccessFiles. Because RandomAccessFile implements the DataInput[1] and DataOutput[2] interfaces, a side benefit is that the filtered stream will also work with other DataInput and DataOutput streams, including some sequential access streams such as DataInputStream and DataOutputStream.

The example CheckedIOTest (page 786) from How to Write Your Own Filter Streams (page 384) implements two filter streams that compute a checksum as data is read from or written to the stream. Those streams are CheckedInputStream (page 783) and CheckedOutputStream (page 783).

In the new example, CheckedDataOutput (page 787) is a rewrite of CheckedOutputStream—it computes a checksum for data written to the stream. However, it operates on DataOutput objects instead of on OutputStreams objects. Similarly, CheckedDataInput (page 788) modifies CheckedInputStream so that it now works on DataInput objects instead of on InputStream objects.

CheckedDataOutput versus CheckedOutputStream

Let's look at how CheckedDataOutput differs from CheckedOutputStream.

The first difference in these two classes is that CheckedDataOutput does *not* extend FilterOutputStream. Instead, it implements the DataOutput interface:

```
public class CheckedDataOutput implements DataOutput
```

Note: To keep the example simple, we did not require that the CheckedDataOutput class in this lesson be declared to implement DataOutput. This was because the DataOutput interface specifies so many methods. However, the CheckedDataOutput class in the example does implement several of DataOutput's methods, to illustrate how it should work.

Next, CheckedDataOutput declares a private variable to hold a DataOutput object:

```
private DataOutput out;
```

This is the object to which data will be written.

---

1 http://java.sun.com/products/jdk/1.1/docs/api/java.io.DataInput.html
2 http://java.sun.com/products/jdk/1.1/docs/api/java.io.DataOutput.html

The constructor for CheckedDataOutput differs from CheckedOutputStream's constructor in that CheckedDataOutput is created on a DataOutput object rather than on an OutputStream:

```
public CheckedDataOutput(DataOutput out, Checksum cksum) {
    this.cksum = cksum;
    this.out = out;
}
```

This constructor does not call super(out) like the CheckedOutputStream constructor did because CheckedDataOutput extends from Object rather than from a stream class.

Those are the only modifications made to CheckedOutputStream to create a filter that works on DataOutput objects.

CheckedDataInput versus CheckedInputStream

CheckedDataInput requires the same changes as CheckedDataOutput, as follows:

- CheckedDataInput does not derive from FilterInputStream. Instead, it implements the DataInput interface.
- CheckedDataInput declares a private variable to hold a DataInput object, which it wraps.
- The constructor for CheckedDataInput requires a DataInput object rather than an InputStream.

In addition to these changes, the read methods are changed. CheckedInputStream from the original example implements two read methods, one for reading a single byte and one for reading a byte array. The DataInput interface has methods that implement the same functionality, but they have different names and different method signatures. Thus the read methods in the CheckedDataInput class have new names and method signatures:

```
public byte readByte() throws IOException {
    byte b = in.readByte();
    cksum.update(b);
    return b;
}

public void readFully(byte[] b) throws IOException {
    in.readFully(b, 0, b.length);
    cksum.update(b, 0, b.length);
}
```

```
public void readFully(byte[] b, int off, int len)
                                throws IOException {
    in.readFully(b, off, len);
    cksum.update(b, off, len);
}
```

Also, the `DataInput` interface declares many other methods that we don't implement for this example.

The Main Programs

Finally, this example has two main programs to test the new filters:

- `CheckedDITest` (page 789), which runs the filters on sequential access files (`DataInputStream` and `DataOutputStream` objects)
- `CheckedRAFTest` (page 790), which runs the filters on random access files (`RandomAccessFile` objects)

These two main programs differ only in the type of object on which they open the checksum filters. `CheckedDITest` creates a `DataInputStream` and `DataOutputStream` and uses the checksum filter on them, as in the following code:

```
in = new CheckedDataInput(new DataInputStream(
        new FileInputStream("farrago.txt")), inChecker);
out = new CheckedDataOutput(new DataOutputStream(
           new FileOutputStream("outagain.txt")), outChecker);
```

`CheckedRAFTest` creates two `RandomAccessFile` objects, one for reading and one for writing, and uses the checksum filter on them:

```
in = new CheckedDataInput(
        new RandomAccessFile("farrago.txt", "r"), inChecker);
out = new CheckedDataOutput(
          new RandomAccessFile("outagain.txt", "rw"),
            outChecker);
```

When you run either of these programs, you should see the following output:

```
Input stream check sum: 736868089
Output stream check sum: 736868089
```

And the Rest . . .

In addition to the classes and interfaces discussed in this lesson, `java.io` contains the following classes and interfaces:

`File`
Represents a file on the native file system. You can create a `File` object for a file on the native file system and then query the object for information about that file (such as its full pathname).

`FileDescriptor`
Represents a file handle (or descriptor) to an open file or an open socket. You will not typically use this class.

`StreamTokenizer`
Breaks the contents of a stream into tokens. Tokens are the smallest unit recognized by a text-parsing algorithm (such as words, symbols, and so on). A `StreamTokenizer` object can be used to parse any text file. For example, you could use it to parse a Java source file into variable names, operators, and so on, or to parse an HTML file into HTML tags.

`FilenameFilter`
Used by the `list` method in the `File` class to determine which files in a directory to list. The `FilenameFilter` accepts or rejects files based on their names. You could use `FilenameFilter` to implement simple regular expression style file search patterns such as `foo`.

You also can find some other input and output streams in the `java.util.zip` package, including these:

`CheckedInputStream` and `CheckedOutputStream`
An input and output stream pair that maintains a checksum as the data is being read or written.

`DeflaterOutputStream` and `InflaterInputStream`
Compresses or uncompresses the data as it is being read or written.

`GZIPInputStream` and `GZIPOutputStream`
Reads and writes compressed data in the GZIP format.

`ZipInputStream` and `ipOutputStream`
Reads and writes compressed data in the ZIP format.

The java.io Classes in Action

Many of the examples in the next trail, Custom Networking (page 581), use the I/O streams described in this lesson to read from and write to `URL`s, `URLConnections`, and `Socket`s.

End of Trail

YOU'VE reached the end of the **Essential Java Classes** trail. Take a break—have a cup of steaming hot java.

What Next?

Once you've caught your breath, you have several choices of where to go next. You can go back to the Trail Map (page xvii) to see all of your choices, or you can go directly to one of the following popular trails:

Writing Applets (page 171): This is the place to read everything about writing applets.

Creating a User Interface (page 403): Once you know how to create applications or applets, follow this trail to read how to create their user interfaces.

Custom Networking (page 581): If you're interested in writing applications or applets that use the network, follow this trail. You'll read about URLs, sockets, datagrams, and multicasting.

http://java.sun.com/docs/books/tutorial/ui/index.html

Creating a User Interface

THIS trail covers everything you need to know to be able to create a user interface (UI) for a Java program.

Note: All the material covered in this trail applies to both applets and applications, except for a few clearly marked exceptions.

Overview of the Java UI (page 407) tells you about the pieces the Java environment provides for building UIs. It introduces you to the graphical UI components and other UI-related classes provided by the Java environment. It also gives an overview of how programs display themselves and how they handle events such as mouse clicks. You should fully understand the information in this lesson before going on to other lessons in this trail.

Using Components, the GUI Building Blocks (page 425) tells you how to use each of the standard UI components and how to implement a custom component. It also has detailed discussions of event handling and the component architecture.

Laying Out Components Within a Container (page 503) tells you how to choose a layout manager, how to use each of the layout manager classes provided by the Java environment, how to use absolute positioning instead of a layout manager, and how to create your own layout manager.

Working with Graphics (page 525) tells you how to do everything from drawing lines and text to loading, displaying, and manipulating images. It includes information on performing animation and on improving graphics performance.

If you have trouble making your program's GUI work well, see **Common Problems (and Their Solutions)** (page 573).

A Note about the Examples: Most of the example programs in this trail are applets. This lets you easily run them just by visiting the relevant pages in the online tutorial. But don't let the fact that the examples are applets confuse you—writing an application with a GUI is similar to writing an applet with a GUI. See page 575 for information on converting an applet into an application.

---

http://java.sun.com/docs/books/Tutorial/ui/overview/index.html

18 Overview of the Java UI

THIS lesson gives an overview of what the Java environment provides to help you create a user interface (UI). *UI* is a broad term that refers to all sorts of communication between a program and its users. UI is not only what the user sees, but what the user hears and feels. Even the speed with which a program interacts with the user is an important part of the program's UI.

The Java environment provides classes for the following UI functionality:

Presenting a graphical UI (GUI)
: This is the preferred UI for most Java programs. This trail concentrates on this topic.

Playing sounds
: Right now, applets can play sounds but applications can't, at least not in a portable way. See Playing Sounds (page 198) for information on playing sounds in applets.

Getting configuration information from the user
: Users can specify configuration information to a program using *command-line arguments* (applications only) and *parameters* (applets only). For information about command line arguments, see Command-Line Arguments (page 264). For information about parameters, see Defining and Using Applet Parameters (page 200).

Saving user preferences using properties
: For information that applications need to save even when they're not running, you can use *properties*. Applets usually can't write properties to the local file system, due to security restrictions. For information on using properties, see System Properties (page 273).

Getting and displaying text using standard input, output, and error streams
Standard input, output, and error are the old-fashioned ways to present a user interface. They still can be useful for testing and debugging programs, as well as for functionality that's not aimed at the typical end user. See The Standard I/O Streams (page 270) for information on using standard input, output, and error.

Applets and applications often present information to the user and invite the user's interaction using a GUI. The part of the Java environment called the Abstract Window Toolkit (AWT) contains a complete set of classes for writing GUI programs.

The AWT provides many standard GUI components such as buttons, lists, menus, and text areas. It also includes containers (such as windows and menu bars) and higher level components (such as a dialog for opening or saving files). AWT Components (page 408) introduces all these AWT-provided components.

Other classes in the AWT include those for working with graphics contexts (including basic drawing operations), images, events, fonts, and colors. Another important group of AWT classes are the layout managers, which manage the size and position of components. Other AWT Classes (page 411) discusses AWT interfaces and classes that aren't components.

The AWT provides a framework for drawing and event handling. The Anatomy of a GUI-Based Program (page 413) explains the AWT architecture by taking you through a program that has a GUI.

AWT Components

The program in the following figure illustrates the graphical UI (GUI) components that the AWT provides. With the exception of menus, every GUI component is implemented with a subclass of the AWT `Component`[1] class.

Implementation Note: The applet has a button that brings up the window showing the components. The window is necessary because the program includes a menu bar, and in 1.1 and earlier releases, menu bars can be used only in windows. If you're curious, look at the source code (page 800) for the window that displays the components. The program has a `main` method so it can run as an application. The `AppletButton` class (page 796) provides an applet framework for the window.

---

[1] http://java.sun.com/products/jdk/1.1/docs/api/java.awt.Component.html

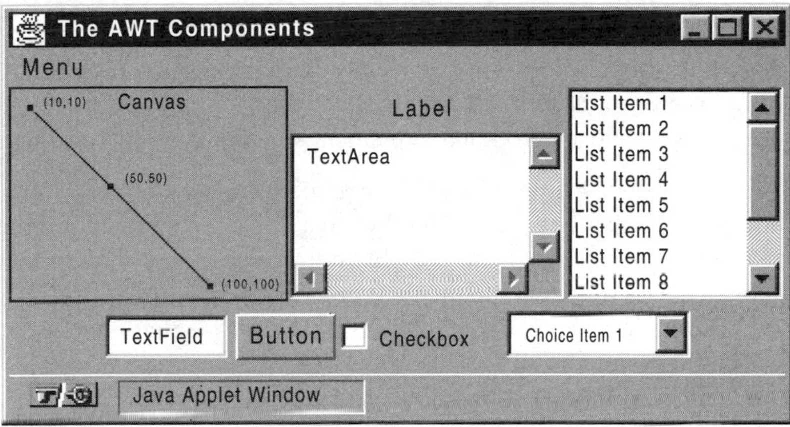

http://java.sun.com/docs/books/tutorial/ui/overview/components.html

The Basic Controls: Buttons, Checkboxes, Choices, Lists, Menus, and Text Fields

The Button (page 430), Checkbox (page 434), Choice (page 436), List (page 444), MenuItem (page 448), and TextField (page 462) classes provide basic controls. These are the most common ways that users give instructions to Java programs. When a user activates one of these controls—by clicking a button or by pressing Return in a text field, for example—it posts an *action event*. See the documentation for each class for examples of handling action events.

Other Ways of Getting User Input: Sliders, Scrollbars, and Text Areas

When the basic controls aren't appropriate, you can sometimes use the Scrollbar (page 457) and TextArea (page 462) classes to get user input. The Scrollbar class is used for both slider and scrollbar functionality. The Anatomy of a GUI-Based Program (page 413) contains an example of sliders. Scrollbars are automatically included in lists and text areas (as shown in the example program) and in ScrollPane (page 459).

The TextArea class provides an area to display or allow editing of several lines of text. As you can see from the example program pictured above, text areas automatically include scrollbars.

Creating Custom Components: Canvases

The `Canvas` class (page 432) lets you write custom components. With your `Canvas` subclass, you can draw custom graphics to the screen—in a paint program, image processor, or game, for example—and implement any kind of event handling.

The 1.1 JDK introduced support for building custom "lightweight" components by extending the `Component` class. However, we don't recommend mixing lightweight components with the "heavyweight" components described in this book. Full support for lightweight components will be in the next major release of the JDK. For information about lightweight components, including how you can download 1.1-compatible, ready-to-use lightweight components, see the Swing discussion in Java Foundation Classes (page 680).

Labels

A `Label` object (page 443) displays an unselectable line of text.

Containers: Windows, Panels, and Scroll Panes

The AWT provides three types of containers, all implemented as subclasses of the `Container`[1] class (which is a `Component` subclass). The `Window` subclasses—`Dialog` (page 438), `FileDialog` (page 438), and `Frame` (page 441)—provide windows to contain components. A `Panel` (page 456) groups components within an area of an existing window. A `ScrollPane` (page 459) is similar to a panel, but its purpose is more specialized: to display a potentially large component in a limited amount of space, generally using scrollbars to control which part of the component is displayed.

`Frame`s create normal, full-fledged windows, as opposed to the windows that `Dialog`s create, which are dependent on `Frame`s and can be modal. When you select the File dialog... item in the menu, the program creates a `FileDialog` object, which is a `Dialog` that can be either an Open or a Save dialog.

Browser Note: Some browsers might not implement the `FileDialog` class if they never allow applets to read or write files on the local file system. Instead of seeing a file dialog, you'll see an error message in the standard output or error stream. See Displaying Diagnostics to the Standard Output and Standard Error Streams (page 216) for information about applets' standard output.

---

1 http://java.sun.com/products/jdk/1.1/docs/api/java.awt.Container.html

Here is a picture of the `FileDialog` window that the Solaris Applet Viewer brings up:

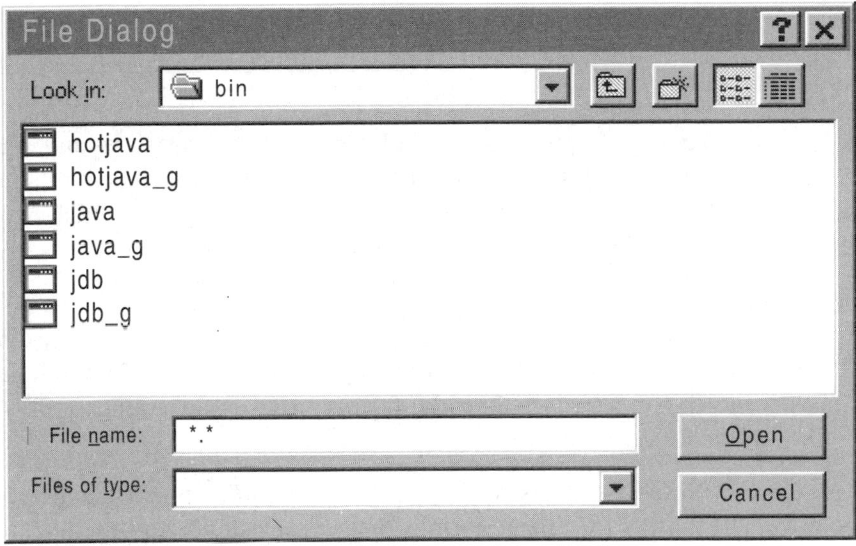

The example program uses a `Panel` to group the label and the text area, another `Panel` to group them with a canvas, and a third `Panel` to group the text field, button, checkbox, and pop-up list of choices. All these `Panels` are grouped by a `Frame` object, which presents the window they're displayed in. The `Frame` also holds a menu and a list.

Summary

This section presented a whirlwind tour of the AWT components. Every component mentioned in this section is described in detail in the lesson Using Components, the GUI Building Blocks (page 425).

Other AWT Classes

The AWT contains more than components. It contains a variety of classes related to drawing and event handling. This section discusses the AWT classes that are in the `java.awt` and `java.awt.event` packages. The AWT contains three other packages—`java.awt.datatransfer`, `java.awt.image`, and `java.awt.peer`—that most programs don't have to use. The classes and interfaces in those packages are discussed as needed elsewhere in this trail.

As you learned in the previous section, components are grouped into containers. What the previous section didn't tell you is that each container uses a *layout manager* to control the on-screen size and position of the components it contains. The `java.awt` package supplies several layout manager classes. You'll learn all about layout managers in the lesson Laying Out Components Within a Container (page 503).

The `java.awt` package supplies several classes to represent sizes and shapes. One is the `Dimension` class, which specifies the size of a rectangular area. Another is the `Insets` class, which is usually used to specify how much padding should exist between the outside edges of a container and the container's display area. Shape classes include `Point`, `Rectangle`, and `Polygon`.

The `Color` class is useful for representing and manipulating colors. It defines constants for commonly used colors, for example, `Color.black`. While it generally uses colors in RGB (red-green-blue) format, it also understands HSB (hue-saturation-brightness) format.

The `Image` class provides a way to represent image data. Applets can get `Image` objects for GIF and JPEG images using the `Applet getImage` methods. Programs that are not applets get images using a different helper class: `Toolkit`. The `Toolkit` class provides a platform-independent interface to the platform-dependent implementation of the AWT. Although that sounds impressive, most programs don't deal with `Toolkit` objects directly, except to get images. Images are loaded asynchronously—you can have a valid `Image` object even if the image data hasn't been loaded yet or doesn't exist. Using a `MediaTracker` object, you can keep track of the status of the image loading. `MediaTracker` currently works only with images, but it might eventually work with other media types, such as sounds. Using Images (page 540) describes how to work with images.

To control the look of the text your program draws, use `Font` and `FontMetrics` objects. The `Font` class lets you get basic information about fonts and create objects representing various fonts. With a `FontMetrics` object, you can get detailed information about the size characteristics of a particular font. You can set the font used by a component using the `Component` and `Graphics setFont` methods. Working with Text (page 534) tells you more about using fonts.

Finally, the `Graphics` class and various types from the `java.awt.event` package are crucial to the AWT drawing and event-handling system. A `Graphics` object represents a drawing context—without a `Graphics` object, no program can draw itself to the screen. The `java.awt.event` package defines classes such as `MouseEvent`, which represents user input made with a mouse or a similar device. You'll learn more about drawing and event handling later in this lesson.

The Anatomy of a GUI-Based Program

This section and the ones that follow pick apart a Java program that has a graphical UI, explaining:

- The classes the program uses
- The program's hierarchy of components
- How components draw themselves
- How events propagate through the hierarchy

The program, which is called Converter, converts distance measurements between metric and U.S. units. If you'd like to look at the complete program, you can find it on page 803. We do *not* expect you to fully understand the source code without reading the rest of this lesson and the relevant pages in Using Components, the GUI Building Blocks (page 425) and Laying Out Components Within a Container (page 503). The following figure shows the program.

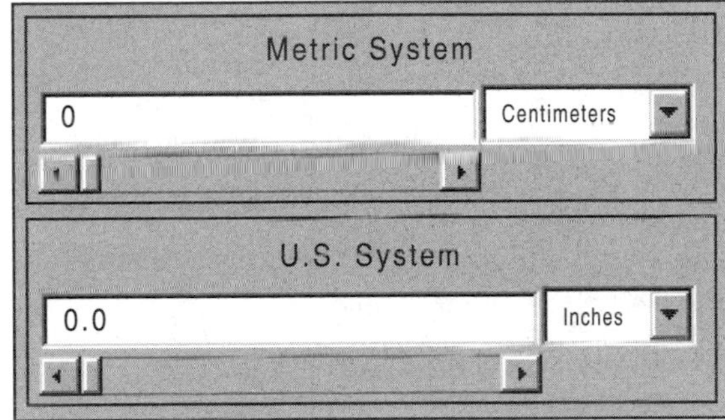

http://java.sun.com/docs/books/tutorial/ui/overview/anatomy.html

The Converter program defines four classes and creates instances of several classes that the AWT provides. One of its custom classes is an `Applet` subclass, which lets the program run as an applet. The Converter program creates components to provide basic controls so that the user can interact with it. Using containers and layout managers, it groups the components. Classes in the Example Program (page 414) describes all the classes that the Converter program uses.

The components in the Converter program are arranged in a hierarchy, with containers defining the structure of the hierarchy. The Containment Hierarchy (page 416) describes how component hierarchies work, as well as the specific hierarchy of the Converter program.

Drawing (page 418) describes how components get drawn and how to perform custom drawing.

User actions result in events, which are delivered to objects that are registered as event listeners. Event Handling (page 420) describes in detail how event handling works, and how the Converter program handles events.

Classes in the Example Program

The Converter program (page 803) defines three classes that inherit from AWT classes. It also defines a data-storing class. However, most of the objects in the program are instances of AWT classes.

Figure 62 shows the Converter program's GUI. Each visible feature is labeled with the class that implements the feature. For example, the `Converter` class implements the object that draws the external box, and which contains every component in the program's GUI. The `Converter` class also happens to implement many features that aren't visible in the snapshot, such as the `main` method that allows the program to run as an application.

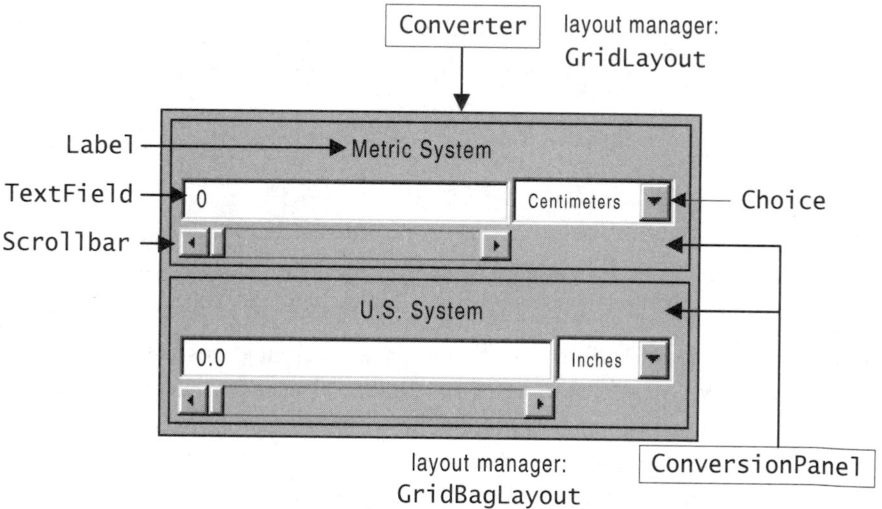

Figure 62: The Converter program's GUI, with visible features labeled.

This section tells you about every object the program creates. Don't worry—we don't expect you to understand everything yet. We just want to convey to you the kinds of objects a GUI program might use.

Classes Defined in the Example Program

The Converter program defines two Panel subclasses (Converter and ConversionPanel), a simple class named Unit, and a class that handles window events.

The Converter class is the heart of the Converter program. It contains the program's main method, which is called if the program is run as an application. The Converter class also contains initialization and startup code, which is called either by the main method or by the application that loads that program as an applet. The Converter class actually extends the Applet class (which itself extends Panel), instead of directly extending Panel. This is necessary because all applets must contain an Applet subclass. However, since the Converter program can also run as an application, the Converter class cannot use any functionality provided by the Applet class. In other words, the Converter class must be implemented as if it extends Panel.

The ConversionPanel class provides a way to group all the controls that describe a particular set of distance measurements. The Converter program creates two ConversionPanel objects, one for metric distance measurements, and the other for U.S. distance measurements.

The Unit class provides objects that group a description (such as "Centimeters") with a multiplier that indicates the number of units per meter (0.01, for example).

When the Converter program is run as an application, it creates an event-handling object (an instance of an anonymous inner class) to help make the application window work correctly.

AWT Objects in the Example Program

The Converter program uses several layout managers, containers, and components provided by the AWT package. It also creates two Insets objects and two GridBagConstraints objects.

The Converter program creates three objects that conform to the LayoutManager interface: a GridLayout and two GridBagLayouts. The GridLayout object manages the layout of the components in the Converter instance. Each ConversionPanel uses a GridBagLayout object to manage its components, and a GridBagConstraints object to specify how to lay out each component. In addition, if the program is run as an application, the program creates a Frame object (the application's window), which is automatically initialized to use the default layout manager for windows: a BorderLayout object.

All the components in the Converter program that are not containers are created by ConversionPanel. Each ConversionPanel contains one instance each of the AWT Label, Choice, TextField, and Scrollbar classes.

Both the Converter and the ConversionPanel classes create Insets instances that specify the padding that should appear around their on-screen representations.

The Containment Hierarchy

The Converter program has several levels in its component containment hierarchy. The parent of each level is a Container (which inherits from Component). Figure 63 shows the hierarchy.

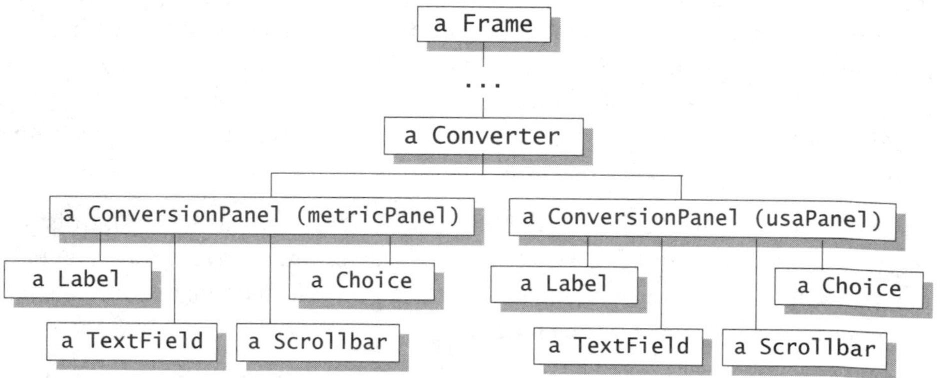

Figure 63: The Converter program's containment hierarchy.

Explanation

At the top of the hierarchy is the window (Frame object) that displays the program. When the Converter program runs as an application, the Frame is created in the program's main method. When the program runs as an applet within a browser, the Frame is the existing browser window.

Under the Frame is a Converter object, which inherits from Applet and thus is a Container. Depending on which viewer the applet is displayed in, one or more Container objects might be between the Converter object and the Frame at the top of the containment hierarchy.

Directly under the Converter object are two ConversionPanels. The following code puts them under the Converter, using the add method. Converter inherits the add method from the Container class.

```
public class Converter extends Applet {
    . . .
    public void init() {
        ...//Create metricPanel and usaPanel, two
                //ConversionPanels.
        //Add metricPanel to this Converter instance:
```

```
        add(metricPanel);
        //Add usaPanel to this Converter instance:
        add(usaPanel);
        . . .
    }
```

Each `ConversionPanel` has four children: a `Label`, a `TextField`, a `Scrollbar`, and a `Choice`. Here's the code that adds the children:

```
class ConversionPanel extends Panel ... {
    . . .
    ConversionPanel(Converter myController, String myTitle,
                    Unit myUnits[]) {
        . . .
        //Add the label.  It displays this panel's title,
        //centered.
        Label label = new Label(myTitle, Label.CENTER);
        ...//Set up GridBagConstraints for this Component.
        gridbag.setConstraints(label, c);
        add(label);

        //Add the text field.  It initially displays "0" and
        //needs to be at least 10 columns wide.
        textField = new TextField("0", 10);
        ...//Set up GridBagConstraints for this Component.
        gridbag.setConstraints(textField, c);
        add(textField);

        //Add the pop-up list (Choice).
        unitChooser = new Choice();
        ...//Populate it with items.
        ...//Set up GridBagConstraints for this Component.
        gridbag.setConstraints(unitChooser, c);
        add(unitChooser);

        //Add the slider...
        slider = new Scrollbar(Scrollbar.HORIZONTAL);
        ...//Initialize the scrollbar.
        ...//Set up GridBagConstraints for this Component.
        gridbag.setConstraints(slider, c);
        add(slider);
        ...
    }
}
```

`GridBagConstraints` is an object that tells the `GridBagLayout` (the layout manager for each `ConversionPanel`) how to place a particular component. `GridBag-`

Layout, along with the other AWT layout managers, is discussed in the lesson Laying Out Components Within a Container (page 503).

Summary

The Converter program's containment hierarchy contains eight non-container components—components that present the graphical UI of the program. These are the labels, text fields, choices, and scrollbars the program displays. There might be additional components such as window controls under the Frame.

This program's containment hierarchy has at least four containers—a Frame object (window), a Converter object (a custom kind of Panel), and two ConversionPanel objects (instances of other custom Panel).

Note that if we add a window—for example, a new Frame that contains a Converter instance that handles volume conversion—the new window will have its own containment hierarchy, unattached to the hierarchy this lesson presents.

Drawing

When a Java program with a GUI needs to draw itself—whether for the first time, or in response to becoming unhidden, or because its appearance needs to change to reflect something happening inside the program—the drawing is orchestrated by the AWT drawing system.

The containment hierarchy affects the components' positions and sizes. Specifically, the container that a component is in helps determine the component's size and position, subject to the container's layout manager and the space allotted to the container.

The containment hierarchy does *not*, however, guarantee the order of drawing. For example, redrawing a container doesn't guarantee that its children will be redrawn.

How Drawing Requests Occur

Programs can draw only when the AWT tells them to. This restriction exists because each occurrence of a component drawing itself must execute without interruption. Otherwise, unpredictable results could occur, such as a button being drawn halfway and then being interrupted by some lengthy animation. The AWT orders drawing requests by making them run in a single thread. Programs use the Component repaint method to request that a component be scheduled for drawing.

The only components you need to invoke the repaint method on are custom components—instances of Canvas, Panel, or Applet subclasses that implement custom drawing code. You don't need to invoke `repaint` on standard AWT components, such as buttons and text fields, since they're painted automatically by platform-dependent code.

The AWT responds to a repaint request by invoking the specified component's `update` method. The default (`Component`) implementation of the `update` method simply clears the component's background (drawing a rectangle over the component's clipping area in the component's background color) and then calls the component's `paint` method. The default implementation of the `paint` method does nothing.

The Graphics Object

The only argument to the `paint` and `update` methods is a `Graphics` object that represents the context in which the component can perform its drawing. The `Graphics` class provides methods for the following:

- Drawing and filling rectangles, arcs, lines, ovals, polygons, text, and images
- Getting or setting the current color, font, or clipping area
- Setting the paint mode

How to Draw

The simplest way for a custom component to draw itself is to put drawing code in its `paint` method. This means that when the AWT makes a drawing request (by calling the component's `update` method), the component's entire area is cleared and then its `paint` method is called. For programs that don't repaint themselves often, the performance of this scheme is fine.

The following example implements the `paint` method. Both the `Converter` and `ConversionPanel` classes draw a box around their area using this code. Both classes also implement a `getInsets` method that specifies the padding around the panels' contents. If they didn't have this method, the box drawn in the `paint` method would overlap the external boundaries of the panels' contents.

```
public void paint(Graphics g) {
    Dimension d = getSize();
    g.drawRect(0,0, d.width - 1, d.height - 1);
}
```

Programs that repaint themselves often can use two techniques to improve their performance: implementing both `update` and `paint`, and using double buffering. These techniques are discussed in Eliminating Flashing (page 561).

For more information on how to draw, see Working with Graphics (page 525).

Event Handling

When the user acts on a component—clicking it or pressing the Return key, for example—the AWT detects the event and notifies any interested objects about the event. The interested objects, which are called *event listeners*, contain code that reacts appropriately to the event. For example, a button might have an event listener that fetches data whenever the user clicks the button.

Note: The event-handling scheme described in this section was introduced in the 1.1 release of the JDK. This scheme is more flexible, powerful, and easy to use than the previous scheme, but it does not work in earlier Java environments. If your programs need to work in 1.0 systems—for example, if you're writing an applet that you want to work even in old browsers—then you should use the 1.0 scheme. You can find the 1.0 event scheme described in How to Convert Code that Uses the AWT (page 655).

An event listener can be an instance of any class. As long as a class implements the appropriate listener interface, its instances can register as event listeners. Here are the three steps for implementing and registering an event listener:

1. In the `class` statement of the event listener, declare that the class implements a listener interface or extends a class that implements a listener interface. For example:

   ```
   public class MyClass implements ActionListener {
   ```

2. In the same class, implement the necessary listener methods. For example:

   ```
   public void actionPerformed(ActionEvent e) {
       ...//code that reacts to a button click...
   }
   ```

3. Register an instance of the class as a listener upon one or more components.

   ```
   someComponent.addActionListener(instanceOfMyClass);
   ```

A Simple Example

Here is a bare-bones applet that illustrates event handling. It contains a single button that beeps when you click it.

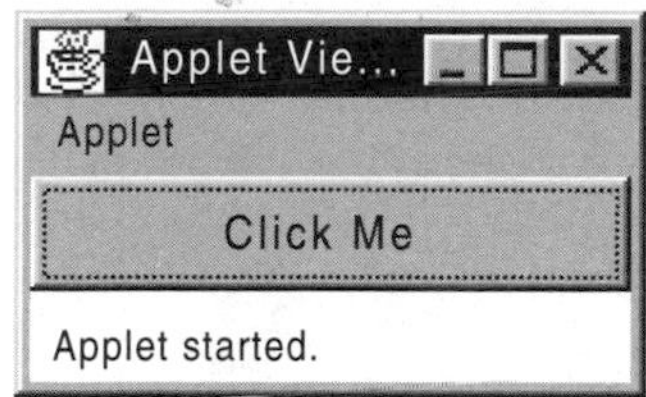

http://java.sun.com/docs/books/tutorial/ui/overview/event.html

You can find the entire program in Beeper.java (page 809). The following code implements the event handling for the button.

```
public class Beeper ... implements ActionListener {
    ...
    //where initialization occurs:
        button.addActionListener(this);
    ...
    public void actionPerformed(ActionEvent e) {
        ...//Make a beep sound...
    }
}
```

Isn't that simple? The Beeper class implements the ActionListener interface, which contains one method: actionPerformed. Since Beeper implements ActionListener, a Beeper object can register as a listener for the action events that buttons generate. Once the Beeper has been registered using the Button addActionListener method, the Beeper's actionPerformed method is called every time the button is clicked.

Standard AWT Events

The AWT defines nearly a dozen kinds of event listeners. You can tell what kinds of events a component can generate by looking at the kinds of event listeners you can register on it. For example, the Component class defines these listener registration methods:

- addComponentListener
- addFocusListener
- addKeyListener
- addMouseListener
- addMouseMotionListener

Thus, every class that inherits from Component supports component, focus, key, mouse, and mouse-motion listeners. However, most Component instances don't

generate these events; a component generates only those events for which listeners have registered on it. For example, if a mouse listener is registered on a particular component, but the component has no other listeners, then the component will generate only mouse events—no component, focus, key, or mouse-motion events.

Here's an overview of the events the AWT defines:

- *Action events*—Buttons and other simple components generate these to indicate that the user wants an action to occur.
- *Adjustment events*—Generated by scrollbars when their values change.
- *Component events*—Can be generated by any `Component` to notify listeners of changes in the component's size, position, or visibility.
- *Container events*—Can be generated by any `Container` to notify listeners that a component has been added to or removed from the container.
- *Focus events*—Can be generated by any `Component` to notify listeners that the component gained or lost the ability to receive keyboard input.
- *Item events*—Generated by checkboxes, pop-up lists of choices, and scrolling lists to indicate that the user has made a choice.
- *Key events*—Can be generated by any `Component` with the current keyboard focus. Notifies the listener of key presses.
- *Mouse events*—Can be generated by any `Component` to notify listeners of mouse clicks and the user moving the cursor into or out of the component's drawing area.
- *Mouse-motion events*—Can be generated by any `Component` to notify listeners of changes in the cursor's position over the component.
- *Text events*—Generated by text components when the text value changes.
- *Window events*—Generated by windows when they're opened, closed, iconified, deiconified, activated, and deactivated.

Writing Event Handlers (page 464) describes each kind of event in detail. You can see examples of handling events both in that section and elsewhere in the lesson Using Components, the GUI Building Blocks (page 425).

Event Handling in the Converter Program

In the Converter program, all the event handling is performed by `ConversionPanel` objects. The `ConversionPanel` class implements the `ActionListener` interface so that `ConversionPanels` can listen to their text fields (`TextField`). `ConversionPanel` also implements `ItemListener` so its instances can listen for pop-up list (`Choice`) changes. To catch events resulting from user actions on the slider (`Scrollbar`), `ConversionPanel` implements the `AdjustmentListener` interface.

Here is the event-handling code from `ConversionPanel`:

```
class ConversionPanel extends Panel
                      implements ActionListener,
                                 AdjustmentListener,
                                 ItemListener {
    TextField textField;
    Choice unitChooser;
    Scrollbar slider;

        ...//in initialization code...
        textField.addActionListener(this);
        ...
        unitChooser.addItemListener(this);
        ...
        slider.addAdjustmentListener(this);
    . . .

    public void actionPerformed(ActionEvent e) {
        setSliderValue(getValue());
        controller.convert(this);
    }

    public void adjustmentValueChanged(AdjustmentEvent e) {
        textField.setText(String.valueOf(e.getValue()));
        controller.convert(this);
    }

    public void itemStateChanged(ItemEvent e) {
        controller.convert(this);
    }
```

The code for each event-handling method simply makes sure that the `ConversionPanel`'s slider and text field both show the same value, and then asks the `Converter` object to update the other `ConversionPanel`.

http://java.sun.com/docs/books/tutorial/ui/components/index.html

19 Using Components, the GUI Building Blocks

THIS lesson describes every component the AWT offers, including the `Canvas` class, which you can use to build your own custom components. This lesson also describes the AWT component architecture.

Start at Using the AWT Components (page 425) to learn the general rules of using components, as well as details on how to use each component the AWT provides.

The next section, Writing Event Handlers (page 464), gives an overview of and general tips on writing event handlers. It then goes on to give details about each kind of event handler you might need to implement.

Details of the Component Architecture (page 501) tells you about peers. A *peer* is an object that provides the look (and part of the feel) for standard components. You usually don't need to know about peer objects, since they're specific to platform implementations. However, sometimes knowing about peers can help you find bugs in event-handling, drawing, or layout code.

Using the AWT Components

Figures 64 and 65 show the inheritance hierarchies for all the AWT component classes. As these figures show, all components except for menu-related components inherit from the AWT `Component` class. Because of cross-platform restrictions such as the inability to set menu background colors, menu-related components aren't full-blown `Component` objects. Instead, menu components inherit from the AWT `MenuComponent` class.

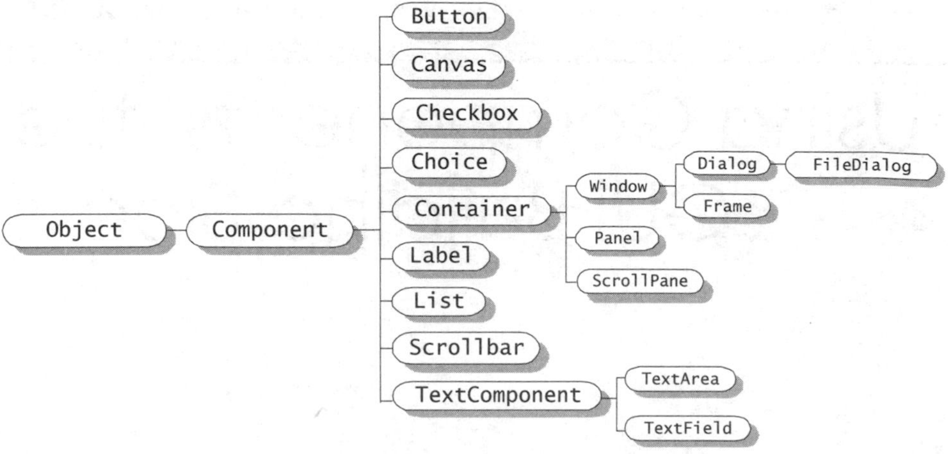

Figure 64: The AWT components that are descendants of `Component`.

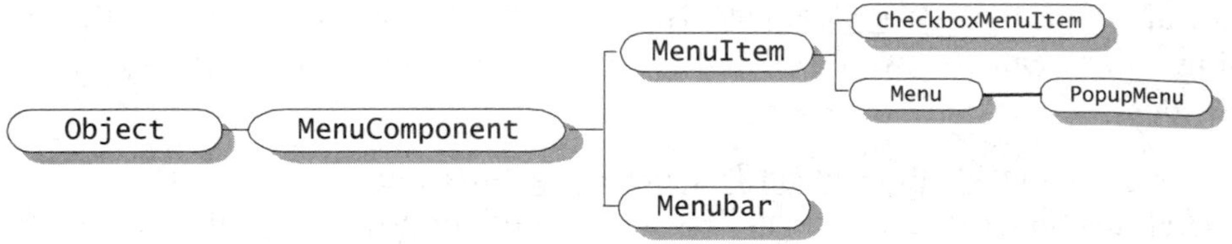

Figure 65: The AWT components that are descendants of `MenuComponent`.

General Rules for Using Components (page 427) tells you what the `Component` class provides and how you can customize components.

The next few sections tells you how to use the components that the AWT provides. Each kind of component has its own section:

- How to Use Buttons (page 430)
- How to Use Canvases (page 432)
- How to Use Checkboxes (page 434)
- How to Use Choices (page 436)
- How to Use Dialogs (page 438)
- How to Use Frames (page 441)
- How to Use Labels (page 443)

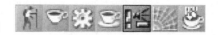

General Rules for Using Components

This section describes what components have in common. It tells you how to add a component to a container. It tells you what functionality components inherit from the `Component` class. It also tells you how you can change the look and feel of components.

How to Add a Component to a Container

As you read on in this lesson, you'll notice code that adds components to containers. This is because for any `Component` object except a `Window` to display itself on screen, you must first add it to a `Container` object. This `Container` is itself a `Component`, and is likely to be added to another `Container`. `Windows` such as `Frames` and `Dialogs` are the top-level containers; they're the only components that aren't added to containers.

To add a component to a container, use one of the several forms of the `Container`[1] add method. Which form you need to use depends on the layout manager the container is using. You'll learn all about layout managers in a later lesson. Right now, we're teaching you just enough to be able to read the code excerpts in this lesson.

Some layout managers require just one argument to the `add` method: the component to add. The `FlowLayout` (page 511), `GridLayout` (page 512), and `GridBagLayout` (page 513) layout managers provided with the AWT all work this way. Here's an example of adding a component to a container that uses `FlowLayout`:

```
container.add(component);
```

Some layout managers require that you specify a string when adding a component. For example, `BorderLayout` (page 508), the default layout manager for `Window` subclasses, requires that you specify "North," "South," "East," "West," or "Center." `CardLayout` (page 509) simply requires that you specify a string

---

1 http://java.sun.com/products/jdk/1.1/docs/api/java.awt.Container.html

that somehow identifies the component being added. Here's an example of adding a component to a container that uses `BorderLayout`:

```
container.add("North", component);
```

Note: Adding a component to a container removes the component from the container it used to be in (if any). For this reason, you can't have one component in two containers, even if the two containers are never shown at the same time.

What the Component Class Provides

All components except menus are implemented as subclasses of the `Component`[1] class. From `Component`, they inherit a huge amount of functionality. By now, you should know that the `Component` class provides the basis for all drawing. Here's a more complete list of the functionality that the `Component` class provides:

Basic drawing support
: `Component` provides the `paint`, `update`, and `repaint` methods, which enable custom components to draw themselves on screen. See Drawing (page 418) for more information.

Event handling
: `Component` supports several kinds of events and has support for keyboard focus, which enables keyboard control of components. See Writing Event Handlers (page 464) for more information.

Appearance control: font
: `Component` provides methods to get and set the current font, and to get information about the current font. See Working with Text (page 534) for information.

Appearance control: color
: `Component` provides the following methods to get and set the foreground and background colors: `setForeground(Color)`, `getForeground()`, `setBackground(Color)`, and `getBackground()`. The foreground color is the color used for all text in the component, as well as for any custom drawing the component performs. The background color is the color behind the text or graphics. For the sake of readability, the background color should contrast with the foreground color.

Appearance control: visibility
: `Component` provides the `setVisible(boolean)` method, which makes the receiving component visible or invisible. Except for `Windows`, components

---

[1] http://java.sun.com/products/jdk/1.1/docs/api/java.awt.Component.html

are generally created visible by default. However, a component can't be drawn on-screen unless its container and all containers above it are in the visible state.

Enabling and disabling components

`Component` provides the `setEnabled(boolean)` method, which enables or disables the receiving component. A disabled component is unresponsive to user input and, in general, looks different from an enabled component.

Image handling

`Component` provides the basis for displaying images. Note that most components can't display images, since their appearance is implemented in platform-specific code. `Canvas` objects and most `Container` objects, however, *can* display images. See Using Images (page 540) for information on working with images.

Cursors

The `Component` `setCursor` and `getCursor` methods set or get the image used while the mouse cursor is over the component. The image is specified as a `Cursor` object. The `Cursor` `getDefaultCursor` method returns the normal cursor for the component. The `Cursor` `getPredefinedCursor` method returns a `Cursor` object corresponding to the specified `Cursor` constant: `CROSSHAIR_CURSOR`, `DEFAULT_CURSOR`, `HAND_CURSOR`, `MOVE_CURSOR`, `TEXT_CURSOR`, `WAIT_CURSOR`, or `X_RESIZE_CURSOR`, where *X* is `SW`, `SE`, `NW`, `NE`, `N`, `S`, `W`, or `E`.

On-screen size and position control

All component sizes and positions (except for those of `Windows`) are subject to the whims of layout managers. Nonetheless, every component has at least some say in its size, if not its position. The `getPreferredSize`, `getMinimumSize`, and `getMaximumSize` methods allow a component to inform a layout manager of the component's preferred, minimum, and maximum sizes. `Component` also provides methods that get or set (subject to layout manager oversight) the component's current size and location. Finally, the `Component` `setVisible` method determines if the component is visible on screen.

Lightweight components

By directly creating a subclass of `Component` or `Container`, you can create a *lightweight component*—a component that has no platform-specific implementation. This book doesn't cover lightweight components, partly because mixing the standard 1.1 components and lightweight components doesn't work very well, and partly because the next release will contain much more support for lightweight components. See the Swing discussion in Java Foundation Classes (page 680) for more information about lightweight components.

How to Change the Appearance and Behavior of Components.

The appearance of most components is platform-specific. Buttons look different on Motif systems than on Mac OS systems, for example. The following figure shows first a Motif button and then its Mac OS equivalent.

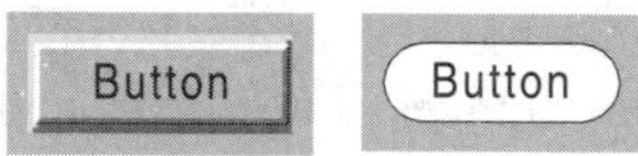

Figure 66: The same Java code results in different looks on different platforms.

You can't easily change most components' appearance in any major way. You can make some minor appearance changes, such as changing the font and the background color, by using the appearance-affecting methods and variables provided by a component's class and superclasses. However, you can't completely change a standard component's appearance, since its platform-specific implementation overrides any drawing the component performs. To change a component's appearance, you must implement a `Canvas` subclass that has the look you want but the behavior that users expect from the component.

Although you can't easily make a major change to a component's appearance, you *can* change component behavior. For example, you can implement a class (perhaps a `TextField` subclass) that makes a text field accept only numeric values. The class might implement this behavior by examining all key events for the text field, detecting and destroying (*consuming*) any that aren't valid. This is possible because event listeners see input events on a component before the component sees the input. See Writing Event Handlers (page 464) for details.

How to Use Buttons

The `Button`[1] class provides a default button implementation. A button is a simple control that generates an action event when the user clicks it.

The on-screen appearance of `Buttons` depends on the platform they're running on and on whether the button is enabled. If you want your program's buttons to look the same for every platform or to otherwise have a special look, you should create a `Canvas` subclass (page 432) to implement this look; you can't change the

---

1 http://java.sun.com/products/jdk/1.1/docs/api/java.awt.Button.html

look using a `Button` subclass. The only facets of a `Button`'s appearance that you can change without creating your own class are the font and text it displays, its foreground and background colors, and (using the `setEnabled` method) whether the button looks enabled or disabled.

The applet in the following figure displays three buttons. When you click the left button, it disables the middle button (and itself, since it's no longer useful) and enables the right button. When you click the right button, it enables the middle button and the left button, and disables itself.

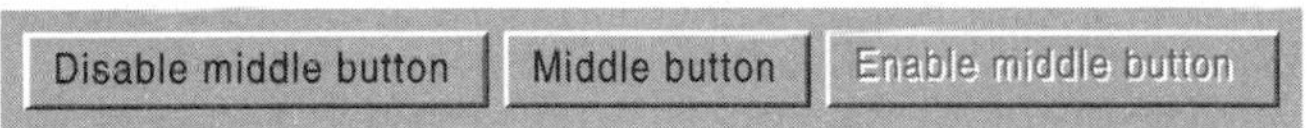

http://java.sun.com/docs/books/tutorial/ui/components/button.html

The following code creates the buttons and reacts to button clicks. You can find the complete program on page 810.

```
public class ButtonDemo ... implements ActionListener  {
    static final String DISABLE = "disable";
    static final String ENABLE = "enable";
    ...//In initialization code:
        b1 = new Button();
        b1.setLabel("Disable middle button");
        b1.setActionCommand(DISABLE);

        b2 = new Button("Middle button");

        b3 = new Button("Enable middle button");
        b3.setEnabled(false);
        b3.setActionCommand(ENABLE);

        //Listen for actions on buttons 1 and 3.
        b1.addActionListener(this);
        b3.addActionListener(this);
    . . .
    public void actionPerformed(ActionEvent e) {
        String command = e.getActionCommand();

        if (command == DISABLE) { //They clicked "Disable..."
            b2.setEnabled(false);
            b1.setEnabled(false);
            b3.setEnabled(true);
        } else { //They clicked "Enable..."
            b2.setEnabled(true);
```

```
            b1.setEnabled(true);
            b3.setEnabled(false);
        }
    }
```

The actionPerformed method in the previous example handles the action events that the buttons generate. For general information about action events, see How to Write an Action Listener (page 470).

In addition to the setLabel, setActionCommand, and setActionListener methods used in the previous example, Button defines getLabel and getActionCommand methods.

How to Use Canvases

The Canvas[1] class exists to be subclassed. It does nothing on its own; it merely provides a way for you to implement a custom component. For example, Canvas objects are useful as display areas for images and custom graphics, whether or not you wish to handle events that occur within the display area.

Canvas objects are also useful when you want a control—a button, for example—that doesn't look like the default implementation of the control. Since you can't change a standard control's appearance by subclassing its corresponding Component (Button, for example), you must instead implement a Canvas subclass to have both the look you want and the same behavior as the default implementation of the control.

When implementing a Canvas subclass, take care to implement the getMinimumSize, and getPreferredSize methods to properly reflect your canvas's size. Otherwise, depending on the layout your canvas's container uses, your canvas could end up too small, perhaps even invisible.

Also take care that the Canvas is repainted whenever its appearance should change. You can do this either by calling the repaint method in the Canvas subclass or by invoking repaint on the Canvas object from another object in the same program.

The applet shown on the next page uses two instances of a Canvas subclass: ImageCanvas.

The code for ImageCanvas follows. (You can find the complete program on page 876.) Because image data is downloaded asynchronously, an ImageCanvas doesn't know how big it should be until some time after it's created. For this rea-

1 http://java.sun.com/products/jdk/1.1/docs/api/java.awt.Canvas.html

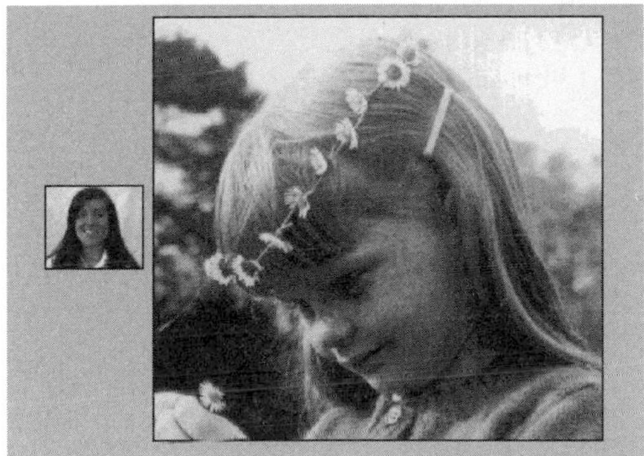

http://java.sun.com/docs/books/tutorial/ui/components/canvas.html

son, `ImageCanvas` uses the initial width and height suggested by its creator until the image size data is available. When the image size data becomes available, the `ImageCanvas` changes the size that its `getPreferredSize` and `getMinimumSize`, methods return, attempts to resize itself, and then requests that its top-level container's layout be adjusted accordingly and redisplayed.

```
class ImageCanvas extends Canvas {
    Container pappy;
    Image image;
    Dimension size;
    int w, h;
    boolean trueSizeKnown;
    MediaTracker tracker;

   public ImageCanvas(Image image, Container highestContainer,
                      int initialWidth, int initialHeight) {
        ...
        this.pappy = highestContainer;

        w = initialWidth;
        h = initialHeight;
        ...
        size = new Dimension(w,h);
    }

    public Dimension getPreferredSize() {
        return getMinimumSize();
    }

    public Dimension getMinimumSize() {
        return size;
    }
```

```
public void paint (Graphics g) {
        if (image != null) {
            if (!trueSizeKnown) {
                ...//Get the image size...

                //Component-initiated resizing.
                if (((imageWidth > 0) && (w != imageWidth)) ||
                   ((imageHeight > 0) && (h != imageHeight))) {
                     w = imageWidth;
                     h = imageHeight;
                     size = new Dimension(w,h);
                     setSize(w, h);
                     pappy.validate();
                }
            }
        }
        ...//Draw the image...
    }
}
```

For an example of implementing a Canvas that both draws custom graphics and handles events, see the RectangleDemo applet in Drawing Shapes (page 528). For another example of an image-displaying canvas, see How to Use Scrollbars (page 457). For more information on drawing graphics, see Working with Graphics (page 525). The MediaTracker class used in this example is discussed in Improving the Appearance and Performance of Image Animation (page 568).

How to Use Checkboxes

The Checkbox[1] class provides *checkboxes*—two-state buttons that can be either "on" or "off." When the user clicks a checkbox, the checkbox state changes and it generates an item event. Other ways of providing groups of items the user can select are reviewed in choices (page 436), lists (page 444), and menus (page 448).

If you want a group of checkboxes in which only one checkbox at a time can be "on," you can add a CheckboxGroup[2] object to oversee the state of the checkboxes. (You might know the resulting UI elements as *radio buttons*.)

The applet in the following two figures has two columns of checkboxes. On the left are three independent checkboxes. You can select all three of the checkboxes, if you like. The three checkboxes on the right are coordinated by a CheckboxGroup object. The CheckboxGroup ensures that no more than one of its

[1] http://java.sun.com/products/jdk/1.1/docs/api/java.awt.Checkbox.html

[2] http://java.sun.com/products/jdk/1.1/docs/api/java.awt.CheckboxGroup.html

checkboxes is selected at a time. To be specific, a checkbox group can come up with no checkboxes selected, but once the user selects a checkbox, exactly one of the checkboxes will be selected forever after.

Here's how the applet looks when it first comes up:

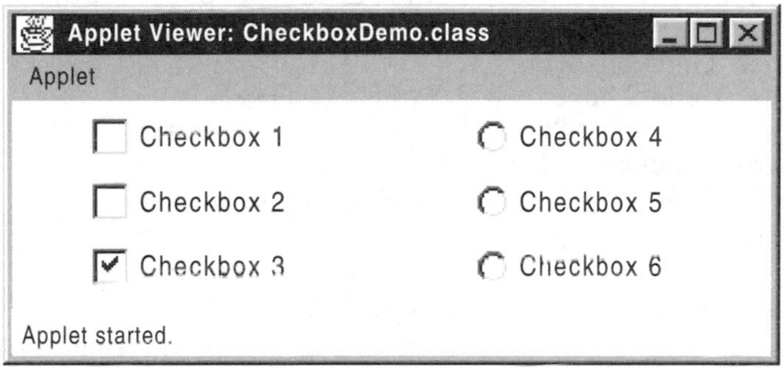

http://java.sun.com/docs/books/tutorial/ui/components/checkbox.html

Here's how the applet looks after the user clicks Checkbox 1, Checkbox 2, Checkbox 2 (again), and then Checkbox 4, Checkbox 5, and Checkbox 5 (again).

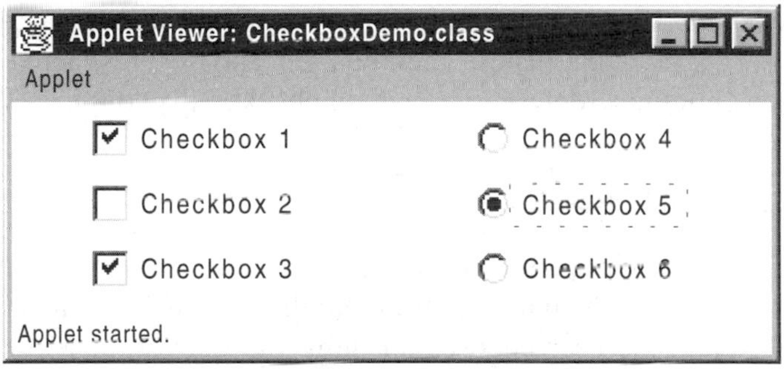

http://java.sun.com/docs/books/tutorial/ui/components/checkbox.html

The following code creates both groups of checkboxes. Note that only the second, mutually-exclusive group of checkboxes is controlled by a `CheckboxGroup`. Also note that for teaching purposes, this program uses all five `Checkbox` constructors. You can find the complete program on page 813.

```
...//in initialization code:
Panel p1, p2;
Checkbox cb1, cb2, cb3; //These are independent checkboxes.
Checkbox cb4, cb5, cb6; //These checkboxes are in a group.
```

```
CheckboxGroup cbg;

cb1 = new Checkbox();   //Default state is "off" (false).
cb1.setLabel("Checkbox 1");
cb2 = new Checkbox("Checkbox 2");
cb3 = new Checkbox("Checkbox 3");
cb3.setState(true);     //Set state to "on" (true).
. . .
cbg = new CheckboxGroup();
//Create 3 checkboxes, all "off" (false).
cb4 = new Checkbox("Checkbox 4", cbg, false);
cb5 = new Checkbox("Checkbox 5", false, cbg);
cb6 = new Checkbox("Checkbox 6", false);
cb6.setCheckboxGroup(cbg);
```

Although the previous example doesn't perform any event handling, checkboxes generate item events when their state changes. For information about item events, see How to Write an Item Listener (page 482).

Besides the `Checkbox` methods shown in the previous example, `Checkbox` has two additional methods you might want to use: `getCheckboxGroup`, `getLabel`, and `getState`.

The `CheckboxGroup` class, besides the single `CheckboxGroup` constructor used in the code example, also defines the following methods: `getSelectedCheckbox` and `setSelectedCheckbox`. These methods get and set, respectively, the currently selected `Checkbox` (determining which checkbox is "on").

How to Use Choices

The `Choice`[1] class provides a menu-like list of choices, accessed by a distinctive button. The user presses the button to bring up the "menu," and then chooses one of the items. When the user chooses an item, the `Choice` generates an action event.

`Choice` objects are useful when you need to display a number of alternatives in a limited amount of space, and the user doesn't need to see all the alternatives all the time. Another name for this UI element is *pop-up list*. Other ways of providing multiple alternatives are described in checkboxes (page 434), lists (page 444), and menus (page 448).

The applet in the following three figures has a `Choice` and a `Label`. When the user chooses an item from the `Choice` list, the `Label` changes to reflect the item chosen. Note that the index of the first item in the `Choice` is 0.

---

1 http://java.sun.com/products/jdk/1.1/docs/api/java.awt.Choice.html

Here's what the applet looks like at first:

ichi Item #0 selected. Text = "ichi".

http://java.sun.com/docs/books/tutorial/ui/components/choice.html

Here's what the applet looks like as you select another item ("san"):

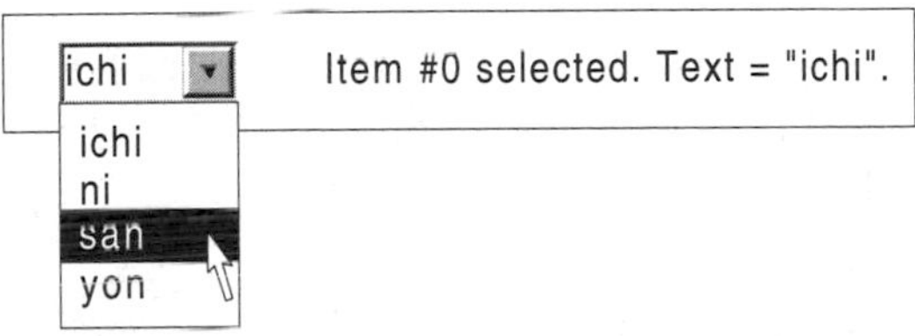

http://java.sun.com/docs/books/tutorial/ui/components/choice.html

Finally, here's what the applet looks like after "san" is selected:

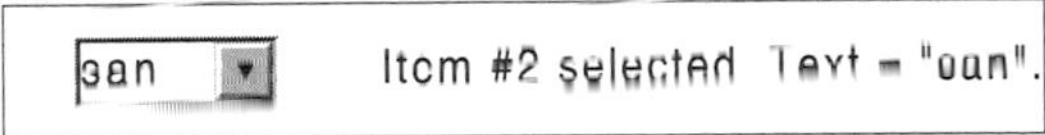

http://java.sun.com/docs/books/tutorial/ui/components/choice.html

The following code creates the `Choice` and handles events from it. You can find the complete program on page 814.

```
public class ChoiceDemo ... implements ItemListener {
    //...Where instance variables are defined:
    Choice choice; //pop-up list of choices

    //...Where initialization occurs:
    choice = new Choice();
    choice.addItem("ichi");
    choice.addItem("ni");
    choice.addItem("san");
    choice.addItem("yon");

    choice.addItemListener(this);

    label = new Label();
    setLabelText(choice.getSelectedIndex(),
                 choice.getSelectedItem());
```

```
. . .

public void itemStageChanged(ItemEvent e) {
    setLabelText(choice.getSelectedIndex(),
                 choice.getSelectedItem());
}
```

The `itemStateChanged` method in the previous example handles the item events that the choices generate. For general information about item events, see How to Write an Item Listener (page 482).

Besides the `addItem`, `getSelectedIndex`, `getSelectedItem`, and `addItemListener` methods used in the previous example, the `Choice` class defines these other useful methods:

`String getItem(int)`
Returns the `String` displayed by the item at the specified index.

`int getItemCount()`
Returns the number of items in the choice.

`void insert(String, int)`
Inserts an item so that it has the specified index. Items previously at that index or higher are shifted up by one.

`void remove(String)`
`void remove(int)`
Removes the specified item from the choice.

`void select(int)`
`void select(String)`
Selects the specified item.

How to Use Dialogs

The AWT provides support for *dialogs*—windows that are dependent on other windows—with the `Dialog`[1] class. It provides a useful subclass, `FileDialog`,[2] that provides dialogs to help the user open and save files.

The one thing that distinguishes dialogs from regular windows (which are implemented with `Frame` objects) is that a dialog is dependent on some other window (a `Frame`). When that other window is destroyed, so are its dependent dialogs. When that other window is iconified—made into an icon—its dependent dialogs disappear from the screen. When the window is returned to its normal state, its

---

1 http://java.sun.com/products/jdk/1.1/docs/api/java.awt.Dialog.html
2 http://java.sun.com/products/jdk/1.1/docs/api/java.awt.FileDialog.html

dependent dialogs return to the screen. The AWT automatically provides this behavior to you.

Because no API currently exists to let applets find the window they're running in, applets generally can't use dialogs in a supported way. The exception is that applets that bring up their own windows (`Frames`) can have dialogs dependent on those windows. For this reason, the applet in the following two figures consists of a button that brings up a window that brings up a dialog.

Here's a snapshot of the window (`Frame`) the button brings up:

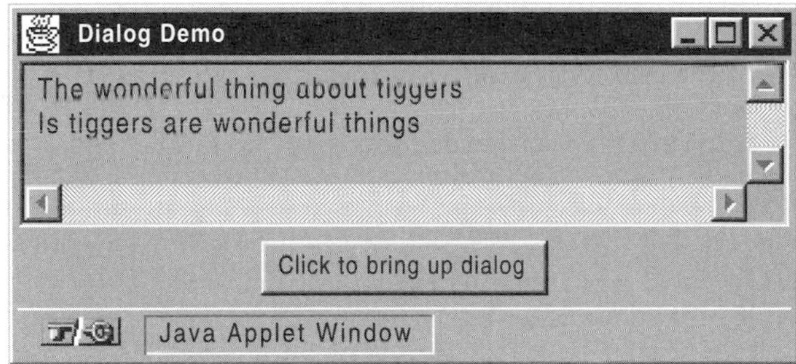

http://java.sun.com/docs/books/tutorial/ui/components/dialog.html

And here's a snapshot of the dialog for the window:

A Simple Dialog
Enter random text here: Is tiggers are wonderful things
Cancel Set
Java Applet Window

http://java.sun.com/docs/books/tutorial/ui/components/dialog.html

Dialogs can be *modal*. Modal dialogs require the user's attention, preventing the user from doing anything else in the dialog's application until the dialog has been dismissed. By default, dialogs are non-modal—the user can keep them up and still work in other windows of the application.

The complete code for the window and dialog that the previous applet brings up is on page 815. This code can be run as a stand-alone application or, with the

help of the AppletButton class as an applet [see AppletButton.java (page 796)]. Here's just the code that implements the Dialog object:

```
class SimpleDialog extends Dialog
                   implements ActionListener {
    TextField field;
    DialogWindow parent;
    Button setButton;

    SimpleDialog(Frame dw, String title) {
        super(dw, title, false); //false = non-modal
        parent = (DialogWindow)dw;

        ...//Create and add components, such as the set button.

        //Initialize this dialog to its preferred size.
        pack();
    }

    public void actionPerformed(ActionEvent e) {
        Object source = e.getSource();
        if ( (source == setButton)
            | (source == field)) {
            parent.setText(field.getText());
        }
        field.selectAll();
        setVisible(false);
    }
}
```

The pack method used in the SimpleDialog constructor above is a method defined by the Window class. It sets the window's size to exactly what's needed to display the window's components. See How to Use Frames (page 441) for more information about pack and other methods that Dialog inherits from the Window class.

Here's the code that displays the dialog:

```
if (dialog == null) {
    dialog = new SimpleDialog(this, "A Simple Dialog");
}
dialog.setVisible(true);
```

For modal dialogs, the setVisible(true) method call doesn't return until the dialog is dismissed. To get data from a modal dialog, you can define a method in your Dialog subclass that gets information from the dialog. For example:

```
myModalDialog.setVisible(true);
state = myModalDialog.getSettings();
```

The `Dialog` class provides four constructors:

`Dialog(Frame)`
`Dialog(Frame, boolean)`
`Dialog(Frame, String)`
`Dialog(Frame, String, boolean)`

The `Frame` argument specifies the window that the dialog depends on. The `String` specifies the dialog's title. The `boolean` argument should be true to specify a modal dialog and should be false for non-modal. The default is non-modal.

The `Dialog` class provides the following methods:

`boolean isModal()`
`void setModal (boolean)`

Gets or sets whether the dialog is modal.

`String getTitle()`
`void setTitle(String)`

Gets or sets the title of the dialog window.

`boolean isResizable()`
`void setResizable(boolean)`

Gets or sets whether the size of the dialog window can change.

How to Use Frames

The `Frame`[1] class provides windows for applets and applications. Every application needs at least one `Frame`. If an application has a window that should be dependent on another window—disappearing when the other window is iconified, for example—then you should use either a `Dialog` [see How to Use Dialogs (page 438)] or (for a no frills window) `Window` instead of a `Frame` for the dependent window. Unfortunately, applets currently can't use dialogs well, so they generally need to use frames instead.

The menu demonstration uses the following code to create its window (a `Frame` subclass) and handle the case where the user closes the window.

---

1 http://java.sun.com/products/jdk/1.1/docs/api/java.awt.Frame.html

```
public class MenuWindow extends Frame ... {
    boolean inAnApplet = true;
    ...
    public MenuWindow {
        ...//This constructor implicitly calls the Frame
           //no-argument constructor
           //and then adds components to the window...

        addWindowListener(new WindowAdapter() {
            public void windowClosing(WindowEvent e) {
                if (inAnApplet) {
                     dispose();
                } else {
                     System.exit(0);
                }
            }
        });
    }

    . . .

    public static void main(String args[]) {
        MenuWindow window = new MenuWindow();
        window.inAnApplet = false;

        window.setTitle("MenuWindow Application");
        window.pack();
        window.setVisible(true);
    }
}
```

Every `Frame` must have a window listener that implements the `windowClosing` method. Otherwise, when the user tries to close the window, nothing will happen. In the previous example, the window listener is implemented in an inner class that extends the AWT `WindowAdapter` class. See How to Write a Window Listener (page 497) for more information and examples.

Besides the no-argument `Frame` constructor implicitly used by the `MenuWindow` constructor shown above, the `Frame` class also provides a one-argument constructor. That argument is a `String` that specifies the title of the frame's window.

Other interesting methods provided by `Frame` include these:

`String getTitle()`
`void setTitle(String)`
Returns or sets, respectively, the title of the frame's window.

`Image getIconImage()`
`void setIconImage(Image)`
Returns or sets the image displayed when the window is iconified.

`MenuBar getMenuBar()`
`void setMenuBar(MenuBar)`
Returns or sets the menu bar for this `Frame`.

`remove(MenuComponent)`
Removes the specified `MenuBar` or `PopupMenu` from this `Frame`.

`boolean isResizable()`
`setResizable(boolean)`
Returns or sets, respectively, whether the user can change the window's size.

From `Window`, `Frame` inherits these useful methods:

`void toBack()`
`void toFront()`
Moves the window behind or in front of all other windows, respectively.

`void pack()`
Resizes the window so that all its contents are at or above their preferred or minimum sizes, depending on the window's layout manager. In general, using pack is preferable to calling the `setSize` method on a window, since pack leaves the window's layout manager in charge of the window's size, and layout managers are good at adjusting to platform dependencies and other factors that affect component size.

Note: You must call either `pack` or `setSize` on a `Frame` before showing it for the first time. Otherwise, the window won't appear on-screen.

From `Component`, `Frame` inherits the `setVisible` method, which lets you show (`setVisible(true)`) or hide (`setVisible(false)`) a window.

How to Use Menus (page 448) and How to Use Dialogs (page 438) contain two of the many examples in this tutorial that use a `Frame`.

How to Use Labels

The `Label`[1] class provides an easy way of putting unselectable text in your program's GUI. Labels are aligned to the left of their drawing area, by default. You can specify that they be centered or right-aligned by specifying `Label.CENTER` or

---

1 http://java.sun.com/products/jdk/1.1/docs/api/java.awt.Label.html

Label.RIGHT either to the Label constructor or to the setAlignment method. As with every Component, you can also specify the font and color of a label. For information on using fonts, see Working with Text (page 534).

Labels are used throughout the examples in this tutorial. For example, the applet in How to Use Choices (page 436) uses a label to display information about the item that's currently chosen.

The following applet demonstrates label alignment.

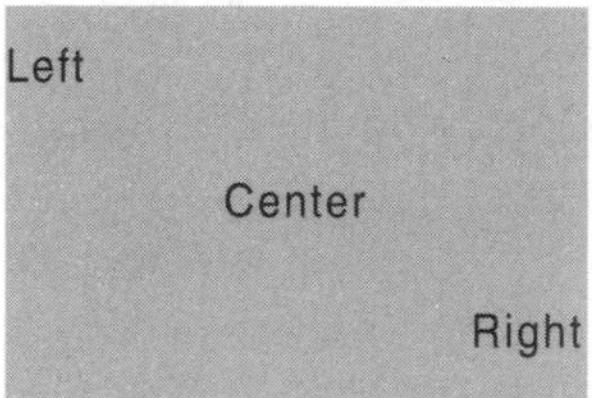

http://java.sun.com/docs/books/tutorial/ui/components/label.html

The applet creates three labels, each with a different alignment. If each label's display area were equal to the width of the text the label displayed, you wouldn't see any difference in the alignment of the labels. Each label's text would simply be displayed using all the available space. However, this applet makes each label's display area as wide as the applet, which is wider than any of the labels' text. As a result, you can see a difference in the horizontal position of the text drawn by the three labels. You can find the complete program on page 818.

The applet uses the following code to create its labels and set their alignment. For teaching purposes only, this applet uses all three Label constructors.

```
Label label1 = new Label();
label1.setText("Left");
Label label2 = new Label("Center");
label2.setAlignment(Label.CENTER);
Label label3 = new Label("Right", Label.RIGHT);
```

Besides the constructors and the setText and setAlignment methods used above, the Label class also provides getText and getAlignment methods.

How to Use Lists

The List[1] class provides a scrollable area containing selectable text items, one per line. Generally, a user selects an item by clicking it, and indicates that an

1 http://java.sun.com/products/jdk/1.1/docs/api/java.awt.List.html

action should occur by double-clicking an item or pressing Return. Lists can allow either multiple selections or just one selection at a time. Other components that allow users to choose from multiple options are checkboxes (page 434), choices (page 436), and menus (page 448).

The applet in the following figure contains two lists, along with a text area that displays information about events. The top list (which lists Spanish numbers) allows multiple selections. The bottom (which lists Italian numbers) allows a maximum of one selection. Note that the first item in each list has index 0.

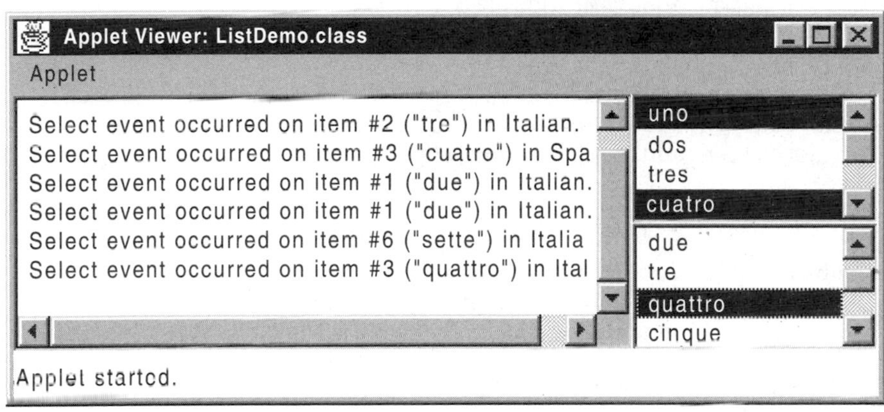

http://java.sun.com/docs/books/tutorial/ui/components/list.html

The following code creates each list and handles events on the lists. You can find the complete program on page 818.

```
public class ListDemo ... implements ActionListener,
                                     ItemListener {
    ...//Where instance variables are declared:
    TextArea output;
    List spanish, italian;

    ...//Where initialization occurs:

    //Build first list, which allows multiple selections.
    //We prefer 4 items visible; true means allow multiple
    //selections.
    spanish = new List(4, true);
    spanish.addItem("uno");
    spanish.addItem("dos");
    spanish.addItem("tres");
    spanish.addItem("cuatro");
    spanish.addItem("cinco");
```

```
        spanish.addItem("seis");
        spanish.addItem("siete");
        spanish.addActionListener(this);
        spanish.addItemListener(this);

        //Build second list, which allows one selection at a time.
        //Defaults to none visible, one selectable
        italian = new List();
        italian.addItem("uno");
        italian.addItem("due");
        italian.addItem("tre");
        italian.addItem("quattro");
        italian.addItem("cinque");
        italian.addItem("sei");
        italian.addItem("sette");
        italian.addActionListener(this);
        italian.addItemListener(this);

    . . .

    public void actionPerformed(ActionEvent e) {
        List list = (List)(e.getSource());
        String language = (list == spanish) ?
                          "Spanish" : "Italian";
        output.append("Action event occurred on \""
                          + list.getSelectedItem()  + "\" in "
                          + language + newline);
    }

    public void itemStateChanged(ItemEvent e) {
        List list = (List)(e.getItemSelectable());
        String language = (list == spanish) ?
                          "Spanish" : "Italian";

        int index = ((Integer)(e.getItem())).intValue();
        if (e.getStateChange() == ItemEvent.SELECTED) {
            output.append("Select event occurred on item #"
                          + index + " (\""
                          + list.getItem(index)  + "\") in "
                          + language + "." + newline);
        } else { //the item was deselected
            output.append("Deselect event occurred on item #"
                          + index + " (\""
                          + list.getItem(index)  + "\") in "
                          + language + "." + newline);
    }
```

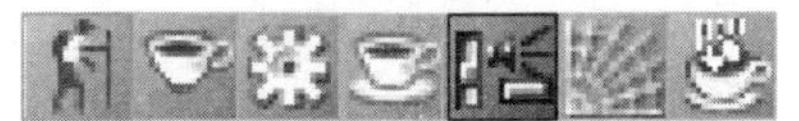

The `itemStateChanged` method in the previous example handles the item events that the lists generate. For general information about item events, see How to Write an Item Listener (page 482).

Besides the two constructors and the `addItem` and `getItem` methods shown in the previous example, the `List` class provides the following handy constructors and methods:

`List(int)`
Creates a single-selection list with the specified number of rows.

`String getItem(int)`
Returns the `String` displayed by the item at the specified index.

`String[] getItems()`
Returns a new array containing the names of each item in the list, in order.

`int getItemCount()`
Returns the number of items in the list.

`int getRows()`
Returns the number of visible lines in the list.

`int getSelectedIndex()`
`String getSelectedItem()`
Returns the index or name of the selected item in the list. Returns -1 or null, respectively, if no item is selected or more than one item is selected.

`int[] getSelectedIndexes()`
`String[] getSelectedItems()`
`Object[] getSelectedObjects()`
Returns an array containing the indexes (for `getSelectedIndexes`) or names of the selected items in the list.

`void select(int)`
`void deselect(int)`
Selects or deselects, respectively, the item at the specified index.

`boolean isIndexSelected(int)`
`boolean isItemSelected(String)`
Returns `true` if the specified item is selected.

`void addItem(String, int)`
Adds the specified item at the specified index.

`void replaceItem(String, int)`
Replaces the item at the specified index with an item with the specified name.

```
void delItem(int)
void remove(int)
void remove(String)
void removeAll()
```

Deletes one or all items from the list. The `delItem` and `remove` methods delete the specified item from the list. The `removeAll` method empties the list.

```
boolean isMultipleMode()
setMultipleMode(boolean)
```

Returns or sets, respectively, whether the list allows multiple items to be selected ("on") at the same time.

```
void makeVisible(int)
int getVisibleIndex()
```

The `makeVisible` method forces the item at the specified index to be visible. The `getVisibleIndex` method gets the index of the item that was last made visible by the `makeVisible` method.

How to Use Menus

The applet shown in the following figures illustrates many of the menu features you're likely to use. The window it brings up has a popup menu and a menu bar that contains five menus. Each menu contains one or more items. When the user chooses any menu item, the window displays a string indicating which item was chosen and which menu it's in.

Menu 1 is a tear-off menu; on platforms that support tear-off menus, the user can create a new window that contains the same menu items as Menu 1. Menu 2's only item has a checkbox. Menu 3 contains a separator between its second and third items. Menu 4 contains a submenu. Menu 5 (labeled "Help Menu") is the window's help menu, which (depending on the platform) generally means that it's set off to the right.

Note: Menu appearance and behavior differ significantly between platforms. For example, under Mac OS menus appear at the top of the screen, instead of within the window to which they're "attached."

Here's a snapshot of the window the applet brings up:

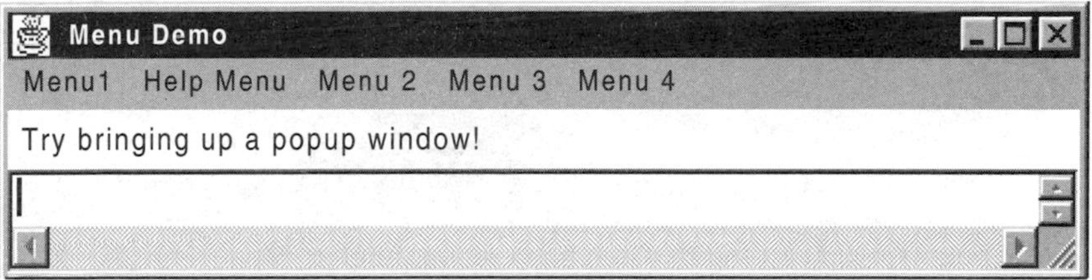

http://java.sun.com/docs/books/tutorial/ui/components/menu.html

Menu 1 has two items that can be selected:

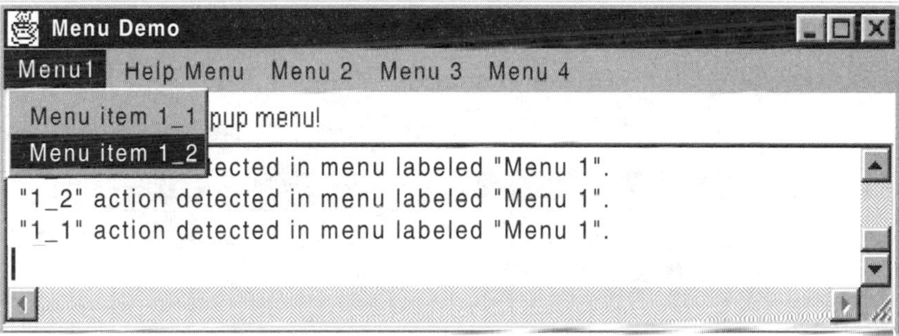

Menu 2's only item has a checkbox, which can be selected and deselected:

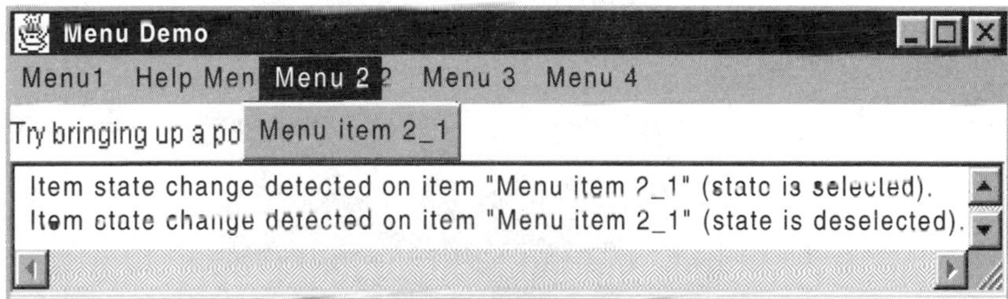

Menu 3 contains a separator between items 3_2 and 3_3:

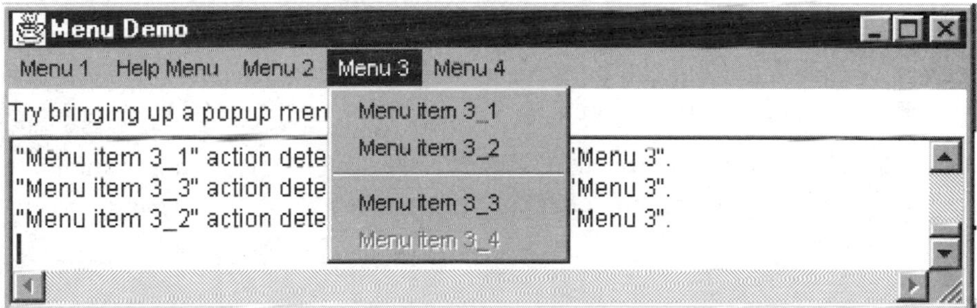

Menu 4 has a submenu:

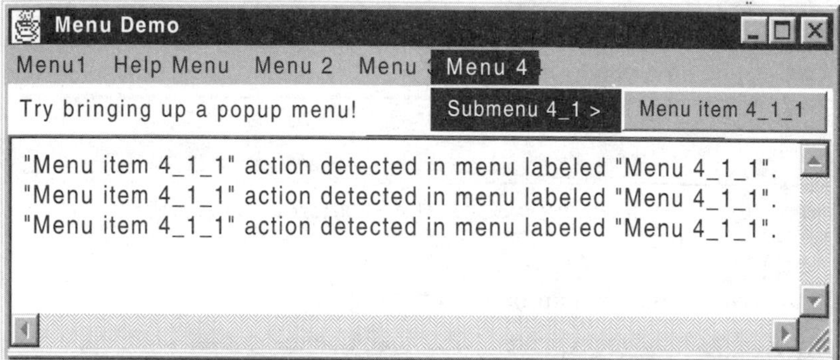

Menu 5 is the designated help menu. It also contains a menu item with a shortcut ("Ctrl+5"):

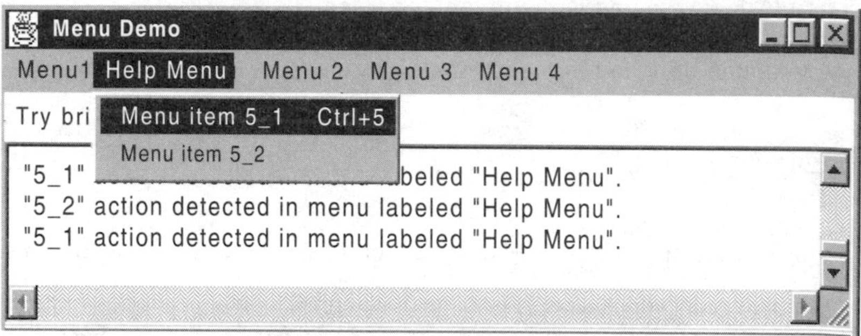

A popup menu appears when the user right-mouse clicks in the label or text area:

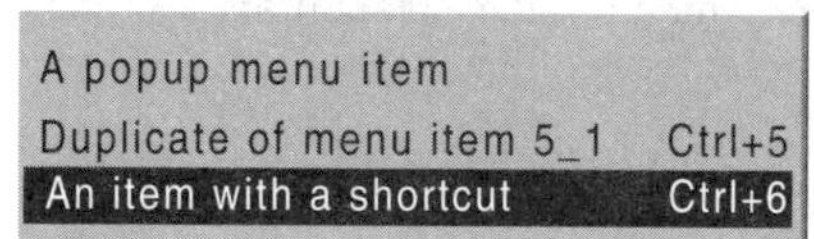

The reason the applet brings up a window to demonstrate menus is that the AWT limits where you can use menus. Except for popup menus and their submenus, menus can exist only in menu bars. Menu bars can be attached only to windows, specifically, only to `Frame` objects.

Menus exist to present the user with a variety of options. Other components that serve a similar purpose include checkboxes (page 434), choices (page 436), and lists (page 444).

Menu functionality in the AWT is provided by several classes. These classes do *not* inherit from `Component` since many platforms place severe limits on menu capabilities. Instead, menu classes inherit from the `MenuComponent`[1] class. The AWT provides the following `MenuComponent` subclasses to support menus:

`MenuItem`[2]
: Each item in a menu is represented by a `MenuItem` object. Each `MenuItem` can generate action events. Unlike all other components, if a menu item has no action listeners, then action events are still sent. These action events go to the action listeners of the containing menu, and the event source is set to the containing menu. You use the `ActionEvent getActionCommand` method to discover which menu item actually generated the event. If you implement a submenu, then you must register an action listener on it or its items, since action events aren't propagated higher than the menu item's actual container.

`CheckboxMenuItem`[3]
: Each menu item that contains a checkbox is represented by a `CheckboxMenuItem` object. `CheckboxMenuItem` is a subclass of `MenuItem`.

`Menu`[4]
: Each menu is represented by a `Menu` object. The `Menu` class is implemented as a subclass of `MenuItem` so that you can easily create a submenu by adding one menu to another.

`PopupMenu`[5]
: Each popup menu is represented by a `PopupMenu` object. The `PopupMenu` class is implemented as a subclass of `Menu`. You can add a `PopupMenu` to any `Component`.

To make a popup menu appear when appropriate, you must implement a mouse listener that shows the popup menu in response to popup trigger events. Then you must register the listener on all components that should be able to generate popup trigger events. Because popup trigger events vary by platform, but generally are the result of mouse-pressed or mouse-released events, you should implement the mouse listener's `mousePressed` and `mouseReleased` methods so that they use the `MouseEvent isPopupTrigger` method to detect the popup trigger event.

Popup menus can display shortcuts, but the shortcuts don't work. To make a popup menu shortcut appear to work, you can create a menu item under the menu bar that implements the shortcut.

---

1 http://java.sun.com/products/jdk/1.1/docs/api/java.awt.MenuComponent.html
2 http://java.sun.com/products/jdk/1.1/docs/api/java.awt.MenuItem.html
3 http://java.sun.com/products/jdk/1.1/docs/api/java.awt.CheckboxMenuItem.html
4 http://java.sun.com/products/jdk/1.1/docs/api/java.awt.Menu.html
5 http://java.sun.com/products/jdk/1.1/docs/api/java.awt.PopupMenu.html

`MenuBar`[1]

Menu bars are implemented by the `MenuBar` class. A `MenuBar` represents the platform-dependent notion of a group of menus attached to a window. `MenuBar`s can *not* be bound to `Panel`s.

A support class named `MenuShortcut`[2] lets you create keyboard alternatives for choosing menu items.

On page 821 you can find the code for the window that the previous applet brings up. This code can be run as a stand-alone application or, with the help of the `AppletButton` class as an applet [see `AppletButton.java` (page 796)]. Here's just the code that creates and adds the menus:

```
public class MenuWindow extends Frame ... {
    . . .
    public MenuWindow() {
        MenuBar mb;
        Menu m1, m2, m3, m4, m4_1, m5;
        MenuItem mi1_1, mi1_2, mi3_1, mi3_2, mi3_3, mi3_4,
                 mi4_1_1, mi5_1, mi5_2,
                 pmi1, pmi2, mi5_1_duplicate;
        CheckboxMenuItem mi2_1;
        ...

        //Build the menu bar.
        mb = new MenuBar();
        setMenuBar(mb);

        //Build first menu in the menu bar.
        //Specifying the second argument as true
        //makes this a tear-off menu.
        m1 = new Menu("Menu 1", true);
        mb.add(m1);
        mi1_1 = new MenuItem("Menu item 1_1");
        m1.add(mi1_1);
        mi1_2 = new MenuItem("Menu item 1_2");
        m1.add(mi1_2);

        //Build help menu.
        m5 = new Menu("Help Menu");
        mb.setHelpMenu(m5);
        mi5_1 = new MenuItem("Menu item 5_1");
        mi5_1.setShortcut(new MenuShortcut(KeyEvent.VK_5));
        m5.add(mi5_1);
```

1 http://java.sun.com/products/jdk/1.1/docs/api/java.awt.MenuBar.html

2 http://java.sun.com/products/jdk/1.1/docs/api/java.awt.MenuContainer.html

```
mi5_2 = new MenuItem("Menu item 5_2");
m5.add(mi5_2);

//Make a popup menu.
popup = new PopupMenu("A Popup Menu");
add(popup);
pmi1 = new MenuItem("A popup menu item");
popup.add(pmi1);
mi5_1_duplicate = new MenuItem(
                      "Duplicate of menu item 5_1",
                      new MenuShortcut(KeyEvent.VK_5));
popup.add(mi5_1_duplicate);
pmi2 = new MenuItem("An item with a shortcut",
                    new MenuShortcut(KeyEvent.VK_6));
popup.add(pmi2);

//Build second menu in the menu bar.
m2 = new Menu("Menu 2");
mb.add(m2);
mi2_1 = new CheckboxMenuItem("Menu item 2_1");
m2.add(mi2_1);

//Build third menu in the menu bar.
m3 = new Menu("Menu 3");
mb.add(m3);
mi3_1 = new MenuItem("Menu item 3_1");
m3.add(mi3_1);
mi3_2 = new MenuItem("Menu item 3_2");
m3.add(mi3_2);
m3.addSeparator();
mi3_3 = new MenuItem("Menu item 3_3");
m3.add(mi3_3);
mi3_4 = new MenuItem("Menu item 3_4");
mi3_4.setEnabled(false);
m3.add(mi3_4);

//Build fourth menu in the menu bar.
m4 = new Menu("Menu 4");
mb.add(m4);
m4_1 = new Menu("Submenu 4_1");
m4.add(m4_1);
mi4_1_1 = new MenuItem("Menu item 4_1_1");
m4_1.add(mi4_1_1);
```

The following snippet contains the event-related code in the example.

```
public class MenuWindow ... implements ActionListener,
                                       ItemListener {
    ...//where the menus are created:
        mi1_1.setActionCommand("1_1");
        mi1_2.setActionCommand("1_2");
        mi5_1.setActionCommand("5_1");
        mi5_2.setActionCommand("5_2");
        pmi1.setActionCommand("popup item #1");
        mi5_1_duplicate.setActionCommand("5_1");
        pmi2.setActionCommand("popup item #2");

        //Register listeners to bring up the popup menu.
        MouseListener listener = new PopupListener();
        addMouseListener(listener);
        output.addMouseListener(listener);
        label.addMouseListener(listener);

        //Register as an ActionListener on all menu items.
        m1.addActionListener(this);
        m2.addActionListener(this);
        m3.addActionListener(this);
        m4.addActionListener(this);
        mi4_1_1.addActionListener(this); //m4 can't detect
                                         //submenu actions
        m5.addActionListener(this);
        popup.addActionListener(this);

       //Register as an ItemListener on the checkbox menu item.
        mi2_1.addItemListener(this);
    }
    . . .
    class PopupListener extends MouseAdapter {
        public void mousePressed(MouseEvent e) {
            maybeShowPopup(e);
        }

        public void mouseReleased(MouseEvent e) {
            maybeShowPopup(e);
        }

        private void maybeShowPopup(MouseEvent e) {
            if (e.isPopupTrigger()) {
                popup.show(e.getComponent(),
                           e.getX(), e.getY());
            }
        }
    }
```

```
public void actionPerformed(ActionEvent e) {
    output.append("\"" + e.getActionCommand()
                  + "\" action detected in menu labeled \""
                  + ((MenuItem)(e.getSource())).getLabel()
                  + "\"." + newline);
}

public void itemStateChanged(ItemEvent e) {
    output.append("Item state change detected on item \""
                  + e.getItem()
                  + "\" (state is "
                  + ((e.getStateChange() ==
                        ItemEvent.SELECTED)?
                        "selected)."
                      : "deselected).")
                  + newline);
}
```

The two different types of user-selectable menu items generate two kinds of events. Checkbox menu items generate item events, which are handled by the `itemStateChanged` method in the previous example. See How to Write an Item Listener (page 482) for more information about item events.

All other menu items (unless they bring up menus) generate action events. Note how some of the menu items in the previous example don't have action commands. In a real program, you'd probably set action commands for every non-checkbox menu item. However, this example sets only a few to demonstrate that if you don't set a menu item's action command, then the action command is the text in the menu item's label. See How to Write an Action Listener (page 470) for more information about action events.

The `MenuItem` class provides the following handy methods:

`boolean isEnabled()`
`void setEnabled(boolean)`
Gets or sets whether the menu item can be chosen.

`String getLabel()`
`void setLabel(String)`
Gets or sets the text displayed by the menu item.

`MenuShortcut getShortcut()`
`void setShortcut(MenuShortcut)`
`void deleteShortcut(MenuShortcut)`
Gets, sets, or deletes the keyboard alternative for a menu item.

`String getActionCommand()`
`void setActionCommand(String)`
Gets or sets the action associated with the menu item.

How to Use Panels

The Panel[1] class is a general-purpose Container subclass. You can use it as-is to hold components, or you can define a subclass to perform special functionality, such as drawing borders or handling events.

The Applet[2] class is a Panel subclass with special hooks to run in a browser or other applet viewer. Whenever you see a program that can run both as an applet and as an application, the chances are that it defines an Applet subclass but doesn't use any of the special Applet capabilities and relies instead on the methods it inherits from the Panel class.

The following example uses a Panel instance to hold some components:

```
Panel p1 = new Panel();
p1.add(new Button("Button 1"));
p1.add(new Button("Button 2"));
p1.add(new Button("Button 3"));
```

The following code contains a Panel subclass that draws a frame around its contents. Versions of this class are used by Examples 1 and 2 in Drawing Shapes (page 528).

```
class FramedArea extends Panel {
    public FramedArea(CoordinatesDemo controller) {
        ...//Set the layout manager.
           //Add any Components this Panel contains...
    }

    //Ensure that no Component is placed on top of the frame.
    //The inset values were determined by trial and error.
    public Insets getInsets() {
        return new Insets(4,4,5,5);
    }

    //Draw the frame at this Panel's edges.
    public void paint(Graphics g) {
        Dimension d = getSize();
        Color bg = getBackground();

        g.setColor(bg);
```

---

1 http://java.sun.com/products/jdk/1.1/docs/api/java.awt.Panel.html
2 http://java.sun.com/products/jdk/1.1/docs/api/java.applet.Applet.html

```
        g.draw3DRect(0, 0, d.width - 1, d.height - 1, true);
        g.draw3DRect(3, 3, d.width - 7, d.height - 7, false);
    }
}
```

How to Use Scrollbars

Scrollbars have two uses:

- A scrollbar can act as a slider that the user manipulates to set a value. An example of this is in the Converter program in The Anatomy of a GUI-Based Program (page 413).
- As controls for scroll panes. The `ScrollPane` class, which was introduced in 1.1, lets you display part of a component that's too large for the available display area. Scrollbars in scroll panes let the user choose exactly which part of the region is visible. To customize scrolling behavior, you sometimes need to invoke methods on a `ScrollPane`'s scrollbars.

If you want to use a scroll pane, you might not need to read this section at all. Instead, read How to Use Scroll Panes (page 459). The following figure shows the parts of a scrollbar:

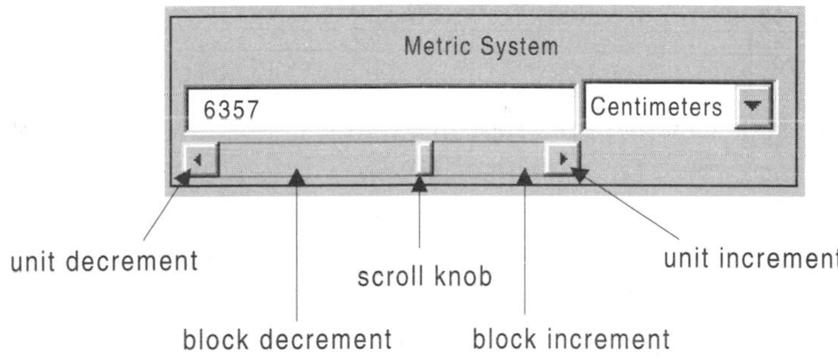

Figure 67: The parts of a scrollbar.

To create a scrollbar that isn't in a scroll pane, you can call the one-argument `Scrollbar`[1] constructor. The argument's value should be either `Scrollbar.HORIZONTAL` (to create a horizontal scrollbar) or `Scrollbar.VERTICAL` (to create a vertical scrollbar). For example:

```
horizontalSB = new Scrollbar(Scrollbar.HORIZONTAL);
verticalSB = new Scrollbar(Scrollbar.VERTICAL);
```

---

1 http://java.sun.com/products/jdk/1.1/docs/api/java.awt.Scrollbar.html

After creating the scrollbar, you should initialize it by calling one or more of the following methods:

`setValues(int, int, int, int)`
Sets the scrollbar's value, visible amount, minimum value, and maximum value. See the descriptions of the `setValue`, `setVisibleAmount`, `setMinimum`, and `setMaximum` methods for more information.

`setValue(int)`
Sets the current value of the scrollbar. Defaults to 0.

`setVisibleAmount(int)`
Sets the relative size of the scroll knob. Because some platforms don't support variable-size scroll knobs, the specified size may or may not be reflected on-screen. The visible amount can't be larger than the scroller's maximum value minus its minimum value. Defaults to 10.

`setMinimum(int)`
Sets the minimum value of the scrollbar. This value can be any integer, positive or not, that is less than the maximum value. Defaults to 0.

`setMaximum(int)`
Sets the maximum value of the scrollbar. Because the knob's width makes the scrollbar's highest values unselectable, you must add the visible amount to the desired maximum value. For example:

```
sb.setMaximum(realMaxValue + sb.getVisibleAmount());
```

Defaults to 100, which results in a maximum choosable value of 90 (after subtracting the default knob width of 10).

`setBlockIncrement(int)`
Specifies the amount to be added to or subtracted from the current value when the user clicks in the block increment or block decrement area of the scrollbar. Defaults to 10.

`setUnitIncrement(int)`
Specifies the amount to be added to or subtracted from the current value when the user clicks in the unit increment or unit decrement area of the scrollbar. Defaults to 10.

Here's an example of scrollbar code, taken from the Converter program featured in The Anatomy of a GUI-Based Program (page 413).

```
class ConversionPanel ... implements AdjustmentListener ... {
    ...
    Scrollbar slider;
    int max = 10000;
    int block = 100;
```

```
    ConversionPanel(...) {
        ...
      //Add the slider.  It's horizontal, and it has the maximum
        //value specified by the instance variable max.  Its
        //initial and minimum values are the default (0).  A
        //click increments the value by block units.
        slider = new Scrollbar(Scrollbar.HORIZONTAL);
        slider.setMaximum(max + 10);
        slider.setBlockIncrement(block);
        ...
        add(slider);
        slider.addAdjustmentListener(this);
    }
    ...
    /** Respond to the slider. */
    public void adjustmentValueChanged(AdjustmentEvent e) {
        textField.setText(String.valueOf(e.getValue()));
        controller.convert(this);
    }
    ...
    /** Set the slider value. */
    void setSliderValue(double f) {
        int sliderValue = (int)f;

        if (sliderValue > max)
               sliderValue = max;
        if (sliderValue < 0)
            sliderValue = 0;
        slider.setValue(sliderValue);
    }
}
```

The `adjustmentValueChanged` method in the previous example handles the adjustment events that the scrollbar generates. For general information about adjustment events, see How to Write an Adjustment Listener (page 472).

How to Use Scroll Panes

The 1.1 AWT introduced the `ScrollPane`[1] class, which makes it easy for you to provide a scrolling area. A `ScrollPane` manages a single child component and displays as much of the component as space permits.

By default, a scroll pane's scrollbars are visible only when they're needed. For example, if a scroll pane is wide enough to show its child's full width, then the

1 http://java.sun.com/products/jdk/1.1/docs/api/java.awt.ScrollPane.html

horizontal scrollbar isn't needed, and by default the horizontal scrollbar will completely disappear. The following picture shows an applet in which both the vertical and horizontal scrollbars are currently needed.

http://java.sun.com/docs/books/tutorial/ui/components/scrollpane.html

Here is the code that creates a scroll pane and puts a child component in it:

```
ScrollPane sp1 = new ScrollPane();
sp1.add(aComponent);
```

When you create a scroll pane (but not later), you can specify when the scroll pane shows scrollbars, using one of these three `ScrollPane` constants:

- `SCROLLBARS_AS_NEEDED`—The default value. Show each scrollbar only when its needed.
- `SCROLLBARS_ALWAYS`—Always show scrollbars.
- `SCROLLBARS_NEVER`—Never show scrollbars. You might use this option if you don't want the user to directly control what part of the child component is shown.

Here's an example of specifying the scrollbar display policy:

```
ScrollPane sp2 = new ScrollPane(ScrollPane.SCROLLBARS_ALWAYS);
```

When you implement a component to be put in a scroll pane, you must take special care:

- You need to implement the child component's `getPreferredSize` method so that it returns the dimensions needed to fully display the component.
- You should implement the child component so that it works well when its drawing area is larger than its preferred size. For example, the component might draw itself in the center of its drawing area, filling the extra space with a solid color.

- When the component is being scrolled, you might notice flashing, or flickering, in the display area. If you don't want this to occur, you'll need to implement the `update` method in the child component, and possibly double buffering as well. These techniques are discussed in Eliminating Flashing (page 561).

Here's the scrolling-related code from the previous applet:

```
//The component that will be scrolled.
class ScrollableCanvas extends Canvas {
    ...
    Dimension preferredSize = new Dimension(600, 320);
    Dimension minimumSize = new Dimension(10, 10);

    public Dimension getMinimumSize() {
        return minimumSize;
    }

    public Dimension getPreferredSize() {
        return preferredSize;
    }

    public void paint(Graphics g) {
        g.drawImage(image, 0, 0, getBackground(), this);
    }
}

public class ImageScroller ... {
    ...//where initialization occurs:
        ScrollableCanvas canvas = new ScrollableCanvas();
        ...
        ScrollPane pane = new ScrollPane();
        setLayout(new BorderLayout());
        pane.add(canvas);
        add("Center", pane);
    }
}
```

Scroll panes don't generate events. If you want to be notified of scrolling activity, then you can get the scroll pane's scrollbars and listen to adjustment events from them. The horizontal scrollbar is returned by the `ScrollPane` `getHAdjustable` method, and the vertical scrollbar by the `getVAdjustable` method.

Another reason you might need to get the scrollbars is to control the scrollbars' appearance or behavior. For example, in a text processor you might need to set the amount scrolled when the user clicks in the scrollbar. For information on setting scrollbar attributes, see How to Use Scrollbars (page 457).

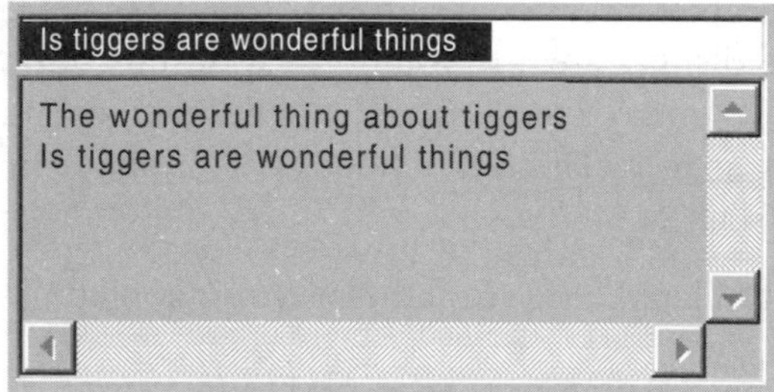

http://java.sun.com/docs/books/tutorial/ui/components/text.html

How to Use Text Areas and Fields

The TextArea[1] and TextField[2] classes display selectable text and, optionally, allow the user to edit the text. You can subclass TextArea and TextField to perform such tasks as checking for errors in the input. As with any component, you can specify the background and foreground colors and font used by TextAreas and TextFields. You cannot, however, change their basic appearance.

Both TextArea and TextField are subclasses of TextComponent.[3] From TextComponent they inherit methods that allow them to set and get the current selection, enable and disable editing, get the currently selected text or all the text, and set the text.

The following applet shows a TextField and then a TextArea. The TextField is editable; the TextArea is not. When the user presses Return in the TextField, its contents are copied to the TextArea and selected in the TextField.

You can find the complete program on page 826. Here's the code that creates, initializes, and handles events in the TextArea and TextField objects:

```
//Where instance variables are defined:
TextField textField;
TextArea textArea;
String newline;

...//where initialization occurs:
    textField = new TextField(20);
    textArea = new TextArea(5, 20);
    textArea.setEditable(false);
```

---

1 http://java.sun.com/products/jdk/1.1/docs/api/java.awt.TextArea.html
2 http://java.sun.com/products/jdk/1.1/docs/api/java.awt.TextField.html
3 http://java.sun.com/products/jdk/1.1/docs/api/java.awt.TextComponent.html

```
    ...//Add the two components to the panel...

        textField.addActionListener(this);
        newline = System.getProperty("line.separator");
    }

    public void actionPerformed(ActionEvent evt) {
        String text = textField.getText();
        textArea.append(text + newline);
        textField.selectAll();
    }
```

The `actionPerformed` method in the previous example handles the action events that the text field generates. For general information about action events, see How to Write an Action Listener (page 470).

The `TextComponent` superclass of `TextArea` and `TextField` supplies the `getText`, `setText`, `setEditable`, and `selectAll` methods used in the previous code example. It also supplies the following useful methods: `getSelectedText`, `isEditable`, `getSelectionStart`, and `getSelectionEnd`. It also provides a `select` method that allows you to select text between beginning and end positions that you specify.

The `TextField` class has four constructors: `TextField()`, `TextField(int` *`columns`*`)`, `TextField(String` *`text`*`)`, and `TextField(String` *`text`*`, int` *`columns`*`)`. The integer argument specifies the number of columns in the text field. The `String` argument specifies the text initially displayed in the text field. The `TextField` class also supplies the following handy methods:

`getColumns()`
Returns the number of columns in the `TextField`.

`setEchoChar(char` *`c`*`)`
Sets the echo character, which is useful for password fields.

`getEchoChar(), echoCharIsSet()`
These methods let you ask about the echo character.

Like the `TextField` class, the `TextArea` class also has four constructors: `TextArea()`, `TextArea(int` *`rows`*`, int` *`columns`*`)`, `TextArea(String` *`text`*`)`, and `TextArea(String` *`text`*`, int` *`rows`*`, int` *`columns`*`)`. The integer arguments specify the number of rows and columns in the text area. The `String` argument specifies the text initially displayed in the text area.

The `TextArea` class supplies the `append` method used in the previous code example. It also supplies the following methods:

`getRows(), getColumns()`
Return the number of rows or columns in the text area.

`insert(String, int)`
Inserts the specified text at the specified position.

`void replaceRange(String, int, int)`
Replaces text from the indicated start position to the indicated end position.

Writing Event Handlers

This section tells you how to write a listener for each kind of event defined in the 1.1 AWT. First, it gives an overview of the AWT events. Then it gives guidelines for writing event listeners. After that, each listener type is discussed in its own subsection. To find out how to handle events for a specific kind of component, you should refer to that component's section—for example, How to Use Checkboxes (page 434)—before looking here.

Table 20 lists the kinds of events each AWT component can generate. For each kind of event a component supports, the component has methods to add and remove listeners. For example, each component that can generate action events has methods named `addActionListener` and `removeActionListener`.

Table 20: Events generated by AWT components.

AWT Component	Kinds of Events It Can Generate										
	action	adjust-ment	com-ponent	con-tainer	focus	item	key	mouse	mouse motion	text	win-dow
`Button`	✔		✔		✔		✔	✔	✔		
`Canvas`			✔		✔		✔	✔	✔		
`Checkbox`			✔		✔	✔	✔	✔	✔		
`Checkbox-MenuItem`[a]	b					✔					
`Choice`			✔		✔	✔	✔	✔	✔		
`Component`			✔		✔		✔	✔	✔		
`Container`			✔	✔	✔		✔	✔	✔		
`Dialog`			✔	✔	✔		✔	✔	✔		✔
`Frame`			✔	✔	✔		✔	✔	✔		✔
`Label`			✔		✔		✔	✔	✔		
`List`	✔		✔		✔	✔	✔	✔	✔		

Table 20: Events generated by AWT components.

AWT Component	Kinds of Events It Can Generate										
	action	adjust-ment	com-ponent	con-tainer	focus	item	key	mouse	mouse motion	text	win-dow
`MenuItem`[c]	✔										
`Panel`			✔	✔	✔		✔	✔	✔		
`Scrollbar`		✔	✔		✔		✔	✔	✔		
`TextArea`			✔		✔		✔	✔	✔	✔	
`TextField`	✔		✔		✔		✔	✔	✔	✔	
`Window`			✔	✔	✔		✔	✔	✔		✔

a. `CheckboxMenuItem` does not inherit from `Component`.
b. Although `CheckboxMenuItem` inherits `addActionListener` from `MenuItem`, it does not generate action events.
c. `MenuItem` does not inherit from `Component`.

In Table 21, each row describes a particular kind of event. The first column gives the name of an event listener interface. The second column names the corresponding adapter class, if any. (An *adapter class* is an abstract class that you can use to avoid providing empty method implementations. Using Adapters and Inner Classes to Handle AWT Events (page 468) has more information.) The third column lists the methods that the listener interface contains. Every type listed in the following table is defined in the `java.awt.event` package.

The AWT events described in the preceding table can be divided into two groups: low-level events and semantic events. Low-level events represent window-system occurrences or low-level input. Clearly, mouse, mouse motion, and key events—all of which result directly from user input—are low-level events. Component, container, focus, and window events are also considered low-level events.

Semantic events include action, adjustment, item, and text events. These events are the result of component-specific user interaction. For example, a button generates an action event when the user clicks it, and a list generates an action event when the user doubleclicks an item in it.

General Rules for Writing Event Listeners (page 467) gives you information you might need when writing any event listener.

Table 21: AWT event listener interfaces.

Listener Interface	Adapter Class	Methods
`ActionListener`	—	`actionPerformed(ActionEvent)`
`Adjustment-Listener`	—	`adjustmentValueChanged(AdjustmentEvent)`

`ComponentListener`	`ComponentAdapter`	`componentHidden(ComponentEvent)`
		`componentMoved(ComponentEvent)`
		`componentResized(ComponentEvent)`
		`componentShown(ComponentEvent)`

`ContainerListener`	`ContainerAdapter`	`componentAdded(ContainerEvent)` `componentRemoved(ContainerEvent)`
`FocusListener`	`FocusAdapter`	`focusGained(FocusEvent)` `focusLost(FocusEvent)`
`ItemListener`	—	`itemStateChanged(ItemEvent)`

`KeyListener`	`KeyAdapter`	`keyPressed(KeyEvent)`
		`keyReleased(KeyEvent)`
		`keyTyped(KeyEvent)`

`MouseListener`	`MouseAdapter`	`mouseClicked(MouseEvent)`
		`mouseEntered(MouseEvent)`
		`mouseExited(MouseEvent)`
		`mousePressed(MouseEvent)`
		`mouseReleased(MouseEvent)`

`MouseMotion-Listener`	`MouseMotion-Adapter`	`mouseDragged(MouseEvent)` `mouseMoved(MouseEvent)`
`TextListener`	—	`textValueChanged(TextEvent)`

`WindowListener`	`WindowAdapter`	`windowActivated(WindowEvent)`
		`windowClosed(WindowEvent)`
		`windowClosing(WindowEvent)`
		`windowDeactivated(WindowEvent)`
		`windowDeiconified(WindowEvent)`
		`windowIconified(WindowEvent)`
		`windowOpened(WindowEvent)`

After that, the next few sections tell you how to write each kind of listener that the AWT defines:

- How to Write an Action Listener (page 470)
- How to Write an Adjustment Listener (page 472)
- How to Write a Component Listener (page 474)
- How to Write a Container Listener (page 477)
- How to Write a Focus Listener (page 479)
- How to Write an Item Listener (page 482)

General Rules for Writing Event Listeners

When the AWT calls an event-listener method, that method executes in the AWT event thread. Because all other event-handling and drawing methods are executed in that same thread, a slow event-listener method can make the program seem unresponsive and slow to repaint itself.

Important: Make sure your event-listener methods execute quickly!

If you need to perform some lengthy operation as the result of an event, do it by starting up another thread (or sending a request to another thread) to perform the operation. For help on using threads, see the lesson Doing Two or More Tasks at Once: Threads (page 327).

The next subsection introduces you to the ancestor of all AWT event classes, the `AWTEvent` class. After that, Using Adapters and Inner Classes to Handle AWT Events (page 468) gives you hints for avoiding clutter in your code.

The AWTEvent Class

Each method in each AWT event listener interface has a single argument: an instance of a class that descends from the `java.awt.AWTEvent`[1] class. The `AWTEvent` class doesn't define any methods or API that you ordinarily need to use. However, it does inherit a useful method from the `java.util.EventObject`[2] class:

`Object getSource()`
Returns the object that generated the event.

Note that the `getSource` method returns an `Object`. Whenever possible, `AWTEvent` subclasses define similar methods with more restricted return types. For example, the `ComponentEvent` class defines a `getComponent` method that returns the `Component` that generated the event.

---

1 http://java.sun.com/products/jdk/1.1/docs/api/java.awt.AWTEvent.html
2 http://java.sun.com/products/jdk/1.1/docs/api/java.util.EventObject.html

Figure 68 shows the class hierarchy for the AWT event classes. As it shows, many but not all of the AWT event classes inherit from the `ComponentEvent` class.

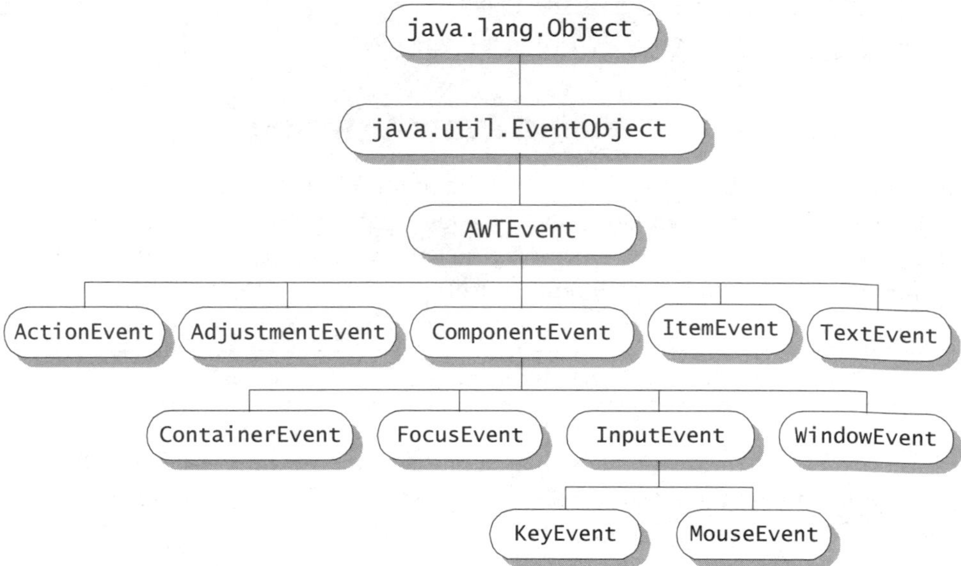

Figure 68: The class hierarchy of the AWT event classes.

Using Adapters and Inner Classes to Handle AWT Events

You can use adapters and inner classes to reduce clutter in your event listener implementations. This section tells you how.

Most AWT listener interfaces contain more than one method. For example, the `MouseListener` interface contains five methods: `mousePressed`, `mouseReleased`, `mouseEntered`, `mouseExited`, and `mouseClicked`. Even if you care only about mouse clicks, if your class directly implements `MouseListener`, then you must implement all five `MouseListener` methods. Methods for those events you don't care about can have empty bodies. Here's an example:

```
//An example with cluttered but valid code.
public class MyClass implements MouseListener {
    ...
        someObject.addMouseListener(this);
    ...
    //Empty method definition.
    public void mousePressed(MouseEvent e) {
    }
```

```
    //Empty method definition.
    public void mouseReleased(MouseEvent e) {
    }

    //Empty method definition.
    public void mouseEntered(MouseEvent e) {
    }

    //Empty method definition.
    public void mouseExited(MouseEvent e) {
    }

    public void mouseClicked(MouseEvent e) {
        ...//Event handler implementation goes here...
    }
```

Unfortunately, the resulting collection of empty method bodies can make code harder to read and maintain. To help you avoid cluttering your code with empty method bodies, the AWT provides an adapter class for each listener interface with more than one method. For example, the `MouseAdapter` class implements the `MouseListener` interface and provides empty versions of all the `MouseListener` methods.

To use an adapter, you create a subclass of it instead of directly implementing a listener interface. For example:

```
//An example of extending an adapter class.
public class MyClass extends MouseAdapter {
    ...
    someObject.addMouseListener(this);
    ...
    public void mouseClicked(MouseEvent e) {
        ...//Event handler implementation goes here...
    }
}
```

What if you don't want your class to inherit from an adapter class? For example, suppose you write an applet, and you want your `Applet` subclass to contain some code to handle mouse events. Since the Java language doesn't permit multiple inheritance, your class can't extend both the `Applet` and `MouseAdapter` classes. The solution is to define an inner class that extends the `MouseAdapter` class. Here's one way of defining an inner class:

```
//An example of using an inner class.
public class MyClass extends Applet {
    ...
        someObject.addMouseListener(new MyAdapter());
    ...
    class MyAdapter extends MouseAdapter {
        public void mouseClicked(MouseEvent e) {
            ...//Event handler implementation goes here...
        }
    }
}
```

Here's another example of using an inner class:

```
//An example of using an anonymous inner class.
public class MyClass extends Applet {
    ...
        someObject.addMouseListener(new MouseAdapter() {
            public void mouseClicked(MouseEvent e) {
                ...//Event handler implementation goes here...
            }
        });
    ...
}
```

Inner classes work well even if your event handler needs access to private instance variables[1] from the enclosing class. As long as you don't declare an inner class to be `static`, the inner class can refer to instance variables and methods just as if its code is in the containing class. To make a local variable available to an inner class, just save a copy of the variable as a `final` local variable.

For more information on inner classes, see Implementing Nested Classes (page 152) in the Learning the Java Language trail.

How to Write an Action Listener

Action listeners are probably the easiest—and most common—event handlers to implement. You implement an action listener to respond to the user's indication that some implementation-dependent action should occur.

When the user clicks a button, double clicks a list item, chooses a menu item, or presses Return in a text field, an action event occurs. The result is that an

---

1 Some 1.1 compilers don't let an inner class use private instance variables of the enclosing class. A workaround is to remove the `private` specifier from the instance variable's declaration.

actionPerformed message is sent to all action listeners that are registered on the relevant component.

Action Event Methods

The ActionListener[1] interface contains a single method, and thus has no corresponding adapter class. Here is the lone ActionListener method:

void actionPerformed(ActionEvent)
Called by the AWT just after the user informs the listened-to component that an action should occur.

Examples of Handling Action Events

Here is the action event handling code from an applet named Beeper:

```
public class Beeper ... implements ActionListener {
    ...
    //where initialization occurs:
        button.addActionListener(this);
    ...
    public void actionPerformed(ActionEvent e) {
        Toolkit.getDefaultToolkit().beep();
    }
}
```

The Beeper applet is described in this trail's introduction to events, Event Handling (page 420). You can find the entire program in Beeper.java (page 809).

Here are some more of the many source files in this book that contain action listeners:

- ShowDocument.java (page 712)
- ButtonDemo.java (page 810)
- DialogWindow.java (page 815)
- ListDemo.java (page 818)
- MenuWindow.java (page 821)
- TextDemo.java (page 826)

---

1 http://java.sun.com/products/jdk/1.1/docs/api/java.awt.event.ActionListener.html

The ActionEvent Class

The `actionPerformed` method has a single parameter: an `ActionEvent`[1] object. The `ActionEvent` class defines two useful methods:

`String getActionCommand()`
Returns the string associated with this action. Most objects that can generate actions support a method called `setActionCommand` that lets you set this string. If you don't set the action command explicitly, then it's generally the text displayed in the component. For objects with multiple items, and thus multiple possible actions, the action command is generally the name of the selected item.

`int getModifiers()`
Returns an integer representing the modifier keys the user was pressing when the action event occurred. You can use the `ActionEvent`-defined constants `SHIFT_MASK`, `CTRL_MASK`, `META_MASK`, `ALT_MASK` to determine which keys were pressed. For example, if the user Shift-selects a menu item, then the following expression is nonzero:

```
actionEvent.getModifiers() & ActionEvent.SHIFT_MASK
```

Also useful is the `getSource` method, which `ActionEvent` inherits from `EventObject`, by way of `AWTEvent`. See The AWTEvent Class (page 467) for more information.

How to Write an Adjustment Listener

Adjustment events notify you of changes in the value of components that implement the `Adjustable`[2] interface. `Adjustable` objects have an integer value, and they generate adjustment events whenever that value changes. The only AWT class that implements `Adjustable` is `Scrollbar`.

There are five kinds of adjustment events:

track
The user explicitly adjusted the value of the component. For a scrollbar, this might be the result of the user dragging the scrollbar knob.

unit increment, unit decrement
The user indicated the wish to slightly adjust the value of the component. For a scrollbar, this might be the result of the user clicking once on an up arrow or down arrow in the scrollbar.

---

1 http://java.sun.com/products/jdk/1.1/docs/api/java.awt.event.ActionEvent.html
2 http://java.sun.com/products/jdk/1.1/docs/api/java.awt.Adjustable.html

block increment, block decrement
The user indicated the wish to adjust the value of the component by a larger amount. For a scrollbar, this might be the result of the user clicking once just above the down arrow or just below the up arrow.

Adjustment Event Methods

The `AdjustmentListener`[1] interface contains a single method, and thus has no corresponding adapter class. Here's the method:

`void adjustmentValueChanged(AdjustmentEvent)`
Called by the AWT just after the listened-to component's value changes.

Examples of Handling Adjustment Events

Here is the adjustment event handling code from the Converter program, which uses two scrollbars to let the user set values:

```
class ConversionPanel ... implements AdjustmentListener ... {
    ...
    Scrollbar slider;
    ...
    ConversionPanel(...) {
        ...
        slider.addAdjustmentListener(this);
    }
    ...
    /** Respond to the slider. */
    public void adjustmentValueChanged(AdjustmentEvent e) {
        textField.setText(String.valueOf(e.getValue()));
        controller.convert(this);
    }
    ...
}
```

You can find the entire program in `Converter.java` (page 803).

The AdjustmentEvent Class

The `adjustmentValueChanged` method has a single parameter: an `AdjustmentEvent`[2] object. The `AdjustmentEvent` class defines the following handy methods:

---

1 http://java.sun.com/products/jdk/1.1/docs/api/java.awt.event.AdjustmentListener.html
2 http://java.sun.com/products/jdk/1.1/docs/api/java.awt.event.AdjustmentEvent.html

`Adjustable getAdjustable()`
Returns the component that generated the event. You can use this instead of the `getSource` method.

`int getAdjustmentType()`
Returns the type of adjustment that occurred. The returned value is one of the following constants defined in the `AdjustmentEvent` class: `UNIT_INCREMENT`, `UNIT_DECREMENT`, `BLOCK_INCREMENT`, `BLOCK_DECREMENT`, `TRACK`.

`int getValue()`
Returns the value of the component just after the adjustment occurred.

How to Write a Component Listener

One or more component events are generated by a `Component` object just after the component is hidden, made visible, moved, or resized. An example of a component listener might be in a GUI builder tool that's displaying information about the size of the currently selected component, and that needs to know when the component's size changes. You shouldn't need to use component events to manage basic layout and rendering.

The component hidden and component visible events occur only as the result of calls to a `Component`'s `setVisible` method (or its equivalents, `show` and `hide`). For example, a window might be miniaturized into an icon (iconified) without a component-hidden event being generated.

Component Event Methods

The `ComponentListener`[1] interface and its corresponding adapter class, `ComponentAdapter`[2], contain four methods:

`void componentHidden(ComponentEvent)`
Called by the AWT after the listened-to component is hidden as the result of the `setVisible` method being called.

`void componentMoved(ComponentEvent)`
Called by the AWT after the listened-to component moves, relative to its container. For example, if a window is moved, the window generates a component-moved event, but the components it contains do not.

`void componentResized(ComponentEvent)`
Called by the AWT after the listened-to component's size (rectangular bounds) changes.

---

1 http://java.sun.com/products/jdk/1.1/docs/api/java.awt.event.ComponentListener.html
2 http://java.sun.com/products/jdk/1.1/docs/api/java.awt.event.ComponentAdapter.html

`void componentShown(ComponentEvent)`
Called by the AWT after the listened-to component becomes visible as the result of the `setVisible` method being called.

Examples of Handling Component Events

The following applet demonstrates component events. The applet contains a button that brings up a window (`Frame`). The window contains a panel that has a label and a checkbox. The checkbox controls whether the label is visible. When you leave the applet's page, the window disappears; it reappears when you return to the applet's page. A text area displays a message every time the window, panel, label, or checkbox generates a component event.

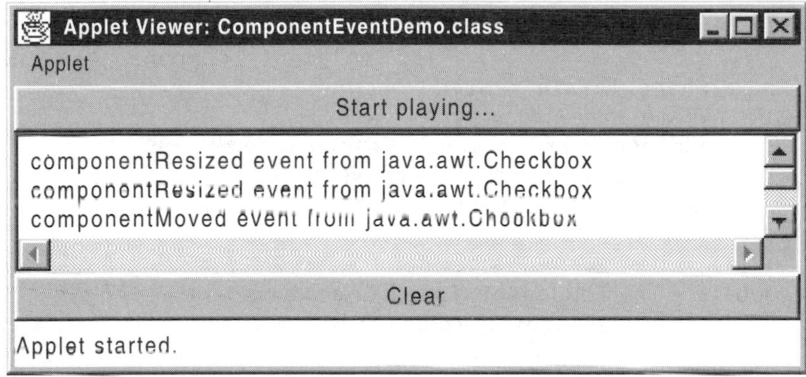

http://java.sun.com/docs/books/tutorial/ui/components/componentlistener.html

---

Try This:

1. Visit the online version of this page in a 1.1 browser.
The URL is `http://java.sun.com/docs/books/tutorial/ui/components/componentlistener.html`. As soon as the applet comes up, you should see several component event messages from the components in the window, due to layout being performed on the still-invisible window.

2. Click the button labeled "Start playing...".
The window comes up, generating one or more component-shown and component-moved events.

3. Click the checkbox to hide the label.
The label generates a component-hidden event.

4. Click the checkbox again to show the label.
The label generates a component-shown event.

5. Iconify and then deiconify the window that contains the label.
You do not get component hidden or shown events. If you want to be notified of iconification events, you should use a window listener.

6. Resize the window that contains the label.
You'll see component-resized (and possibly component-moved) events from all four components—label, checkbox, panel, and window. If the window and panel's layout managers didn't make every component as wide as possible, the panel, label, and checkbox wouldn't have been resized.

You can find the applet's code in ComponentEventDemo.java (page 827). Here is just the code related to handling component events:

```
public class ComponentEventDemo ...
                                  implements ComponentListener {
    ...//where initialization occurs:
        aFrame = new Frame("A Frame");
        ComponentPanel p = new ComponentPanel(this);
        aFrame.addComponentListener(this);
        p.addComponentListener(this);
    ...

    public void componentHidden(ComponentEvent e) {
        displayMessage("componentHidden event from "
                     + e.getComponent().getClass().getName());
    }

    public void componentMoved(ComponentEvent e) {
        displayMessage("componentMoved event from "
                     + e.getComponent().getClass().getName());
    }

    public void componentResized(ComponentEvent e) {
        displayMessage("componentResized event from "
                     + e.getComponent().getClass().getName());
    }

    public void componentShown(ComponentEvent e) {
        displayMessage("componentShown event from "
                     + e.getComponent().getClass().getName());
    }
}

class ComponentPanel extends Panel ... {
    ...
    ComponentPanel(ComponentEventDemo listener) {
        ...//after creating the label and checkbox:
```

```
        label.addComponentListener(listener);
        checkbox.addComponentListener(listener);
    }
    ...
}
```

The ComponentEvent Class

Each component event method has a single parameter: a ComponentEvent[1] object. The ComponentEvent class defines the following useful method:

Component getComponent()
Returns the component that generated the event. You can use this instead of the getSource method.

How to Write a Container Listener

Container events are generated by a Container just after a component is added to or removed from the container. These events are for notification *only*—no container listener need be present for components to be successfully added or removed.

Container Event Methods

The ContainerListener[2] interface and its corresponding adapter class, ContainerAdapter[3], contain two methods:

void componentAdded(ContainerEvent)
Called by the AWT after a component is added to the listened-to container.

void componentRemoved(ContainerEvent)
Called by the AWT just after a component is removed from the listened-to container.

Examples of Handling Container Events

The following applet demonstrates container events. By clicking "Add a button" or "Remove a button," you can add components to or remove them from a panel at the bottom of the applet. Each time a component is added to or removed from the panel, the panel fires off a container event, and the panel's container listener is notified. The listener displays descriptive messages in the text area at the top of the applet.

---

[1] http://java.sun.com/products/jdk/1.1/docs/api/java.awt.event.ComponentEvent.html
[2] http://java.sun.com/products/jdk/1.1/docs/api/java.awt.event.ContainerListener.html
[3] http://java.sun.com/products/jdk/1.1/docs/api/java.awt.event.ContainerAdapter.html

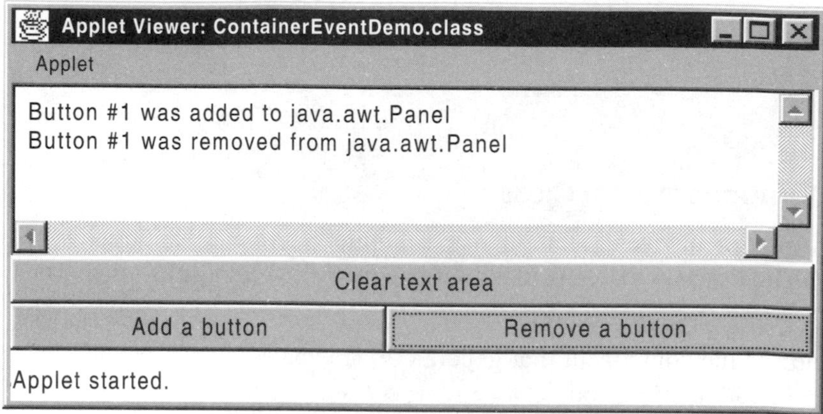

http://java.sun.com/docs/books/tutorial/ui/components/containerlistener.html

---

Try This:

1. Visit the online version of this page in a 1.1 browser.
The URL is `http://java.sun.com/docs/books/tutorial/ui/components/containerlistener.html`.

2. Click the button labeled "Add a button."
You'll see a button appear near the bottom of the applet. The container listener (in this example, an instance of `ContainerEventDemo`) reacts to the resulting component-added event by displaying "Button #1 was added to java.awt.Panel" at the top of the applet.

3. Click the button labeled "Remove a button."
This removes the most recently added button from the panel and causes the container listener to receive a component-removed event.

You can find the applet's code in `ContainerEventDemo.java` (page 830). Here is the applet's container-event handling code:

```
public class ContainerEventDemo ...
                                implements ContainerListener {
    ...//where initialization occurs:
        buttonPanel = new Panel();
        buttonPanel.addContainerListener(this);
    ...
    public void componentAdded(ContainerEvent e) {
        displayMessage(" added to ", e);
    }
```

```
public void componentRemoved(ContainerEvent e) {
        displayMessage(" removed from ", e);
    }

    void displayMessage(String action, ContainerEvent e) {
        display.append(((Button)e.getChild()).getLabel()
                       + " was"
                       + action
                       + e.getContainer().getClass().getName()
                       + newline);
    }
    ...
}
```

The ContainerEvent Class

Each component event method has a single parameter: a `ContainerEvent`[1] object. The `ContainerEvent` class defines the two useful methods:

`Container getComponent()`
: Returns the component whose addition or removal triggered this event.

`Container getContainer()`
: Returns the container that generated the event. You can use this instead of the `getSource` method.

How to Write a Focus Listener

Many components—even those primarily operated with the mouse, such as buttons—can be operated by the keyboard. For a keypress to affect a component, the component must have the keyboard focus.

From the user's point of view, the component with the keyboard focus is generally prominent—with a thicker border than usual, for example—and the window containing the component is also more prominent than other windows on-screen. These visual cues let the user know to which component any typing will go. At most one component in the window system can have the keyboard focus.

Focus events are generated whenever a component gains or loses the keyboard focus. Exactly how components gain the focus depends on the window system. Typically, the user sets the focus by clicking a window or component, by tabbing between components, or by otherwise interacting with a component. Once the focus is in a window (the window is *activated*), a program can use the `Component requestFocus` method to request that a specific component get the focus.

---

1 http://java.sun.com/products/jdk/1.1/docs/api/java.awt.event.ContainerEvent.html

Focus Event Methods

The `FocusListener`[1] interface and its corresponding adapter class, `FocusAdapter`[2], contain two methods:

`void focusGained(FocusEvent)`
Called by the AWT just after the listened-to component gets the focus.

`void focusLost(FocusEvent)`
Called by the AWT just after the listened-to component loses the focus.

Examples of Handling Focus Events

The following applet demonstrates focus events. By clicking the top button in the applet, you can bring up a window that contains a variety of components. A focus listener listens for focus events on each component in the window, including the window itself (which is an instance of a `Frame` subclass called `FocusFrame`).

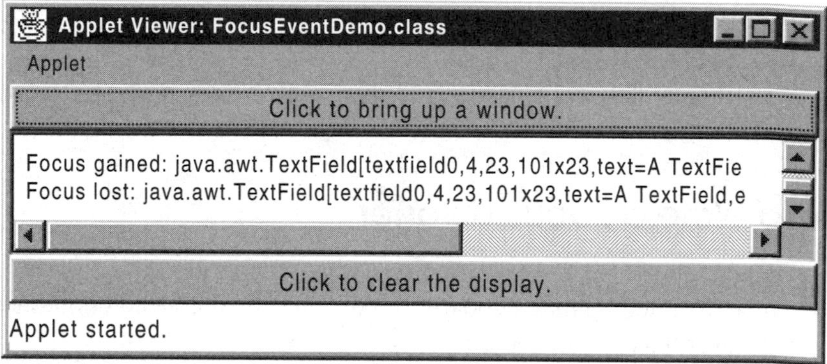

http://java.sun.com/docs/books/tutorial/ui/components/focuslistener.html

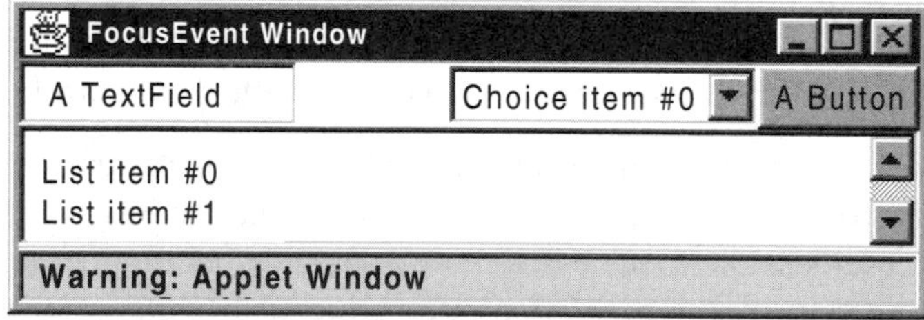

http://java.sun.com/docs/books/tutorial/ui/components/focuslistener.html

---

1 http://java.sun.com/products/jdk/1.1/docs/api/java.awt.event.FocusListener.html
2 http://java.sun.com/products/jdk/1.1/docs/api/java.awt.event.FocusAdapter.html

---

Try This:

1. **Visit the online version of this page in a 1.1 browser.**
   The URL is `http://java.sun.com/docs/books/tutorial/ui/components/focuslistener.html`.

2. **Bring up the Focus Event Window by clicking the top button in the applet.**
   If necessary, click the Focus Event Window so that its contents can gain the keyboard focus. You'll see a "Focus gained" message in the applet's display area. The way in which its window gets the focus and which components get the focus are system dependent by default. You can detect when the window gets or loses the focus by implementing a window listener and listening for window activation or deactivation events.

3. **Click the button at the right of the Focus Event Window, and then click in another component, such as the text field.**
   Notice that when the focus changes from one component to another, the first component generates a focus-lost event before the second component generates a focus-gained event.

4. **Try changing the focus by pressing Tab or Shift-Tab.**
   Most systems let you use the Tab key to cycle through components that are able to get the focus.

5. **Iconify the Focus Event Window.**
   You should see a "Focus lost" message for the last component that had focus.

You can find the applet's code in `FocusEventDemo.java` (page 833). Here is the applet's focus-event handling code:

```
public class FocusEventDemo ...
                          implements FocusListener {
    ...//where initialization occurs:
        //Create but don't show window.
        window = new FocusWindow(this);
    }
    ...
    public void focusGained(FocusEvent e) {
        displayMessage("Focus gained", e);
    }

    public void focusLost(FocusEvent e) {
        displayMessage("Focus lost", e);
```

```
    }
void displayMessage(String prefix, FocusEvent e) {
        display.append(prefix
                       + ": "
                       + e.getComponent()
                       + newline);
    }
    ...
}

class FocusWindow extends Frame {
    ...
    public FocusWindow(FocusListener listener) {
        super("Focus Event Window");
        ...
        this.addFocusListener(listener);
        textField.addFocusListener(listener);
        label.addFocusListener(listener);
        choice.addFocusListener(listener);
        button.addFocusListener(listener);
        list.addFocusListener(listener);
        ...
    }
}
```

The FocusEvent Class

Each component event method has a single parameter: a `FocusEvent`[1] object. The `FocusEvent` class defines the following method:

`boolean isTemporary()`
Returns true if a focus loss is temporary. You'll need to use this method if you're implementing a component that can indicate that it will get the focus if its window regains the focus.

The `getComponent` method, which `FocusEvent` inherits from `ComponentEvent`[2], returns the component that generated the focus event.

How to Write an Item Listener

Item events are generated by components that implement the `ItemSelectable`[3] interface. These are components that maintain state—generally the on/off state for one or more items. The 1.1 AWT components that generate item events are checkboxes, checkbox menu items, choices, and lists.

---

1 http://java.sun.com/products/jdk/1.1/docs/api/java.awt.event.FocusEvent.html
2 http://java.sun.com/products/jdk/1.1/docs/api/java.awt.event.ComponentEvent.html
3 http://java.sun.com/products/jdk/1.1/docs/api/java.awt.event.ItemSelectable.html

Item Event Methods

The ItemListener[1] interface contains a single method, so it has no corresponding adapter class. Here's the method:

void itemStateChanged(ItemEvent)
Called by the AWT just after a state change in the listened-to component.

Examples of Handling Item Events

Here is some item-event handling code taken from ComponentEventDemo.java (page 827):

```
public void itemStateChanged(ItemEvent e) {
    if (e.getStateChange() == ItemEvent.SELECTED) {
        label.setVisible(true);
    } else {
        label.setVisible(false);
    }
}
```

You can find examples of item listeners in the following source files:

- CardWindow.java (page 848)
- Converter.java (page 803)
- ChoiceDemo.java (page 814)
- ListDemo.java (page 818)
- MenuWindow.java (page 821)

The ItemEvent Class

The itemStateChanged method has a single parameter: an ItemEvent[2] object. The ItemEvent class defines the following handy methods:

Object getItem()
Returns the component-specific object associated with the item whose state has changed. Often this is a String containing the text on the selected item. For an item event generated by a List, this is an Integer that specifies the index of the selected item.

ItemSelectable getItemSelectable()
Returns the component that generated the item event. You can use this instead of the getSource method.

---

1 http://java.sun.com/products/jdk/1.1/docs/api/java.awt.event.ItemListener.html
2 http://java.sun.com/products/jdk/1.1/docs/api/java.awt.event.ItemEvent.html

`int getStateChange()`
Returns the new state of the item. The `ItemEvent` class defines two states: `SELECTED` and `DESELECTED`.

How to Write a Key Listener

Key events tell you when the user is typing at the keyboard. Specifically, key events are generated by the component with the keyboard focus when the user presses or releases keyboard keys. [For information about focus, see How to Write a Focus Listener (page 479).]

You can be notified about two basic kinds of key events: the typing of a Unicode character, and the pressing or releasing of a key on the keyboard. The first kind of event is called a *key-typed* event. The second kind are *key-pressed* and *key-released* events.

In general, you should try to handle only key-typed events unless you need to know when the user presses keys that don't correspond to characters. For example, if you want to know when the user types some Unicode character—whether as the result of pressing one key such as 'a' or from pressing several keys in sequence—you should handle key-typed events. On the other hand, if you need to know when the user presses the F1 key, you need to handle key-pressed events.

Note: To generate key events, a component *must* have the keyboard focus.

To make a component get the keyboard focus, follow these steps:

1. Make sure the component can get the keyboard focus. For example, on some systems labels might not be able to get the keyboard focus.
2. Make sure that the component requests the focus when appropriate. For custom components, you'll probably need to implement a `MouseListener` that calls the `requestFocus` method when the component is clicked.
3. If you're writing a custom component, implement the component's `isFocusTraversable` method so that it returns true when the component is enabled. This lets the user tab to your component.

Key Event Methods

The `KeyListener`[1] interface and its corresponding adapter class, `KeyAdapter`[2], contain three methods:

`void keyTyped(KeyEvent)`
: Called by the AWT just after the user types a Unicode character into the listened-to component.

`void keyPressed(KeyEvent)`
: Called by the AWT just after the user presses a key while the listened-to component has the focus.

`void keyReleased(KeyEvent)`
: Called by the AWT just after the user releases a key while the listened-to component has the focus.

Examples of Handling Key Events

The following applet demonstrates key events. It consists of a text field that you can type into, followed by a text area that displays a message every time the text field fires a key event. A button at the bottom of the applet lets you clear both the text field and the text area.

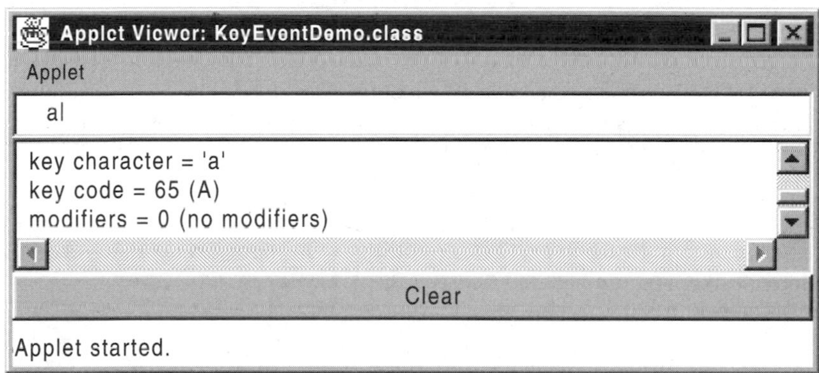

http://java.sun.com/docs/books/tutorial/ui/components/keylistener.html

---

Try This:

1. Visit the online version of this page in a 1.1 browser.
The URL is `http://java.sun.com/docs/books/tutorial/ui/components/keylistener.html`.

2. Click in the applet's text field so that it gets the keyboard focus.

---

1 http://java.sun.com/products/jdk/1.1/docs/api/java.awt.event.KeyListener.html
2 http://java.sun.com/products/jdk/1.1/docs/api/java.awt.event.KeyAdapter.html

3. Type a lowercase 'a' by pressing and releasing the A key on the keyboard.
The text field fires three events: a key-pressed event, a key-typed event, and a key-released event. Note that the key-typed event doesn't have key-code information; key-typed events also don't have modifier information.

4. Press the Clear button.
You might want to do this after each of the following steps.

5. Press and release the Shift key.
The text field fires two events: a key press and a key release. The text field doesn't generate a key-typed event because Shift, by itself, doesn't correspond to any character.

6. Type an uppercase 'A' by pressing the Shift and A keys.
You'll see the following events: key pressed (Shift), key pressed (A), key typed ('A'), key released (A), key released (Shift).

7. Type an uppercase 'A' by pressing and releasing the Caps Lock key, and then pressing the A key.
You'll see the following events: key pressed (Caps Lock), key pressed (A), key typed ('A'), key released (A). Notice that the Caps Lock key doesn't generate a key-released event until you press and release it again. The same is true of other two-state keys, such as Scroll Lock and Num Lock.

8. Press and hold the A key.
Does it automatically repeat? If so, you'll see the same events that you would have seen if you pressed and released the A key repeatedly.

You can find the applet's code in `KeyEventDemo.java` (page 836). Here is the applet's key-event handling code:

```
public class KeyEventDemo ... implements KeyListener {
    ...//where initialization occurs:
        typingArea = new TextField(20);
        typingArea.addKeyListener(this);
    ...
    /** Handle the key typed event from the text field. */
    public void keyTyped(KeyEvent e) {
        displayInfo(e, "KEY TYPED: ");
    }

    /** Handle the key pressed event from the text field. */
    public void keyPressed(KeyEvent e) {
        displayInfo(e, "KEY PRESSED: ");
```

```
        }

        /** Handle the key released event from the text field. */
        public void keyReleased(KeyEvent e) {
            displayInfo(e, "KEY RELEASED: ");
        }

        protected void displayInfo(KeyEvent e, String s) {
            ...
            char c = e.getKeyChar();
            int keyCode = e.getKeyCode();
            int modifiers = e.getModifiers();
            ...//Display the char, key code, and modifiers...
        }
    }
```

The KeyEvent Class

Each component event method has a single parameter: a `KeyEvent`[1] object. The `KeyEvent` class defines the following useful methods:

`int getKeyChar()`
`void setKeyChar(int)`
Get or set the Unicode character associated with this event.

`int getKeyCode()`
`void setKeyCode(int)`
Get or set the key code associated with this event. The key code identifies the particular key on the keyboard that the user pressed or released. The `KeyEvent` class defines many key code constants for common keys. For example, `VK_A` specifies the A key, and `VK_ESCAPE` specifies the Escape key.

`void setModifiers(int)`
Sets the state of the modifier keys for this event. You can get the state of the modifier keys using the `InputEvent` `getModifiers` method.

`String getKeyText()`
`String getKeyModifiersText()`
Return text descriptions of the event's key code and modifier keys, respectively.

The `KeyEvent` class inherits many useful methods from `InputEvent`[2] and `ComponentEvent`.[3] The following methods are described in The MouseEvent Class (page 490):

---

1 http://java.sun.com/products/jdk/1.1/docs/api/java.awt.event.KeyEvent.html
2 http://java.sun.com/products/jdk/1.1/docs/api/java.awt.event.InputEvent.html
3 http://java.sun.com/products/jdk/1.1/docs/api/java.awt.event.ComponentEvent.html

- `Component getComponent()`
- `void consume()`
- `int getWhen()`
- `boolean isAltDown()`
- `boolean isControlDown()`
- `boolean isMetaDown()`
- `boolean isShiftDown()`
- `int getModifiers()`

How to Write a Mouse Listener

Mouse events tell you when the user uses the mouse (or similar input device) to interact with a component. Mouse events occur when the cursor enters or exits a component's on-screen area and the user presses or releases the mouse button.

Because tracking the cursor's motion involves much more system overhead than tracking other mouse events, mouse-motion events are separated into a separate listener type [see How to Write a Mouse-Motion Listener (page 492)].

Mouse Event Methods

The `MouseListener`[1] interface and its corresponding adapter class, `MouseAdapter`[2], contain these methods:

`void mouseClicked(MouseEvent)`
Called by the AWT just after the user clicks the listened-to component.

`void mouseEntered(MouseEvent)`
Called by the AWT just after the cursor enters the bounds of the listened-to component.

`void mouseExited(MouseEvent)`
Called by the AWT just after the cursor exits the bounds of the listened-to component.

`void mousePressed(MouseEvent)`
Called by the AWT just after the user presses a mouse button while the cursor is over the listened-to component.

`void mouseReleased(MouseEvent)`
Called by the AWT just after the user releases a mouse button after a mouse press over the listened-to component.

---

1 http://java.sun.com/products/jdk/1.1/docs/api/java.awt.event.MouseListener.html
2 http://java.sun.com/products/jdk/1.1/docs/api/java.awt.event.MouseAdapter.html

One complication affects mouse-entered, mouse-exited, and mouse-released events. When the user drags (presses and holds the mouse button and then moves the mouse), then the component that the cursor was over when the drag started is the one that receives all subsequent mouse and mouse-motion events up to and including the mouse button release. That means that no other component will receive a single mouse event—not even a mouse-released event—while the drag is occurring.

Examples of Handling Mouse Events

The following applet contains a mouse listener. At the top of the applet is a blank area (implemented, strangely enough, by a class named `BlankArea`). A mouse listener listens for events both on the `BlankArea` instance and on its container, which is an instance of `MouseEventDemo`. Each time a mouse event occurs, a descriptive message appears under the blank area. By moving the cursor on top of the blank area and occasionally pressing mouse buttons, you can generate mouse events. You can find the applet's code in `MouseEventDemo.java` (page 838).

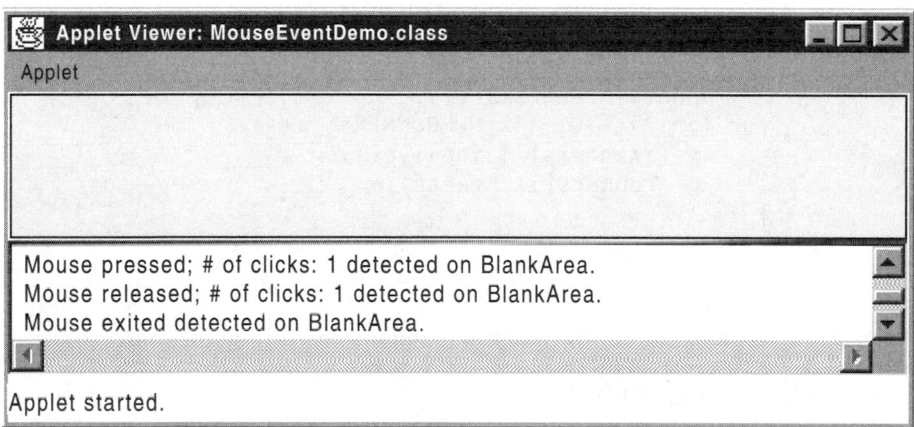

http://java.sun.com/docs/books/tutorial/ui/components/mouselistener.html

---

Try This:

1. **Visit the online version of this page in a 1.1 browser.**
The URL is `http://java.sun.com/docs/books/tutorial/ui/components/mouselistener.html`.

2. **Move the cursor into the yellow rectangle at the top of the applet.**
You'll see one or more mouse-entered events.

3. Press and hold the mouse button.
You'll see a mouse-pressed event. You might see some extra mouse events, such as mouse-exited and then mouse-entered.

4. Release the mouse button.
You'll see a mouse-released event. If you didn't move the mouse, a mouse-clicked event will follow.

5. Press and hold the mouse button, and then drag the mouse so that the cursor ends up outside the applet's area. Release the mouse button.
You'll see a mouse-pressed event, followed by a mouse-exited event, followed by a mouse-released event. You are not notified of the cursor's motion. To get mouse-motion events, you must implement a mouse-motion listener.

Here's an example of creating and registering a mouse listener, taken from `RaceApplet.java` (page 765).

```
...//where initialization occurs:
    addMouseListener(new MyAdapter());
...
class MyAdapter extends MouseAdapter {
    public void mouseClicked(MouseEvent evt) {
        if (!updateThread.isAlive())
            updateThread.start();
        for (int i = 0; i < NUMRUNNERS; i++) {
            if (!runners[i].isAlive())
                runners[i].start();
        }
    }
}
```

You can find more examples of mouse listeners in the following source files:

- `SimpleClick.java` (page 709)
- `CoordinatesDemo.java` (page 861)
- `RectangleDemo.java` (page 863)
- `AnimatorApplet.java` (page 883)
- `AnimatorApplication.java` (page 885)

The MouseEvent Class

Each mouse event method has a single parameter: a `MouseEvent`[1] object. The `MouseEvent` class defines the following useful methods:

---

1 http://java.sun.com/products/jdk/1.1/docs/api/java.awt.event.MouseEvent.html

`int getClickCount()`

Returns the number of quick, consecutive clicks the user has made (including this event).

`int getX()`
`int getY()`
`int getPoint()`

Returns the (x,y) position at which the event occurred, relative to the component that generated the event.

`boolean isPopupTrigger()`

Returns true if the mouse event should cause a popup menu to appear. Because popup triggers are platform dependent, if your program uses popup menus, you should call `isPopupTrigger` for all mouse-pressed and mouse-released events generated by components over which the popup can appear. See How to Use Menus (page 448) for more information about popup menus.

The `MouseEvent` class inherits the following handy method from `ComponentEvent`[1]:

`Component getComponent()`

Returns the component that generated the event. You can use this instead of the `getSource` method.

The `MouseEvent` class inherits many useful methods from `InputEvent`[2]:

`void consume()`

Causes the event not to be processed by the component's peer. You might use this method to discard letters typed into a text field that accepts only numbers.

`int getWhen()`

Returns a timestamp indicating when this event occurred. The higher the timestamp, the more recently the event occurred

`boolean isAltDown()`
`boolean isControlDown()`
`boolean isMetaDown()`
`boolean isShiftDown()`

Returns the state of individual modifier keys at the time the event was generated.

---

1 http://java.sun.com/products/jdk/1.1/docs/api/java.awt.event.ComponentEvent.html
2 http://java.sun.com/products/jdk/1.1/docs/api/java.awt.event.InputEvent.html

`int getModifiers()`
: Returns the state of all the modifier keys and mouse buttons when the event was generated. You can use this method to determine which mouse button was pressed (or newly released) when a mouse event was generated. The `InputEvent` class defines these constants for use with the `getModifiers` method: `ALT_MASK`, `BUTTON1_MASK`, `BUTTON2_MASK`, `BUTTON3_MASK`, `CTRL_MASK`, `META_MASK`, `SHIFT_MASK`. For example, the following expression is true if the right button was pressed:

```
(evt.getModifiers()
 & InputEvent.BUTTON3_MASK) == InputEvent.BUTTON3_MASK
```

How to Write a Mouse-Motion Listener

Mouse-motion events tell you when the user uses the mouse (or similar input device) to move the onscreen cursor. For information on listening for other kinds of mouse events, such as clicks, see How to Write a Mouse Listener (page 488).

Mouse-Motion Event Methods

The `MouseMotionListener`[1] interface and its corresponding adapter class, `MouseMotionAdapter`[2], contain these methods:

`void mouseDragged(MouseEvent)`
: Called by the AWT in response to the user moving the mouse while holding a mouse button down. This event is fired by the component that fired the most recent mouse-pressed event, even if the cursor is no longer over that component.

`void mouseMoved(MouseEvent)`
: Called by the AWT in response to the user moving the mouse with no mouse buttons pressed. This event is fired by the component that's currently under the cursor.

Examples of Handling Mouse-Motion Events

The following applet contains a mouse-motion listener. It's exactly like the applet in How to Write a Mouse Listener (page 488), except it substitutes `MouseMotionListener` for `MouseListener`, and implements the `mouseDragged` and `mouseMoved` methods instead of the mouse-listener methods. You can find the applet's code in `MouseMotionEventDemo.java` (page 840).

---

1 http://java.sun.com/products/jdk/1.1/docs/api/java.awt.event.MouseMotionListener.html
2 http://java.sun.com/products/jdk/1.1/docs/api/java.awt.event.MouseMotionAdapter.html

Applet Viewer: MouseMotionEventDemo.class
Applet
Mouse moved; # of clicks: 0 detected on BlankArea.
Mouse dragged; # of clicks: 0 detected on BlankArea.
Applet started.

http://java.sun.com/docs/books/tutorial/ui/components/mousemotionlistener.html

---

Try This:

1. Visit the online version of this page in a 1.1 browser.
The URL is `http://java.sun.com/docs/books/tutorial/ui/components/mousemotionlistener.html`.

2. Move the cursor into the yellow rectangle at the top of the applet.
You'll see one or more mouse-moved events.

3. Press and hold the mouse button, and then move the mouse so that the cursor is outside the yellow rectangle.
You'll see mouse-dragged events.

The following code is from an event handling class in the source file `RectangleDemo.java` (page 863). This class handles three kinds of events: mouse presses, mouse drags, and mouse releases. These events correspond to the `mousePressed` method (from `MouseListener`), `mouseDragged` (from `MouseMotionListener`), and `mouseReleased` (from `MouseListener`). Thus, this class must implement both `MouseListener` and `MouseMotionListener`. To avoid having to define too many empty methods, this class doesn't implement `MouseListener` directly. Instead, it extends `MouseAdapter` and implements only `MouseMotionListener` directly.

```
...//where initialization occurs:
    MyListener myListener = new MyListener();
    addMouseListener(myListener);
    addMouseMotionListener(myListener);
```

```
...
class MyListener extends MouseAdapter
                 implements MouseMotionListener {
    public void mousePressed(MouseEvent e) {
        int x = e.getX();
        int y = e.getY();
        currentRect = new Rectangle(x, y, 0, 0);
        repaint();
    }

    public void mouseDragged(MouseEvent e) {
        updateSize(e);
    }

    public void mouseMoved(MouseEvent e) {
        //Do nothing.
    }

    public void mouseReleased(MouseEvent e) {
        updateSize(e);
    }

    void updateSize(MouseEvent e) {
        int x = e.getX();
        int y = e.getY();
        currentRect.setSize(x - currentRect.x,
                            y - currentRect.y);
        repaint();
    }
}
```

Event Methods Used by Mouse-Motion Listeners

Each mouse-motion event method has a single parameter—and it's *not* called `MouseMotionEvent`! Instead, each mouse-motion event method has a `MouseEvent` argument. See The MouseEvent Class (page 490) for information about using `MouseEvent` objects.

How to Write a Text Listener

Text events are generated after the text in a text component has somehow changed. To get earlier notification of text changes—for example, to intercept incorrect characters—you should write a key listener [see How to Write a Key Listener (page 484)]. The 1.1 AWT components that generate text events are text fields and text areas.

Text Event Methods

The `TextListener`[1] interface contains a single method, so it has no corresponding adapter class. Here's the method:

`void textValueChanged(TextEvent)`
Called by the AWT just after the text in the listened-to component changes.

Examples of Handling Text Events

The following applet demonstrates text events. It contains two editable text components, a text field and a text area. Pressing Return in the text field causes the field's contents to be appended to the text area. Each of the editable text components has a text listener. The two text listeners, which are instances of a single class, append a message to an uneditable text area at the right of the applet. A button at the bottom right of the applet lets you clear the message display area.

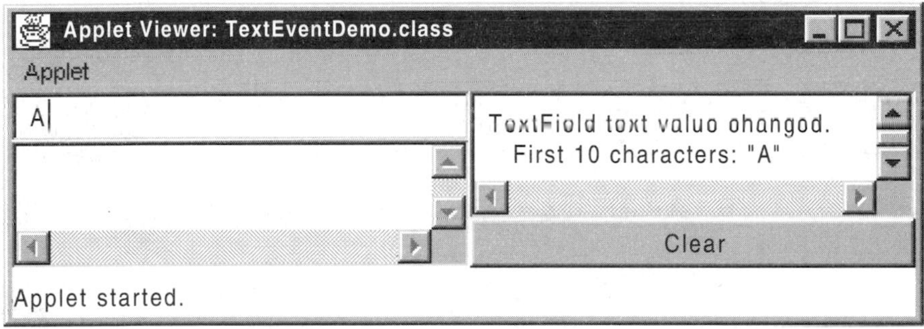

http://java.sun.com/docs/books/tutorial/ui/components/textlistener.html

---

Try This:

1. Visit the online version of this page in a 1.1 browser.
The URL is `http://java.sun.com/docs/books/tutorial/ui/components/textlistener.html`.

2. Click the text field at the upper left of the applet, then press the A key on the keyboard.
A text event occurs, and you'll see a message in the display area at the right of the applet.

3. Type a few more characters.
A text event occurs each time you type a character.

---

1 http://java.sun.com/products/jdk/1.1/docs/api/java.awt.event.TextListener.html

4. Press Return.
The text field does not generate a text event. Instead, it generates an action event, and the action listener copies the text field's contents into the editable text area. The editable text area reacts by generating a single text event, no matter how many characters are copied into it.

5. Click the editable text area—the large area at the bottom left of the applet—and then press a character key on the keyboard.
The text area fires a text event.

You can find the applet's code in TextDemo.java (page 826). This applet implements its text-event handling inside an inner class named `MyTextListener`. It creates and registers two instances of `MyTextListener`, one for each editable text component. Here is the applet's text-event handling code:

```
...//where initialization occurs:
    textField.addTextListener(new MyTextListener(
                                        "Text Field"));
    textArea.addTextListener(new MyTextListener(
                                        "Text Area"));
...

class MyTextListener implements TextListener {
    String preface;
    String newline;

    public MyTextListener(String source) {
        newline = System.getProperty("line.separator");
        preface = source
                  + " text value changed."
                  + newline
                  + "   First 10 characters: \"";
    }

    public void textValueChanged(TextEvent e) {
        TextComponent tc = (TextComponent)e.getSource();
        String s = tc.getText();
        try {
            s = s.substring(0, 10);
        } catch (StringIndexOutOfBoundsException ex) {
        }

        displayArea.append(preface + s + "\"" + newline);
        ...
    }
}
```

The TextEvent Class

The `textValueChanged` method has a single parameter: a `TextEvent`[1] object. The `TextEvent` class defines no generally useful methods. The only method you'll typically invoke on a `TextEvent` is the `getSource` method, which `ActionEvent` inherits from `EventObject`, by way of `AWTEvent`. See The AWTEvent Class (page 467) for more information.

How to Write a Window Listener

Window events are generated by a `Window` object just after the window is opened, closed, iconified, deiconified, activated, or deactivated. *Opening* a window means showing it for the first time; *closing* it means removing the window from the screen. *Iconifying* it means substituting a small icon on the desktop for the window; *deiconifying* it means the opposite. A window is *activated* if it or a component it contains has the keyboard focus; *deactivation* occurs when the window and all of its contents lose the keyboard focus.

The most common use of window listeners is closing windows. If a program doesn't handle window-closing events, then nothing happens when the user attempts to close a window. An application that features a single window might react to window-closing events from that window by exiting. Other programs usually react to window-closing events by disposing of the window or making it invisible. See How to Use Frames (page 441) for an example of a handler for window-closing events.

Another common use of window listeners is to stop threads and release resources when a window is iconified, and to start up again when the window is deiconified. This way, you can avoid unnecessarily using the processor or other resources. For example, when a window that contains animation is iconified, it should stop its animation thread and free any large buffers. When the window is deiconified, it can start the thread again and recreate the buffers.

Window Event Methods

The `WindowListener`[2] interface and its corresponding adapter class, `WindowAdapter`[3], contain these methods:

`void windowOpened(WindowEvent)`
Called by the AWT just after the listened-to window has been shown for the first time.

---

1 http://java.sun.com/products/jdk/1.1/docs/api/java.awt.event.TextEvent.html
2 http://java.sun.com/products/jdk/1.1/docs/api/java.awt.event.WindowListener.html
3 http://java.sun.com/products/jdk/1.1/docs/api/java.awt.event.WindowAdapter.html

`void windowClosing(WindowEvent)`
Called by the AWT in response to a user request that the listened-to window be closed. To actually close the window, the listener should invoke the window's `dispose` or `setVisible(false)` method.

`void windowClosed(WindowEvent)`
Called by the AWT just after the listened-to window has closed.

`void windowIconified(WindowEvent)`
`void windowDeiconified(WindowEvent)`
Called by the AWT just after the listened-to window is iconified or deiconified, respectively.

`void windowActivated(WindowEvent)`
`void windowDeactivated(WindowEvent)`
Called by the AWT just after the listened-to window is activated or deactivated, respectively.

Examples of Handling Window Events

The following applet demonstrates window events. By clicking the top button in the applet, you can bring up a small window. The controlling class listens for window events from the window, printing a message whenever it detects a window event. You can find the applet's code in `WindowEventDemo.java` (page 844).

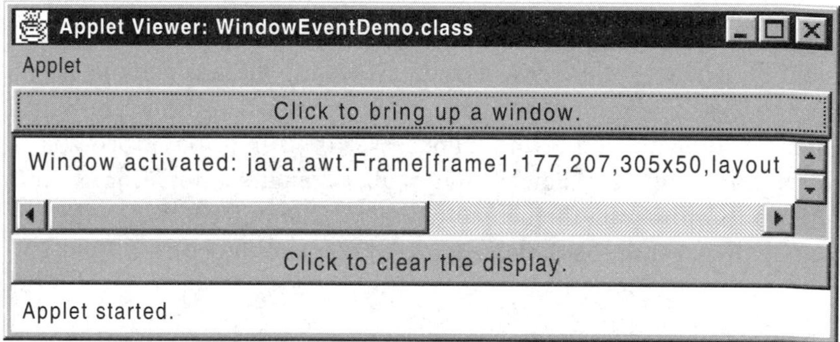

http://java.sun.com/docs/books/tutorial/ui/components/windowlistener.html

http://java.sun.com/docs/books/tutorial/ui/components/windowlistener.html

---

Try This:

1. **Visit the online version of this page in a 1.1 browser.**
The URL is `http://java.sun.com/docs/books/tutorial/ui/components/windowlistener.html`.

2. **Bring up the Window Demo Window by clicking the applet's top button.**
You'll see a "Window opened" message in the applet's display area.

3. **Click the window if it doesn't already have the focus.**
Do you see a "Window activated" message in the applet's display area?

4. **Iconify the window, using the window controls.**
You'll see a "Window iconified" message in the applet's display area.

5. **Deiconify the window.**
You'll see a "Window deiconified" message in the applet's display area.

6. **Close the window, using the window controls.**
You'll see at least two messages appear in the applet's display area: "Window closing" and "Window closed."

Here is the applet's window-event handling code:

```
public class WindowEventDemo ... implements WindowListener {
    ...//where initialization occurs:
        //Create but don't show window.
        window = new Frame("Window Event Window");
        window.addWindowListener(this);
        window.add("Center",
                 new Label("The applet listens to this window"
                           " for window events."));
        window.pack();
    }

    public void windowClosing(WindowEvent e) {
            window.setVisible(false);
        displayMessage("Window closing", e);
    }

    public void windowClosed(WindowEvent e) {
        displayMessage("Window closed", e);
    }

    public void windowOpened(WindowEvent e) {
```

```
            displayMessage("Window opened", e);
        }

        public void windowIconified(WindowEvent e) {
            displayMessage("Window iconified", e);
        }

        public void windowDeiconified(WindowEvent e) {
            displayMessage("Window deiconified", e);
        }

        public void windowActivated(WindowEvent e) {
            displayMessage("Window activated", e);
        }

        public void windowDeactivated(WindowEvent e) {
            displayMessage("Window deactivated", e);
        }

        void displayMessage(String prefix, WindowEvent e) {
            display.append(prefix
                           + ": "
                           + e.getWindow()
                           + newline);
        }
        ...
    }
```

Here are some of the source files that contain window listeners:

- `ShowDocument.java` (page 712)
- `ComponentEventDemo.java` (page 827)
- `FlowWindow.java` (page 849)
- `AnimatorApplication.java` (page 885)

The WindowEvent Class

Each window event method has a single parameter: a `WindowEvent`[1] object. The `WindowEvent` class defines one useful method:

`Window getWindow()`
Returns the window that generated the event. You can use this instead of the `getSource` method.

1 http://java.sun.com/products/jdk/1.1/docs/api/java.awt.event.WindowEvent.html

Details of the Component Architecture

The AWT is designed to have a platform-independent API and yet to preserve each platform's look and feel. For example, the AWT has just one API for buttons (provided by the `Button` class), but a button in Mac OS looks different from one in Windows 95/NT.

The AWT achieves its seemingly contradictory goals by providing classes (*components*) that provide a platform-independent API but that make use of platform-specific implementations (*peers*). In particular, every AWT component class (`Component`, `MenuComponent`, and their subclasses) has an equivalent peer class, and every component object has a peer object that controls the component's look and feel.

Figure 69 illustrates how a typical AWT component (a `Button`) is mapped to a peer. `Button` peers are implemented in platform-specific classes that implement the `java.awt.peer ButtonPeer` interface. The `java.awt Toolkit` class defines methods that choose exactly which class to use for the peer implementation.

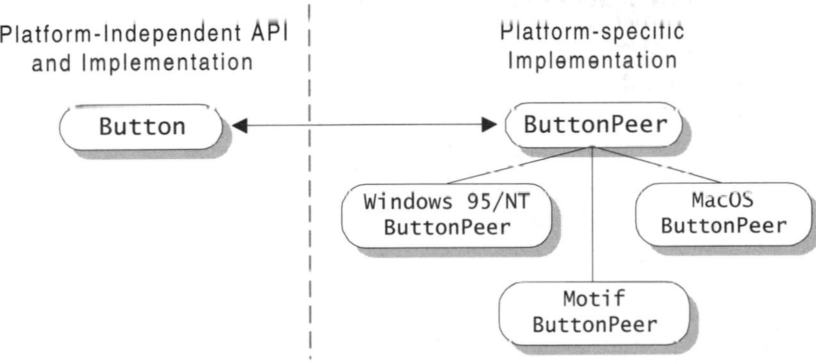

Figure 69: How Button is mapped to ButtonPeer.

Peers are created lazily, often just before their corresponding component object is drawn for the first time. Notice one side effect of this: The size of a component is not usually valid until after the component has been shown for the first time.

A component's peer is created when one of the following happens:

- The `pack`, `show`, or `setVisible(true)` method is invoked on a window that contains the component.
- The component is added to a container that is already visible.

If you add a component to a visible container, you need to explicitly tell the AWT to show the component and recalculate the layout of its container. You do this by calling the `validate` method. Although you can invoke `validate` directly on the component you're adding, it's usually invoked on the container, instead. The reason is that invoking `validate` on a container causes a chain reaction—every component under the container gets validated, as well. For example, after you add components to an `Applet` object, you call `validate` on the `Applet`, which makes it lay out and show all the new components.

Before you can get the correct size of a component, you need to make sure the component has a peer and (if you added the component to a visible container) call the `validate` method.

How Peers Handle Events

Peers implement the feel (and, indirectly, the look) of UI components by reacting to user input events. For example, when the user clicks a button, the peer reacts by causing the button's appearance to change and by forwarding an action event to the AWT, which notifies the button's action listeners.

Peers are at the end of the event chain for input events such as mouse clicks and key presses. When the user presses a key while a text field has the focus, for example, all key listeners registered on the `TextField` component are notified of the key-pressed event. If any of the key listeners calls the event's `consume` method, the peer never gets to see and react to the event. Normally, none of the key listeners consumes the event, and the peer is notified of the key press.

http://java.sun.com/docs/books/tutorial/ui/layout/index.html

20

Laying Out Components Within a Container

THE following figures show two programs, each of which displays five buttons. The Java code for both programs is almost identical. So why do they look so different? Because they use different *layout managers* to control the layout of the buttons.

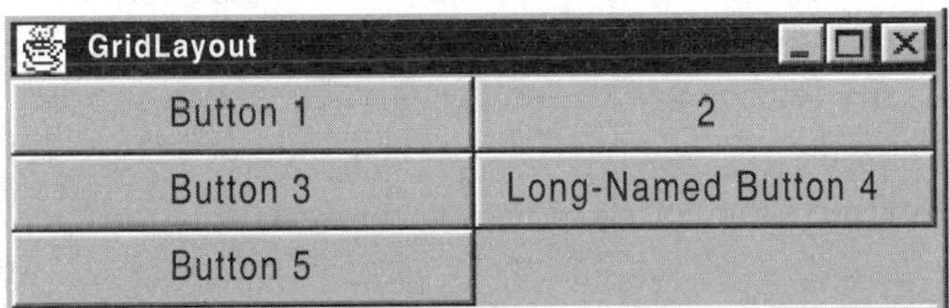

A layout manager is an object that controls the size and position of components in a container. Layout managers adhere to the `LayoutManager` interface. By default, every `Container` object has a `LayoutManager` object that controls its layout. For `Panel` objects, the default layout manager is an instance of the `FlowLayout` class. For `Window` objects, the default layout manager is an instance of the `BorderLayout` class.

This lesson has examples of every kind of layout manager. Each example can run either as an applet or as an application. The examples bring up windows that you can resize to see how resizing affects the layout.

Using Layout Managers (page 504) tells you how to use layout managers. It gives both general rules and detailed instructions on using each of the layout managers that the AWT provides.

Instead of using one of the AWT's layout managers, you can write your own. Layout managers must implement the `LayoutManager` interface, which specifies the five methods every layout manager must define. Creating a Custom Layout Manager (page 521) describes how to write a layout manager.

You can position components without using a layout manager. Generally, this solution is used to specify absolute positions for components, and only for programs that are executed on only one platform or that use custom components. Absolute positioning is often *unsuitable* for platform-independent programs, since the size of components can be different on different platforms. Laying Out Components Without a Layout Manager (Absolute Positioning) (page 522) gives you details.

Using Layout Managers

Every container, by default, has a layout manager—an object that implements the `LayoutManager` interface. If a container's default layout manager doesn't suit your needs, you can easily replace it with another one. The AWT supplies layout managers that range from the very simple (`FlowLayout` and `GridLayout`) to the special purpose (`BorderLayout` and `CardLayout`) to the very flexible (`GridBagLayout`).

This section gives you an overview of the layout managers the AWT provides, gives you some general rules for using layout managers, and then tells you how to use each of theAWT layout managers.

`BorderLayout` (page 508), shown on the next page, is the default layout manager for all `Window` objects, such as `Frames` and `Dialogs`. It uses five areas to hold components: north, south, east, west, and center. All extra space is placed in the center area. The following program, shown on page 505, puts one button in each area.

Use `CardLayout` (page 509) when you have an area that can contain different components at different times. A `CardLayout` is often controlled by a `Choice`, with the state of the `Choice` determining which `Panel` (group of components) the `CardLayout` displays. Shown after the `BorderLayout` applet, the following page displays two screenshots of a program that uses a `Choice` and a `CardLayout` in this way.

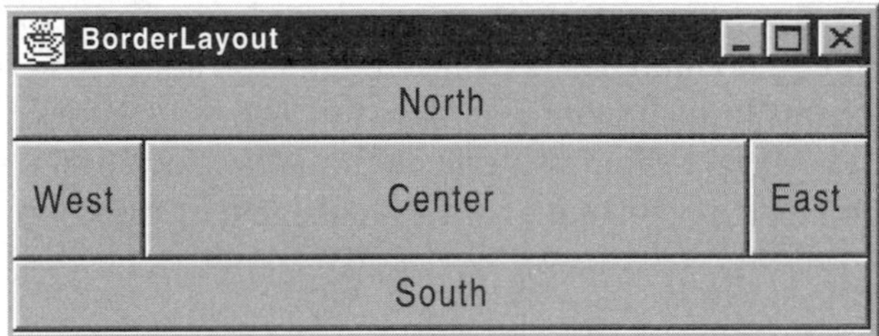

http://java.sun.com/docs/books/tutorial/ui/layout/using.html

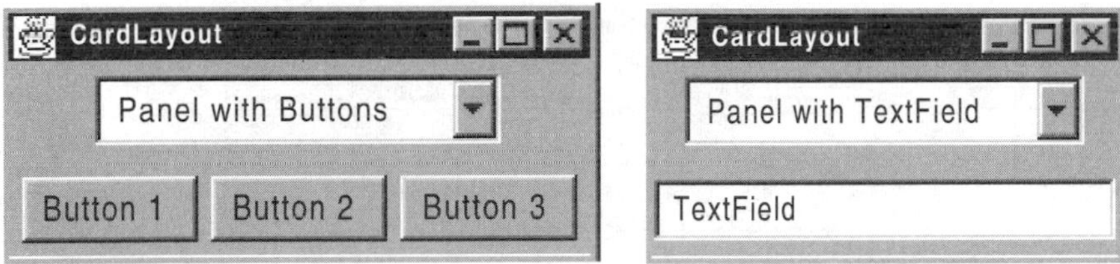

http://java.sun.com/docs/books/tutorial/ui/layout/using.html

`FlowLayout` (page 511) is the default layout manager for every `Panel`. It simply lays out components from left to right, starting new rows if necessary. Both panels in the `CardLayout` figure use `FlowLayout`. The following program also uses a `FlowLayout`:

http://java.sun.com/docs/books/tutorial/ui/layout/using.html

`GridLayout` (page 512) simply makes a bunch of components equal in size and displays them in the requested number of rows and columns. The following program uses a `GridLayout` to control the display of five buttons:

http://java.sun.com/docs/books/tutorial/ui/layout/using.html

GridBagLayout (page 513) is the most sophisticated, flexible layout manager the AWT provides. It aligns components by placing them within a grid of cells, allowing some components to span more than one cell. The rows in the grid aren't necessarily all the same height; similarly, grid columns can have different widths. The following program uses a GridBagLayout to manage ten buttons in a panel:

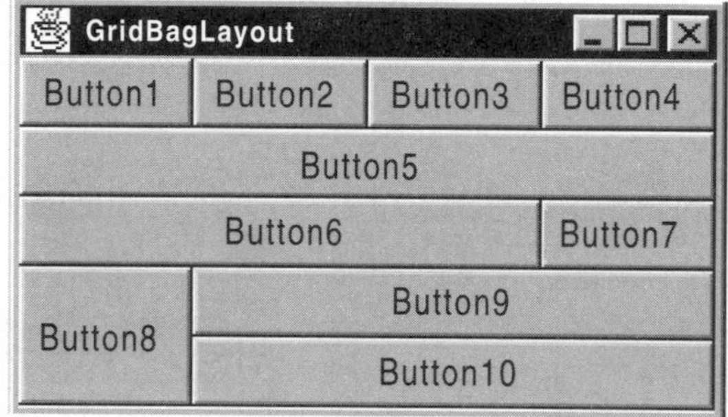

http://java.sun.com/docs/books/tutorial/ui/layout/using.html

General Rules for Using Layout Managers

Unless you explicitly tell a container not to use a layout manager, it is associated with its very own instance of a layout manager. This layout manager is automatically consulted each time the container might need to change its appearance. Most layout managers don't require programs to directly call their methods.

How to Choose a Layout Manager

The layout managers provided by the AWT have different strengths and weaknesses. This section discusses some common layout scenarios and which AWT layout managers might work for each scenario. If none of the AWT layout managers is right for your situation, feel free to use other layout managers, such as the freely available PackerLayout.

Scenario: You need to display a component in as much space as it can get.
Consider using BorderLayout (page 508) or GridBagLayout (page 513). If you use BorderLayout, you'll need to put the space-hungry component in the center. With GridBagLayout, you'll need to set the constraints for the component so that fill=GridBagConstraints.BOTH. Or, if you don't mind every other component in the same container being just as large as your space-hungry component, you can use a GridLayout (page 512).

Scenario: You need to display a few components in a compact row at their natural size.

Consider using a `Panel` to hold the components and using the `Panel`'s default `FlowLayout` manager (page 511).

Scenario: You need to display a few components of the same size in rows and columns.

`GridLayout` (page 512) is perfect for this.

How to Create a Layout Manager and Associate It with a Container

Each container has a default layout manager associated with it. All `Panel` objects (including `Applets`) are initialized to use a `FlowLayout`. All `Window` objects, except special-purpose ones like `FileDialog`, are initialized to use a `BorderLayout`.

If you want to use a container's default layout manager, you don't have to do a thing. The constructor for each container creates a layout manager instance and initializes the container to use it.

To use a layout manager other than the default layout manager, you must create an instance of the desired layout manager class and tell the container to use it. The following Java statement creates a `CardLayout` manager and sets it up as the layout manager for a container.

```
aContainer.setLayout(new CardLayout());
```

Rules of Thumb for Using Layout Managers

The `Container` methods that might result in calls to the container's layout manager are `add`, `remove`, `removeAll`, `doLayout`, `invalidate`, `getAlignmentX`, `getAlignmentY`, `getPreferredSize`, `getMinimumSize`, and `getMaximumSize`. The `add`, `remove`, and `removeAll` methods add and remove components from a container; you can call them at any time. The `doLayout` method, which is called as the result of any paint request to a container or of a `validate` call on the container, requests that the container place and size itself and the components it contains; you don't call the `doLayout` method directly.

If you change the size of a component by indirect means, such as changing its font, you should invoke the `invalidate` method on the component. Then you should call `validate` on its container so that `doLayout` will be executed.

The `getAlignmentX` and `getAlignmentY` methods are called by layout managers that try to align groups of components. None of the layout managers in the 1.1 JDK calls these methods.

The `getPreferredSize`, `getMinimumSize`, and `getMaximumSize` methods return the container's ideal, minimum, and maximum sizes, respectively. The values returned are just hints; a layout manager can ignore them.

Take special care when calling a container's `getPreferredSize` and `getMinimumSize` methods. The values these methods return are meaningless unless the container and its components have valid peer objects. See Details of the Component Architecture (page 501) for information on when peers are created.

How to Use BorderLayout

The following figure shows a `BorderLayout`[1] object in action.

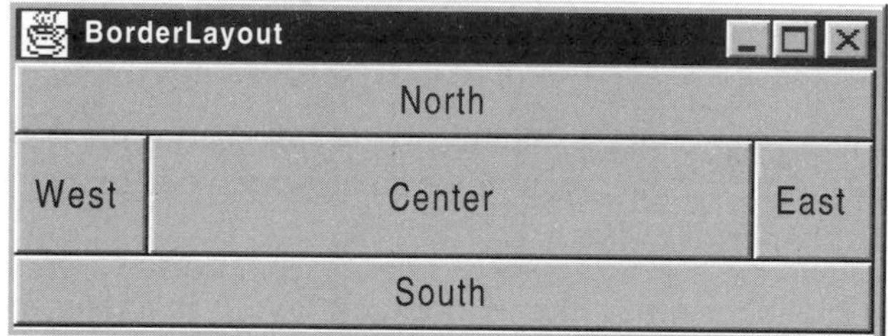

http://java.sun.com/docs/books/tutorial/ui/layout/using.html

A `BorderLayout` has five areas: north, south, east, west, and center. If you enlarge the window, the center area gets as much of the available space as possible. The other areas expand only as much as necessary to fill all available space.

The following code creates the `BorderLayout` and the components it manages. You can find the complete program on page 847. The program runs either within an applet, with the help of `AppletButton` (page 796), or as an application. The first line of this code is actually unnecessary for this example, since it's in a `Window` subclass and each `Window` already has an associated `BorderLayout` instance. However, the first line would be necessary if the code were in a `Panel` instead of a `Window`.

```
setLayout(new BorderLayout());
...
add("North", new Button("North"));
add("South", new Button("South"));
add("East", new Button("East"));
add("West", new Button("West"));
add("Center", new Button("Center"));
```

[1] http://java.sun.com/products/jdk/1.1/docs/api/java.awt.BorderLayout.html

By default, a `BorderLayout` puts no gap between the components it manages. In this section's example, any apparent gaps are the result of the `Buttons` reserving extra space around their apparent display area. You can specify gaps (in pixels) using the following constructor:

```
BorderLayout(int horizontalGap, int verticalGap)
```

How to Use CardLayout

The following two figures show a `CardLayout`[1] object in action.

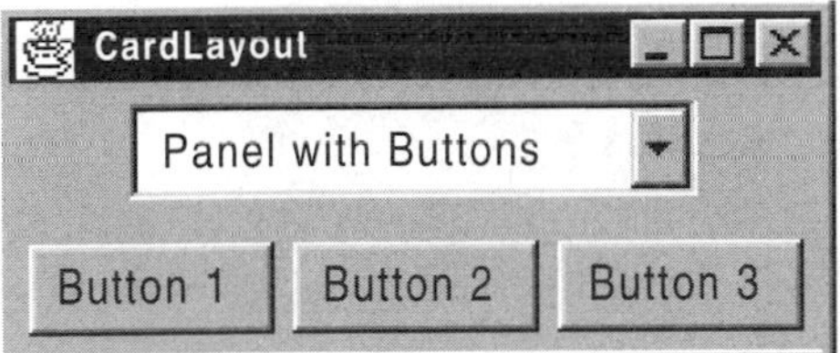

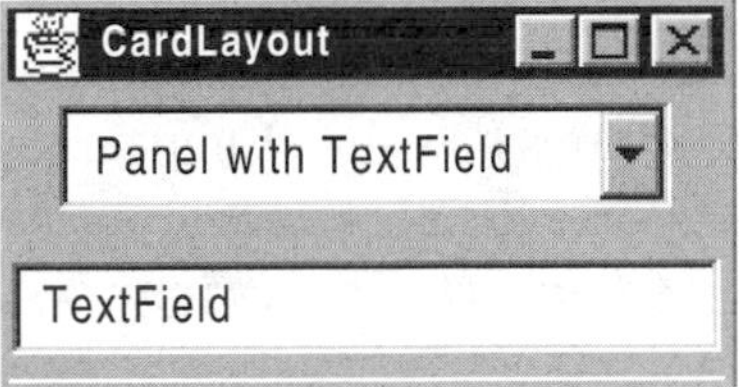

http://java.sun.com/docs/books/tutorial/ui/layout/using.html

The `CardLayout` class helps you manage two or more components (usually `Panel` objects) that share the same display space. Conceptually, each component a `CardLayout` manages is like a playing card or trading card in a stack, where only the top card is visible at any time. You can choose the card that's showing in any of the following ways:

- By asking for either the first or the last card, in the order it was added to the container.
- By flipping through the deck backwards or forwards.
- By specifying a card with a specific name. This is the scheme this section's example program uses. Specifically, the user can choose a card (component) by selecting it by name from a pop-up list of choices.

The following code creates the `CardLayout` and the components it manages. You can find the complete program on page 848. The program runs either within an applet, with the help of `AppletButton` (page 796), or as an application. As the example shows, when you add a component to a container that a `CardLayout` manages, you must specify a string that somehow identifies the component being added.

---

[1] http://java.sun.com/products/jdk/1.1/docs/api/java.awt.CardLayout.html

```
//Where instance variables are declared:
Panel cards;
final static String BUTTONPANEL = "Panel with Buttons";
final static String TEXTPANEL = "Panel with TextField";
...//Where the container is initialized:
cards = new Panel();
cards.setLayout(new CardLayout());

...//Create a Panel named p1. Put buttons in it.
...//Create a Panel named p2. Put a text field in it.

cards.add(BUTTONPANEL, p1);
cards.add(TEXTPANEL, p2);
```

To choose which component a `CardLayout` shows, you need some additional code. Here's how the example program does this:

```
//Where the container is initialized:
. . .
    //Put the Choice in a Panel to get a nicer look.
    Panel cp = new Panel();
    Choice c = new Choice();
    c.addItem(BUTTONPANEL);
    c.addItem(TEXTPANEL);
    c.addItemListener(this);
    cp.add(c);
    add("North", cp);

. . .

public void itemStateChanged(ItemEvent evt) {
    CardLayout cl = (CardLayout)cards.getLayout();
    cl.show(cards, (String)evt.getItem());
}
```

This example shows that you can use the `CardLayout` `show` method to set the currently showing component. The first argument to the `show` method is the container the `CardLayout` controls, that is, the container of the components the `CardLayout` manages. The second argument is the string that identifies the component to show. This string is the same as the one specified when adding the component to the container.

The following methods are all the `CardLayout` methods that let you choose a component. For each method, the first argument is the container for which the `CardLayout` is the layout manager (the container of the cards the `CardLayout` controls).

```
void first(Container)
void next(Container)
void previous(Container)
void last(Container)
void show(Container, String)
```

How to Use FlowLayout

The following figure shows a `FlowLayout`[1] in action.

http://java.sun.com/docs/books/tutorial/ui/layout/using.html

`FlowLayout` puts components in a row, sized at their preferred size. If the horizontal space in the container is too small to put all the components in one row, `FlowLayout` uses multiple rows. (`FlowLayout` reserves only enough vertical space for one row, however.) Within each row, components are centered (the default), left-aligned, or right-aligned as specified when the `FlowLayout` is created.

The following code from this section's example program creates the `FlowLayout` and the components it manages. You can find the complete program on page 849. The program runs either within an applet, with the help of `AppletButton` (page 796), or as an application.

```
setLayout(new FlowLayout());
...
add(new Button("Button 1"));
add(new Button("2"));
add(new Button("Button 3"));
add(new Button("Long-Named Button 4"));
add(new Button("Button 5"));
```

The `FlowLayout` class has three constructors:

```
FlowLayout()
FlowLayout(int alignment)
FlowLayout(int alignment, int horizontalGap, int verticalGap)
```

---

1 http://java.sun.com/products/jdk/1.1/docs/api/java.awt.FlowLayout.html

The *alignment* argument must have the value `FlowLayout.LEFT`, `FlowLayout.CENTER`, or `FlowLayout.RIGHT`. The *horizontalGap* and *verticalGap* arguments specify the number of pixels to put between components. If you don't specify a gap value, `FlowLayout` uses 5 for the default gap value.

How to Use GridLayout

The following figure shows a `GridLayout`[1] object in action.

http://java.sun.com/docs/books/tutorial/ui/layout/using.html

A `GridLayout` places components in a grid of cells. Each component takes all the available space within its cell, and each cell is exactly the same size. If you resize the `GridLayout` window, the `GridLayout` changes the cell size so that the cells are as large as possible, given the space available to the container.

The following code creates the `GridLayout` and the components it manages. You can find the complete program on page 851. The program runs either within an applet, with the help of `AppletButton` (page 796), or as an application.

```
//Construct a GridLayout with 2 columns
//and an unspecified number of rows.
setLayout(new GridLayout(0,2));
...
add(new Button("Button 1"));
add(new Button("2"));
add(new Button("Button 3"));
add(new Button("Long-Named Button 4"));
add(new Button("Button 5"));
```

The constructor tells the `GridLayout` class to create an instance that has two columns and as many rows as necessary. It's one of two constructors for `GridLayout`. Here are both constructors:

---

1 http://java.sun.com/products/jdk/1.1/docs/api/java.awt.GridLayout.html

```
GridLayout(int rows, int columns)
GridLayout(int rows, int columns,
           int horizontalGap, int verticalGap)
```

At least one of the `rows` and `columns` arguments must be nonzero. The `horizontalGap` and `verticalGap` arguments to the second constructor allow you to specify the number of pixels between cells. If you don't specify gaps, their values default to zero. In the program, any apparent gaps between buttons are the result of the buttons reserving extra space around their apparent display area.

How to Use GridBagLayout

The following figure shows a `GridBagLayout`[1] object in action.

http://java.sun.com/docs/books/tutorial/ui/layout/using.html

`GridBagLayout` is the most flexible—and complex—layout manager the AWT provides. A `GridBagLayout` places components in a grid of rows and columns, allowing specified components to span multiple rows or columns. Not all rows necessarily have the same height. Similarly, not all columns necessarily have the same width. Essentially, `GridBagLayout` places components in squares (cells) in a grid, and then uses the components' preferred sizes to determine how big the cells should be.

Figure 70 illustrates what happens if you enlarge the window the program brings up.

As you can see, the last row gets all the new vertical space, and the new horizontal space is split evenly among all the columns. This resizing behavior is based on weights that the program assigns to individual components in the `GridBagLayout`. Note also that each component takes up as much space as it can. This behavior is also specified by the program.

---

1 http://java.sun.com/products/jdk/1.1/docs/api/java.awt.GridBagLayout.html

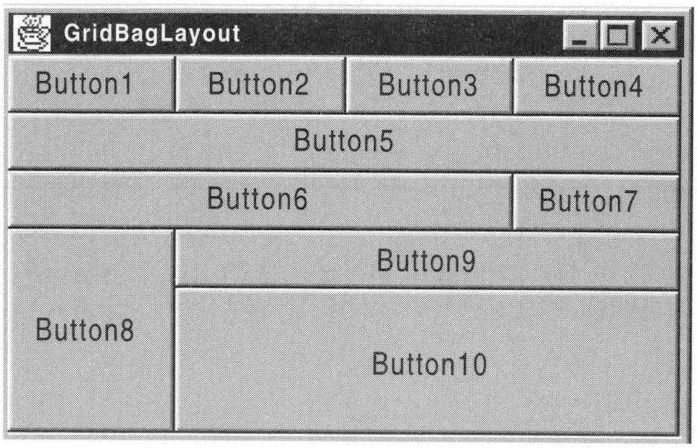

Figure 70: The same window, enlarged.

The way the program specifies the size and position characteristics of its components is by specifying *constraints* for each component. To specify constraints, you set instance variables in a `GridBagConstraints` object and tell the `GridBagLayout` (with the `setConstraints` method) to associate the constraints with the component.

The following sections explain the constraints you can set and provide examples:

Specifying Constraints for GridBagLayout (page 514) tells you what instance variables `GridBagConstraints` has, what values you can set them to, and how to associate the resulting `GridBagConstraints` with a component.

The GridBagLayout Applet Example Explained (page 516) puts it all together, explaining the code for the program in this section.

More GridBagLayout Examples (page 520) tells you where you can find some more examples of using `GridBagLayout`.

Specifying Constraints for GridBagLayout

The following code is typical of what you'll see in a container that uses a `GridBagLayout`. (You'll see a more detailed example in the next section.)

```
GridBagLayout gridbag = new GridBagLayout();
GridBagConstraints c = new GridBagConstraints();
setLayout(gridbag);

//For each component to be added to this container:
//...Create the component...
//...Set instance variables in GridBagConstraints instance...
gridbag.setConstraints(theComponent, c);
add(theComponent);
```

As you might have guessed from the above example, you can reuse the same `GridBagConstraints` instance for multiple components, even if the components have different constraints. The `GridBagLayout` extracts the constraint values and doesn't use the `GridBagConstraints` object again. You must be careful, however, to reset the `GridBagConstraints` instance variables to their default values when necessary.

You can set the following `GridBagConstraints`[1] instance variables:

`gridx, gridy`
: Specify the row and column at the upper left of the component. The leftmost column has the address `gridx=0` and the top row has the address `gridy=0`. Use `GridBagConstraints.RELATIVE` (the default value) to specify that the component be placed just to the right of (for `gridx`) or just below (for `gridy`) the component that was added to the container just before this component was added.

`gridwidth, gridheight`
: Specify the number of columns (for `gridwidth`) or rows (for `gridheight`) in the component's display area. These constraints specify the number of cells the component uses, *not* the number of pixels it uses. The default value is 1. Use `GridBagConstraints.REMAINDER` to specify that the component be the last one in its row (for `gridwidth`) or column (for `gridheight`). Use `GridBagConstraints.RELATIVE` to specify that the component be the next to last one in its row (for `gridwidth`) or column (for `gridheight`).

Note: A `GridBagLayout` bug prevents you from using `gridheight` to specify that a component span multiple rows unless the component is in the leftmost column or you've specified positive `gridx` and `gridy` values for the component.

`fill`
: Used when the component's display area is larger than the component's requested size to determine whether and how to resize the component. Valid values (defined as `GridBagConstraints` constants) are `NONE` (the default), `HORIZONTAL` (make the component wide enough to fill its display area horizontally, but don't change its height), `VERTICAL` (make the component tall enough to fill its display area vertically, but don't change its width), and `BOTH` (make the component fill its display area entirely).

`ipadx, ipady`
: Specify the internal padding: how much to add to the minimum size of the component. The default value is zero. The width of the component will be at

---

[1] http://java.sun.com/products/jdk/1.1/docs/api/java.awt.GridBagConstraints.html

least its minimum width plus `ipadx*2` pixels, since the padding applies to both sides of the component. Similarly, the height of the component will be at least its minimum height plus `ipady*2` pixels.

`insets`

Specifies the external padding of the component—the minimum amount of space between the component and the edges of its display area. The value is specified as an `Insets`[1] object. By default, each component has no external padding.

`anchor`

Used when the component is smaller than its display area to determine where (within the area) to place the component. Valid values (defined as `GridBagConstraints` constants) are `CENTER` (the default), `NORTH`, `NORTHEAST`, `EAST`, `SOUTHEAST`, `SOUTH`, `SOUTHWEST`, `WEST`, and `NORTHWEST`.

`weightx, weighty`

Specifying weights is an art that can have a significant impact on the appearance of the components a `GridBagLayout` controls. Weights are used to determine how to distribute space among columns (`weightx`) and among rows (`weighty`); this is important for specifying resizing behavior.

Unless you specify at least one nonzero value for `weightx` or `weighty`, all the components clump together in the center of their container. This is because when the weight is 0.0 (the default), the `GridBagLayout` puts any extra space between its grid of cells and the edges of the container.

Generally weights are specified with 0.0 and 1.0 as the extremes: the numbers in between are used as necessary. Larger numbers indicate that the component's row or column should get more space. For each column, the weight is related to the highest `weightx` specified for a component within that column, with each multicolumn component's weight being split somehow between the columns the component is in. Similarly, each row's weight is related to the highest `weighty` specified for a component within that row. Extra space tends to go toward the rightmost column and bottom row.

The following section discusses constraints in depth, in the context of explaining how the example applet works.

The GridBagLayout Applet Example Explained

Here, again, is the applet that shows a `GridBagLayout` in action.

---

1 http://java.sun.com/products/jdk/1.1/docs/api/java.awt.Insets.html

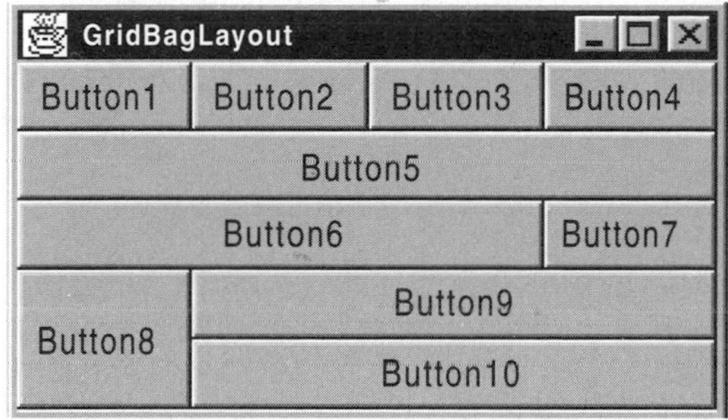

http://java.sun.com/docs/books/tutorial/ui/layout/gridbagExample.html

The following code creates the `GridBagLayout` and the components it manages. You can find the complete program on page 852. The program runs either within an applet, with the help of `AppletButton` (page 796), or as an application.

```
protected void makebutton(String name,
                          GridBagLayout gridbag,
                          GridBagConstraints c) {
    Button button = new Button(name);
    gridbag.setConstraints(button, c);
    add(button);
}

public GridBagWindow() {
    GridBagLayout gridbag = new GridBagLayout();
    GridBagConstraints c = new GridBagConstraints();

    setFont(new Font("SansSerif", Font.PLAIN, 14));
    setLayout(gridbag);

    c.fill = GridBagConstraints.BOTH;
    c.weightx = 1.0;
    makebutton("Button1", gridbag, c);
    makebutton("Button2", gridbag, c);
    makebutton("Button3", gridbag, c);

    c.gridwidth = GridBagConstraints.REMAINDER; //end of row
    makebutton("Button4", gridbag, c);

    c.weightx = 0.0;                    //reset to the default
    makebutton("Button5", gridbag, c); //another row

    c.gridwidth = GridBagConstraints.RELATIVE; //next to last
                                            // end of the row

    makebutton("Button6", gridbag, c);
```

```
        c.gridwidth = GridBagConstraints.REMAINDER; //end of row
        makebutton("Button7", gridbag, c);
        c.gridwidth = 1;                           //reset to the default
        c.gridheight = 2;
        c.weighty = 1.0;
        makebutton("Button8", gridbag, c);

        c.weighty = 0.0;                           //reset to the default
        c.gridwidth = GridBagConstraints.REMAINDER; //end of row
        c.gridheight = 1;                          //reset to the default
        makebutton("Button9", gridbag, c);
        makebutton("Button10", gridbag, c);
    }
```

This example uses one `GridBagConstraints` instance for all the components the `GridBagLayout` manages. Just before each component is added to the container, the code sets (or resets to the default values) the appropriate instance variables in the `GridBagConstraints` object. It then uses the `setConstraints` method to record all the constraint values for that component.

For example, just before adding a component that ends a row, you see this code:

```
c.gridwidth = GridBagConstraints.REMAINDER; //end of row
```

And just before adding the next component, if the next component doesn't take up a whole row, you see the same instance variable reset to its default value:

```
c.gridwidth = 1;                           //reset to the default
```

For clarity, Table 22 shows all the constraints for each component that the `GridBagLayout` handles. Values that are not the default values are marked in bold. Values that are different from those in the previous table entry are in italic.

All the components in this container are as large as possible, given their row and column. The program accomplishes this by setting the `GridBagConstraints` `fill` instance variable to `GridBagConstraints.BOTH`, leaving it at that setting for all the components. If the program didn't specify the fill, the buttons would be at their natural size, as in Figure 71.

This program has four components that span multiple columns (`Button5`, `Button6`, `Button9`, and `Button10`) and one that spans multiple rows (`Button8`). In only one of these cases (`Button8`) is the height or width of the component explicitly specified. In all the other cases, the width of the component is specified as either `GridBagConstraints.RELATIVE` or `GridBagConstraints.REMAINDER`, which lets the `GridBagLayout` determine the component's size, taking into account the size of other components in the row.

Table 22: The constraints for each component handled by `GridBagLayout`.

Component	Constraints

All components	`gridx = GridBagConstraints.RELATIVE`
	`gridy = GridBagConstraints.RELATIVE`
	`fill = GridBagConstraints.BOTH`
	`ipadx = 0, ipady = 0`
	`insets = new Insets(0,0,0,0)`
	`anchor = GridBagConstraints.CENTER`

`Button1`
`Button2`
`Button3`
	`gridwidth = 1`
	`gridheight = 1`
	`weightx = 1.0`
	`weighty = 0.0`

`Button4`	***`gridwidth = GridBagConstraints.REMAINDER`***
	`gridheight = 1`
	`weightx = 1.0`
	`weighty = 0.0`

`Button5`	**`gridwidth = GridBagConstraints.REMAINDER`**
	`gridheight = 1`
	`weightx = 0.0`
	`weighty = 0.0`

`Button6`	***`gridwidth = GridBagConstraints.RELATIVE`***
	`gridheight = 1`
	`weightx = 0.0`
	`weighty = 0.0`

`Button7`	***`gridwidth = GridBagConstraints.REMAINDER`***
	`gridheight = 1`
	`weightx = 0.0`
	`weighty = 0.0`

`Button8`	*`gridwidth = 1`* ***`gridheight = 2`*** `weightx = 0.0` ***`weighty = 1.0`***

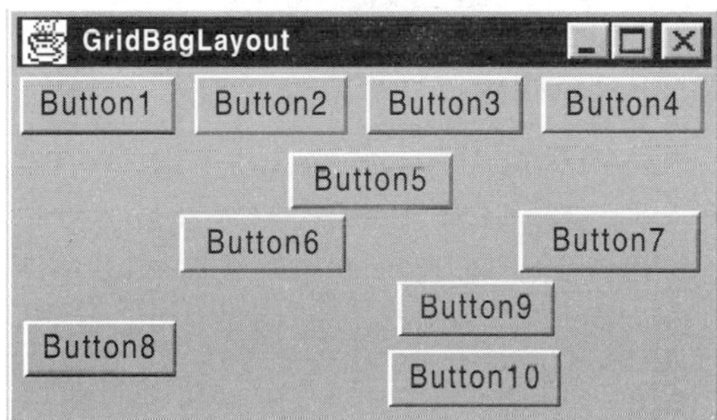

Figure 71: The example with the fill unspecified.

When you enlarge the window the program brings up, the columns stay equal in width as they grow. This is because each component in the first row, where each component is one column wide, has `weightx = 1.0`. The actual value of these components' `weightx` is unimportant. What matters is that all the components, and consequently, all the columns, have an equal weight that is greater than 0. If no component managed by the `GridBagLayout` had `weightx` set, then when the components' container was made wider, the components would stay clumped together in the center of the container, as in Figure 72.

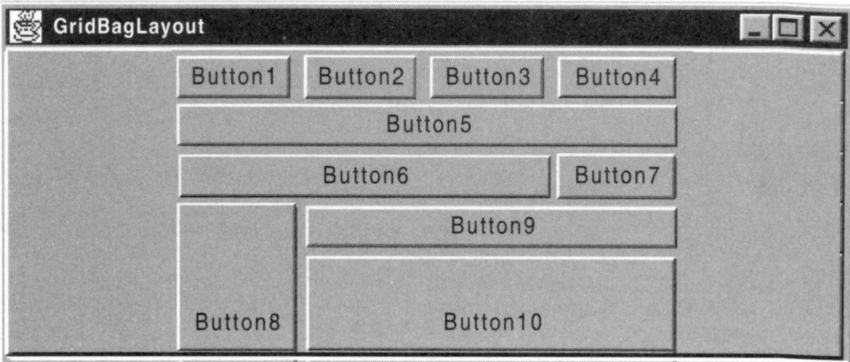

Figure 72: The example with no `weightx` values set.

Note that if you enlarge the window, the last row is the only one that gets taller. This is because only `Button8` has `weighty` greater than zero. `Button8` spans two rows, and the `GridBagLayout` happens to allocate all `Button8`'s weight to the lowest row that `Button8` occupies.

More GridBagLayout Examples

You can find more examples of using `GridBagLayout` throughout this tutorial. Here are a few programs that use `GridBagLayout`:

- `DialogWindow.java` (page 815)
- `ListDemo.java` (page 818)
- `TextDemo.java` (page 826)
- `CoordinatesDemo.java` (page 861)
- `ShowDocument.java` (page 712)

Creating a Custom Layout Manager

Before you start creating a custom layout manager, make sure that no existing layout manager will work. In particular, `GridBagLayout` (page 513) is flexible enough to work in many cases. You can also find layout managers from other sources, such as from the Internet.

To create a custom layout manager, you must create a class that implements the `LayoutManager`[1] interface. `LayoutManager` requires its adherents to implement five methods:

`void addLayoutComponent(String, Component)`
Called only by the `Container add(String, Component)` method. Layout managers that don't require that their components have names generally do nothing in this method.

`void removeLayoutComponent(Component)`
Called by the `Container remove` and `removeAll` methods. Layout managers that don't require that their components have names generally do nothing in this method, since they can query the container for its components using the `Container getComponents` method.

`Dimension preferredLayoutSize(Container)`
Called by the `Container getPreferredSize` method, which is itself called under a variety of circumstances. This method should calculate and return the ideal size of the parent, assuming that the components it contains will be at or above their preferred sizes. This method must take into account the parent's internal borders, which are returned by the `Container getInsets` method.

`Dimension minimumLayoutSize(Container)`
Called by the `Container getMinimumSize` method, which is itself called under a variety of circumstances. This method should calculate and return the minimum size of the parent, assuming that the components it contains will be at or above their minimum sizes. This method must take into account the parent's internal borders, which are returned by the `Container getInsets` method. Like `preferredLayoutSize`, this method returns a `Dimension` object.

`void layoutContainer(Container)`
Called when the container is first displayed, and each time its size changes. A layout manager's `layoutContainer` method doesn't actually draw components. It simply invokes each component's `setSize`, `setLocation`, and `set-`

---

1 http://java.sun.com/products/jdk/1.1/docs/api/java.awt.LayoutManager.html

`Bounds` methods to set the component's size and position. This method must take into account the parent's internal borders, which are returned by the `Container getInsets` method. You can't assume that the `preferredLayoutSize` or `minimumLayoutSize` method will be called before `layoutContainer` is called.

Besides implementing the five methods required by `LayoutManager`, layout managers generally implement at least one public constructor and the `Object toString`[1] method. Instead of implementing layout manager `LayoutManager` directly, some layout managers implement the `LayoutManager2`[2] interface. The `LayoutManager2` interface extends `LayoutManager` by adding methods that take components' maximum sizes and alignments into account, a more general form of the `addLayoutComponent` method, and a method that tells the layout manager to discard any cached layout information.

The complete code for a custom layout manager named `DiagonalLayout` is on page 854. `DiagonalLayout` lays out components diagonally, from left to right, with one component per row. An example of a program that uses it is on page 858.

Here's `DiagonalLayout` in action:

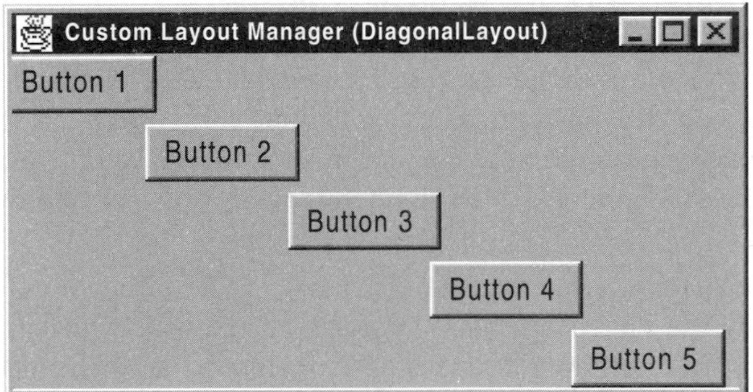

http://java.sun.com/docs/books/tutorial/ui/layout/custom.html

Laying Out Components Without a Layout Manager (Absolute Positioning)

Although it's possible to lay out components without a layout manager, you should use a layout manager if at all possible. Layout managers make it easy to

---

1 http://java.sun.com/products/jdk/1.1/docs/api/java.lang.Object.html

2 http://java.sun.com/products/jdk/1.1/docs/api/java.awt.LayoutManager2.html

resize a container and adjust to platform-dependent component appearance and to different font sizes. They also can be reused easily by other containers as well as other programs. If your custom container won't be reused, can't be resized, and completely controls normally system-dependent factors like font size and component appearance (implementing its own controls if necessary), then absolute positioning might make sense.

The window in the following figure uses absolute positioning.

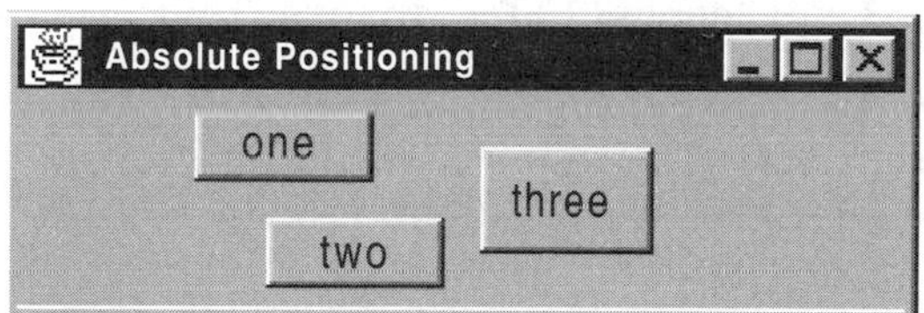

http://java.sun.com/docs/books/tutorial/ui/layout/none.html

The following code contains the instance variable declarations, constructor implementation, and `paint` method implementation of the window class. You can find the complete program on page 859. The program runs either within an applet, with the help of `AppletButton` (page 796), or as an application.

```
public class NoneWindow extends Frame {
    . . .
    private boolean laidOut = false;
    private Button b1, b2, b3;

    public NoneWindow() {
        setLayout(null);
        setFont(new Font("SansSerif", Font.PLAIN, 14));

        b1 = new Button("one");
        add(b1);
        b2 = new Button("two");
        add(b2);
        b3 = new Button("three");
        add(b3);
    }

    public void paint(Graphics g) {
        if (!laidOut) {
            Insets insets = getInsets();
            /*
             * We're guaranteed that getInsets will return a
             * valid Insets if called from paint -- it isn't
```

```
             * valid when called from the constructor.
             *
             * We could perhaps cache this in an ivar, but
             * insets can change, and when they do,
             * the AWT creates a whole new
             * Insets object; the old one is invalid.
             */
            b1.setBounds(50 + insets.left, 5 + insets.top, 50, 20);
            b2.setBounds(70 + insets.left, 35 + insets.top,
                         50, 20);
            b3.setBounds(130 + insets.left, 15 + insets.top,
                         50, 30);

            laidOut = true;
        }
    }

    . . .
}
```

Working with Graphics

THIS lesson teaches you everything you need to make your program draw to the screen. You'll learn how to create simple geometric shapes, display text, and display images. You'll also learn how to animate these shapes and images. This lesson assumes that you've read the Overview of the Java UI (page 407), especially The Anatomy of a GUI-Based Program (page 413).

Overview of AWT Graphics Support (page 526) gives an overview of the AWT support for drawing, with links to where you can find more information.

Using Graphics Primitives (page 528) teaches you how to draw simple shapes and display text effectively. It includes examples of using the `Graphics`, `Font`, and `FontMetrics` classes. One rectangle-drawing example can be used as the basis for implementing selection in a paint program.

Using Images (page 540) discusses the Java support for images and tells you how to load, display, and manipulate images.

Performing Animation (page 554) describes how to perform animation well. Many Java programs (especially applets) perform animation, whether it's the classic, cartoon-style animation of Duke waving (visible at the beginning of the online tutorial's Getting Started trail[1]), program-generated graphics such as a scrolling checkerboard, or simply moving static images across the screen. This section includes tips on improving graphics, performance, and appearance, using techniques such as implementing the `update` method and double buffering.

---

[1] http://java.sun.com/docs/books/tutorial/getStarted/index.html

Overview of AWT Graphics Support

As you learned from the first lesson in this trail, in Drawing (page 418), the AWT drawing system controls when and how programs can draw. In response to a call to a component's `repaint` method, the AWT invokes that component's `update` method to request that the component redraw itself. By default, the `update` method in turn invokes the component's `paint` method.

An additional wrinkle in this scenario is that sometimes the AWT calls the `paint` method directly, instead of calling `update`. This almost always happens as a result of the AWT reacting to an external stimulus, such as the component first appearing on screen, or the component being uncovered by another window. You'll learn more about `paint` and `update` in Eliminating Flashing (page 561), later in this lesson.

Important: The `paint` and `update` methods must execute very quickly! Otherwise, they'll destroy the perceived performance of your program. If you need to perform some lengthy operation as the result of a paint request, do it by starting up another thread (or somehow sending a request to another thread) to perform the operation. For help on using threads, see the lesson Doing Two or More Tasks at Once: Threads (page 327).

The Graphics Object

The lone argument to the `paint` and `update` methods is a `Graphics`[1] object. `Graphics` objects are the key to all drawing. They support the two basic kinds of drawing: primitive graphics (lines, rectangles, and text) and images. You'll learn about primitive graphics in Using Graphics Primitives (page 528). You'll learn about images in Using Images (page 540).

Besides supplying methods to draw primitive graphics and images to the screen, a `Graphics` object provides a drawing context by maintaining state such as the current drawing area and the current drawing color. You can decrease the current drawing area by *clipping* it, but you can never increase the drawing area. In this way, a `Graphics` object ensures that a component can draw only within its own drawing area. You'll learn more about clipping in Overriding the update Method (page 561).

---

[1] http://java.sun.com/products/jdk/1.1/docs/api/java.awt.Graphics.html

The Coordinate System

Each `Component` object has its own integer coordinate system, ranging from (0, 0) to (*width* - 1, *height* - 1), with each unit representing the size of one pixel. As the following figure shows, the upper left corner of the component's drawing area is (0, 0). The X coordinate increases to the right, and the Y coordinate increases downward.

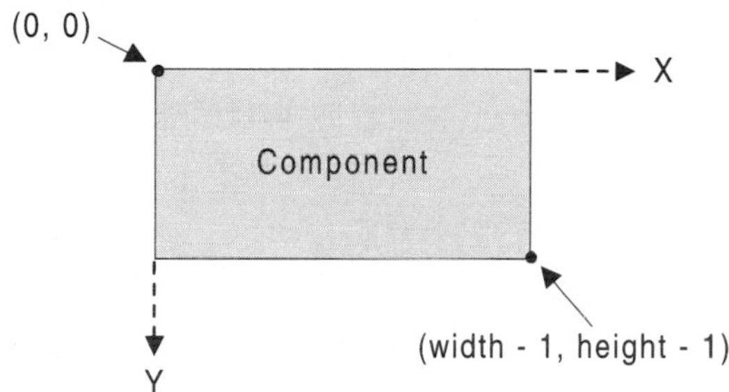

Figure 73: A component's coordinate system.

Here's an applet that we'll build on later in this lesson. Whenever you click within the framed area, the applet draws a dot where you clicked and displays a string describing where the click occurred.

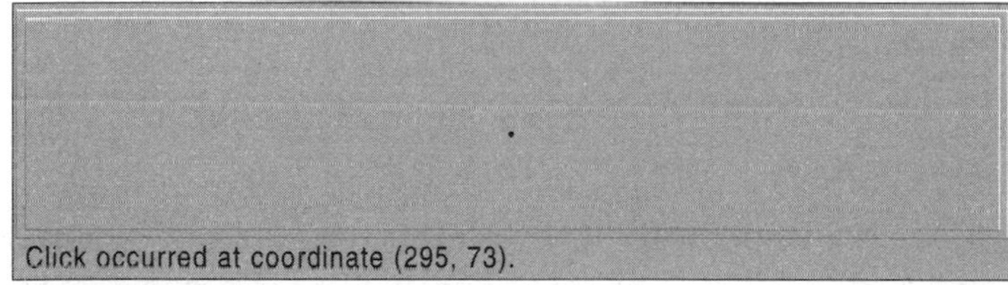

http://java.sun.com/docs/books/tutorial/ui/drawing/overview.html

The Four Forms of the repaint Method

Remember that programs can call a component's `repaint` method to request that the AWT call the component's `update` method. Here are descriptions of the four forms of the `repaint` method:

`repaint()`
: Requests that the AWT call the component's `update` method as soon as possible. This is the most frequently used form of `repaint`.

`repaint(long` *time*`)`
: Requests that the AWT call the component's `update` method as much as *`time`* milliseconds from now.

`repaint(int` *x*`, int` *y*`, int` *width*`, int` *height*`)`
: Requests that the AWT call the component's `update` method as soon as possible, but repaint only the specified part of the component.

`repaint(long` *time*`, int` *x*`, int` *y*`, int` *width*`, int` *height*`)`
: Requests that the AWT call the component's `update` method as much as *`time`* milliseconds from now, but repaint only the specified part of the component.

Using Graphics Primitives

The next few sections provide the details you'll need to generate primitive graphics and text.

Drawing Shapes (page 528) tells you how to draw shapes, such as lines, rectangles, ovals, arcs, and polygons.

Working with Text (page 534) tells you how to draw text using the `Graphics` `drawString` method. It also tells you how to use `Font` and `FontMetrics` objects to get information about a font's size characteristics.

Drawing Shapes

The `Graphics`[1] class defines methods for drawing the following kinds of shapes:

- Lines—`drawLine`, which draws a line in the `Graphics` object's current color, which is initialized to the component's foreground color
- Rectangles—`drawRect`, `fillRect`, and `clearRect`, where `drawRect` draws an unfilled rectangle in the `Graphics` object's current color, `fillRect` fills a rectangle with the `Graphics` object's current color, and `clearRect` fills a rectangle with the component's background color
- Raised or lowered rectangles—`draw3DRect` and `fill3DRect`
- Round-edged rectangles—`drawRoundRect` and `fillRoundRect`
- Ovals—`drawOval` and `fillOval`
- Arcs—`drawArc` and `fillArc`
- Polygons—`drawPolygon`, `drawPolyline`, and `fillPolygon`

---

1 http://java.sun.com/products/jdk/1.1/docs/api/java.awt.Graphics.html

Except for polygons and lines, all shapes are specified using their bounding rectangle. Once you understand rectangles, drawing other shapes is relatively easy. For this reason, this section concentrates on rectangle drawing.

Example 1: Simple Rectangle Drawing

The applet on page 527 uses the `draw3DRect` and `fillRect` methods to draw its interface. Here's the applet again:

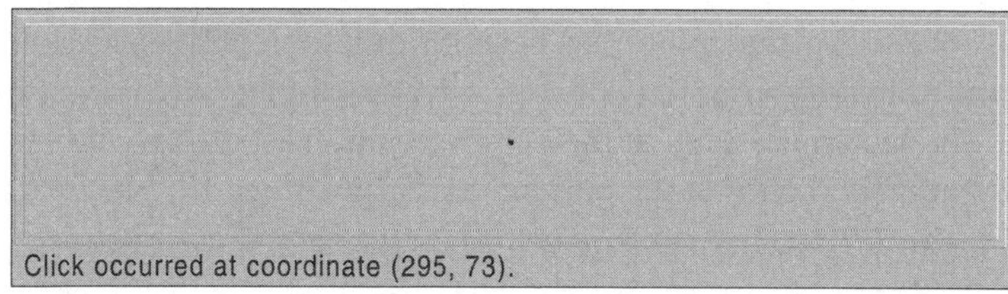
Click occurred at coordinate (295, 73).

http://java.sun.com/docs/books/tutorial/ui/drawing/drawingShapes.html

You can find the complete program on page 861. Here is just the drawing code:

```
//In FramedArea (a Panel subclass):
public void paint(Graphics g) {
    Dimension d = getSize();
    Color bg = getBackground();

    //Draw a fancy frame around the applet.
    g.setColor(bg);
    g.draw3DRect(0, 0, d.width - 1, d.height - 1, true);
    g.draw3DRect(3, 3, d.width - 7, d.height - 7, false);
}

//In CoordinateArea (a Canvas subclass):
public void paint(Graphics g) {
    //If user has clicked, paint a tiny rectangle where click
    //occurred
    if (point != null) {
        g.fillRect(point.x - 1, point.y - 1, 2, 2);
    }
}
```

This applet creates and contains a `FramedArea` object, which in turn creates and contains a `CoordinateArea` object. The first call to `draw3DRect` creates a rectangle as big as the `FramedArea`'s drawing area. The `true` argument specifies that the rectangle should appear to be raised. The second call to `draw3DRect` creates a second rectangle just a bit smaller, with `false` specifying that the rectangle

should appear to be sunken. Together, the two calls produce the effect of a raised frame that contains the `CoordinateArea`. (`FramedArea` implements the `getInsets` method so that the `CoordinateArea`'s drawing area is a few pixels inside of the `FramedArea`.)

The `CoordinateArea` uses `fillRect` to draw a rectangle whose size is two pixels square at the position where the user clicks.

Example 2: Using a Rectangle to Indicate a Selected Area

You can use the following applet as a basis for implementing selection in a drawing program. When the user drags the mouse, the applet continuously displays a rectangle. The rectangle starts at the cursor position where the user first pressed the mouse button and ends at the current cursor position.

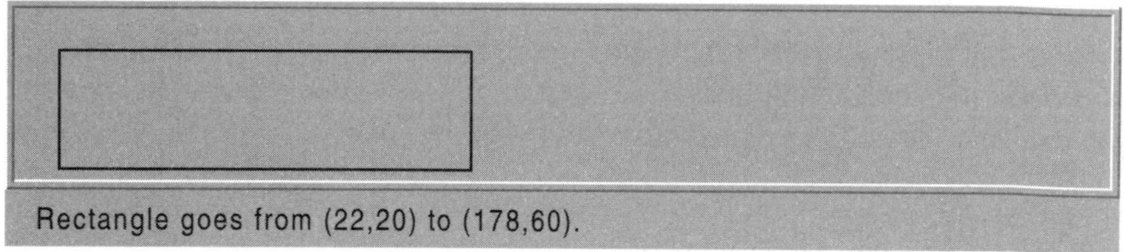
Rectangle goes from (22,20) to (178,60).

http://java.sun.com/docs/books/tutorial/ui/drawing/drawingShapes.html

You can find the complete program on page 863. Here is the code that's significantly different from the code of the previous applet:

```
class SelectionArea extends Canvas {
    Rectangle currentRect = null;
    RectangleDemo controller;

    public SelectionArea(RectangleDemo controller) {
        super();
        this.controller = controller;

        MyListener myListener = new MyListener();
        addMouseListener(myListener);
        addMouseMotionListener(myListener);
    }

    class MyListener extends MouseAdapter
                     implements MouseMotionListener {
        public void mousePressed(MouseEvent e) {
            int x = e.getX();
            int y = e.getY();
```

```
            currentRect = new Rectangle(x, y, 0, 0);
            repaint();
        }

        public void mouseDragged(MouseEvent e) {
            updateSize(e);
        }

        public void mouseMoved(MouseEvent e) {
            //Do nothing.
        }

        public void mouseReleased(MouseEvent e) {
            updateSize(e);
        }

        void updateSize(MouseEvent e) {
            int x = e.getX();
            int y = e.getY();
            currentRect.setSize(x - currentRect.x,
                                y - currentRect.y);
            repaint();
        }
    }

    public void paint(Graphics g) {
        //update has already cleared the previous rectangle,
        //so we don't need to here.

        //If currentRect exists, paint a rectangle on top.
        if (currentRect != null) {
            Dimension d = getSize();
            Rectangle box = getDrawableRect(currentRect, d);
            controller.updateLabel(box);

            //Draw the box outline.
            g.drawRect(box.x, box.y,
                       box.width - 1, box.height - 1);
        }
    }

    Rectangle getDrawableRect(Rectangle originalRect,
                              Dimension drawingArea) {
        ...//Make rectangle width and height positive...
        ...//Make the rectangle smaller if necessary...
    }
}
```

The `SelectionArea` keeps track of the currently selected rectangle, using a `Rectangle` object called `currentRect`. As implemented, the `currentRect` keeps the same origin (`currentRect.x`, `currentRect.y`) for as long as the user drags the mouse. This means that the height and width of the rectangle can be negative.

However, the `draw`*`Xxx`* and `fill`*`Xxx`* methods don't draw anything if either the height or width is negative. For this reason, when the `SelectionArea` draws the rectangle, it must specify the upper left vertex of the rectangle so that the width and height are positive. The `SelectionArea` class defines a `getDrawableRect` method to perform the necessary calculations to find the upper left vertex. The `getDrawableRect` method also makes sure that the rectangle doesn't extend beyond the boundaries of its drawing area. The definition of `getDrawableRect` is near the end of the file that starts on page 863.

Note: It's perfectly legal to specify x, y, height, or width values that are negative or cause a result larger than the drawing area. Values outside the drawing area don't matter too much because they're clipped to the drawing area. You just won't see part of the shape. Negative height or width results in the shape not being drawn at all.

Example 3: A Shape Sampler

The applet in the following figure demonstrates all the shapes you can draw and fill.

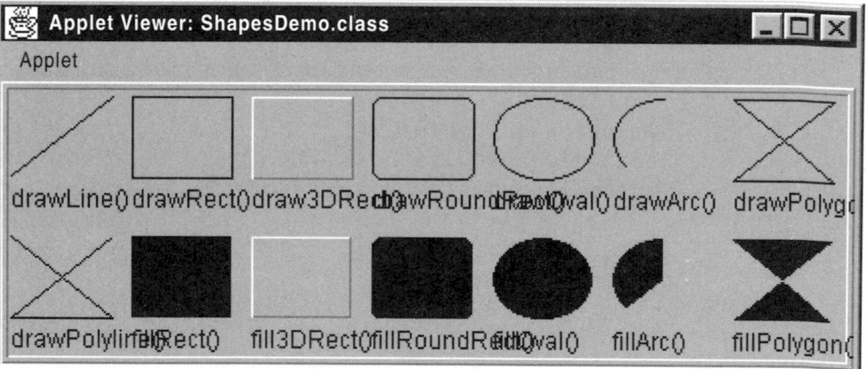

http://java.sun.com/docs/books/tutorial/ui/drawing/drawingShapes.html

Unless your applet viewer's default font is very small, the text displayed in this applet might look ugly in places. Words might be drawn on top of each other. And because this applet doesn't use the `getInsets` method to protect its boundaries, text might be drawn on top of the frame around the applet. Setting the Font (page 535) improves on this example, teaching you how to make sure text fits within a given space.

You can find the complete code for the shape-drawing applet on page 867. The following code draws the geometric shapes. The `rectHeight` and `rectWidth` variables specify the size in pixels of the area each shape must be drawn in. The `x` and `y` variables change for each shape, so that the shapes aren't drawn on top of each other.

```
Color fg3d = Color.lightGray;
. . .
// drawLine(x1, y1, x2, y2)
g.drawLine(x, y+rectHeight-1, x + rectWidth, y);
. . .
// drawRect(x, y, w, h)
g.drawRect(x, y, rectWidth, rectHeight);
. . .
// draw3DRect(x, y, w, h, raised)
g.setColor(fg3D);
g.draw3DRect(x, y, rectWidth, rectHeight, true);
g.setColor(fg);
. . .
// drawRoundRect(x, y, width, height, arcw, arch)
g.drawRoundRect(x, y, rectWidth, rectHeight, 10, 10);
. . .
// drawOval(x, y, w, h)
g.drawOval(x, y, rectWidth, rectHeight);
. . .
// drawArc(x, y, w, h)
g.drawArc(x, y, rectWidth, rectHeight, 90, 135);
. . .
// drawPolygon(xPoints, yPoints, numPoints)
int x1Points[] = {x, x+rectWidth, x, x+rectWidth};
int y1Points[] = {y, y+rectHeight, y+rectHeight, y};
g.drawPolygon(x1Points, y1Points, x1Points.length);
. . .
// NEW ROW
. . .
// drawPolyline(xPoints, yPoints, numPoints)
// Note: drawPolygon would close the polygon.
int x2Points[] = {x, x+rectWidth, x, x+rectWidth};
int y2Points[] = {y, y+rectHeight, y+rectHeight, y};
g.drawPolyline(x2Points, y2Points, x2Points.length);
. . .
// fillRect(x, y, w, h)
g.fillRect(x, y, rectWidth, rectHeight);
. . .
```

```
// fill3DRect(x, y, w, h, raised)
g.setColor(fg3D);
g.fill3DRect(x, y, rectWidth, rectHeight, true);
g.setColor(fg);
. . .

// fillRoundRect(x, y, w, h, arcw, arch)
g.fillRoundRect(x, y, rectWidth, rectHeight, 10, 10);
. . .

// fillOval(x, y, w, h)
g.fillOval(x, y, rectWidth, rectHeight);
. . .

// fillArc(x, y, w, h)
g.fillArc(x, y, rectWidth, rectHeight, 90, 135);
. . .
// fillPolygon(xPoints, yPoints, numPoints)
int x3Points[] = {x, x+rectWidth, x, x+rectWidth};
int y3Points[] = {y, y+rectHeight, y+rectHeight, y};
g.fillPolygon(x3Points, y3Points, x3Points.length);
```

Working with Text

Support for working with primitive text is spread between the AWT `Graphics`[1], `Font`[2], and `FontMetrics` [3] classes.

Drawing Text

When you're writing code to draw text, first consider whether you can use a text-oriented component, such as the `Label`, `TextField`, or `TextArea` class. If a text-oriented component isn't appropriate, you can use the `Graphics` `drawBytes`, `drawChars`, or `drawString` method.

Here is an example of code that draws a string to the screen:

```
g.drawString("Hello World!", x, y);
```

For the text-drawing methods, `x` and `y` are integers that specify the position of the *lower left* corner of the text. To be precise, the `y` coordinate specifies the *baseline* of the text—the line that most letters rest on. This doesn't include room for the

---

1 http://java.sun.com/products/jdk/1.1/docs/api/java.awt.Graphics.html
2 http://java.sun.com/products/jdk/1.1/docs/api/java.awt.Font.html
3 http://java.sun.com/products/jdk/1.1/docs/api/java.awt.FontMetrics.html

tails (*descenders*) on letters such as "y." Be sure to make y large enough to allow vertical space for the text, but small enough to allow room for descenders.

Figure 74 shows the baseline, as well as the ascender and descender lines. You'll learn more about ascenders and descenders a bit later.

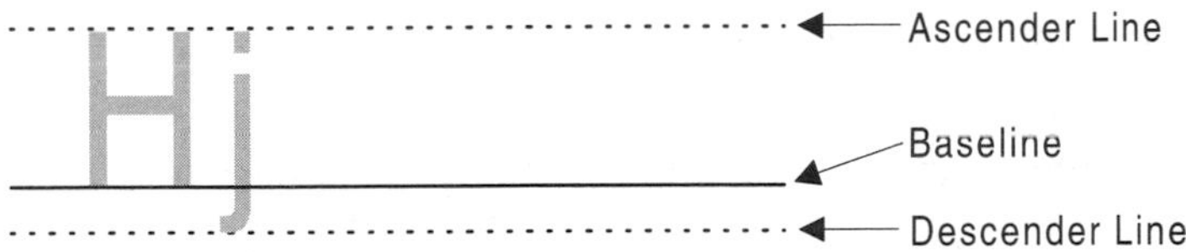

Figure 74: The baseline, ascender and descender lines.

The following applet illustrates what can happen when you're not careful about where you position your text:

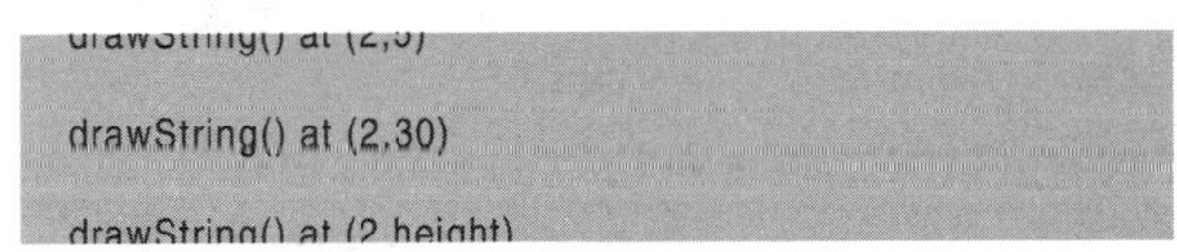

http://java.sun.com/docs/books/tutorial/ui/drawing/drawingText.html

The top string is cut off, since its y argument is 5, which leaves only 5 pixels above the baseline for the string—not enough for most fonts. The middle string shows up just fine, unless you have a huge default font. Most of the letters in the bottom string display fine, except for letters with descenders. All descenders in the bottom string are cut off, since the code that displays this string doesn't allow room for them. You can find this applet's source code on page 870.

Note: The text-drawing methods' interpretation of x and y is different from that of the shape-drawing methods. When drawing a shape (such as a rectangle), x and y specify the upper left corner of the shape's bounding rectangle, instead of the lower left corner.

Setting the Font

In the AWT, each font is represented by a `Font` object. Both `Component` and `Graphics` objects have `getFont` and `setFont` methods that you can use to get and set the object's font. To create a `Font` object, you can invoke the `Font` constructor, specifying the logical font name, style, and size. For example:

```
Font defaultNormalFont = new Font("Serif", Font.PLAIN, 12);
Font defaultBigFont = new Font("SansSerif", Font.BOLD, 24);
```

The logical name of a font can be any of the following values:

`"Serif"`
: Specifies a font with variable-width characters that have serifs. Example: Times (the font used in this book for normal text).

`"SansSerif"`
: Specifies a font with variable-width characters that have no serifs. Example: Helvetica.

`"Monospaced"`
: Specifies a font with fixed-width characters. Example: `Courier`.

`"Dialog"` *or* `"DialogInput"`
: Specifies a font used in dialogs.

The font style can have any of these values:

- `Font.PLAIN`
- `Font.BOLD`
- `Font.ITALIC`
- `Font.BOLD|Font.ITALIC` (both bold and italic; other ORed combinations are also legal)

The font size must be a positive integer. Note that the font size is an abstract measurement. Typically, font size is measured in *points*, which are approximately 1/72 of an inch. However, each font designer decides exactly how tall a 12-point font (for example) is. For example, 12-point Times is often slightly shorter than 12-point Helvetica.

You can get information about a `Font` object by invoking its `getName`, `getSize`, and `getStyle` methods. You can also ask about the font's style using the `isBold`, `isItalic`, and `isPlain` methods. For example:

```
if (!aFont.isItalic()) {
    Font italicFont = new Font(aFont.getName(),
                               aFont.getStyle()|Font.ITALIC,
                                defaultNormalFont.getSize());
```

For information about creating fonts based on system properties, see the `getFont` method in the `Font`[1] API documentation.

---

[1] http://java.sun.com/products/jdk/1.1/docs/api/java.awt.Font.html

Getting Information About a Font: FontMetrics

The shape-drawing example (page 528) can sometimes be improved by choosing a font that's smaller than the usual default font. The following example does this and also enlarges the shapes to take up the space freed by the font's smaller height. This figure contains the improved applet. You can find its source code on page 870.

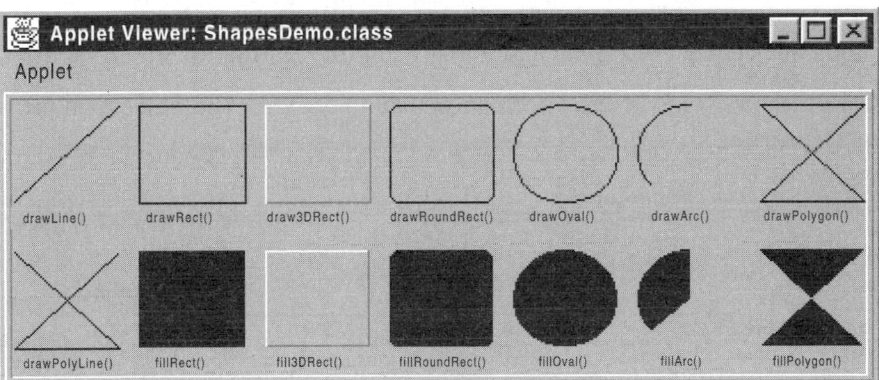

http://java.sun.com/docs/books/tutorial/ui/drawing/drawingText.html

The following code chooses the appropriate font by using a `FontMetrics` object to get details of the font's size. For example, the following loop in the `paint` method ensures that the longest string displayed by the applet ("`drawRound-Rect()`") fits within the space each shape is allotted.

```
boolean fontFits = false;
Font font = g.getFont();
FontMetrics fontMetrics = g.getFontMetrics();
int size = font.getSize();
String name = font.getName();
int style = font.getStyle();

while (!fontFits) {
    if ( (fontMetrics.getHeight() <= maxCharHeight)
      && (fontMetrics.stringWidth(longString) <= xSpace)) {
        fontFits = true;
    } else {
        if (size <= minFontSize) {
            fontFits = true;
        } else {
            g.setFont(font = new Font(name,
                                      style,
                                      --size));
```

```
                fontMetrics = g.getFontMetrics();
            }
        }
    }
```

This code uses the Graphics getFont, setFont, and getFontMetrics methods to get and set the current font and to get the FontMetrics object that corresponds to the font. From the FontMetrics getHeight and getStringWidth methods, the code gets vertical and horizontal size information about the font.

Figure 75 shows some of the information that a FontMetrics object can provide about a font's size.

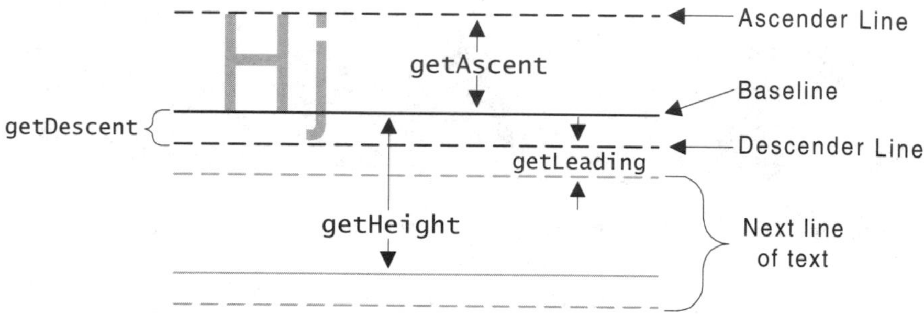

Figure 75: Some of the information FontMetrics can provide about a font's size.

In theory, a font's size (as returned by the Font getSize method) corresponds to the ascent plus the descent. Practically, however, fonts vary slightly in how they define sizes. Here's a summary of the FontMetrics methods that return information about a font's vertical size:

int getAscent()
int getMaxAscent()

The getAscent method returns the number of pixels between the ascender line and the baseline. Generally, the ascender line represents the typical height of capital letters. Specifically, the ascent and descent values are chosen by the font's designer to represent the correct text "color," or density of ink, so that the text appears as the designer planned it. The ascent typically provides enough room for almost all of the characters in the font, except perhaps for accents on capital letters. The getMaxAscent method accounts for these exceptionally tall characters.

`int getDescent()`
`int getMaxDescent()`

The `getDescent` method returns the number of pixels between the baseline and the descender line. In most fonts, all characters fall within the descender line at their lowest point. Just in case, though, you can use the `getMaxDescent` method to get a distance guaranteed to encompass all characters.

`int getHeight()`

Returns the number of pixels normally found between the baseline of one line of text and the baseline of the next line of text. Note that this includes an allowance for leading.

`int getLeading()`

Returns the suggested distance in pixels between one line of text and the next. Specifically the leading is the distance between the descender line of one line of text and the ascender line of the next line of text. By the way, "leading" is pronounced "LEDDing."

`FontMetrics` provides the following methods to return information about the horizontal size of a font's characters. These methods take into account the spacing around each character. More precisely, each method returns *not* the number of pixels taken up by a particular character (or characters), but the number of pixels by which the *current point* will be advanced when that character (or characters) is shown. We call this the *advance width* to distinguish it from the character or text width.

`int getMaxAdvance()`

The advance width in pixels of the widest character in the font.

`int bytesWidth(byte[], int, int)`

The advance width of the text represented by the specified array of bytes. The first integer argument specifies the starting offset of the data within the byte array. The second integer argument specifies the maximum number of bytes to check.

`int charWidth(int), charWidth(char)`

The advance width of the specified character.

`int charsWidth(char[], int, int)`

The advance width of the string represented by the specified character array.

`int stringWidth(String)`

The advance width of the specified string.

`int[] getWidths()`

The advance width of each of the first 256 characters in the font.

Using Images

This is an image:

The next few sections provide the details you'll need to work with images. You'll learn how to load, display, and manipulate them.

Support for using images is spread across the `java.applet`, `java.awt`, and `java.awt.image` packages. Every image is represented by a `java.awt.Image` object. In addition to the `Image` class, the `java.awt` package provides other basic image support, such as the `Graphics drawImage` methods, the `Toolkit getImage` methods, and the `MediaTracker` class. In `java.applet`, the `Applet getImage` methods make it easy for applets to load images using URLs. Finally, the `java.awt.image` package provides interfaces and classes that let you create, manipulate, and observe images.

The AWT makes it easy to load images in either of two formats: GIF and JPEG. Loading Images (page 541) describes how to use the `Applet` and `Toolkit getImage` methods to load images. By default, the data for an image is loaded in the background the first time you try to draw the image. This section describes how to change or monitor this default image loading behavior by using the `MediaTracker` class or by implementing the `imageUpdate` method, which is defined by the `ImageObserver` interface. This section also tells you how to create images on the fly using the `MemoryImageSource` class.

It's easy to display an image using the `Graphics` object that's passed into your `update` or `paint` method. You simply invoke a `drawImage` method on the `Graphics` object. Displaying Images (page 544) explains the four forms of `drawImage`, two of which scale the image. Like `getImage`, `drawImage` is asynchronous, returning immediately even if the image hasn't been fully loaded or drawn yet.

Manipulating Images (page 545) gives you an overview of how to change images, using filters.

Loading Images

This section describes how to get the `Image` object corresponding to an image. As long as the image data is in GIF or JPEG format and you know its filename or URL, it's easy to get an `Image` object for it: just use one of the `Applet` or `Toolkit` `getImage` methods. The `getImage` methods return immediately, without checking whether the image data exists. The actual loading of image data normally doesn't start until the first time the program tries to draw the image.

For many programs, this invisible background loading works well. Other programs, though, need to keep track of the progress of the image loading. This section explains how to do so using the `MediaTracker` class and the `ImageObserver` interface.

Finally, this section tells you how to create images on the fly, using a class such as `MemoryImageSource`.

Using the getImage Methods

This section discusses first the `Applet` `getImage` methods and then the `Toolkit` `getImage` methods.

The `Applet` class supplies two `getImage` methods:

- `getImage(URL` *url*`)`
- `getImage(URL` *url*`, String` *name*`)`

Only applets can use the `Applet` `getImage` methods. Moreover, the `Applet` `getImage` methods don't work until the applet has a full context. For this reason, these methods *do not work* if called in a constructor or in a statement that declares an instance variable. Instead, you must call `getImage` from a method such as `init`.

The following code examples show you how to use the `Applet` `getImage` methods. See Taking Advantage of the Applet API (page 189) for an explanation of the `getCodeBase` and `getDocumentBase` methods.

```
//In a method in an Applet subclass:
Image image1 = getImage(getCodeBase(), "imageFile.gif");
Image image2 = getImage(getDocumentBase(), "anImageFile.jpeg");
Image image3 = getImage(imageURL);
```

The `Toolkit` class declares two more `getImage` methods:

- `getImage(URL` *url*`)`
- `getImage(String` *filename*`)`

You can get a `Toolkit` object either by invoking `Toolkit`'s `getDefaultToolkit` class method or by invoking the Component `getToolkit` instance method. The `Component getToolkit` method returns the toolkit that was used (or will be used) to implement the component.

The following examples show how to use the `Toolkit getImage` methods. Every Java application and applet can use these methods, with applets subject to the usual security restrictions. You can read about applet security in Practical Considerations of Writing Applets (page 211).

```
Toolkit toolkit = Toolkit.getDefaultToolkit();
Image image1 = toolkit.getImage("imageFile.gif");
Image image2 = toolkit.getImage(new URL(
      "http://java.sun.com/graphics/people.gif"));
```

Requesting and Tracking Image Loading: MediaTracker and ImageObserver

The AWT provides two ways for you to track image loading: the `MediaTracker`[1] class and the `ImageObserver`[2] interface. The `MediaTracker` class is sufficient for many programs. You create a `MediaTracker` instance, tell it to track one or more images, and then ask the `MediaTracker` the status of those images as needed. An example is explained in Improving the Appearance and Performance of Image Animation (page 568).

The animation example shows two particularly useful `MediaTracker` features: requesting that the data for a group of images be loaded, and waiting for a group of images to be loaded. To request that the image data for a group of images be loaded, use the forms of `checkID` and `checkAll` that take a boolean argument. Setting the boolean argument to `true` starts loading the data for any images that aren't yet being loaded. Alternatively, you can request that the image data be loaded and wait for it using the `waitForID` and `waitForAll` methods.

If you browse the `MediaTracker` API documentation, you might notice that the `Component` class defines two useful-looking methods: `checkImage` and `prepareImage`. The `MediaTracker` class has made calling these methods directly largely unnecessary.

The `ImageObserver` interface lets you keep even closer track of image loading than `MediaTracker` allows. The `Component` class uses it so that components are repainted as the images they display are loaded. To use the `ImageObserver` inter-

---

1 http://java.sun.com/products/jdk/1.1/docs/api/java.awt.MediaTracker.html
2 http://java.sun.com/products/jdk/1.1/docs/api/java.awt.image.ImageObserver.html

face, you implement the `ImageObserver imageUpdate` method and make sure that the implementing object is registered as the image observer. Usually, this registration happens when you specify an `ImageObserver` to the `drawImage` method, as described in the next section. The `imageUpdate` method is called whenever information about an image becomes available.

The following example implements the `Image Observer` interface's `imageUpdate` method. This example uses `imageUpdate` to position two images as soon as their size is known, and to repaint every 100 milliseconds until both images are loaded. You can find the complete program on page 874.

```
public boolean imageUpdate(Image theimg, int infoflags,
                           int x, int y, int w, int h) {
    if ((infoflags & (ERROR)) != 0) {
        errored = true;
    }
    if ((infoflags & (WIDTH | HEIGHT)) != 0) {
        positionImages();
    }
    boolean done = ((infoflags & (ERROR | FRAMEBITS |
                       ALLBITS)) != 0);
    // Repaint immediately if we are done, otherwise repaint
    // in 100 milliseconds.
    repaint(done ? 0 : 100);
    return !done; //If done, no further updates required.
}
```

Creating Images with MemoryImageSource

With the help of an image producer such as the `MemoryImageSource`[1] class, you can construct images from scratch. The following code example calculates a 100 x 100 image representing a fade from black to blue along the X axis and a fade from black to red along the Y axis.

```
int w = 100;
int h = 100;
int[] pix = new int[w * h];
int index = 0;
for (int y = 0; y < h; y++) {
    int red = (y * 255) / (h - 1);
    for (int x = 0; x < w; x++) {
        int blue = (x * 255) / (w - 1);
```

1 http://java.sun.com/products/jdk/1.1/docs/api/java.awt.image.MemoryImageSource.html

```
            pix[index++] = (255 << 24) | (red << 16) | blue;
        }
    }
    Image img = createImage(new MemoryImageSource(w, h, pix, 0, w));
```

Displaying Images

The following statement displays an image at its normal size in the upper left corner of the component area (0, 0):

```
g.drawImage(image, 0, 0, this);
```

This statement displays an image scaled to be 300 pixels wide and 62 pixels tall, starting at the coordinates (90, 0):

```
g.drawImage(myImage, 90, 0, 300, 62, this);
```

The following applet loads a single image and displays it twice, using both code examples that you see above. You can find the complete program on page 876.

http://java.sun.com/docs/books/tutorial/ui/drawing/drawingImages.html

The `Graphics` class declares the following `drawImage` methods. They all return a boolean value, although this value is rarely used. The return value is `true` if the image has been completely loaded and completely drawn; otherwise, the return value is `false`.

- `drawImage(Image` *img*`, int` *x*`, int` *y*`, ImageObserver` *observer*`)`
- `drawImage(Image` *img*`, int` *x*`, int` *y*`, int` *width*`, int` *height*`, ImageObserver` *observer*`)`
- `drawImage(Image` *img*`, int` *x*`, int` *y*`, Color` *bgcolor*`, ImageObserver` *observer*`)`
- `drawImage(Image` *img*`, int` *x*`, int` *y*`, int` *width*`, int` *height*`, Color` *bgcolor*`, ImageObserver` *observer*`)`

The `drawImage` methods have the following arguments:

`Image` ***img***
The image to draw.

`int` *x*, `int` *y*
The coordinates of the upper left corner of the image.

`int` *width*, `int` *height*
The width and height (in pixels) of the image.

`Color` *bgcolor*
The color to draw underneath the image. This argument can be useful if the image contains transparent pixels and you know that the image will be displayed against a solid background of the indicated color.

`ImageObserver` *observer*
An object that implements the `ImageObserver` interface. This argument registers the object as the image observer so that it is notified whenever new information about the image becomes available. Most components can simply specify `this`. The reason why `this` works as the image observer is that the `Component` class implements the `ImageObserver` interface. Its implementation invokes the `repaint` method as the image data is loaded, which is usually what you want to happen.

The `drawImage` method returns after displaying the image data that has been loaded so far. To make sure that `drawImage` draws only complete images, you must track image loading. See Loading Images (page 541) for information on tracking image loading.

Manipulating Images

Figure 76 illustrates how image data is created behind the scenes. An *image producer*—an object that adheres to the `ImageProducer`[1] interface—produces the raw data for an `Image` object. The image producer provides this data to an *image consumer*—an object that adheres to the `ImageConsumer`[2] interface. Unless you need to manipulate or create custom images, you don't usually need to know about image producers and consumers. The AWT automatically uses image producers and consumers behind the scenes.

Figure 76: How image data is created.

---

1 http://java.sun.com/products/jdk/1.1/docs/api/java.awt.image.ImageProducer.html
2 http://java.sun.com/products/jdk/1.1/docs/api/java.awt.image.ImageConsumer.html

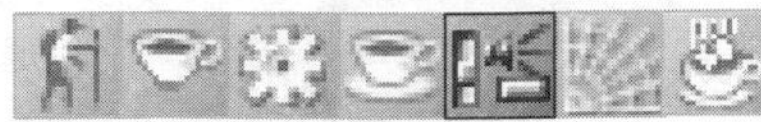

The AWT supports image manipulation by letting you insert image filters between image producers and image consumers. An *image filter* is an `ImageFilter`[1] object that sits between a producer and a consumer and modifies the image data before the consumer gets it. The `ImageFilter` class implements the `ImageConsumer` interface, since image filters intercept messages that the producer sends to the consumer. The following figure shows how an image filter sits between the image producer and consumer.

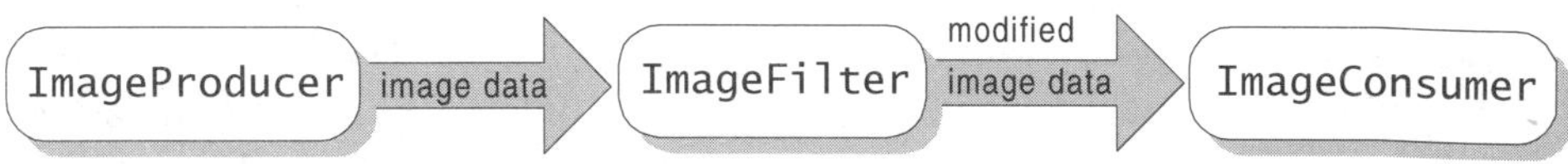

Figure 77: An image filter sits between a producer and a consumer, modifying the image data before the consumer gets it.

Using an existing image filter is easy. Simply use the following code and modifies the image filter constructor as necessary:

```
Image sourceImage;
...//Initialize sourceImage, using the Toolkit or Applet
   //getImage() method.
ImageFilter filter = new SomeImageFilter();
ImageProducer producer = new
                    FilteredImageSource(sourceImage.getSource(),

Image resultImage = createImage(producer);
```

The next section explains how this code works and tells you where to find some image filters.

What if you can't find an image filter that does what you need? You can write your own image filter. How to Write an Image Filter (page 550) gives you some tips on how to do so, including pointers to examples and an explanation of a custom filter that rotates images.

How to Use an Image Filter

The following applet uses a filter to rotate an image. The filter is a custom filter named `RotateFilter` that you'll see discussed a bit later. All you need to know about the filter to use it is that its constructor takes a single `double` argument: the rotation angle in radians. This applet converts the number the user enters from degrees into radians, so that the applet can construct a `RotateFilter`.

---

[1] http://java.sun.com/products/jdk/1.1/docs/api/java.awt.image.ImageFilter.html

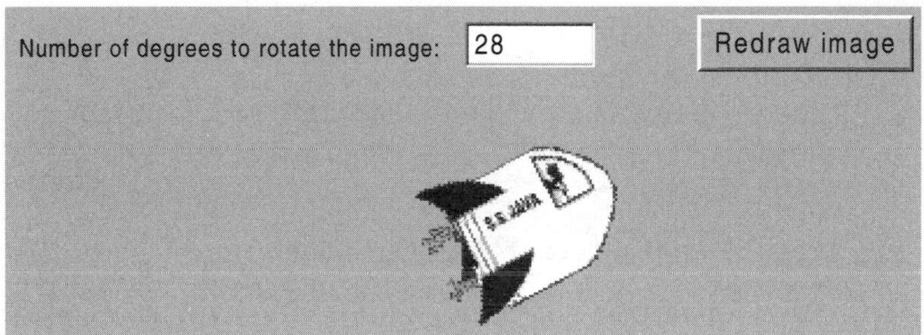

http://java.sun.com/docs/books/tutorial/ui/drawing/useFilter.html

Here's the source code that uses the filter. You can find the complete program on page 877.

```
public class ImageRotator extends Applet ... {
    . . .
    RotatorCanvas rotator;
    double radiansPerDegree = Math.PI / 180;

    public void init() {
        //Load the image.
        Image image = getImage(getCodeBase(),
                               "rocketship.gif");

        ...//Create the component that uses the image filter:
        rotator = new RotatorCanvas(image);
        ...
        add(rotator);
        ...
    }

    public void actionPerformed(ActionEvent evt) {
        int degrees;

        ...//Get the number of degrees to rotate the image by.

        //Convert to radians.
        rotator.rotateImage((double)degrees * radiansPerDegree);
    }
}

class RotatorCanvas extends Canvas {
    Image sourceImage;
    Image resultImage;

    public RotatorCanvas(Image image) {
        sourceImage = image;
        resultImage = sourceImage;
```

```
    }

    public void rotateImage(double angle) {
        ImageFilter filter = new RotateFilter(angle);
        ImageProducer producer = new FilteredImageSource(
                                               sourceImage.getSource(),

        resultImage = createImage(producer);
        repaint();
    }

    public void paint(Graphics g) {
        Dimension d = getSize();
        int x = (d.width - resultImage.getWidth(this)) / 2;
        int y = (d.height - resultImage.getHeight(this)) / 2;

        g.drawImage(resultImage, x, y, this);
    }
}
```

How the Code Works. To use an image filter, a program goes through the following steps:

1. Get an `Image` object (usually done with a `getImage` method).
2. Using the `getSource` method, get the data source (an `ImageProducer`) for the `Image` object.
3. Create an instance of the image filter and initializes the filter as necessary.
4. Create a `FilteredImageSource` object and passes the constructor the image source and filter objects.
5. With the `Component` `createImage` method, create a new `Image` object that has the `FilteredImageSource` as its image producer.

This might sound complex, but it's actually easy to implement. The real complexity is behind the scenes, as we'll explain a bit later. First, we'll explain the code in the example applet that uses the image filter.

In the example applet, the `RotatorCanvas` `rotateImage` method performs most of the tasks associated with using the image filter. The one exception is the first step, getting the original `Image` object, which is performed by the applet's `init` method. This `Image` object is passed to the `RotatorCanvas`, which refers to it as `sourceImage`.

The `rotateImage` method instantiates the image filter by calling the filter's constructor. The single argument to the constructor is the angle, in radians, to rotate the image by.

```
ImageFilter filter = new RotateFilter(angle);
```

Next, the rotateImage method creates a FilteredImageSource instance. The first argument to the FilteredImageSource constructor is the image source, obtained with the getSource method. The second argument is the filter object.

```
ImageProducer producer = new FilteredImageSource(
                                sourceImage.getSource(),
                                filter);
```

Finally, the code creates a second Image, resultImage, by invoking the Component createImage method. The lone argument to createImage is the FilteredImageSource created in the previous statement.

```
resultImage = createImage(producer);
```

What Happens Behind the Scenes. This section explains how image filtering works, behind the scenes. If you don't care about these implementation details, feel free to skip ahead to Where to Find Image Filters (page 550).

The first thing you need to know is that the AWT uses ImageConsumers behind the scenes, in response to drawImage requests. So the component that displays the image isn't the image consumer—some object deep in the AWT is the image consumer.

The createImage call in the previous statement sets up an Image (resultImage), that expects to get image data from its producer, the FilteredImageSource instance. Here's what the path for the image data looks like from the perspective of resultImage:

Figure 78: The path for the image data from the perspective of resultImage.

The dotted line indicates that the image consumer never actually gets data from the FilteredImageSource. Instead, when the image consumer requests image data, in response to g.drawImage(resultImage,...), the FilteredImageSource performs some sleight of hand and then steps out of the way. The FilteredImageSource performs that "magic" by taking the following steps:

- It creates a new image filter object by invoking the `getFilterInstance` method on the filter object that you gave to the `FilteredImageSource` constructor. By default, `getFilterInstance` clones the filter object.
- It connects the new image filter object to the image consumer.
- It connects the image data source, which you gave to the `FilteredImageSource` constructor, to the image filter.

Here is the result:

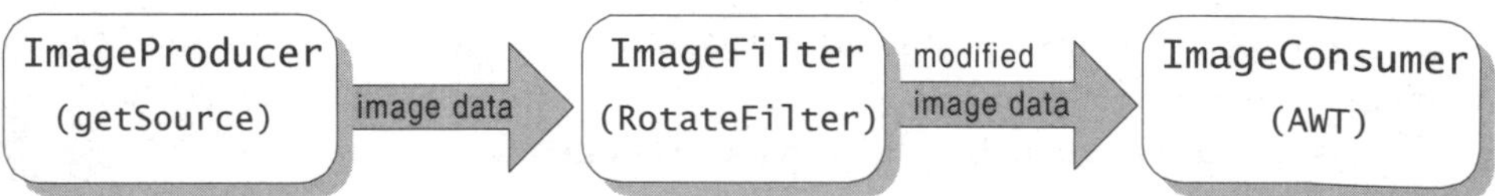

Figure 79: The intermediary step performed by the `FilteredImageSource`.

Where to Find Image Filters. So where can you find existing image filters? The `java.awt.image` package includes one ready-to-use filter, `CropImageFilter`[1], which produces an image consisting of a rectangular region of a larger image. You can also find several image filters used by applets at our Web site.[2]

How to Write an Image Filter

All image filters must be subclasses of the `ImageFilter`[3] class. If your image filter will modify the colors or transparency of an image, then instead of creating a direct subclass of `ImageFilter`, you should probably create a subclass of `RGBImageFilter`.[4]

Before writing an image filter, you should first find others, studying any that are similar to what you plan to write. You should also study the `ImageProducer` and `ImageConsumer` interfaces, and become thoroughly familiar with them.

Finding Examples. You can find examples of image filters on our Web site.[5] Later in this section, you'll see an example of a direct `ImageFilter` subclass, `RotateFilter`.

---

1 http://java.sun.com/products/jdk/1.1/docs/api/java.awt.image.CropImageFilter.html
2 For an up-to-date list of filters at our Website, visit this book's Web page: http://java.sun.com/docs/books/tutorial/2e/book.html
3 http://java.sun.com/products/jdk/1.1/docs/api/java.awt.image.ImageFilter.html
4 http://java.sun.com/products/jdk/1.1/docs/api/java.awt.image.RGBImageFilter.html
5 For a list of `ImageFilter` subclasses whose source code is available on our Web site, see this book's Web page: http://java.sun.com/docs/books/tutorial/2e/book.html

Creating an ImageFilter Subclass. As we mentioned before, image filters implement the `ImageConsumer`[1] interface. This lets them intercept data intended for the image consumer. `ImageConsumer` defines the following methods:

```
setDimensions(int width, int height);
setProperties(Hashtable props);
setColorModel(ColorModel model);
setHints(int hintflags);
setPixels(int x, int y, int w, int h,
              ColorModel model, byte pixels[],
              int offset, int scansize);
setPixels(int x, int y, int w, int h,
              ColorModel model, int pixels[],
              int offset, int scansize);
imageComplete(int status);
```

The `ImageFilter` class implements all the above methods so that they forward the method data to the filter's consumer. For example, `ImageFilter` implements the `setDimensions` method as follows:

```
public void setDimensions(int width, int height) {
    consumer.setDimensions(width, height);
}
```

Thanks to these `ImageFilter` methods, your subclass probably doesn't need to implement every `ImageConsumer` method. You need to implement only the methods that transmit data you want to change.

For example, the `CropImageFilter`[2] class implements four of the `ImageConsumer` methods: `setDimensions`, `setProperties`, and both varieties of `setPixels`. It also implements a constructor with arguments that specify the rectangle to be cropped. As another example, the `RGBImageFilter`[3] class implements some helper methods, defines an abstract helper method to perform the actual color modifications of each pixel, and implements the following `ImageConsumer` methods: `setColorModel` and both varieties of `setPixels`.

Most, if not all, filters implement the `setPixels` methods. These methods determine exactly what image data is used to construct the `Image`. One or both of the `setPixels` methods may be called multiple times during the construction of a single image. Each call gives the `ImageConsumer` information about a rectangle of pixels within the image. When the `ImageConsumer`'s `imageComplete` method

---

1 http://java.sun.com/products/jdk/1.1/docs/api/java.awt.image.ImageConsumer.html
2 http://java.sun.com/products/jdk/1.1/docs/api/java.awt.image.CropImageFilter.html
3 http://java.sun.com/products/jdk/1.1/docs/api/java.awt.image.RGBImageFilter.html

is called with any status except `SINGLEFRAMEDONE` (which implies that data for more frames will appear), then the `ImageConsumer` can assume that it will receive no further `setPixels` calls. An `imageComplete` status of `STATICIMAGE-DONE` specifies that not only is the image data complete, but that no errors have been detected.

The following figure illustrates the arguments to the `setPixels` methods. A further explanation of the arguments follows the figure.

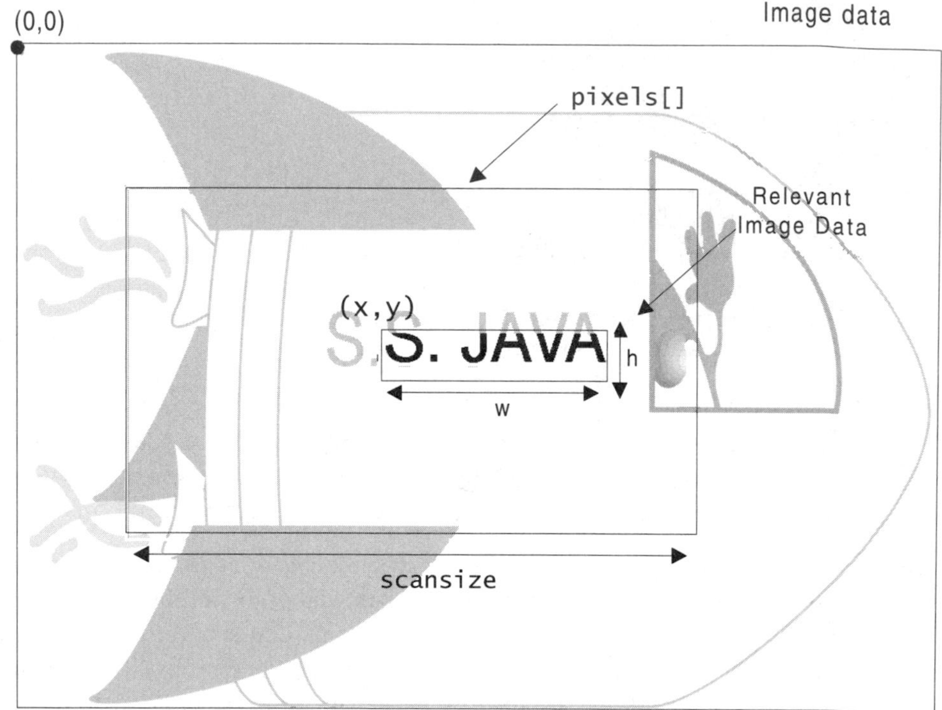

Figure 80: Arguments to the `setPixel` methods.

`x, y`
Specify the location within the image, relative to its upper left corner, where this rectangle begins.

`w, h`
Specify the width and height, in pixels, of this rectangle.

`model`
Specifies the color model used by the data in the pixels array.

`pixels[]`

Specifies an array of pixels. The rectangle of image data is contained in this array, but the array might contain more than `w*h` entries, depending on the values of `offset` and `scansize`. Here's the formula for determining what entry in the `pixels` array contains the data for the pixel at (`x+i`, `y+j`), where (0 <= `i` < `w`) and (0 <= `j` < `h`):

```
offset + (j * scansize) + i
```

The following illustration of the `pixels` array should make this clearer. It shows how a specific pixel—for example, (x,y)—maps to an entry in the `pixels` array.

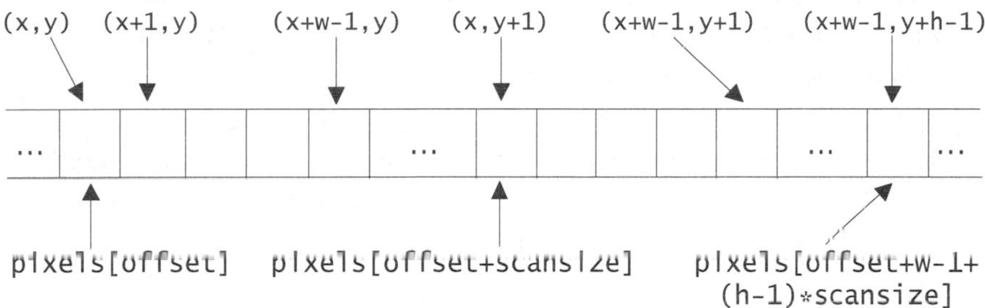

`offset`

Specifies the index (in the `pixels` array) of the first pixel in the rectangle.

`scansize`

Specifies the width of each row in the `pixels` array. Due to efficiency considerations, this might be greater than `w`.

The RotateFilter Image Filter. The `RotateFilter` class (page 879) implements a filter that rotates an image by the specified angle. It relies on the following graphics formulas to calculate the new position of each pixel:

```
newX = oldX*cos(angle) - oldY*sin(angle)
newY = oldX*sin(angle) + oldY*cos(angle)
```

`RotateFilter` implements the following `ImageConsumer` methods:

`setDimensions`

Records the unfiltered image's width and height for use in the `setPixels` and `imageComplete` methods. Calculates the filtered image's final width and height, records it for use in its `imageComplete` method, creates a buffer to store the image data as it comes in, and calls the consumer's `setDimensions` method to set the new width and height.

`setColorModel`
Tells the consumer to expect pixels in the default RGB color model.

`setHints`
Tells the consumer to expect the image data in top-down-left-right order (the order in which you're reading this page), in complete scan lines, and with every pixel sent exactly once.

`setPixels`
Both varieties of this method convert the pixels to the default RGB model, if necessary, and copy the pixels into a storage buffer. Most image filters would simply modify the pixel data and forward it to the consumer, but because the sides of a rotated rectangle are no longer horizontal and vertical (for most angles), this filter cannot efficiently forward pixels from its `setPixels` method. Instead, `RotateFilter` stores all the pixel data until it receives an `imageComplete` message.

`imageComplete`
Rotates the image and then invokes `consumer.setPixels` repeatedly to send each line of the image to the consumer. After sending the whole image, this method invokes `consumer.imageComplete`.

Performing Animation

Once you've learned how to draw graphics to the screen, you can learn how to animate those graphics.

What all forms of animation have in common is that they create some kind of perceived motion by showing successive frames at a relatively high speed. Computer animation usually shows 10–20 frames per second. By comparison, traditional hand-drawn animation uses anywhere from 8 frames per second (for poor quality animation) to 12 frames per second (for standard animation) to 24 frames per second (for short bursts of smooth, realistic motion). The next few sections describe everything you need to know to write a Java program that performs animation.

Before you start: Check out existing animation tools and applets, such as the `Animator applet`,[1] to see whether you can use one of them instead of writing your own program.

---

[1] To find the Animator applet, visit the Web page for this book: http://java.sun.com/docs/books/tutorial/2e/book.html

The most important step in creating a program that animates is to set up the framework correctly. Except for animation performed only in direct response to external events, such as the user dragging an onscreen object, a program that performs animation needs an animation loop.

Creating the Animation Loop (page 555) tells you exactly what you need in an animation loop. The animation loop is responsible for keeping track of the current frame and for requesting periodic screen updates. For applets and many applications, you need a separate thread to run the animation loop. This section contains an example applet and an example application that you can use as templates for all animation.

Animating Graphics (page 560) features an example that animates primitive graphics.

The example featured in Animating Graphics (page 560) is imperfect because its flashing is distracting. Eliminating Flashing (page 561) tells you how to use two techniques to eliminate flashing:

- Overriding the `update` method
- Double buffering (also known as *using a backbuffer*)

The simplest form of image animation involves moving an unchanging image across the screen. In the traditional animation world, this is known as *cutout animation*, since it's traditionally accomplished by cutting a shape out of paper and moving the shape in front of the camera. In computer programs, this technique is often used for drag and drop interfaces. Moving an Image Across the Screen (page 565) gives an example of performing this type of animation.

Displaying a Sequence of Images (page 567) tells you how to perform classic, cartoon-style animation, given a sequence of images.

Improving the Appearance and Performance of Image Animation (page 568) tells you how to use the `MediaTracker` class so that you can delay displaying an animation until all its images are loaded. You'll also get some hints on improving applet animation performance by combining image files and by using a compression scheme such as Flic.

Creating the Animation Loop

Every program that performs animation by drawing at regular intervals needs an animation loop. Generally, this loop should be in its own thread. The animation loop should *never* be in the `paint` or `update` method, since that would take over the main AWT thread, which is in charge of all drawing and event handling.

This section provides two templates for performing animation, one for applets and another for applications. Here's what a single frame of the animation produced by the template looks like:

Frame 33

http://java.sun.com/docs/books/tutorial/ui/drawing/animLoop.html

The animation the template performs is a bit boring: It simply displays the current frame number, using a default rate of 10 frames per second. The next few sections build on this example and shows you how to animate primitive graphics and images.

The complete code for the applet animation template is on page 883. The code for the equivalent application animation template is on page 885. The rest of this section explains the templates' code. Here is a summary of what both templates accomplish:

```
public class AnimatorClass extends AComponentClass
                             implements Runnable {

    //In initialization code:
        //From user-specified frames-per-second value,
        //determine how long to delay between frames.

    //In a method that does nothing but start the animation:
        //Create and start the animating thread.

    //In a method that does nothing but stop the animation:
        //Stop the animating thread.

    public void run() {
        //Lower this thread's priority so it can't interfere
        //with other processing going on.

        //Remember the starting time.

        //Here's the animation loop:
        while (/* animation thread is still running */) {
            //Advance the animation frame.
            //Display it.
            //Delay depending on how far we are behind.
        }
    }
```

```
public void paint(Graphics g) {
    //Draw the current frame of animation.
}
. . .
//In a mouse listener registered upon this component:
public void mousePressed(MouseEvent e) {
    if (/* animation is currently frozen */) {
        //Call the method that starts the animation.
    } else {
        //Call the method that stops the animation.
    }
}
```

Initializing Instance Variables

The animation templates use four instance variables. The first instance variable, `frameNumber`, represents the current frame. It is initialized to -1, even though the first frame number is 0, because the frame number is incremented at the start of the animation loop before any frames are painted. As a result, the first frame to be painted is frame 0.

The second instance variable, `delay`, is the number of milliseconds between frames. It is initialized using a *frames per second* number provided by the user. If the user provides no valid number, then the templates default to 10 frames per second. The following Java statement converts frames per second into the number of milliseconds between frames:

```
delay = (fps > 0) ? (1000 / fps) : 100;
```

The `? :` notation in the previous code snippet is shorthand for `if else`. If the user provides a number of frames per second greater than 0, then the delay is 1000 milliseconds divided by the number of frames per second. Otherwise, the delay between frames is 100 milliseconds.

The third instance variable, `animatorThread`, is a `Thread` object representing the thread in which the animation loop runs. If you're not familiar with threads, see Doing Two or More Tasks at Once: Threads (page 327) for an overview of their use.

The fourth instance variable, `frozen`, is a boolean value that is initialized to `false`. The templates set `frozen` to `true` to indicate that the user has requested that the animation stop. You'll see more about this later in this section.

The Animation Loop

The animation loop (the `while` loop in the animation thread) does the following, over and over again:

1. Advances the frame number.
2. Calls the `repaint` method to request that the current frame of animation be drawn.
3. Sleeps for up to `delay` milliseconds (more on this later).

The following code performs these tasks:

```
while (/* animation thread is still running */) {
    //Advance the animation frame.
    frameNumber++;

    //Display it.
    repaint();

    ...//Delay depending on how far we are behind.
}
```

Ensuring a Constant Frame Rate

The most obvious way to implement the delay in the animation loop is to sleep for `delay` milliseconds. However, this can cause the thread to sleep too long since you lose a certain amount of time just by executing the animation loop.

The solution to this problem is to remember when the animation loop starts, add `delay` milliseconds to arrive at a wakeup time, and then sleep until the wakeup time. Here's the code that implements this:

```
long startTime = System.currentTimeMillis();
while (/* animation thread is still running */) {
    ...//Advance the animation frame and display it.
    try {
        startTime += delay;
        Thread.sleep(Math.max(0,
                     startTime-System.currentTimeMillis()));
    } catch (InterruptedException e) {
        break;
    }
}
```

Behaving Politely

Two more features of the animation templates belong in the category of polite behavior.

The first feature is allowing the user to explicitly stop and restart the animation while the applet or application is still visible. Animation can be quite distracting, and it's a good idea to give the user the power to stop the animation so that the user can concentrate on something else. This feature is implemented with a mouse listener that's registered on the animation component. The mouse listener implements the `mousePressed` method so that it stops or starts the animation thread, depending on the thread's current state. Here's the code that implements this:

```
...//In initialization code:
boolean frozen = false;
addMouseListener(theMouseListener);

...//In the method that starts the animation thread:
    if (frozen) {
        //Do nothing.  The user has requested that we
        //stop changing the image.
    } else {
        //Start animating!
       ...//Create and start the animating thread.
    }
}

. . .
...//In the mouse listener:
public void mousePressed(MouseEvent e) {
    if (frozen) {
        frozen = false;
        //Call the method that stops the animation.
    } else {
        frozen = true;
        //Call the method that stops the animation.
    }
}
```

The second polite feature is to suspend the animation whenever the applet or application is known not to be visible. For the applet animation template, this is achieved by implementing the `Applet` `stop` and `start` methods. For the application animation template, this is achieved by implementing an event handler for the `WINDOW_ICONIFY` and `WINDOW_DEICONIFY` events. In both templates, if the user hasn't frozen the animation, then when the program detects that the animation is not visible, it stops the animation thread. When the user revisits the animation, the program restarts the animation thread unless the user has explicitly requested that the animation be stopped.

You might be wondering why the frame number is incremented at the beginning of the loop rather than at the end. The reason has to do with what happens

when the user freezes the animation, then leaves it, and then revisits it. When the user freezes the animation, the animation loop completes before exiting. If the frame number is incremented at the bottom of the loop instead of at the top of the loop, then when the loop exits, the frame number is one more than the number of the frame being displayed. When the user revisits the animation, the animation is frozen on a different frame than the one the user left. This is disconcerting and annoying when the user stops the animation to look at a particular frame.

Animating Graphics

This section features an applet that creates a moving checkerboard effect by painting alternate squares. The squares are drawn by the `Graphics` `fillRect` method. The following figure shows the applet in action:

http://java.sun.com/docs/books/tutorial/ui/drawing/animGraphics.html

If you run this applet, you might notice that the graphics aren't animated perfectly smoothly; occasionally part or all of the drawing area flashes noticeably. The next section will explain the cause of this flashing and tell you how to eliminate it.

The complete code for the checkerboard applet is on page 888. The major difference between this applet and the animation template is that the `paint` method now draws filled rectangles, using an algorithm that depends on the current frame number. This applet also introduces two instance variables, one that holds the square size and another that keeps track of whether the next column to be drawn begins with a black square. The user can set the square size by means of a new applet parameter. An application version of this applet would have similar differences from the animation template, except that square size would be set using a command-line argument or property.

The following code contains the `paint` code that performs the actual drawing. Note that the program draws only the black boxes, indicated by `fillSquare` being `true`, not the other boxes. It can get away with this because, by default, a component's drawing area is cleared (set to the background color) just before the `paint` method is called.

```
// Draw the rectangle if necessary.
if (fillSquare) {
    g.fillRect(x, y, w, h);
    fillSquare = false;
} else {
    fillSquare = true;
}
```

Eliminating Flashing

The flashing in the example in the previous section is a common problem with animation (and occasionally with static graphics). The flashing effect is the result of two facts:

- By default, the background of the animation is cleared (its whole area is redrawn in the background color) before the `paint` method is called.
- The computation in the previous example's `paint` method is so complex that it takes longer to compute and draw each frame of animation than the video screen's refresh rate. As a result, the first part of the frame is drawn on one video refresh pass, and the rest of the frame is drawn on the next (or even the pass after that). The result is that although the first part of the frame is usually animated smoothly, you can see a break between the first and second parts, since the second part is blank until the second pass.

You can use two techniques to eliminate flashing: overriding the `update` method and implementing double buffering.

To eliminate flashing, whether or not you use double buffering, you must override the `update` method. This is necessary because it is the only way to prevent the entire background of the component from being cleared every time the component is drawn. Overriding the update Method (page 561) discusses how to implement the `update` method.

Double buffering involves performing multiple graphics operations on an undisplayed graphics buffer, and then displaying the resulting image onscreen. Double buffering prevents incomplete images from being drawn to the screen. Implementing Double Buffering (page 563) discusses how to implement double buffering.

Overriding the update Method

To eliminate flashing, you must override the `update` method. The reason lies in the way the AWT requests that a component (such as an `Applet`, `Canvas`, or `Frame`) repaint itself.

The AWT requests a repaint by calling the component's update method. The default implementation of update clears the component's background before calling paint. Because eliminating flashing requires that you eliminate all unnecessary drawing, your first step is always to override update so that it clears the entire background only when necessary. When moving drawing code from the paint method to update, you might need to modify the drawing code so that it doesn't depend on the background being cleared.

Note: Even if your implementation of update doesn't call paint, you must still implement a paint method. The reason: When an area that your component displays is suddenly revealed after being hidden (behind another window, for example), the AWT calls paint directly, without calling update. An easy way to implement paint is to have it call update.

On page 891 you can find the code for a modified version of the previous example that implements update to eliminate flashing. The following figure shows this applet.

http://java.sun.com/docs/books/tutorial/ui/drawing/update.html

Here's the new version of the paint method, along with the new update method. All of the drawing code that used to be in the paint method is now in the update method. Significant changes in the drawing code are in bold.

```
public void paint(Graphics g) {
    update(g);
}

public void update(Graphics g) {
    Color bg = getBackground();
    Color fg = getForeground();

    ...//same as old paint method until we draw the rectangle:
            if (fillSquare) {
                g.fillRect(x, y, w, h);
                fillSquare = false;
            } else {
                g.setColor(bg);
                g.fillRect(x, y, w, h);
                g.setColor(fg);
```

```
                fillSquare = true;
            }
        ...//same as old paint method
    }
```

Note that since the background is no longer automatically cleared, the drawing code must now draw the rectangles that are not black, as well as the black ones.

Clipping the Drawing Area. One technique you might be able to use in your `update` method is *clipping* the area you draw. This doesn't work for the example applet, since the entire drawing area changes with every frame. Clipping works well, though, when only a small part of the drawing area changes, such as when the user drags an object across a background.

You perform clipping using the `clipRect` method. An example of using `clipRect` is in Improving the Appearance and Performance of Image Animation (page 568).

Implementing Double Buffering

The previous section showed you how to eliminate flashing by implementing the `update` method. If you run the applet, you might notice (depending on the performance of your computer) that the resulting applet, although it probably doesn't flash, appears to crawl a bit. That is, instead of the whole drawing area (or frame) being updated at once, sometimes one part is updated before the part just to its right, which causes noticeably uneven drawing between columns.

You can use double buffering to avoid this crawling effect by forcing the entire frame to be drawn at once. To implement double buffering, to create an undisplayed buffer (often called a *backbuffer* or *off-screen buffer*), draw to it, and then display the resulting image on-screen.

On page 895 you'll find the code for the graphics animation example, modified so that it implements double buffering. Below is the resulting applet.

http://java.sun.com/docs/books/tutorial/ui/drawing/doubleBuffer.html

To create an off-screen buffer with the AWT, you need to first create an image of the proper size and then get a graphics context to manipulate the image. Here is the code that does this:

```
//Where instance variables are declared:
Dimension offDimension;
Image offImage;
Graphics offGraphics;
. . .
//In the update method, where d holds the size of the
//onscreen drawing area:
if ( (offGraphics == null)
  || (d.width != offDimension.width)
  || (d.height != offDimension.height) ) {
    offDimension = d;
    offImage = createImage(d.width, d.height);
    offGraphics = offImage.getGraphics();
}
```

Below, in bold, is the new drawing code in the `update` method. Note that the drawing code now clears the entire background, but it doesn't cause flashing because the code is drawing to the off-screen buffer, not to the screen. Note also that all the calls to `fillRect` are performed to the off-screen buffer. The final result is drawn to the screen just before the `update` method returns.

```
public void update(Graphics g) {
    ...//First, initialize variables and create the
       //offscreen buffer as shown above. Then erase the
       //previous image:
        offGraphics.setColor(getBackground());
        offGraphics.fillRect(0, 0, d.width, d.height);
        offGraphics.setColor(Color.black);

    ...//Do everything the old paint method did --
       //until we draw the rectangle.
            if (fillSquare) {
                offGraphics.fillRect(x, y, w, h);
                fillSquare = false;
            } else {
                fillSquare = true;
            }

    ...//The rest is exactly like the old paint method
       //until the very end, when we add the following:
    //Paint the image onto the screen.
    g.drawImage(offImage, 0, 0, this);
}
```

It's not necessary for the `update` method to call the `paint` method. All that's necessary is that the `update` method somehow draw its off-screen buffer to the screen, and that the `paint` method be able to draw the proper image when it's called directly by the AWT.

You might wonder why the off-screen image and graphics context are created in the `update` method, instead of in, for example, the `start` method. The reason is that the image and graphics context depend on the size of the applet `Panel`'s drawing area, and the size of any component's drawing area is not reliably valid until the component is just about to be drawn to the screen for the first time.

Moving an Image Across the Screen

This section features an applet that moves one image (a rocketship) in front of a background image (a field of stars). This section shows only applet code. The code for an application would be similar, except you would use different code to load the images, as described in Loading Images (page 541).

Below are the two images this applet uses.

rocketship.gif:

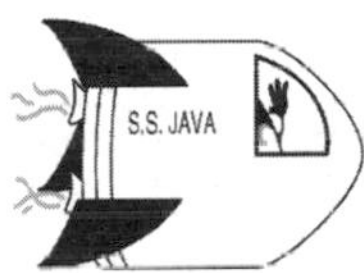

starfield.gif:

Note: The rocketship image has a transparent background. The transparent background makes the rocketship image appear to have a rocketship shape, no matter what color background it's drawn on top of. If the rocketship background weren't transparent, then instead of the illusion of a rocketship moving through space, you'd see a rocketship on top of a rectangle moving through space.

Here's what the applet looks like:

http://java.sun.com/docs/books/tutorial/ui/drawing/movingImage.html

The code for performing this animation isn't complex. Essentially, it's the applet animation template, plus the double buffering code you saw in the previous section, plus a few additional lines of code. The additional code loads the images, draws the background image, and then uses a simple algorithm to determine where to draw the moving image. Here is the additional code:

```
...//Where instance variables are declared:
Image stars;
Image rocket;

...//In the init method:
stars = getImage(getCodeBase(), "starfield.gif");
rocket = getImage(getCodeBase(), "rocketship.gif");

...//In the update method:
//Paint the frame into the image.
paintFrame(offGraphics);

...//A new method:
void paintFrame(Graphics g) {
    Dimension d = getSize();
    int w;
    int h;

    //If we have a valid width and height for the background
    //image, draw it.
    w = stars.getWidth(this);
    h = stars.getHeight(this);
    if ((w > 0) && (h > 0)) {
        g.drawImage(stars, (d.width - w)/2,
                    (d.height - h)/2, this);
    }

    //If we have a valid width and height for the foreground
    //image, draw it.
    w = rocket.getWidth(this);
    h = rocket.getHeight(this);
```

```
        if ((w > 0) && (h > 0)) {
            g.drawImage(rocket, ((frameNumber*5) % (w + d.width))
                        - w, (d.height - h)/2, this);
        }
    }
```

You might think that this program doesn't need to clear the background since it uses a background image. However, clearing the background is still necessary. One reason is that the applet usually starts drawing before the images are fully loaded. If the rocketship image loaded before the background image, you would see parts of multiple rocketships until the background image loaded. Another reason is that if the applet drawing area were wider than the background image, for some reason, then you'd see multiple rocketships on either side of the background image.

You could solve the first problem by delaying all drawing until both images are fully loaded. The second problem could be solved by scaling the background image to fit the entire applet area. You'll learn how to wait for images to be fully loaded in Improving the Appearance and Performance of Image Animation (page 568). Scaling is described in Displaying Images (page 544).

Displaying a Sequence of Images

This section features the same animation that you see at the beginning of the online tutorial's Getting Started trail[1]: our mascot, Duke, waving. The example in this section describes the basic techniques for displaying an image sequence. The next section has hints for improving the appearance and performance of this animation. This section uses only applet code. The code for an application would be similar, except you would use different code to load the images, as described in Loading Images (page 541).

The applet looks something like this:

http://java.sun.com/docs/books/tutorial/ui/drawing/imageSequence.html

---

1 http://java.sun.com/docs/books/tutorial/getStarted/index.html

Here are the ten images that this applet uses:

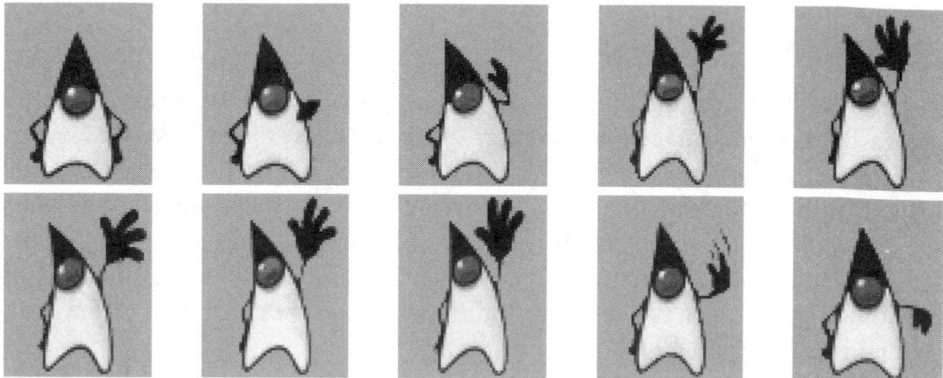

http://java.sun.com/docs/books/tutorial/ui/drawing/imageSequence.html

The code for this example (which you can find on page 903) is even simpler than for the previous example, which moved an image. Here is the code that differs from the previous example:

```
. . .//Where instance variables are declared:
Image duke[10];

. . .//In the init method:
for (int i = 1; i <= 10; i++) {
    images[i-1] = getImage(getCodeBase(),
                           "T"+i+".gif");
}

. . .//In the update method, instead of calling drawFrame:
offGraphics.drawImage(images[frameNumber % 10], 0, 0, this);
```

Improving the Appearance and Performance of Image Animation

If you run the previous applet, you might notice two things:

- While the images are loading, the program might display some images partially and others not at all.
- Loading the images takes a long time.

The problem of displaying partial images is easy to fix using the `MediaTracker` class. `MediaTracker` also can decrease the amount of time that loading images takes. Another way to deal with the problem of slow image loading is to change the image format somehow; this section gives you some suggestions for doing this.

Using MediaTracker to Download Images and Delay Image Display

The `MediaTracker` class lets you easily download data for a group of images and find out when the images are fully loaded. Ordinarily, an image's data isn't downloaded until the image is drawn for the first time. To request that the data for a group of images be preloaded asynchronously, use the forms of `checkID` and `checkAll` that take a boolean argument, setting the argument to `true`. To load data synchronously (waiting for the data to arrive), use the `waitForID` and `waitForAll` methods. The `MediaTracker` methods that load data use several background threads to download the data, resulting in increased speed.

To check on the status of image loading, you can use the `MediaTracker` `statusID` and `statusAll` methods. To simply check whether any image data remains to be loaded, use the `checkID` and `checkAll` methods.

On page 907 you can find a modified version of the example applet that uses the MediaTracker `waitForAll` and `checkAll` methods. Until every image is fully loaded, this applet simply displays a "Please wait . . ." message. See the `MediaTracker`[1] documentation for an example that draws a background image immediately, but delays drawing the animated images.

The applet, again, looks something like this:

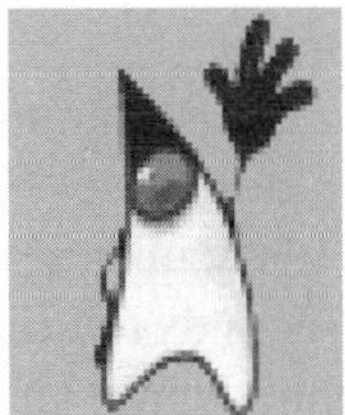

http://java.sun.com/docs/books/tutorial/ui/drawing/imageSequence.html

Below is the changed code, which uses a `MediaTracker` to help delay image display. Differences are marked in bold.

---

1 http://java.sun.com/products/jdk/1.1/docs/api/java.awt.MediaTracker.html

```
...//Where instance variables are declared:
MediaTracker tracker;

...//In the init method:
tracker = new MediaTracker(this);
for (int i = 1; i <= 10; i++) {
    images[i-1] = getImage(getCodeBase(),
                           "images/duke/T"+i+".gif");
    tracker.addImage(images[i-1], 0);
}

...//At the beginning of the run method:
try {
    //Start downloading the images. Wait until they're loaded.
    tracker.waitForAll();
} catch (InterruptedException e) {}

...//At the beginning of the update method:
//If not all the images are loaded, just clear the background
//and display a status string.
if (!tracker.checkAll()) {
    g.clearRect(0, 0, d.width, d.height);
    g.drawString("Please wait...", 0, d.height/2);
}

//If all images are loaded, draw.
else {
    ...//same code as before...
}
```

Speeding Up Image Loading

Whether or not you use `MediaTracker`, loading images using URLs (as applets usually do) usually takes a long time. Most of the time is taken up by initiating HTTP connections. Each image file requires a separate HTTP connection, and each connection can take several seconds to initiate. The key to avoiding this performance hit is to combine the images in a single file. You can further improve performance by using some sort of compression scheme, especially one that's designed for moving images.

One simple way to combine images in a single file is to create an *image strip*, a file that contains several images in a row. The following figure shows an image strip:

To draw an image from the strip, first set the clipping area to the size of one image. Then draw the image strip, shifted to the left (if necessary) so that only the image you want appears within the clipping area. For example:

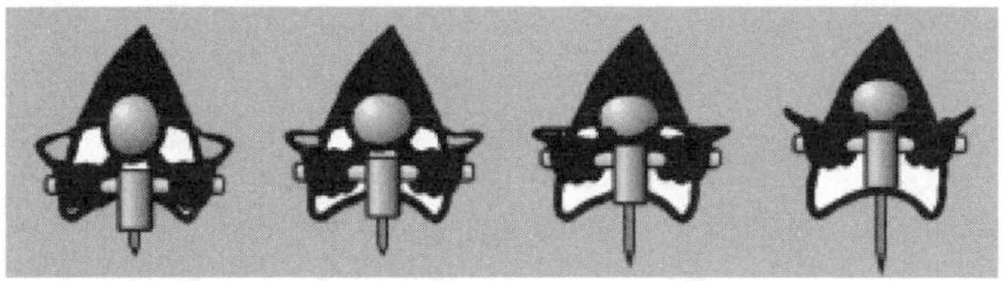

```
//imageStrip is the Image object representing the image strip.
//imageWidth is the size of an individual image in the strip.
//imageNumber is the number (0 to numImages)
//of the image to draw.
int stripWidth = imageStrip.getWidth(this);
int stripHeight = imageStrip.getHeight(this);
int imageWidth = stripWidth / numImages;
g.clipRect(0, 0, imageWidth, stripHeight);
g.drawImage(imageStrip, -imageNumber*imageWidth, 0, this);
```

If you want image loading to be faster still, you should look into image compression schemes, especially ones like Flic that perform inter-frame compression.

Common Problems (and Their Solutions)

THIS section lists problems that people frequently run into when writing and using components. The first two subsections, Component Problems (page 573) and Layout Problems (page 575), contain information that's useful for any program that uses components. The third subsection, Graphics Problems (page 576), applies only to components that perform custom drawing.

If this section doesn't list the solution to your problem, you might get some insight by reading Details of the Component Architecture (page 501). If your program is an applet, check the Writing Applets trail's common problems section (page 235). If you still don't find the solution, check the online version of this page:

```
http://java.sun.com/docs/books/tutorial/ui/problems/index.html
```

Component Problems

Problem: How do I increase or decrease the number of components in a container?

- To add a component to a container, use the `Container` add method. See How to Add a Component to a Container (page 427) for information. To remove a component from a container, use the `Container` `remove` or `removeAll` method. Alternatively, just add the component to another container, since that automatically removes the component from its previous container.

Problem: My component never shows up!

- If the component is a window, did you invoke `pack` or `setSize` on it before showing the window for the first time? Did you make the window visible (by invoking `setVisible(true)` on it)?
- Did you add the component to its container using the right `add` method for the container's layout manager? See Laying Out Components Within a Container (page 503) for examples of using the `add` method.
- If you're not using the default layout manager, did you successfully create an instance of the right layout manager and call the `setLayout` method on the container?
- If the component is added properly, but added to a container that might already be visible, did you call `validate` on the container after adding the component?
- If your component is a custom component (a `Canvas` subclass, for example), does it implement the `getMinimumSize` and `getPreferredSize` methods so that they return the correct size of the component?
- If you use a non-AWT layout manager, or none at all, does the component have a reasonable size and reasonable display coordinates? In particular, if you use absolute positioning (no layout manager), you must explicitly set the size of your components, or they just won't show up. See Laying Out Components Without a Layout Manager (Absolute Positioning) (page 522).

Problem: My custom component doesn't get updated when it should.

- Make sure that the component's `repaint` method is called every time the component's appearance should change. For standard components, this isn't a problem, since platform-specific code takes care of all the drawing of the component. For custom components, however, you have to explicitly call the `repaint` method on the component whenever the component's appearance should change. Invoking `repaint` on a container of the component is *not* good enough. See How to Use Canvases (page 432) for more information.

Problem: My event listener isn't getting a particular event.

- Check whether the event listener is getting any events. If it isn't, make sure you've used the appropriate `add`*`Xxx`*`Listener` method to register it with the right component.

Problem: Nothing happens when a user tries to close my window.

- You need to implement a window listener and put the appropriate code in its `windowClosing` method. See How to Use Frames (page 441) for more information.

Problem: All your examples are for applets. How do I apply them to applications?

- Except where noted, anywhere in this trail that you see a subclass of the `Applet` class, you can substitute a subclass of the `Panel` class. If the subclass isn't used as a container, you can substitute a subclass of the `Canvas` class. In general, it's easy to convert an applet into an application, as long as the applet doesn't rely on any special applet abilities, such as using methods defined in the `Applet` class.
- To convert an applet into an application, add a `main` method that creates a `Frame` object, creates an instance of the `Applet` (or `Panel` or `Canvas`) subclass, adds the instance to the `Frame`, and then calls the `init` and `start` methods of the instance. The `Frame` should have a window listener that implements the `windowClosing` method in the appropriate way.

  See `AnimatorApplet.java` (page 883) and `AnimatorApplication.java` (page 885) for examples of an applet and an application that implement the same functionality.

Problem: Whenever I execute a Java application with a GUI, I get this annoying error message:

```
Warning:
    Cannot allocate colormap entry for default background
```

- This message occurs only on Motif systems. It occurs when the Motif library is initialized and finds that there's no room in the default colormap to allocate its GUI colors. The solution is to run fewer "colormap hogging" applications on your desktop. The Java runtime system adapts itself to whatever colors are in the default palette, but the Motif library is less forgiving.

Layout Problems

Problem: How do I specify a component's exact size?

- First, make sure that you really need to set the component's exact size. The standard components have different sizes, depending on the platform they're running on and the font they use, so it usually doesn't make sense to specify their exact size.

  For custom components whose contents do not change size (such as images), specifying the exact size makes sense. For custom components, you need to override the `Component` `getMinimumSize` and `getPreferredSize` methods to return the correct size of the component. You can also override the `getMaximumSize` method to return the largest reasonable size of the component. Next, be sure that your component's container uses a layout manager that respects the specified size of the component.

  To change the size of a component that's already been displayed, see the next problem.

Note: All component sizes are subject to layout manager approval. The `FlowLayout` and `GridBagLayout` layout managers use the component's natural size (the latter depending on the constraints that you set), but `BorderLayout` and `GridLayout` usually don't. Other options are writing or finding a custom layout manager or using absolute positioning.

Problem: How do I resize a component?

- Once a component has been displayed, you can change its size using the `Component` `setSize` method. You then need to call the `validate` method on the component's container to make sure the container is laid out again.

Problem: My custom component is being sized too small.

- Does the component implement the `getPreferredSize` and `getMinimumSize` methods? If so, do they return the right values?
- Are you using a layout manager that can use as much space as is available? See General Rules for Using Layout Managers (page 506) for some tips on choosing a layout manager and specifying that it use the maximum available space for a particular component.

Graphics Problems

Problem: I don't know where to put my drawing code.

- Drawing code belongs in the `paint` method of a custom component. You can create a custom component by creating a subclass of the `Canvas`, `Panel`, or `Applet` class. See How to Use Canvases (page 432) for information on implementing a custom component. For efficiency, once you have your drawing code working, you can modify it to go in the `update` method, although you must still implement the `paint` method, as described in Eliminating Flashing (page 561).

Problem: The stuff I draw doesn't show up.

- Check whether your component is showing up at all. Common Problems (and Their Solutions) (page 573) should help you with this.

Problem: I'm using the exact same drawing code as a tutorial example, but it doesn't work. Why?

- Is the code executed in the exact same method as the tutorial example? For example, when the tutorial example has the code in the example's `paint` or `update` method, then those two methods might be the only places where the code is guaranteed to work.

Problem: How do I draw thick lines? Patterns?

- The 1.1 AWT's API for primitive graphics is rather limited. For example, it supports only one line width. You can simulate thick lines by drawing multiple times at one-pixel offsets or by drawing filled rectangles. Also, the AWT doesn't currently support fill or line patterns. See the Java2D discussion in Java Foundation Classes (page 680) for a preview of graphics and imaging support in a future JDK release.

End of Trail

YOU'VE reached the end of the **Creating a User Interface** trail. Take a break—have a cup of steaming hot java.

What Next?

Once you've caught your breath, you have several choices of where to go next. You can go back to the Trail Map (page xvii) to see all of your choices, or you can go directly to one of the following popular trails:

Writing Applets (page 171): This is the starting point for learning everything about writing applets.

Essential Java Classes (page 241): By taking this trail, you can find out about strings, exceptions, threads, and other Java features that are used in all kinds of Java programs.

Custom Networking (page 581): If you like, you can forge onward to learn about the Java environment's support for networking.

http://java.sun.com/docs/books/tutorial/networking/index.html

Custom Networking

THE Java platform is highly regarded in part because of its suitability for writing programs that use and interact with the resources on the Internet and the World Wide Web. In fact, Java-compatible browsers use this ability of the Java platform to the extreme to transport and run applets over the Internet.

This trail walks you through the complexities of writing Java applications and applets that can be used on the Internet.

Overview of Networking (page 585) has two sections. The first describes the networking capabilities of the Java platform that you may already be using without realizing that you are using the network. The second provides a brief overview of networking to familiarize you with terms and concepts that you should understand before reading how to use URLs, sockets, and datagrams.

Working with URLs (page 591) discusses how your Java programs can use URLs to access information on the Internet. A *URL* (Uniform Resource Locator) is the address of a resource on the Internet. Your Java programs can use URLs to connect to and retrieve information over a network. This lesson provides a more complete definition of a URL and shows you how to create and parse a URL, how to open a connection to a URL, and how to read from and write to that connection.

All About Sockets (page 605) explains how to use sockets so that your programs can communicate with other programs on the network. A *socket* is one endpoint of a two-way communication link between two programs running on the network. This lesson shows you how a client can connect to a standard server, the Echo server, and communicate with it via a socket. It then walks you through the details of a complete client/server example, which shows you how to implement both the client side and the server side of a client/server pair.

All About Datagrams (page 619) takes you step by step through a simple client/server example that uses datagrams to communicate. It then challenges you to rewrite the example using multicast socket instead.

Security Considerations: Note that communications over the network are subject to approval by the current security manager. (Providing Your Own Security Manager (page 279) describes what a security manager is and how to write a customized security manager for your applications.) The example programs in the following lessons that cover URLs, sockets, and datagrams are standalone applications, which, by default, have no security manager. If you convert these applications to applets, they may be unable to communicate over the network, depending on the browser or viewer in which they are running. See Practical Considerations of Writing Applets (page 211) for information about the security restrictions placed on applets.

Overview of Networking

BEFORE working through the examples in the next several lessons, you need to understand some networking basics.

To boost your confidence, this trail starts with What You May Already Know about Networking in Java (page 585) which reviews what you may already know about networking in Java without even realizing it. If you have worked on the other trails in this tutorial, by now you probably have loaded an applet over the Internet. You also have probably loaded images from the network into applets running over the network. And you already know how to use the network.

The second section of this lesson, Networking Basics (page 586), discusses TCP, UDP, sockets, datagrams, and ports. You need to know about these in order to get the most out of the remaining lessons in this trail. If you are already familiar with these concepts, feel free to skip this section.

What You May Already Know about Networking in Java

The word *networking* strikes fear in the hearts of many programmers. Fear not! Using the networking capabilities provided in the Java platform is quite easy.

Loading Applets from the Network

If you have access to a Java-compatible browser, you have undoubtedly already executed many applets. The applets you've run are referenced by a special tag in an HTML file—the <APPLET> tag. Applets can be located anywhere, whether on your local machine or somewhere on the Internet. The location of the applet is encoded within the <APPLET> tag, which the browser decodes to locate and run the applet. If the applet is on some machine other than yours, the browser must download the applet before the applet can be run. The browser does all of the grunt work of connecting to the network and getting data from it, thereby enabling you to run applets from anywhere in the world.

For More Information about Applets

- The "Hello World" Applet (page 19) is a brief lesson that shows you how to write your first applet and run it.
- Writing Applets (page 171) describes how to write Java applets, from A to Z.

Loading Images from URLs

If you've ventured into writing your own Java applets and applications, you may have encountered a class in the `java.net` package called `URL`. This class represents a Uniform Resource Locator and is the address of a resource on the network. Your applets and applications can use a `URL` to reference and even connect to resources on the Internet. For example, to load an image from the Internet, your Java program must first create a `URL` object that contains the address of the image.

For More Information about Images and URLs

- Loading Images (page 541) shows you how to load an image into your Java program (whether applets or applications) when you have its `URL`. Before you can load the image, you must create a `URL` object that contains the address of the resource.
- Working with URLs (page 591), the next lesson in this trail, provides a complete discussion about URLs, including how your program establishes a connection to a URL and how it reads from and writes to that connection.

Networking Basics

Computers running on the Internet communicate to each other using either the Transport Control Protocol (TCP) or the User Datagram Protocol (UDP), as Figure 81 illustrates.

When you write Java programs that communicate over the network, you are programming at the application layer. Typically, you don't need to concern yourself with the TCP and UDP layers. Instead, you can use the classes in the `java.net` package. These classes provide system-independent network communication. However, to decide which Java classes your programs should use, you do need to understand how TCP and UDP differ.

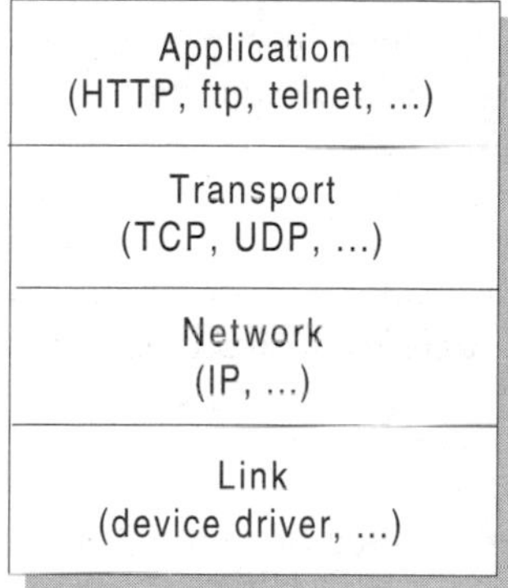

Figure 81: Computers communicate with one another across the Internet using either TCP or UDP.

TCP

When two applications want to communicate to each other reliably, they establish a connection and send data back and forth over that connection. This is analogous to making a telephone call. If you want to speak to Aunt Beatrice in Kentucky, a connection is established when you dial her phone number and she answers. You send data back and forth over the connection by speaking to one another over the phone lines. Like the phone company, TCP guarantees that data sent from one end of the connection actually gets to the other end and in the same order it was sent. Otherwise, an error is reported.

TCP provides a point-to-point channel for applications that require reliable com munications. The Hypertext Transfer Protocol (HTTP), File Transfer Protocol (FTP), and Telnet are all examples of applications that require a reliable communication channel. The order in which the data is sent and received over the network is critical to the success of these applications. When HTTP is used to read from a URL, the data must be received in the order in which it was sent. Otherwise, you end up with a jumbled HTML file, a corrupt zip file, or some other invalid information.

Definition: *TCP (Transport Control Protocol)* is a connection-based protocol that provides a reliable flow of data between two computers.

UDP

The UDP protocol provides for communication that is not guaranteed between two applications on the network. UDP is not connection-based like TCP. Rather, it sends independent packets of data, called *datagrams*, from one application to another. Sending datagrams is much like sending a letter through the postal service: The order of delivery is not important and is not guaranteed, and each message is independent of any other.

Definition: *UDP (User Datagram Protocol)* is a protocol that sends independent packets of data, called *datagrams,* from one computer to another with no guarantees about arrival. UDP is not connection-based like TCP.

For many applications, the guarantee of reliability is critical to the success of the transfer of information from one end of the connection to the other. However, other forms of communication don't require such strict standards. In fact, they may be slowed down by the extra overhead or the reliable connection may invalidate the service altogether.

Consider, for example, a clock server that sends the current time to its client when requested to do so. If the client misses a packet, it doesn't really make sense to resend it because the time will be incorrect when the client receives it on the second try. If the client makes two requests and receives packets from the server out of order, it doesn't really matter because the client can figure out that the packets are out of order and make another request. The reliability of TCP is unnecessary in this instance because it causes performance degradation and may hinder the usefulness of the service.

Another example of a service that doesn't need the guarantee of a reliable channel is the `ping` command. The purpose of the `ping` command is to test the communication between two programs over the network. In fact, `ping` *needs to know* about dropped or out-of-order packets to determine how good or bad the connection is. A reliable channel would invalidate this service altogether.

The UDP protocol provides for communication that is not guaranteed between two applications on the network. UDP is not connection-based like TCP. Rather, it sends independent packets of data, called *datagrams,* from one application to another. Sending datagrams is much like sending a letter through the mail service: The order of delivery is not important and is not guaranteed, and each message is independent of any others.

Note: Many firewalls and routers have been configured not to allow UDP packets. If you're having trouble connecting to a service outside your firewall, or if clients are having trouble connecting to your service, ask your system administrator if UDP is permitted.

Understanding Ports

Generally speaking, a computer has a single physical connection to the network. All data destined for a particular computer arrives through that connection. However, the data may be intended for different applications running on the computer. So how does the computer know to which application to forward the data? Through the use of *ports*.

Data transmitted over the Internet is accompanied by addressing information that identifies the computer and the port for which it is destined. The computer is identified by its 32-bit IP address, which IP uses to deliver data to the right computer on the network. Ports are identified by a 16-bit number, which TCP and UDP use to deliver the data to the right application.

In connection-based communication such as TCP, a server application binds a socket to a specific port number. This has the effect of registering the server with the system to receive all data destined for that port. A client can then rendezvous with the server at the server's port, as illustrated in Figure 82.

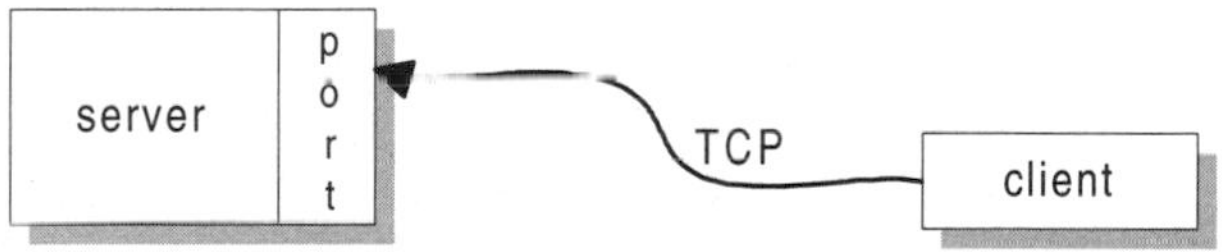

Figure 82: A client and server rendezvous at the server's port.

Definition: The TCP and UDP protocols use *ports* to map incoming data to a particular process running on a computer.

In datagram-based communication such as UDP, the datagram packet contains the port number of its destination and UDP routes the packet to the appropriate application, as illustrated in Figure 83.

Port numbers range from 0 to 65,535 because ports are represented by 16-bit numbers. The port numbers ranging from 0–1023 are restricted; they are reserved for use by well-known services such as HTTP and FTP and other sys-

tem services. These ports are called *well-known ports*. Your applications should not attempt to bind to them.

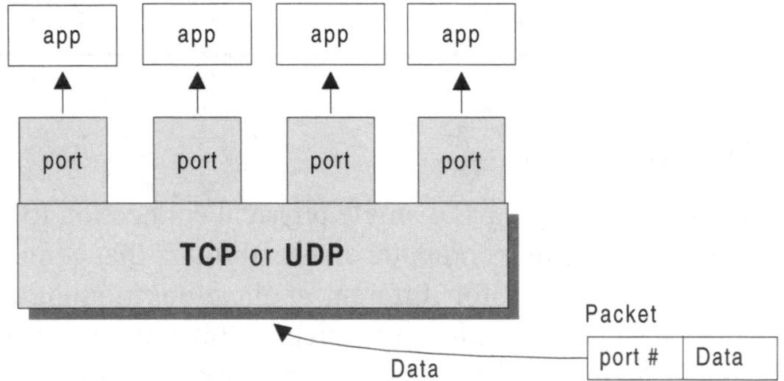

Figure 83: The datagram packet contains the port number of its destination.

Networking Classes in the JDK

Through the classes in `java.net`, Java programs can use TCP or UDP to communicate over the Internet. The `URL`, `URLConnection`, `Socket`, and `ServerSocket` classes all use TCP to communicate over the network. The `DatagramPacket`, `DatagramSocket`, and `MulticastSocket` classes are for use with UDP.

http://java.sun.com/docs/books/tutorial/networking/urls/index.html

23 Working with URLs

URL is the acronym for Uniform Resource Locator. It is a reference (an address) to a resource on the Internet. You provide URLs to your favorite Web browser so that it can locate files on the Internet in the same way that you provide addresses on letters so that the post office can locate your correspondents.

Java programs that interact with the Internet also may use URLs to find the resources on the Internet they wish to access. Java programs can use a class called `URL`[1] in the `java.net` package to represent a URL address.

Terminology Note: The term *URL* can be ambiguous. It can refer to an Internet address or a `URL` object in a Java program. Where the meaning of URL needs to be specific, this text uses "URL address" to mean an Internet address and "`URL` object" to refer to an instance of the `URL` class in a program.

A URL takes the form of a string that describes how to find a resource on the Internet. URLs have two main components: the protocol needed to access the resource and the location of the resource. What Is a URL? (page 592) looks in depth at a URL and its components. Within your Java programs, you can create a `URL` object that represents a URL address. The `URL` object always refers to an absolute URL. However, it can be constructed from an absolute URL, a relative URL, or URL components. See Creating a URL (page 593) to learn how.

Once you've created a `URL` object in your Java program, you can use its methods to find out its host name, filename, and other information. With a valid `URL` object, you can call any of its accessor methods to get all of that information.

---

[1] http://java.sun.com/products/jdk/1.1/docs/api/java.net.URL.html

This is just like the Parsing a URL (page 596) section, without all of the string manipulations.

Your Java programs also can read directly from a URL by using the openStream method. And, if you want to do more than just read from a URL, you can connect to it by calling openConnection on the URL object. The openConnection method returns a URLConnection object that you can use for more general communications with the URL, such as reading from it, writing to it, or querying it for content and other information. The sections Reading Directly from a URL (page 597), Connecting to a URL (page 599), and Reading from and Writing to a URL Connection (page 599) show you how to do all of these things.

What Is a URL?

If you've been surfing the Web, you have undoubtedly heard the term URL and have used URLs to access HTML pages from the Web.

It's often easiest, although not entirely accurate, to think of a URL as the name of a file on the World Wide Web because most URLs refer to a file on some machine on the network. However, remember that URLs also can point to other resources on the network, such as database queries and command output.

Definition: URL is an acronym for *Uniform Resource Locator* and is a reference (an address) to a resource on the Internet.

The following is an example of a URL which addresses the Java Web site hosted by Sun Microsystems:

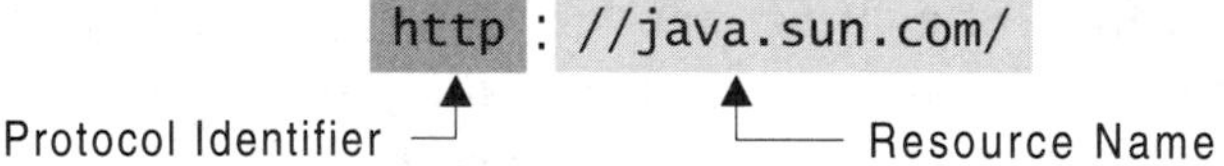

Figure 84: A URL has two main components.

As in Figure 84, all URLs, has two main components:

- Protocol identifier
- Resource name

Note that the protocol identifier and the resource name are separated by a colon and two forward slashes. The protocol identifier indicates the name of the protocol to be used to fetch the resource. The example uses the Hypertext Transfer Protocol (HTTP), which is typically used to serve up hypertext documents. HTTP is just one of many different protocols used to access different types of resources on the net. Other protocols include File Transfer Protocol (FTP), Gopher, File, and News.

The resource name is the complete address to the resource. The format of the resource name depends entirely on the protocol used, but for many protocols, including HTTP, the resource name contains one or more of the components listed in Table 23.

Table 23: Components the resource name may contain.

Host Name	The name of the machine on which the resource lives.
Filename	The pathname to the file on the machine.
Port Number	The port number to which to connect (typically optional).
Reference	A reference to a named anchor within a resource that usually identifies a specific location within a file (typically optional).

For many protocols, the host name and the filename are required, while the port number and reference are optional. For example, the resource name for an HTTP URL must specify a server on the network (Host Name) and the path to the document on that machine (Filename); it also can specify a port number and a reference. In the URL shown in Figure 84, `java.sun.com` is the host name and the trailing slash is shorthand for the file named `/index.html`.

Creating a URL

The easiest way to create a `URL` object is from a `String` that represents the human-readable form of the URL address. This is typically the form that another person will use for a URL. For example, the URL for the Gamelan site, which is a directory of Java resources, takes the following form:

```
http://www.gamelan.com/
```

In your Java program, you can use a `String` containing this text to create a `URL` object:

```
URL gamelan = new URL("http://www.gamelan.com/");
```

The URL object created by this statement represents an *absolute URL*. An absolute URL contains all of the information necessary to reach the resource in question. You can also create URL objects from a relative URL address.

Creating a URL Relative to Another

A *relative URL* contains only enough information to reach the resource relative to (or in the context of) another URL.

Relative URL specifications are often used within HTML files. For example, suppose you write an HTML file called JoesHomePage.html. This page contains links to two other pages, PicturesOfMe.html and MyKids.html, that are on the same machine and in the same directory as JoesHomePage.html. The links to PicturesOfMe.html and MyKids.html from JoesHomePage.html can be specified as filenames, as follows:

```
<A HREF="PicturesOfMe.html">Pictures of Me</A>
<A HREF="MyKids.html">Pictures of My Kids</A>
```

The URL addresses specified after the HREF tag are relative URLs. The URLs are specified relative to the file in which they are contained—JoesHomePage.html.

In your Java programs, you can create a URL object from a relative URL specification. For example, suppose you know two URLs at the Gamelan site:

```
http://www.gamelan.com/pages/Gamelan.game.html
http://www.gamelan.com/pages/Gamelan.net.html
```

You can create URL objects for these pages relative to their common base URL: http://www.gamelan.com/pages/ like this:

```
URL gamelan = new URL("http://www.gamelan.com/pages/");
URL gamelanGames = new URL(gamelan, "Gamelan.game.html");
URL gamelanNetwork = new URL(gamelan, "Gamelan.net.html");
```

This code snippet uses the URL constructor that lets you create a URL object from another URL object (the base) and a relative URL specification. The general form of this constructor is:

```
URL(URL baseURL, String relativeURL)
```

The first argument is a URL object that specifies the base of the new URL. The second argument is a String that specifies the rest of the resource name relative to

the base. If `baseURL` is `null`, then this constructor treats `relativeURL` like an absolute URL specification. Conversely, if `relativeURL` is an absolute URL specification, then the constructor ignores `baseURL`.

This constructor is also useful for creating `URL` objects for named anchors (also called *references*) within a file. For example, suppose the `Gamelan.network.html` file has a named anchor called `BOTTOM` at the bottom of the file. You can use the relative URL constructor to create a `URL` object for it like this:

```
URL gamelanNetworkBottom = new URL(gamelanNetwork, "#BOTTOM");
```

Other URL Constructors

The `URL` class provides two additional constructors for creating a `URL` object. These constructors are useful when you are working with URLs, such as HTTP URLs, that have host name, filename, port number, and reference components in the resource name portion of the URL. These two constructors are useful when you do not have a `String` containing the complete URL specification, but you do know various components of the URL.

For example, suppose you design a network browsing panel similar to a file browsing panel that allows users to choose the protocol, host name, port number, and filename. You can construct a `URL` from the panel's components. The first constructor creates a `URL` object from a protocol, host name, and filename. The following code snippet creates a `URL` to the `Gamelan.net.html` file at the Gamelan site:

```
new URL("http", "www.gamelan.com", "/pages/Gamelan.net.html");
```

This is equivalent to

```
new URL("http://www.gamelan.com/pages/Gamelan.net.html");
```

The first argument is the protocol, the second is the host name, and the last is the pathname of the file. Note that the filename contains a forward slash at the beginning. This indicates that the filename is specified from the root of the host.

The final `URL` constructor adds the port number to the list of arguments used in the previous constructor:

```
URL gamelan = new URL("http", "www.gamelan.com", 80,
                      "pages/Gamelan.network.html");
```

This creates a `URL` object for the following URL:

```
http://www.gamelan.com:80/pages/Gamelan.network.html
```

If you construct a URL object using one of these constructors, you can get a String containing the complete URL address by using the URL object's toString method or the equivalent toExternalForm method.

MalformedURLException

Each of the four URL constructors throws a MalformedURLException if the arguments to the constructor refer to a null or unknown protocol. Typically, you want to catch and handle this exception by embedding your URL constructor statements in a try/catch pair, like this:

```
try {
    URL myURL = new URL(. . .)
} catch (MalformedURLException e) {
    . . .
    // exception handler code here
    . . .
}
```

See Handling Errors with Exceptions (page 293) for information about handling exceptions.

Note: URLs are "write-once" objects. Once you've created a URL object, you cannot change any of its attributes (protocol, host name, filename, or port number).

Parsing a URL

The URL class provides several methods that let you query URL objects. You can get the protocol, host name, port number, and filename from a URL object using the following accessor methods:

getProtocol Returns the protocol identifier component of the URL.

getHost Returns the host name component of the URL.

getPort Returns an integer that is the port number of the URL. If the port is not set, getPort returns -1.

getFile Returns the filename component of the URL.

getRef Returns the reference component of the URL.

Note: Remember that not all URL addresses contain these components. The `URL` class provides these methods because HTTP URLs do contain these components and that type of URL is perhaps the most commonly used URL. The `URL` class is somewhat HTTP-centric.

You can use these `get`*XXX* methods to get information about the `URL` regardless of the constructor you used to create the `URL` object.

The `URL` class, along with these accessor methods, frees you from ever having to parse URLs again. Given any string specification of a URL, you just create a new `URL` object and call any of the accessor methods for the information you need. The following program creates a `URL` from a string specification and then uses the `URL` object's accessor methods to parse the URL:

```
import java.net.*;
import java.io.*;

public class ParseURL {
    public static void main(String[] args) throws Exception {
        URL aURL = new URL("http://java.sun.com:80/docs/" +
                           "books/tutorial/intro.html#" +
                           "DOWNLOADING");
       System.out.println("protocol = "  + aURL.getProtocol());
        System.out.println("host = " + aURL.getHost());
        System.out.println("filename = " + aURL.getFile());
        System.out.println("port = " + aURL.getPort());
        System.out.println("ref = " + aURL.getRef());
    }
}
```

Here's the output displayed by this program:

```
protocol = http
host = java.sun.com
filename = /docs/books/tutorial/intro.html
port = 80
ref = DOWNLOADING
```

Reading Directly from a URL

After you've successfully created a `URL` object, you can call the `URL` object's `openStream` method to get a stream from which you can read the contents of the

URL. The `openStream` method returns a `java.io.InputStream`[1] object, so reading from a URL is as easy as reading from an input stream.

The following small Java program uses `openStream` to get an input stream on the URL `http://www.yahoo.com/`. It then opens a `BufferedReader` on the input stream and reads from the `BufferedReader` thereby reading from the URL. Everything read is copied to the standard output stream:

```
import java.net.*;
import java.io.*;

public class URLReader {
    public static void main(String[] args) throws Exception {
        URL yahoo = new URL("http://www.yahoo.com/");
        BufferedReader in = new BufferedReader(
                                new InputStreamReader(
                                yahoo.openStream()));
        String inputLine;

        while ((inputLine = in.readLine()) != null)
            System.out.println(inputLine);
        in.close();
    }
}
```

When you run the program, you should see, scrolling by in your command window, the HTML commands and textual content from the HTML file located at `http://www.yahoo.com/`. Alternatively, the program might hang or you might see an exception stack trace. If either of the latter two events occurs, you may have to set your proxy host so that the program can find the Yahoo server.

Platform-specific Details: Setting the Proxy Host

You can set the proxy host through the command line. Depending on your network configuration, you might also need to set the proxy port. If necessary, ask your system administrator for the name of the proxy host on your network.

UNIX:

```
java -Dhttp.proxyHost=hostName
      [-Dhttp.proxyPort=portNumber]URLReader
```

DOS shell (Windows 95/NT):

```
java -Dhttp.proxyHost=hostName
      [-Dhttp.proxyPort=portNumber]URLReader
```

---

1 http://java.sun.com/products/JDK/1.1/api/java.io.InputStream.html

Connecting to a URL

After you've successfully created a URL object, you can call the URL object's openConnection method to connect to it. When you connect to a URL, you are initializing a communication link between your Java program and the URL over the network. For example, you can open a connection to the Yahoo site with the following code:

```
try {
    URL yahoo = new URL("http://www.yahoo.com/");
    URL Connection = yahoo.openConnection();
} catch (MalformedURLException e) { // new URL failed
    . . .
} catch (IOException e) {           // openConnection failed
    . . .
}
```

If possible, the openConnection method creates a new URLConnection (if an appropriate one does not already exist), initializes it, connects to the URL, and returns the URLConnection[1] object. If something goes wrong—for example, the Yahoo server is down—then the openConnection method throws an IOException.

Now that you've successfully connected to your URL, you can use the URLConnection object to perform actions such as reading from or writing to the connection. The next section shows you how.

Reading from and Writing to a URLConnection Object

If you've successfully used openConnection to initiate communications with a URL, then you have a reference to a URLConnection object. The URLConnection class contains many methods that let you communicate with the URL over the network. URLConnection is an HTTP-centric class; that is, many of its methods are useful only when you are working with HTTP URLs. However, most URL protocols allow you to read from and write to the connection. This section describes both functions.

---

1 http://java.sun.com/products/JDK/1.1/api/java.net.URLConnection.html

Reading from a URLConnection

The following program performs the same function as the `URLReader` program shown in Reading Directly from a URL (page 597).

However, rather than getting an input stream directly from the `URL`, this program explicitly opens a connection to a `URL` and gets an input stream from the connection. Then, like `URLReader`, this program creates a `BufferedReader` on the input stream and reads from it. The bold statements highlight the differences between this example and the previous

```
import java.net.*;
import java.io.*;

public class URLConnectionReader {
    public static void main(String[] args) throws Exception {
        URL yahoo = new URL("http://www.yahoo.com/");
        URLConnection yc = yahoo.openConnection();
        BufferedReader in = new BufferedReader(
                                new InputStreamReader(
                                yc.getInputStream()));
        String inputLine;

        while ((inputLine = in.readLine()) != null)
            System.out.println(inputLine);
        in.close();
    }
}
```

The output from this program is identical to the output from the program that opens a stream directly from the `URL`. You can use either way to read from a `URL`. However, reading from a `URLConnection` instead of reading directly from a `URL` might be more useful. This is because you can use the `URLConnection` object for other tasks (like writing to the `URL`) at the same time.

Again, if the program hangs or you see an error message, you may have to set the proxy host so that the program can find the Yahoo server.

Writing to a URLConnection

Many HTML pages contain *forms*—text fields and other GUI objects that let you enter data to send to the server. After you type in the required information and initiate the query by clicking a button, your Web browser writes the data to the URL over the network. At the other end, a `cgi-bin` script (usually) on the server receives the data, processes it, and then sends you a response, usually in the form of a new HTML page.

Many `cgi-bin` scripts use the `POST METHOD` for reading the data from the client. Thus writing to a URL is often called *posting to a URL.* Server-side scripts use the `POST METHOD` to read from their standard input.

Note: Some server-side `cgi-bin` scripts use the `GET METHOD` to read your data. The `POST METHOD` is quickly making the `GET METHOD` obsolete because it's more versatile and has no limitations on the amount of data that can be sent through the connection.

A Java program can interact with `cgi-bin` scripts also on the server side. It simply must be able to write to a URL, thus providing data to the server. It can do this by following these steps:

1. Create a `URL`.
2. Open a connection to the `URL`.
3. Set output capability on the `URLConnection`.
4. Get an output stream from the connection. This output stream is connected to the standard input stream of the `cgi-bin` script on the server.
5. Write to the output stream.
6. Close the output stream.

Hassan Schroeder, a member of the Java development team, wrote a small `cgi-bin` script named backwards (page 914) and made it available at the Java Web site, `http://java.sun.com/cgi-bin/backwards`. You can use this script to test the following example program. You can also put the script on your network, name it `backwards`, and test the program locally.

The script at our Web site reads a string from its standard input, reverses the string, and writes the result to its standard output. The script requires input of the form `string=string_to_reverse`, where `string_to_reverse` is the string whose characters you want displayed in reverse order.

Here's an example program that runs the `backwards` script over the network through a `URLConnection`:

```
import java.io.*;
import java.net.*;

public class Reverse {
    public static void main(String[] args) throws Exception {
```

```
            if (args.length != 1) {
                System.err.println("Usage: java Reverse " +
                                   "string_to_reverse");
                System.exit(1);
            }
            String stringToReverse = URLEncoder.encode(args[0]);

            URL url = new URL("http://java.sun.com/cgi-bin" +
                              "backwards");
            URLConnection c = url.openConnection();
            c.setDoOutput(true);

            PrintWriter out = new PrintWriter(c.getOutputStream());
            out.println("string=" + stringToReverse);
            out.close();

            BufferedReader in = new BufferedReader(
                                    new InputStreamReader(
                                    c.getInputStream()));
            String inputLine;

            while ((inputLine = in.readLine()) != null)
                System.out.println(inputLine);
            in.close();
        }
    }
```

Let's examine the program and see how it works. First, the program processes its command-line arguments:

```
if (args.length != 1) {
    System.err.println("Usage:  java Reverse " +
                       "string_to_reverse");
    System.exit(-1);
}
String stringToReverse = URLEncoder.encode(args[0]);
```

These statements ensure that the user provides one and only one command-line argument to the program, and then encodes it. The command-line argument is the string that will be reversed by the `cgi-bin` script `backwards`. It may contain spaces or other nonalphanumeric characters. These characters must be encoded because the string is processed on its way to the server. The `URLEncoder` class methods encode the characters.

Next, the program creates the `URL` object—the URL for the `backwards` script on `java.sun.com`—opens a `URLConnection`, and sets the connection so that it can write to it:

```
URL url = new URL("http://java.sun.com/cgi-bin/backwards");
URLConnection c = url.openConnection();
c.setDoOutput(true);
```

The program then creates an output stream on the connection and opens a `PrintWriter` on it:

```
PrintWriter out = new PrintWriter(c.getOutputStream());
```

If the URL does not support output, `getOutputStream` method throws an `UnknownServiceException`. If the URL does support output, then this method returns an output stream that is connected to the standard input stream of the URL on the server side—the client's output is the server's input.

Next, the program writes the required information to the output stream and closes the stream:

```
out.println("string=" + stringToReverse);
out.close();
```

This code writes to the output stream using the `println` method. So you can see that writing data to a URL is as easy as writing data to a stream. The data written to the output stream on the client side is the input for the `backwards` script on the server side. The `Reverse` program constructs the input in the form required by the script by concatenating `string=` to the encoded string to be reversed.

Often, when you are writing to a URL, you are passing information to a `cgi-bin` script, as in this example. This script reads the information you write, performs some action, and then sends information back to you via the same URL. So it's likely that you will want to read from the URL after you've written to it. The `Reverse` program does this:

```
BufferReader in = new BufferedReader(
                      new InputStreamReader(c.getInputStream()));
String inputLine;

while ((inputLine = in.readLine()) != null)
    System.out.println(inputLine);
in.close();
```

When you run the `Reverse` program using "`Reverse Me`" as an argument, you should see this output:

```
Reverse Me
 reversed is:
eM esreveR
```

http://java.sun.com/docs/books/tutorial/networking/sockets/index.html

24 All About Sockets

`URLs` and `URLConnections` provide a relatively high-level mechanism for accessing resources on the Internet. Sometimes your programs require lower-level network communication, for example, when you want to write a client-server application.

In client server applications, the server provides some service, such as processing database queries or sending out current stock prices. The client uses the service provided by the server, either displaying database query results to the user or making stock purchase recommendations to an investor. The communication that occurs between the client and the server must be reliable. That is, no data can be dropped and it must arrive on the client side in the same order in which the server sent it.

TCP provides a reliable, point-to-point communication channel that client-server applications on the Internet use to communicate with each other. To communicate over TCP, a client program and a server program establish a connection to one another. Each program binds a socket to its end of the connection. To communicate, the client and the server each reads from and writes to the socket bound to the connection.

This lesson begins with What Is a Socket? (page 606) which takes a closer look at what a socket is. It then walks you through two examples that use sockets. The first example in Reading from and Writing to a Socket (page 607) illustrates how a client program can read from and write to a socket that is connected to a well-known server. The second example in Writing a Client/Server Pair (page 610) shows you how to write both sides of a client/server connection.

What Is a Socket?

Normally, a server runs on a specific computer and has a socket that is bound to a specific port number. The server just waits, listening to the socket for a client to make a connection request.

On the client-side: The client knows the hostname of the machine on which the server is running and the port number to which the server is connected. To make a connection request, the client tries to rendezvous with the server on the server's machine and port.

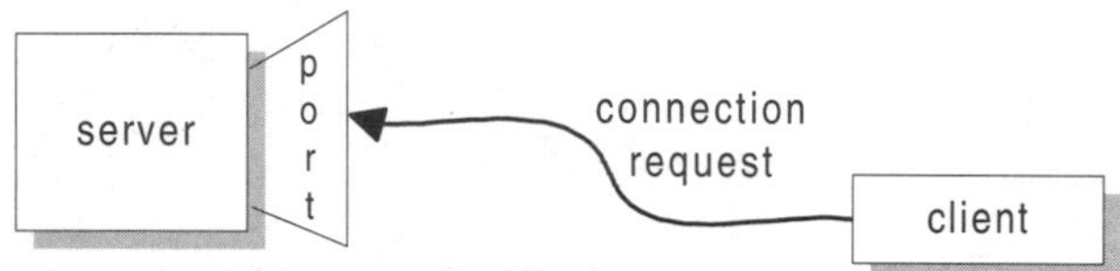

Figure 85: A client requests a connection to a server using a predetermined port number and host computer to identify the server.

If everything goes well, the server accepts the connection. Upon acceptance, the server gets a new socket bound to a different port. It needs a new socket (and consequently a different port number) so that it can continue to listen to the original socket for connection requests while tending to the needs of the connected client.

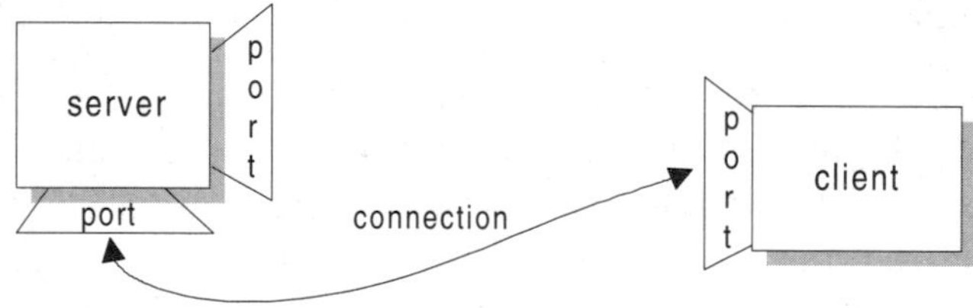

Figure 86: A connection is established with sockets bound to new port numbers.

On the client side, if the connection is accepted, a socket is successfully created and the client can use the socket to communicate with the server. Note that the socket on the client side is not bound to the port number used to rendezvous with the server. Rather, the client is assigned a port number local to the machine on which the client is running.

The client and server can now communicate by writing to or reading from their sockets.

Definition: A *socket* is one endpoint of a two-way communication link between two programs running on the network. A socket is bound to a port number so that the TCP layer can identify the application that data is destined to be sent.

The `java.net` package in the Java platform provides a class, `Socket`,[1] that implements one side of a two-way connection between your Java program and another program on the network. The `Socket` class sits on top of a platform-dependent implementation, hiding the details of any particular system from your Java program. By using the `java.net.Socket` class instead of relying on native code, your Java programs can communicate over the network in a platform-independent fashion.

Additionally, `java.net` includes the `ServerSocket`[2] class, which implements a socket that servers can use to listen for and accept connections to clients. This lesson shows you how to use the `Socket` and `ServerSocket` classes.

If you are trying to connect to the Web, the `URL` class and related classes (`URLConnection`, `URLEncoder`) are probably more appropriate than the socket classes. In fact, `URL`s are a relatively high-level connection to the Web and use sockets as part of the underlying implementation. See Working with URLs (page 591) for information about connecting to the Web via `URL`s.

Reading from and Writing to a Socket

Let's look at a simple example that illustrates how a program can establish a connection to a server program using the `Socket` class and then, how the client can send data to and receive data from the server through the socket.

The example program implements a client, `EchoClient`, that connects to the Echo server. The Echo server simply receives data from its client and echoes it back. The Echo server is a well-known service that clients can rendezvous with on port 7.

`EchoClient` creates a socket thereby getting a connection to the Echo server. It reads input from the user on the standard input stream, and then forwards that text to the Echo server by writing the text to the socket. The server echoes the input back through the socket to the client. The client program reads and displays the data passed back to it from the server:

---

1 http://java.sun.com/products/JDK/1.1/api/java.net.Socket.html
2 http://java.sun.com/products/JDK/1.1/api/java.net.ServerSocket.html

```
import java.io.*;
import java.net.*;

public class EchoClient {
    public static void main(String[] args) throws IOException {
        Socket echoSocket = null;
        DataOutputStream out = null;
        BufferedReader in = null;

        try {
            echoSocket = new Socket("taranis", 7);
            out = new PrintWriter(
                        echoSocket.getOutputStream(), true);
            in = new BufferedReader(newInputStreamReader(
                      echoSocket.getInputStream()));
        } catch (UnknownHostException e) {
            System.err.println("Don't know about host: taranis");
            System.exit(-1);
        } catch (IOException e) {
            System.err.println("Couldn't get I/O for the " +
                                 "connection to: taranis");
            System.exit(-1);
        }

        BufferedReader stdIn = new BufferedReader(
                                newInputStreamReader(System.in));
        String userInput;

        while ((userInput = stdIn.readLine()) != null) {
            out.writeBytes(userInput);
            System.out.println("echo: " + in.readLine());
        }
        out.close();
        in.close();
        stdIn.close();
        echoSocket.close();
    }
}
```

Note that `EchoClient` both writes to and reads from its socket, thereby sending data to and receiving data from the Echo server.

Let's walk through the program and investigate the interesting parts. The three statements in the `try` block of the `main` method are critical. These lines establish the socket connection between the client and the server and open a `PrintWriter` and a `BufferedReader` on the socket:

```
echoSocket = new Socket("taranis", 7);
out = new PrintWriter(echoSocket.getOutputStream(), true);
in = new BufferedReader(new InputStreamReader(
                            echoSocket.getInputStream()));
```

The first statement in this sequence creates a new `Socket` object and names it `echoSocket`. The `Socket` constructor used here requires the name of the machine and the port number to which you want to connect. The example program uses the host name `taranis`. This is the name of a hypothetical machine on our local network. When you type in and run this program on your machine, change the host name to the name of a machine on your network. Make sure that the name you use is the fully qualified IP name of the machine to which you want to connect. The second argument is the port number. Port number 7 is the port on which the Echo server listens.

The second statement gets the socket's output stream and opens a `PrintWriter` on it. Similarly, the third statement gets the socket's input stream and opens a `BufferedReader` on it. The example uses readers and writers so that it can write Unicode characters over the socket.

To send data through the socket to the server, `EchoClient` simply needs to write to the `PrintWriter`. To get the server's response, `EchoClient` reads from the `BufferedReader`. The rest of the program achieves this. If you are not yet familiar with the Java platform's I/O classes, you may wish to read The Standard I/O Streams (page 270).

The next interesting part of the program is the `while` loop. The loop reads a line at a time from the standard input stream and immediately sends it to the server by writing it to the `PrintWriter` connected to the socket:

```
String userInput;

while ((userInput = stdIn.readLine()) != null) {
    out.println(userInput);
    System.out.println("echo: " + in.readLine());
}
```

The last statement in the `while` loop reads a line of information from the `BufferedReader` connected to the socket. The `readLine` method waits until the server echoes the information back to `EchoClient`. When `readline` returns, `EchoClient` prints the information to the standard output.

The `while` loop continues until the user types an end-of-input character. That is, `EchoClient` reads input from the user, sends it to the Echo server, gets a response from the server, and displays it, until it reaches the end-of-input. The while loop then terminates and the program continues, executing the next four lines of code:

```
out.close();
in.close();
stdIn.close();
echoSocket.close();
```

These lines of code fall into the category of housekeeping. A well-behaved program always cleans up after itself, and this program is well-behaved. These statements close the readers and writers connected to the socket and to the standard input stream, and close the socket connection to the server. The order here is important. You should close any streams connected to a socket before you close the socket itself.

This client program is straightforward and simple because the Echo server implements a simple protocol. The client sends text to the server, and the server echoes it back. When your client programs are talking to a more complicated server such as an HTTP server, your client program will also be more complicated. However, the basics are much the same as they are in this program:

1. Open a socket.
2. Open an input stream and output stream to the socket.
3. Read from and write to the stream according to the server's protocol.
4. Close the streams.
5. Close the socket.

Only step 3 differs from client to client, depending on the server. The other steps remain largely the same.

Writing a Client/Server Pair

This section shows you how to write a server and the client that goes with it. The server in the client/server pair serves up Knock Knock jokes. Knock Knock jokes are favored by children and are usually vehicles for bad puns. They go like this:

Server: "Knock! Knock!"
Client: "Who's there?"
Server: "Dexter."
Client: "Dexter who?"
Server: "Dexter halls with boughs of holly."
Client: "(Groan)."

The example consists of two independently running Java programs: the client program and the server program. The client program is implemented by a single class, `KnockKnockClient`, and is very similar to the `EchoClient` (page 915) example from the previous section. The server program is implemented by two classes: `KnockKnockServer` and `KnockKnockProtocol`, `KnockKnockServer` contains the `main` method for the server program and performs the work of listening to the port, establishing connections, and reading from and writing to the socket. `KnockKnockProtocol` serves up the jokes. It keeps track of the current joke, the current state (sent knock knock, sent clue, and so on), and returns the various text pieces of the joke depending on the current state. This object implements the *protocol*—the language that the client and server have agreed to use to communicate.

The following section looks in detail at each class in both the client and the server and then shows you how to run them.

The Knock Knock Server

This section walks through the code that implements the Knock Knock server program. The complete source for the `KnockKnockServer` is in the Appendix (page 916).

The server program begins by creating a new `ServerSocket` object to listen on a specific port (see the statement in bold in the following code segment). When writing a server, choose a port that is not already dedicated to some other service. `KnockKnockServer` listens on port 4444 because 4 happens to be my favorite number and port 4444 is not being used for anything else in my environment:

```
ServerSocket serverSocket = null;
try {
    serverSocket = new ServerSocket(4444);
} catch (IOException e) {
    System.out.println("Could not listen on port: 4444.");
    System.exit(-1);
}
```

`ServerSocket` is a `java.net` class that provides a system-independent implementation of the server side of a client/server socket connection. The constructor for `ServerSocket` throws an exception if it can't listen on the specified port (for example, the port is already being used). In this case, the `KnockKnockServer` has no choice but to exit.

If the server successfully connects to its port, then the ServerSocket object is successfully created and the server continues to the next step—accepting a connection from a client (shown in bold):

```
Socket clientSocket = null;
try {
    clientSocket = serverSocket.accept();
} catch (IOException e) {
    System.out.println("Accept failed.");
    System.exit(-1);
}
```

The accept method waits until a client starts up and requests a connection on the host and port of this server (in this example, the server is running on the hypothetical machine taranis on port 4444). When a connection is requested and successfully established, the accept method returns a new Socket object which is bound to a new port. The server can communicate with the client over this new Socket and continue to listen for client connection requests on the ServerSocket bound to the original, predetermined port. This particular version of the program doesn't listen for more client connection requests. However, a modified version of the program is provided in Supporting Multiple Clients (page 617).

After the server successfully establishes a connection with a client, it communicates with the client using this code:

```
PrintWriter out = new PrintWriter(
                      clientSocket.getOutputStream(), true);
BufferedReader in = new BufferedReader(
                        new BufferedOutputStream(
                        clientSocket.getInputStream())),
String inputLine, outputLine;

// initiate conversation with client
KnockKnockProtocol kkp = new KnockKnockProtocol();
outputLine = kkp.processInput(null);
out.println(outputLine);

while ((inputLine - in.readLine()) != null) {
    outputLine = kkp.processInput(inputLine);
    out.println(outputLine);
    if outputLine.equals("Bye."))
        break;
}
```

This code:

1. Gets the socket's input and output stream and opens readers and writers on them.
2. Initiates communication with the client by writing to the socket (shown in bold).
3. Communicates with the client by reading from and writing to the socket (the `while` loop).

Step 1 is already familiar. Step 2 is shown in bold and is worth a few comments. The bold statements in the code segment above initiate the conversation with the client. The code creates a `KnockKnockProtocol` object—the object that keeps track of the current joke, the current state within the joke, and so on.

After the `KnockKnockProtocol` is created, the code calls `KnockKnockProtocol`'s `processInput` method to get the first message that the server sends to the client. For this example, the first thing that the server says is "Knock! Knock!" Next, the server writes the information to the `PrintWriter` connected to the client socket, thereby sending the message to the client.

Step 3 is encoded in the `while` loop. As long as the client and server still have something to say to each other, the server reads from and writes to the socket, sending messages back and forth between the client and the server.

The server initiated the conversation with a "Knock! Knock!" so afterwards the server must wait for the client to say "Who's there?" As a result, the `while` loop iterates on a read from the input stream. The `readLine` method waits until the client responds by writing something to its output stream (the server's input stream). When the client responds, the server passes the client's response to the `KnockKnockProtocol` object and asks the `KnockKnockProtocol` object for a suitable reply. The server immediately sends the reply to the client via the output stream connected to the socket, using a call to `println`. If the server's response generated from the `KnockKnockServer` object is "Bye." this indicates that the client doesn't want any more jokes and the loop quits.

The `KnockKnockServer` class is a well-behaved server, so the last several lines of this section of `KnockKnockServer` clean up by closing all of the input and output streams, the client socket, and the server socket:

```
out.close();
in.close();
clientSocket.close();
serverSocket.close();
```

The Knock Knock Protocol

KnockKnockServer.java (page 916) implements the protocol that the client and server use to communicate. This class keeps track of where the client and the server are in their conversation and serves up the server's response to the client's statements. The KnockKnockServer object contains the text of all the jokes and makes sure that the client gives the proper response to the server's statements. It wouldn't do to have the client say "Dexter who?" when the server says "Knock! Knock!"

All client/server pairs must have some protocol by which they speak to each other; otherwise, the data that passes back and forth would be meaningless. The protocol that your own clients and servers use depends entirely on the communication required by them to accomplish the task.

The Knock Knock Client

KnockKnockClient.java (page 919) implements the client program that speaks to the KnockKnockServer. KnockKnockClient is based on the EchoClient.java (page 915) program in the previous section, Reading from and Writing to a Socket (page 607), and should be somewhat familiar to you. But we'll go over the program anyway and look at what's happening in the client in the context of what's going on in the server.

When you start the client program, the server should already be running and listening to the port, waiting for a client to request a connection. So, the first thing the client program does is to open a socket that is connected to the server running on the hostname and port specified:

```
kkSocket = new Socket("taranis", 4444);
out = new PrintWriter(kkSocket.getOutputStream(), true);
in = new BufferedReader(new InputStreamReader(
                              kkSocket.getInputStream()));
```

When creating its socket, KnockKnockClient uses the host name taranis, the name of a hypothetical machine on our network. When you type in and run this program, change the host name to the name of a machine on your network. This is the machine on which you will run the KnockKnockServer.

The KnockKnockClient program also specifies the port number 4444 when creating its socket. This is a *remote port number*—the number of a port on the server machine—and is the port to which KnockKnockServer is listening. The client's socket is bound to any available *local port*—a port on the client machine.

Remember that the server gets a new socket as well. That socket is bound to a local port number (not port 4444) on its machine. The server's socket and the client's socket are connected.

Next comes the `while` loop that implements the communication between the client and the server. The server speaks first, so the client must listen first. The client does this by reading from the input stream attached to the socket. If the server does speak, it says "Bye." and the client exits the loop. Otherwise, the client displays the text to the standard output and then reads the response from the user, who types into the standard input. After the user types a carriage return, the client sends the text to the server through the output stream attached to the socket.

```
while ((fromServer = in.readLine()) != null) {
    System.out.println("Server: " + fromServer);
    if (fromServer.equals("Bye."))
        break;
    fromUser = stdIn.readLine();
    if (fromUser != null) {
        System.out.println("Client: " + fromUser);
        out.println(fromUser);
    }
}
```

The communication ends when the server asks if the client wishes to hear another joke, the client says no, and the server says "Bye."

In the interest of good housekeeping, the client closes its input and output streams and the socket:

```
out.close();
in.close();
stdIn.close();
kkSocket.close();
```

Running the Programs

You must start the server program first. To do this, run the server program using the Java interpreter, just as you would any other Java application. Remember to run the server on the machine that the client program specifies when it creates the socket.

Next, run the client program. Note that you can run the client on any machine on your network; it does not have to run on the same machine as the server.

If you are too quick, you might start the client before the server has a chance to initialize itself and begin listening on the port. If this happens, you will see a stack trace from the client. If this happens, just restart the client.

If you forget to change the host name in the source code for the `KnockKnockClient` program, you will see the following error message:

```
Don't know about host: taranis
```

To fix this, modify the `KnockKnockClient` program and provide a valid host name for your network. Recompile the client program and try again.

If you try to start a second client while the first client is connected to the server, the second client just hangs. The next section, Supporting Multiple Clients (page 617), talks about dealing with multiple clients.

When you successfully get a connection between the client and server, you will see the following text displayed on your screen:

```
Server: Knock! Knock!
```

Now, you must respond with

```
Who's there?
```

The client echoes what you type and sends the text to the server. The server responds with the first line of one of the many Knock Knock jokes in its repertoire. Now your screen should contain this (the text you typed is in bold):

```
Server: Knock! Knock!
Who's there?
Client: Who's there?
Server: Turnip
```

Now, you respond with

```
Turnip who?
```

Again, the client echoes what you type and sends the text to the server. The server responds with the punch line. Now your screen should contain this:

```
Server: Knock! Knock!
Who's there?
Client: Who's there?
Server: Turnip
Turnip who?
Client: Turnip who?
Server: Turnip the heat, it's cold in here! Want another? (y/n)
```

If you want to hear another joke, type **y**; if not, type **n**. If you type **y**, the server begins again with "Knock! Knock!" If you type **n**, the server says "Bye." thus causing both the client and the server to exit.

If at any point you make a typing mistake, the `KnockKnockServer` object catches it and the server responds with a message similar to this:

```
Server: You're supposed to say "Who's there?"!
```

The server then starts the joke over again:

```
Server: Try again. Knock! Knock!
```

Note that the `KnockKnockServer` object is particular about spelling and punctuation but not about capitalization.

Supporting Multiple Clients

To keep the `KnockKnockServer` example simple, we designed it to listen for and handle a single connection request. However, multiple client requests can come into the same port and, consequently, into the same `ServerSocket`. Client connection requests are queued at the port, so the server must accept the connections sequentially. However, the server can service them simultaneously through the use of threads—one thread per each client connection.

The basic flow of logic in such a server is this:

```
while (true) {
    accept a connection ;
    create a thread to deal with the client ;
end while
```

The thread reads from and writes to the client connection as necessary.

Try This: Modify the `KnockKnockServer` so that it can service multiple clients at the same time. Two classes compose our solution: `KKMultiServer` (page 920) and `KKMultiServerThread` (page 920). `KKMultiServer` loops forever, listening for client connection requests on a `ServerSocket`. When a request comes in, `KKMultiServer` accepts the connection, creates a new `KKMultiServerThread` object to process it, hands it the socket returned from `accept`, and starts the thread. Then the server goes back to listening for connection requests. The `KKMultiServerThread` object communicates to the client by reading from and writing to the socket. Run the new Knock Knock server and then run several clients in succession.

---

http://java.sun.com/docs/books/tutorial/networking/datagrams/index.html

25 All About Datagrams

SOME applications that you write to communicate over the network will not require the reliable, point-to-point channel provided by TCP. Rather, your applications might benefit from a mode of communication that delivers independent packages of information whose arrival and order of arrival are not guaranteed.

The UDP protocol provides a mode of network communication whereby applications send packets of data, called *datagrams,* to one another. A datagram is an independent, self-contained message sent over the network whose arrival, arrival time, and content are not guaranteed. The `DatagramPacket` and `DatagramSocket` classes in the `java.net` package implement system-independent datagram communication using UDP.

This lesson begins with a closer look at datagrams in What Is a Datagram? (page 620). The next and final section of this lesson, Writing a Datagram Client and Server (page 620), walks you through an example that contains two Java programs that use datagrams to communicate. The server side is a quote server that listens to its `DatagramSocket` and sends a quotation to a client whenever the client requests it. The client side is a simple program that simply makes a request of the server.

Broadcasting to Multiple Recipients (page 625) modifies the quote server so that instead of sending a quotation to a single client upon request, the quote server broadcasts a quote every minute to as many clients as are listening. The client program must be modified accordingly.

Note: Many firewalls and routers are configured not to allow UDP packets. If you have trouble connecting to a service outside your firewall, or if clients have trouble connecting to your service, ask your system administrator if UDP is permitted.

What Is a Datagram?

Clients and servers that communicate via a reliable channel, such as a URL or a socket, have a dedicated point-to-point channel between themselves, or at least the illusion of one. To communicate, they establish a connection, transmit the data, and then close the connection. All data sent over the channel is received in the same order in which it was sent. This is guaranteed by the channel.

In contrast, applications that communicate via datagrams send and receive completely independent packets of information. These clients and servers do not have and do not need a dedicated point-to-point channel. The delivery of datagrams to their destinations is not guaranteed. Nor is the order of their arrival.

Definition: A *datagram* is an independent, self-contained message sent over the network whose arrival, arrival time, and content are not guaranteed.

The `java.net` package contains two classes to help you write Java programs that use datagrams to send and receive packets over the network: `DatagramSocket`[1], `DatagramPacket`[2], and `MulticastSocket`.[3] An application can send and receive `DatagramPackets` through a `DatagramSocket`. In addition, `DatagramPackets` can be broadcast to multiple recipients all listening to a `MulticastSocket`.

Writing a Datagram Client and Server

The example featured in this section consists of two applications: a client and a server. The server continuously receives datagram packets over a datagram socket. Each datagram packet received by the server indicates a client request for a quotation. When the server receives a datagram, it replies by sending a datagram packet that contains a one-line "quote of the moment" back to the client.

The client application in this example is fairly simple. It sends a single datagram packet to the server indicating that the client would like to receive a quote of the moment. The client then waits for the server to send a datagram packet in response.

Two classes implement the server application: `QuoteServer` and `QuoteServerThread`. A single class implements the client application: `QuoteClient`.

---

1 http://java.sun.com/products/JDK/1.1/api/java.net.DatagramSocket.html
2 http://java.sun.com/products/JDK/1.1/api/java.net.DatagramPacket.html
3 http://java.sun.com/products/JDK/1.1/api/java.net.MulticastSocket.html

Let's investigate these classes, starting with class that contains the main method for the server application. A Simple Network Client Applet (page 227) contains an applet version of the QuoteClient class.

The QuoteServer Class

The QuoteServer class, shown here in its entirety, contains a single method: the main method for the quote server application. The main method simply creates a new QuoteServerThread object and starts it:

```
import java.io.*;
public class QuoteServer {
    public static void main(String[] args) throws IOException {
        new QuoteServerThread().start();
    }
}
```

The QuoteServerThread class implements the main logic of the quote server.

The QuoteServerThread Class

When created, QuoteServerThread (page 922) creates a DatagramSocket on port 4445 (arbitrarily chosen). This is the DatagramSocket through which the server communicates with all of its clients.

```
public QuoteServerThread() throws IOException {
    this.("QuoteServer");
}
public QuoteServerThread(String name) throws IOException {
    super(name);
    socket = new DatagramSocket(4445);

    try {
        in = new BufferedReader(
                  new FileReader("one-liners.txt"));
    } catch (FileNotFoundException e)
        System.err.println("Couldn't open quote file. " +
                           "Serving time instead.");
    }
}
```

Remember that certain ports are dedicated to well-known services and you cannot use them. If you specify a port that is in use, the creation of the DatagramSocket will fail.

The constructor also opens a `BufferedReader` on a file named `one-liners.txt` (page 924) which contains a list of quotes. Each quote in the file is on a line by itself.

Now for the interesting part of `QuoteServerThread` (page 922): its `run` method. The `run` method overrides `run` in the `Thread` class and provides the implementation for the thread. For information about threads, see Doing Two or More Tasks at Once: Threads (page 327).

The `run` method contains a while loop that continues as long as there are more quotes in the file. During each iteration of the loop, the thread waits for a `DatagramPacket` to arrive over the `DatagramSocket`. The packet indicates a request from a client. In response to the client's request, the `QuoteServerThread` gets a quote from the file, puts it in a `DatagramPacket` and sends it over the `DatagramSocket` to the client that asked for it.

Let's look first at the section that receives the requests from clients:

```
byte[] buf = new byte[256];
DatagramPacket packet = new DatagramPacket(buf, buf.length);
socket.receive(packet);
```

The first statement creates an array of bytes which is then used to create a `DatagramPacket`. The `DatagramPacket` will be used to receive a datagram from the socket because of the constructor used to create it. This constructor requires only two arguments: a byte array that contains client-specific data and the length of the byte array. When constructing a `DatagramPacket` to send over the `DatagramSocket`, you also must supply the Internet address and port number of the packet's destination. You'll see this later when we discuss how the server responds to a client request.

The last statement in the previous code snippet receives a datagram from the socket (the information received from the client gets copied into the packet). The `receive` method waits forever until a packet is received. If no packet is received, the server makes no further progress and just waits.

Now assume that, the server has received a request from a client for a quote. Now the server must respond. This section of code in the `run` method constructs the response:

```
String dString = null;
if (in == null)
    dString = new Date().toString();
else
    dString = getNextQuote();
buf = dString.getBytes();
```

If the quote file did not get opened for some reason, then `in` equals `null`. If this is the case, the quote server serves up the time of day instead. Otherwise, the quote server gets the next quote from the already opened file. Finally, the code converts the string to an array of bytes.

Now, the run method sends the response to the client over the `DatagramSocket` with this code:

```
InetAddress address = packet.getAddress();
int port = packet.getPort();
packet = new DatagramPacket(buf, buf.length, address, port);
socket.send(packet);
```

The first two statements in this code segment get the Internet address and the port number, respectively, from the datagram packet received from the client. The Internet address and port number indicate where the datagram packet came from. This is where the server must send its response. In this example, the byte array of the datagram packet contains no relevant information. The arrival of the packet itself indicates a request from a client that can be found at the Internet address and port number indicated in the datagram packet.

The third statement creates a new `DatagramPacket` object intended for sending a datagram message over the datagram socket. You can tell that the new `DatagramPacket` is intended to send data over the socket because of the constructor used to create it. This constructor requires four arguments. The first two arguments are the same required by the constructor used to create receiving datagrams: a byte array containing the message from the sender to the receiver and the length of this array. The next two arguments are different: an Internet address and a port number. These two arguments are the complete address of the destination of the datagram packet and must be supplied by the sender of the datagram. The last line of code sends the `DatagramPacket` on its way.

When the server has read all the quotes from the quote file, the `while` loop terminates and the `run` method cleans up:

```
socket.close();
```

The QuoteClient Class

The `QuoteClient` class (page 923) implements a client application for the `QuoteServer`. This application sends a request to the `QuoteServer`, waits for the response, and, when the response is received, displays it to the standard output. Let's look at the code in detail.

The `QuoteClient` class contains one method, the `main` method for the client application. The top of the `main` method declares several local variables for its use:

```
int port;
InetAddress address;
DatagramSocket socket = null;
DatagramPacket packet;
byte[] sendBuf = new byte[256];
```

First, the `main` method processes the command-line arguments used to invoke the `QuoteClient` application:

```
if (args.length != 1) {
     System.out.println("Usage: java QuoteClient <hostname>");
     return;
}
```

The `QuoteClient` application requires one command-line arguments: the name of the machine on which the `QuoteServer` is running.

Next, the `main` method creates a `DatagramSocket`:

```
DatagramSocket socket = new DatagramSocket();
```

The client uses a constructor that does not require a port number. This constructor just binds the `DatagramSocket` to any available local port. It doesn't matter what port the client is connected to because the `DatagramPackets` contain the addressing information. The server gets the port number from the `DatagramPackets` and send its response to that port.

Next, the `QuoteClient` program sends a request to the server:

```
byte[] buf = new byte[256];
InetAddress address = InetAddress.getByName(args[0]);
DatagramPacket packet = new DatagramPacket(buf, buf.length,
                                            address, 4445);
socket.send(packet);
```

The code segment gets the Internet address for the host named on the command line (presumably the name of the machine on which the server is running). This `InetAddress` and the port number 4445 (the port number that the server used to create its `DatagramSocket`) are then used to create `DatagramPacket` destined for that Internet address and port number. Therefore the `DatagramPacket` will be delivered to the quote server.

Note that the code creates a `DatagramPacket` with an empty byte array. The byte array is empty because this datagram packet is simply a request to the server for information. All the server needs to know to send a response—the address and port number to which reply—is automatically part of the packet.

Next, the client gets a response from the server and displays it:

```
packet = new DatagramPacket(buf, buf.length);
socket.receive(packet);
String received = new String(packet.getData());
System.out.println("Quote of the Moment: " + received);
```

To get a response from the server, the client creates a "receive" packet and uses the `DatagramSocket` `receive` method to receive the reply from the server. The `receive` method waits until a datagram packet destined for the client comes through the socket. Note that if the server's reply is somehow lost, the client will wait forever because of the no-guarantee policy of the datagram model. Normally, a client sets a timer so that it doesn't wait forever for a reply; if no reply arrives, the timer goes off and the client retransmits.

When the client receives a reply from the server, the client uses the `getData` method to retrieve that data from the packet. The client then converts the data to a string and displays it.

Running the Server and Client

After you've successfully compiled the server and the client programs, you run them. You have to run the server program first. Just use the Java interpreter and specify the `QuoteServer` class name.

Once the server has started, you can run the client program. Remember to run the client program with one command-line argument: the name of the host on which the `QuoteServer` is running.

After the client sends a request and receives a response from the server, you should see output similar to this:

```
Quote of the Moment: Good programming is 99% sweat and 1% coffee.
```

Broadcasting to Multiple Recipients

In addition to `DatagramSocket`, which lets programs send packets to one another, `java.net` includes a class called `MulticastSocket`. This kind of socket

is used on the client-side to listen for packets that the server broadcasts to multiple clients.

Let's rewrite the quote server so that it broadcasts `DatagramPackets` to multiple recipients. Instead of sending quotes to a specific client that makes a request, the new server now needs to broadcast quotes at a regular interval. The client needs to be modifies sot that it passively listens for quotes and does so on a `MulticastSocket`.

This example is comprised of three classes which are modifications of the three classes from the previous example: `MulticastServer`, `MulticastServerThread`, and `MulticastClient`. This discussion highlights the interesting parts of these classes. The entire code is shown in Appendix A (page 926).

Here is the new version of the server's main program. The differences between this code and the previous version, `QuoteServer`, are shown in bold:

```
import java.io.*;
public class MulticastServer {
    public static void main(String[] args) throws IOException {
        new MulticastServerThread().start();
    }
}
```

Basically, the server got a new name and creates a `MulticastServerThread` instead of a `QuoteServerThread`. Now let's look at the `MulticastServerThread` which contains the heart of the server. Here's its class declaration:

```
public class MulticastServerThread extends QuoteServerThread {
    ...
}
```

We've made this class a subclass of `QuoteServerThread` so that it can use the constructor, and inherit some member variable and the `getNextQuote` method. Recall that `QuoteServerThread` creates a `DatagramSocket` bound to port 4445 and opens the quote file. The `DatagramSocket`'s port number doesn't actually matter in this example because the client never send anything to the server.

The only method explicitly implemented in `MulticastServerThread` is its `run` method. The differences between this `run` method and the one in `QuoteServerThread` are shown in bold:

```
public void run() {
    while (moreQuotes) {
        try {
            byte[] buf new byte[256];
```

```
            // don't wait for request...just send a quote

            String dString = null;
            if (in == null)
                dString = new Date().toString();
            else
                dString = getNextQuote();
            buf = dString.getBytes();

            InetAddress group = InetAddress.getByName(
                                          "230.0.0.1");
            DatagramPacket packet;
            packet = new DatagramPacket(buf, buf.length,
                                      group, 4446);
            socket.send(packet);

            try {
                sleep((long)Math.random() * FIVE_SECONDS);
            } catch (InterruptedException e) { }
        } catch (IOException e) {
            e.printStackTrace();
            moreQuotes = false;
        }
    }
    socket.close();
}
```

The interesting change is how the DatagramPacket is constructed, in particular, the InetAddress and port used to construct the DatagramPacket. Recall that the previous example retrieved the InetAddress and port number from the packet sent to the server from the client. This was because the server needed to reply directly to the client. Now, the server needs to address multiple clients. So this time both the InetAddress and the port number are hard-coded.

The hard-coded port number is 4446 (the client must have a MulticastSocket bound to this port). The hard-coded InetAddress of the DatagramPacket is "230.0.0.1" and is a group identifier (rather than the Internet address of the machine on which a single client is running). This particular address was arbitrarily chosen from the reserved for this purpose.

Created in this way, the DatagramPacket is destined for all clients listening to port number 4446 who are member of the "230.0.0.1" group.

To listen to port number 4446, the new client program just created its MulticastSocket with that port number. To become a member of the "230.0.0.1" group, the client calls the MulticastSocket's joinGroup method with the InetAddress that identifies the group. Now, the client is set up to receive Data-

gramPackets destined for the port and group specified. Here's the relevant code from the new client program (which was also rewritten to passively receive quotes rather than actively request them). The bold statements are the ones that interact with the MulticastSocket:

```
MulticastSocket socket = new MulticastSocket(4446);
InetAddress group = InetAddress.getByName("230.0.0.1");
socket.joinGroup(group);

DatagramPacket packet;
for (int i = 0; i < 5; i++) {
    byte[] buf = new byte[256];
    packet = new DatagramPacket(buf, buf.length);
    socket.receive(packet);

    String received = new String(packet.getData());
    System.out.println("Quote of the Moment: " + received);
}
socket.leaveGroup(group);
socket.close();
```

Notice that the server uses a DatagramSocket to broadcast packet received by the client over a MulticastSocket. Alternatively, it could have used a MulticastSocket. The socket used by the server to send the DatagramPacket is not important. What's important when broadcasting packets is the addressing information contained in the DatagramPacket, and the socket used by the client to listen for it.

Try this: Run the MulticastServer and several clients. Watch how the clients all get the same quotes.

End of Trail

YOU'VE reached the end of the **Custom Networking** trail. Take a break—have a cup of steaming hot java.

What Next?

Once you've caught your breath, you have several choices of where to go next. You can go back to the Trail Map (page xvii) to see all of your choices, or you can go directly to one of the following popular trails:

Writing Applets (page 171): For information about writing applets that use the network. In particular, check out Sending Messages to Other Applets (page 194).

To 1.1— and Beyond! (page 631): In the next trail, you will learn which features were added to the JDK for 1.1 and how to upgrade from 1.0 to 1.1.

To 1.1—and Beyond!

UNTIL now, the lessons and examples in this tutorial have documented the Java language and platform as they exist in the JDK 1.1 release. While this snapshot approach provides new Java programmers a clear path to learning, it ignores the history and future of the language and API.

This trail steps back and looks at the JDK 1.1 release in the light of what came before and what is likely to come after. This wide-angle perspective can help you make decisions about your Java development.

First, this trail discusses how 1.1 differs from 1.0. Then it moves into how and when to upgrade your programs from 1.0 to 1.1. Finally, the end of this trail includes a preview of the next major release of the JDK, which is likely to be called JDK 1.2.

The sources for much of this trail were collected from documents written by various Java team members. We are indebted to our colleagues.

Note: Since the JDK 1.1 release shipped in December 1996, Sun has made several bug-fix releases. Bug-fix releases don't generally add new features, but they might enable functionality that was impossible before due to bugs. For example, the JDK 1.1.2 release has the same API as JDK 1.1, but lightweight components work much better in 1.1.2 and subsequent releases.

What's New in 1.1 (page 635) provides a summary of new features for JDK 1.1. This might be your first stop if you used 1.0. Even if you didn't use 1.0, you might find this lesson handy as an overview of many of the capabilities that the JDK provides.

Migrating to 1.1 (page 643) is the place to go if you developed programs for JDK 1.0, and you're wondering how and when to upgrade them. This lesson provides specific information about the API that changed from 1.0 to 1.1 and gives tips about how to migrate your 1.0 code to 1.1.

A Preview of Things to Come (page 679) describes the features we expect the next major release of the JDK to contain. Some of the most eagerly awaited 1.2 features are in the Java Foundation Classes (JFC), which extend the GUI capabilities provided by the Java platform. This lesson tells you where to find information on getting 1.1-compatible versions of the new JFC components.

What's New in 1.1

FROM internationalization to performance improvements, this lesson provides a brief description of each feature that was added to the JDK for its 1.1 release. Besides describing a particular feature, each section provides pointers to any API documentation and tutorial pages that discuss the feature. Many of the features are further described in specifications and other documents on the Java Web site. To find pointers to these Web site documents, you can visit the Web page for this book:

```
http://java.sun.com/docs/books/tutorial/2e/book.html
```

Internationalization

One of the more comprehensive changes to the JDK provides support for programmers to easily write programs that are independent of the user's culture and language: We call these programs "global programs." The process of writing a global program and ensuring that it can be used without change by anyone in the world is a process known as *internationalization* (often called "I18N" by those who don't care to type the full 20-letter word). Internationalization support is fully integrated into the classes and packages that provide language- or culture-dependent functionality. With internationalization completely built into the JDK, it becomes easy for programmers to write global applets and applications from the design phase forward.

Features added to the JDK to support internationalization include the display of Unicode characters, a locale mechanism, localized message support, character set converters, locale-sensitive date, time, time zone, and number handling, collation services, parameter formatting, and support for finding boundaries of characters, words, and sentences.

One of the trails in the online version of this tutorial, Writing Global Programs[1], documents the internationalization features of JDK 1.1 and shows you how to internationalize an existing program.

Security and Signed Applets

The Java Security API is designed to allow developers to incorporate both low-level and high-level security into their Java applications. The first release of Java Security in JDK 1.1 contains a subset of this functionality, including an API for digital signatures and message digests. In addition, JDK 1.1 contains abstract interfaces for key management, certificate management, and access control. API to support specific certificate formats and richer functionality in the area of access control will follow in subsequent JDK releases.

JDK 1.1 provides a tool that can sign Java ARchive (JAR) files. The JDK Applet Viewer allows any downloaded applets in JAR files signed (using the tool) by a trusted entity to run with the same full rights as local applications. That is, such applets are not subject to the "sandbox" restrictions of the original Java security model. Later releases will provide more sophisticated security policies, including greater granularity in the allowable trust levels.

Mary Dageforde, a guest author for the tutorial, has written about 1.1's new security API. You can find her work in the online tutorial's Java Security[2] trail. Also, you can read a preview of the Security Enhancements (page 679) planned for the next major release of the JDK.

AWT Enhancements

The AWT has changed in three ways:

The architecture has been improved to make large-scale GUI development more feasible and basic functionality that was missing was added.
Architectural support has been added for event handling by non-components ("delegation"), data transfer (such as cut-copy-paste), desktop color schemes

1 http://java.sun.com/docs/books/tutorial/intl/index.html
2 http://java.sun.com/docs/books/tutorial/security1.1/index.html

(to improve consistency of appearance), printing, mouseless operation, component-specific cursors, and lightweight components.

Method names, arguments, and functionality have been made consistent.
These changes make it possible for programs such as GUI builders to query components to determine the components' properties. They also make it easier for programmers to learn and use the AWT API.

Overall quality improvements have been made and new features added.
For example, image and graphics functionality has improved, with font support made more flexible to accommodate internationalization. The new `PopupMenu` class makes it possible to have a menu that is not attached to a menu bar. The new `ScrollPane` class makes implementing scrolling areas easy, as well as increasing the speed of scrolling.

Creating a User Interface (page 214) describes the new AWT event architecture and other commonly used 1.1 features. Read about the changes planned for GUI API for the next major release of the JDK: Java Foundation Classes (page 680).

JavaBeans Architecture

The JavaBeans architecture defines Java's reusable software component model. The JavaBeans API allows third-party software vendors (ISVs) to create and ship reusable Java components (Beans), such as text, spreadsheet, or graphing widgets, that can be composed together into applications by non-programmers.

Check out our online JavaBeans Tutorial[1], which contains task-oriented documentation and includes several examples. See what Enhancements to the JavaBeans Architecture (page 681) are planned for the next major release.

JAR File Format

JAR (Java ARchive) is a platform-independent file format that allows you to bundle a Java applet and its requisite components (`.class` files, images and sounds) into a single file. Using the new `ARCHIVE` attribute of the `<APPLET>` tag, this JAR file can be downloaded to a browser in a single HTTP transaction, greatly improving the download speed. In addition, JAR supports compression, which reduces the file size, further improving the download time.

---

1 http://java.sun.com/docs/books/tutorial/javabeans/index.html

Finally, the applet author can digitally sign individual entries in a JAR file to authenticate their origin. You read about this in Security and Signed Applets (page 636).

To help you get started, here's a brief introduction to some of the basics of using JAR files.

You create and manipulate JAR files with the `jar` utility program. The command-line arguments to `jar` are similar to those of the UNIX `tar` program. Table 24 lists the most common manipulations of a JAR file along with the `jar` command or HTML tags for doing them.

Table 24: Commands and HTML tags for manipulating JAR files.

To create a JAR file:	`jar cvf` *`jarFilename listOfFiles`*
To list the contents of a JAR file:	`jar tvf` *`jarFilename`*
To extract the entire contents of a JAR file:	`jar xvf` *`jarFilename`*
To extract a specific file from a JAR file:	`jar xvf` *`jarFilename fileToExtract`*

To specify the use of a JAR file with an applet:	`<applet code="AppletClassName.class"`
	`archive="jarFileName"`
	`width=width height=height>`
	`</applet>`

Combining an Applet's Files into a Single File (page 209) shows you how to use JAR files with your applets and talks about the benefits of doing so.

Networking Enhancements

The JDK 1.1 release made several enhancements to the networking package, `java.net`: Support was added for selected BSD-style socket options; `Socket` and `ServerSocket` are now non-`final`, extendable classes; new subclasses of `SocketException` have been added for finer granularity in reporting and handling network errors; and support was added for multicasting.

The JDK 1.1 release also includes general performance improvements and bug fixes.

I/O Enhancements

To support internationalization, the JDK 1.1 release adds character streams to the `java.io` package. Character streams are like the byte streams that appeared in JDK 1.0 except that they operate on 16-bit Unicode characters rather than 8-bit bytes. In addition, two new byte streams were added to `java.io` to support object serialization.

The new character streams are documented in Reading and Writing (but No 'rithmetic) (page 365) which also contains a section on Object Serialization (page 388). For information about converting 1.0 programs that use byte streams to use character streams instead, refer to How to Convert Code that Uses I/O (page 650).

Math Package

A new package, `java.math`, was added to the JDK 1.1 release. The math package contains two new classes: `BigInteger`[1] and `BigDecimal`[2].

`BigInteger` numbers are immutable arbitrary-precision integers. They provide analogs to all of Java's primitive integer operators and all relevant static methods from the `java.lang.Math` class. Additionally, `BigInteger` numbers provide operations for modular arithmetic, GCD calculation, primality testing, prime generation, single-bit manipulation, and a few other odds and ends.

`BigDecimal` numbers are immutable, arbitrary-precision signed decimal numbers, suitable for monetary calculations. `BigDecimal` numbers provide operations for basic arithmetic, scale manipulation, comparison, format conversion, and hashing.

Remote Method Invocation

Remote Method Invocation (RMI) enables programmers to create distributed Java-to-Java applications, in which the methods of remote Java objects can be invoked from other Java virtual machines, possibly on different hosts. A Java program can make a call on a remote object once it obtains a reference to the remote object, either by looking up the remote object in the bootstrap naming

---

1 http://java.sun.com/products/jdk/1.1/api/java.math.BigIntger.html
2 http://java.sun.com/products/jdk/1.1/api/java.math.BigDecimal.html

service provided by RMI or by receiving the reference as an argument or a return value. A client can call a remote object in a server, and that server can also be a client of other remote objects. RMI uses object serialization to marshal and unmarshal parameters and does not truncate types, thereby supporting true object-oriented polymorphism.

For an example that uses RMI, refer to Putting It All Together[1] in the online tutorial. RMI Enhancements (page 682) provides a preview of the enhancements planned for RMI in the next major release of the JDK.

Reflection

Reflection enables Java code to discover information about the fields, methods and constructors of loaded classes, and to use reflected fields, methods, and constructors to operate on their underlying counterparts on objects, within security restrictions. The reflection API accommodates applications that need access to either the public members of a target object (based on its runtime class) or the members declared by a given class.

You should avoid the temptation to use reflection when other tools more natural to the language would suffice. If you are accustomed to using function pointers in another language, for example, you might think that `Method` objects are a natural replacement for them. However, usually an object-oriented tool—such as an interface that is implemented by objects that perform the needed action—is better. Reflection is intended for use by language tools such as debuggers and class browsers.

Java Database Connectivity (JDBC)

JDBC is a standard SQL database access interface that provides uniform access to a wide range of relational databases. It also provides a common base on which higher level tools and interfaces can be built. This comes with an ODBC Bridge. The Bridge is a library that implements JDBC in terms of the ODBC standard C API.

---

[1] http://java.sun.com/docs/books/tutorial/together/index.html

Inner Classes

Previous releases of the Java language required that all classes be *top-level classes*—classes declared as members of a package. The JDK 1.1 release removes this restriction and now allows classes to be declared in any scope. Classes declared inside other classes are called *nested classes*, and one common type of nested class is called an *inner class*.

You can get a first glimpse of an inner class in the `Spot` applet found in Reality Break! The Spot Applet (page 125). Nested and inner classes are covered thoroughly in Implementing Nested Classes (page 152).

Java Native Interface (JNI)

Native methods—methods used by a Java program but written in a different language—have been in the JDK since the beginning. As promised, the native methods interface from 1.0 has been completely rewritten and formalized. This interface is now named the Java Native Interface, or JNI for short.

The JNI is documented in Using the JNI to Integrate Native Code and Java Programs.[1] If you're interested in the pre-1.1 API, you can read Integrating Native Methods into Java Programs.[2]

Performance Enhancements

The following list describes the performance enhancements made to the JDK for the 1.1 release:

Interpreter loop in assembly code on Win32 and Solaris/SPARC
: Since portions of the Java VM have been rewritten in assembly language, the resulting VM now runs up to five times faster on certain operations.

Monitor speedups
: Synchronized methods enable operations to run more quickly and efficiently.

Garbage collection of classes
: This enhancement automatically discards unused classes. Improved overall VM memory usage enables Java to operate more efficiently, and with less memory.

---

1 http://java.sun.com/docs/books/tutorial/native1.1/index.html
2 http://java.sun.com/docs/books/tutorial/native/index.html

AWT peer class rewrite for Win32

To achieve higher performance, AWT peer native classes have been completely rewritten to be hosted running on top of Win32.

JAR (Java ARchive) bundling of resources for a single HTTP transaction

JAR is a new JDK 1.1 platform-independent file format that aggregates many files into one. See JAR File Format (page 637).

You might also be interested in the Performance Enhancements (page 684) planned for the next major release of the JDK.

Miscellaneous

The following changes were also made to the JDK 1.1 release.

`Byte`, `Short`, and `Void` classes

Bytes and shorts are accommodated as wrapped numbers by adding new classes `Byte`[1] and `Short`[2]. The abstract class `Number` gets two new concrete methods: `byteValue` and `shortValue`; the default implementations of these use the `intValue` method. A new class, `Void`[3], is an uninstantiable placeholder.

The `@deprecated` tag

Used in documentation comments for unambiguously marking classes, methods, and fields that have been superseded by new API. The compiler issues a warning when it processes source code that uses deprecated API.

Accessing resource files

JDK 1.1 provides a new mechanism for locating a resource file independently of its location. For example, this mechanism can locate a resource file whether it is an applet loaded from the net using multiple HTTP connects, an applet loaded using JAR files, or a "library" installed in the class path.

Additions to the `<APPLET>` tag

Enhancements of the `<APPLET>` tag used in HTML.

---

1 http://java.sun.com/products/jdk/1.1/docs/api/java.lang.Byte.html
2 http://java.sun.com/products/jdk/1.1/docs/api/java.lang.Short.html
3 http://java.sun.com/products/jdk/1.1/docs/api/java.lang.Void.html

http://java.sun.com/docs/books/tutorial/post1.0/converting/index.html 27

Migrating to 1.1

USUALLY, converting a 1.0 program to 1.1 is fairly easy. In fact, making the decision of when to migrate can be more difficult than actually changing the program's code. This lesson discusses what to consider as you decide when to upgrade. It then presents information to help upgrade programs quickly.

The first section of this lesson, When Should the Great Migration Occur? (page 644), helps you determine if and when a program should be upgraded to the JDK 1.1 release.

Some of the 1.0 API is *deprecated*, which means that it's no longer recommended. If you try to compile a program that uses deprecated API, the compiler gives you a warning. What Does Deprecation Mean? (page 645) gives you more information about deprecation.

How to Convert Your Program (page 646) provides step-by-step instructions on what to do if your program uses deprecated API. Besides giving you general instructions, this section pays special attention to the common situations of converting code that uses deprecated I/O and AWT API.

As you convert your program to 1.1, you need to determine what code to substitute for deprecated API. Lists and Tables (page 664) provides many resources to help you, including several tables that list deprecated methods and their alternatives.

When Should the Great Migration Occur?

Before deciding when to convert a 1.0 program to 1.1, you must answer two questions:

- What version of the Java runtime environment do the program's users have?
- How eager are you to upgrade the program to 1.1?

Version Compatibility

As a rule, 1.0 programs run in any Java runtime environment, but programs that use 1.1 features don't run in 1.0 runtimes. Here are a couple of exceptions to the rule:

- 1.0 programs that depend on bugs in the 1.0 implementation might not work correctly in 1.1 runtime environments. You can find a list of incompatible bug fixes in JDK 1.1 Compatibility (page 933) in Appendix B.
- Programs that use only 1.0 features but are compiled under 1.1 often run in 1.0 runtime systems. You can take advantage of this fact to conditionally use 1.1 features, as described in Special Coding Techniques (page 648).

For example, assume you have a 1.0 program. Unless your program depends on a 1.0 bug, your program should work just fine in 1.1 runtimes. You can almost certainly use the 1.1 compiler to recompile that program, although you might see a few compiler warnings. The resulting 1.1 class files work in all 1.1-based runtime environments and probably will work in 1.0 runtimes. However, if you change the program to rely on any 1.1 API, the program won't run in 1.0 environments.

If some of your users have 1.0 environments and others have 1.1, you might choose to avoid upgrading until all the users have 1.1 runtime environments. Your program won't be able to rely on 1.1 features, but all your users should be able to run the program.

If your program is an applet that you want anyone on the Internet to be able to use, then you have to consider how many Web surfers have 1.1-compatible browsers. By the time you read this section, it's possible that very few users will still have 1.0 browsers. However, at the time of this writing, many users have browsers that support 1.0 applets but not 1.1 applets. For that reason, the online version of this book runs 1.0 versions of applets, unless the applet depends on a 1.1 feature.

If your program is an application and you distribute a runtime environment with it, then you can upgrade the program whenever you like. Similarly, if your program is an applet distributed only within your company, and everyone in your company uses a 1.1-compatible browser such as HotJava, then you can upgrade the program whenever you like.

Reasons to Convert to 1.1

Here are a few possible reasons to convert a 1.0 program to 1.1:

1.1 contains features that make the program better.
For example, if you want your program's custom components to work in GUI builders, then you should rewrite them to use the API necessary for JavaBeans components. Or you might want to use object serialization or inner classes. What's New in 1.1 (page 635) lists all the new 1.1 features.

1.1 introduces new API for an old feature, and the new API will be used in all foreseen releases.
For example, the AWT event system has been rearchitected in 1.1. Although existing AWT components work with both the 1.0 and 1.1 event APIs, new components, such as the new 1.2 lightweight components, won't work with the 1.0 event API. If you upgrade your event code to 1.1, then you'll probably have less work to do when you switch to the 1.2 lightweight components.

The 1.1 implementation of some 1.0 API is incompatible with the 1.0 implementation.
This case is rare. When it happens, it's usually because the 1.0 implementation had a possible security problem, varied from platform to platform, or was simply buggy. For example, in 1.1 the `System.out` class variable is now `final`, to close a possible security hole. If a 1.0 program sets the value of `System.out`, then it won't work in 1.1 runtimes unless you change it to use the new `System.setOut` method.

You want to use the 1.1 compiler, and you want the program to compile cleanly.
You might want to upgrade a program simply to avoid compiler warnings about deprecated methods.

What Does Deprecation Mean?

You might have heard of the term "self-deprecating humor." It describes humor that minimizes one's own importance.

Similarly, when a class or method is deprecated, it means that the class or method is no longer considered important. It is *so* unimportant, in fact, that it should no longer be used at all, as it might well cease to exist in the future.

The need for deprecation comes about because as a class evolves, its API changes. Methods are renamed for consistency. New and better methods are added. Attributes change. But making such changes introduces a problem: You need to keep the old API around until people make the transition to the new one, but you don't want developers to continue programming to the old API.

The ability to mark a class or method as "deprecated" solves the problem. Existing classes that use the old API continue to work, but the compiler can issue a warning when it finds references to deprecated items. Meanwhile, API documentation can warn the user against using the deprecated item and tell the user how to avoid doing so. To mark API as deprecated, the implementer of the API uses a special tag in doc comments: `@deprecated`.

Note: "Deprecated" and "depreciated" are not the same. "Depreciated" is a financial term that means "lowered value." Although the meanings are similar, classes and methods are deprecated, not depreciated.

How to Convert Your Program

This section tells you how to convert programs that use deprecated API. This section does not tell you how to use the JDK's new features unless a new feature's API replaces deprecated API. For example, this section doesn't discuss substituting RMI for your existing networking code, since the original networking code is still valid. However, this section does tell you how to update to the new AWT event system, since the API for the old AWT event system is deprecated.

This section has four subsections:

- General Instructions (page 647)
  Provides step-by-step instructions on how to convert your programs.
- Special Coding Techniques (page 648)
  Describes a couple of techniques for writing code that works in both 1.0 and 1.1.
- How to Convert Code that Uses I/O (page 650)
  Demonstrates how to convert code that uses deprecated API in `java.io`.

- How to Convert Code that Uses the AWT (page 655)
  Gives detailed directions on converting programs that have a GUI.

General Instructions

1. First, save a copy of the original program—both the Java source code (`.java` files) and the Java bytecodes (`.class` files). You'll need the copy until all of the program's users have 1.1-compatible or later Java runtime systems. Here's an example of saving a copy of a program on a UNIX system:

```
% cp MyClass.java MyClass.java.orig
% cp MyClass.class MyClass.class.orig
```

2. Get a list of the deprecated API the program uses by compiling the program with deprecation warnings turned on. Make sure you're using a 1.1 compiler. Here's an example of compiling on a UNIX or Windows system:

```
% javac -deprecation MyClass.java
```

If your program calls or overrides any deprecated methods, the compiler displays a warning. For example:

```
MyClass.java:18: Note: The method boolean
handleEvent(java.awt.Event) in class java.awt.Component
has been deprecated, and class MyClass overrides it.
   public boolean handleEvent(Event event) {
                  ^
MyClass.java:26: Note: The method boolean
handleEvent(java.awt.Event) in class java.awt.Component
has been deprecated.
   return super.handleEvent(event);
                           ^
Note: MyClass.java uses a deprecated API. Please consult
the documentation for a better alternative.
2 warnings
```

Note: The original JDK 1.1 compiler warns you only when a program *calls* a deprecated method, not when it *overrides* it. Starting with 1.1.1, the Java compiler warns you of both overridden and called deprecated methods.

---

3. Now that you have identified where your program uses deprecated API, modify the program to use alternative API instead. The following sections can help you find the best alternative API:

- How to Convert Code that Uses I/O (page 650), for programs that use deprecated `java.io` API.
- How to Convert Code that Uses the AWT (page 655), for programs with GUIs.
- Alternatives to Deprecated API in java.lang, java.net, and java.util (page 664), for programs that use deprecated API in the remaining 1.0 packages. (Note that `java.applet` contains no deprecated methods or classes.)
- Lists and Tables (page 664), for reference material that lists all of the deprecated API and alternatives.

4. Once your program compiles without warnings, test it by running it. It should work as well as or better than it worked before.

   If your program doesn't work the way you expected it to, then you have probably either used a new feature incorrectly or encountered an incompatible change. See the relevant section in this tutorial for help implementing any new features. See JDK 1.1 Compatibility (page 933) in Appendix B for a list of incompatible changes between 1.0 and 1.1.

Special Coding Techniques

This section discusses two techniques for writing code that can optionally use 1.1 API while remaining compatible with 1.0. If 1.0 compatibility isn't an issue for you, then skip this section.

The first technique lets your program dynamically determine whether to invoke 1.0 or 1.1 API. The second technique lets you override deprecated methods without causing compiler warnings.

Mixing 1.0 and 1.1 Code in a 1.0-Compatible Program

This technique consists of enclosing a 1.1 method invocation in a `try` statement and putting alternative 1.0 code in the corresponding `catch` statement. Here's an example:

```
//Draw an unclosed polygon.
try {
    g.drawPolyline(xPoints, yPoints, numPoints); //1.1 API
} catch (NoSuchMethodError e) {
   g.drawPolygon(xPoints, yPoints, numPoints); //1.0 equivalent
}
```

When the above code runs in a 1.1 runtime, then the `drawPolyline` method is called and no exception is generated. When the code runs in a 1.0 runtime, the attempt to call `drawPolyline` fails, causing a `NoSuchMethodError` exception. The exception handler is then executed, and it calls the 1.0 equivalent method, `drawPolygon`.

Overriding Deprecated Methods

You might find yourself in the following situation:

- You're writing 1.1-based code.
- It can be called by 1.0 code.
- You need to override a method that has been deprecated.

In this situation, you might wonder which version of the method you should override: the deprecated method or its replacement. If you simply override the replacement, then your code won't work correctly with 1.0 code that calls it. (If no 1.0 code will call the method, then this solution is fine.) If you simply override the deprecated version, then you'll see compilation warnings and you'll have 1.0 dependencies embedded in your code.

The solution is to override both methods. Override the deprecated method so that it calls the replacement method, and override the replacement method to provide the appropriate functionality. In your implementation of the deprecated method, use the `@deprecated` documentation tag to indicate that you are intentionally overriding the method to provide backwards compatibility. For example:

```
/** @deprecated */
public Dimension preferredSize() {
    return getPreferredSize();
}
public Dimension getPreferredSize() {
    ...//implementation goes here...
}
```

This solution takes advantage of a loophole: The compiler doesn't warn you when you override a deprecated method and you mark the overriding method as deprecated. For example, the preceding code results in no warnings when compiled. However, if a program that calls the preceding `preferredSize` method is compiled, a deprecation warning occurs.

The solution described in this section helps you write code that is backward compatible, compiles cleanly, and is easy to understand. When you no longer have to provide 1.0 compatibility, it'll be easy to find and remove the deprecated code.

How to Convert Code that Uses I/O

To support internationalization, the JDK 1.1 release adds character streams to the `java.io` package. In addition, a few of the package's classes and methods have been deprecated because they did not properly support internationalization. Converting a 1.0 program that uses `java.io` API usually requires two steps:

1. If the program uses a byte stream to read or write data, decide whether the byte stream is still appropriate for the data being read or written by the program. If not, convert the program so that it uses a character stream instead.
2. Make sure that the program does not use any deprecated API.

The following two sections provide details and examples to help you with these two steps.

Step 1: If Appropriate, Switch from Byte Streams to Character Streams

Does the program use a byte stream (an object that inherits from `InputStream` or `OutputStream`)? If so, does the stream truly contain byte data, or does it contain characters? If the stream contains characters, then you should seriously consider changing the program to use character streams, which were introduced in 1.1. With character streams, you can write programs that don't depend upon a specific character encoding and are therefore easy to internationalize.

Another advantage of character streams is that they are potentially much more efficient than byte streams. The implementations of many of Java's original byte streams are oriented around byte-at-a-time read and write operations. The character-stream classes, in contrast, are oriented around buffer-at-a-time read and write operations. This difference, in combination with a more efficient locking scheme, allows the character stream classes to make up for the added overhead of encoding conversion in many cases.

Character streams are implemented by the `java.io` package's `Reader` and `Writer` classes and their subclasses. Most of the functionality available for byte streams is also provided for character streams. This is reflected in the name of each character stream class, whose prefix is usually shared with the name of the corresponding byte stream class. For example, there is a `PushbackReader` class that provides the same functionality for character streams that is provided by `PushbackInputStream` for byte streams. Thus to switch from a byte stream to a character stream, just find the byte stream used by the code you're converting in Table 37 on page 670 and change your program to use the corresponding character stream instead.

Step 2: Remove Calls to Deprecated Classes and Methods

Two classes and five methods were deprecated in `java.io`. Of these, only one seems to give programmers trouble: `DataInputStream`'s `readLine` method. This section talks about the alternatives to this method and provides examples. For alternatives to the other classes and methods that were deprecated in `java.io`, consult Alternatives to Deprecated API in java.io (page 668).

Many programs that use `DataInputStream`'s `readLine` method can be converted to use `BufferedReader`'s `readLine` method instead. Sometimes, this change is straightforward. A programmer can simply modify the program so that it creates and uses a `BufferedReader` instead of a `DataInputStream`. Thus code like this:

```
DataInputStream d = new DataInputStream(in); //1.0
```

changes to:

```
BufferedReader d = new BufferedReader(new
                          InputStreamReader(in)); //1.1
```

Let's look at an example from Reading from a URLConnection (page 600). That section features the `URLReader` program, which calls the `DataInputStream` `readLine` method. Here's the program in its original 1.0 form with the call to the deprecated API shown in bold:

```
import java.net.*;
import java.io.*;
class URLReader {
    public static void main(String[] args) throws Exception {
        URL yahoo = new URL("http://www.yahoo.com/");
        DataInputStream in = new DataInputStream(
                                yahoo.openStream());
        String inputLine;
        while ((inputLine = in.readLine()) != null)
            System.out.println(inputLine);
        in.close();
    }
}
```

To change this program so that it no longer uses deprecated API, modify the program to use a `BufferedReader` instead of a `DataInputStream`. Here's the new 1.1 version of this program with the changes shown in bold:

```
import java.net.*;
import java.io.*;
class URLReader {
    public static void main(String[] args) throws Exception {
        URL yahoo = new URL("http://www.yahoo.com/");
        BufferedReader in = new BufferedReader(
                                new InputStreamReader(
                                yahoo.openStream()));
        String inputLine;
        while ((inputLine = in.readLine()) != null)
            System.out.println(inputLine);
        in.close();
    }
}
```

This simple change can be made in this case because `readLine` is the only `DataInputStream` method used by this program.

However, `DataInputStream` and `BufferedReader` do not support all of the same methods. If your program uses `DataInputStream` methods that are not supported by `BufferedReader`, then your conversion may not be this simple.

For instance, one example in this book, `DataIOTest` from Using the Processing Streams (page 376), uses not only `readLine`, but also three of `DataInputStream`'s other `read`*XXX* methods: `readDouble`, `readInt`, and `readChar`. Here's the 1.0 version of `DataIOTest` with these method calls shown in bold:

```
import java.io.*;
class DataIOTest {
    public static void main(String[] args) throws IOException {
        // write the data out
        DataOutputStream out = new DataOutputStream(new
                                FileOutputStream("invoice1.txt"));
        double[] prices = { 19.99, 9.99, 15.99, 3.99, 4.99 };
        int[] units = { 12, 8, 13, 29, 50 };
        String[] descs = { "Java T-shirt",
                           "Java Mug",
                           "Duke Juggling Dolls",
                           "Java Pin",
                           "Java Key Chain" };
        for (int i = 0; i < prices.length; i ++) {
            out.writeDouble(prices[i]);
            out.writeChar('\t');
```

```
            out.writeInt(units[i]);
            out.writeChar('\t');
            out.writeChars(descs[i]);
            out.writeChar('\n');
        }
        out.close();
        // read it in again
        DataInputStream in = new DataInputStream(new
                              FileInputStream("invoice1.txt"));
        double price;
        int unit;
        String desc;
        double total = 0.0;
        try {
            while (true) {
                price = in.readDouble();
                in.readChar();        // throws out the tab
                unit = in.readInt();
                in.readChar();        // throws out the tab
                desc = in.readLine();
                System.out.println("You've ordered " +
                                   unit + " units of " +
                                   desc + " at $" + price);
                total = total + unit * price;
            }
        } catch (EOFException e) {
        }
        System.out.println("For a TOTAL of: $" + total);
        in.close();
    }
}
```

The solution of swapping a `BufferedReader` for the `DataInputStream` won't work in this program because `BufferedReader` does not support `readDouble`, `readInt`, or `readChar`.

In this situation, you have three choices:

1. Change the algorithm so that the program doesn't need to read lines.
2. Use an `ObjectInputStream` in place of the `DataInputStream`. (`ObjectInputStream` provides methods for reading all of Java's primitive data types and so supports `readDouble`, `readInt`, or `readChar` as well as `readLine`.)
3. Call `DataInputStream`'s `readChar` method iteratively.

Option #1 isn't reasonable for most programs. For this example, option #2 isn't reasonable either because `DataIOTest` is an example of how to use `DataInput-`

Stream; it doesn't really make sense to use an ObjectInputStream instead. However, this situation is a bit unusual and it's likely that ObjectInputStream will serve most programmers better (who wants to rewrite readLine all the time especially given that a newline character differs by platform?). So we'll show you two solutions for the DataIOTest example, one implementing option #2, and one implementing option #3.

Here's DataIOTest modified to use an ObjectInputStream instead of a DataInputStream. Note that the DataOutputStream had to be changed to an ObjectInputStream so that the data written by it could be read by the ObjectInputStream.

```
import java.io.*;
class DataIOTest {
    public static void main(String[] args) throws IOException {
        // write the data out
        ObjectOutputStream out = new ObjectOutputStream(new
                                 FileOutputStream("invoice1.txt"));
       ...// unchanged code removed for the sake of brevity...
        // read it in again
        ObjectInputStream in = new ObjectInputStream(new
                                 FileInputStream("invoice1.txt"));
       ...// unchanged code removed for the sake of brevity...
    }
}
```

And here's another version modified to use DataInputStream's readChar method iteratively instead of readLine:

```
import java.io.*;
class DataIOTest {
    public static void main(String[] args) throws IOException {
       ...// unchanged code removed for the sake of brevity...
        double price;
        int unit;
        StringBuffer desc;
        double total = 0.0;
        try {
            while (true) {
                price = in.readDouble();
                in.readChar();       // throws out the tab
                unit = in.readInt();
                in.readChar();       // throws out the tab
                char chr;
                desc = new StringBuffer(20);
                char lineSep = System.getProperty(
```

```
                    "line.separator").charAt(0);
            while ((chr = in.readChar()) != lineSep)
                desc.append(chr);
            System.out.println("You've ordered " +
                                unit + " units of " +
                                desc + " at $" + price);
            total = total + unit * price;
        }
    } catch (EOFException e) {
    }
    System.out.println("For a TOTAL of: $" + total);
    in.close();
  }
}
```

How to Convert Code that Uses the AWT

Why should you update a program to the 1.1 AWT API? Here are five possible reasons:

- The 1.1 version of AWT has some new features you want to use. See AWT Enhancements (page 636) for a summary of new features.
- The new AWT architecture enables faster, more robust implementations of the AWT, which means that the updated program might work better.
- You plan to use the Swing components, which rely on the new event architecture. See Java Foundation Classes (page 680) for information on the Swing components.
- The program is one of the rare ones that is affected by incompatible AWT changes. You can find a list of possibly incompatible bug fixes in JDK 1.1 Compatibility (page 933).
- You want the 1.1 Java compiler to compile the program without deprecation warnings.

Converting a 1.0 program to the 1.1 AWT API usually requires two steps:

1. Replace deprecated methods with their 1.1 equivalents.
2. Convert the program's event-handling code to use the new AWT event system.

The following two sections describe each step in detail and show an example.

Step 1: Replace Deprecated Methods with Their 1.1 Equivalents

Because so many AWT methods were deprecated, Sun provides a script to help you convert 1.0 programs to the 1.1 versions. This script, called `updateAWT`, uses a UNIX utility called `sed` to change the names of many deprecated 1.0 AWT methods into their 1.1 equivalents. If you're developing on a PC, you might be able to run the script using a product such as MKS Toolkit, which provides PC versions of UNIX tools.

Platform-specific Details: Using the `updateAWT` Script

Here's an example of using the `updateAWT` script to help convert a 1.0 AWT program to the 1.1 API. The example shows the commands you might enter at a shell prompt on a UNIX system.

- Get the script. You can find it in the online tutorial at the following URL:

  `http://java.sun.com/docs/books/tutorial/post1.0/converting/updateAWT`

- Run the script:

```
% cp MyClass.java OldMyClass.java
% updateAWT MyClass.java > tmp.java
```

- Check the changes to make sure nothing obviously bad happened. For example, on a UNIX system, you might execute the following command:

```
% diff MyClass.java tmp.java
```

- After confirming that the changes look OK, save the new version of the program:

```
% mv tmp.java MyClass.java
```

- Try recompiling the program to make sure that the script didn't incorrectly convert a method name. Be *sure* to use a 1.1 compiler.

```
% javac MyClass.java
```

You might still get a few deprecation warnings, but you shouldn't get any compile errors. If the program doesn't compile, you probably will have to undo a change the script made. See Simple Name Changes in the AWT[1] in the online tutorial for help.

You'll probably have to make some changes by hand, whether or not you use the `updateAWT` script. As described in How to Convert Your Program (page 646),

[1] http://java.sun.com/docs/books/tutorial/post1.0/converting/nameChangesAWT.html

you can get a list of the deprecated methods in the program by compiling its files with the `-deprecation` flag.

Once you know which deprecated methods the program uses, look up each method in the section Alternatives to Deprecated API in the AWT (page 671). Then replace each deprecated method with its 1.1 alternative. Most of the changes you need to make are straightforward, except those to event-handling code, which are described in the next section.

Step 2: Convert Event-Handling Code

In 1.0, the `Component` `handleEvent` method (along with the methods it called, such as `action`) was the center of event handling. Only `Component` objects could handle events, and the component that handled an event had to be either the component in which the event occurred or a component above it in the component containment hierarchy.

In 1.1, event handling is no longer restricted to objects in the component containment hierarchy, and the `handleEvent` method is no longer the center of event handling. Instead, objects of any type can register as event listeners. Event listeners receive notification only about the types of events they've registered their interest in. Never again will you have to create a `Component` subclass just to handle events. You can get more information about 1.1 event handling from Event Handling (page 420).

When upgrading to the 1.1 release, the simplest way to convert event-handling code is to leave it in the same class, making that class a listener for the appropriate type of event. That's the scheme this section illustrates.

Another possibility is to centralize event-handling code in one or more non-`Component` listeners. This approach lets you separate the GUI of your program from implementation details. It requires that you modify your existing code so that the listeners can get whatever state information they require from the components. This approach can be worth your while if you're trying to keep your program's architecture clean.

Note: We recommend that you do not mix the 1.0 event model with the 1.1 event model in the same program. The results would be unpredictable and might be difficult to debug.

Making a Component a Listener. The process of making a `Component` a listener can be straightforward, once you figure out which events a program handles and which components generate the events. If you're using a Java compiler from JDK 1.1.1 or later, then compiling with the `-deprecation` flag generates a list that includes all old-style event handling methods. (Before 1.1.1, the compiler didn't generate a complete list, so you had to search for "Event" in a source file.) While you're looking at the code, you should note whether any classes exist solely for the purpose of handling events; you might be able to eliminate such classes.

Here are the steps to follow when converting a 1.0 component into a listener:

1. Figure out which components generate each event type. The Event-Conversion Table (page 674) can help you know what to look for. For example, if you're converting event code that's in an action method, the table tells you to look for `Button`, `List`, `MenuItem`, `TextField`, `Checkbox`, and `Choice` objects.
2. By looking up each event type in this table, note which listener interfaces the listener should implement, and which methods within each interface should contain event-handling code. For example, if you're trying to handle an action event generated by a `Button`, the table tells you to implement the `ActionListener` interface, putting the event-handling code in the `actionPerformed` method.
3. Change the class declaration so that the class imports the necessary types and implements the appropriate listener interfaces. For example:

```
import java.awt.event.*;
...
public class MyClass extends SomeComponent
                          implements ActionListener {
```

   Alternative: Instead of implementing an interface, you can declare an inner class that extends an event adapter class. Inner classes are useful when you need to implement only one method of an interface that contains many other methods. See Using Adapters and Inner Classes to Handle AWT Events (page 468) for more information.

4. Create empty implementations of all the methods in the listener interfaces your class must implement. Copy the event-handling code into the appropriate methods. For example, `ActionListener` has just one method, `actionPerformed`. So as a shortcut way of creating the new method and copying the event-handling code to it, you can simply change the signature of an action method from this:

```
public boolean action(Event event, Object arg) {
```

   to this:

```
public void actionPerformed(ActionEvent event) {
```

Alternative: If you use an adapter subclass to handle the events, you don't need to create empty implementations of methods. See Using Adapters and Inner Classes to Handle AWT Events (page 468) for more information.

5. Modify the event-handling code in these ways:
   - Delete all `return` statements.
   - Change references to `event.target` to be `event.getSource()`.
   - Delete any code that unnecessarily tests for which component the event came from. Now that events are forwarded only if the generating component has a listener, you don't have to worry about receiving events from an unwanted component.
   - Perform any other modifications required to make the program compile cleanly and execute correctly.
6. Determine where the components that generate the events are created. Just after the code that creates each component, register this as the appropriate type of listener. For example:

   ```
   newComponentObject.addActionListener(this);
   ```

   Alternative: If you use an inner class to handle the events, register an instance of that inner class instead. See Using Adapters and Inner Classes to Handle AWT Events (page 468) for more information.
7. Compile and test your program. If your program is ignoring some events, make sure you added the correct event-listener object as a listener to the correct event-generating object.

Example: Converting DialogWindow

This section shows how to convert a program called `DialogWindow` from the 1.0 API to the 1.1 API. `DialogWindow` is an application, but it can also run as an applet, with the help of a class named `AppletButton`. The `DialogWindow` program is featured in the section How to Use Dialogs (page 438).

You can find the 1.0 `DialogWindow` source code (`DialogWindow.java`[1]) in the online version of this tutorial.

Step 1: Replace Deprecated Methods with Their 1.1 Equivalents.

1. Move the 1.0 source and bytecode files to a safe place, and keep a copy of the source file that you modify. For example, on a UNIX system:

---

1 http://java.sun.com/docs/books/tutorial/ui/components/example/DialogWindow.java

```
% mkdir 1.0example
% mv DialogWindow.class 1.0example
% cp DialogWindow.java 1.0example
```

2. Perform as much automatic conversion as possible. For example:

```
% updateAWT DialogWindow.java > tmp.java
% diff DialogWindow.java tmp.java
33c33
< dialog.show();
---
> dialog.setVisible(true);
38c38
< textArea.appendText(text + "\n");
---
> textArea.append(text + "\n");
47c47
< window.show();
---
> window.setVisible(true);
87c87
< hide();
---
> setVisible(false);
% mv tmp.java DialogWindow.java
```

3. Compile `DialogWindow`, making sure to use the 1.1 compiler. For example:

```
% which javac
/usr/local/java/jdk1.1.1/solaris/bin/javac
% javac DialogWindow.java
Note: DialogWindow.java uses a deprecated API. Recompile
with "-deprecation" for details. 1 warning
%

% javac -deprecation DialogWindow.java
DialogWindow.java:18: Note: The method boolean
handleEvent(java.awt.Event) in class java.awt.Component
has been deprecated, and class DialogWindow overrides it.
   public boolean handleEvent(Event event) {
                  ^
DialogWindow.java:26: Note: The method boolean
handleEvent(java.awt.Event) in class java.awt.Component
has been deprecated.
   return super.handleEvent(event);
                           ^
DialogWindow.java:29: Note: The method boolean
action(java.awt.Event, java.lang.Object) in class
```

```
java.awt.Component has been deprecated, and class
DialogWindow overrides it.
   public boolean action(Event event, Object arg) {
                  ^
DialogWindow.java:81: Note: The method boolean
action(java.awt.Event, java.lang.Object) in class
java.awt.Component has been deprecated, and class
SimpleDialog overrides it.
   public boolean action(Event event, Object arg) {
                  ^
Note: DialogWindow.java uses a deprecated API. Please
consult the documentation for a better alternative.
5 warnings
%
```

As you can see, the example compiles successfully. However, a few calls or overrides of deprecated methods remain. The `Event` arguments to these methods are a tell-tale sign that the methods contain event-handling code.

Step 2: Convert Event-Handling Code. To convert the event-handling code in `DialogWindow`, follow the sequence described previously in Making a Component a Listener (page 657).

1. The first and hardest task is determining which components generate events that must be handled. Compiling with the `-deprecation` flag tells us that `DialogWindow` has three 1.0-style event-handling methods:
   - `handleEvent` in `DialogWindow`
   - `action` in `DialogWIndow`
   - `action` in `SimpleDialog`

   Studying `DialogWindow`'s code tells us these things about its event handling architecture:
   - `DialogWindow` handles `WINDOW_DESTROY` events for itself.
   - `DialogWindow` handles action events for the components it contains. Upon closer inspection, we can see that it contains only one component that can generate action events: a `Button`.
   - `SimpleDialog` handles action events for the components it contains. Upon closer inspection, we can see that it contains three components that can generate action events: two `Buttons` (`Cancel` and `Set`) and a `TextField`.
   - Both `DialogWindow` and `SimpleDialog` contain non-event-handling code, so you can't eliminate them by moving their event-handling code elsewhere.

2. Now that we know which objects generate which events, it's easy to determine which interfaces the event handlers should implement. Consulting the Event-Conversion Table (page 674) tells us that `WINDOW_DESTROY` corresponds to the `windowClosing` method of `WindowListener`, and that action events generated by buttons and text fields are handled by the `actionPerformed` method of `ActionListener`.
3. Now all that's left is to implement the event-handling methods and register the event listener. The following example gives the highlights of the event-related code in the converted `DialogWindow` program. Significant changes are in bold.

```
import java.awt.event.*;
public class DialogWindow extends Frame
                                 implements WindowListener,
                                            ActionListener{
    ...
    public DialogWindow() {
        ...
        Button button = new Button(
                             "Click to bring up dialog");
        button.addActionListener(this);
        ...
        addWindowListener(this);
    }
    public void windowClosed(WindowEvent event) { }
    public void windowDeiconified(WindowEvent event) { }
    public void windowIconified(WindowEvent event) { }
    public void windowActivated(WindowEvent event) { }
    public void windowDeactivated(WindowEvent event) { }
    public void windowOpened(WindowEvent event) { }
    public void windowClosing(WindowEvent event) {
        if (inAnApplet) {
            dispose();
        } else {
            System.exit(0);
        }
    }
    public void actionPerformed(ActionEvent event) {
        if (dialog == null) {
            dialog = new SimpleDialog(this,
                                      "A Simple Dialog");
        }
        dialog.setVisible();
    }
    ...
}
```

```
class SimpleDialog extends Dialog
                    implements ActionListener {
    ...
    SimpleDialog(Frame dw, String title) {
        ...
        field = new TextField(40);
        field.addActionListener(this);
        ...
        Button b = new Button("Cancel");
        b.addActionListener(this);
        setButton = new Button("Set");
        setButton.addActionListener(this);
        ...
    }
    public void actionPerformed(ActionEvent event) {
        Object source = event.getSource();
        if ( (source == setButton) | (source == field)) {
            parent.setText(field.getText());
        }
        field.selectAll();
        setVisible(false);
    }
}
```

Instead of implementing the `WindowListener` interface, `DialogWindow` could simply contain an inner class that extends `WindowAdapter`. This change makes the empty method bodies unnecessary.

4. The following are the highlights of a `DialogWindow` class that uses an inner class to handle window events. Significant changes from the 1.1 window listener version are in bold. To see the whole program, go to DialogWindow.java (page 815).

```
public class DialogWindow extends Frame
                          implements ActionListener {
    ...
    public DialogWindow() {
        ...
        Button button = new Button("Click to bring up dialog");
        button.addActionListener(this);
        ...
        addWindowListener(new WindowAdapter(){
            public void windowClosing(WindowEvent event) {
                if (inAnApplet) {
                    dispose();
                } else {
                    System.exit(0);
                }
```

```
                }
            });
        }
        ...//No empty windowXXX method implementations! ...
        ...
    }
```

By using the DialogWindow program, both as an applet and as an application, we can see that it handles all events properly.

Lists and Tables

The lists and tables in this section can help you convert your programs by showing you the alternatives to deprecated API and describing the changes made to the Java language.

Alternatives to Deprecated API in java.lang, java.net, and java.util

This section lists alternatives to deprecated classes and methods in all packages except for `java.io` and `java.awt.*`.

The java.lang.String Class

The following constructors and methods in `java.lang.String` (see Table 25) were deprecated in favor of replacements that better support internationalization. These constructors and methods did not properly convert bytes into characters. The new constructors and methods use a named character encoding or the default character encoding to do the conversion. Creating Strings and StringBuffers (page 249) covers the `String` class thoroughly.

Table 25: Deprecated constructors and methods in `java.lang.String`.

Deprecated API	Alternatives

`String(byte[], int)`	`String(byte[])`
	or
	`String(byte[], String)`

`String(byte[], int, int, int)`	`String(byte[], int, int)`
	or
	`String(byte[], int, int, String)`

`getBytes(int, int, byte[], int)`	`byte[] getBytes(String)`
	or
	`byte[] getBytes()`

The java.lang.System Class

The `getenv` method has been out of use for several releases of the JDK. The 1.1 release formalizes this change by deprecating the method (Table 26). Programmers should use `Properties` to store information between invocations of a program.

Table 26: Deprecated method in `java.lang`.

Deprecated API	Alternatives
`String getenv(String)`	`String getProperty(String)`

Setting Up Your Properties Object (page 262) talks about how to use the `Properties` class and in one of our online trails, the Managing Locale-Sensitive Data[1] section shows you how to use `Properties` to help internationalize your Java programs.

The java.lang.Runtime Class

The following methods in the `java.lang.Runtime` class (Table 27) have been deprecated because the JDK 1.1 introduced new internationalization features that replaced them. The new internationalization API includes I/O classes that translate a byte stream into a character stream based on a character encoding. [You can learn more about the `Runtime` class in The Runtime Object (page 291).]

Table 27: Methods in the `java.lang.Runtime` class.

Deprecated API	Alternatives
`InputStream getLocalizedInputStream(InputStream)`	`InputStreamReader`[a] *or* `BufferedReader`[b]
`OutputStream getLocalizedOutputStream(OutputStream)`	`OutputStreamReader`[c] *or* `BufferedWriter`[d] *or* `PrintWriter`[e]

a. http://java.sun.com/products/jdk/1.1/api/java.io.InputStreamReader.html
b. http://java.sun.com/products/jdk/1.1/api/java.io.BufferedReader.html
c. http://java.sun.com/products/jdk/1.1/api/java.io.OutputStreamReader.html
d. http://java.sun.com/products/jdk/1.1/api/java.io.BufferedWriter.html
e. http://java.sun.com/products/jdk/1.1/api/java.io.PrintWriter.html

1 http://java.sun.com/docs/books/tutorial/intl/datamgmt/bundles.html

The java.lang.Character Class

The following methods in the `java.lang.Character` class were deprecated in favor of alternatives that better support internationalization (Table 28).

Table 28: Deprecated methods in `java.lang.Character`.

Deprecated API	Alternatives
`boolean isJavaLetter(char)`	`boolean isJavaIdentifierStart(char)`
`boolean isJavaLetterOrDigit(char)`	`boolean isJavaIdentifierPart(char)`
`boolean isSpace(char)`	`boolean isWhitespace(char)`

The java.lang.ClassLoader Class

The following method in `java.lang.ClassLoader` has been deprecated in favor of the version that takes a `String` as a first argument because the latter is more secure (Table 29).

Table 29: Deprecated methods in `java.lang.ClassLoader`.

Deprecated API	Alternatives
`Class defineClass(byte[], int, int)`	`Class defineClass(String,byte[], int, int)`

The java.net.Socket Class

Two constructors in the `java.net.Socket` class were deprecated (Table 30). These constructors allowed programmers to create a `DatagramSocket`. Now programmers should explicitly construct a `DatagramSocket` if they want one.

You can learn about `Socket` and `DatagramSocket` in All About Sockets (page 605) and All About Datagrams (page 619), respectively.

Table 30: Deprecated constructors in `java.net.Socket`.

Deprecated API	Alternatives
`Socket(InetAddress, int, boolean)`	One of `DatagramSocket`'s constructors
`Socket(String, int, boolean)`	One of `DatagramSocket`'s constructors

The java.util.Date Class

Many of the methods in `java.util.Date` have been deprecated in favor of another API that better supports internationalization (Table 31). The following table provides a list of these methods and their alternatives.

Table 31: Deprecated constructors and methods in `java.util.Date`.

Deprecated API	Alternatives

`Date(int, int, int)`
`Date(int, int, int, int)`
`Date(int, int, int,`
`int, int, int)`
`Date(String)`
	Create a `java.util.GregorianCalendar` object and use its `getTime` method to convert it to a `Date`.

`int getYear()`
`int getMonth()`
`int getDate()`
`int getHours()`
`int getMinutes()`
`int getSeconds()`
`int getDay()`
`int getTimezoneOffset()`
`setYear(int)`
`setMonth(int)`
`setDate(int)`
`setHours(int)`
`setMinutes(int)`
`setSeconds(int)`
`UTC(int, int, int,`
`int, int, int)`
	Create a `java.util.GregorianCalendar` object and use its setters and getters instead.

`parse(String)`
`String toLocaleString()`
`String toGMTString()`
	Use `java.text.DateFormat` and its subclasses to parse and format dates.

Instinctively, when programmers want to create the current date, they immediately look at the `Date` class. While intuitive, this is usually the wrong choice. For storing date and time information, most programmers should use the `Calendar` class, and to format dates and times they should use the `java.text.DateFormat` class. This is all described with task-oriented documentation and examples in Writing Global Programs.[1]

1 http://java.sun.com/docs/books/tutorial/intl/index.html

Alternatives to Deprecated API in java.io

This section lists alternatives to deprecated `java.io` classes and methods.

Deprecated Classes in java.io

The following two classes have been deprecated in `java.io` (Table 32). `LineNumberInputStream` was deprecated because it incorrectly assumes that bytes adequately represent characters. `StringBufferInputStream` was deprecated because it does not properly convert characters into bytes. As of JDK 1.1, the preferred way to operate on character streams is with the new set of character stream classes, which provide character-based alternatives to both `LineNumberInputStream` and `StringBufferInputStream`.

Table 32: Deprecated classes in `java.io`.

Deprecated API	Alternative
`LineNumberInputStream`	`LineNumberReader`
`StringBufferInputStream`	`StringReader`

The java.io.ByteArrayOutputStream Class

The following method in `java.io.ByteArrayOutputStream` was deprecated because it does not properly convert bytes into characters (Table 33). As of JDK 1.1, the preferred way to do this is with one of the other two `toString` methods, which either allow the caller to specify the character encoding to use to convert bytes to characters or use the platform's default character encoding.

Table 33: Deprecated method in `java.io.ByteArrayOutputStream`.

Deprecated API	Alternative

`String toString(int)`	`String toString()`
	or
	`String toString(String)`

The java.io.DataInputStream Class

The following method in `java.io.DataInputStream` has been deprecated because it does not properly convert bytes to characters (Table 34).

Table 34: Deprecated method in java.io.DataInputStream.

Deprecated API	Alternative
String readLine()	String readLine() in the BufferedReader class

The alternative shown here will not work for all programs. For examples and discussion about other choices, see How to Convert Code that Uses I/O (page 650).

The java.io.PrintStream Class

The java.io.PrintStream class has been superseded by the character-based java.io.PrintWriter class. To discourage its use, all constructors for java.io.PrintStream have been deprecated (Table 35).

Table 35: Deprecated constructors for java.io.PrintStream.

Deprecated API	Alternative
PrintStream(OutputStream)	PrintWriter(OutputStream)
PrintStream(OutputStream, boolean)	PrintWriter(OutputStream, boolean)

Note: The PrintStream class has been modified to use the platform's default character encoding and the platform's default line terminator. Thus each PrintStream incorporates an OutputStreamWriter, and it passes all characters through this writer to produce bytes for output. The println methods use the platform's default line terminator, which is defined by the system property line.separator and is not necessarily a single newline character ('\n'). Bytes and byte arrays written with the existing write methods are not passed through the writer.

The primary motivation for changing the PrintStream class is that it will make System.out and System.err more useful to people writing Java programs on platforms where the local encoding is something other than ASCII. PrintStream is, in other words, provided primarily for use in debugging and for compatibility with existing code. Therefore, its two constructors have been deprecated.

Deprecating the constructors rather than the entire class allows existing uses of System.out and System.err to be compiled without generating deprecation warnings. Thus programmers just learning Java, or programmers inserting System.err.println calls for debugging purposes, will not be bothered by such warnings. Programmers writing code that explicitly constructs a PrintStream will see a deprecation warning when that code is compiled. Code that produces textual output should use the new `PrintWriter` class, which allows the character encoding to be specified or the default encoding to be accepted. For convenience, the `PrintWriter` class provides constructors that take an `OutputStream` object and create an intermediate `OutputStreamWriter` object that uses the default encoding.

The java.io.StreamTokenizer Class

The constructor for `java.io.StreamTokenizer` that operates on an `InputStream` has been deprecated in favor of the constructor that operates on a `Reader` (Table 36). You can still tokenize an `InputStream` by converting it to a `Reader`:

```
Reader r = new BufferedReader(new InputStreamReader(is));
StreamTokenizer st = new StreamTokenizer(r);
```

Table 36: Deprecated constructor for `java.io.StreamTokenizer`.

Deprecated API	Alternative
`StreamTokenizer(InputStream)`	`StreamTokenizer(Reader)`

Character Streams and Their Corresponding Byte Streams

The first column of Table 37 lists the character streams that were added to the JDK 1.1 release. The second column provides a brief description of the class, and the third column indicates the byte stream class that performs the same operation but for bytes instead of characters.

Table 37 : The character stream classes and their corresponding byte classes.

Character Stream Class	Description	Corresponding Byte Class
`Reader`	Abstract class for character-input streams	`InputStream`
`BufferedReader`	Buffers input, parses lines	`BufferedInputStream`
`LineNumberReader`	Keeps track of line numbers	`LineNumberInputStream`
`CharArrayReader`	Reads from a character array	`ByteArrayInputStream`
`InputStreamReader`	Translates a byte stream into a character stream	*(none)*

Table 37 : The character stream classes and their corresponding byte classes.

Character Stream Class	Description	Corresponding Byte Class
`FileReader`	Translates bytes from a file into a character stream	`FileInputStream`
`FilterReader`	Abstract class for filtered character input	`FilterInputStream`
`PushbackReader`	Allows characters to be pushed back	`PushbackInputStream`
`PipedReader`	Reads from a `PipedWriter`	`PipedInputStream`
`StringReader`	Reads from a `String`	`StringBufferInputStream`
`Writer`	Abstract class for character-output streams	`OutputStream`
`BufferedWriter`	Buffers output, uses platform's line separator	`BufferedOutputStream`
`CharArrayWriter`	Writes to a character array	`ByteArrayOutputStream`
`FilterWriter`	Abstract class for filtered character output	`FilterOutputStream`
`OutputStreamWriter`	Translates a character stream into a byte stream	*(none)*
`FileWriter`	Translates a character stream into a byte file	`FileOutputStream`
`PrintWriter`	Prints values and objects to a `Writer`	`PrintStream`
`PipedWriter`	Writes to a `PipedReader`	`PipedOutputStream`
`StringWriter`	Writes to a `String`	*(none)*

Alternatives to Deprecated API in the AWT

This section lists all the deprecated AWT methods and their 1.1 replacements. A script named `updateAWT` can make the simplest replacements for you. See How to Convert Code that Uses the AWT (page 655) for instructions and examples of using the script.

A table similar to Table 38, called Simple Name Changes in the AWT[1], is available online; however, the online table contains less information and is alphabet-

[1] http://java.sun.com/docs/books/tutorial/post1.0/converting/nameChangesAWT.html

ized by the 1.1 column to help you easily undo incorrect changes that the script has made.

Deprecated event-handling methods aren't quite as easy to replace as are other deprecated AWT methods. See Step 2: Convert Event-Handling Code (page 657) for help updating event-handling code.

Table 38: Deprecated AWT methods and their replacements.

Deprecated Method	Class Where Deprecated	1.1 Replacement
action	Component	*
addLayoutComponent (String, Component)	BorderLayout, CardLayout	addLayoutComponent (Component, Object)
allowsMultipleSelec-tions	List	isMultipleMode
appendText	TextArea	append
bounds	Component	getBounds
clear	List	removeAll
countComponents	Container	getComponentCount
countItems	Choice, List, Menu	getItemCount
countMenus	MenuBar	getMenuCount
deliverEvent	Component, Container	dispatchEvent
disable()	MenuItem	setEnabled(false)
enable()	Component, MenuItem	setEnabled(true)
enable(expression)	Component	setEnabled(expression)
getBoundingBox	Polygon	getBounds
getClipRect	Graphics	getClipBounds
getCurrent	CheckboxGroup	getSelectedCheckbox
getCursorType	Frame	getCursor method in Component
getLineIncrement	Scrollbar	getUnitIncrement
getMaxDecent	FontMetrics	getMaxDescent
getPageIncrement	Scrollbar	getBlockIncrement
getPeer	Component	*(none)*
getVisible	Scrollbar	getVisibleAmount

Table 38: Deprecated AWT methods and their replacements.

Deprecated Method	Class Where Deprecated	1.1 Replacement
gotFocus	Component	*
handleEvent	Component	*
hide	Component	setVisible(false)
insertText	TextArea	insert
insets	Container	getInsets
inside	Component, Polygon, Rectangle	contains
isSelected	List	isIndexSelected
keyDown	Component	*
keyUp	Component	*
layout	Component, Container, ScrollPane	doLayout
locate	Component, Container	getComponentAt
location	Component	getLocation
lostFocus	Component	*
minimumSize	Component, Container, TextArea, TextField	getMinimumSize
mouseDown	Component	*
mouseDrag	Component	*
mouseEnter	Component	*
mouseExit	Component	*
mouseMove	Component	*
mouseUp	Component	*
move	Component, Rectangle	setLocation
nextFocus	Component, Container, Window	transferFocus
postEvent	Component, Window	dispatchEvent
preferredSize	Component, Container, TextArea, TextField	getPreferredSize
replaceText	TextArea	replaceRange
reshape	Component, Rectangle	setBounds
resize	Component, Rectangle	setSize
setCurrent	CheckboxGroup	setSelectedCheckbox

Table 38: Deprecated AWT methods and their replacements.

Deprecated Method	Class Where Deprecated	1.1 Replacement
`setCursor`	`Frame`	`getCursor` method in `Component`
`setEchoCharacter`	`TextField`	`setEchoChar`
`setLineIncrement`	`Scrollbar`	`setUnitIncrement`
`setMultipleSelections`	`List`	`setMultipleMode`
`setPageIncrement`	`Scrollbar`	`setBlockIncrement`
`show()`	`Component`	`setVisible(true)`
`show(expression)`	`Component`	`setVisible(expression)`
`size`	`Component`	`getSize`

* See Step 2: Convert Event-Handling Code (page 657) for information on handling events.

Event-Conversion Table

Table 39 maps 1.0 events to their 1.1 counterparts. The first column lists each 1.0 event type, along with the name of the method (if any) that's specific to the event. Where no method is listed, the event is always handled in the `handleEvent` method. The second column lists the 1.0 components that can generate the event type. The third column lists the listener interface that helps you handle the 1.1 equivalents of the listed events. The fourth column lists the methods in each listener interface. The methods in these table cells are listed in the same order as the corresponding event type in the cells of the first column.

Table 39: Event-Conversion Table.

<table>
<tr><th colspan="2">1.0</th><th colspan="2">1.1</th></tr>
<tr><th>Event Source</th><th>Event/Method</th><th>Method</th><th>Interface</th></tr>
<tr><td><code>Button, List, MenuItem, TextField</code></td><td rowspan="2"><code>ACTION_EVENT/action</code></td><td><code>actionPerformed</code></td><td><code>ActionListener</code></td></tr>
<tr><td><code>Checkbox, CheckboxMenuItem, Choice</code></td><td><code>itemStateChanged</code></td><td><code>ItemListener</code></td></tr>
</table>

Table 39: Event-Conversion Table.

1.0		1.1	
Event Source	**Event/Method**	**Method**	**Interface**
Dialog, Frame	WINDOW_DESTROY WINDOW_EXPOSE WINDOW_ICONIFY WINDOW_DEICONIFY	windowClosing windowOpened windowIconified windowDeiconified windowClosed* windowActivated* windowDeactivated*	Window- Listener
Dialog, Frame	WINDOW_MOVED	componentMoved componentHidden* componentResized * componentShown*	Component- Listener
Scrollbar	SCROLL_LINE_UP SCROLL_LINE_DOWN SCROLL_PAGE_UP SCROLL_PAGE_DOWN SCROLL_ABSOLUTE SCROLL_BEGIN SCROLL_END	adjustment- ValueChanged	Adjustment- Listener (or use the new Scroll Pane class)
Checkbox, CheckboxMenu- Item, Choice, List	LIST_SELECT LIST_DESELECT	itemStateChanged	ItemListener
Canvas, Dialog, Frame, Panel, Window	MOUSE_DRAG/mouseDrag MOUSE_MOVE/mouseMove	mouseDragged mouseMoved	MouseMotion- Listener
Canvas, Dialog, Frame, Panel, Window	MOUSE_DOWN/mouseDown MOUSE_UP/mouseUp MOUSE_ENTER/mouseEnter MOUSE_EXIT/mouseExit	mousePressed mouseReleased mouseEntered mouseExited mouseClicked*	Mouse- Listener
Component	KEY_PRESS/keyDown KEY_ACTION/keyDown KEY_RELEASE/keyUp KEY_ACTION_RELEASE/ keyUp	keyPressed keyReleased keyTyped*	KeyListener
Component	GOT_FOCUS/gotFocus LOST_FOCUS/lostFocus	focusGained focusLost	Focus- Listener
No 1.0 equivalent.		componentAdded* componentRemoved*	Container- Listener
No 1.0 equivalent.		textValueChanged*	TextListener

* These methods have no 1.0 equivalent.

Changes to the Java Language

A few additions have been made to the Java language.

Inner Classes

Probably the single most significant change to the Java language for JDK 1.1 is the ability to define classes as members of other classes. Such classes are called *nested classes*. Inner classes are one type of nested class. Read about nested and inner classes in Implementing Nested Classes (page 152).

Anonymous Classes

When you are writing simple subclasses or implementations of interfaces, creating a bunch of classes for each trivial class can be awkward. Anonymous classes are a convenient short form of inner classes that have no name, only an implementation that is specified right along with the `new`.

For a brief discussion of anonymous classes and an example that uses one, refer to Anonymous Classes (page 130).

Instance Initializers

In JDK 1.0, the Java language supported `static` initializers that let you initialize class variables.

```
class ClassWithStaticInitializer {
    static {
        // ... initialization code ...
    }
}
```

JDK 1.1 adds a similar syntax for performing instance initialization:

```
class ClassWithInstanceInitializer {
    {
        // ... initialization code ...
    }
}
```

Initialization code introduced without the `static` keyword is executed by every constructor, just after the superclass constructor is called, in the same order that they appear in the source code, along with any instance variable initializations.

An instance initializer may not return, nor throw a checked exception, unless that exception is explicitly declared in the `throws` clause of each constructor. An instance initializer in an anonymous class *can* throw any exceptions.

Instance initializers are useful when instance variables (including blank `finals`) must be initialized by code which must catch exceptions, or perform other kinds of control flow which cannot be expressed in a single initializer expression. Instance initializers are required if an anonymous class is to initialize itself, since an anonymous class cannot declare any constructors.

Initializing Instance and Class Members (page 122) discusses the use of static and instance initializers.

Array Initialization

You can initialize the contents of an array in a `new` statement. For example, the following would be a flexible way to create an array of strings:

```
String[] tutorialTeam = new String[] {
    "Alison", "Kathy", "Mary"
};
```

The array allocation syntax is extended to support initialization of the elements of anonymous arrays.

Class Literals

A *class literal* is an expression consisting of the name of a class, interface, array, or primitive type followed by a period (`.`) and the token `class`. It evaluates to an object of type `Class`, the class object for the named type (or for void).

For reference types, a class literal is equivalent to a call to `Class.forName` with the appropriate string, except that it does not raise any checked exceptions. (Its efficiency is likely to be comparable to that of a field access, rather than a method call.) The class literal of a reference type can raise `NoClassDefFoundError`, in much the same way that a class variable reference can raise that error if the variable's class is not available.

The class literal of a primitive type or void is equivalent to a `static` variable reference to a pre-installed primitive type descriptor, according to Table 40.

New Uses for final

Method parameters and local variables can be declared `final`. If you do not expect to change the value of a parameter or variable inside the method, you can declare it `final` to let the compiler enforce that. The compiler can also optimize uses of a `final` parameter or variable since it knows the value will never change.

Table 40: Class literal equivalents.

`boolean.class`
`char.class`
`byte.class`
	`Boolean.TYPE`
	`Character.TYPE`
	`Byte.TYPE`

`short.class`
`int.class`
`long.class`
	`Short.TYPE`
	`Integer.TYPE`
	`Long.TYPE`

`float.class`	`Float.TYPE`
`double.class` `void.class`	`Double.TYPE` `Void.TYPE`

The `final`-ness of a parameter is not part of the method signature—it is simply a detail of the implementation. A subclass can override a method and add or drop any `final` parameter modifiers you wish. You can also add or drop `final` modifiers in a method's parameters without causing any harm to existing compiled code that uses that method. The `final` declaration does not show up in the documentation generated from doc comments.

You can defer initialization of a `final` field or variable, as long as you initialize it before it is used and assign a value to it exactly once. The compiler will check for proper assignment, as will the verifier before code is executed. Deferred initialization can be useful when the proper value can only be calculated by a loop or other code that is hard or impossible to encode in a variable initializer, such as code that throws exceptions that must be caught and handled.

Transient Defined in 1.1

The `transient` keyword, which was undefined in 1.0, is now defined. In 1.1, `transient` is used to mark member variables that should not be saved during object serialization.

28 A Preview of Things to Come

THE Java engineering team plans to add many features to the JDK in an upcoming release. As of this writing, the release name is 1.2. As you read this preview, please keep in mind that it's always possible that a feature we tell you about will be changed or moved to a different release. Such is the nature of *soft*ware!

The following sections briefly describe the features that are planned for the JDK 1.2 release. In addition to the features in the following list, the Java engineering team plans to add a standard extensions architecture and enhance JAR, JNI, and reflection.

Security Enhancements

The next release introduces three new major security enhancements:

Policy-based, easily-configurable, fine-grained access control.
When code is loaded, it is assigned "permissions" based on the security policy currently in effect. Each permission specifies a permitted access to a particular resource (such as "read" and "write" access to a specified file or directory, "connect" access to a given host and port, etc.). The policy, specifying which permissions are available for code from various signers/locations, can be initialized from an external configurable policy file. Unless a permission is explicitly granted to code, it cannot access the resource that is guarded by that permission. These new concepts of permission and policy enable the JDK to offer fine-

grained, highly configurable, flexible, and extensible access control. Such access control can now be specified not only for applets, but also for all Java code, including applications, Beans, and servlets.

Certificates

JDK 1.1 includes certificate interfaces for parsing and managing certificates and X.509 v3 implementation of the certificate interfaces.

Three new tools

- `keytool` is used to create public/private keys; to display, import, and export certificates; and to generate X.509 v1 self-signed certificates.
- `jarsigner` signs JAR (Java ARchive) files, and verifies the signatures of signed JAR files.
- `policytool` creates and modifies the external policy configuration files that define your installation's Java security policy.

Java Foundation Classes

The Java Foundation Classes (JFC) extend the AWT to provide richer GUI functionality. We expect the next major release to include the following new JFC functionality:

Swing

Swing is the part of the JFC that implements a new set of GUI components with a pluggable look and feel. Swing is implemented completely in Java code, and is based on the JDK 1.1 Lightweight UI Framework. The pluggable look and feel lets you design a single set of GUI components that can automatically have the look and feel of any OS platform. Swing components include both Java-language versions of the existing AWT component set (`Button`, `Scrollbar`, `Label`, etc.), plus a rich set of higher-level components (such as tree view, list box, and tabbed panes).

You can download the latest 1.1-compatible version of Swing from the Java web site.[1]

[1] For information on how to download the latest 1.1-compatible Swing release, see the Web page for this book: http://java.sun.com/docs/books/tutorial/2e/book.html

Java 2D

The Java 2D API is a set of classes for advanced 2D graphics and imaging. It encompasses line art, text, and images in a single comprehensive model. The API provides extensive support for image compositing and alpha channel images, a set of classes to provide accurate color space definition and conversion, and a rich set of display-oriented imaging operators.

Accessibility

Through the Java Accessibility API, developers can create Java applications that can interact with assistive technologies such as screen readers, speech recognition systems and Braille terminals. Accessibility-enabled Java applications are not dependent on machines that require assistive technology support, rather these applications run on any Java-enabled machine with or without assistive technologies.

Drag and Drop

Drag and Drop enables data transfer across Java and native applications, between Java applications, and within a single Java application.

Collections

The Java Collections API is a unified framework for representing and manipulating collections, allowing them to be manipulated independent of the details of their representation. It allows for interoperability among unrelated APIs, reduces the effort in designing and learning new APIs that would otherwise have their own collection interfaces, and fosters software reuse. The API includes interfaces, concrete implementations, abstract implementations, and a few polymorphic algorithms.

Enhancements to the JavaBeans Architecture

Glasgow is the codename for the next release of the JavaBeans component model specification. Glasgow provides developers with standard means to create more sophisticated Java components and applications that offer their customers more seamless integration with the rest of their runtime environment, such as the desk-

top of the underlying OS or the browser. To achieve this, Glasgow adds three new capabilities to the JavaBeans component model:

- An extensible runtime containment and services protocol
- A drag-and-drop subsystem for JFC
- The JavaBeans activation framework

Input Method Framework

The input method framework enables all text editing components to receive Japanese, Chinese, or Korean text input through input methods. An input method lets users enter thousands of different characters using keyboards with far fewer keys. Typically a sequence of several characters needs to be typed and then converted to create one or more characters. Components can actively use the API to support the on-the-spot input style; otherwise the framework provides root-window style input as a fallback.

Package Version Identification

Versioning introduces package level version control where applications and applets can identify at runtime the version of a specific Java Runtime Environment, VM, and class package.

RMI Enhancements

Remote Method Invocation (RMI) has several new enhancements. Remote Object Activation introduces support for persistent references to remote objects and automatic object activation via these references. Custom Socket Types allow a remote object to specify the custom socket type that RMI will use for remote calls to that object. RMI over a secure transport (such as SSL) can be supported using custom socket types. Minor API enhancements allow the following:

- Unexporting a remote object
- Obtaining the stub for an object implementation
- Obtaining a local object implementation from a stub
- Exporting an object on a specific port

Serialization Enhancements

Serialization now includes an API that allows the persistent data of an object to be specified independently of the fields of the class and allows those persistent data fields to be written to and read from the stream using the existing protocol to ensure compatibility with the default writing and reading mechanisms.

Weak References

Weak references allow a program to maintain a reference to an object that does not prevent the object from being considered for reclamation by the garbage collector. They also allow a program to be notified when the collector has determined that an object has become eligible for reclamation. Weak references are useful for building simple caches as well as caches that are flushed only when memory is low, for implementing mappings that do not prevent their keys (or values) from being reclaimed, and for scheduling post-mortem cleanup actions in a more flexible way than is possible with the Java finalization mechanism.

Audio Enhancements

Audio enhancements include a new sound engine and a new method.

Java Sound replaces the existing sound engine with a new sound engine that provides playback for MIDI files and the full range of `.wav`, `.aiff` and `.au` files. It also provides much higher sound quality. This introduces no new API in the `Applet` class.

The `Applet` class includes a new class method that allows applications to create `AudioClips` without requiring an `AppletContext`.

Java IDL

Java IDL adds CORBA (Common Object Request Broker Architecture) capability to Java, providing standards-based interoperability and connectivity. Java IDL enables distributed Web-enabled Java applications to transparently invoke operations on remote network services using the industry standard OMG IDL (Object Management Group Interface Definition Language) and IIOP (Internet Inter-ORB Protocol) defined by the Object Management Group. Runtime components include a fully-compliant Java ORB for distributed computing using IIOP communication. The `idltojava` compiler generates portable client stubs and server skeletons that work with any CORBA-compliant ORB implementation.

Performance Enhancements

Some of the performance enhancements expected in the next major release include the following:

Solaris Native Thread Support
: In a multi-processor environment, the Solaris kernel can schedule native threads on the parallel processors for increased performance. The native threads VM integrates better with native code than the default green threads VM. The VM can avoid some inefficient remapping of I/O system calls that are otherwise necessary.

Reduced Memory Usage for Loaded Classes
: Constant strings are shared among different classes, resulting in reduced memory consumption for Java applications.

Faster Memory Allocation and Garbage Collection
: The thread-local heap cache eliminates the need of locking for the majority of heap allocations. Memory allocation speed is drastically increased. Garbage collection pauses are shorter. The garbage collector no longer excessively consumes the C stack.

Monitor Speedups
: The thread-local monitor cache enables synchronized methods to run closer to the speed of normal methods.

Native Library JNI Port
: Native libraries supporting core Java classes (such as the AWT) have been rewritten using the Java Native Interface (JNI). The resulting code is more efficient and can run unmodified on different Java Virtual Machines.

Just In Time (JIT) Compilers
: JIT compilers are being included with the JDK.

Thread Changes

The `Thread` `stop`, `suspend`, and `resume` methods are deprecated in the next major release of the JDK.

The Thread stop Method is Deprecated

The `stop` method is being deprecated because it is inherently unsafe. Stopping a thread causes it to unlock all the monitors that it has locked. (The monitors are unlocked as the `ThreadDeath` exception propagates up the stack.) If any of the objects previously protected by these monitors were in an inconsistent state, other threads may now view these objects in an inconsistent state. Such objects are said to be *damaged*. When threads operate on damaged objects, arbitrary behavior can result. This behavior may be subtle and difficult to detect, or it may be pronounced. Unlike other unchecked exceptions, `ThreadDeath` kills threads silently; thus, the user has no warning that the program may be corrupted. The corruption can manifest itself at any time after the actual damage occurs, even hours or days in the future.

This tutorial has always recommended against using the `Thread stop` method. So, hopefully, this change will not affect your programs.

If, however, you've been using the `Thread stop` method in your programs, you should provide for a gentler termination of those threads. Most uses of `stop` can and should be replaced by code that simply modifies some variable to indicate that the target thread should stop running. The target thread should check this variable regularly, and return from its `run` method in an orderly fashion if the variable indicates that it is to stop running.

For example, suppose your applet contains the following `start`, `stop`, and `run` methods:

```
public void start() {
    blinker = new Thread(this);
    blinker.start();
}
public void stop() {
    blinker.stop();  // UNSAFE!
}
public void run() {
    Thread thisThread = Thread.currentThread();
    while (true) {
        try {
            Thread.sleep(interval);
        } catch (InterruptedException e){
        }
        repaint();
    }
}
```

You can avoid the use of the Thread stop method by replacing the applet's stop and run methods with:

```
public void stop() {
    blinker = null;
}
public void run() {
    Thread thisThread = Thread.currentThread();
    while (blinker == thisThread) {
        try {
            Thread.sleep(interval);
        } catch (InterruptedException e){
        }
        repaint();
    }
}
```

The Thread suspend and resume Methods Are Deprecated

The Thread suspend method is inherently deadlock-prone so it is also being deprecated, thereby necessitating the deprecation of the Thread resume method. If the target thread holds a lock on the monitor protecting a critical system resource when it is suspended, no thread can access this resource until the target thread is resumed. If the thread that would resume the target thread attempts to lock this monitor prior to calling resume, deadlock results. Such deadlocks typically manifest themselves as "frozen" processes.

As with the Thread stop method, the prudent approach is to have the "target thread" poll a variable that indicates the desired state of the thread (active or suspended). When the desired state is suspended, the thread waits using the Object wait method. When the thread is resumed, the target thread is notified using Object notify method.

For example, suppose your applet contains the following mousePressed event handler, which toggles the state of a thread called blinker:

```
Public void mousePressed(MouseEvent e) {
    e.consume();
    if (threadSuspended)
        blinker.resume();
    else
        blinker.suspend();  // DEADLOCK-PRONE!
    threadSuspended = !threadSuspended;
}
```

You can avoid the use of Thread's suspend and resume methods by replacing the event handler above with:

```
public synchronized void mousePressed(MouseEvent e) {
    e.consume();
    threadSuspended = !threadSuspended;
    if (!threadSuspended)
        notify();
}
```

and adding the following code to the "run loop":

```
synchronized(this) {
    while (threadSuspended)
        wait();
}
```

The wait method throws the InterruptedException, so it must be inside a try ... catch clause. It's fine to put it in the same clause as the sleep. The check should follow (rather than precede) the sleep so the window is immediately repainted when the thread is "resumed." The resulting run method follows:

```
public void run() {
    while (true) {
        try {
            Thread.sleep(interval);
            synchronized(this) {
                while (threadSuspended)
                    wait();
            }
        } catch (InterruptedException e){
        }
        repaint();
    }
}
```

Note that the notify in the mousePressed method and the wait in the run method are inside synchronized blocks. This is required by the language, and ensures that wait and notify are properly serialized. In practical terms, this eliminates race conditions that could cause the "suspended" thread to miss a notify and remain suspended.

Note: Don't wait for the next major release of the JDK. These are changes that you can make to improve your programs NOW!

End of Trail

YOU'VE reached the end of the **To 1.1—And Beyond!** trail. Take a break—have a cup of steaming hot java.

What Next?

Well, you made it through this book! If you still have some energy, why not head to our online tutorial and see what's new:

```
http://java.sun.com/docs/books/tutorial/2e/index.html
```

Appendixes

APPENDIX A

Code Examples

THIS appendix lists every complete Java example program featured in this tutorial. It also includes a few HTML and data files that you might need to copy. Here's a typical example:

EXAMPLE: The Character-Counting Application

Where Explained: *The Nuts and Bolts of the Java Language* (page 49)

Count.java

SOURCE CODE: *http://java.sun.com/docs/books/tutorial/java/nutsandbolts/example-1dot1/Count.java*

1.0 SOURCE CODE: *http://java.sun.com/docs/books/tutorial/java/nutsandbolts/example/Count.java*

```
import java.io.*;
public class Count {
    public static void countChars(Reader in) throws IOException
    {
        int count = 0;

        while (in.read() != -1)
            count++;
        System.out.println("Counted " + count + " chars.");
    }
    public static void main(String[] args) throws Exception
    {
        if (args.length >=1)
            countChars(new FileReader(args[0]));
        else
            System.err.println("Usage: Count filename");
    }
}
```

Each example lists the section(s) in which it is explained, the names of the source files that comprise the example, and the location of each source file on our Web site.

Most applets have an additional field that lists the HTML pages on which you can find the applet running. Here's a typical example of this field:

HTML PAGES CONTAINING APPLET: *http://java.sun.com/docs/books/tutorial/applet/overview/lifeCycle.html*

Getting Started

LESSON 2: The "Hello World" Application

EXAMPLE: The "Hello World" Application

Where Explained:
The Anatomy of a Java Application (page 11)

HelloWorldApp.java

SOURCE CODE: *http://java.sun.com/docs/books/tutorial/getStarted/application/example/HelloWorldApp.java*

```
/**
 * The HelloWorldApp class implements an application that
 * simply displays "Hello World!" to the standard output.
 */
class HelloWorldApp {
    public static void main(String[] args) {
        System.out.println("Hello World!"); //Display the string.
    }
}
```

LESSON 3: The "Hello World" Applet

EXAMPLE: The "Hello World" Applet

Where Explained:
The Anatomy of a Java Applet (page 22)

HelloWorld.java

SOURCE CODE: *http://java.sun.com/docs/books/tutorial/getStarted/applet/example/HelloWorld.java*

```
import java.applet.Applet;
import java.awt.Graphics;

public class HelloWorld extends Applet {
    public void paint(Graphics g) {
        g.drawString("Hello world!", 50, 25);
    }
}
```

Hello.html

SOURCE CODE: *http://java.sun.com/docs/books/tutorial/getStarted/applet/example/Hello.html*

```
<HTML>
<HEAD>
<TITLE> A Simple Program </TITLE>
</HEAD>
<BODY>

Here is the output of my program:
<APPLET CODE="HelloWorld.class" WIDTH=150 HEIGHT=25>
</APPLET>
</BODY>
</HTML>
```

Learning the Java Language

LESSON 5: The Nuts and Bolts of the Java Language

EXAMPLE: The Character-Counting Application

Where Explained: *The Nuts and Bolts of the Java Language* (page 49)

Count.java

SOURCE CODE: *http://java.sun.com/docs/books/tutorial/java/nutsandbolts/example-1dot1/Count.java*

1.0 SOURCE CODE: *http://java.sun.com/docs/books/tutorial/java/nutsandbolts/example/Count.java*

```
import java.io.*;
public class Count {
    public static void countChars(Reader in) throws IOException
    {
        int count = 0;

        while (in.read() != -1)
            count++;
        System.out.println("Counted " + count + " chars.");
    }
    public static void main(String[] args) throws Exception
    {
        if (args.length >=1)
            countChars(new FileReader(args[0]));
        else
            System.err.println("Usage: Count filename");
    }
}
```

testing

SOURCE CODE: *http://java.sun.com/docs/books/tutorial/java/nutsandbolts/example-1dot1/testing*

1.0 SOURCE CODE: *http://java.sun.com/docs/books/tutorial/java/nutsandbolts/example/testing*

```
Ich bin ein Berliner.
I am a jelly doughnut.
```

LESSON 6: Objects and Classes in Java

EXAMPLE: Point and Rectangle Classes

Where Explained:
A Brief Introduction to Classes (page 82)

SimplePoint.java

SOURCE CODE: *http://java.sun.com/docs/books/tutorial/java/javaOO/example/SimplePoint.java*

```
public class SimplePoint {
    public int x = 0;
    public int y = 0;
}
```

SimpleRectangle.java

SOURCE CODE: *http://java.sun.com/docs/books/tutorial/java/javaOO/example/SimpleRectangle.java*

```
public class SimpleRectangle {
    public int width = 0;
    public int height = 0;
    public SimplePoint origin = new SimplePoint();
}
```

Point.java

SOURCE CODE: *http://java.sun.com/docs/books/tutorial/java/javaOO/example/Point.java*

```
public class Point {
    public int x = 0;
    public int y = 0;
    public Point(int x, int y) {
        this.x = x;
        this.y = y;
    }
}
```

Rectangle.java

SOURCE CODE: *http://java.sun.com/docs/books/tutorial/java/javaOO/example/Rectangle.java*

```
public class Rectangle {
    public int width = 0;
    public int height = 0;
    public Point origin;
```

```
        // four constructors
        public Rectangle() {
            origin = new Point(0, 0);
        }
        public Rectangle(Point p) {
            origin = p;
        }
        public Rectangle(int w, int h) {
            this(new Point(0, 0), w, h);
        }
        public Rectangle(Point p, int w, int h) {
            origin = p;
            width = w;
            height = h;
        }
        // a method for moving the rectangle
        public void move(int x, int y) {
            origin.x = x;
            origin.y = y;
        }
        // a method for computing the area of the rectangle
        public int area {
            return width * height;
        }
        // clean up!
        protected void finalize() throws Throwable {
            origin = null;
            super.finalize();
        }
    }
```

EXAMPLE: A Stack Class

Where Explained: *Creating Classes* (page 93)

Stack.java

SOURCE CODE: *http://java.sun.com/docs/books/tutorial/java/javaOO/example/Stack.java*

```
    public class Stack
    {
        private Vector items;
        public Stack() {
            items = new Vector(10);
        }
        public Object push(Object item) {
            items.addElement(item);
            return item;
        }
        public synchronized Object pop() {
```

```
        int len = items.size();
        Object obj = null;
        if (len == 0)
            throw new EmptyStackException();
        obj = items.elementAt(len - 1);
        items.removeElementAt(len - 1);
        return obj;
    }
    public boolean isEmpty() {
        if (items.size() == 0)
            return true;
        else
            return false;
    }
    protected void finalize() throws Throwable {
        items = null;
        super.finalize();
    }
}
```

EXAMPLE: The Spot Applet

Where Explained:
Reality Break! The Spot Applet (page 125)

HTML PAGES CONTAINING APPLET: *http://java.sun.com/docs/books/tutorial/java/javaOO/spot.html*

Spot.java

SOURCE CODE: *http://java.sun.com/docs/books/tutorial/java/javaOO/example-1dot1/Spot.java*

1.0 SOURCE CODE: *http://java.sun.com/docs/books/tutorial/java/javaOO/example/Spot.java*

```
import java.applet.Applet;
import java.awt.*;
import java.awt.event.*;

public class Spot extends Applet implements MouseListener {
    private Point clickPoint = null;
    private static final int RADIUS = 7;

    public void init() {
        addMouseListener(this);
    }
    public void paint(Graphics g) {
        g.drawRect(0, 0,
                   getSize().width - 1,
                   getSize().height - 1);
        if (clickPoint != null)
            g.fillOval(clickPoint.x - RADIUS,
```

```
                        clickPoint.y - RADIUS,
                        RADIUS * 2, RADIUS * 2);
        }
        public void mousePressed(MouseEvent event) {
            clickPoint = event.getPoint();
            repaint();
        }
        public void mouseClicked(MouseEvent event) {}
        public void mouseReleased(MouseEvent event) {}
        public void mouseEntered(MouseEvent event) {}
        public void mouseExited(MouseEvent event) {}
    }
```

HTML PAGES CONTAINING APPLET: *http://java.sun.com/docs/books/tutorial/java/javaOO/innerClassAdapter.html*

AdapterSpot.java

SOURCE CODE: *http://java.sun.com/docs/books/tutorial/java/javaOO/example-1dot1/AdapterSpot.java*

```
import java.applet.Applet;
import java.awt.*;
import java.awt.event.*;

public class AdapterSpot extends Applet // no implements clause
{
    private Point clickPoint = null;
    private static final int RADIUS = 7;

    public void init() {
        addMouseListener(new MyMouseAdapter());
    }
    public void paint(Graphics g) {
        g.drawRect(0, 0,
                   getSize().width - 1,
                   getSize().height - 1);
        if (clickPoint != null)
            g.fillOval(clickPoint.x-RADIUS,
                       clickPoint.y-RADIUS,
                       RADIUS*2, RADIUS*2);
    }
    class MyMouseAdapter extends MouseAdapter {
        public void mousePressed(MouseEvent event) {
            clickPoint = event.getPoint();
            repaint();
```

```
        }
    }
    /* no empty methods! */
}
```

HTML PAGES CONTAINING APPLET: *http://java.sun.com/docs/books/tutorial/java/javaOO/innerClassAdapter.html*

AnonymousSpot.java

SOURCE CODE: *http://java.sun.com/docs/books/tutorial/java/javaOO/example-1dot1/AnonymousSpot.java*

```
import java.applet.Applet;
import java.awt.*;
import java.awt.event.*;

public class AnonymousSpot extends Applet {
    private Point clickPoint = null;
    private static final int RADIUS = 7;
    public void init() {
        addMouseListener(new MouseAdapter() {
            public void mousePressed(MouseEvent event) {
                clickPoint = event.getPoint();
                repaint();
            }
        } );
    }
    public void paint(Graphics g) {
        g.drawRect(0, 0,
                   getSize().width - 1,
                   getSize().height - 1);
        if (clickPoint != null)
            g.fillOval(clickPoint.x-RADIUS,
                       clickPoint.y-RADIUS,
                       RADIUS*2, RADIUS*2);
    }
}
```

LESSON 7: More Features of the Java Language

EXAMPLE: The AlarmClock Class and the Sleeper Interface

Where Explained:
Creating Interfaces (page 145)

AlarmClock.java

SOURCE CODE: *http://java.sun.com/docs/books/tutorial/java/more/example-1dot1/AlarmClock.java*

1.0 SOURCE CODE: *http://java.sun.com/docs/books/tutorial/java/more/example/AlarmClock.java*

1.0 SOURCE CODE: *http://java.sun.com/docs/books/tutorial/java/more/example/AlarmThread.java*

```
public class AlarmClock {

    private static final int MAX_CAPACITY = 10;
    private static final int UNUSED = -1;
    private static final int NOROOM = -1;

    private Sleeper[] sleepers = new Sleeper[MAX_CAPACITY];
    private long[] sleepFor = new long[MAX_CAPACITY];

    public AlarmClock () {
        for (int i = 0; i < MAX_CAPACITY; i++)
            sleepFor[i] = UNUSED;
    }

    public synchronized boolean letMeSleepFor(Sleeper s,
                                              long time) {
        int index = findNextSlot();
        if (index == NOROOM) {
            return false;
        } else {
            sleepers[index] = s;
            sleepFor[index] = time;
            new AlarmThread(index).start();
            return true;
        }
    }

    private synchronized int findNextSlot() {
        for (int i = 0; i < MAX_CAPACITY; i++) {
            if (sleepFor[i] == UNUSED)
                return i;
        }
        return NOROOM;
    }
```

```
    private synchronized void wakeUpSleeper(int sleeperIndex) {
        sleepers[sleeperIndex].wakeUp();
        sleepers[sleeperIndex] = null;
        sleepFor[sleeperIndex] = UNUSED;
    }

    private class AlarmThread extends Thread {
        int mySleeper;
        AlarmThread(int sleeperIndex) {
            super();
            mySleeper = sleeperIndex;
        }
        public void run() {
            try {
                sleep(sleepFor[mySleeper]);
            } catch (InterruptedException e) {}
            wakeUpSleeper(mySleeper);
        }
    }
}
```

Sleeper.java

SOURCE CODE: *http://java.sun.com/docs/books/tutorial/java/more/example-1dot1/Sleeper.java*

1.0 SOURCE CODE: *http://java.sun.com/docs/books/tutorial/java/more/example/Sleeper.java*

```
public interface Sleeper {
    public void wakeUp();
    public long ONE_SECOND = 1000;
    public long ONE_MINUTE = 60000;
}
```

HTML PAGES CONTAINING APPLET: *http://java.sun.com/docs/books/tutorial/java/more/implementing.html*

GUIClock.java

SOURCE CODE: *http://java.sun.com/docs/books/tutorial/java/more/example-1dot1/GUIClock.java*

1.0 SOURCE CODE: *http://java.sun.com/docs/books/tutorial/java/more/example/GUIClock.java*

```
import java.applet.Applet;
import java.awt.Graphics;
import java.util.*;
import java.text.DateFormat;
public class GUIClock extends Applet implements Sleeper {

    private AlarmClock clock;

    public void init() {
        clock = new AlarmClock();
    }
    public void start() {
        clock.letMeSleepFor(this, ONE_MINUTE);
    }
    public void paint(Graphics g) {
        Calendar cal = Calendar.getInstance();
        Date date = cal.getTime();
       DateFormat dateFormatter = DateFormat.getTimeInstance();
        g.drawString(dateFormatter.format(date), 5, 10);
    }
    public void wakeUp() {
        repaint();
        clock.letMeSleepFor(this, ONE_MINUTE);
    }
}
```

Writing Applets

LESSON 8: Overview of Applets

EXAMPLE: The Simple Applet

Where Explained: *Overview of Applets* (page 175); *The Life Cycle of an Applet* (page 177)

HTML PAGES CONTAINING APPLET: *http://java.sun.com/docs/books/tutorial/applet/overview/lifeCycle.html*

Simple.java

SOURCE CODE: *http://java.sun.com/docs/books/tutorial/applet/overview/example-1dot1/Simple.java*

1.0 SOURCE CODE: *http://java.sun.com/docs/books/tutorial/applet/overview/example/Simple.java*

```
import java.applet.Applet;
import java.awt.Graphics;

public class Simple extends Applet {

    StringBuffer buffer;

    public void init() {
        buffer = new StringBuffer();
        addItem("initializing... ");
    }

    public void start() {
        addItem("starting... ");
    }

    public void stop() {
        addItem("stopping... ");
    }

    public void destroy() {
        addItem("preparing for unloading...");
    }

    void addItem(String newWord) {
        System.out.println(newWord);
```

```
        buffer.append(newWord);
        repaint();
    }

    public void paint(Graphics g) {
        //Draw a Rectangle around the applet's display area.
        g.drawRect(0, 0,
                   getSize().width - 1,
                   getSize().height - 1);

        //Draw the current string inside the rectangle.
        g.drawString(buffer.toString(), 5, 15);
    }
}
```

EXAMPLE: The Simple Applet with Event Handling

Where Explained: *Methods for Drawing and Event Handling* (page 181)

HTML PAGES CONTAINING APPLET: *http://java.sun.com/docs/books/tutorial/applet/overview/componentMethods.html*

SimpleClick.java

SOURCE CODE: *http://java.sun.com/docs/books/tutorial/applet/overview/example-1dot1/SimpleClick.java*

1.0 SOURCE CODE: *http://java.sun.com/docs/books/tutorial/applet/overview/example/SimpleClick.java*

```
import java.applet.Applet;
import java.awt.Graphics;

import java.awt.event.MouseListener;
import java.awt.event.MouseEvent;

public class SimpleClick extends Applet
                         implements MouseListener {

    StringBuffer buffer;

    public void init() {
        buffer = new StringBuffer();
        addItem("initializing... ");
        addMouseListener(this);
    }

    public void start() {
        addItem("starting... ");
    }

    public void stop() {
```

```
            addItem("stopping... ");
        }

        public void destroy() {
            addItem("preparing for unloading...");
        }

        void addItem(String newWord) {
            System.out.println(newWord);
            buffer.append(newWord);
            repaint();
        }

        public void paint(Graphics g) {
            //Draw a Rectangle around the applet's display area.
            g.drawRect(0, 0,
                       getSize().width - 1,
                       getSize().height - 1);

            //Draw the current string inside the rectangle.
            g.drawString(buffer.toString(), 5, 15);
        }

        //The following empty methods can be removed
        //by implementing a MouseAdapter (usually done
        //using an inner class).
        public void mouseEntered(MouseEvent event) {
        }
        public void mouseExited(MouseEvent event) {
        }
        public void mousePressed(MouseEvent event) {
        }
        public void mouseReleased(MouseEvent event) {
        }

        public void mouseClicked(MouseEvent event) {
            addItem("click!... ");
        }
    }
```

EXAMPLE: The Simple Applet with a Text Field

HTML PAGES CONTAINING APPLET: *http://java.sun.com/docs/books/tutorial/applet/overview/containerMethods.html*

Where Explained:
Methods for Adding UI Components (page 183)

ScrollingSimple.java

SOURCE CODE: *http://java.sun.com/docs/books/tutorial/applet/overview/example/ScrollingSimple.java*

```
import java.applet.Applet;
import java.awt.TextField;

public class ScrollingSimple extends Applet {

    TextField field;

    public void init() {
        //Create the text field and make it uneditable.
        field = new TextField();
        field.setEditable(false);

        //Set the layout manager so that the text field will
        //be as wide as possible.
        setLayout(new java.awt.GridLayout(1,0));

        //Add the text field to the applet.
        add(field);

        addItem("initializing... ");
    }

    public void start() {
        addItem("starting... ");
    }

    public void stop() {
        addItem("stopping... ");
    }

    public void destroy() {
        addItem("preparing for unloading...");
    }

    void addItem(String newWord) {
        String t = field.getText();
        System.out.println(newWord);
        field.setText(t + newWord);
    }
}
```

LESSON 9: Taking Advantage of the Applet API

EXAMPLE: Telling the Browser to Show a Document

Where Explained:
Displaying Documents in the Browser (page 192)

HTML PAGES CONTAINING APPLET: *http://java.sun.com/docs/books/tutorial/applet/appletsonly/browser.html*

ShowDocument.java

SOURCE CODE: *http://java.sun.com/docs/books/tutorial/applet/appletsonly/example-1dot1/ShowDocument.java*

1.0 SOURCE CODE: *http://java.sun.com/docs/books/tutorial/applet/appletsonly/example/ShowDocument.java*

```
import java.applet.*;
import java.awt.*;
import java.awt.event.*;
import java.net.URL;
import java.net.MalformedURLException;

public class ShowDocument extends Applet
                             implements ActionListener {
    URLWindow urlWindow;

    public void init() {
        Button button = new Button("Bring up URL window");
        button.addActionListener(this);
        add(button);

        urlWindow = new URLWindow(getAppletContext());
        urlWindow.pack();
    }

    public void destroy() {
        urlWindow.setVisible(false);
        urlWindow = null;
    }

    public void actionPerformed(ActionEvent event) {
        urlWindow.setVisible(true);
    }
}

class URLWindow extends Frame
                implements ActionListener {
    TextField urlField;
    Choice choice;
    AppletContext appletContext;
```

```
public URLWindow(AppletContext appletContext) {
    super("Show a Document!");

    this.appletContext = appletContext;

    GridBagLayout gridBag = new GridBagLayout();
    GridBagConstraints c = new GridBagConstraints();
    setLayout(gridBag);

    Label label1 = new Label("URL of document to show:",
                             Label.RIGHT);
    gridBag.setConstraints(label1, c);
    add(label1);

    urlField = new TextField("http://java.sun.com/", 40);
    urlField.addActionListener(this);
    c.gridwidth = GridBagConstraints.REMAINDER;
    c.fill = GridBagConstraints.HORIZONTAL;
    c.weightx = 1.0;
    gridBag.setConstraints(urlField, c);
    add(urlField);

    Label label2 = new Label("Window/frame to show it in:",
                             Label.RIGHT);
    c.gridwidth = 1;
    c.weightx = 0.0;
    gridBag.setConstraints(label2, c);
    add(label2);

    choice = new Choice();
    choice.addItem("(browser's choice)"); //don't specify
    choice.addItem("My Personal Window"); //a window named
                                      //"My Personal Window"
    choice.addItem("_blank"); //a new, unnamed window
    choice.addItem("_self");
    choice.addItem("_parent");
    choice.addItem("_top"); //the Frame that contained this
                            //applet
    c.fill = GridBagConstraints.NONE;
    c.gridwidth = GridBagConstraints.REMAINDER;
    c.anchor = GridBagConstraints.WEST;
    gridBag.setConstraints(choice, c);
    add(choice);

    Button button = new Button("Show document");
    button.addActionListener(this);
    c.weighty = 1.0;
```

```
            c.ipadx = 10;
            c.ipady = 10;
            c.insets = new Insets(5,0,0,0);
            c.anchor = GridBagConstraints.SOUTH;
            gridBag.setConstraints(button, c);
            add(button);

            addWindowListener(new WindowAdapter() {
                public void windowClosing(WindowEvent event) {
                    setVisible(false);
                }
            });
        }

        public void actionPerformed(ActionEvent event) {
            String urlString = urlField.getText();
            URL url = null;
            try {
                url = new URL(urlString);
            } catch (MalformedURLException e) {
                System.err.println("Malformed URL: " + urlString);
            }

            if (url != null) {
                if (choice.getSelectedIndex() == 0) {
                    appletContext.showDocument(url);
                } else {
                    appletContext.showDocument(url,
                                       choice.getSelectedItem());
                }
            }
        }
    }
```

EXAMPLE: Communication Between Two Applets

HTML PAGES CONTAINING APPLET: *http://java.sun.com/docs/books/tutorial/applet/appletsonly/iac.html*

Where Explained:
Sending Messages to Other Applets (page 194)

Sender.java

SOURCE CODE: *http://java.sun.com/docs/books/tutorial/applet/appletsonly/example-1dot1/Sender.java*

1.0 SOURCE CODE: *http://java.sun.com/docs/books/tutorial/applet/appletsonly/example/Sender.java*

```
import java.applet.*;
import java.awt.*;
import java.awt.event.*;
import java.util.Enumeration;

public class Sender extends Applet
                    implements ActionListener {
    private String myName;
    private TextField nameField;
    private TextArea status;
    private String newline;

    public void init() {
        GridBagLayout gridBag = new GridBagLayout();
        GridBagConstraints c = new GridBagConstraints();

        setLayout(gridBag);

        Label receiverLabel = new Label("Receiver name:",
                                        Label.RIGHT);
        gridBag.setConstraints(receiverLabel, c);
        add(receiverLabel);

        nameField = new TextField(getParameter("RECEIVERNAME"),
                                              10);
        c.fill = GridBagConstraints.HORIZONTAL;
        gridBag.setConstraints(nameField, c);
        add(nameField);
        nameField.addActionListener(this);

        Button button = new Button("Send message");
        c.gridwidth = GridBagConstraints.REMAINDER; //end row
        c.anchor = GridBagConstraints.WEST; //stick to the
                                            //text field
        c.fill = GridBagConstraints.NONE; //keep the button
                                          //small
        gridBag.setConstraints(button, c);
```

```
        add(button);
        button.addActionListener(this);

        status = new TextArea(5, 60);
        status.setEditable(false);
        c.anchor = GridBagConstraints.CENTER; //reset to default
        c.fill = GridBagConstraints.BOTH; //make this big
        c.weightx = 1.0;
        c.weighty = 1.0;
        gridBag.setConstraints(status, c);
        add(status);

        myName = getParameter("NAME");
        Label senderLabel = new Label("(My name is " + myName
                                      + ".)",
                                      Label.CENTER);
        c.weightx = 0.0;
        c.weighty = 0.0;
        gridBag.setConstraints(senderLabel, c);
        add(senderLabel);

        newline = System.getProperty("line.separator");
    }

    public void actionPerformed(ActionEvent event) {
        Applet receiver = null;
        String receiverName = nameField.getText(); //Get name to
                                                   //search for.
        receiver = getAppletContext().getApplet(receiverName);
        if (receiver != null) {
            //Use the instanceof operator to make sure the
            //applet we found is a Receiver object.
            if (!(receiver instanceof Receiver)) {
                status.append("Found applet named "
                              + receiverName + ", "
                              + "but it's not a Receiver "
                              + "object." + newline);
            } else {
                status.append("Found applet named "
                              + receiverName + newline
                              + "  Sending message to it."
                              + newline);
                //Cast the receiver to be a Receiver object
                //(instead of just an Applet object) so that the
                //compiler will let us call a Receiver method.
                ((Receiver)receiver).processRequestFrom(myName);
```

```
            }
        } else {
            status.append("Couldn't find any applet named "
                          + receiverName + "." + newline);
        }
    }

    public Insets getInsets() {
        return new Insets(3,3,3,3);
    }

    public void paint(Graphics g) {
        g.drawRect(0, 0,
                   getSize().width - 1, getSize().height - 1);
    }

    public String getAppletInfo() {
        return "Sender by Kathy Walrath";
    }
}
```

Receiver.java

SOURCE CODE: *http://java.sun.com/docs/books/tutorial/applet/appletsonly/example-1dot1/Receiver.java*

1.0 SOURCE CODE: *http://java.sun.com/docs/books/tutorial/applet/appletsonly/example/Receiver.java*

```
import java.applet.*;
import java.awt.*;
import java.awt.event.*;

public class Receiver extends Applet
                      implements ActionListener {
    private final String waitingMessage =
            "Waiting for a message...           ";
    private Label label = new Label(waitingMessage,
                                    Label.RIGHT);

    public void init() {
        Button button = new Button("Clear");
        add(label);
        add(button);
        button.addActionListener(this);
        add(new Label("(My name is " + getParameter("name")
                      + ".)",
                      Label.LEFT));
    }

    public void actionPerformed(ActionEvent event) {
        label.setText(waitingMessage);
```

```
    }

    public void processRequestFrom(String senderName) {
        label.setText("Received message from "
                              + senderName + "!");
    }

    public void paint(Graphics g) {
        g.drawRect(0, 0,
                   getSize().width - 1, getSize().height - 1);
    }

    public String getAppletInfo() {
        return "Receiver (named " + getParameter("name") +
               ") by Kathy Walrath";
    }
}
```

EXAMPLE: Finding All of the Applets on a Page

Where Explained: *Finding All of the Applets on a Page: the getApplets Method* (page 197)

HTML PAGES CONTAINING APPLET: *http://java.sun.com/docs/books/tutorial/applet/appletsonly/iac.html*

GetApplets.java

SOURCE CODE: *http://java.sun.com/docs/books/tutorial/applet/appletsonly/example-1dot1/GetApplets.java*

1.0 SOURCE CODE: *http://java.sun.com/docs/books/tutorial/applet/appletsonly/example/GetApplets.java*

```
import java.applet.*;
import java.awt.*;
import java.awt.event.*;
import java.util.Enumeration;

public class GetApplets extends Applet
                        implements ActionListener {
    private TextArea textArea;
    private String newline;

    public void init() {
        Button b = new Button("Click to call getApplets()");
        b.addActionListener(this);

        setLayout(new BorderLayout());
        add("North", b);

        textArea = new TextArea(5, 40);
        textArea.setEditable(false);
```

```
        add("Center", textArea);

        newline = System.getProperty("line.separator");
    }

    public void actionPerformed(ActionEvent event) {
        printApplets();
    }

    public String getAppletInfo() {
        return "GetApplets by Kathy Walrath";
    }

    public void printApplets() {
        //Enumeration will contain all applets on this page
        //(including this one) that we can send messages to.
        Enumeration e = getAppletContext().getApplets();

        textArea.append("Results of getApplets():" + newline);

        while (e.hasMoreElements()) {
            Applet applet = (Applet)e.nextElement();
            String info = ((Applet)applet).getAppletInfo();
            if (info != null) {
                textArea.append("- " + info + newline);
            } else {
                textArea.append("- "
                               + applet.getClass().getName()
                               + newline);
            }
        }
        textArea.append("________________________"
                        + newline + newline);
    }
}
```

EXAMPLE: A Framework for Playing Sounds in Applets

Where Explained:
Playing Sounds (page 198); *Threads in Applets* (page 219)

HTML PAGES CONTAINING APPLET: *http://java.sun.com/docs/books/tutorial/applet/appletsonly/sound.html*

SoundExample.java

SOURCE CODE: *http://java.sun.com/docs/books/tutorial/applet/appletsonly/example-1dot1/SoundExample.java*

1.0 SOURCE CODE: *http://java.sun.com/docs/books/tutorial/applet/appletsonly/example/SoundExample.java*

```
import java.applet.*;
import java.awt.*;
import java.awt.event.ActionListener;
import java.awt.event.ActionEvent;

public class SoundExample extends Applet
                             implements ActionListener {
    SoundList soundList;
    String onceFile = "bark.au";
    String loopFile = "train.au";
    AudioClip onceClip;
    AudioClip loopClip;

    Button playOnce;
    Button startLoop;
    Button stopLoop;
    Button reload;

    boolean looping = false;

    public void init() {
        playOnce = new Button("Bark!");
        playOnce.addActionListener(this);
        add(playOnce);

        startLoop = new Button("Start sound loop");
        stopLoop = new Button("Stop sound loop");
        stopLoop.setEnabled(false);
        startLoop.addActionListener(this);
        add(startLoop);
        stopLoop.addActionListener(this);
        add(stopLoop);

        reload = new Button("Reload sounds");
        reload.addActionListener(this);
        add(reload);
```

```
        startLoadingSounds();
    }

    void startLoadingSounds() {
        //Start asynchronous sound loading.
        soundList = new SoundList(this, getCodeBase());
        soundList.startLoading(loopFile);
        soundList.startLoading(onceFile);
   }

    public void stop() {
        onceClip.stop();         //Cut short the one-time sound.
        if (looping) {
            loopClip.stop();    //Stop the sound loop.
        }
    }

    public void start() {
        if (looping) {
            loopClip.loop();    //Restart the sound loop.
        }
    }

    public void actionPerformed(ActionEvent event) {
        //PLAY BUTTON
        Object source = event.getSource();
        if (source == playOnce) {
            if (onceClip == null) {
                //Try to get the AudioClip.
                onceClip = soundList.getClip(onceFile);
            }

            if (onceClip != null) {  //If the sound is loaded:
                onceClip.play();     //Play it once.
                showStatus("Playing sound " + onceFile + ".");
            } else {
                showStatus("Sound " + onceFile
                           + " not loaded yet.");
            }
            return;
        }

        //START LOOP BUTTON
        if (source == startLoop) {
            if (loopClip == null) {
                //Try to get the AudioClip.
                loopClip = soundList.getClip(loopFile);
            }
```

```
            if (loopClip != null) {  //If the sound is loaded:
                looping = true;
                loopClip.loop();     //Start the sound loop.
              stopLoop.setEnabled(true);  //Enable stop button.
              startLoop.setEnabled(false); //Disable start btn.
                showStatus("Playing sound " + loopFile
                           + " continuously.");
            } else {
                showStatus("Sound " + loopFile
                           + " not loaded yet.");
            }
            return;
        }

        //STOP LOOP BUTTON
        if (source == stopLoop) {
            if (looping) {
                looping = false;
                loopClip.stop();    //Stop the sound loop.
            startLoop.setEnabled(true); //Enable start button.
            stopLoop.setEnabled(false); //Disable stop button.
            }
          showStatus("Stopped playing sound " + loopFile + ".");
            return;
        }

        //RELOAD BUTTON
        if (source == reload) {
            if (looping) {              //Stop the sound loop.
                looping = false;
                loopClip.stop();
            startLoop.setEnabled(true); //Enable start button.
            stopLoop.setEnabled(false); //Disable stop button.
            }
            loopClip = null;            //Reset AudioClip to null.
            onceClip = null;            //Reset AudioClip to null.
            startLoadingSounds();
            showStatus("Reloading all sounds.");
            return;
        }
    }
}
```

SoundList.java

SOURCE CODE: *http://java.sun.com/docs/books/tutorial/applet/appletsonly/example-1dot1/SoundList.java*

1.0 SOURCE CODE: *http://java.sun.com/docs/books/tutorial/applet/appletsonly/example/SoundList.java*

```
import java.applet.*;
import java.net.URL;

//Loads and holds a bunch of audio files whose locations are
//specified relative to a fixed base URL.
class SoundList extends java.util.Hashtable {
    Applet applet;
    URL baseURL;

    public SoundList(Applet applet, URL baseURL) {
        super(5); //Initialize Hashtable with capacity of 5.
        this.applet = applet;
        this.baseURL = baseURL;
    }

    public void startLoading(String relativeURL) {
        new SoundLoader(applet, this,
                        baseURL, relativeURL);
    }

    public AudioClip getClip(String relativeURL) {
        return (AudioClip)get(relativeURL);
    }

    public void putClip(AudioClip clip, String relativeURL) {
        put(relativeURL, clip);
    }
}
```

SoundLoader.java

SOURCE CODE: *http://java.sun.com/docs/books/tutorial/applet/appletsonly/example-1dot1/SoundLoader.java*

1.0 SOURCE CODE: *http://java.sun.com/docs/books/tutorial/applet/appletsonly/example/SoundLoader.java*

```
import java.applet.*;
import java.net.URL;

class SoundLoader extends Thread {
```

```
    Applet applet;
    SoundList soundList;
    URL baseURL;
    String relativeURL;

    public SoundLoader(Applet applet, SoundList soundList,
                       URL baseURL, String relativeURL) {
        this.applet = applet;
        this.soundList = soundList;
        this.baseURL = baseURL;
        this.relativeURL = relativeURL;
        setPriority(MIN_PRIORITY);
        start();
    }

    public void run() {
        AudioClip audioClip = applet.getAudioClip(baseURL,
                                                   relativeURL);

        //AudioClips load too fast for me!
       //Simulate slow loading by adding delay of up to 10 secs.
        try {
            sleep((int)(Math.random()*10000));
        } catch (InterruptedException e) {}

        soundList.putClip(audioClip, relativeURL);
    }
}
```

LESSON 10: Practical Considerations for Writing Applets

EXAMPLE: Getting System Properties

Where Explained:
System Properties That Applets Can Get (page 218), *Threads in Applets* (page 219)

HTML PAGES CONTAINING APPLET: *http://java.sun.com/docs/books/tutorial/applet/practical/properties.html*

GetOpenProperties.java

SOURCE CODE: *http://java.sun.com/docs/books/tutorial/applet/practical/example/GetOpenProperties.java*

```
/**
  * @author  Marianne Mueller
  * @author  Kathy Walrath
  */
```

```
import java.awt.*;
import java.applet.*;

public class GetOpenProperties extends Applet
                               implements Runnable {
    String[] propertyNames = {"file.separator",
                               "line.separator",
                               "path.separator",
                               "java.class.version",
                               "java.vendor",
                               "java.vendor.url",
                               "java.version",
                               "os.name",
                               "os.arch",
                               "os.version"};
    final int numProperties = propertyNames.length;
    Label[] values;

    public void init() {
        //Set up the layout.
        GridBagLayout gridbag = new GridBagLayout();
        setLayout(gridbag);
        GridBagConstraints labelConstraints =
                new GridBagConstraints();
        GridBagConstraints valueConstraints =
                new GridBagConstraints();
        labelConstraints.anchor = GridBagConstraints.WEST;
        labelConstraints.ipadx = 10;
        valueConstraints.fill = GridBagConstraints.HORIZONTAL;
        valueConstraints.gridwidth =
                GridBagConstraints.REMAINDER;
       valueConstraints.weightx = 1.0; //Extra space to values
                                       //column.

        //Set up the Label arrays.
        Label[] names = new Label[numProperties];
        values = new Label[numProperties];
        String firstValue = "not read yet";

        for (int i = 0; i < numProperties; i++) {
            names[i] = new Label(propertyNames[i]);
          gridbag.setConstraints(names[i], labelConstraints);
            add(names[i]);

            values[i] = new Label(firstValue);
         gridbag.setConstraints(values[i], valueConstraints);
            add(values[i]);
        }

        new Thread(this, "Loading System Properties").start();
```

```
    }

    /*
     * This method runs in a separate thread, loading
     * properties one by one.
     */
    public void run() {
        String value = null;

      Thread.currentThread().setPriority(Thread.MIN_PRIORITY);

        //Pause to let the reader see the default strings.
        pause(3000);

        for (int i = 0; i < numProperties; i++) {
            //Pause for dramatic effect.
            pause(250);

            try {
                value = System.getProperty(propertyNames[i]);
                values[i].setText(value);
            } catch (SecurityException e) {
                values[i].setText("Could not read: "
                                  + "SECURITY EXCEPTION!");
            }
        }
    }

    synchronized void pause(int millis) {
        try {
            wait(millis);
        } catch (InterruptedException e) {
        }
    }
}
```

EXAMPLE: Threads in Applets

HTML PAGES CONTAINING APPLET: *http://java.sun.com/docs/books/tutorial/applet/practical/threads.html*

Where Explained:

Threads in Applets (page 219)

PrintThread.java

SOURCE CODE: *http://java.sun.com/docs/books/tutorial/applet/practical/example-1dot1/PrintThread.java*

1.0 SOURCE CODE: *http://java.sun.com/docs/books/tutorial/applet/practical/example/PrintThread.java*

```
import java.applet.Applet;
import java.awt.Graphics;
import java.awt.TextArea;

public class PrintThread extends Applet {

    java.awt.TextArea display = new java.awt.TextArea(1, 80);
    int paintCount = 0;
    String newline;

    public void init() {
        //Create the text area and make it uneditable.
            display = new TextArea(1, 80);
        display.setEditable(false);

        //Set the layout manager so that the text area
        //will be as wide as possible.
        setLayout(new java.awt.GridLayout(1,0));

        //Add the text area to the applet.
        add(display);

        newline = System.getProperty("line.separator");

       addItem("init: " + threadInfo(Thread.currentThread()));
    }

    public void start() {
      addItem("start: " + threadInfo(Thread.currentThread()));
    }

    public void stop() {
       addItem("stop: " + threadInfo(Thread.currentThread()));
    }

    public void destroy() {
        addItem("destroy: "
```

```
                + threadInfo(Thread.currentThread()));
    }

    String threadInfo(Thread t) {
        return "thread=" + t.getName() + ", "
              + "thread group=" + t.getThreadGroup().getName();
    }

    void addItem(String newWord) {
        System.out.println(newWord);
        display.append(newWord + newline);
        display.repaint();
        //A hack to get the applet update() method called
        //occasionally:
        if (++paintCount % 4 == 0) {
            repaint();
        }
    }

    public void update(Graphics g) {
        addItem("update: " +
                threadInfo(Thread.currentThread()));
        super.update(g);
    }
}
```

Where Explained: *A Simple Network Client Applet* (page 227)

EXAMPLE: A Simple Network Client Applet

For the application version of this example, see QuoteClient.java (page 923).

QuoteClientApplet.java

SOURCE CODE: *http://java.sun.com/docs/books/tutorial/applet/practical/example-1dot1/QuoteClientApplet.java*

1.0 SOURCE CODE: *http://java.sun.com/docs/books/tutorial/applet/practical/example/QuoteClientApplet.java*

```
import java.applet.Applet;
import java.awt.*;
import java.awt.event.*;
import java.io.*;
import java.net.*;
import java.util.*;

public class QuoteClientApplet extends Applet
                               implements ActionListener {
```

```
boolean DEBUG = false;
InetAddress address;
TextField portField;
Label display;
DatagramSocket socket;

public void init() {
    //Initialize networking stuff.
    String host = getCodeBase().getHost();

    try {
        address = InetAddress.getByName(host);
    } catch (UnknownHostException e) {
       System.out.println("Couldn't get Internet address:
                            Unknown host");
        // What should we do?
    }

    try {
        socket = new DatagramSocket();
    } catch (IOException e) {
        System.out.println("Couldn't create new
                            DatagramSocket");
        return;
    }

    //Set up the UI.
    GridBagLayout gridBag = new GridBagLayout();
    GridBagConstraints c = new GridBagConstraints();
    setLayout(gridBag);

    Label l1 = new Label("Quote of the Moment:",
                         Label.CENTER);
    c.anchor = GridBagConstraints.SOUTH;
    c.gridwidth = GridBagConstraints.REMAINDER;
    gridBag.setConstraints(l1, c);
    add(l1);

    display = new Label("(no quote received yet)",
                         Label.CENTER);
    c.anchor = GridBagConstraints.NORTH;
    c.weightx = 1.0;
    c.fill = GridBagConstraints.HORIZONTAL;
    gridBag.setConstraints(display, c);
    add(display);

    Label l2 = new Label("Enter the port (on host " +
                            host + ") + to send the
```

```
                                          request to: ",    Label.RIGHT);
            c.anchor = GridBagConstraints.SOUTH;
            c.gridwidth = 1;
            c.weightx = 0.0;
            c.weighty = 1.0;
            c.fill = GridBagConstraints.NONE;
            gridBag.setConstraints(l2, c);
            add(l2);

            portField = new TextField(6);
            gridBag.setConstraints(portField, c);
            add(portField);

            Button button = new Button("Send");
            gridBag.setConstraints(button, c);
            add(button);

            portField.addActionListener(this);
            button.addActionListener(this);
        }

        public Insets getInsets() {
            return new Insets(4,4,5,5);
        }

        public void paint(Graphics g) {
            Dimension d = getSize();
            Color bg = getBackground();

            g.setColor(bg);
            g.draw3DRect(0, 0, d.width - 1, d.height - 1, true);
            g.draw3DRect(3, 3, d.width - 7, d.height - 7, false);
        }

        void doIt(int port) {
            DatagramPacket packet;
            byte[] sendBuf = new byte[256];

             packet = new DatagramPacket(sendBuf, 256, address,
                                             port);
            try { // send request
                if (DEBUG) {
                    System.out.println("Applet about to send "
                                   + "packet to address "
                                   + address + " at port " + port);
                }
                socket.send(packet);
                if (DEBUG) {
```

```
                System.out.println("Applet sent packet.");
            }
        } catch (IOException e) {
            System.out.println("Applet socket.send failed:");
            e.printStackTrace();
            return;
        }

        packet = new DatagramPacket(sendBuf, 256);

        try { // get response
            if (DEBUG) {
                System.out.println("Applet about to call
                                    socket.receive().");
            }
            socket.receive(packet);
            if (DEBUG) {
                System.out.println("Applet returned from
                                    socket.receive().");
            }
        } catch (IOException e) {
          System.out.println("Applet socket.receive failed:");
            e.printStackTrace();
            return;
        }

        String received = new String(packet.getData());
        if (DEBUG) {
            System.out.println("Quote of the Moment: " +
                               received);
        }
        display.setText(received);
    }

    public void actionPerformed(ActionEvent event) {
        int port;

        try {
            port = Integer.parseInt(portField.getText());
            doIt(port);
        } catch (NumberFormatException e) {
            //No integer entered.  Should warn the user.

        }
    }
}
```

quoteApplet.html

SOURCE CODE: *http://java.sun.com/docs/books/tutorial/applet/practical/example/quoteApplet.html*

```
<HTML>
<TITLE>
QuoteClientApplet
</TITLE>

<BODY>
<APPLET CODE=QuoteClientApplet.class
        CODEBASE=example/
        WIDTH=500 HEIGHT=100>
</APPLET>
</BODY>
</HTML>
```

QuoteServer.java

See QuoteServer.java (page 921).

QuoteServerThread.java

See QuoteServerThread.java (page 922).

EXAMPLE: A Talk Client and Server

Where Explained: *Using a Server to Work Around Security Restrictions* (page 228)

TalkClientApplet.java

SOURCE CODE: *http://java.sun.com/docs/books/tutorial/applet/practical/example-1dot1/TalkClientApplet.java*

1.0 SOURCE CODE: *http://java.sun.com/docs/books/tutorial/applet/practical/example/TalkClientApplet.java*

```
import java.applet.Applet;
import java.awt.*;
import java.awt.event.*;
import java.io.*;
import java.net.*;
import java.util.*;

public class TalkClientApplet extends Applet
                              implements Runnable,
                                         ActionListener  {
    Socket socket;
    BufferedWriter os;
```

```
BufferedReader is;
TextField portField, message;
TextArea display;
Button button;
int dataPort;
boolean trysted;
Thread receiveThread;
String host;
boolean DEBUG = false;

public void init() {
    //Get the address of the host we came from.
    host = getCodeBase().getHost();

    //Set up the UI.
    GridBagLayout gridBag = new GridBagLayout();
    GridBagConstraints c = new GridBagConstraints();
    setLayout(gridBag);

    message = new TextField("");
    c.fill = GridBagConstraints.HORIZONTAL;
    c.gridwidth = GridBagConstraints.REMAINDER;
    gridBag.setConstraints(message, c);
    message.addActionListener(this);
    add(message);

    display = new TextArea(10, 40);
    display.setEditable(false);
    c.weightx = 1.0;
    c.weighty = 1.0;
    c.fill = GridBagConstraints.BOTH;
    gridBag.setConstraints(display, c);
    add(display);

    Label l = new Label("Enter the port (on host " + host
                        + ") to send the request to:",
                        JLabel.RIGHT);
    c.fill = GridBagConstraints.HORIZONTAL;
    c.gridwidth = 1;
    c.weightx = 0.0;
    c.weighty = 0.0;
    gridBag.setConstraints(l, c);
    add(l);

    portField = new TextField(6);
    c.fill = GridBagConstraints.NONE;
    gridBag.setConstraints(portField, c);
    portField.addActionListener(this);
```

```
        add(portField);

        button = new Button("Connect");
        gridBag.setConstraints(button, c);
        button.addActionListener(this);
        add(button);
    }

    public synchronized void start() {
        if (DEBUG) {
            System.out.println("In start() method.");
        }
        if (receiveThread == null) {
            trysted = false;
            portField.setEditable(true);
            button.setEnabled(true);
            os = null;
            is = null;
            socket = null;
            receiveThread = new Thread(this);
            receiveThread.start();
            if (DEBUG) {
                System.out.println(" Just set everything to "
                                   + "null and started thread.");
            }
        } else if (DEBUG) {
            System.out.println(
                       " receiveThread not null! Did nothing!");
        }
    }

    public synchronized void stop() {
        if (DEBUG) {
            System.out.println("In stop() method.");
        }
        receiveThread = null;
        trysted = false;
        portField.setEditable(true);
        button.setEnabled(true);
        notify();

        try { //Close input stream.
            if (is != null) {
                is.close();
                is = null;
            }
        } catch (Exception e) {} //Ignore exceptions.

        try { //Close output stream.
```

```
            if (os != null) {
                os.close();
                os = null;
            }
        } catch (Exception e) {} //Ignore exceptions.

        try { //Close socket.
            if (socket != null) {
                socket.close();
                socket = null;
            }
        } catch (Exception e) {} //Ignore exceptions.
    }

    public Insets getInsets() {
        return new Insets(4,4,5,5);
    }

    public void paint(Graphics g) {
        Dimension d = getSize();
        Color bg = getBackground();

        g.setColor(bg);
        g.draw3DRect(0, 0, d.width - 1, d.height - 1, true);
        g.draw3DRect(3, 3, d.width - 7, d.height - 7, false);
    }

    public synchronized void actionPerformed(ActionEvent e) {
        int port;

        if (DEBUG) {
            System.out.println("In action() method.");
        }

        if (receiveThread == null) {
            start();
        }

        if (!trysted) {
        //We need to attempt a rendezvous.

            if (DEBUG) {
                System.out.println(" trysted = false. "
                         + "About to attempt a rendezvous.");
            }

            //Get the port the user entered...
            try {
```

```
                port = Integer.parseInt(portField.getText());
            } catch (NumberFormatException e) {
                //No integer entered.
                display.append("Please enter an integer "
                                + "below.\n");
                return;
            }
            //...and rendezvous with it.
            rendezvous(port);

        } else { //We've already rendezvoused.
                 //Just send data over.
            if (DEBUG) {
                System.out.println("  trysted = true. "
                                   + "About to send data.");
            }
            String str = message.getText();
            message.selectAll();

            try {
                os.write(str);
                os.newline();
                os.flush();
            } catch (IOException e) {
                display.append("ERROR: Applet couldn't write "
                               + "to socket.\n");
                display.append("...Disconnecting.\n");
                stop();
                return;
            } catch (NullPointerException e) {
                display.append("ERROR: No output stream!\n");
                display.append("...Disconnecting.\n");
                stop();
                return;
            }
            display.append("Sent: " + str + "\n");
        }
        return;
    }

    synchronized void waitForTryst() {
        //Wait for notify() call from action().
        try {
            wait();
        } catch (InterruptedException e) {}

        if (DEBUG) {
            System.out.println("waitForTryst about to return. "
```

```
                              + "trysted = " + trysted + ".");
        }

        return;
    }

    public void run() {
        String received = null;

        waitForTryst();

        //OK, now we can send messages.
        while (Thread.currentThread() == receiveThread) {
            try {
                //Wait for data from the server.
                received = is.readLine();

                //Display it.
                if (received != null) {
                   display.append("Received: " + received
                                 + "\n");
                } else { //success but no data...
                   System.err.println("readLine returned "
                                     + "no data");
                }
                    } catch (IOException e) { //Perhaps a
                                      //temporary problem?
                display.append("NOTE: Couldn't read from "
                           + "socket.\n") ;
                return;
            }
        }
    }

    private void rendezvous(int port) {
        //Try to open a socket to the port.
        try {
            socket = new Socket(host, port);
        } catch (UnknownHostException e) {
            display.append("ERROR: Can't find host: " + host
                          + ".\n");
            return;
        } catch (IOException e) {
            display.append("ERROR: Can't open socket "
                          + "on rendezvous port "
                          + port + " (on host " +
                          host + ").\n");
            return;
```

```
            }

            //Try to open streams to read and write from the socket.
            try {
                os = new BufferedWriter(
                         new OutputStreamWriter(
                         socket.getOutputStream()));
                is = new BufferedReader(
                        new InputStreamReader(
                        socket.getInputStream()));
            } catch (IOException e) {
                display.append("ERROR: Created data socket "
                               + "but can't open stream on "
                               + "it.\n");
                display.append("...Disconnecting.\n");
                stop();
                return;
            }

            if ((os != null) & (is != null)) {
                if (DEBUG) {
                    System.out.println("Successful rendezvous.");
                    System.out.println("socket = " + socket);
                    System.out.println("output stream = " + os);
                    System.out.println("input stream = " + is);
                }
                //Let the main applet thread know we've
                //successfully rendezvoused.
                portField.setEditable(false);
                button.setEnabled(false);
                trysted = true;
                notify();
            } else {
                display.append("ERROR: Port is valid but "
                               + "communication failed. "
                               + "Please TRY AGAIN.\n");
            }
        }

    }
```

talk.html

SOURCE CODE: *http://java.sun.com/docs/books/tutorial/applet/practical/example/talk.html*

```
<HTML>
<TITLE>
TalkClientApplet
</title>

<BODY>
<APPLET CODE=TalkClientApplet.class
        CODEBASE=example/
        WIDTH=550 HEIGHT=200>
</APPLET>
</BODY>
</HTML>
```

TalkServer.java

SOURCE CODE: *http://java.sun.com/docs/books/tutorial/applet/practical/example-1dot1/TalkServer.java*

1.0 SOURCE CODE: *http://java.sun.com/docs/books/tutorial/applet/practical/example/TalkServer.java*

```
import java.net.*;
import java.io.*;

class TalkServer {
    TalkServerThread[] tstList = new TalkServerThread[2];
    boolean DEBUG = false;

    public static void main(String[] args) {
        new TalkServer().start();
    }

    public void start() {
        ServerSocket serverRSocket = null;
        int numConnected = 0;

        try {
            serverRSocket = new ServerSocket(0);
            System.out.println("TalkServer listening on "
                              + "rendezvous port: "
                              + serverRSocket.getLocalPort());
        } catch (IOException e) {
           System.err.println("Server could not create server "
                              + "socket for rendezvous.");
```

```
            return;
        }

        while (true) {

            //Connect to two clients.
            while (numConnected < 2) {
                TalkServerThread tst;
                tst = connectToClient(serverRSocket);
                if (tst != null) {
                    numConnected++;
                    if (tstList[0] == null) {
                        tstList[0] = tst;
                    } else {
                        tstList[1] = tst;
                    }
                }
            } //end while (numConnected < 2) loop

            if (DEBUG) {
                try {
                    System.out.println("tst #0 = " + tstList[0]);
                } catch (Exception e) {}
                try {
                    System.out.println("tst #1 = " + tstList[1]);
                } catch (Exception e) {}
            }

            //If they're really OK, tell them to start writing.
            if (everythingIsOK(0) & everythingIsOK(1)) {
                for (int i = 0; i < 2; i++) {
                    writeToStream("START WRITING!" +
                                  "\n-----------------------"
                                  + "-------------", tstList[i].os);
                }
            } else {
                System.err.println("2 server threads created, "
                                  + "but not everything is OK");
            }

            while (numConnected == 2) {
                if (!everythingIsOK(0)) {
                    if (DEBUG) {
                    System.out.println("Applet #0 is hosed; "
                                       + "disconnecting.");
                    }
                    numConnected--;
                    cleanup(tstList[0]);
```

```
                tstList[0] = null;
            }
            if (!everythingIsOK(1)) {
                if (DEBUG) {
                System.out.println("Applet #1 is hosed; "
                                   + "disconnecting.");
                }
                numConnected--;
                cleanup(tstList[1]);
                tstList[1] = null;
            }
                    try {
                Thread.sleep(1000);
            } catch (InterruptedException e) {
            }
        } //end while(numConnected==2) loop

        if (DEBUG) {
            try {
                System.out.println("Number of connections = " +
                                   numConnected);
                System.out.println("tst #0 = " + tstList[0]);
                System.out.println("tst #1 = " + tstList[1]);
            } catch (Exception e) {}
        }

    } //end while (true) loop
}

protected TalkServerThread connectToClient(ServerSocket
                                            serverRSocket) {

    Socket rendezvousSocket = null;
    TalkServerThread tst = null;

   //Listen for client connection on the rendezvous socket.
    try {
        rendezvousSocket = serverRSocket.accept();
    } catch (IOException e) {
        System.err.println("Accept failed.");
        e.printStackTrace();
        return null;
    }

    //Create a thread to handle this connection.
    try {
        tst = new TalkServerThread(rendezvousSocket,this);
        tst.start();
```

```
        } catch (Exception e) {
             System.err.println("Couldn't create "
                                  + "TalkServerThread:");
            e.printStackTrace();
            return null;
        }

        writeToStream("Successful connection. "
                      + "Please wait for second applet to "
                      + "connect...",
                      tst.os);
        return tst;
    }

    boolean everythingIsOK(int tstNum) {
        TalkServerThread tst = tstList[tstNum];

        if (tst == null) {
            if (DEBUG) {
               System.out.println("TalkServerThread #" + tstNum
                                  + " is null");
            }
            return false;
        } else {
            if (tst.os == null) {
                if (DEBUG) {
                      System.out.println("TalkServerThread #"
                                         + tstNum
                                        + " output stream is null.");
                }
                return false;
            }
            if (tst.is == null) {
                if (DEBUG) {
                      System.out.println("TalkServerThread #"
                                         +tstNum
                                        + " input stream is null.");
                }
                return false;
            }
            if (tst.socket == null) {
                if (DEBUG) {
                      System.out.println("TalkServerThread #"
                                         + tstNum
                                         + " socket is null.");
                }
                return false;
            }
```

```
        }
        return true;
    }

    void cleanup(TalkServerThread tst) {
        if (tst != null) {
            try {
                if (tst.os != null) {
                    tst.os.close();
                    tst.os = null;
                }
            } catch (Exception e) {} //Ignore errors
            try {
                if (tst.is != null) {
                    tst.is.close();
                    tst.is = null;
                }
            } catch (Exception e) {} //Ignore errors
            try {
                if (tst.socket != null) {
                    tst.socket.close();
                    tst.socket = null;
                }
            } catch (Exception e) {} //Ignore errors
        }
    }

    public void forwardString(String string,
                              TalkServerThread requestor) {
        BufferedWriter clientStream = null;

        if (tstList[0] == requestor) {
            if (tstList[1] != null) {
                clientStream = tstList[1].os;
            } else {
                if (DEBUG) {
                System.out.println("Applet #0 has a "
                                   + "string to forward, "
                                   + "but Applet #1 is gone...");
                }
                //cleanup();
                return;
            }
        } else {
            if (tstList[0] != null) {
                clientStream = tstList[0].os;
            } else {
                if (DEBUG) {
```

```
                    System.out.println("Applet #1 has a "
                                       + "string to forward, "
                                     + "but Applet #0 is gone...");
                    }
                    //cleanup();
                    return;
                }
            }

            if (clientStream != null) {
                writeToStream(string, clientStream);
            } else if (DEBUG) {
                System.out.println("Can't forward string -- no "
                                   + "output stream.");
            }
        }

        public void writeToStream(String string,
                                  BufferedWriter stream) {
            if (DEBUG) {
                System.out.println(
                     "TalkServer about to forward data: + string);
            }

            try {
                stream.write(string);
                stream.writeLine();
                stream.flush();
                if (DEBUG) {
                    System.out.println("TalkServer forwarded "
                                       + "string.");
                }
            } catch (IOException e) {
                System.err.println("TalkServer failed to "
                                   + "forward string:");
                e.printStackTrace();
                return;
            } catch (NullPointerException e) {
              System.err.println("TalkServer can't forward string "
                               + "since output stream is null.") ;
                return;
            }
        }

    }
```

TalkServerThread.java

SOURCE CODE: *http://java.sun.com/docs/books/tutorial/applet/practical/example-1dot1/TalkServerThread.java*

1.0 SOURCE CODE: *http://java.sun.com/docs/books/tutorial/applet/practical/example/TalkServerThread.java*

```
import java.io.*;
import java.net.*;
import java.util.*;

class TalkServerThread extends Thread {
    public Socket socket;
    public BufferedReader is;
    public BufferedWriter os;
    TalkServer server;
    boolean DEBUG = false;

    public String toString() {
        return "TalkServerThread: socket = " + socket
              + "; is = " + is
              + "; os = " + os;
    }

    TalkServerThread(Socket socket, TalkServer server) throws
                     IOException {
        super("TalkServer");

        is = new BufferedReader(
                new InputStreamReader(
                socket.getInputStream()));
        os = new BufferedWriter(
                new OutputStreamWriter(
                socket.getOutputStream()));

        if (is == null) {
            System.err.println("TalkServerThread: Input stream "
                              + "seemed "
                              + "to be created successfully, "
                              + "but it's null.");
            throw new IOException();
        }

        if (os == null) {
            System.err.println("TalkServerThread: Output "
                              + "stream seemed "
                              + "to be created successfully, "
                              + "but it's null.");
```

```
            throw new IOException();
        }

        this.socket = socket;
        this.server = server;
    }

    public void run() {
        while (socket != null) {
            try {
                //Read data.
                String str = is.readLine();

                //Pass it on.
                if (str != null) {
                    server.forwardString(str, this);
                }
              } catch (EOFException e) {
              //No more data on this socket...
                server.forwardString("SERVER SAYS other applet "
                                   + "disconnected", this);
                cleanup();
                return;
              } catch (NullPointerException e) {
              //Socket doesn't exist...
                server.forwardString("SERVER SAYS no socket to "
                                   + "other applet", this);
                cleanup();
                return;
            } catch (IOException e) { //Read problem.
              server.forwardString("SERVER SAYS socket "
                                   + "trouble with other "
                                   + "applet",this);
                cleanup();
                return;
        } catch (Exception e) { //Unknown exception. Complain
                                //and quit.
              System.err.println("Exception on is.readUTF():");
                e.printStackTrace();
                cleanup();
                return;
            }
        }
    }

    protected void finalize() {
        cleanup();
    }
```

```
    void cleanup() {
        try {
            if (is != null) {
                is.close();
                is = null;
            }
        } catch (Exception e) {} //Ignore errors.

        try {
            if (os != null) {
                os.close();
                os = null;
            }
        } catch (Exception e) {} //Ignore errors.

        try {
            if (socket != null) {
                socket.close();
                socket = null;
            }
        } catch (Exception e) {} //Ignore errors.
    }

}
```

Essential Java Classes

LESSON 12: Using String and StringBuffer

EXAMPLE: Reversing a String

The `reverseIt` method is featured throughout the lesson on the `String` and `StringBuffer` classes. The second file, `ReverseStringTest.java`, defines a class with a `main` method that you can use to test the `reverseIt` method.

Where Explained: *Using String and String-Buffer* (page 247)

ReverseString.java

SOURCE CODE: *http://java.sun.com/docs/books/tutorial/essential/strings/example/ReverseString.java*

```
public class ReverseString {
    public static String reverseIt(String source) {
        int i, len = source.length();
        StringBuffer dest = new StringBuffer(len);

        for (i = (len - 1); i >= 0; i--)
```

```
            dest.append(source.charAt(i));
        return dest.toString();
    }
}
```

ReverseStringTest.java

SOURCE CODE: *http://java.sun.com/docs/books/tutorial/essential/strings/example/ReverseStringTest.java*

```
public class ReverseStringTest {
    public static void main(String[] args) {
        String str = "What's going on?";
        System.out.println(ReverseString.reverseIt(str));
    }
}
```

EXAMPLE: Extracting Components of a Filename

Where Explained: *More Accessor Methods* (page 251)

The `Filename` class contains several methods that parse a `String` for filename components such as the directory name and the filename extension. The second example file, `FilenameTest.java`, defines a class that has a `main` method that you can use to test the methods in the `Filename` class.

Filename.java

SOURCE CODE: *http://java.sun.com/docs/books/tutorial/essential/strings/example/Filename.java*

```
// This class assumes that the string used to initialize
// fullPath has a directory path, filename, and extension.
// The methods won't work if it doesn't.
public class Filename {
    private String fullPath;
    private char fileSeparator, extensionSeparator;

    public Filename(String str, char sep, char ext) {
        fullPath = str;
        pathSeparator = sep;
        extensionSeparator = ext;
    }

    public String extension() {
        int dot = fullPath.lastIndexOf(extensionSeparator);
        return fullPath.substring(dot + 1);
    }

    public String filename() {
        int dot = fullPath.lastIndexOf(extensionSeparator);
```

```
        int sep = fullPath.lastIndexOf(pathSeparator);
        return fullPath.substring(sep + 1, dot);
    }

    public String path() {
        int sep = fullPath.lastIndexOf(pathSeparator);
        return fullPath.substring(0, sep);
    }
}
```

FilenameTest.java

SOURCE CODE: *http://java.sun.com/docs/books/tutorial/essential/strings/example/FilenameTest.java*

```
public class FilenameTest {
    public static void main(String[] args) {
        Filename myHomePage = new
            Filename("/home/mem/index.html", '/', '.');
        System.out.println("Extension = " +
            myHomePage.extension());
        System.out.println("Filename = " +
            myHomePage.filename());
        System.out.println("Path = " + myHomePage.path());
    }
}
```

LESSON 13: Setting Program Attributes

EXAMPLE: Echoing Command-Line Arguments

Echo.java

SOURCE CODE: *http://java.sun.com/docs/books/tutorial/essential/attributes/example/Echo.java*

Where Explained:
Echoing Command-Line Arguments (page 266)

```
public class Echo {
    public static void main (String[] args) {
        for (int i = 0; i < args.length; i++)
            System.out.println(args[i]);
    }
}
```

LESSON 14: Accessing System Resources

EXAMPLE: Getting the Current User's Name

Where Explained: *Using the System Class* (page 269)

UserNameTest.java

SOURCE CODE: *http://java.sun.com/docs/books/tutorial/essential/system/example/UserNameTest.java*

```
public class UserNameTest {
    public static void main(String[] args) {
        String name = System.getProperty("user.name");
        System.out.println(name);
    }
}
```

EXAMPLE: Printing Various Data Types

Where Explained: *The Standard I/O Streams* (page 270)

DataTypePrintTest.java

SOURCE CODE: *http://java.sun.com/docs/books/tutorial/essential/system/example/DataTypePrintTest.java*

```
public class DataTypePrintTest {
    public static void main(String[] args) {

        Thread objectData = new Thread();
        String stringData = "Java Mania";
        char[] charArrayData = { 'a', 'b', 'c' };
        int integerData = 4;
        long longData = Long.MIN_VALUE;
        float floatData = Float.MAX_VALUE;
        double doubleData = Math.PI;
        boolean booleanData = true;

        System.out.println(objectData);
        System.out.println(stringData);
        System.out.println(charArrayData);
        System.out.println(integerData);
        System.out.println(longData);
        System.out.println(floatData);
        System.out.println(doubleData);
        System.out.println(booleanData);
    }
}
```

EXAMPLE: Displaying System Properties

Where Explained: *System Properties* (page 273)

DisplaySystemProps.java

SOURCE CODE: *http://java.sun.com/docs/books/tutorial/essential/system/example/DisplaySystemProps.java*

```
public class DisplaySystemProps {
    public static void main(String[] args) {
        System.getProperties().list(System.out);
    }
}
```

EXAMPLE: Setting System Properties

Where Explained: *Setting System Properties* (page 275)

PropertiesTest.java

SOURCE CODE: *http://java.sun.com/docs/books/tutorial/essential/system/example/PropertiesTest.java*

```
import java.io.FileInputStream;
import java.util.Properties;

public class PropertiesTest {
    public static void main(String[] args)  throws Exception {
        // set up new properties object from
        // file "myProperties.txt"
        FileInputStream propFile = new FileInputStream(
                                          "myProperties.txt");
        Properties p = new Properties(System.getProperties());
        p.load(propFile);

        // set the system properties
        System.setProperties(p);
        // display the system properties
        System.getProperties().list(System.out);
    }
}
```

myProperties.txt

SOURCE CODE: *http://java.sun.com/docs/books/tutorial/essential/system/example/myProperties.txt*

```
subliminal.message=Buy Java Now!
```

EXAMPLE: Providing Your Own Security Manager

Where Explained: *Providing Your Own Security Manager* (page 279)

PasswordSecurityManager.java

SOURCE CODE: *http://java.sun.com/docs/books/tutorial/essential/system/example-1dot1/PasswordSecurityManager.java*

1.0 SOURCE CODE: *http://java.sun.com/docs/books/tutorial/essential/system/example/PasswordSecurityManager.java*

```
import java.io.*;

public class PasswordSecurityManager extends SecurityManager {

    private String password;
    private BufferedReader buffy;

   public PasswordSecurityManager(String p, BufferedReader b) {
        super();
        this.password = p;
        this.buffy = b;
    }

    private boolean accessOK() {
        int c;
        String response;

        System.out.println("What's the secret password?");
        try {
            response = buffy.readLine();
            if (response.equals(password))
                return true;
            else
                return false;
        } catch (IOException e) {
            return false;
        }
    }
    public void checkRead(FileDescriptor filedescriptor) {
        if (!accessOK())
            throw new SecurityException("Not a Chance!");
    }
    public void checkRead(String filename) {
        if (!accessOK())
            throw new SecurityException("No Way!");
    }
    public void checkRead(String filename,
                               Object executionContext) {
        if (!accessOK())
```

```
            throw new SecurityException("Forget It!");
    }
    public void checkWrite(FileDescriptor filedescriptor) {
        if (!accessOK())
            throw new SecurityException("Not!");
    }
    public void checkWrite(String filename) {
        if (!accessOK())
            throw new SecurityException("Not Even!");
    }
    public void checkPropertyAccess(String s) {}
    public void checkPropertiesAccess() {}
}
```

SecurityManagerTest.java

SOURCE CODE: *http://java.sun.com/docs/books/tutorial/essential/system/example-1dot1/SecurityManagerTest.java*

1.0 SOURCE CODE: *http://java.sun.com/docs/books/tutorial/essential/system/example/SecurityManagerTest.java*

Where Explained:
Installing Your Security Manager (page 284)

```
import java.io.*;

public class SecurityManagerTest {
    public static void main(String[] args) throws Exception {
        BufferedReader buffy = new BufferedReader(
                                    new InputStreamReader(
                                    System.in));
        try {
            System.setSecurityManager(
                    new PasswordSecurityManager("Booga Booga",
                                                buffy));
        } catch (SecurityException se) {
           System.err.println("SecurityManager already set!");
        }

        BufferedReader in = new BufferedReader(
                                new FileReader("inputtext.txt"));
        PrintWriter out = new PrintWriter(
                                new FileWriter("outputtext.txt"));
        String inputString;
        while ((inputString = in.readLine()) != null)
            out.println(inputString);
        in.close();
        out.close();
    }
}
```

inputtext.txt

Where Explained:

Installing Your Security Manager (page 284)

SOURCE CODE: *http://java.sun.com/docs/books/tutorial/essential/system/example-1dot1/inputtext.txt*

1.0 SOURCE CODE: *http://java.sun.com/docs/books/tutorial/essential/system/example/inputtext.txt*

```
Now is the time for all good men
to come to the aid of their country.
```

EXAMPLE: Copying Arrays

Where Explained:

Copying Arrays (page 288)

ArrayCopyTest.java

SOURCE CODE: *http://java.sun.com/docs/books/tutorial/essential/system/example/ArrayCopyTest.java*

```
public class ArrayCopyTest {
    public static void main(String[] args) {
        char[] copyFrom = { 'd', 'e', 'c', 'a', 'f', 'f', 'e',
                            'i', 'n', 'a', 't', 'e', 'd' };
        char[] copyTo = new char[7];

        System.arraycopy(copyFrom, 2, copyTo, 0, 7);
        System.out.println(new String(copyTo));
    }
}
```

EXAMPLE: Timing Is Everything

Where Explained:

Getting the Current Time (page 289)

HTML PAGES CONTAINING APPLET: *http://java.sun.com/docs/books/tutorial/essential/system/misc.html*

TimingIsEverything.java

SOURCE CODE: *http://java.sun.com/docs/books/tutorial/essential/system/example-1dot1/TimingIsEverything.java*

1.0 SOURCE CODE: *http://java.sun.com/docs/books/tutorial/essential/system/example/TimingIsEverything.java*

```
import java.awt.*;
import java.awt.event.*;

public class TimingIsEverything extends java.applet.Applet {

    public long firstClickTime = 0;
    public String displayStr;

    public void init() {
```

```
            displayStr = "Double Click Me";
            addMouseListener(new MyAdapter());
        }
        public void paint(Graphics g) {
          g.drawRect(0, 0, getSize().width-1, getSize().height-1);
            g.drawString(displayStr, 40, 30);
        }
        class MyAdapter extends MouseAdapter {
            public void mouseClicked(Event evt) {
                long clickTime = System.currentTimeMillis();
                long clickInterval = clickTime - firstClickTime;
                if (clickInterval < 200) {
                    displayStr = "Double Click!! (Interval = " +
                                 clickInterval + ")";
                    firstClickTime = 0;
                } else {
                    displayStr = "Single Click!!";
                    firstClickTime = clickTime;
                }
                repaint();
            }
        }
    }
```

LESSON 15: Handling Errors with Exceptions

EXAMPLE: Catching or Specifying Exceptions

The `InputFile` class demonstrates what the compiler will do if a method in your Java program contains code that can throw an exception and the exception is neither caught nor specified in the method declaration. This file will not compile. See the next file, `InputFileDeclared.java`, for a version that specifies the exceptions in the method declaration and therefore will compile.

Where Explained: *Your First Encounterwith Java Exceptions* (page 301)

InputFile.java

SOURCE CODE: *http://java.sun.com/docs/books/tutorial/essential/exceptions/example-1dot1/InputFile.java*

1.0 SOURCE CODE: *http://java.sun.com/docs/books/tutorial/essential/exceptions/example/InputFile.java*

```
// Note: This class won't compile by design!
import java.io.*;

public class InputFile {
```

```
        private FileReader in;

        public InputFile(String filename) {
            in = new FileReader(filename);
        }

        public String getWord() {
            int c;
            StringBuffer buf = new StringBuffer();

            do {
                c = in.read();
                if (Character.isWhitespace((char)c))
                    return buf.toString();
                else
                    buf.append((char)c);
            } while (c != -1);
            return buf.toString();
        }
    }
```

InputFileDeclared.java

1.0 SOURCE CODE: *http://java.sun.com/docs/books/tutorial/essential/exceptions/example-1dot1/InputFileDeclared.java*

SOURCE CODE: *http://java.sun.com/docs/books/tutorial/essential/exceptions/example/InputFileDeclared.java*

```
    import java.io.*;

    public class InputFileDeclared {

        private FileReader in;

        public InputFileDeclared(String filename)
                                    throws FileNotFoundException {
            in = new FileReader(filename);
        }

        public String getWord() throws IOException {
            int c;
            StringBuffer buf = new StringBuffer();

            do {
                c = in.read();
                if (Character.isWhitespace((char)c))
                    return buf.toString();
                else
```

```
            buf.append((char)c);
        } while (c != -1);
        return buf.toString();
    }
}
```

EXAMPLE: The ListOfNumbers Class

The `ListOfNumbers` class defined in `ListOfNumbersWOHandler.java` can throw an exception, and the exception is neither caught nor specified in the method declaration. This file will not compile. See the next file, `ListOfNumbers.java`, for a version that catches and handles the exceptions and therefore will compile.

Where Explained: *Dealing with Exceptions* (page 305)

ListOfNumbersWOHandler.java

SOURCE CODE: *http://java.sun.com/docs/books/tutorial/essential/exceptions/example-1dot1/ListOfNumbersWOHandler.java*

1.0 SOURCE CODE: *http://java.sun.com/docs/books/tutorial/essential/exceptions/example/ListOfNumbersWOHandler.java*

```
// Note: This class won't compile by design!
import java.io.*;
import java.util.Vector;

public class ListOfNumbers {
    private Vector victor;
    private static final int size = 10;

    public ListOfNumbers () {
        victor = new Vector(size);
        for (int i = 0; i < size; i++)
            victor.addElement(new Integer(i));
    }
    public void writeList() {
        PrintWriter out = new PrintWriter(
                              new FileWriter("OutFile.txt"));

        for (int i = 0; i < size; i++)
            out.println("Value at: " + i + " = "
           + victor.elementAt(i));

        out.close();
    }
}
```

ListOfNumbers.java

SOURCE CODE: *http://java.sun.com/docs/books/tutorial/essential/exceptions/example-1dot1/ListOfNumbers.java*

1.0 SOURCE CODE: *http://java.sun.com/docs/books/tutorial/essential/exceptions/example/ListOfNumbers.java*

```
import java.io.*;
import java.util.Vector;

public class ListOfNumbers {
    private Vector victor;
    private static final int size = 10;

    public ListOfNumbers () {
        victor = new Vector(size);
        for (int i = 0; i < size; i++)
            victor.addElement(new Integer(i));
    }
    public void writeList() {
        PrintWriter out = null;

        try {
            System.out.println("Entering try statement");
            out = new PrintWriter(
                        new FileWriter("OutFile.txt"));

            for (int i = 0; i < size; i++)
                out.println("Value at: " + i + " = "
                             + victor.elementAt(i));
        } catch (ArrayIndexOutOfBoundsException e) {
            System.err.println(
                  "Caught ArrayIndexOutOfBoundsException: "
                  + e.getMessage());
        } catch (IOException e) {
            System.err.println("Caught IOException: "
                               + e.getMessage());
        } finally {
            if (out != null) {
                System.out.println("Closing PrintWriter");
                out.close();
            } else {
                System.out.println("PrintWriter not open");
            }
        }
    }
}
```

LESSON 16: Doing Two or More Tasks at Once: Threads

EXAMPLE: The Vacation Destination Decision-maker

Where Explained:
Subclassing Thread and Overriding run (page 330)

SimpleThread.java

SOURCE CODE: *http://java.sun.com/docs/books/tutorial/essential/threads/example/SimpleThread.java*

```
public class SimpleThread extends Thread {
    public SimpleThread(String str) {
        super(str);
    }
    public void run() {
        for (int i = 0; i < 10; i++) {
            System.out.println(i + " " + getName());
            try {
                sleep((int)(Math.random() * 1000));
            } catch (InterruptedException e) {}
        }
        System.out.println("DONE! " + getName());
    }
}
```

TwoThreadsTest.java

SOURCE CODE: *http://java.sun.com/docs/books/tutorial/essential/threads/example/TwoThreadsTest.java*

```
public class TwoThreadsTest {
    public static void main (String[] args) {
        new SimpleThread("Jamaica").start();
        new SimpleThread("Fiji").start();
    }
}
```

ThreeThreadsTest.java

SOURCE CODE: *http://java.sun.com/docs/books/tutorial/essential/threads/example/ThreeThreadsTest.java*

```
public class ThreeThreadsTest {
    public static void main (String[] args) {
        new SimpleThread("Jamaica").start();
        new SimpleThread("Fiji").start();
        new SimpleThread("Bora Bora").start();
    }
}
```

EXAMPLE: Does Anybody Really Know What Time It Is?

Where Explained:
Implementing the Runnable Interface (page 332)

HTML PAGES CONTAINING APPLET: *http://java.sun.com/docs/books/tutorial/essential/threads/clock.html*

Clock.java

SOURCE CODE: *http://java.sun.com/docs/books/tutorial/essential/threads/example-1dot1/Clock.java*

1.0 SOURCE CODE: *http://java.sun.com/docs/books/tutorial/essential/threads/example/Clock.java*

```
import java.awt.Graphics;
import java.util.*;
import java.text.DateFormat;
import java.applet.Applet;

public class Clock extends Applet implements Runnable {
    private Thread clockThread = null;
    public void start() {
        if (clockThread == null) {
            clockThread = new Thread(this, "Clock");
            clockThread.start();
        }
    }
    public void run() {
        Thread myThread = Thread.currentThread();
        while (clockThread == myThread) {
            repaint();
            try {
                Thread.sleep(1000);
            } catch (InterruptedException e) {
                // the VM doesn't want us to sleep anymore,
                // so get back to work
            }
        }
    }
    public void paint(Graphics g) {
        // get the time and convert it to a date
        Calendar cal = Calendar.getInstance();
        Date date = cal.getTime();
        // format it and display it
       DateFormat dateFormatter = DateFormat.getTimeInstance();
        g.drawString(dateFormatter.format(date), 5, 10);
    }
    // overrides Applet's stop method, not Thread's
```

```
    public void stop() {
        clockThread = null;
    }
}
```

EXAMPLE: The 400,000 Micron Thread Race

HTML PAGES CONTAINING APPLET: *http://java.sun.com/docs/books/tutorial/essential/threads/priority.html*

Where Explained: *Understanding Thread Priority* (page 340)

RaceApplet.java

SOURCE CODE: *http://java.sun.com/docs/books/tutorial/essential/threads/example-1dot1/RaceApplet.java*

1.0 SOURCE CODE: *http://java.sun.com/docs/books/tutorial/essential/threads/example/RaceApplet.java*

```
import java.awt.*;
import java.awt.event.*;
import java.applet.Applet;

public class RaceApplet extends Applet implements Runnable {

    private final static int NUMRUNNERS = 2;
    private final static int SPACING = 20;

    private Runner[] runners = new Runner[NUMRUNNERS];

    private Thread updateThread = null;

    public void init() {
        String raceType = getParameter("type");
        for (int i = 0; i < NUMRUNNERS; i++) {
            runners[i] = new Runner();
            if (raceType.compareTo("unfair") == 0)
                    runners[i].setPriority(i+2);
            else
                    runners[i].setPriority(2);
        }
        if (updateThread == null) {
            updateThread = new Thread(this, "Thread Race");
            updateThread.setPriority(NUMRUNNERS+2);
        }
        addMouseListener(new MyAdapter());
    }

    class MyAdapter extends MouseAdapter {
        public void mouseClicked(MouseEvent evt) {
            if (!updateThread.isAlive())
```

```
                updateThread.start();
            for (int i = 0; i < NUMRUNNERS; i++) {
                if (!runners[i].isAlive())
                    runners[i].start();
            }
        }
    }

    public void paint(Graphics g) {
        g.setColor(Color.lightGray);
        g.fillRect(0, 0, getSize().width, getSize().height);
        g.setColor(Color.black);
        for (int i = 0; i < NUMRUNNERS; i++) {
            int pri = runners[i].getPriority();
            g.drawString(new Integer(pri).toString(), 0,
                         (i+1)*SPACING);
        }
        update(g);
    }

    public void update(Graphics g) {
        for (int i = 0; i < NUMRUNNERS; i++) {
            g.drawLine(SPACING, (i+1)*SPACING,
                       SPACING + (runners[i].tick)/1000,
                       (i+1)*SPACING);
        }
    }

    public void run() {
        Thread myThread = Thread.currentThread();
        while (updateThread == myThread) {
            repaint();
            try {
                updateThread.sleep(10);
            } catch (InterruptedException e) { }
        }
    }

    public void stop() {
        for (int i = 0; i < NUMRUNNERS; i++) {
            if (runners[i].isAlive())
                runners[i] = null;
        }
        if (updateThread.isAlive())
            updateThread = null;
    }
}
```

Runner.java

SOURCE CODE: *http://java.sun.com/docs/books/tutorial/essential/threads/example-1dot1/Runner.java*

1.0 SOURCE CODE: *http://java.sun.com/docs/books/tutorial/essential/threads/example/Runner.java*

```
public class Runner extends Thread {
    public int tick = 1;
    public void run() {
        while (tick < 400000)
            tick++;
    }
}
```

RaceTest.java

SOURCE CODE: *http://java.sun.com/docs/books/tutorial/essential/threads/example/RaceTest.java*

```
public class RaceTest {

    private final static int NUMRUNNERS = 2;

    public static void main(String[] args) {

       SelfishRunner[] runners = new SelfishRunner[NUMRUNNERS];

        for (int i = 0; i < NUMRUNNERS; i++) {
            runners[i] = new SelfishRunner(i);
            runners[i].setPriority(2);
        }
        for (int i = 0; i < NUMRUNNERS; i++)
            runners[i].start();
    }
}
```

SelfishRunner.java

SOURCE CODE: *http://java.sun.com/docs/books/tutorial/essential/threads/example/SelfishRunner.java*

```
public class SelfishRunner extends Thread {

    private int tick = 1;
    private int num;

    public SelfishRunner(int num) {
```

```
            this.num = num;
        }

        public void run() {
            while (tick < 400000) {
                tick++;
                if ((tick % 50000) == 0)
                   System.out.println("Thread #" + num + ", tick = "
                                                 + tick);
            }
        }
    }
```

PoliteRunner.java

SOURCE CODE: *http://java.sun.com/docs/books/tutorial/essential/threads/example/PoliteRunner.java*

```
    public class PoliteRunner extends Thread {

        private int tick = 1;
        private int num;

        public PoliteRunner(int num) {
            this.num = num;
        }

        public void run() {
            while (tick < 400000) {
                tick++;
                if ((tick % 50000) == 0) {
                   System.out.println("Thread #" + num + ", tick = "
                                                 + tick);
                    yield();
                }
            }
        }
    }
```

RaceTest2.java

SOURCE CODE: *http://java.sun.com/docs/books/tutorial/essential/threads/example/RaceTest2.java*

```
    public class RaceTest2 {

        private final static int NUMRUNNERS = 2;
```

```
    public static void main(String[] args) {

        PoliteRunner[] runners = new PoliteRunner[NUMRUNNERS];

        for (int i = 0; i < NUMRUNNERS; i++) {
            runners[i] = new PoliteRunner(i);
            runners[i].setPriority(2);
        }
        for (int i = 0; i < NUMRUNNERS; i++)
            runners[i].start();
    }
}
```

EXAMPLE: Producer/Consumer

Where Explained:
Synchronizing Threads (page 346)

Producer.java

SOURCE CODE: *http://java.sun.com/docs/books/tutorial/essential/threads/example/Producer.java*

```
public class Producer extends Thread {
    private CubbyHole cubbyhole;
    private int number;

    public Producer(CubbyHole c, int number) {
        cubbyhole = c;
        this.number = number;
    }

    public void run() {
        for (int i = 0; i < 10; i++) {
            cubbyhole.put(i);
            System.out.println("Producer #" + this.number
                               + " put: " + i);
            try {
                sleep((int)(Math.random() * 100));
            } catch (InterruptedException e) { }
        }
    }
}
```

Consumer.java

SOURCE CODE: *http://java.sun.com/docs/books/tutorial/essential/threads/example/Consumer.java*

```
public class Consumer extends Thread {
    private CubbyHole cubbyhole;
    private int number;

    public Consumer(CubbyHole c, int number) {
        cubbyhole = c;
        this.number = number;
    }

    public void run() {
        int value = 0;
        for (int i = 0; i < 10; i++) {
            value = cubbyhole.get();
            System.out.println(" Consumer #" + this.number
                                 + " got: " + value);
        }
    }
}
```

CubbyHole.java

SOURCE CODE: *http://java.sun.com/docs/books/tutorial/essential/threads/example/CubbyHole.java*

```
public class CubbyHole {
    private int contents;
    private boolean available = false;

    public synchronized int get() {
        while (available == false) {
            try {
                wait();
            } catch (InterruptedException e) { }
        }
        available = false;
        notify();
        return contents;
    }

    public synchronized void put(int value) {
        while (available == true) {
            try {
                wait();
```

```
            } catch (InterruptedException e) { }
        }
        contents = value;
        available = true;
        notify();
    }
}
```

ProducerConsumerTest.java

SOURCE CODE: *http://java.sun.com/docs/books/tutorial/essential/threads/example/ProducerConsumerTest.java*

```
public class ProducerConsumerTest {
    public static void main(String[] args) {
        CubbyHole c = new CubbyHole();
        Producer p1 = new Producer(c, 1);
        Consumer c1 = new Consumer(c, 1);

        p1.start();
        c1.start();
    }
}
```

EXAMPLE: A Test for Reentrant Locks

Where Explained:
Reaquiring a Lock (page 350)

Reentrant.java

SOURCE CODE: *http://java.sun.com/docs/books/tutorial/essential/threads/example/Reentrant.java*

```
public class Reentrant {
    public synchronized void a() {
        b();
        System.out.println("here I am, in a()");
    }
    public synchronized void b() {
        System.out.println("here I am, in b()");
    }
}
```

ReentrantTest.java

SOURCE CODE: *http://java.sun.com/docs/books/tutorial/essential/threads/example/ReentrantTest.java*

```
public class ReentrantTest {
    public static void main(String[] args) {
        new Reentrant().a();
    }
}
```

EXAMPLE: Listing All of the Threads in a Group

Where Explained: *Using the ThreadGroup Class* (page 358)

EnumerateTest.java

SOURCE CODE: *http://java.sun.com/docs/books/tutorial/essential/threads/example/EnumerateTest.java*

```
public class EnumerateTest {
    public void listCurrentThreads() {
        ThreadGroup currentGroup = Thread.currentThread().
                                         getThreadGroup();
        int numThreads = currentGroup.activeCount();
        Thread[] listOfThreads = new Thread[numThreads];

        currentGroup.enumerate(listOfThreads);
        for (int i = 0; i < numThreads; i++)
            System.out.println("Thread #" + i + " = "
                                 + listOfThreads[i].getName());
    }
}
```

EXAMPLE: Tricking a Thread Group's Maximum Priority

Where Explained: *Using the ThreadGroup Class* (page 358)

MaxPriorityTest.java

SOURCE CODE: *http://java.sun.com/docs/books/tutorial/essential/threads/example/MaxPriorityTest.java*

```
public class MaxPriorityTest {
    public static void main(String[] args) {

        ThreadGroup groupNORM = new ThreadGroup(
                                "A group with normal priority");
        Thread priorityMAX = new Thread(groupNORM,
                               "A thread with maximum priority");

        // set Thread's priority to max (10)
        priorityMAX.setPriority(Thread.MAX_PRIORITY);
```

```
        // set ThreadGroup's max priority to normal (5)
        groupNORM.setMaxPriority(Thread.NORM_PRIORITY);

        System.out.println("Group's maximum priority = "
                           + groupNORM.getMaxPriority());
        System.out.println("Thread's priority = "
                           + priorityMAX.getPriority());
    }
}
```

LESSON 17: Reading and Writing (but No 'rithmetic)

EXAMPLE: Copying Files

The two classes in this example do the same thing: copy the contents of the file name `farrago.txt` into another file named `outagain.txt`. The first class uses `FileReader` and `FileWriter`; the second uses `FileInputStream` and `FileOutputStream`.

Copy.java

SOURCE CODE: *http://java.sun.com/docs/books/tutorial/essential/io/example-1dot1/Copy.java*

Where Explained:
How to Use File Streams (page 372)

```
import java.io.*;

public class Copy {
    public static void main(String[] args) throws IOException {
        File inputFile = new File("farrago.txt");
        File outputFile = new File("outagain.txt");

        FileReader in = new FileReader(inputFile);
        FileWriter out = new FileWriter(outputFile);
        int c;

        while ((c = in.read()) != -1)
           out.write(c);
        in.close();
        out.close();
    }
}
```

CopyBytes.java

1.0 SOURCE CODE: *http://java.sun.com/docs/books/tutorial/essential/io/example/CopyBytes.java*

```
import java.io.*;

public class CopyBytes {
    public static void main(String[] args) throws IOException {
        File inputFile = new File("farrago.txt");
        File outputFile = new File("outagain.txt");

        FileInputStream in = new FileInputStream(inputFile);
        FileOutputStream out = new FileOutputStream(
                                 outputFile);
        int c;

        while ((c = in.read()) != -1)
               out.write(c);

        in.close();
        out.close();
    }
}
```

farrago.txt

SOURCE CODE: *http://java.sun.com/docs/books/tutorial/essential/io/example-1dot1/farrago.txt*

```
So she went into the garden to cut a cabbage-leaf, to
make an apple-pie; and at the same time a great
she-bear, coming up the street, pops its head into the
shop. 'What! no soap?' So he died, and she very
imprudently married the barber; and there were
present the Picninnies, and the Joblillies, and the
Garyalies, and the grand Panjandrum himself, with the
little round button at top, and they all fell to playing
the game of catch as catch can, till the gun powder ran
out at the heels of their boots.

Samuel Foote 1720-1777
```

EXAMPLE: Creating a List of Rhyming Words

RhymingWords.java

Where Explained:
How to Use Pipe Streams (page 374)

SOURCE CODE: *http://java.sun.com/docs/books/tutorial/essential/io/example-1dot1/RhymingWords.java*

1.0 SOURCE CODE: *http://java.sun.com/docs/books/tutorial/essential/io/example/RhymingWords.java*

```
import java.io.*;

public class RhymingWords {
    public static void main(String[] args) throws IOException {

        FileReader words = new FileReader("words.txt"));

        // do the reversing and sorting
        Reader rhyming = reverse(sort(reverse(words)));

        // write new list to standard out
        BufferedReader in = new BufferedReader(rhyming);
        String input;

        while ((input = in.readLine()) != null)
            System.out.println(input);
        in.close();
    }

    public static Reader reverse(Reader source)
                                      throws IOException {
        BufferedReader in = new BufferedReader(source);

        PipedWriter pipeOut = new PipedWriter();
        PipedReader pipeIn = new PipedReader(pipeOut);
        PrintWriter out = new PrintWriter(pipeOut);

        new ReverseThread(out, in).start();

        return pipeIn;
    }

    public static Reader sort(Reader source)
                                   throws IOException {
        BufferedReader in = new BufferedReader(source);

        PipedWriter pipeOut = new PipedOutputStream();
        PipedReader pipeIn new PipedInputStream(pipeOut);
        PrintWriter out = new PrintWriter(pipeOut);
```

```
            new SortThread(out, in).start();

            return pipeIn;
        }
    }
```

ReverseThread.java

SOURCE CODE: *http://java.sun.com/docs/books/tutorial/essential/io/example-1dot1/ReverseThread.java*

1.0 SOURCE CODE: *http://java.sun.com/docs/books/tutorial/essential/io/example/ReverseThread.java*

```
import java.io.*;

public class ReverseThread extends Thread {
    private PrintWriter out = null;
    private BufferedReader in = null;

    public ReverseThread(PrintWriter out, BufferedReader in) {
        this.out = out;
        this.in = in;
    }

    public void run() {
        if (out != null && in != null) {
            try {
                String input;
                while ((input = in.readLine()) != null) {
                    out.println(reverseIt(input));
                    out.flush();
                }
                out.close();
            } catch (IOException e) {
                System.err.println("ReverseThread run: "
                                   + e);
            }
        }
    }

    protected void finalize() throws IOException {
        if (out != null) {
            out.close();
            out = null;
        }
        if (in != null) {
            in.close();
            in = null;
```

```
        }
    }

    private String reverseIt(String source) {
        int i, len = source.length();
        StringBuffer dest = new StringBuffer(len);

        for (i = (len - 1); i >= 0; i--)
            dest.append(source.charAt(i));
        return dest.toString();
    }
}
```

SortThread.java

SOURCE CODE: *http://java.sun.com/docs/books/tutorial/essential/io/example-1dot1/SortThread.java*

1.0 SOURCE CODE: *http://java.sun.com/docs/books/tutorial/essential/io/example/SortThread.java*

```
import java.io.*;

public class SortThread extends Thread {
    private PrintWriter out = null;
    private BufferedReader in = null;

    public SortThread(PrintWriter out, BufferedReader in) {
        this.out = out;
        this.in = in;
    }

    public void run() {
        int MAXWORDS = 50;

        if (out != null && in != null) {
            try {
                String[] listOfWords = new String[MAXWORDS];
                int numwords = 0, i = 0;

                while ((listOfWords[numwords] = in.readLine())
                        != null)
                    numwords++;
                quicksort(listOfWords, 0, numwords-1);
                for (i = 0; i < numwords; i++)
                    out.println(listOfWords[i]);
                out.close();
            } catch (IOException e) {
                System.err.println("SortThread run: " + e);
```

```
                }
            }
        }

        protected void finalize() throws IOException {
            if (out != null) {
                out.close();
                out = null;
            }
            if (in != null) {
                in.close();
                in = null;
            }
        }

        private static void quicksort(String[] a, int lo0, int hi0) {
            int lo = lo0;
            int hi = hi0;
            if (lo >= hi)
                return;
            String mid = a[(lo + hi) / 2];
            while (lo < hi) {
                while (lo<hi && a[lo].compareTo(mid) < 0)
                    lo++;
                while (lo<hi && a[hi].compareTo(mid) > 0)
                    hi--;
                if (lo < hi) {
                    String T = a[lo];
                    a[lo] = a[hi];
                    a[hi] = T;
                }
            }
            if (hi < lo) {
                int T = hi;
                hi = lo;
                lo = T;
            }
            quicksort(a, lo0, lo);
            quicksort(a, lo == lo0 ? lo+1 : lo, hi0);
        }
    }
```

words.txt

SOURCE CODE: *http://java.sun.com/docs/books/tutorial/essential/io/example-1dot1/words.txt*

1.0 SOURCE CODE: *http://java.sun.com/docs/books/tutorial/essential/io/example/words.txt*

```
anatomy
animation
applet
application
argument
bolts
class
communicate
component
container
development
environment
exception
graphics
image
input
integrate
interface
Java
language
native
network
nuts
object
output
primer
program
security
stream
string
threads
tools
user
```

EXAMPLE: Concatenating a List of Files

Where Explained:
How to Concatenate Files (page 378)

Concatenate.java

SOURCE CODE: *http://java.sun.com/docs/books/tutorial/essential/io/example/Concatenate.java*

```
import java.io.*;

public class Concatenate {
    public static void main(String[] args) throws IOException {
        ListOfFiles mylist = new ListOfFiles(args);

        SequenceInputStream s = new SequenceInputStream(mylist);
        int c;

        while ((c = s.read()) != -1)
           System.out.write(c);

        s.close();
    }
}
```

ListOfFiles.java

SOURCE CODE: *http://java.sun.com/docs/books/tutorial/essential/io/example/ListOfFiles.java*

```
import java.util.*;
import java.io.*;

public class ListOfFiles implements Enumeration {

    private String[] listOfFiles;
    private int current = 0;

    public ListOfFiles(String[] listOfFiles) {
        this.listOfFiles = listOfFiles;
    }

    public boolean hasMoreElements() {
        if (current < listOfFiles.length)
            return true;
        else
            return false;
    }

    public Object nextElement() {
        InputStream in = null;
```

```
        if (!hasMoreElements())
            throw new NoSuchElementException("No more files.");

        else {
            String nextElement = listOfFiles[current];
            current++;
            try {
                in = new FileInputStream(nextElement);
            } catch (FileNotFoundException e) {
                System.err.println("ListOfFiles: Can't open" +
                                   nextElement);
            }
        }
        return in;
    }
}
```

EXAMPLE: An Invoice for Java Merchandise

Where Explained: *How to Use DataInput-Stream and DataOutput-Stream* (page 382)

DataIOTest.java

SOURCE CODE: *http://java.sun.com/docs/books/tutorial/essential/io/example-1dot1/DataIOTest.java*

SOURCE CODE: *http://java.sun.com/docs/books/tutorial/essential/io/example-1dot1/DataIOTest2.java*

1.0 SOURCE CODE: *http://java.sun.com/docs/books/tutorial/essential/io/example/DataIOTest.java*

```
import java.io.*;

public class DataIOTest {
    public static void main(String[] args) throws IOException {

        // write the data out
        DataOutputStream out = new DataOutputStream(
                        new FileOutputStream("invoice1.txt"));

        double[] prices = { 19.99, 9.99, 15.99, 3.99, 4.99 };
        int[] units = { 12, 8, 13, 29, 50 };
        String[] descs = { "Java T-shirt", "Java Mug",
                           "Duke Juggling Dolls",
                           "Java Pin", "Java Key Chain" };

        for (int i = 0; i < prices.length; i ++) {
            out.writeDouble(prices[i]);
            out.writeChar('\t');
            out.writeInt(units[i]);
            out.writeChar('\t');
```

```
                out.writeChars(descs[i]);
                out.writeChar('\n');
            }
            out.close();

            // read it in again
            DataInputStream in = new DataInputStream(new
                                    FileInputStream("invoice1.txt"));

            double price;
            int unit;
            StringBuffer desc;
            double total = 0.0;

            try {
                while (true) {
                    price = in.readDouble();
                    in.readChar();        // throws out the tab
                    unit = in.readInt();
                    in.readChar();        // throws out the tab
                    char chr;
                    desc = new StringBuffer(20);
                    char lineSep = System.getProperty(
                                      "line.separator").charAt(0);
                    while ((chr = in. readChar()) != lineSep)
                         desc.append(chr);
                    System.out.println("You've ordered "
                                        + unit + " units of "
                                        + desc + " at $"
                                        + price);
                    total = total + unit * price;
                }
            } catch (EOFException e) {
            }
            System.out.println("For a TOTAL of: $" + total);
            in.close();
        }
    }
```

EXAMPLE: Filtered Streams That Compute a Checksum

CheckedOutputStream.java

Where Explained: *How to Write Your Own Filter Streams* (page 384)

SOURCE CODE: *http://java.sun.com/docs/books/tutorial/essential/io/example/CheckedOutputStream.java*

```
import java.io.*;

public class CheckedOutputStream extends FilterOutputStream {
    private Checksum cksum;
    public CheckedOutputStream(OutputStream out,
                               Checksum cksum) {
        super(out);
        this.cksum = cksum;
    }

    public void write(int b) throws IOException {
        out.write(b);
        cksum.update(b);
    }

    public void write(byte[] b) throws IOException {
        out.write(b, 0, b.length);
        cksum.update(b, 0, b.length);
    }

    public void write(byte[] b, int off, int len)
                                    throws IOException {
        out.write(b, off, len);
        cksum.update(b, off, len);
    }

    public Checksum getChecksum() {
        return cksum;
    }
}
```

CheckedInputStream.java

SOURCE CODE: *http://java.sun.com/docs/books/tutorial/essential/io/example/CheckedInputStream.java*

```
import java.io.FilterInputStream;
import java.io.InputStream;
import java.io.IOException;

public class CheckedInputStream extends FilterInputStream {
    private Checksum cksum;
```

```
    public CheckedInputStream(InputStream in, Checksum cksum) {
        super(in);
        this.cksum = cksum;
    }

    public int read() throws IOException {
        int b = in.read();
        if (b != -1)
            cksum.update(b);
        return b;
    }

    public int read(byte[] b) throws IOException {
        int len;
        len = in.read(b, 0, b.length);
        if (len != -1)
            cksum.update(b, 0, b.length);
        return len;
    }

    public int read(byte[] b, int off, int len)
                                          throws IOException
    {
        len = in.read(b, off, len);
        if (len != -1)
            cksum.update(b, off, len);
        return len;
    }

    public Checksum getChecksum() {
        return cksum;
    }
}
```

Checksum.java

SOURCE CODE: *http://java.sun.com/docs/books/tutorial/essential/io/example/Checksum.java*

```
public interface Checksum {
    /**
     * Updates the current checksum with the specified byte.
     */
    public void update(int b);

    /**
     * Updates the current checksum with the
```

```
     * specified array of bytes.
     */
    public void update(byte[] b, int off, int len);

    /**
     * Returns the current checksum value.
     */
    public long getValue();

    /**
     * Resets the checksum to its initial value.
     */
    public void reset();
}
```

Adler32.java

SOURCE CODE: *http://java.sun.com/docs/books/tutorial/essential/io/example/Adler32.java*

```
public class Adler32 implements Checksum {
    private int value = 1;

    /*
     * BASE is the largest prime number smaller than 65536
     * NMAX is the largest n such that:
     *      255n(n+1)/2 + (n+1)(BASE-1) <= 2^32-1
     */
    private static final int BASE = 65521;
    private static final int NMAX = 5552;

    /**
    * Update current Adler-32 checksum given the specified byte.
     */
    public void update(int b) {
        int s1 = value & 0xffff;
        int s2 = (value >> 16) & 0xffff;
        s1 += b & 0xff;
        s2 += s1;
        value = ((s2 % BASE) << 16) | (s1 % BASE);
    }

    /**
     * Update current Adler-32 checksum given the specified
     * byte array.
     */
    public void update(byte[] b, int off, int len) {
        int s1 = value & 0xffff;
```

```
            int s2 = (value >> 16) & 0xffff;

            while (len > 0) {
                int k = len < NMAX ? len : NMAX;
                len -= k;
                while (k-- > 0) {
                    s1 += b[off++] & 0xff;
                    s2 += s1;
                }
                s1 %= BASE;
                s2 %= BASE;
            }
            value = (s2 << 16) | s1;
        }

        /**
         * Reset Adler-32 checksum to initial value.
         */
        public void reset() {
            value = 1;
        }

        /**
         * Returns current checksum value.
         */
        public long getValue() {
            return (long)value & 0xffffffff;
        }
    }
```

CheckedIOTest.java

SOURCE CODE: *http://java.sun.com/docs/books/tutorial/essential/io/example/CheckedIOTest.java*

```
import java.io.*;

public class CheckedIOTest {
    public static void main(String[] args) throws IOException {

        Adler32 inChecker = new Adler32();
        Adler32 outChecker = new Adler32();
        CheckedInputStream in = null;
        CheckedOutputStream out = null;

        try {
            in = new CheckedInputStream(
                new FileInputStream("farrago.txt"), inChecker);
```

```
            out = new CheckedOutputStream(
                  new FileOutputStream("outagain.txt"), outChecker);
        } catch (FileNotFoundException e) {
            System.err.println("CheckedIOTest: " + e);
            System.exit(-1);
        } catch (IOException e) {
            System.err.println("CheckedIOTest: " + e);
            System.exit(-1);
        }

        int c;

        while ((c = in.read()) != -1)
           out.write(c);

        System.out.println("Input stream check sum: "
                           + inChecker.getValue());
        System.out.println("Output stream check sum: "
                           + outChecker.getValue());

        in.close();
        out.close();
    }
}
```

EXAMPLE: DataInput and DataOutput Filtered Streams

CheckedDataOutput.java

Where Explained: *Writing Filters for Random Access Files* (page 397)

SOURCE CODE: *http://java.sun.com/docs/books/tutorial/essential/io/example/CheckedDataOutput.java*

```
/*
 * This class is an example only. A "final" version of
 * this class should implement the DataOutput interface
 * and provide implementations for the methods declared in
 * DataOutput.
 */

import java.io.*;

public class CheckedDataOutput {
    private Checksum cksum;
    private DataOutput out;

    public CheckedDataOutput(DataOutput out, Checksum cksum) {
        this.cksum = cksum;
        this.out = out;
    }
```

```
    public void write(int b) throws IOException {
        out.write(b);
        cksum.update(b);
    }

    public void write(byte[] b) throws IOException {
        out.write(b, 0, b.length);
        cksum.update(b, 0, b.length);
    }
    public void write(byte[] b, int off, int len)
                                            throws IOException {
        out.write(b, off, len);
        cksum.update(b, off, len);
    }

    public Checksum getChecksum() {
        return cksum;
    }
}
```

CheckedDataInput.java

SOURCE CODE: *http://java.sun.com/docs/books/tutorial/essential/io/example/CheckedDataInput.java*

```
/*
 * This class is an example only. A "final" version of
 * this class should implement the DataInput interface
 * and provide implementations for the methods declared in
 * DataInput.
 */
import java.io.*;

public class CheckedDataInput {
    private Checksum cksum;
    private DataInput in;

    public CheckedDataInput(DataInput in, Checksum cksum) {
        this.cksum = cksum;
        this.in = in;
    }

    public byte readByte() throws IOException {
        byte b = in.readByte();
        cksum.update(b);
        return b;
```

```
    }

    public void readFully(byte[] b) throws IOException {
        in.readFully(b, 0, b.len);
        cksum.update(b, 0, b.len);
    }

    public void readFully(byte[] b, int off, int len)
                                        throws IOException {
        in.readFully(b, off, len);
        cksum.update(b, off, len);
    }

    public Checksum getChecksum() {
        return cksum;
    }
}
```

CheckedDITest.java

SOURCE CODE: *http://java.sun.com/docs/books/tutorial/essential/io/example/CheckedDITest.java*

```
import java.io.*;

public class CheckedDITest {
    public static void main(String[] args) throws IOException {

        Adler32 inChecker = new Adler32();
        Adler32 outChecker = new Adler32();
        CheckedDataInput in = null;
        CheckedDataOutput out = null;

        try {
            in = new CheckedDataInput(new DataInputStream(
                                     new FileInputStream(
                                     "farrago.txt")),
                                     inChecker);
            out = new CheckedDataOutput(new DataOutputStream(
                                       newFileOutputStream(
                                       "outagain.txt")),
                                       outChecker);
        } catch (FileNotFoundException e) {
            System.err.println("CheckedIOTest: " + e);
            System.exit(-1);
        } catch (IOException e) {
            System.err.println("CheckedIOTest: " + e);
            System.exit(-1);
```

```
        }

        boolean EOF = false;

        while (!EOF) {
            try {
                int c = in.readByte();
                out.write(c);
            } catch (EOFException e) {
                EOF = true;
            }
        }

        System.out.println("Input stream check sum: " +
            in.getChecksum().getValue());
        System.out.println("Output stream check sum: " +
            out.getChecksum().getValue());
    }
}
```

CheckedRAFTest.java

SOURCE CODE: *http://java.sun.com/docs/books/tutorial/essential/io/example/CheckedRAFTest.java*

```
import java.io.*;

public class CheckedRAFTest {
    public static void main(String[] args) throws IOException {

        Adler32 inChecker = new Adler32();
        Adler32 outChecker = new Adler32();
        CheckedDataInput in = null;
        CheckedDataOutput out = null;

        try {
          in = new CheckedDataInput(new
               RandomAccessFile("farrago.txt", "r"), inChecker);
          out = new CheckedDataOutput(new
              RandomAccessFile("outagain.txt", "rw"), outChecker);
        } catch (FileNotFoundException e) {
            System.err.println("CheckedIOTest: " + e);
            System.exit(-1);
        } catch (IOException e) {
            System.err.println("CheckedIOTest: " + e);
            System.exit(-1);
        }

        boolean EOF = false;
```

```
        while (!EOF) {
            try {
                int c = in.readByte();
                out.write(c);
            } catch (EOFException e) {
                EOF = true;
            }
        }

        System.out.println("Input stream check sum: " +
                           in.getChecksum().getValue());
        System.out.println("Output stream check sum: " +
                           out.getChecksum().getValue());
    }
}
```

Creating a User Interface

LESSON 18: Overview of the Java UI

EXAMPLE: The AppletButton Applet

Where Explained:
Defining and Using Applet Parameters (page 200)

HTML PAGES CONTAINING APPLET:
http://java.sun.com/docs/books/tutorial/ui/overview/components.html
http://java.sun.com/docs/books/tutorial/ui/components/dialog.html
http://java.sun.com/docs/books/tutorial/ui/components/menu.html
http://java.sun.com/docs/books/tutorial/ui/layout/using.html (multiple instances)
http://java.sun.com/docs/books/tutorial/ui/layout/border.html
http://java.sun.com/docs/books/tutorial/ui/layout/card.html
http://java.sun.com/docs/books/tutorial/ui/layout/flow.html
http://java.sun.com/docs/books/tutorial/ui/layout/grid.html
http://java.sun.com/docs/books/tutorial/ui/layout/gridbag.html
http://java.sun.com/docs/books/tutorial/ui/layout/gridbagExample.html
http://java.sun.com/docs/books/tutorial/ui/layout/custom.html
http://java.sun.com/docs/books/tutorial/ui/layout/none.html

The `AppletButton` applet is a highly configurable applet used to bring up windows.

AppletButton.java

SOURCE CODE: *http://java.sun.com/docs/books/tutorial/ui/overview/example-1dot1/AppletButton.java*

1.0 SOURCE CODE: *http://java.sun.com/docs/books/tutorial/ui/overview/example/AppletButton.java*

```
import java.awt.*;
import java.awt.event.*;
import java.util.*;
import java.applet.Applet;

public class AppletButton extends Applet
                          implements Runnable,
                                     ActionListener {
    int frameNumber = 1;
    String windowClass;
    String buttonText;
    String windowTitle;
    int requestedWidth = 0;
    int requestedHeight = 0;
    Button button;
    Thread windowThread;
    Label label;
    boolean pleaseShow = false;
    boolean shouldInitialize = true;
```

```
Class windowClassObject;

public void init() {
    //Look up the parameters we need right away.
    windowClass = getParameter("WINDOWCLASS");
    if (windowClass == null) {
        windowClass = "TestWindow";
    }
    buttonText = getParameter("BUTTONTEXT");
    if (buttonText == null) {
     buttonText = "Click here to bring up a " + windowClass;
    }

    //Set up the button this applet displays.
    setLayout(new GridLayout(2,0));
    add(button = new Button(buttonText));
    button.setFont(new Font("SansSerif", Font.PLAIN, 14));
    button.addActionListener(this);
    add(label = new Label("", Label.CENTER));
}

public void start() {
    if (windowThread == null) {
        windowThread = new Thread(this, "Bringing Up "
                                        + windowClass);
        windowThread.start();
    }
}

public void stop() {
    windowThread = null;
}

public synchronized void run() {
    Object object = null;
    Frame window = null;
    String name = null;

    if (shouldInitialize) {
        //Look up the rest of the parameters.
        windowTitle = getParameter("WINDOWTITLE");
        if (windowTitle == null) {
            windowTitle = windowClass;
        }
        String windowWidthString = getParameter(
                                      "WINDOWWIDTH");
        if (windowWidthString != null) {
            try {
```

```
                    requestedWidth =
                        Integer.parseInt(windowWidthString);
                } catch (NumberFormatException e) {
                    //Use default width.
                }
            }
            String windowHeightString =
                    getParameter("WINDOWHEIGHT");
            if (windowHeightString != null) {
                try {
                    requestedHeight =
                        Integer.parseInt(windowHeightString);
                } catch (NumberFormatException e) {
                    //Use default height.
                }
            }

            // Make sure the window class exists.
            try {
                windowClassObject = Class.forName(windowClass);
            } catch (Exception e) {
                // The class isn't anywhere that we can find.
            label.setText("Bad parameter: Couldn't find class "
                                + windowClass);
                button.setEnabled(false);
                return;
            }

            // Create an invisible instance.
            window = createWindow(windowTitle);
            if (window == null) {
                return;
            }

            shouldInitialize = false;
        }

        Thread currentThread = Thread.currentThread();
        while (currentThread == windowThread) {

            //Wait until we're asked to show a window.
            while (pleaseShow == false) {
                try {
                    wait();
                } catch (InterruptedException e) {
                }
            }
```

```
            //We've been asked to bring up a window.
            pleaseShow = false;

            //Create another window if necessary.
            if (window == null) {
                window = createWindow(windowTitle + ": "
                                      + ++frameNumber);
            }

            window.setVisible(true);
            label.setText("");
            window = null;
        } //end thread loop
    }

    private Frame createWindow(String title) {
        Object object = null;
        Frame window = null;

        //Instantiate the window class.
        try {
            object = windowClassObject.newInstance();
        } catch (Exception e) {
            label.setText("Bad parameter: Can't instantiate "
                          + windowClassObject);
            button.setEnabled(false);
            return null;
        }

        //Make sure it's a frame.
        try {
            window = (Frame)object;
        } catch (Exception e) {
            label.setText("Bad parameter: "
                          + windowClassObject +
                          " isn't a Frame subclass.");
            button.setEnabled(false);
            return null;
        }

        window.setTitle(title);

        //Set its size.
        window.pack();
        if ((requestedWidth > 0)
          | (requestedHeight > 0)) {
            window.setSize(Math.max(requestedWidth,
                                    window.getSize().width),
```

```
                                Math.max(requestedHeight,
                                         window.getSize().height));
        }

        return window;
    }

    /* Signal the window thread to build a window. */
    public synchronized void actionPerformed(ActionEvent event)
    {
        label.setText(
                "Please wait while the window comes up...");
        pleaseShow = true;
        notify();
    }
}

class TestWindow extends Frame {
    public TestWindow() {
        addWindowListener(new WindowAdapter() {
            public void windowClosing(WindowEvent e) {
                dispose();
            }
        });
    }
}
```

EXAMPLE: Introduction to the AWT Components

Where Explained: *AWT Components* (page 408)

HTML PAGES CONTAINING APPLET: *http://java.sun.com/docs/books/tutorial/ui/overview/components.html*

This program can run either as an application or, with the help of AppletButton.java (page 796), as an applet.

GUIWindow.java

SOURCE CODE: *http://java.sun.com/docs/books/tutorial/ui/overview/example-1dot1/GUIWindow.java*

1.0 SOURCE CODE: *http://java.sun.com/docs/books/tutorial/ui/overview/example/GUIWindow.java*

```
import java.awt.*;
import java.awt.event.*;

public class GUIWindow extends Frame
                       implements ActionListener {
    boolean inAnApplet = true;
    final String FILEDIALOGMENUITEM = "File dialog...";
```

```
public GUIWindow() {
    Panel bottomPanel = new Panel();
    Panel centerPanel = new Panel();
    setLayout(new BorderLayout());

    //Set up the menu bar.
    MenuBar mb = new MenuBar();
    Menu m = new Menu("Menu");
    m.add(new MenuItem("Menu item 1"));
    m.add(new CheckboxMenuItem("Menu item 2"));
    m.add(new MenuItem("Menu item 3"));
    m.add(new MenuItem("-"));

  MenuItem fileMenuItem = new MenuItem(FILEDIALOGMENUITEM);
    fileMenuItem.addActionListener(this);
    m.add(fileMenuItem);

    mb.add(m);
    setMenuBar(mb);

    //Add small things at the bottom of the window.
    bottomPanel.add(new TextField("TextField"));
    bottomPanel.add(new Button("Button"));
    bottomPanel.add(new Checkbox("Checkbox"));
    Choice c = new Choice();
    c.add("Choice Item 1");
    c.add("Choice Item 2");
    c.add("Choice Item 3");
    bottomPanel.add(c);
    add("South", bottomPanel);

    //Add big things to the center area of the window.
    centerPanel.setLayout(new GridLayout(1,2));
    //Put a canvas in the left column.
    centerPanel.add(new MyCanvas());
    //Put a label and a text area in the right column.
    Panel p = new Panel();
    p.setLayout(new BorderLayout());
    p.add("North", new Label("Label", Label.CENTER));
    p.add("Center", new TextArea("TextArea", 5, 20));
    centerPanel.add(p);
    add("Center", centerPanel);

    //Put a list on the right side of the window.
    List l = new List(3, false);
    for (int i = 1; i <= 10; i++) {
        l.add("List item " + i);
    }
```

```
        add("East", l);

        addWindowListener(new WindowAdapter() {
            public void windowClosing(WindowEvent e) {
                if (inAnApplet) {
                    dispose();
                } else {
                    System.exit(0);
                }
            }
        });
    }

    public void actionPerformed(ActionEvent event) {
        //The only action event we get is when the
        //user requests we bring up a FileDialog.
        FileDialog fd = new FileDialog(this, "FileDialog");
        fd.setVisible(true);
    }

    public static void main(String[] args) {
        GUIWindow window = new GUIWindow();
        window.inAnApplet = false;

        window.setTitle("The AWT Components");
        window.pack();
        window.setVisible(true);
    }

}

//We can't just instantiate Canvas, since its default
//implementation gives us nothing interesting to look at or do.
//So here's a Canvas subclass that draws something slightly
//interesting.
class MyCanvas extends Canvas {

    public void paint(Graphics g) {
        int w = getSize().width;
        int h = getSize().height;
        g.drawRect(0, 0, w - 1, h - 1);
        g.drawString("Canvas",
                     (w - g.getFontMetrics().stringWidth(
                                                  "Canvas"))/2,
                     10);

        g.setFont(new Font("SansSerif", Font.PLAIN, 8));
        g.drawLine(10,10, 100,100);
```

```
        g.fillRect(9,9,3,3);
        g.drawString("(10,10)", 13, 10);
        g.fillRect(49,49,3,3);
        g.drawString("(50,50)", 53, 50);
        g.fillRect(99,99,3,3);
        g.drawString("(100,100)", 103, 100);
    }

    //If we don't specify this, the canvas might not show up at
    //all (depending on the layout manager).
    public Dimension getMinimumSize() {
        return new Dimension(150,130);
    }

    //If we don't specify this, the canvas might not show up at
    //all (depending on the layout manager).
    public Dimension getPreferredSize() {
        return getMinimumSize();
    }
}
```

EXAMPLE: The Converter Applet/Application

HTML PAGES CONTAINING APPLET: *http://java.sun.com/docs/books/tutorial/ui/overview/anatomy.html*

Where Explained: *The Anatomy of a GUI-Based Program* (page 413)

This program can run either as an applet or as an application.

Converter.java

SOURCE CODE: *http://java.sun.com/docs/books/tutorial/ui/overview/example-1dot1/Converter.java*

1.0 SOURCE CODE: *http://java.sun.com/docs/books/tutorial/ui/overview/example/Converter.java*

```
import java.awt.*;
import java.awt.event.*;
import java.util.*;
import java.applet.Applet;

public class Converter extends Applet {
    ConversionPanel metricPanel, usaPanel;
    Unit[] metricDistances = new Unit[3];
    Unit[] usaDistances = new Unit[4];

    /**
     * Create the ConversionPanels (one for metric, another for
     * U.S.).  I used "U.S." because although Imperial and U.S.
     * distance measurements are the same, this program could
```

```
     * be extended to include volume measurements, which aren't
     * the same.
     */
    public void init() {
        //Use a GridLayout with 2 rows, as many columns as
        //necessary, and 5 pixels of padding around all edges
        //of each cell.
        setLayout(new GridLayout(2,0,5,5));

        //Create Unit objects for metric distances, and then
        //instantiate a ConversionPanel with these Units.
        metricDistances[0] = new Unit("Centimeters", 0.01);
        metricDistances[1] = new Unit("Meters", 1.0);
        metricDistances[2] = new Unit("Kilometers", 1000.0);
       metricPanel = new ConversionPanel(this, "Metric System",
                                          metricDistances);

        //Create Unit objects for U.S. distances, and then
        //instantiate a ConversionPanel with these Units.
        usaDistances[0] = new Unit("Inches", 0.0254);
        usaDistances[1] = new Unit("Feet", 0.305);
        usaDistances[2] = new Unit("Yards", 0.914);
        usaDistances[3] = new Unit("Miles", 1613.0);
        usaPanel = new ConversionPanel(this, "U.S. System",
                                       usaDistances);

        //Add both ConversionPanels to the Converter.
        add(metricPanel);
        add(usaPanel);
    }

    /**
     * Does the conversion from metric to U.S., or vice versa, and
     * updates the appropriate ConversionPanel.
     */
    void convert(ConversionPanel from) {
        ConversionPanel to;

        if (from == metricPanel)
            to = usaPanel;
        else
            to = metricPanel;

        double multiplier = from.getMultiplier()
                            / to.getMultiplier();
        to.setValue(multiplier * from.getValue());
    }

    /** Draws a box around this panel. */
```

```
    public void paint(Graphics g) {
        Dimension d = getSize();
        g.drawRect(0,0, d.width - 1, d.height - 1);
    }

    /**
     * Puts a little breathing space between
     * the panel and its contents, which lets us draw a box
     * in the paint() method.
     */
    public Insets getInsets() {
        return new Insets(5,5,5,5);
    }

    //Executed only when this program runs as an application.
    public static void main(String[] args) {
        //Create a new window.
        Frame f = new Frame("Converter Applet/Application");
        f.addWindowListener(new WindowAdapter() {
            public void windowClosing(WindowEvent e) {
                System.exit(0);
            }
        });

        //Create a Converter instance.
        Converter converter = new Converter();

        //Initialize the Converter instance.
        converter.init();

       //Add the Converter to the window and display the window.
        f.add("Center", converter);
       f.pack();       //Resizes the window to its natural size.
        f.setVisible(true);
    }
}

class ConversionPanel extends Panel
                      implements ActionListener,
                                 AdjustmentListener,
                                 ItemListener {
    TextField textField;
    Choice unitChooser;
    Scrollbar slider;
    int max = 10000;
    int block = 100;
    Converter controller;
```

```
    Unit[] units;

    ConversionPanel(Converter myController, String myTitle,
                    Unit[] myUnits) {
        //Initialize this ConversionPanel to use a GridBagLayout.
        GridBagConstraints c = new GridBagConstraints();
        GridBagLayout gridbag = new GridBagLayout();
        setLayout(gridbag);

        //Save arguments in instance variables.
        controller = myController;
        units = myUnits;

        //Set up default layout constraints.
        c.fill = GridBagConstraints.HORIZONTAL;

        //Add the label.  It displays this panel's title,
        //centered.
        Label label = new Label(myTitle, Label.CENTER);
        c.gridwidth = GridBagConstraints.REMAINDER; //Ends row
        gridbag.setConstraints(label, c);
        add(label);

        //Add the text field.  It initially displays "0" and needs
        //to be at least 10 columns wide.
        textField = new TextField("0", 10);
        c.weightx = 1.0;  //Use maximum horizontal space...
        c.gridwidth = 1; //The default value.
        gridbag.setConstraints(textField, c);
        add(textField);
        textField.addActionListener(this);

        //Add the pop-up list (Choice).
        unitChooser = new Choice();
        for (int i = 0; i < units.length; i++) { //Populate it.
            unitChooser.add(units[i].description);
        }
        c.weightx = 0.0; //The default value.
        c.gridwidth = GridBagConstraints.REMAINDER; //End a row.
        gridbag.setConstraints(unitChooser, c);
        add(unitChooser);
        unitChooser.addItemListener(this);

        //Add the slider.  It's horizontal, and it has the maximum
        //value specified by the instance variable max.  Its
        //initial and minimum values are the default (0).  A click
        //increments the value by block units.
        slider = new Scrollbar(Scrollbar.HORIZONTAL);
```

```
        slider.setMaximum(max + 10);
        slider.setBlockIncrement(block);
        c.gridwidth = 1; //The default value.
        gridbag.setConstraints(slider, c);
        add(slider);
        slider.addAdjustmentListener(this);
    }

    /**
     * Returns the multiplier (units/meter) for the currently
     * selected unit of measurement.
     */
    double getMultiplier() {
        int i = unitChooser.getSelectedIndex();
        return units[i].multiplier;
    }

    /** Draws a box around this panel. */
    public void paint(Graphics g) {
        Dimension d = getSize();
        g.drawRect(0,0, d.width - 1, d.height - 1);
    }

    /**
     * Puts a little breathing space between
     * the panel and its contents, which lets us draw a box
     * in the paint() method.
     * We add more pixels to the right, to work around a
     * Choice bug.
     */
    public Insets getInsets() {
        return new Insets(5,5,5,8);
    }

    /**
     * Gets the current value in the text field.
     * It's guaranteed to be the same as the value
     * in the scroller (subject to rounding, of course).
     */
    double getValue() {
        double f;
        try {
            f = (double)Double.valueOf(textField.getText(
                                               )).doubleValue();
        } catch (java.lang.NumberFormatException e) {
            f = 0.0;
        }
        return f;
```

```
    }

    public void actionPerformed(ActionEvent e) {
        setSliderValue(getValue());
        controller.convert(this);
    }

    /** Respond to the slider. */
    public void adjustmentValueChanged(AdjustmentEvent e) {
        textField.setText(String.valueOf(slider.getValue()));
        controller.convert(this);
    }

    public void itemStateChanged(ItemEvent e) {
        controller.convert(this);
    }

    /** Set the values in the slider and text field. */
    void setValue(double f) {
        setSliderValue(f);
        textField.setText(String.valueOf((float)f));
    }

    /** Set the slider value. */
    void setSliderValue(double f) {
        int sliderValue = (int)f;

        if (sliderValue > max)
                sliderValue = max;
        if (sliderValue < 0)
            sliderValue = 0;
        slider.setValue(sliderValue);
    }
}


class Unit {
    String description;
    double multiplier;

    Unit(String description, double multiplier) {
        super();
        this.description = description;
        this.multiplier = multiplier;
    }

    public String toString() {
```

```
        String s = "Meters/" + description + " = " + multiplier;
        return s;
    }
}
```

EXAMPLE: A Simple Event Example

HTML PAGES CONTAINING APPLET: *http://java.sun.com/docs/books/tutorial/ui/overview/event.html*

Where Explained:
Event Handling (page 420)

Beeper.java

SOURCE CODE: *http://java.sun.com/docs/books/tutorial/ui/overview/example-1dot1/Beeper.java*

```
import java.applet.Applet;
import java.awt.Button;
import java.awt.Toolkit;
import java.awt.BorderLayout;
import java.awt.event.ActionListener;
import java.awt.event.ActionEvent;

public class Beeper extends Applet
                    implements ActionListener {
    Button button;

    public void init() {
        setLayout(new BorderLayout());
        button = new Button("Click Me");
        add("Center", button);

        button.addActionListener(this);
    }

    public void actionPerformed(ActionEvent e) {
        Toolkit.getDefaultToolkit().beep();
    }
}
```

LESSON 19: Using Components, the GUI Building Blocks

EXAMPLE: Button Demo Applet

Where Explained:
How to Use Buttons (page 430)

HTML PAGES CONTAINING APPLET: *http://java.sun.com/docs/books/tutorial/ui/components/button.html*

ButtonDemo.java

SOURCE CODE: *http://java.sun.com/docs/books/tutorial/ui/components/example-1dot1/ButtonDemo.java*

1.0 SOURCE CODE: *http://java.sun.com/docs/books/tutorial/ui/components/example/ButtonDemo.java*

```
import java.awt.*;
import java.awt.event.ActionListener;
import java.awt.event.ActionEvent;
import java.applet.Applet;

public class ButtonDemo extends Applet
                        implements ActionListener {

    Button b1, b2, b3;
    static final String DISABLE = "disable";
    static final String ENABLE = "enable";

    public void init() {
        b1 = new Button();
        b1.setLabel("Disable middle button");
        b1.setActionCommand(DISABLE);

        b2 = new Button("Middle button");

        b3 = new Button("Enable middle button");
        b3.setEnabled(false);
        b3.setActionCommand(ENABLE);

        //Listen for actions on buttons 1 and 3.
        b1.addActionListener(this);
        b3.addActionListener(this);

        //Add Components, using the default FlowLayout.
        add(b1);
        add(b2);
        add(b3);
    }
```

```
    public void actionPerformed(ActionEvent e) {
        String command = e.getActionCommand();

        if (command == DISABLE) { //They clicked "Disable..."
            b2.setEnabled(false);
            b1.setEnabled(false);
            b3.setEnabled(true);
        } else { //They clicked "Enable..."
            b2.setEnabled(true);
            b1.setEnabled(true);
            b3.setEnabled(false);
        }
    }
}
```

EXAMPLE: Canvas Demo Applet

HTML PAGES CONTAINING APPLET: *http://java.sun.com/docs/books/tutorial/ui/components/canvas.html*

Where Explained:
How to Use Canvases (page 432)

ImageApplet.java

SOURCE CODE: *http://java.sun.com/docs/books/tutorial/ui/components/example-1dot1/ImageApplet.java*

1.0 SOURCE CODE: *http://java.sun.com/docs/books/tutorial/ui/components/example/ImageApplet.java*

```
import java.awt.*;
import java.applet.Applet;

class ImageCanvas extends Canvas {
    Container pappy;
    Image image;
    Dimension size;
    int w, h;
    boolean trueSizeKnown;
    MediaTracker tracker;

   public ImageCanvas(Image image, Container highestContainer,
                      int initialWidth, int initialHeight) {
        if (image == null) {
            System.err.println("Canvas got invalid image"
                               + " object!");
            return;
        }

        this.image = image;
        this.pappy = highestContainer;
```

```
            w = initialWidth;
            h = initialHeight;

            tracker = new MediaTracker(this);
            tracker.addImage(image, 0);

            size = new Dimension(w,h);
        }

        public Dimension getPreferredSize() {
            return getMinimumSize();
        }

        public synchronized Dimension getMinimumSize() {
            return size;
        }

        public void paint (Graphics g) {
            if (image != null) {
                if (!trueSizeKnown) {
                    int imageWidth = image.getWidth(this);
                    int imageHeight = image.getHeight(this);

                    if (tracker.checkAll(true)) {
                        trueSizeKnown = true;
                        if (tracker.isErrorAny()) {
                         System.err.println("Error loading image: "
                                            + image);
                        }
                    }

                    //Component-initiated resizing.
                    if (((imageWidth > 0) && (w != imageWidth)) ||
                       ((imageHeight > 0) && (h != imageHeight))) {
                        w = imageWidth;
                        h = imageHeight;
                        size = new Dimension(w,h);
                        setSize(w, h);
                        pappy.validate();
                    }
                }
            }

            g.drawImage(image, 0, 0, this);
            g.drawRect(0, 0, w - 1, h - 1);
        }
    }
```

```
public class ImageApplet extends Applet {
    public void init() {
        Image image1 = getImage(getCodeBase(),
                               "kwalrath.gif");
        Image image2 = getImage(getCodeBase(),
                                 "innocence_small.gif");
        ImageCanvas ic1 = new ImageCanvas(image1, this,
                                          50, 50);
        ImageCanvas ic2 = new ImageCanvas(image2, this,
                                          100, 100);
        add(ic1);
        add(ic2);
    }
}
```

EXAMPLE: Checkbox Demo Applet

HTML PAGES CONTAINING APPLET: *http://java.sun.com/docs/books/tutorial/ui/components/checkbox.html*

Where Explained:
How to Use Checkboxes (page 434)

CheckboxDemo.java

SOURCE CODE: *http://java.sun.com/docs/books/tutorial/ui/components/example/CheckboxDemo.java*

```
import java.awt.*;
import java.applet.Applet;

public class CheckboxDemo extends Applet {

    public void init() {
        Panel p1, p2;
        Checkbox cb1, cb2, cb3; //These are independent
                                //checkboxes.
        Checkbox cb4, cb5, cb6; //These checkboxes are part
                                //of a group
        CheckboxGroup cbg;

        //Build first panel,
        //which contains independent checkboxes
        cb1 = new Checkbox(); //Default state is "off"(false).
        cb1.setLabel("Checkbox 1");
        cb2 = new Checkbox("Checkbox 2");
        cb3 = new Checkbox("Checkbox 3");
        cb3.setState(true); //Set state to "on"(true).
        p1 = new Panel();
        p1.setLayout(new FlowLayout());
        //Using a GridLayout didn't work
        //--kept box and text too far apart.
```

```
            p1.add(cb1);
            p1.add(cb2);
            p1.add(cb3);

            //Build second panel, which contains a checkbox group.
            cbg = new CheckboxGroup();
            cb4 = new Checkbox("Checkbox 4", cbg, false);
                                 //initial state: off
            cb5 = new Checkbox("Checkbox 5", cbg, false);
                                 //initial state: off
            cb6 = new Checkbox("Checkbox 6", cbg, false);
                                 //initial state: off
            p2 = new Panel();
            p2.setLayout(new FlowLayout());
            p2.add(cb4);
            p2.add(cb5);
            p2.add(cb6);

            //Add panels to the Applet.
            setLayout(new GridLayout(0, 2));
            add(p1);
            add(p2);
        }
    }
```

EXAMPLE: Choice Demo Applet

Where Explained: *How to Use Choices* (page 436)

HTML PAGES CONTAINING APPLET: *http://java.sun.com/docs/books/tutorial/ui/components/choice.html*

ChoiceDemo.java

SOURCE CODE: *http://java.sun.com/docs/books/tutorial/ui/components/example-1dot1/ChoiceDemo.java*

1.0 SOURCE CODE: *http://java.sun.com/docs/books/tutorial/ui/components/example/ChoiceDemo.java*

```
import java.awt.*;
import java.awt.event.ItemListener;
import java.awt.event.ItemEvent;
import java.applet.Applet;

public class ChoiceDemo extends Applet
                        implements ItemListener {
    Choice choice; //pop-up list of choices
    Label label;
```

```
    public void init() {
        choice = new Choice();
        choice.addItem("ichi");
        choice.addItem("ni");
        choice.addItem("san");
        choice.addItem("yon");

        choice.addItemListener(this);

        label = new Label();
        setLabelText(choice.getSelectedIndex(),
                     choice.getSelectedItem());

        //Add components to the Applet.
        add(choice);
        add(label);
    }

    void setLabelText(int num, String text) {
        label.setText("Item #" + num + " selected. "
                    + "Text = \"" + text + "\".");
    }

    public void itemStateChanged(ItemEvent e) {
        setLabelText(choice.getSelectedIndex(),
                     choice.getSelectedItem());
    }
}
```

EXAMPLE: Dialog Demo Applet/Application

HTML PAGES CONTAINING APPLET: *http://java.sun.com/docs/books/tutorial/ui/components/dialog.html*

Where Explained:
How to Use Dialogs (page 438)

This program can run either as an application or, with the help of `AppletButton.java` (page 796), as an applet.

DialogWindow.java

SOURCE CODE: *http://java.sun.com/docs/books/tutorial/ui/components/example-1dot1/DialogWindow.java*

1.0 SOURCE CODE: *http://java.sun.com/docs/books/tutorial/ui/components/example/DialogWindow.java*

```
import java.awt.*;
import java.awt.event.*;

public class DialogWindow extends Frame
```

```
                            implements ActionListener {
    boolean inAnApplet = true; //should be private
    private SimpleDialog dialog;
    private TextArea textArea;

    public DialogWindow() {
        textArea = new TextArea(5, 40);
        textArea.setEditable(false);
        add("Center", textArea);
        Button button = new Button("Click to bring up dialog");
        button.addActionListener(this);
        Panel panel = new Panel();
        panel.add(button);
        add("South", panel);

        addWindowListener(new WindowAdapter() {
            public void windowClosing(WindowEvent e) {
                if (inAnApplet) {
                    setVisible(false);
                    dispose();
                } else {
                    System.exit(0);
                }
            }
        });
    }

    public void actionPerformed(ActionEvent event) {
        if (dialog == null) {
            dialog = new SimpleDialog(this, "A Simple Dialog");
        }
        dialog.setVisible(true);
    }

    public void setText(String text) {
        textArea.append(text + "\n");
    }

    public static void main(String args[]) {
        DialogWindow window = new DialogWindow();
        window.inAnApplet = false;

        window.setTitle("DialogWindow Application");
        window.pack();
        window.setVisible(true);
    }
}
```

```
class SimpleDialog extends Dialog implements ActionListener {
    TextField field;
    DialogWindow parent;
    Button setButton;

    SimpleDialog(Frame dw, String title) {
        super(dw, title, false);
        parent = (DialogWindow)dw;

        //Create middle section.
        Panel p1 = new Panel();
        Label label = new Label("Enter random text here:");
        p1.add(label);
        field = new TextField(40);
        field.addActionListener(this);
        p1.add(field);
        add("Center", p1);

        //Create bottom row.
        Panel p2 = new Panel();
        p2.setLayout(new FlowLayout(FlowLayout.RIGHT));
        Button b = new Button("Cancel");
        b.addActionListener(this);
        setButton = new Button("Set");
        setButton.addActionListener(this);
        p2.add(b);
        p2.add(setButton);
        add("South", p2);

        //Initialize this dialog to its preferred size.
        pack();
    }

    public void actionPerformed(ActionEvent event) {
        Object source = event.getSource();
        if ( (source == setButton)
           | (source == field)) {
            parent.setText(field.getText());
        }
        field.selectAll();
        setVisible(false);
    }
}
```

EXAMPLE: Label Demo Applet

Where Explained:
How to Use Labels (page 443)

HTML PAGES CONTAINING APPLET: *http://java.sun.com/docs/books/tutorial/ui/components/label.html*

LabelAlignDemo.java

SOURCE CODE: *http://java.sun.com/docs/books/tutorial/ui/components/example/LabelAlignDemo.java*

```
import java.awt.*;
import java.applet.Applet;

public class LabelAlignDemo extends Applet {

    public void init() {
        Label label1 = new Label();
        label1.setText("Left");
        Label label2 = new Label("Center");
        label2.setAlignment(Label.CENTER);
        Label label3 = new Label("Right", Label.RIGHT);

        //Add Components to the Applet.
        setLayout(new GridLayout(0, 1));
        add(label1);
        add(label2);
        add(label3);
    }
}
```

EXAMPLE: List Demo Applet

HTML PAGES CONTAINING APPLET: *http://java.sun.com/docs/books/tutorial/ui/components/list.html*

Where Explained:
How to Use Lists (page 444)

ListDemo.java

SOURCE CODE: *http://java.sun.com/docs/books/tutorial/ui/components/example-1dot1/ListDemo.java*

1.0 SOURCE CODE: *http://java.sun.com/docs/books/tutorial/ui/components/example/ListDemo.java*

```
import java.awt.*;
import java.awt.event.*;
import java.applet.Applet;

public class ListDemo extends Applet
                      implements ActionListener,
                                 ItemListener {
    TextArea output;
```

```
List spanish, italian;
String newline;

public void init() {
    newline = System.getProperty("line.separator");

    //Build first list, which allows multiple selections.
    spanish = new List(4, true); //prefer 4 items visible
    spanish.add("uno");
    spanish.add("dos");
    spanish.add("tres");
    spanish.add("cuatro");
    spanish.add("cinco");
    spanish.add("seis");
    spanish.add("siete");
    spanish.addActionListener(this);
    spanish.addItemListener(this);

    //Build second list, which allows one selection at a time.
    //Defaults to none visible, one selectable.
    italian = new List();
    italian.add("uno");
    italian.add("due");
    italian.add("tre");
    italian.add("quattro");
    italian.add("cinque");
    italian.add("sei");
    italian.add("sette");
    italian.addActionListener(this);
    italian.addItemListener(this);

    //Add lists to the Applet.
    GridBagLayout gridBag = new GridBagLayout();
    setLayout(gridBag);

    //Can't put text area on right due to GBL bug
    //(can't span rows in any column but the first).
    output = new TextArea(10, 40);
    output.setEditable(false);
    GridBagConstraints tc = new GridBagConstraints();
    tc.fill = GridBagConstraints.BOTH;
    tc.weightx = 1.0;
    tc.weighty = 1.0;
    tc.gridheight = 2;
    gridBag.setConstraints(output, tc);
    add(output);

    GridBagConstraints lc = new GridBagConstraints();
```

```
        lc.fill = GridBagConstraints.VERTICAL;
        lc.gridwidth = GridBagConstraints.REMAINDER; //end row
        gridBag.setConstraints(spanish, lc);
        add(spanish);
        gridBag.setConstraints(italian, lc);
        add(italian);
    }

    public void actionPerformed(ActionEvent e) {
        List list = (List)(e.getSource());
        String language = (list == spanish) ?
                          "Spanish" : "Italian";
        output.append("Action event occurred on \""
                          + list.getSelectedItem()  + "\" in "
                          + language + ".\n");
    }

    public void itemStateChanged(ItemEvent e) {
        List list = (List)(e.getItemSelectable());
        String language = (list == spanish) ?
                          "Spanish" : "Italian";

        int index = ((Integer)(e.getItem())).intValue();
        if (e.getStateChange() == ItemEvent.SELECTED) {
            int sIndex = ((Integer)e.getItem()).intValue();
            output.append("Select event occurred on item #"
                             + index + " (\""
                            + list.getItem(index)  + "\") in "
                             + language + "." + newline);
        } else { //the item was deselected
            output.append("Deselect event occurred on item #"
                             + index + " (\""
                            + list.getItem(index)  + "\") in "
                             + language + "." + newline);
        }
    }
}
```

EXAMPLE: Menu Demo Applet/Application

Where Explained:
How to Use Menus (page 448)

HTML PAGES CONTAINING APPLET: *http://java.sun.com/docs/books/tutorial/ui/components/menu.html*

This program can run either as an application or, with the help of `AppletButton.java` (page 796), as an applet.

MenuWindow.java

SOURCE CODE: *http://java.sun.com/docs/books/tutorial/ui/components/example-1dot1/MenuWindow.java*

1.0 SOURCE CODE: *http://java.sun.com/docs/books/tutorial/ui/components/example/MenuWindow.java*

```
import java.awt.*;
import java.awt.event.*;
public class MenuWindow extends Frame
                        implements ActionListener,
                                   ItemListener {
    boolean inAnApplet = true;
    TextArea output;
    PopupMenu popup;
    String newline;

    public MenuWindow() {
        MenuBar mb;
        Menu m1, m2, m3, m4, m4_1, m5;
        MenuItem mi1_1, mi1_2, mi3_1, mi3_2, mi3_3, mi3_4,
                 mi4_1_1, mi5_1, mi5_2,
                 pmi1, pmi2, mi5_1_duplicate;
        CheckboxMenuItem mi2_1;
        addWindowListener(new WindowAdapter() {
            public void windowClosing(WindowEvent e) {
                if (inAnApplet) {
                    dispose();
                } else {
                    System.exit(0);
                }
            }
        });

        newline = System.getProperty("line.separator");

        //Add regular components to the window.
        setLayout(new BorderLayout()); //max space: output
        output = new TextArea(5, 30);
        output.setEditable(false);
        add("Center", output);
        Label label = new Label("Try bringing up"
                                + " a popup menu!");

        add("North", label);

        //Build the menu bar.
        mb = new MenuBar();
        setMenuBar(mb);
```

```
//Build first menu in the menu bar.
//Specifying the second argument as true
//makes this a tear-off menu.
m1 = new Menu("Menu 1", true);
mb.add(m1);
mi1_1 = new MenuItem("Menu item 1_1");
m1.add(mi1_1);
mi1_2 = new MenuItem("Menu item 1_2");
m1.add(mi1_2);

//Build help menu.
m5 = new Menu("Help Menu");
mb.setHelpMenu(m5);
mi5_1 = new MenuItem("Menu item 5_1");
mi5_1.setShortcut(new MenuShortcut(KeyEvent.VK_5));
m5.add(mi5_1);
mi5_2 = new MenuItem("Menu item 5_2");
m5.add(mi5_2);

//Make a popup menu.
popup = new PopupMenu("A Popup Menu");
add(popup);
pmi1 = new MenuItem("A popup menu item");
popup.add(pmi1);
mi5_1_duplicate =
       new MenuItem("Duplicate of menu item 5_1",
                    new MenuShortcut(KeyEvent.VK_5));
popup.add(mi5_1_duplicate);
pmi2 = new MenuItem("An item with a shortcut",
                    new MenuShortcut(KeyEvent.VK_6));
popup.add(pmi2);

//Build second menu in the menu bar.
m2 = new Menu("Menu 2");
mb.add(m2);
mi2_1 = new CheckboxMenuItem("Menu item 2_1");
m2.add(mi2_1);

//Build third menu in the menu bar.
m3 = new Menu("Menu 3");
mb.add(m3);
mi3_1 = new MenuItem("Menu item 3_1");
m3.add(mi3_1);
mi3_2 = new MenuItem("Menu item 3_2");
m3.add(mi3_2);
m3.addSeparator();
mi3_3 = new MenuItem("Menu item 3_3");
m3.add(mi3_3);
mi3_4 = new MenuItem("Menu item 3_4");
```

```
        mi3_4.setEnabled(false);
        m3.add(mi3_4);
        //Build fourth menu in the menu bar.
        m4 = new Menu("Menu 4");
        mb.add(m4);
        m4_1 = new Menu("Submenu 4_1");
        m4.add(m4_1);
        mi4_1_1 = new MenuItem("Menu item 4_1_1");
        m4_1.add(mi4_1_1);

        //Register as an ActionListener for all menu items.
        m1.addActionListener(this);
        m2.addActionListener(this);
        m3.addActionListener(this);
        m4.addActionListener(this);
        mi4_1_1.addActionListener(this); //m4 can't detect
                                         //submenu actions
        m5.addActionListener(this);
        popup.addActionListener(this);

        //Set action commands for a few menu items.
        mi1_1.setActionCommand("1_1");
        mi1_2.setActionCommand("1_2");
        mi5_1.setActionCommand("5_1");
        mi5_2.setActionCommand("5_2");
        pmi1.setActionCommand("popup item #1");
        mi5_1_duplicate.setActionCommand("5_1");
        pmi2.setActionCommand("popup item #2");

        //Register as ItemListener on checkbox menu item.
        mi2_1.addItemListener(this);

        //Listen for when the popup menu should be shown.
        MouseListener listener = new PopupListener();
        addMouseListener(listener);
        output.addMouseListener(listener);
        label.addMouseListener(listener);
    }

    class PopupListener extends MouseAdapter {
        public void mousePressed(MouseEvent e) {
            maybeShowPopup(e);
        }

        public void mouseReleased(MouseEvent e) {
            maybeShowPopup(e);
```

```
        }

    private void maybeShowPopup(MouseEvent e) {
        if (e.isPopupTrigger()) {
            popup.show(e.getComponent(),
                           e.getX(), e.getY());
            }
        }
    }

    public void actionPerformed(ActionEvent e) {
        output.append("\"" + e.getActionCommand()
                    + "\" action detected in menu labeled \""
                      + ((MenuItem)(e.getSource())).getLabel()
                      + "\"." + newline);
    }

    public void itemStateChanged(ItemEvent e) {
        output.append("Item state change detected on item \""
                      + e.getItem()
                      + "\" (state is "
                      + ((e.getStateChange() ==
                            ItemEvent.SELECTED)?
                            "selected)."
                          : "deselected).")
                      + newline);
    }

    public static void main(String[] args) {
        MenuWindow window = new MenuWindow();
        window.inAnApplet = false;
        window.setTitle("MenuWindow Application");
        window.setSize(450, 200);
        window.setVisible(true);
    }
}
```

EXAMPLE: Scroll Pane Demo Applet

HTML PAGES CONTAINING APPLET: *http://java.sun.com/docs/books/tutorial/ui/components/scrollpane.html*

ImageScroller.java

SOURCE CODE: *http://java.sun.com/docs/books/tutorial/ui/components/example-1dot1/ImageScroller.java*

1.0 SOURCE CODE: *http://java.sun.com/docs/books/tutorial/ui/components/example/ImageScroller.java*

Where Explained:
How to Use Scroll Panes (page 459)

```
import java.awt.*;
import java.applet.*;
import java.net.URL;

class ScrollableCanvas extends Canvas {
    Image image;
    public String imageFile = "people.gif";
    Dimension preferredSize = new Dimension(600, 320);
    Dimension minimumSize = new Dimension(10, 10);

    public void setImage(Image img) {
        image = img;
    }

    public Dimension getMinimumSize() {
        return minimumSize;
    }

    public Dimension getPreferredSize() {
        /*
         * If we didn't hard code the preferred size,
         * then we'd have to inform the scrollpane
         * when we got the real size data.
         */
        return preferredSize;
    }

    public void paint(Graphics g) {
        g.drawImage(image, 0, 0, getBackground(), this);
    }
```

```
}

public class ImageScroller extends Applet {
    public void init() {
        ScrollableCanvas canvas = new ScrollableCanvas();
        canvas.setImage(getImage(getCodeBase(),
                                 canvas.imageFile));

        setLayout(new BorderLayout());
        ScrollPane pane = new ScrollPane();
        pane.add(canvas);
        add("Center", pane);
    }
}
```

EXAMPLE: Text Demo Applet

Where Explained: *How to Use Text Areas and Fields* (page 462)

HTML PAGES CONTAINING APPLET: *http://java.sun.com/docs/books/tutorial/ui/components/text.html*

TextDemo.java

SOURCE CODE: *http://java.sun.com/docs/books/tutorial/ui/components/example-1dot1/TextDemo.java*

1.0 SOURCE CODE: *http://java.sun.com/docs/books/tutorial/ui/components/example/TextDemo.java*

```
import java.awt.*;
import java.awt.event.*;
import java.applet.Applet;

public class TextDemo extends Applet
                      implements ActionListener {
    TextField textField;
    TextArea textArea;
    String newline;

    public void init() {
        textField = new TextField(20);
        textArea = new TextArea(5, 20);
        textArea.setEditable(false);

        //Add Components to the Applet.
        GridBagLayout gridBag = new GridBagLayout();
        setLayout(gridBag);
        GridBagConstraints c = new GridBagConstraints();
        c.gridwidth = GridBagConstraints.REMAINDER;
```

```
        c.fill = GridBagConstraints.HORIZONTAL;
        gridBag.setConstraints(textField, c);
        add(textField);

        c.fill = GridBagConstraints.BOTH;
        c.weightx = 1.0;
        c.weighty = 1.0;
        gridBag.setConstraints(textArea, c);
        add(textArea);

        textField.addActionListener(this);
        newline = System.getProperty("line.separator");
    }

    public void actionPerformed(ActionEvent evt) {
        String text = textField.getText();
        textArea.append(text + newline);
        textField.selectAll();
    }
}
```

EXAMPLE: Component Event Demo Applet

HTML PAGES CONTAINING APPLET: *http://java.sun.com/docs/books/tutorial/ui/components/componentlistener.html*

Where Explained:
How to Write a Component Listener (page 474)

ComponentEventDemo.java

SOURCE CODE: *http://java.sun.com/docs/books/tutorial/ui/components/example-1dot1/ComponentEventDemo.java*

```
import java.applet.Applet;
import java.awt.*;
import java.awt.event.*;

public class ComponentEventDemo extends Applet
                                implements ComponentListener,
                                           ActionListener {
    TextArea display;
    Frame aFrame;
    public boolean showIt = false;
    final static String SHOW = "show";
    final static String CLEAR = "clear";
    String newline;

    public void init() {
        newline = System.getProperty("line.separator");
        setLayout(new BorderLayout());
```

```
        display = new TextArea(5, 20);
        display.setEditable(false);
        add("Center", display);

        Button b1 = new Button("Start playing...");
        b1.setActionCommand(SHOW);
        b1.addActionListener(this);
        add("North", b1);

        Button b2 = new Button("Clear");
        b2.setActionCommand(CLEAR);
        b2.addActionListener(this);
        add("South", b2);

        aFrame = new Frame("A Frame");
        ComponentPanel p = new ComponentPanel(this);
        aFrame.addComponentListener(this);
        p.addComponentListener(this);
        aFrame.add("Center", p);
        aFrame.pack();

        aFrame.addWindowListener(new WindowAdapter() {
            public void windowClosing(WindowEvent e) {
                showIt = false;
                aFrame.setVisible(false);
            }
        });
    }

    public void actionPerformed(ActionEvent e) {
        if (e.getActionCommand() == SHOW) {
            showIt = true;
            aFrame.setVisible(true);
        } else { //CLEAR
            display.setText("");
        }
    }

    public void stop() {
        aFrame.setVisible(false);
    }

    public void start() {
        if (showIt) {
            aFrame.setVisible(true);
        }
    }
```

```
    protected void displayMessage(String message) {
        try {
            display.append(message + newline);
        } catch (Exception e) {
        }
    }

    public void componentHidden(ComponentEvent e) {
        displayMessage("componentHidden event from "
                    + e.getComponent().getClass().getName());
    }

    public void componentMoved(ComponentEvent e) {
        displayMessage("componentMoved event from "
                    + e.getComponent().getClass().getName());
    }

    public void componentResized(ComponentEvent e) {
        displayMessage("componentResized event from "
                    + e.getComponent().getClass().getName());
    }

    public void componentShown(ComponentEvent e) {
        displayMessage("componentShown event from "
                    + e.getComponent().getClass().getName());
    }
}

class ComponentPanel extends Panel
                    implements ItemListener {
    Label label;
    Checkbox checkbox;

    ComponentPanel(ComponentEventDemo listener) {
        setLayout(new BorderLayout());

        label = new Label("This is a Label", Label.CENTER);
        add("Center", label);

        checkbox = new Checkbox("Label visible", true);
        checkbox.addItemListener(this);
        add("South", checkbox);

        label.addComponentListener(listener);
        checkbox.addComponentListener(listener);
    }

    public void itemStateChanged(ItemEvent e) {
        if (e.getStateChange() == ItemEvent.SELECTED) {
            label.setVisible(true);
```

```
            } else {
                label.setVisible(false);
            }
        }
    }
```

EXAMPLE: Container Event Demo Applet

Where Explained:
How to Write a Container Listener (page 477)

HTML PAGES CONTAINING APPLET: *http://java.sun.com/docs/books/tutorial/ui/components/containerlistener.html*

ContainerEventDemo.java

SOURCE CODE: *http://java.sun.com/docs/books/tutorial/ui/components/example-1dot1/ContainerEventDemo.java*

```
import java.applet.Applet;
import java.awt.*;
import java.awt.event.ContainerEvent;
import java.awt.event.ContainerListener;
import java.awt.event.ActionEvent;
import java.awt.event.ActionListener;
import java.util.Vector;

public class ContainerEventDemo extends Applet
                                implements ContainerListener,
                                           ActionListener {
    TextArea display;
    Panel buttonPanel;
    Button addButton, removeButton, clearButton;
    Vector buttonList;
    static final String ADD = "add";
    static final String REMOVE = "remove";
    static final String CLEAR = "clear";
    String newline;

    public void init() {
        newline = System.getProperty("line.separator");

        //Initialize an empty list of buttons.
        buttonList = new Vector(10, 10);

        //Create all the components.

        addButton = new Button("Add a button");
        addButton.setActionCommand(ADD);
        addButton.addActionListener(this);

        removeButton = new Button("Remove a button");
```

```
        removeButton.setActionCommand(REMOVE);
        removeButton.addActionListener(this);

        buttonPanel = new Panel();
        buttonPanel.addContainerListener(this);

        display = new TextArea(5, 20);
        display.setEditable(false);

        clearButton = new Button("Clear text area");
        clearButton.setActionCommand(CLEAR);
        clearButton.addActionListener(this);

        //Lay out the components.
        GridBagLayout gridbag = new GridBagLayout();
        GridBagConstraints c = new GridBagConstraints();
        setLayout(gridbag);
        c.fill = GridBagConstraints.BOTH; //Fill entire cell.

        c.weighty = 1.0;  //Button & message area are same height.
        c.gridwidth = GridBagConstraints.REMAINDER; //end of row
        gridbag.setConstraints(display, c);
        add(display);

        c.weighty = 0.0;
        gridbag.setConstraints(clearButton, c);
        add(clearButton);

        c.weightx = 1.0;  //Add/remove buttons have equal width.
        c.gridwidth = 1;  //NOT end of row
        gridbag.setConstraints(addButton, c);
        add(addButton);

        c.gridwidth = GridBagConstraints.REMAINDER; //end of row
        gridbag.setConstraints(removeButton, c);
        add(removeButton);

        c.weighty = 1.0;  //Button & message area are same height.
        gridbag.setConstraints(buttonPanel, c);
        add(buttonPanel);
    }

    public void componentAdded(ContainerEvent e) {
        displayMessage(" added to ", e);
    }

    public void componentRemoved(ContainerEvent e) {
        displayMessage(" removed from ", e);
    }
```

```
    void displayMessage(String action, ContainerEvent e) {
        display.append(((Button)e.getChild()).getLabel()
                       + " was"
                       + action
                       + e.getContainer().getClass().getName()
                       + newline);
    }

    /*
     * This could have been implemented as two or three
     * classes or objects, for clarity.
     */
    public void actionPerformed(ActionEvent e) {
        String command = e.getActionCommand();

        if (command == ADD) {
            Button newButton = new Button("Button #"
                                 + (buttonList.size() + 1));
            buttonList.addElement(newButton);
            buttonPanel.add(newButton);
            buttonPanel.validate(); //Make the button show up.
        } else if (command == REMOVE) {
            int lastIndex = buttonList.size() - 1;
            try {
                Button nixedButton =
                     (Button)buttonList.elementAt(lastIndex);
                buttonPanel.remove(nixedButton);
                buttonList.removeElementAt(lastIndex);
                buttonPanel.validate(); //Make it disappear.
            } catch (ArrayIndexOutOfBoundsException exc) {
            }
        } else if (command == CLEAR) {
            display.setText("");
        }
    }
}
```

EXAMPLE: Focus Event Demo Applet

HTML PAGES CONTAINING APPLET: *http://java.sun.com/docs/books/tutorial/ui/components/focuslistener.html*

Where Explained:
How to Write a Focus Listener (page 479)

FocusEventDemo.java

SOURCE CODE: *http://java.sun.com/docs/books/tutorial/ui/components/example-1dot1/FocusEventDemo.java*

```
import java.applet.Applet;
import java.awt.*;
import java.awt.event.FocusListener;
import java.awt.event.FocusEvent;
import java.awt.event.ActionListener;
import java.awt.event.ActionEvent;
import java.awt.event.WindowEvent;
import java.awt.event.WindowAdapter;

public class FocusEventDemo extends Applet
                             implements FocusListener,
                                        ActionListener {

    TextArea display;
    FocusWindow window;
    Button b1, b2;
    static final String SHOW = "show";
    static final String CLEAR = "clear";
    String newline;

    public void init() {
        newline = System.getProperty("line.separator");

        b1 = new Button("Click to bring up a window.");
        b1.setActionCommand(SHOW);
        b1.addActionListener(this);

        b2 = new Button("Click to clear the display.");
        b2.setActionCommand(CLEAR);
        b2.addActionListener(this);

        display = new TextArea(5, 20);
        display.setEditable(false);

        setLayout(new BorderLayout());
        add("North", b1);
        add("Center", display);
        add("South", b2);
```

```
            //Create but don't show window.
            window = new FocusWindow(this);
        }

        public void stop() {
            window.setVisible(false);
        }

        public void focusGained(FocusEvent e) {
            displayMessage("Focus gained", e);
        }

        public void focusLost(FocusEvent e) {
            displayMessage("Focus lost", e);
        }

        void displayMessage(String prefix, FocusEvent e) {
            display.append(prefix
                           + ": "
                           + e.getComponent()
                           + newline);
        }

        public void actionPerformed(ActionEvent e) {
            if (e.getActionCommand() == SHOW) {
                window.pack();
                window.setVisible(true);
            } else { //CLEAR
                display.setText("");
            }
        }
    }

    class FocusWindow extends Frame {
        class FocusWindowListener extends WindowAdapter {
            public void windowClosing(WindowEvent e) {
                    setVisible(false);
            }
        }

        public FocusWindow(FocusListener listener) {
            super("Focus Event Window");
            this.addFocusListener(listener);
            this.addWindowListener(new FocusWindowListener());

            GridBagLayout gridbag = new GridBagLayout();
            GridBagConstraints c = new GridBagConstraints();
```

```
        setLayout(gridbag);

        c.fill = GridBagConstraints.HORIZONTAL;
        c.weightx = 1.0;  //Make column as wide as possible.
        TextField textField = new TextField("A TextField");
        textField.addFocusListener(listener);
        gridbag.setConstraints(textField, c);
        add(textField);

      c.weightx = 0.1;  //Widen every other col, when possible.
        c.fill = GridBagConstraints.NONE;
        Label label = new Label("A Label");
        label.addFocusListener(listener);
        gridbag.setConstraints(label, c);
        add(label);

        Choice choice = new Choice();
        String choiceprefix = "Choice item #";
        for (int i = 0; i < 10; i++) {
            choice.addItem(choiceprefix + i);
        }
        choice.addFocusListener(listener);
        gridbag.setConstraints(choice, c);
        add(choice);

        c.gridwidth = GridBagConstraints.REMAINDER;
        Button button = new Button("A Button");
        button.addFocusListener(listener);
        gridbag.setConstraints(button, c);
        add(button);

       c.weighty = 1.0;   //Make this row as tall as possible.
        c.weightx = 0.0;
        c.fill = GridBagConstraints.BOTH;
        List list = new List();
        String listprefix = "List item #";
        for (int i = 0; i < 10; i++) {
            list.addItem(listprefix + i);
        }
        list.addFocusListener(listener);
        gridbag.setConstraints(list, c);
        add(list);
    }
}
```

EXAMPLE: Key Event Demo Applet

Where Explained:
How to Write a Key Listener (page 484)

HTML PAGES CONTAINING APPLET: *http://java.sun.com/docs/books/tutorial/ui/components/keylistener.html*

KeyEventDemo.java

SOURCE CODE: *http://java.sun.com/docs/books/tutorial/ui/components/example-1dot1/KeyEventDemo.java*

```
import java.applet.Applet;
import java.awt.*;
import java.awt.event.*;

public class KeyEventDemo extends Applet
                          implements KeyListener,
                                     ActionListener {
    TextArea displayArea;
    TextField typingArea;
    String newline;

    public void init() {
        Button button = new Button("Clear");
        button.addActionListener(this);

        typingArea = new TextField(20);
        typingArea.addKeyListener(this);

        displayArea = new TextArea(5, 20);
        displayArea.setEditable(false);

        setLayout(new BorderLayout());
        add("Center", displayArea);
        add("North", typingArea);
        add("South", button);

        newline = System.getProperty("line.separator");
    }

    /** Handle the key typed event from the text field. */
    public void keyTyped(KeyEvent e) {
        displayInfo(e, "KEY TYPED: ");
    }

    /** Handle the key pressed event from the text field. */
    public void keyPressed(KeyEvent e) {
        displayInfo(e, "KEY PRESSED: ");
    }
```

```
    /** Handle the key released event from the text field. */
    public void keyReleased(KeyEvent e) {
        displayInfo(e, "KEY RELEASED: ");
    }

    /** Handle the button click. */
    public void actionPerformed(ActionEvent e) {
        //Clear the text components.
        displayArea.setText("");
        typingArea.setText("");

        //Return the focus to the typing area.
        typingArea.requestFocus();
    }

    /*
     * We have to jump through some hoops to avoid
     * trying to print non-printing characters
     * such as Shift.  (Not only do they not print,
     * but if you put them in a String, the characters
     * afterward won't show up in the text area.)
     */
    protected void displayInfo(KeyEvent e, String s){
       String charString, keyCodeString, modString, tmpString;

        char c = e.getKeyChar();
        int keyCode = e.getKeyCode();
        int modifiers = e.getModifiers();

        if (Character.isISOControl(c)) {
         charString = "key character = (an unprintable control
character)";
        } else {
            charString = "key character = '" + c + "'";
        }

        keyCodeString = "key code = " + keyCode
                        + " ("
                        + KeyEvent.getKeyText(keyCode)
                        + ")";

        modString = "modifiers = " + modifiers;
        tmpString = KeyEvent.getKeyModifiersText(modifiers);
        if (tmpString.length() > 0) {
            modString += " (" + tmpString + ")";
        } else {
            modString += " (no modifiers)";
        }
```

```
            displayArea.append(s
                               + newline + "    "
                               + charString
                               + newline + "    "
                               + keyCodeString
                               + newline + "    "
                               + modString
                               + newline);
        }
    }
```

Where Explained: *How to Write a Mouse Listener* (page 488)

EXAMPLE: Mouse Event Demo Applet

HTML PAGES CONTAINING APPLET: *http://java.sun.com/docs/books/tutorial/ui/components/mouselistener.html*

MouseEventDemo.java

SOURCE CODE: *http://java.sun.com/docs/books/tutorial/ui/components/example-1dot1/MouseEventDemo.java*

```
import java.applet.Applet;
import java.awt.*;
import java.awt.event.MouseListener;
import java.awt.event.MouseEvent;

public class MouseEventDemo extends Applet
                            implements MouseListener {
    BlankArea blankArea;
    TextArea textArea;
    static final int maxInt = java.lang.Integer.MAX_VALUE;
    String newline;

    public void init() {
        newline = System.getProperty("line.separator");

        GridBagLayout gridbag = new GridBagLayout();
        GridBagConstraints c = new GridBagConstraints();
        setLayout(gridbag);

        c.fill = GridBagConstraints.BOTH;
        c.gridwidth = GridBagConstraints.REMAINDER;
        c.weightx = 1.0;
        c.weighty = 1.0;

        c.insets = new Insets(1, 1, 1, 1);
        blankArea = new BlankArea(new Color(0.98f, 0.97f,
                                            0.85f));
        gridbag.setConstraints(blankArea, c);
```

```
        add(blankArea);

        c.insets = new Insets(0, 0, 0, 0);
        textArea = new TextArea(5, 20);
        textArea.setEditable(false);
        gridbag.setConstraints(textArea, c);
        add(textArea);

        //Register for mouse events on blankArea and applet.
        blankArea.addMouseListener(this);
        addMouseListener(this);
    }

    public void mousePressed(MouseEvent e) {
       saySomething("Mouse pressed; # of clicks: "
                    + e.getClickCount(), e);
    }

    public void mouseReleased(MouseEvent e) {
       saySomething("Mouse released; # of clicks: "
                    + e.getClickCount(), e);
    }

    public void mouseEntered(MouseEvent e) {
       saySomething("Mouse entered", e);
    }

    public void mouseExited(MouseEvent e) {
       saySomething("Mouse exited", e);
    }

    public void mouseClicked(MouseEvent e) {
       saySomething("Mouse clicked (# of clicks: "
                    + e.getClickCount() + ")", e);
    }

    void saySomething(String eventDescription, MouseEvent e) {
        textArea.append(eventDescription + " detected on "
                        + e.getComponent().getClass().getName()
                        + newline);
        textArea.setCaretPosition(maxInt); //scroll to bottom
    }
}
```

BlankArea.java

SOURCE CODE: *http://java.sun.com/docs/books/tutorial/ui/components/example-1dot1/BlankArea.java*

```
import java.awt.*;

public class BlankArea extends Canvas {
    Dimension minSize = new Dimension(100, 100);

    public BlankArea(Color color) {
        setBackground(color);
    }

    public Dimension getMinimumSize() {
        return minSize;
    }

    public Dimension getPreferredSize() {
        return minSize;
    }

    public void paint(Graphics g) {
        Dimension size = getSize();
        g.drawRect(0, 0, size.width - 1, size.height - 1);
    }
}
```

EXAMPLE: Mouse-Motion Event Demo Applet

Where Explained: *How to Write a Mouse-Motion Listener* (page 492)

HTML PAGES CONTAINING APPLET: *http://java.sun.com/docs/books/tutorial/ui/components/mousemotionlistener.html*

MouseMotionEventDemo.java

SOURCE CODE: *http://java.sun.com/docs/books/tutorial/ui/components/example-1dot1/MouseMotionEventDemo.java*

```
import java.applet.Applet;
import java.awt.*;
import java.awt.event.MouseMotionListener;
import java.awt.event.MouseEvent;

public class MouseMotionEventDemo extends Applet
                                  implements MouseMotionListener {
    BlankArea blankArea;
    TextArea textArea;
    static final int maxInt = java.lang.Integer.MAX_VALUE;
    String newline;
```

```
    public void init() {
        newline = System.getProperty("line.separator");

        GridBagLayout gridbag = new GridBagLayout();
        GridBagConstraints c = new GridBagConstraints();
        setLayout(gridbag);

        c.fill = GridBagConstraints.BOTH;
        c.gridwidth = GridBagConstraints.REMAINDER;
        c.weightx = 1.0;
        c.weighty = 1.0;

        c.insets = new Insets(1, 1, 1, 1);
        blankArea = new BlankArea(new Color(0.98f, 0.97f,
                                            0.85f));
        gridbag.setConstraints(blankArea, c);
        add(blankArea);

        c.insets = new Insets(0, 0, 0, 0);
        textArea = new TextArea(5, 20);
        textArea.setEditable(false);
        gridbag.setConstraints(textArea, c);
        add(textArea);

        //Register for events on blankArea and applet (panel).
        blankArea.addMouseMotionListener(this);
        addMouseMotionListener(this);
    }

    public void mouseMoved(MouseEvent e) {
       saySomething("Mouse moved; # of clicks: "
                    + e.getClickCount(), e);
    }

    public void mouseDragged(MouseEvent e) {
       saySomething("Mouse dragged; # of clicks: "
                    + e.getClickCount(), e);
    }

    void saySomething(String eventDescription, MouseEvent e) {
        textArea.append(eventDescription + " detected on "
                        + e.getComponent().getClass().getName()
                        + newline);
        textArea.setCaretPosition(maxInt); //scroll to bottom
    }
}
```

EXAMPLE: Text Event Demo Applet

HTML PAGES CONTAINING APPLET: *http://java.sun.com/docs/books/tutorial/ui/components/textlistener.html*

Where Explained:
How to Write a Text Listener (page 494)

TextEventDemo.java

SOURCE CODE: *http://java.sun.com/docs/books/tutorial/ui/components/example-1dot1/TextEventDemo.java*

```
import java.applet.Applet;
import java.awt.*;
import java.awt.event.*;

public class TextEventDemo extends Applet
                           implements ActionListener {
    TextField textField;
    TextArea textArea;
    TextArea displayArea;

    public void init() {
        Button button = new Button("Clear");
        button.addActionListener(this);

        textField = new TextField(20);
      textField.addActionListener(new MyTextActionListener());
        textField.addTextListener(new MyTextListener(
                                             "Text Field"));

        textArea = new TextArea(5, 20);
        textArea.addTextListener(new MyTextListener(
                                                "Text Area"));

        displayArea = new TextArea(5, 20);
        displayArea.setEditable(false);

        GridBagLayout gridbag = new GridBagLayout();
        GridBagConstraints c = new GridBagConstraints();
        setLayout(gridbag);
        c.fill = GridBagConstraints.BOTH;
        c.weightx = 1.0;

        Panel leftPanel = new Panel();
        leftPanel.setLayout(new BorderLayout());
        leftPanel.add("North", textField);
        leftPanel.add("Center", textArea);

        c.gridheight = 2;
        gridbag.setConstraints(leftPanel, c);
```

```
        add(leftPanel);

        c.weighty = 1.0;
        c.gridwidth = GridBagConstraints.REMAINDER;
        c.gridheight = 1;
        gridbag.setConstraints(displayArea, c);
        add(displayArea);

        c.weighty = 0.0;
        gridbag.setConstraints(button, c);
        add(button);

        textField.requestFocus();
    }

    class MyTextListener implements TextListener {
        String preface;
        String newline;

        public MyTextListener(String source) {
            newline = System.getProperty("line.separator");
            preface = source
                    + " text value changed."
                    + newline
                    + "   First 10 characters: \"";
        }

        public void textValueChanged(TextEvent e) {
            TextComponent tc = (TextComponent)e.getSource();
            String s = tc.getText();
            try {
                s = s.substring(0, 10);
            } catch (StringIndexOutOfBoundsException ex) {
            }

            displayArea.append(preface + s + "\"" + newline);

            //Scroll down, unless the peer doesn't exist yet.
            if (displayArea.isValid()) {
                displayArea.setCaretPosition(
                                java.lang.Integer.MAX_VALUE);
            }
        }
    }

    class MyTextActionListener implements ActionListener {
        /** Handle the text field Return. */
        public void actionPerformed(ActionEvent e) {
```

```
                int selStart = textArea.getSelectionStart();
                int selEnd = textArea.getSelectionEnd();

                textArea.replaceRange(textField.getText(),
                                      selStart, selEnd);
                textField.selectAll();
            }
        }

        /** Handle button click. */
        public void actionPerformed(ActionEvent e) {
            displayArea.setText("");
            textField.requestFocus();
        }
    }
```

EXAMPLE: Window Event Demo Applet

Where Explained: *How to Write a Window Listener* (page 497)

HTML PAGES CONTAINING APPLET: *http://java.sun.com/docs/books/tutorial/ui/components/windowlistener.html*

WindowEventDemo.java

SOURCE CODE: *http://java.sun.com/docs/books/tutorial/ui/components/example-1dot1/WindowEventDemo.java*

```
import java.applet.Applet;
import java.awt.*;
import java.awt.event.ActionListener;
import java.awt.event.ActionEvent;
import java.awt.event.WindowEvent;
import java.awt.event.WindowListener;

public class WindowEventDemo extends Applet
                             implements WindowListener,
                                        ActionListener {

    TextArea display;
    Frame window;
    Button b1, b2;
    static final String SHOW = "show";
    static final String CLEAR = "clear";
    String newline;

    public void init() {
        newline = System.getProperty("line.separator");

        b1 = new Button("Click to bring up a window.");
        b1.setActionCommand(SHOW);
```

```
        b1.addActionListener(this);

        b2 = new Button("Click to clear the display.");
        b2.setActionCommand(CLEAR);
        b2.addActionListener(this);

        display = new TextArea(5, 20);
        display.setEditable(false);

        setLayout(new BorderLayout());
        add("North", b1);
        add("Center", display);
        add("South", b2);

        //Create but don't show window.
        window = new Frame("Window Event Window");
        window.addWindowListener(this);
        window.add("Center",
                 new Label("The applet listens to this window"
                           " for window events."));
        window.pack();
    }

    public void stop() {
        window.setVisible(false);
    }

    public void windowClosing(WindowEvent e) {
            window.setVisible(false);
        displayMessage("Window closing", e);
    }

    public void windowClosed(WindowEvent e) {
        displayMessage("Window closed", e);
    }

    public void windowOpened(WindowEvent e) {
        displayMessage("Window opened", e);
    }

    public void windowIconified(WindowEvent e) {
        displayMessage("Window iconified", e);
    }

    public void windowDeiconified(WindowEvent e) {
        displayMessage("Window deiconified", e);
    }
```

```
    public void windowActivated(WindowEvent e) {
        displayMessage("Window activated", e);
    }

    public void windowDeactivated(WindowEvent e) {
        displayMessage("Window deactivated", e);
    }

    void displayMessage(String prefix, WindowEvent e) {
        display.append(prefix
                       + ": "
                       + e.getWindow()
                       + newline);
    }

    public void actionPerformed(ActionEvent e) {
        if (e.getActionCommand() == SHOW) {
            window.pack();
            window.setVisible(true);
        } else {
            display.setText("");
        }
    }
}
```

LESSON 20: Laying Out Components Within a Container

EXAMPLE: BorderLayout Applet/Application

Where Explained:
How to Use BorderLayout (page 508)

HTML PAGES CONTAINING APPLET: *http://java.sun.com/docs/books/tutorial/ui/layout/using.html, http://java.sun.com/docs/books/tutorial/ui/layout/border.html*

This program can run either as an application or, with the help of `AppletButton.java` (page 796), as an applet.

BorderWindow.java

SOURCE CODE: *http://java.sun.com/docs/books/tutorial/ui/layout/example-1dot1/BorderWindow.java*

1.0 SOURCE CODE: *http://java.sun.com/docs/books/tutorial/ui/layout/example/BorderWindow.java*

```
import java.awt.*;
import java.awt.event.*;

public class BorderWindow extends Frame {
    boolean inAnApplet = true;

    public BorderWindow() {
        setLayout(new BorderLayout());
        setFont(new Font("SansSerif", Font.PLAIN, 14));

        add("North", new Button("North"));
        add("South", new Button("South"));
        add("East", new Button("East"));
        add("West", new Button("West"));
        add("Center", new Button("Center"));

        addWindowListener(new WindowAdapter() {
            public void windowClosing(WindowEvent e) {
                if (inAnApplet) {
                    dispose();
                } else {
                    System.exit(0);
                }
            }
        });
    }

    public static void main(String args[]) {
        BorderWindow window = new BorderWindow();
        window.inAnApplet = false;

        window.setTitle("BorderWindow Application");
        window.pack();
        window.setVisible(true);
    }
}
```

EXAMPLE: CardLayout Applet/Application

Where Explained:
How to use CardLayout (page 509)

HTML PAGES CONTAINING APPLET:
http://java.sun.com/docs/books/tutorial/ui/layout/using.html
http://java.sun.com/docs/books/tutorial/ui/layout/card.html

This program can run either as an application or, with the help of `AppletButton.java` (page 796), as an applet.

CardWindow.java

SOURCE CODE: *http://java.sun.com/docs/books/tutorial/ui/layout/example-1dot1/CardWindow.java*

1.0 SOURCE CODE: *http://java.sun.com/docs/books/tutorial/ui/layout/example/CardWindow.java*

```
import java.awt.*;
import java.awt.event.*;

public class CardWindow extends Frame
                        implements ItemListener {
    boolean inAnApplet = true;

    Panel cards;
    final static String BUTTONPANEL = "Panel with Buttons";
    final static String TEXTPANEL = "Panel with TextField";

    public CardWindow() {
        setLayout(new BorderLayout());
        setFont(new Font("SansSerif", Font.PLAIN, 14));

        //Put the Choice in a Panel to get a nicer look.
        Panel cp = new Panel();
        Choice c = new Choice();
        c.add(BUTTONPANEL);
        c.add(TEXTPANEL);
        c.addItemListener(this);
        cp.add(c);
        add("North", cp);

        cards = new Panel();
        cards.setLayout(new CardLayout());

        Panel p1 = new Panel();
        p1.add(new Button("Button 1"));
        p1.add(new Button("Button 2"));
        p1.add(new Button("Button 3"));

        Panel p2 = new Panel();
```

```
        p2.add(new TextField("TextField", 20));

        cards.add(BUTTONPANEL, p1);
        cards.add(TEXTPANEL, p2);
        add("Center", cards);

        addWindowListener(new WindowAdapter() {
            public void windowClosing(WindowEvent e) {
                if (inAnApplet) {
                   dispose();
                } else {
                   System.exit(0);
                }
            }
        });
    }

    public void itemStateChanged(ItemEvent evt) {
        CardLayout cl = (CardLayout)(cards.getLayout());
        cl.show(cards, (String)evt.getItem());
    }

    public static void main(String args[]) {
        CardWindow window = new CardWindow();
        window.inAnApplet = false;

        window.setTitle("CardWindow Application");
        window.pack();
        window.setVisible(true);
    }
}
```

EXAMPLE: FlowLayout Applet/Application

HTML PAGES CONTAINING APPLET: *http://java.sun.com/docs/books/tutorial/ui/layout/using.html, http://java.sun.com/docs/books/tutorial/ui/layout/flow.html*

This program can run either as an application or, with the help of `AppletButton.java` (page 796), as an applet.

Where Explained:
How to Use FlowLayout (page 511)

FlowWindow.java

SOURCE CODE: *http://java.sun.com/docs/books/tutorial/ui/layout/example-1dot1/FlowWindow.java*

1.0 SOURCE CODE: *http://java.sun.com/docs/books/tutorial/ui/layout/example/FlowWindow.java*

```
import java.awt.*;
import java.awt.event.*;

public class FlowWindow extends Frame {
    boolean inAnApplet = true;

    public FlowWindow() {
        setLayout(new FlowLayout());
        setFont(new Font("SansSerif", Font.PLAIN, 14));

        add(new Button("Button 1"));
        add(new Button("2"));
        add(new Button("Button 3"));
        add(new Button("Long-Named Button 4"));
        add(new Button("Button 5"));

        addWindowListener(new WindowAdapter() {
            public void windowClosing(WindowEvent e) {
                if (inAnApplet) {
                    dispose();
                } else {
                    System.exit(0);
                }
            }
        });
    }

    public static void main(String args[]) {
        FlowWindow window = new FlowWindow();
        window.inAnApplet = false;

        window.setTitle("FlowWindow Application");
        window.pack();
        window.setVisible(true);
    }
}
```

EXAMPLE: GridLayout Applet/Application

Where Explained: *How to Use GridLayout* (page 512)

HTML PAGES CONTAINING APPLET: *http://java.sun.com/docs/books/tutorial/ui/layout/using.html, http://java.sun.com/docs/books/tutorial/ui/layout/grid.html*

This program can run either as an application or, with the help of `AppletButton.java` (page 796), as an applet.

GridWindow.java

SOURCE CODE: *http://java.sun.com/docs/books/tutorial/ui/layout/example-1dot1/GridWindow.java*

1.0 SOURCE CODE: *http://java.sun.com/docs/books/tutorial/ui/layout/example/GridWindow.java*

```
import java.awt.*;
import java.awt.event.*;

public class GridWindow extends Frame {
    boolean inAnApplet = true;

    public GridWindow() {
        setLayout(new GridLayout(0,2));
        setFont(new Font("SansSerif", Font.PLAIN, 14));

        add(new Button("Button 1"));
        add(new Button("2"));
        add(new Button("Button 3"));
        add(new Button("Long-Named Button 4"));
        add(new Button("Button 5"));

        addWindowListener(new WindowAdapter() {
            public void windowClosing(WindowEvent e) {
                if (inAnApplet) {
                    dispose();
                } else {
                    System.exit(0);
                }
            }
        });
    }

    public static void main(String args[]) {
        GridWindow window = new GridWindow();
        window.inAnApplet = false;

        window.setTitle("GridWindow Application");
        window.pack();
        window.setVisible(true);
    }
}
```

EXAMPLE: GridBagLayout Applet/Application

Where Explained: *The GridBag-Layout Applet Example Explained* (page 516)

HTML PAGES CONTAINING APPLET: *http://java.sun.com/docs/books/tutorial/ui/layout/using.html, http://java.sun.com/docs/books/tutorial/ui/layout/gridbag.html*

This program can run either as an application or, with the help of `AppletButton.java` (page 796), as an applet.

GridBagWindow.java

SOURCE CODE: *http://java.sun.com/docs/books/tutorial/ui/layout/example-1dot1/GridBagWindow.java*

1.0 SOURCE CODE: *http://java.sun.com/docs/books/tutorial/ui/layout/example/GridBagWindow.java*

```
import java.awt.*;
import java.awt.event.*;

public class GridBagWindow extends Frame {
    boolean inAnApplet = true;

    protected void makebutton(String name,
                              GridBagLayout gridbag,
                              GridBagConstraints c) {
        Button button = new Button(name);
        gridbag.setConstraints(button, c);
        add(button);
    }

    public GridBagWindow() {
        GridBagLayout gridbag = new GridBagLayout();
        GridBagConstraints c = new GridBagConstraints();

        setFont(new Font("SansSerif", Font.PLAIN, 14));
        setLayout(gridbag);

        c.fill = GridBagConstraints.BOTH;
        c.weightx = 1.0;
        makebutton("Button1", gridbag, c);
        makebutton("Button2", gridbag, c);
        makebutton("Button3", gridbag, c);

        c.gridwidth = GridBagConstraints.REMAINDER; //end of row
        makebutton("Button4", gridbag, c);

        c.weightx = 0.0;                    //reset to the default
        makebutton("Button5", gridbag, c); //another row
```

```
        c.gridwidth = GridBagConstraints.RELATIVE;//next-to-last
        makebutton("Button6", gridbag, c);

        c.gridwidth = GridBagConstraints.REMAINDER; //end of row
        makebutton("Button7", gridbag, c);

        c.gridwidth = 1;                      //reset to the default
        c.gridheight = 2;
        c.weighty = 1.0;
        makebutton("Button8", gridbag, c);

        c.weighty = 0.0;                      //reset to the default
        c.gridwidth = GridBagConstraints.REMAINDER; //end of row
        c.gridheight = 1;                     //reset to the default
        makebutton("Button9", gridbag, c);
        makebutton("Button10", gridbag, c);

        addWindowListener(new WindowAdapter() {
            public void windowClosing(WindowEvent e) {
                if (inAnApplet) {
                    dispose();
                } else {
                    System.exit(0);
                }
            }
        });
    }

    public static void main(String args[]) {
        GridBagWindow window = new GridBagWindow();
        window.inAnApplet = false;

        window.setTitle("GridBagWindow Application");
        window.pack();
        window.setVisible(true);
    }
}
```

EXAMPLE: Custom Layout Manager Applet/Application

Where Explained:
Creating a Custom Layout Manager (page 521)

HTML PAGES CONTAINING APPLET: *http://java.sun.com/docs/books/tutorial/ui/layout/gridbag.html*

This program can run either as an application or, with the help of AppletButton.java (page 796), as an applet. DiagonalLayout.java implements a layout manager. CustomWindow.java (page 858) uses DiagonalLayout as a layout manager.

DiagonalLayout.java

SOURCE CODE: *http://java.sun.com/docs/books/tutorial/ui/layout/example-1dot1/DiagonalLayout.java*

1.0 SOURCE CODE: *http://java.sun.com/docs/books/tutorial/ui/layout/example/DiagonalLayout.java*

```
import java.awt.*;
import java.util.Vector;

public class DiagonalLayout implements LayoutManager {

    private int vgap;
    private int minWidth = 0, minHeight = 0;
    private int preferredWidth = 0, preferredHeight = 0;
    private boolean sizeUnknown = true;

    public DiagonalLayout() {
        this(5);
    }

    public DiagonalLayout(int v) {
        vgap = v;
    }

    /* Required by LayoutManager. */
    public void addLayoutComponent(String n, Component c) {
    }

    /* Required by LayoutManager. */
    public void removeLayoutComponent(Component comp) {
    }

    private void setSizes(Container parent) {
        int nComps = parent.getComponentCount();
        Dimension d = null;

        //Reset preferred/minimum width and height.
        preferredWidth = 0;
        preferredHeight = 0;
        minWidth = 0;
        minHeight = 0;

        for (int i = 0; i < nComps; i++) {
            Component c = parent.getComponent(i);
            if (c.isVisible()) {
                d = c.getPreferredSize();
```

```
            if (i > 0) {
                preferredWidth += d.width/2;
                preferredHeight += vgap;
            } else {
                preferredWidth = d.width;
            }
            preferredHeight += d.height;

            minWidth = Math.max(c.getMinimumSize().width,
                                minWidth);
            minHeight = preferredHeight;
        }
    }
}


/* Required by LayoutManager. */
public Dimension preferredLayoutSize(Container parent) {
    Dimension dim = new Dimension(0, 0);
    int nComps = parent.getComponentCount();

    setSizes(parent);

    //Always add the container's insets!
    Insets insets = parent.getInsets();
    dim.width = preferredWidth
              + insets.left + insets.right;
    dim.height = preferredHeight
               + insets.top + insets.bottom;

    sizeUnknown = false;

    return dim;
}

/* Required by LayoutManager. */
public Dimension minimumLayoutSize(Container parent) {
    Dimension dim = new Dimension(0, 0);
    int nComps = parent.getComponentCount();

    //Always add the container's insets!
    Insets insets = parent.getInsets();
    dim.width = minWidth
              + insets.left + insets.right;
    dim.height = minHeight
               + insets.top + insets.bottom;
```

```
        sizeUnknown = false;

        return dim;
    }

    /* Required by LayoutManager. */
    /*
     * This is called when the panel is first displayed,
     * and every time its size changes.
     * Note: You CAN'T assume preferredLayoutSize or
     * minimumLayoutSize will be called -- in the case
     * of applets, at least, they probably won't be.
     */
    public void layoutContainer(Container parent) {
        Insets insets = parent.getInsets();
        int maxWidth = parent.getSize().width
                       - (insets.left + insets.right);
        int maxHeight = parent.getSize().height
                         - (insets.top + insets.bottom);
        int nComps = parent.getComponentCount();
        int previousWidth = 0, previousHeight = 0;
        int x = 0, y = insets.top;
        int rowh = 0, start = 0;
        int xFudge = 0, yFudge = 0;
        boolean oneColumn = false;

        // Go through the components' sizes, if neither
        // preferredLayoutSize nor minimumLayoutSize has
        // been called.
        if (sizeUnknown) {
            setSizes(parent);
        }

        if (maxWidth <= minWidth) {
            oneColumn = true;
        }

        if (maxWidth != preferredWidth) {
            xFudge = (maxWidth - preferredWidth)/(nComps - 1);
        }

        if (maxHeight > preferredHeight) {
           yFudge = (maxHeight - preferredHeight)/(nComps - 1);
        }

        for (int i = 0 ; i < nComps ; i++) {
            Component c = parent.getComponent(i);
            if (c.isVisible()) {
```

```
                Dimension d = c.getPreferredSize();

                 // increase x and y, if appropriate
                if (i > 0) {
                    if (!oneColumn) {
                         x += previousWidth/2 + xFudge;
                    }
                    y += previousHeight + vgap + yFudge;
                }

                // If x is too large,
                if ((!oneColumn) &&
                    (x + d.width) >
                    (parent.getSize().width - insets.right)) {
                    // reduce x to a reasonable number.
                    x = parent.getSize().width
                         - insets.bottom - d.width;
                }

                // If y is too large,
                if ((y + d.height)
                 > (parent.getSize().height - insets.bottom)) {
                    // do nothing.
                // Another choice would be to do what we do to x.
                }

                // Set the component's size and position.
                c.setBounds(x, y, d.width, d.height);

                previousWidth = d.width;
                previousHeight = d.height;
            }
        }
    }

    public String toString() [
         String str = "";
      return getClass().getName() + "[vgap=" + vgap + str + "]";
    }
}
```

CustomWindow.java

SOURCE CODE: *http://java.sun.com/docs/books/tutorial/ui/layout/example-1dot1/CustomWindow.java*

1.0 SOURCE CODE: *http://java.sun.com/docs/books/tutorial/ui/layout/example/CustomWindow.java*

```
import java.awt.*;
import java.awt.event.*;

public class CustomWindow extends Frame {
    boolean inAnApplet = true;

    public CustomWindow() {
        setLayout(new DiagonalLayout());
        setFont(new Font("SansSerif", Font.PLAIN, 14));

        add(new Button("Button 1"));
        add(new Button("Button 2"));
        add(new Button("Button 3"));
        add(new Button("Button 4"));
        add(new Button("Button 5"));

        addWindowListener(new WindowAdapter() {
            public void windowClosing(WindowEvent e) {
                if (inAnApplet) {
                    dispose();
                } else {
                    System.exit(0);
                }
            }
        });
    }

    public static void main(String args[]) {
        CustomWindow window = new CustomWindow();
        window.inAnApplet = false;

        window.setTitle("CustomWindow Application");
        window.pack();
        window.setVisible(true);
    }
}
```

EXAMPLE: Absolute Positioning Applet/Application

HTML PAGES CONTAINING APPLET: *http://java.sun.com/docs/books/tutorial/ui/layout/none.html*

This program can run either as an application or, with the help of `AppletButton.java` (page 796), as an applet.

Where Explained: *Laying Out Components Without a Layout Manager (Absolute Positioning)* (page 522)

NoneWindow.java

SOURCE CODE: *http://java.sun.com/docs/books/tutorial/ui/layout/example-1dot1/NoneWindow.java*

1.0 SOURCE CODE: *http://java.sun.com/docs/books/tutorial/ui/layout/example/NoneWindow.java*

```
import java.awt.*;
import java.awt.event.*;

public class NoneWindow extends Frame {
    boolean inAnApplet = true;
    private boolean laidOut = false;
    private Button b1, b2, b3;

    public NoneWindow() {
        setLayout(null);
        setFont(new Font("SansSerif", Font.PLAIN, 14));

        b1 = new Button("one");
        add(b1);
        b2 = new Button("two");
        add(b2);
        b3 = new Button("three");
        add(b3);

        addWindowListener(new WindowAdapter() {
            public void windowClosing(WindowEvent e) {
                if (inAnApplet) {
                    dispose();
                } else {
                    System.exit(0);
                }
            }
        });
    }

    public void paint(Graphics g) {
        if (!laidOut) {
            Insets insets = getInsets();
            /*
```

```
             * We're guaranteed that getInsets will return a
             * valid Insets if called from paint -- it isn't
             * valid when called from the constructor.
             *
             * We could perhaps cache this in an ivar, but
             * insets can change, and when they do, the AWT
             * creates a whole new Insets object; the old one
             * is invalid.
             */
            b1.setBounds(50 + insets.left, 5 + insets.top,
                         50, 20);
            b2.setBounds(70 + insets.left, 35 + insets.top,
                         50, 20);
            b3.setBounds(130 + insets.left, 15 + insets.top,
                         50, 30);

            laidOut = true;
        }
    }

    public static void main(String args[]) {
        NoneWindow window = new NoneWindow();
        Insets insets = window.getInsets();
        window.inAnApplet = false;

        window.setTitle("NoneWindow Application");
        window.setSize(250 + insets.left + insets.right,
                       90 + insets.top + insets.bottom);
        window.setVisible(true);
    }
}
```

LESSON 21: Working with Graphics

EXAMPLE: Coordinates Demo Applet

Where Explained: *Drawing Shapes* (page 528)

HTML PAGES CONTAINING APPLET: *http://java.sun.com/docs/books/tutorial/ui/drawing/overview.html, http://java.sun.com/docs/books/tutorial/ui/drawing/drawingShapes.html*

When you click the mouse in this applet's display area, the applet displays the coordinates that the click occurred at.

CoordinatesDemo.java

SOURCE CODE: *http://java.sun.com/docs/books/tutorial/ui/drawing/example-1dot1/CoordinatesDemo.java*

1.0 SOURCE CODE: *http://java.sun.com/docs/books/tutorial/ui/drawing/example/CoordinatesDemo.java*

```
import java.awt.*;
import java.awt.event.*;
import java.applet.Applet;

// Displays a framed area.  When the user clicks within
// the area, this program displays a dot and a string indicating
// the coordinates where the click occurred.
public class CoordinatesDemo extends Applet {
    FramedArea framedArea;
    Label label;

    public void init() {
        GridBagLayout gridBag = new GridBagLayout();
        GridBagConstraints c = new GridBagConstraints();

        setLayout(gridBag);

        framedArea = new FramedArea(this);
        c.fill = GridBagConstraints.BOTH;
        c.weighty = 1.0;
        c.gridwidth = GridBagConstraints.REMAINDER; //end row
        gridBag.setConstraints(framedArea, c);
        add(framedArea);

        label = new Label("Click within the framed area.");
        c.fill = GridBagConstraints.HORIZONTAL;
        c.weightx = 1.0;
        c.weighty = 0.0;
        gridBag.setConstraints(label, c);
        add(label);
    }

    public void updateLabel(Point point) {
        label.setText("Click occurred at coordinate ("
                      + point.x + ", " + point.y + ").");
    }
}

// This class exists solely to put a frame around the coordinate
// area.
```

```
class FramedArea extends Panel {
    public FramedArea(CoordinatesDemo controller) {
        super();

        //Set layout to make contents as big as possible.
        setLayout(new GridLayout(1,0));

        add(new CoordinateArea(controller));
    }

    public Insets getInsets() {
        return new Insets(4,4,5,5);
    }

    public void paint(Graphics g) {
        Dimension d = getSize();
        Color bg = getBackground();

        g.setColor(bg);
        g.draw3DRect(0, 0, d.width - 1, d.height - 1, true);
        g.draw3DRect(3, 3, d.width - 7, d.height - 7, false);
    }
}

class CoordinateArea extends Canvas {
    Point point = null;
    CoordinatesDemo controller;

    public CoordinateArea(CoordinatesDemo controller) {
        super();
        this.controller = controller;

        addMouseListener(new MouseAdapter() {
            public void mousePressed(MouseEvent e) {
                int x = e.getX();
                int y = e.getY();
                if (point == null) {
                    point = new Point(x, y);
                } else {
                    point.x = x;
                    point.y = y;
                }
                repaint();
            }
        });
    }

    public void paint(Graphics g) {
```

```
        //If user has chosen a point, paint tiny rectangle on top.
          if (point != null) {
              controller.updateLabel(point);
              g.fillRect(point.x - 1, point.y - 1, 2, 2);
          }
      }
}
```

EXAMPLE: Rectangle Demo Applet

HTML PAGES CONTAINING APPLET: *http://java.sun.com/docs/books/tutorial/ui/drawing/drawingShapes.html*

Where Explained: *Drawing Shapes* (page 528)

RectangleDemo.java

SOURCE CODE: *http://java.sun.com/docs/books/tutorial/ui/drawing/example-1dot1/RectangleDemo.java*

1.0 SOURCE CODE: *http://java.sun.com/docs/books/tutorial/ui/drawing/example/RectangleDemo.java*

```
import java.awt.*;
import java.awt.event.*;
import java.applet.Applet;

/*
 * This displays a framed area.  When the user clicks within
 * the area, this program displays a dot and a string indicating
 * the coordinates where the click occurred.
 */

public class RectangleDemo extends Applet {
    RFramedArea framedArea;
    Label label;

    public void init() {
        GridBagLayout gridBag = new GridBagLayout();
        GridBagConstraints c = new GridBagConstraints();

        setLayout(gridBag);

        framedArea = new RFramedArea(this);
        c.fill = GridBagConstraints.BOTH;
        c.weighty = 1.0;
        c.gridwidth = GridBagConstraints.REMAINDER; //end row
        gridBag.setConstraints(framedArea, c);
        add(framedArea);
```

```
        label = new Label("Drag within the framed area.");
        c.fill = GridBagConstraints.HORIZONTAL;
        c.weightx = 1.0;
        c.weighty = 0.0;
        gridBag.setConstraints(label, c);
        add(label);
    }

    public void updateLabel(Rectangle rect) {
        label.setText("Rectangle goes from ("
                      + rect.x + ", " + rect.y + ") to ("
                      + (rect.x + rect.width - 1) + ", "
                      + (rect.y + rect.height - 1) + ").");
    }
}

/* This class exists solely to put a frame around the coordinate
area. */
class RFramedArea extends Panel {
    public RFramedArea(RectangleDemo controller) {
        super();

        //Set layout to make contents as big as possible.
        setLayout(new GridLayout(1,0));

        add(new SelectionArea(controller));
    }

    public Insets getInsets() {
        return new Insets(4,4,5,5);
    }

    public void paint(Graphics g) {
        Dimension d = getSize();
        Color bg = getBackground();

        g.setColor(bg);
        g.draw3DRect(0, 0, d.width - 1, d.height - 1, true);
        g.draw3DRect(3, 3, d.width - 7, d.height - 7, false);
    }
}

class SelectionArea extends Canvas {
    Rectangle currentRect = null;
    RectangleDemo controller;

    public SelectionArea(RectangleDemo controller) {
        super();
```

```
        this.controller = controller;

        MyListener myListener = new MyListener();
        addMouseListener(myListener);
        addMouseMotionListener(myListener);
    }

    class MyListener extends MouseAdapter
                     implements MouseMotionListener {
        public void mousePressed(MouseEvent e) {
            int x = e.getX();
            int y = e.getY();
            currentRect = new Rectangle(x, y, 0, 0);
            repaint();
        }

        public void mouseDragged(MouseEvent e) {
            updateSize(e);
        }

        public void mouseMoved(MouseEvent e) {
            //Do nothing.
        }

        public void mouseReleased(MouseEvent e) {
            updateSize(e);
        }

        void updateSize(MouseEvent e) {
            int x = e.getX();
            int y = e.getY();
            currentRect.setSize(x - currentRect.x,
                                y - currentRect.y);
            repaint();
        }
    }

    public void paint(Graphics g) {
        //update has already cleared the previous rectangle,
        //so we don't need to here.

        //If currentRect exists, paint a rectangle on top.
        if (currentRect != null) {
            Dimension d = getSize();
            Rectangle box = getDrawableRect(currentRect, d);
            controller.updateLabel(box);

            //Draw the box outline.
```

```
            g.drawRect(box.x, box.y,
                       box.width - 1, box.height - 1);
        }
    }

    Rectangle getDrawableRect(Rectangle originalRect,
                              Dimension drawingArea) {
        int x = originalRect.x;
        int y = originalRect.y;
        int width = originalRect.width;
        int height = originalRect.height;

        //Make sure rectangle width and height are positive.
        if (width < 0) {
            width = 0 - width;
            x = x - width + 1;
            if (x < 0) {
                width += x;
                x = 0;
            }
        }
        if (height < 0) {
            height = 0 - height;
            y = y - height + 1;
            if (y < 0) {
                height += y;
                y = 0;
            }
        }

        //The rectangle shouldn't extend past the drawing area.
        if ((x + width) > drawingArea.width) {
            width = drawingArea.width - x;
        }
        if ((y + height) > drawingArea.height) {
            height = drawingArea.height - y;
        }

        //If the width or height is 0, make it 1
        //so that the box is visible.
        if (width == 0) {
            width = 1;
        }
        if (height == 0) {
            height = 1;
```

```
        }
        return new Rectangle(x, y, width, height);
    }
}
```

EXAMPLE: Shape-Drawing Applet

HTML PAGES CONTAINING APPLET: *http://java.sun.com/docs/books/tutorial/ui/drawing/drawingShapes.html*

ShapesDemo.java

SOURCE CODE: *http://java.sun.com/docs/books/tutorial/ui/drawing/example-1dot1/ShapesDemo.java*

1.0 SOURCE CODE: *http://java.sun.com/docs/books/tutorial/ui/drawing/example/ShapesDemo.java*

Where Explained:
Drawing Shapes (page 528)

```
import java.awt.*;
import java.applet.Applet;

/*
 * This displays a framed area containing one of
 * each shape you can draw.
 */

public class ShapesDemo extends Applet {
    final static int maxCharHeight = 15;
    final static Color bg = Color.lightGray;
    final static Color fg = Color.black;

    public void init() {
        //Initialize drawing colors
        setBackground(bg);
        setForeground(fg);
    }

    public void paint(Graphics g) {
        Dimension d = getSize();
        int x = 5;
        int y = 7;
        int gridWidth = d.width / 7;
        int gridHeight = d.height / 2;
        int stringY = gridHeight - 7;
        int rectWidth = gridWidth - 2*x;
        int rectHeight = stringY - maxCharHeight - y;

        Color fg3D = Color.lightGray;
```

```
// Draw the border.
 g.setColor(fg3D);
 g.draw3DRect(0, 0, d.width - 1, d.height - 1, true);
 g.draw3DRect(3, 3, d.width - 7, d.height - 7, false);
 g.setColor(fg);

 // drawLine(x1, y1, x2, y2)
 g.drawLine(x, y+rectHeight-1, x + rectWidth, y);
 g.drawString("drawLine()", x, stringY);
 x += gridWidth;

 // drawRect(x, y, w, h)
 g.drawRect(x, y, rectWidth, rectHeight);
 g.drawString("drawRect()", x, stringY);
 x += gridWidth;

 // draw3DRect(x, y, w, h, raised)
 g.setColor(fg3D);
 g.draw3DRect(x, y, rectWidth, rectHeight, true);
 g.setColor(fg);
 g.drawString("draw3DRect()", x, stringY);
 x += gridWidth;

 // drawRoundRect(x, y, w, h, arcw, arch)
 g.drawRoundRect(x, y, rectWidth, rectHeight, 10, 10);
 g.drawString("drawRoundRect()", x, stringY);
 x += gridWidth;

 // drawOval(x, y, w, h)
 g.drawOval(x, y, rectWidth, rectHeight);
 g.drawString("drawOval()", x, stringY);
 x += gridWidth;

 // drawArc(x, y, w, h)
 g.drawArc(x, y, rectWidth, rectHeight, 90, 135);
 g.drawString("drawArc()", x, stringY);
 x += gridWidth;

 // drawPolygon(xPoints, yPoints, numPoints)
 int x1Points[] = {x, x+rectWidth, x, x+rectWidth};
 int y1Points[] = {y, y+rectHeight, y+rectHeight, y};
 g.drawPolygon(x1Points, y1Points, x1Points.length);
 g.drawString("drawPolygon()", x, stringY);

 // NEW ROW
 x = 5;
 y += gridHeight;
 stringY += gridHeight;
```

```
        // drawPolyline(xPoints, yPoints, numPoints)
        // Note: drawPolygon would close the polygon.
        int x2Points[] = {x, x+rectWidth, x, x+rectWidth};
        int y2Points[] = {y, y+rectHeight, y+rectHeight, y};
        g.drawPolyline(x2Points, y2Points, x2Points.length);
        g.drawString("drawPolyline()", x, stringY);
        x += gridWidth;

        // fillRect(x, y, w, h)
        g.fillRect(x, y, rectWidth, rectHeight);
        g.drawString("fillRect()", x, stringY);
        x += gridWidth;

        // fill3DRect(x, y, w, h, raised)
        g.setColor(fg3D);
        g.fill3DRect(x, y, rectWidth, rectHeight, true);
        g.setColor(fg);
        g.drawString("fill3DRect()", x, stringY);
        x += gridWidth;

        // fillRoundRect(x, y, w, h, arcw, arch)
        g.fillRoundRect(x, y, rectWidth, rectHeight, 10, 10);
        g.drawString("fillRoundRect()", x, stringY);
        x += gridWidth;

        // fillOval(x, y, w, h)
        g.fillOval(x, y, rectWidth, rectHeight);
        g.drawString("fillOval()", x, stringY);
        x += gridWidth;

        // fillArc(x, y, w, h)
        g.fillArc(x, y, rectWidth, rectHeight, 90, 135);
        g.drawString("fillArc()", x, stringY);
        x += gridWidth;

        // fillPolygon(xPoints, yPoints, numPoints)
        int x3Points[] = {x, x+rectWidth, x, x+rectWidth};
        int y3Points[] = {y, y+rectHeight, y+rectHeight, y};
        g.fillPolygon(x3Points, y3Points, x3Points.length);
        g.drawString("fillPolygon()", x, stringY);
    }
}
```

EXAMPLE: Simple Text-Drawing Applet

Where Explained:
Working with Text (page 534)

HTML PAGES CONTAINING APPLET: *http://java.sun.com/docs/books/tutorial/ui/drawing/drawingText.html*

TextXY.java

SOURCE CODE: *http://java.sun.com/docs/books/tutorial/ui/drawing/example-1dot1/TextXY.java*

1.0 SOURCE CODE: *http://java.sun.com/docs/books/tutorial/ui/drawing/example/TextXY.java*

```
import java.awt.*;
import java.applet.Applet;

public class TextXY extends Applet {
    public void paint(Graphics g) {
        Dimension d = getSize();

        g.drawString("drawString() at (2, 5)", 2, 5);
        g.drawString("drawString() at (2, 30)", 2, 30);
      g.drawString("drawString() at (2, height)", 2, d.height);
    }
}
```

EXAMPLE: Shapes Demo with Font Manipulation

HTML PAGES CONTAINING APPLET: *http://java.sun.com/docs/books/tutorial/ui/drawing/drawingText.html*

This enhanced version of ShapesDemo.java (page 867) adjusts its fonts so that they fit within the allotted space.

FontDemo.java

Where Explained:
Working with Text (page 534)

SOURCE CODE: *http://java.sun.com/docs/books/tutorial/ui/drawing/example-1dot1/FontDemo.java*

1.0 SOURCE CODE: *http://java.sun.com/docs/books/tutorial/ui/drawing/example/FontDemo.java*

```
import java.awt.*;
import java.applet.Applet;

/*
 * This is like the ShapesDemo applet, except that it
 * handles fonts more carefully.
 */

public class FontDemo extends Applet {
```

```
    final static int maxCharHeight = 15;
    final static int minFontSize = 6;
    final static Color bg = Color.lightGray;
    final static Color fg = Color.black;

    Dimension totalSize;
    FontMetrics fontMetrics;

    public void init() {
        //Initialize drawing colors
        setBackground(bg);
        setForeground(fg);
    }

    FontMetrics pickFont(Graphics g,
                         String longString,
                         int xSpace) {
        boolean fontFits = false;
        Font font = g.getFont();
        FontMetrics fontMetrics = g.getFontMetrics();
        int size = font.getSize();
        String name = font.getName();
        int style = font.getStyle();

        while (!fontFits) {
            if ( (fontMetrics.getHeight() <= maxCharHeight)
              && (fontMetrics.stringWidth(longString) <= xSpace))
{
                fontFits = true;
            } else {
                if (size <= minFontSize) {
                    fontFits = true;
                } else {
                    g.setFont(font = new Font(name,
                                              style,
                                              --size));
                    fontMetrics = g.getFontMetrics();
                }
            }
        }

        return fontMetrics;
    }

    public void paint(Graphics g) {
        Dimension d = getSize();
        int gridWidth = d.width / 7;
        int gridHeight = d.height / 2;
```

```
if ( (totalSize == null)
  || (totalSize.width != d.width)
  || (totalSize.height != d.height) ) {
    totalSize = d;
    fontMetrics = pickFont(g, "drawRoundRect()",
                            gridWidth);
}

Color fg3D = Color.lightGray;

g.setColor(fg3D);
g.draw3DRect(0, 0, d.width - 1, d.height - 1, true);
g.draw3DRect(3, 3, d.width - 7, d.height - 7, false);
g.setColor(fg);

int x = 5;
int y = 7;
int rectWidth = gridWidth - 2*x;
int stringY = gridHeight - 5 -
              fontMetrics.getDescent();
int rectHeight = stringY - fontMetrics.getMaxAscent()
                 - y - 2;

// drawLine(x1, y1, x2, y2)
g.drawLine(x, y+rectHeight-1, x + rectWidth, y);
g.drawString("drawLine()", x, stringY);
x += gridWidth;

// drawRect(x, y, w, h)
g.drawRect(x, y, rectWidth, rectHeight);
g.drawString("drawRect()", x, stringY);
x += gridWidth;

// draw3DRect(x, y, w, h, raised)
g.setColor(fg3D);
g.draw3DRect(x, y, rectWidth, rectHeight, true);
g.setColor(fg);
g.drawString("draw3DRect()", x, stringY);
x += gridWidth;

// drawRoundRect(x, y, w, h, arcw, arch)
g.drawRoundRect(x, y, rectWidth, rectHeight, 10, 10);
g.drawString("drawRoundRect()", x, stringY);
x += gridWidth;

// drawOval(x, y, w, h)
g.drawOval(x, y, rectWidth, rectHeight);
```

```
g.drawString("drawOval()", x, stringY);
x += gridWidth;

// drawArc(x, y, w, h)
g.drawArc(x, y, rectWidth, rectHeight, 90, 135);
g.drawString("drawArc()", x, stringY);
x += gridWidth;

// drawPolygon(xPoints, yPoints, numPoints)
int x1Points[] = {x, x+rectWidth, x, x+rectWidth};
int y1Points[] = {y, y+rectHeight, y+rectHeight, y};
g.drawPolygon(x1Points, y1Points, x1Points.length);
g.drawString("drawPolygon()", x, stringY);

// NEW ROW
x = 5;
y += gridHeight;
stringY += gridHeight;

// drawPolyline(xPoints, yPoints, numPoints)
// Note: drawPolygon would close the polygon.
int x2Points[] = {x, x+rectWidth, x, x+rectWidth};
int y2Points[] = {y, y+rectHeight, y+rectHeight, y};
g.drawPolyline(x2Points, y2Points, x2Points.length);
g.drawString("drawPolyline()", x, stringY);
x += gridWidth;

// fillRect(x, y, w, h)
g.fillRect(x, y, rectWidth, rectHeight);
g.drawString("fillRect()", x, stringY);
x += gridWidth;

// fill3DRect(x, y, w, h, raised)
g.setColor(fg3D);
g.fill3DRect(x, y, rectWidth, rectHeight, true);
g.setColor(fg);
g.drawString("fill3DRect()", x, stringY);
x += gridWidth;

// fillRoundRect(x, y, w, h, arcw, arch)
g.fillRoundRect(x, y, rectWidth, rectHeight, 10, 10);
g.drawString("fillRoundRect()", x, stringY);
x += gridWidth;

// fillOval(x, y, w, h)
g.fillOval(x, y, rectWidth, rectHeight);
g.drawString("fillOval()", x, stringY);
x += gridWidth;
```

```
            // fillArc(x, y, w, h)
            g.fillArc(x, y, rectWidth, rectHeight, 90, 135);
            g.drawString("fillArc()", x, stringY);
            x += gridWidth;

            // fillPolygon(xPoints, yPoints, numPoints)
            int x3Points[] = {x, x+rectWidth, x, x+rectWidth};
            int y3Points[] = {y, y+rectHeight, y+rectHeight, y};
            g.fillPolygon(x3Points, y3Points, x3Points.length);
            g.drawString("fillPolygon()", x, stringY);
        }
    }
```

EXAMPLE: Image-Loading Applet

Where Explained: *Loading Images* (page 541)

ImageUpdater.java

SOURCE CODE: *http://java.sun.com/docs/books/tutorial/ui/drawing/example-1dot1/ImageUpdater.java*

1.0 SOURCE CODE: *http://java.sun.com/docs/books/tutorial/ui/drawing/example/ImageUpdater.java*

```
import java.applet.*;
import java.awt.*;
import java.awt.image.ImageObserver;

public class ImageUpdater extends Applet {
    /*
     * Written by Jim Graham.
     * This applet draws a big image scaled to its width
     * and height as specified in the <APPLET> tag, and a
     * small image scaled by the same ratio as the big
     * image and positioned in the center of it.
     */
    Image bigimg, smallimg;
    int smallx, smally, smallw, smallh;
    boolean sizeknown = false;
    boolean errored = false;

    public void init() {
        bigimg = getImage(getCodeBase(), "bigimg.gif");
        smallimg = getImage(getCodeBase(), "smallimg.gif");
        positionImages();
    }

    public boolean imageUpdate(Image theimg, int infoflags,
                               int x, int y, int w, int h) {
        if ((infoflags & (ERROR)) != 0) {
```

```
            errored = true;
        }
        if ((infoflags & (WIDTH | HEIGHT)) != 0) {
            positionImages();
        }
        boolean done = ((infoflags & (ERROR | FRAMEBITS |
                                      ALLBITS)) != 0);
        // Repaint immediately if we are done,
        // otherwise batch up repaint requests every
        // 100 milliseconds
        repaint(done ? 0 : 100);
        return !done;
    }

    public synchronized void positionImages() {
        Dimension d = getSize();
        int bigw = bigimg.getWidth(this);
        int bigh = bigimg.getHeight(this);
        smallw = smallimg.getWidth(this);
        smallh = smallimg.getHeight(this);
        if (bigw < 0 || bigh < 0 || smallw < 0 || smallh < 0) {
            return;
        }
        smallw = smallw * d.width / bigw;
        smallh = smallh * d.height / bigh;
        smallx = (d.width - smallw) / 2;
        smally = (d.height - smallh) / 2;
        sizeknown = true;
    }

    public synchronized void paint(Graphics g) {
        Dimension d = getSize();
        int appw = d.width;
        int apph = d.height;
        if (errored) {
            // The images had a problem - just draw a
            // big red rectangle
            g.setColor(Color.red);
            g.fillRect(0, 0, appw, apph);
            return;
        }
        // Scale the big image to the width and height
        // of the applet
        g.drawImage(bigimg, 0, 0, appw, apph, this);
        if (sizeknown) {
            // Scale the small image to the central
            // region calculated above.
            g.drawImage(smallimg, smallx, smally,
```

```
                                        smallw, smallh, this);
            }
        }
    }
```

EXAMPLE: Image-Displaying Applet

Where Explained: *Displaying Images* (page 544)

HTML PAGES CONTAINING APPLET: *http://java.sun.com/docs/books/tutorial/ui/drawing/drawingImages.html*

ImageDisplayer.java

SOURCE CODE: *http://java.sun.com/docs/books/tutorial/ui/drawing/example/ImageDisplayer.java*

```
import java.awt.*;
import java.applet.Applet;

/*
 * This applet displays a single image twice,
 * once at its normal size and once much wider.
 */

public class ImageDisplayer extends Applet {
    Image image;

    public void init() {
        image = getImage(getCodeBase(), "rocketship.gif");
    }

    public void paint(Graphics g) {
        //Draw image at its natural size first.
        g.drawImage(image, 0, 0, this); //85x62 image

        //Now draw the image scaled.
        g.drawImage(image, 90, 0, 300, 62, this);
    }
}
```

EXAMPLE: An Applet That Uses an Image Filter

HTML PAGES CONTAINING APPLET: *http://java.sun.com/docs/books/tutorial/ui/drawing/useFilter.html*

Where Explained:
How to Use an Image Filter (page 546)

ImageRotator.java

SOURCE CODE: *http://java.sun.com/docs/books/tutorial/ui/drawing/example-1dot1/ImageRotator.java*

1.0 SOURCE CODE: *http://java.sun.com/docs/books/tutorial/ui/drawing/example/ImageRotator.java*

```
import java.awt.*;
import java.awt.event.*;
import java.awt.image.*;
import java.applet.Applet;

/*
 * This applet displays an image. When the user enters
 * an angle, the image is rotated to the specified angle.
 */

public class ImageRotator extends Applet
                          implements ActionListener {
    TextField degreeField;
    RotatorCanvas rotator;
    double radiansPerDegree = Math.PI / 180;

    public void init() {
        // Load the image.
        Image image = getImage(getCodeBase(),
                               "rocketship.gif");

        //Set up the UI.
        GridBagLayout gridBag = new GridBagLayout();
        GridBagConstraints c = new GridBagConstraints();
        setLayout(gridBag);

        Label l = new Label("Number of degrees to "
                            + "rotate the image:");
        gridBag.setConstraints(l, c);
        add(l);

        degreeField = new TextField(5);
        degreeField.addActionListener(this);
        gridBag.setConstraints(degreeField, c);
        add(degreeField);

        Button b = new Button("Redraw image");
```

```
        b.addActionListener(this);
        c.gridwidth = GridBagConstraints.REMAINDER;
        gridBag.setConstraints(b, c);
        add(b);

        rotator = new RotatorCanvas(image);
        c.fill = GridBagConstraints.BOTH;
        c.weightx = 1.0;
        c.weighty = 1.0;
        gridBag.setConstraints(rotator, c);
        add(rotator);
    }

    public void actionPerformed(ActionEvent e) {
        int degrees;

        try {
            degrees = Integer.parseInt(degreeField.getText());
        } catch (NumberFormatException exc) {
            degrees = 0;
        }

        //Convert to radians.
       rotator.rotateImage((double)degrees * radiansPerDegree);
    }
}

class RotatorCanvas extends Canvas {
    Image sourceImage;
    Image resultImage;

    public RotatorCanvas(Image image) {
        sourceImage = image;
        resultImage = sourceImage;
    }

    public void rotateImage(double angle) {
        ImageFilter filter = new RotateFilter(angle);
        ImageProducer producer = new FilteredImageSource(
                                        sourceImage.getSource(),
                                          filter);
        resultImage = createImage(producer);
        repaint();
    }

    public void paint(Graphics g) {
        Dimension d = getSize();
        int x = (d.width - resultImage.getWidth(this)) / 2;
```

```
        int y = (d.height - resultImage.getHeight(this)) / 2;

        g.drawImage(resultImage, x, y, this);
    }
}
```

EXAMPLE: A Filter that Rotates Images

HTML PAGES CONTAINING APPLET: *http://java.sun.com/docs/books/tutorial/ui/drawing/useFilter.html*

RotateFilter.java

SOURCE CODE: *http://java.sun.com/docs/books/tutorial/ui/drawing/example/RotateFilter.java*

Where Explained:
How to Write an Image Filter (page 550)

```
import java.awt.image.ColorModel;
import java.awt.image.ImageFilter;
import java.util.Hashtable;
import java.awt.Rectangle;

public class RotateFilter extends ImageFilter {

    private static ColorModel defaultRGB =
         ColorModel.getRGBdefault();

    private double angle;
    private double sin;
    private double cos;
    private double coord[] = new double[2];

    private int raster[];
    private int xoffset, yoffset;
    private int srcW, srcH;
    private int dstW, dstH;

    public RotateFilter(double angle) {
        this.angle = angle;
        sin = Math.sin(angle);
        cos = Math.cos(angle);
    }

    public void transform(double x, double y,
                          double[] retcoord) {
        // Remember that the coordinate system is
        // upside down so apply the transform
        // as if the angle were negated.
        // cos(-angle) =  cos(angle)
        // sin(-angle) = -sin(angle)
```

```
            retcoord[0] = cos * x + sin * y;
            retcoord[1] = cos * y - sin * x;
        }

    public void itransform(double x, double y, double[] retcoord) {
            // Remember that the coordinate system is upside down
            // so apply the transform as if the angle were
            // negated. Since inverting the transform is also the
            // same as negating the angle, itransform is
            // calculated the way you would expect to
            // calculate transform.
            retcoord[0] = cos * x - sin * y;
            retcoord[1] = cos * y + sin * x;
        }

        public void transformBBox(Rectangle rect) {
            double minx = Double.POSITIVE_INFINITY;
            double miny = Double.POSITIVE_INFINITY;
            double maxx = Double.NEGATIVE_INFINITY;
            double maxy = Double.NEGATIVE_INFINITY;
            for (int y = 0; y <= 1; y++) {
                for (int x = 0; x <= 1; x++) {
                    transform(rect.x + x * rect.width,
                              rect.y + y * rect.height,
                              coord);
                    minx = Math.min(minx, coord[0]);
                    miny = Math.min(miny, coord[1]);
                    maxx = Math.max(maxx, coord[0]);
                    maxy = Math.max(maxy, coord[1]);
                }
            }
            rect.x = (int) Math.floor(minx);
            rect.y = (int) Math.floor(miny);
            rect.width = (int) Math.ceil(maxx) - rect.x + 1;
            rect.height = (int) Math.ceil(maxy) - rect.y + 1;
        }

        public void setDimensions(int width, int height) {
            Rectangle rect = new Rectangle(0, 0, width, height);
            transformBBox(rect);
            xoffset = -rect.x;
            yoffset = -rect.y;
            srcW = width;
            srcH = height;
            dstW = rect.width;
            dstH = rect.height;
            raster = new int[srcW * srcH];
            consumer.setDimensions(dstW, dstH);
```

```
}

public void setColorModel(ColorModel model) {
    consumer.setColorModel(defaultRGB);
}

public void setHints(int hintflags) {
    consumer.setHints(TOPDOWNLEFTRIGHT
                     | COMPLETESCANLINES
                     | SINGLEPASS
                     | (hintflags & SINGLEFRAME));
}

public void setPixels(int x, int y, int w, int h,
                      ColorModel model, byte pixels[],
                      int off, int scansize) {
    int srcoff = off;
    int dstoff = y * srcW + x;
    for (int yc = 0; yc < h; yc++) {
        for (int xc = 0; xc < w; xc++) {
            raster[dstoff++] = model.getRGB(
                 pixels [srcoff++] & 0xff);
        }
        srcoff += (scansize - w);
        dstoff += (srcW - w);
    }
}

public void setPixels(int x, int y, int w, int h,
                      ColorModel model,
                     int pixels[], int off, int scansize) {
    int srcoff = off;
    int dstoff = y * srcW + x;
    if (model == defaultRGB) {
        for (int yc = 0; yc < h; yc++) {
            System.arraycopy(pixels, srcoff,
                             raster, dstoff, w);
            srcoff += scansize;
            dstoff += srcW;
        }
    } else {
        for (int yc = 0; yc < h; yc++) {
            for (int xc = 0; xc < w; xc++) {
               raster[dstoff++] = model.getRGB(
                                  pixels[srcoff++]);
            }
            srcoff += (scansize - w);
            dstoff += (srcW - w);
```

```
            }
        }
    }

    public void imageComplete(int status) {
        if (status == IMAGEERROR || status == IMAGEABORTED) {
            consumer.imageComplete(status);
            return;
        }
        int pixels[] = new int[dstW];
        for (int dy = 0; dy < dstH; dy++) {
            itransform(0 - xoffset, dy - yoffset, coord);
            double x1 = coord[0];
            double y1 = coord[1];
            itransform(dstW - xoffset, dy - yoffset, coord);
            double x2 = coord[0];
            double y2 = coord[1];
            double xinc = (x2 - x1) / dstW;
            double yinc = (y2 - y1) / dstW;
            for (int dx = 0; dx < dstW; dx++) {
                int sx = (int) Math.round(x1);
                int sy = (int) Math.round(y1);
                if (sx < 0 || sy < 0 || sx >=
                        srcW || sy >= srcH) { pixels[dx] = 0;
                } else {
                        pixels[dx] = raster[sy * srcW + sx];
                }
                x1 += xinc;
                y1 += yinc;
            }
            consumer.setPixels(0, dy, dstW, 1, defaultRGB,
                                pixels, 0, dstW);
        }
        consumer.imageComplete(status);
    }
}
```

Where Explained: *Creating the Animation Loop* (page 555)

EXAMPLE: Applet Animation Template

HTML PAGES CONTAINING APPLET: *http://java.sun.com/docs/books/tutorial/ui/drawing/animLoop.html*

Also see AnimatorApplication.java (page 885), which implements an application that does the same thing as this applet.

AnimatorApplet.java

SOURCE CODE: *http://java.sun.com/docs/books/tutorial/ui/drawing/example-1dot1/AnimatorApplet.java*

1.0 SOURCE CODE: *http://java.sun.com/docs/books/tutorial/ui/drawing/example/AnimatorApplet.java*

```
import java.awt.*;
import java.awt.event.*;
import java.applet.Applet;

/*
 * Based on Arthur van Hoff's animation examples, this applet
 * can serve as a template for all animation applets.
 */

public class AnimatorApplet extends Applet
                            implements Runnable {
    int frameNumber = -1;
    int delay;
    Thread animatorThread;
    boolean frozen = false;

    public void init() {
        String str;
        int fps = 10;

        //How many milliseconds between frames?
        str = getParameter("fps");
        try {
            if (str != null) {
                fps = Integer.parseInt(str);
            }
        } catch (Exception e) {}
        delay = (fps > 0) ? (1000 / fps) : 100;

        addMouseListener(new MouseAdapter() {
            public void mousePressed(MouseEvent e) {
                if (frozen) {
                    frozen = false;
                    start();
                } else {
                    frozen = true;
                    stop();
                }
            }
        });
    }
```

```
public void start() {
    if (frozen) {
        //Do nothing.  The user has requested that we
        //stop changing the image.
    } else {
        //Start animating!
        if (animatorThread == null) {
            animatorThread = new Thread(this);
        }
        animatorThread.start();
    }
}

public void stop() {
    //Stop the animating thread.
    animatorThread = null;
}

public void run() {
    //Just to be nice, lower this thread's priority
    //so it can't interfere with other processing going on.
  Thread.currentThread().setPriority(Thread.MIN_PRIORITY);

    //Remember the starting time.
    long startTime = System.currentTimeMillis();

    //Remember which thread we are.
    Thread currentThread = Thread.currentThread();

    //This is the animation loop.
    while (currentThread == animatorThread) {
        //Advance the animation frame.
        frameNumber++;

        //Display it.
        repaint();

        //Delay depending on how far we are behind.
        try {
            startTime += delay;
            Thread.sleep(Math.max(0,
                    startTime-System.currentTimeMillis()));
        } catch (InterruptedException e) {
            break;
        }
    }
}
```

```
    //Draw the current frame of animation.
    public void paint(Graphics g) {
        g.drawString("Frame " + frameNumber, 0, 30);
    }
}
```

EXAMPLE: Application Animation Template

Also see AnimatorApplet.java (page 883), which implements an applet that does the same thing as this application.

AnimatorApplication.java

SOURCE CODE: *http://java.sun.com/docs/books/tutorial/ui/drawing/example-1dot1/AnimatorApplication.java*

1.0 SOURCE CODE: *http://java.sun.com/docs/books/tutorial/ui/drawing/example/AnimatorApplication.java*

Where Explained: *Creating the Animation Loop* (page 555)

```
import java.awt.*;
import java.awt.event.*;

/*
 * Based on Arthur van Hoff's animation examples, this
 * application can serve as a template for all animation
 * applications.
 */
public class AnimatorApplication extends Frame
                                 implements Runnable {
    int frameNumber = -1;
    int delay;
    Thread animatorThread;
    boolean frozen = false;

    AnimatorApplication(int fps, String windowTitle) {
        super(windowTitle);
        delay = (fps > 0) ? (1000 / fps) : 100;

        addMouseListener(new MouseAdapter() {
            public void mousePressed(MouseEvent e) {
                if (frozen) {
                    frozen = false;
                    startAnimation();
                } else {
                    frozen = true;
                    stopAnimation();
                }
            }
        });
```

```
        addWindowListener(new WindowAdapter() {
            public void windowIconified(WindowEvent e) {
                stopAnimation();
            }
            public void windowDeiconified(WindowEvent e) {
                startAnimation();
            }
            public void windowClosing(WindowEvent e) {
                System.exit(0);
            }
        });
    }

    public void startAnimation() {
        if (frozen) {
            //Do nothing.  The user has requested that we
            //stop changing the image.
        } else {
            //Start animating!
            if (animatorThread == null) {
                animatorThread = new Thread(this);
            }
            animatorThread.start();
        }
    }

    public void stopAnimation() {
        //Stop the animating thread.
        animatorThread = null;
    }

    public void run() {
        //Just to be nice, lower this thread's priority
        //so it can't interfere with other processing going on.
      Thread.currentThread().setPriority(Thread.MIN_PRIORITY);

        //Remember the starting time.
        long startTime = System.currentTimeMillis();

        //Remember which thread we are.
        Thread currentThread = Thread.currentThread();

        //This is the animation loop.
        while (currentThread == animatorThread) {
            //Advance the animation frame.
            frameNumber++;

            //Display it.
```

```
            repaint();

            //Delay depending on how far we are behind.
            try {
                startTime += delay;
                Thread.sleep(Math.max(0,
                       startTime-System.currentTimeMillis()));
            } catch (InterruptedException e) {
                break;
            }
        }
    }

    //Draw the current frame of animation.
    public void paint(Graphics g) {
        g.drawString("Frame " + frameNumber, 5, 50);
    }

    public static void main(String args[]) {
        AnimatorApplication animator = null;
        int fps = 10;

       // Get frames per second from the command line argument
        if (args.length > 0) {
            try {
                fps = Integer.parseInt(args[0]);
            } catch (Exception e) {}
        }
        animator = new AnimatorApplication(fps, "Animator");
        animator.setSize(200, 60);
        animator.setVisible(true);
        animator.startAnimation();
    }
}
```

EXAMPLE: A First Try at Animating Graphics

Where Explained:
Animating Graphics
(page 560)

HTML PAGES CONTAINING APPLET: *http://java.sun.com/docs/books/tutorial/ui/drawing/animGraphics.html*

This applet animates some primitive graphics. It's not the best example, since its display flashes. The next two examples improve on this one.

FlashingGraphics.java

SOURCE CODE: *http://java.sun.com/docs/books/tutorial/ui/drawing/example-1dot1/FlashingGraphics.java*

1.0 SOURCE CODE: *http://java.sun.com/docs/books/tutorial/ui/drawing/example/FlashingGraphics.java*

```
import java.awt.*;
import java.awt.event.*;
import java.applet.Applet;

/*
 * This applet animates graphics that it generates.  This
 * example isn't a good one to copy -- it flashes.  The
 * next couple of examples will show how to eliminate the
 * flashing.
 */

public class FlashingGraphics extends Applet
                               implements Runnable {
    int frameNumber = -1;
    int delay;
    Thread animatorThread;
    boolean frozen = false;

    int squareSize = 20;
    boolean fillColumnTop = true;

    public void init() {
        String str;
        int fps = 10;

        //How many milliseconds between frames?
        str = getParameter("fps");
        try {
            if (str != null) {
                fps = Integer.parseInt(str);
            }
        } catch (Exception e) {}
        delay = (fps > 0) ? (1000 / fps) : 100;

        //How many pixels wide is each square?
        str = getParameter("squareWidth");
        try {
            if (str != null) {
                squareSize = Integer.parseInt(str);
            }
        } catch (Exception e) {}
```

```
        addMouseListener(new MouseAdapter() {
            public void mousePressed(MouseEvent e) {
                if (frozen) {
                    frozen = false;
                    start();
                } else {
                    frozen = true;
                    stop();
                }
            }
        });
    }

    public void start() {
        if (frozen) {
            //Do nothing.  The user has requested that we
            //stop changing the image.
        } else {
            //Start animating!
            if (animatorThread == null) {
                animatorThread = new Thread(this);
            }
            animatorThread.start();
        }
    }

    public void stop() {
        //Stop the animating thread.
        animatorThread = null;
    }

    public void run() {
        //Just to be nice, lower this thread's priority
        //so it can't interfere with other processing going on.
        Thread.currentThread().setPriority(Thread.MIN_PRIORITY);

        //Remember the starting time.
        long startTime = System.currentTimeMillis();

        //Remember which thread we are.
        Thread currentThread = Thread.currentThread();

        //This is the animation loop.
        while (currentThread == animatorThread) {
            //Advance the animation frame.
            frameNumber++;

            //Display it.
```

```
                repaint();

                //Delay depending on how far we are behind.
                try {
                    startTime += delay;
                    Thread.sleep(Math.max(0,
                            startTime-System.currentTimeMillis()));
                } catch (InterruptedException e) {
                    break;
                }
            }
        }

        //Draw the current frame of animation.
        public void paint(Graphics g) {
            Dimension d = getSize();
            boolean fillSquare;
            boolean fillNextFrame;
            int rowWidth = 0;
            int x = 0, y = 0;
            int w, h;
            int tmp;

          //Set width of first "square". Decide whether to fill it.
            fillSquare = fillColumnTop;
            fillColumnTop = !fillColumnTop;
            tmp = frameNumber % squareSize;
            if (tmp == 0) {
                w = squareSize;
                fillNextFrame = !fillSquare;
            } else {
                w = tmp;
                fillNextFrame = fillSquare;
            }

            //Draw from left to right.
            while (x < d.width) {
                int colHeight = 0;

                //Draw the column.
                while (y < d.height) {
                    colHeight += squareSize;

                    //If no room for a full square, cut it off.
                    if (colHeight > d.height) {
                        h = d.height - y;
                    } else {
                        h = squareSize;
```

```
                }

                //Draw the rectangle if necessary.
                if (fillSquare) {
                   g.fillRect(x, y, w, h);
                   fillSquare = false;
                } else {
                   fillSquare = true;
                }

                y += h;
            } //while y

            //Determine x, y, and w for the next go around.
            x += w;
            y = 0;
            w = squareSize;
            rowWidth += w;
            if (rowWidth > d.width) {
                w = d.width - x;
            }
            fillSquare = fillColumnTop;
            fillColumnTop = !fillColumnTop;
        } //while x
        fillColumnTop = fillNextFrame;
    }
}
```

EXAMPLE: Implementing the update Method

HTML PAGES CONTAINING APPLET: *http://java.sun.com/docs/books/tutorial/ui/drawing/update.html*

This applet animates some primitive graphics, implementing the `update` method to avoid flashing.

Where Explained:
Overriding the update Method (page 561)

Update.java

SOURCE CODE: *http://java.sun.com/docs/books/tutorial/ui/drawing/example-1dot1/Update.java*

1.0 SOURCE CODE: *http://java.sun.com/docs/books/tutorial/ui/drawing/example/Update.java*

```
import java.awt.*;
import java.awt.event.*;
import java.applet.Applet;

/*
 * This applet animates graphics that it generates.  This
```

```
 * example eliminates flashing by overriding the update
 * method.  For the graphics this example generates,
 * overriding update isn't quite good enough -- on some
 * systems, you can still see a crawling effect.
 */

public class Update extends Applet
                               implements Runnable {
    int frameNumber = -1;
    int delay;
    Thread animatorThread;
    boolean frozen = false;

    int squareSize = 20;
    boolean fillColumnTop = true;

    public void init() {
        String str;
        int fps = 10;

        //How many milliseconds between frames?
        str = getParameter("fps");
        try {
            if (str != null) {
                fps = Integer.parseInt(str);
            }
        } catch (Exception e) {}
        delay = (fps > 0) ? (1000 / fps) : 100;

        //How many pixels wide is each square?
        str = getParameter("squareWidth");
        try {
            if (str != null) {
                squareSize = Integer.parseInt(str);
            }
        } catch (Exception e) {}

        addMouseListener(new MouseAdapter() {
            public void mousePressed(MouseEvent e) {
                if (frozen) {
                    frozen = false;
                    start();
                } else {
                    frozen = true;
                    stop();
                }
            }
        });
```

```
}

public void start() {
    if (frozen) {
        //Do nothing.  The user has requested that we
        //stop changing the image.
    } else {
        //Start animating!
        if (animatorThread == null) {
            animatorThread = new Thread(this);
        }
        animatorThread.start();
    }
}

public void stop() {
    //Stop the animating thread.
    animatorThread = null;
}

public void run() {
    //Just to be nice, lower this thread's priority
   //so it can't interfere with other processing going on.
  Thread.currentThread().setPriority(Thread.MIN_PRIORITY);

    //Remember the starting time.
    long startTime = System.currentTimeMillis();

    //Remember which thread we are.
    Thread currentThread = Thread.currentThread();

    //This is the animation loop.
    while (currentThread == animatorThread) {
        //Advance the animation frame.
        frameNumber++;

        //Display it.
        repaint();

        //Delay depending on how far we are behind.
        try {
            startTime += delay;
            Thread.sleep(Math.max(0,
                    startTime-System.currentTimeMillis()));
        } catch (InterruptedException e) {
            break;
        }
    }
```

```
    }

    //Draw the current frame of animation.
    public void paint(Graphics g) {
        update(g);
    }

    public void update(Graphics g) {
        Color bg = getBackground();
        Color fg = getForeground();
        Dimension d = getSize();
        boolean fillSquare;
        boolean fillNextFrame;
        int rowWidth = 0;
        int x = 0, y = 0;
        int w, h;
        int tmp;

      //Set width of first "square". Decide whether to fill it.
        fillSquare = fillColumnTop;
        fillColumnTop = !fillColumnTop;
        tmp = frameNumber % squareSize;
        if (tmp == 0) {
            w = squareSize;
            fillNextFrame = !fillSquare;
        } else {
            w = tmp;
            fillNextFrame = fillSquare;
        }

        //Draw from left to right.
        while (x < d.width) {
            int colHeight = 0;

            //Draw the column.
            while (y < d.height) {
                colHeight += squareSize;

                //If no room for a full square, cut it off.
                if (colHeight > d.height) {
                    h = d.height - y;
                } else {
                    h = squareSize;
                }

                //Draw the rectangle.
                if (fillSquare) {
                    g.fillRect(x, y, w, h);
```

```
                    fillSquare = false;
                } else {
                    g.setColor(bg);
                    g.fillRect(x, y, w, h);
                    g.setColor(fg);
                    fillSquare = true;
                }

                y += h;
            } //while y

            //Determine x, y, and w for the next go around.
            x += w;
            y = 0;
            w = squareSize;
            rowWidth += w;
            if (rowWidth > d.width) {
                w = d.width - x;
            }
            fillSquare = fillColumnTop;
            fillColumnTop = !fillColumnTop;
        } //while x
        fillColumnTop = fillNextFrame;
    }
}
```

EXAMPLE: Implementing Double Buffering

HTML PAGES CONTAINING APPLET: *http://java.sun.com/docs/books/tutorial/ui/drawing/doubleBuffer.html*

This applet animates some primitive graphics, implementing double buffering to avoid flashing.

Where Explained:
Implementing Double Buffering (page 563)

DoubleBuffer.java

SOURCE CODE: *http://java.sun.com/docs/books/tutorial/ui/drawing/example-1dot1/DoubleBuffer.java*

1.0 SOURCE CODE: *http://java.sun.com/docs/books/tutorial/ui/drawing/example/DoubleBuffer.java*

```
import java.awt.*;
import java.awt.event.*;
import java.applet.Applet;

/*
 * This applet animates graphics that it generates.  This
 * example eliminates flashing by double buffering.
 */
```

```
public class DoubleBuffer extends Applet
                              implements Runnable {
    int frameNumber = -1;
    int delay;
    Thread animatorThread;
    boolean frozen = false;

    int squareSize = 20;
    boolean fillColumnTop = true;

    Dimension offDimension;
    Image offImage;
    Graphics offGraphics;

    public void init() {
        String str;
        int fps = 10;

        //How many milliseconds between frames?
        str = getParameter("fps");
        try {
            if (str != null) {
                fps = Integer.parseInt(str);
            }
        } catch (Exception e) {}
        delay = (fps > 0) ? (1000 / fps) : 100;

        //How many pixels wide is each square?
        str = getParameter("squareWidth");
        try {
            if (str != null) {
                squareSize = Integer.parseInt(str);
            }
        } catch (Exception e) {}

        addMouseListener(new MouseAdapter() {
            public void mousePressed(MouseEvent e) {
                if (frozen) {
                    frozen = false;
                    start();
                } else {
                    frozen = true;

                  //Instead of calling stop(), which destroys the
                  //backbuffer, just stop the animating thread.
                    animatorThread = null;
                }
            }
```

```
    });
}

public void start() {
    if (frozen) {
        //Do nothing.  The user has requested that we
        //stop changing the image.
    } else {
        //Start animating!
        if (animatorThread == null) {
            animatorThread = new Thread(this);
        }
        animatorThread.start();
    }
}

public void stop() {
    //Stop the animating thread.
    animatorThread = null;

   //Get rid of the objects necessary for double buffering.
    offGraphics = null;
    offImage = null;
}

public void run() {
    //Just to be nice, lower this thread's priority
   //so it can't interfere with other processing going on.
  Thread.currentThread().setPriority(Thread.MIN_PRIORITY);

    //Remember the starting time.
    long startTime = System.currentTimeMillis();

    //Remember which thread we are.
    Thread currentThread = Thread.currentThread();

    //This is the animation loop.
    while (currentThread == animatorThread) {
        //Advance the animation frame.
        frameNumber++;

        //Display it.
        repaint();

        //Delay depending on how far we are behind.
        try {
            startTime += delay;
            Thread.sleep(Math.max(0,
```

```
                              startTime-System.currentTimeMillis()));
                } catch (InterruptedException e) {
                    break;
                }
            }
        }

        //Draw the current frame of animation.
        public void paint(Graphics g) {
            update(g);
        }

        public void update(Graphics g) {
            Dimension d = getSize();
            boolean fillSquare;
            boolean fillNextFrame;
            int rowWidth = 0;
            int x = 0, y = 0;
            int w, h;
            int tmp;

            //Create the offscreen graphics context,
            //if no good one exists.
            if ( (offGraphics == null)
              || (d.width != offDimension.width)
              || (d.height != offDimension.height) ) {
                offDimension = d;
                offImage = createImage(d.width, d.height);
                offGraphics = offImage.getGraphics();
            }

            //Erase the previous image.
            offGraphics.setColor(getBackground());
            offGraphics.fillRect(0, 0, d.width, d.height);
            offGraphics.setColor(Color.black);

          //Set width of first "square". Decide whether to fill it.
            fillSquare = fillColumnTop;
            fillColumnTop = !fillColumnTop;
            tmp = frameNumber % squareSize;
            if (tmp == 0) {
                w = squareSize;
                fillNextFrame = !fillSquare;
            } else {
                w = tmp;
                fillNextFrame = fillSquare;
            }
```

```
        //Draw from left to right.
        while (x < d.width) {
            int colHeight = 0;

            //Draw the column.
            while (y < d.height) {
                colHeight += squareSize;

                //If no room for a full square, cut it off.
                if (colHeight > d.height) {
                   h = d.height - y;
                } else {
                   h = squareSize;
                }

                //Draw the rectangle if necessary.
                if (fillSquare) {
                   offGraphics.fillRect(x, y, w, h);
                   fillSquare = false;
                } else {
                   fillSquare = true;
                }

                y += h;
            } //while y

            //Determine x, y, and w for the next go around.
            x += w;
            y = 0;
            w = squareSize;
            rowWidth += w;
            if (rowWidth > d.width) {
                w = d.width - x;
            }
            fillSquare = fillColumnTop;
            fillColumnTop = !fillColumnTop;
        } //while x
        fillColumnTop = fillNextFrame;

        //Paint the image onto the screen.
        g.drawImage(offImage, 0, 0, this);
    }
}
```

EXAMPLE: Performing Cutout Animation

HTML PAGES CONTAINING APPLET: *http://java.sun.com/docs/books/tutorial/ui/drawing/movingImage.html*

MovingImage.java

SOURCE CODE: *http://java.sun.com/docs/books/tutorial/ui/drawing/example-1dot1/MovingImage.java*

1.0 SOURCE CODE: *http://java.sun.com/docs/books/tutorial/ui/drawing/example/MovingImage.java*

Where Explained: *Moving an Image Across the Screen* (page 565)

```
import java.awt.*;
import java.awt.event.*;
import java.applet.Applet;

/*
 * This applet moves an image in front of a background image.
 * It eliminates flashing by double buffering.
 */

public class MovingImage extends Applet
                         implements Runnable {
    int frameNumber = -1;
    int delay;
    Thread animatorThread;
    boolean frozen = false;

    Image stars;
    Image rocket;

    Dimension offDimension;
    Image offImage;
    Graphics offGraphics;

    public void init() {
        String str;
        int fps = 10;

        //How many milliseconds between frames?
        str = getParameter("fps");
        try {
            if (str != null) {
                fps = Integer.parseInt(str);
            }
        } catch (Exception e) {}
        delay = (fps > 0) ? (1000 / fps) : 100;

        //Get the images.
```

```
        stars = getImage(getCodeBase(),
                         "starfield.gif");
        rocket = getImage(getCodeBase(),
                         "rocketship.gif");

        addMouseListener(new MouseAdapter() {
            public void mousePressed(MouseEvent e) {
                if (frozen) {
                    frozen = false;
                    start();
                } else {
                    frozen = true;

                //Instead of calling stop(), which destroys the
                  //backbuffer, just stop the animating thread.
                    animatorThread = null;
                }
            }
       });
    }

    public void start() {
        if (frozen) {
            //Do nothing.  The user has requested that we
            //stop changing the image.
        } else {
            //Start animating!
            if (animatorThread == null) {
                animatorThread = new Thread(this);
            }
            animatorThread.start();
        }
    }

    public void stop() {
        //Stop the animating thread.
        animatorThread = null;

       //Get rid of the objects necessary for double buffering.
        offGraphics = null;
        offImage = null;
    }

    public void run() {
        //Just to be nice, lower this thread's priority
       //so it can't interfere with other processing going on.
      Thread.currentThread().setPriority(Thread.MIN_PRIORITY);
```

```
        //Remember the starting time.
        long startTime = System.currentTimeMillis();

        //Remember which thread we are.
        Thread currentThread = Thread.currentThread();

        //This is the animation loop.
        while (currentThread == animatorThread) {
            //Advance the animation frame.
            frameNumber++;

            //Display it.
            repaint();

            //Delay depending on how far we are behind.
            try {
                startTime += delay;
                Thread.sleep(Math.max(0,
                        startTime-System.currentTimeMillis()));
            } catch (InterruptedException e) {
                break;
            }
        }
    }

    //Draw the current frame of animation.
    public void paint(Graphics g) {
        update(g);
    }

    public void update(Graphics g) {
        Dimension d = getSize();

        //Create the offscreen graphics context,
        //if no good one exists.
        if ( (offGraphics == null)
          || (d.width != offDimension.width)
          || (d.height != offDimension.height) ) {
            offDimension = d;
            offImage = createImage(d.width, d.height);
            offGraphics = offImage.getGraphics();
        }

        //Erase the previous image.
        offGraphics.setColor(getBackground());
        offGraphics.fillRect(0, 0, d.width, d.height);
        offGraphics.setColor(Color.black);
```

```
            //Paint the frame into the image.
            paintFrame(offGraphics);

            //Paint the image onto the screen.
            g.drawImage(offImage, 0, 0, this);
        }

        void paintFrame(Graphics g) {
            Dimension d = getSize();
            int w;
            int h;

            //If we have a valid width and height for the
            //background image, draw it.
            w = stars.getWidth(this);
            h = stars.getHeight(this);
            if ((w > 0) && (h > 0)) {
                g.drawImage(stars,
                            (d.width - w)/2,
                            (d.height - h)/2, this);
            }

            //If we have a valid width and height for the
            //foreground image, draw it.
            w = rocket.getWidth(this);
            h = rocket.getHeight(this);
            if ((w > 0) && (h > 0)) {
                g.drawImage(rocket,
                            ((frameNumber*5) % (w + d.width)) - w,
                            (d.height - h)/2, this);
            }
        }
    }
```

EXAMPLE: Performing Classic Animation

HTML PAGES CONTAINING APPLET: *http://java.sun.com/docs/books/tutorial/ui/drawing/imageSequence.html*

ImageSequence.java

SOURCE CODE: *http://java.sun.com/docs/books/tutorial/ui/drawing/example-1dot1/ImageSequence.java*

1.0 SOURCE CODE: *http://java.sun.com/docs/books/tutorial/ui/drawing/example/ImageSequence.java*

Where Explained:
Displaying a Sequence of Images (page 567)

```
import java.awt.*;
import java.awt.event.*;
import java.applet.Applet;

/*
 * This applet displays several images in a row.  It prevents
 * flashing by double buffering.  However, it doesn't wait
 * for the images to fully load before drawing them, which
 * causes the weird effect of the animation appearing from
 * the top down.
 */

public class ImageSequence extends Applet
                          implements Runnable {
    int frameNumber = -1;
    int delay;
    Thread animatorThread;
    boolean frozen = false;

    Image images[];

    Dimension offDimension;
    Image offImage;
    Graphics offGraphics;

    public void init() {
        String str;
        int fps = 10;

        //How many milliseconds between frames?
        str = getParameter("fps");
        try {
            if (str != null) {
                fps = Integer.parseInt(str);
            }
        } catch (Exception e) {}
        delay = (fps > 0) ? (1000 / fps) : 100;

        //Get the images.
        images = new Image[10];
        for (int i = 1; i <= 10; i++) {
            images[i-1] = getImage(getCodeBase(),
                                   "T"+i+".gif");
        }

        addMouseListener(new MouseAdapter() {
            public void mousePressed(MouseEvent e) {
                if (frozen) {
```

```
                frozen = false;
                start();
            } else {
                frozen = true;

            //Instead of calling stop(), which destroys the
              //backbuffer, just stop the animating thread.
                animatorThread = null;
            }
        }
    });
}

public void start() {
    if (frozen) {
        //Do nothing.  The user has requested that we
        //stop changing the image.
    } else {
        //Start animating!
        if (animatorThread == null) {
            animatorThread = new Thread(this);
        }
        animatorThread.start();
    }
}

public void stop() {
    //Stop the animating thread.
    animatorThread = null;

   //Get rid of the objects necessary for double buffering.
    offGraphics = null;
    offImage = null;
}

public void run() {
    //Just to be nice, lower this thread's priority
   //so it can't interfere with other processing going on.
  Thread.currentThread().setPriority(Thread.MIN_PRIORITY);

    //Remember the starting time.
    long startTime = System.currentTimeMillis();

    //Remember which thread we are.
    Thread currentThread = Thread.currentThread();

    //This is the animation loop.
    while (currentThread == animatorThread) {
```

```
            //Advance the animation frame.
            frameNumber++;

            //Display it.
            repaint();

            //Delay depending on how far we are behind.
            try {
                startTime += delay;
                Thread.sleep(Math.max(0,
                        startTime-System.currentTimeMillis()));
            } catch (InterruptedException e) {
                break;
            }
        }
    }

    //Draw the current frame of animation.
    public void paint(Graphics g) {
        update(g);
    }

    public void update(Graphics g) {
        Dimension d = getSize();

        //Create the offscreen graphics context,
        //if no good one exists.
        if ( (offGraphics == null)
          || (d.width != offDimension.width)
          || (d.height != offDimension.height) ) {
            offDimension = d;
            offImage = createImage(d.width, d.height);
            offGraphics = offImage.getGraphics();
        }

        //Erase the previous image.
        offGraphics.setColor(getBackground());
        offGraphics.fillRect(0, 0, d.width, d.height);
        offGraphics.setColor(Color.black);

        //Paint the frame into the image.
        try {
            offGraphics.drawImage(images[frameNumber%10],
                                  0, 0, this);
        } catch(ArrayIndexOutOfBoundsException e) {
            //On rare occasions, this method can be called
            //when frameNumber is still -1.  Do nothing.
            return;
```

```
        }

        //Paint the image onto the screen.
        g.drawImage(offImage, 0, 0, this);
    }
}
```

EXAMPLE: Using MediaTracker to Improve Image Animation

HTML PAGES CONTAINING APPLET: *http://java.sun.com/docs/books/tutorial/ui/drawing/improvingImageAnim.html*

Where Explained:
Improving the Appearance and Performance of Image Animation (page 568)

MTImageSequence.java

SOURCE CODE: *http://java.sun.com/docs/books/tutorial/ui/drawing/example-1dot1/MTImageSequence.java*

1.0 SOURCE CODE: *http://java.sun.com/docs/books/tutorial/ui/drawing/example/MTImageSequence.java*

```
import java.awt.*;
import java.awt.event.*;
import java.applet.Applet;

/*
 * This applet displays several images in a row.  It prevents
 * flashing by double buffering.  It preloads the images using
 * MediaTracker, which uses multiple background threads to
 * download the images.  The program displays a "Please wait"
 * message until all the images are fully loaded.
 */

public class MTImageSequence extends Applet
                            implements Runnable {
    int frameNumber = -1;
    int delay;
    Thread animatorThread;
    boolean frozen = false;

    Image images[];
    MediaTracker tracker;

    Dimension offDimension;
    Image offImage;
    Graphics offGraphics;

    public void init() {
        String str;
        int fps = 10;
```

```
        //How many milliseconds between frames?
        str = getParameter("fps");
        try {
            if (str != null) {
                fps = Integer.parseInt(str);
            }
        } catch (Exception e) {}
        delay = (fps > 0) ? (1000 / fps) : 100;

        //Load the images.
        images = new Image[10];
        tracker = new MediaTracker(this);
        for (int i = 1; i <= 10; i++) {
            images[i-1] = getImage(getCodeBase(),
                                   "T"+i+".gif");
            tracker.addImage(images[i-1], 0);
        }

        addMouseListener(new MouseAdapter() {
            public void mousePressed(MouseEvent e) {
                if (frozen) {
                    frozen = false;
                    start();
                } else {
                    frozen = true;

                    //Instead of calling stop(), which destroys the
                    //backbuffer, just stop the animating thread.
                    animatorThread = null;
                }
            }
        });
    }

    public void start() {
        if (frozen) {
            //Do nothing.  The user has requested that we
            //stop changing the image.
        } else {
            //Start animating!
            if (animatorThread == null) {
                animatorThread = new Thread(this);
            }
            animatorThread.start();
        }
    }

    public void stop() {
```

```
        //Stop the animating thread.
        animatorThread = null;

       //Get rid of the objects necessary for double buffering.
        offGraphics = null;
        offImage = null;
    }

    public void run() {
        //Start downloading the images. Wait until they're
        //loaded before requesting repaints.
        try {
            tracker.waitForAll();
        } catch (InterruptedException e) {}

        //Just to be nice, lower this thread's priority
       //so it can't interfere with other processing going on.
      Thread.currentThread().setPriority(Thread.MIN_PRIORITY);

        //Remember the starting time.
        long startTime = System.currentTimeMillis();

        //Remember which thread we are.
        Thread currentThread = Thread.currentThread();

        //This is the animation loop.
        while (currentThread == animatorThread) {
            //Advance the animation frame.
            frameNumber++;

            //Display it.
            repaint();

            //Delay depending on how far we are behind.
            try {
                startTime += delay;
                Thread.sleep(Math.max(0,
                        startTime-System.currentTimeMillis()));
            } catch (InterruptedException e) {
                break;
            }
        }
    }

    //Draw the current frame of animation.
    public void paint(Graphics g) {
        update(g);
    }
```

```
    public void update(Graphics g) {
        Dimension d = getSize();

        //If not all the images are loaded,
        //just clear the background
        //and display a status string.
        if (!tracker.checkAll()) {
            g.clearRect(0, 0, d.width, d.height);
            g.drawString("Please wait...", 0, d.height/2);
            return;
        }

        //Create the offscreen graphics context,
        //if no good one exists.
        if ( (offGraphics == null)
          || (d.width != offDimension.width)
          || (d.height != offDimension.height) ) {
            offDimension = d;
            offImage = createImage(d.width, d.height);
            offGraphics = offImage.getGraphics();
        }

        //Erase the previous image.
        offGraphics.setColor(getBackground());
        offGraphics.fillRect(0, 0, d.width, d.height);
        offGraphics.setColor(Color.black);

        //Paint the frame into the image.
        offGraphics.drawImage(images[frameNumber%10],
                              0, 0, this);

        //Paint the image onto the screen.
        g.drawImage(offImage, 0, 0, this);
    }
}
```

Custom Networking

LESSON 23: Working with URLs

EXAMPLE: Parsing a URL

ParseURL.java

Where Explained: *Parsing a URL* (page 596)

SOURCE CODE: *http://java.sun.com/docs/books/tutorial/networking/urls/example/ParseURL.java*

```
import java.net.*;
import java.io.*;

public class ParseURL {
    public static void main(String[] args) throws Exception {
        URL aURL = new URL("http://java.sun.com:80/docs/" +
                           "books/tutorial/intro.html#" +
                           "DOWNLOADING");
        System.out.println("protocol = " + aURL.getProtocol());
        System.out.println("host = " + aURL.getHost());
        System.out.println("filename = " + aURL.getFile());
        System.out.println("port = " + aURL.getPort());
        System.out.println("ref = " + aURL.getRef());
    }
}
```

EXAMPLE: Reading from a URL

URLReader.java

Where Explained: *Reading Directly from a URL* (page 597)

SOURCE CODE: *http://java.sun.com/docs/books/tutorial/networking/urls/example-1dot1/URLReader.java*

1.0 SOURCE CODE: *http://java.sun.com/docs/books/tutorial/networking/urls/example/URLReader.java*

```
import java.net.*;
import java.io.*;

public class URLReader {
    public static void main(String[] args) throws Exception {
        URL yahoo = new URL("http://www.yahoo.com/");
        BufferedReader in = new BufferedReader(
                                new InputStreamReader(
                                yahoo.openStream()));
        String inputLine;

        while ((inputLine = in.readLine()) != null)
```

```
                System.out.println(inputLine);
        in.close();
    }
}
```

EXAMPLE: Reading from a URLConnection

URLConnectionReader.java

SOURCE CODE: *http://java.sun.com/docs/books/tutorial/networking/urls/example-1dot1/URLConnectionReader.java*

1.0 SOURCE CODE: *http://java.sun.com/docs/books/tutorial/networking/urls/example/URLConnectionReader.java*

Where Explained:
Reading from and Writing to a URLConnection Object (page 599)

```
import java.net.*;
import java.io.*;

public class URLConnectionReader {
    public static void main(String[] args) throws Exception {
        URL yahoo = new URL("http://www.yahoo.com/");
        URLConnection yahooConnection = yahoo.openConnection();
        BufferedReader in = new BufferedReader(
                                new InputStreamReader(
                                yahooConnection.getInputStream()));
        String inputLine;

        while ((inputLine = in.readLine()) != null)
            System.out.println(inputLine);
        in.close();
    }
}
```

EXAMPLE: Reading from and Writing to a URLConnection

Reverse.java

SOURCE CODE: *http://java.sun.com/docs/books/tutorial/networking/urls/example-1dot1/Reverse.java*

1.0 SOURCE CODE: *http://java.sun.com/docs/books/tutorial/networking/urls/example/Reverse.java*

Where Explained:
Reading from and Writing to a URLConnection Object (page 599)

```
import java.io.*;
import java.net.*;

public class Reverse {
    public static void main(String[] args) throws Exception {
        if (args.length != 1) {
            System.err.println("Usage: java Reverse " +
```

```
                                    "string_to_reverse");
            System.exit(-1);
        }
        String stringToReverse = URLEncoder.encode(args[0]);

        URL url = new URL("http://java.sun.com/" +
                          "cgi-bin/backwards");
        URLConnection connection = url.openConnection();
        connection.setDoOutput(true);

        PrintWriter out = new PrintWriter(
                              connection.getOutputStream());
        out.println("string=" + stringToReverse);
        out.close();

        BufferedReader in = new BufferedReader(
                                new InputStreamReader(
                                connection.getInputStream()));
        String inputLine;

        while ((inputLine = in.readLine()) != null)
            System.out.println(inputLine);
        in.close();
    }
}
```

backwards

SOURCE CODE: *http://java.sun.com/docs/books/tutorial/networking/urls/example-1dot1/backwards*

1.0 SOURCE CODE: *http://java.sun.com/docs/books/tutorial/networking/urls/example/backwards*

```
#!/opt/internet/bin/perl
read(STDIN, , {'CONTENT_LENGTH'});
@pairs = split(/&/, );
foreach  (@pairs)
{
    (, ) = split(/=/, );
     =~ tr/+/ /;
     =~ s/%([a-fA-F0-9][a-fA-F0-9])/pack("C", hex())/eg;
    # Stop people from using subshells to execute commands
     =~ s/~!/ ~!/g;
    {} = ;
}

print "Content-type: text/plain\n\n";
```

```
print "{'string'} reversed is: ";
=reverse({'string'});
print "\n";
exit 0;
```

LESSON 24: All About Sockets

EXAMPLE: The Echo Server Client

EchoClient.java

SOURCE CODE: *http://java.sun.com/docs/books/tutorial/networking/sockets/example-1dot1/EchoClient.java*

1.0 SOURCE CODE: *http://java.sun.com/docs/books/tutorial/networking/sockets/example/EchoClient.java*

Where Explained:
Reading from and Writing to a Socket (page 607)

```
import java.io.*;
import java.net.*;

public class EchoClient {
    public static void main(String[] args) throws IOException {
        Socket echoSocket = null;
        BufferedWriter out = null;
        BufferedReader in = null;

        try {
            echoSocket = new Socket("taranis", 7);
            out = new PrintWriter(
                     echoSocket.getOutputStream(), true);
            in = new BufferedReader(
                    new InputStreamReader(
                    echoSocket.getInputStream()));
        } catch (UnknownHostException e) {
            System.err.println("Don't know about host: taranis.");
            System.exit(-1);
        } catch (IOException e) {
            System.err.println("Couldn't get I/O for the " +
                               "connection to: taranis.");
            System.exit(-1);
        }

        BufferedReader stdIn = new BufferedReader(
                                   new InputStreamReader(
                                   System.in ));
        String userInput;
```

```
            while ((userInput = stdIn.readLine()) != null) {
                out.println(userInput);
                System.out.println("echo: " + in.readLine());
            }
            out.close();
            in.close();
            stdIn.close();
            echoSocket.close();
        }
    }
```

EXAMPLE: The Knock Knock Joke Client and Server

Where Explained: *Writing a Client/Server Pair* (page 610)

KnockKnockServer.java

SOURCE CODE: *http://java.sun.com/docs/books/tutorial/networking/sockets/example-1dot1/KnockKnockServer.java*

1.0 SOURCE CODE: *http://java.sun.com/docs/books/tutorial/networking/sockets/example/KnockKnockServer.java*

```
import java.net.*;
import java.io.*;

public class KnockKnockServer {
    public static void main(String[] args) throws IOException {

        ServerSocket serverSocket = null;
        try {
            serverSocket = new ServerSocket(4444);
        } catch (IOException e) {
          System.out.println("Could not listen on port: 4444.");
            System.exit(-1);
        }

        Socket clientSocket = null;
        try {
            clientSocket = serverSocket.accept();
        } catch (IOException e) {
            System.out.println("Accept failed.");
            System.exit(-1);
        }

        PrintWriter out = new PrintWriter(
                         clientSocket.getOutputStream(), true);
        BufferedReader in = new BufferedReader(
                                new InputStreamReader(
                                clientSocket.getInputStream()));
        String inputLine, outputLine;
```

```
        // initiate conversation with client
        KnockKnockProtocol kkp = new KnockKnockProtocol();
        outputLine = kkp.processInput(null);
        out.println(outputLine);

        while ((inputLine = in.readLine()) != null) {
            outputLine = kkp.processInput(inputLine);
            out.println(outputLine);
            if (outputLine.equals("Bye."))
                break;
        }
        out.close();
        in.close();
        clientSocket.close();
        serverSocket.close();
    }
}
```

KnockKnockProtocol.java

SOURCE CODE: *http://java.sun.com/docs/books/tutorial/networking/sockets/example-1dot1/KnockKnockProtocol.java*

1.0 SOURCE CODE: *http://java.sun.com/docs/books/tutorial/networking/sockets/example/KnockKnockProtocol.java*

```
import java.net.*;
import java.io.*;

public class KnockKnockProtocol {
    private static final int WAITING = 0;
    private static final int SENTKNOCKKNOCK = 1;
    private static final int SENTCLUE = 2;
    private static final int ANOTHER = 3;

    private static final int NUMJOKES = 5;

    private int state = WAITING;
    private int currentJoke = 0;

    private String[] clues = { "Turnip", "Little Old Lady",
                               "Atch", "Who", "Who" };
    private String[] answers = { "Turnip the heat, " +
                                   "it's cold in here!",
                              "I didn't know you could yodel!",
                                   "Bless you!",
                                   "Is there an owl in here?",
                                   "Is there an echo in here?" };
```

```
    public String processInput(String theInput) {
        String theOutput = null;

        if (state == WAITING) {
            theOutput = "Knock! Knock!";
            state = SENTKNOCKKNOCK;
        } else if (state == SENTKNOCKKNOCK) {
            if (theInput.equalsIgnoreCase("Who's there?")) {
                theOutput = clues[currentJoke];
                state = SENTCLUE;
            } else {
                theOutput = "You're supposed to say \"Who's "
                            + "there?\"! Try again. "
                            + "Knock! Knock!";
            }
        } else if (state == SENTCLUE) {
            if (theInput.equalsIgnoreCase(clues[currentJoke]
                                          + " who?")) {
                theOutput = answers[currentJoke] +
                            " Want another? (y/n)";
                state = ANOTHER;
            } else {
                theOutput = "You're supposed to say \""
                            + clues[currentJoke] + " who?\""
                            + "! Try again. Knock! Knock!";
                state = SENTKNOCKKNOCK;
            }
        } else if (state == ANOTHER) {
            if (theInput.equalsIgnoreCase("y")) {
                theOutput = "Knock! Knock!";
                if (currentJoke == (NUMJOKES - 1))
                    currentJoke = 0;
                else
                    currentJoke++;
                state = SENTKNOCKKNOCK;
            } else {
                theOutput = "Bye.";
                state = WAITING;
            }
        }
        return theOutput;
    }
}
```

KnockKnockClient.java

SOURCE CODE: *http://java.sun.com/docs/books/tutorial/networking/sockets/example-1dot1/KnockKnockClient.java*

1.0 SOURCE CODE: *http://java.sun.com/docs/books/tutorial/networking/sockets/example/KnockKnockClient.java*

```
import java.io.*;
import java.net.*;

public class KnockKnockClient {
    public static void main(String[] args) throws IOException {
        Socket kkSocket = null;
        PrintWriter out = null;
        BufferedReader in = null;

        try {
            kkSocket = new Socket("taranis", 4444);
            out = new PrintWriter(
                      kkSocket.getOutputStream(), true);
            in = new BufferedReader(
                      new InputStreamReader(
                      kkSocket.getInputStream()));
        } catch (UnknownHostException e) {
         System.err.println("Don't know about host: taranis.");
        } catch (IOException e) {
            System.err.println("Couldn't get I/O for the " +
                               "connection to: taranis.");
        }

        BufferedReader stdIn = new BufferedReader(
                           new InputStreamReader(System.in));
        String fromServer;
        String fromUser;

        while ((fromServer = in.readLine()) != null) {
            System.out.println("Server: " + fromServer);
            if (fromServer.equals("Bye."))
                break;
            fromUser = stdIn.readLine();
            if (fromUser != null) {
                System.out.println("Client: " + fromUser);
                out.println(fromUser);
            }
        }
        out.close();
        in.close();
```

```
            stdIn.close();
            kkSocket.close();
        }
    }
```

EXAMPLE: The Knock Knock Joke Multiclient Server

KKMultiServer.java

Where Explained: *Supporting Multiple Clients* (page 617)

SOURCE CODE: *http://java.sun.com/docs/books/tutorial/networking/sockets/example-1dot1/KKMultiServer.java*

1.0 SOURCE CODE: *http://java.sun.com/docs/books/tutorial/networking/sockets/example/KKMultiServer.java*

```
import java.net.*;
import java.io.*;

public class KKMultiServer {
    public static void main(String[] args) throws IOException {
        ServerSocket serverSocket = null;
        boolean listening = true;

        try {
            serverSocket = new ServerSocket(4444);
        } catch (IOException e) {
          System.err.println("Could not listen on port: 4444");
            System.exit(-1);
        }

        while (listening)
            new KKMultiServerThread(
                serverSocket.accept()).start();

        serverSocket.close();
    }
}
```

KKMultiServerThread.java

SOURCE CODE: *http://java.sun.com/docs/books/tutorial/networking/sockets/example-1dot1/KKMultiServerThread.java*

1.0 SOURCE CODE: *http://java.sun.com/docs/books/tutorial/networking/sockets/example/KKMultiServerThread.java*

```
import java.net.*;
import java.io.*;

public class KKMultiServerThread extends Thread {
```

```
    private Socket socket = null;

    public KKMultiServerThread(Socket socket) {
        super("KKMultiServerThread");
        this.socket = socket;
    }

    public void run() {
        try {
            BufferedReader in = new BufferedReader(
                                    new InputStreamReader(
                                    socket.getInputStream()));
            PrintWriter out = new PrintWriter(
                                socket.getOutputStream(), true);

            String inputLine, outputLine;
            KnockKnockProtocol kkp = new KnockKnockProtocol();
            outputLine = kkp.processInput(null);
            out.println(outputLine);

            while ((inputLine = in.readLine()) != null) {
                outputLine = kkp.processInput(inputLine);
                out.println(outputLine);
                if (outputLine.equals("Bye"))
                   break;
            }
            out.close();
            in.close();
            socket.close();
        } catch (IOException e) {
            e.printStackTrace();
        }
    }
}
```

LESSON 25: All About Datagrams

Where Explained:

Writing a Datagram Client and Server (page 620)

EXAMPLE: The Quote-of-the-Moment Client and Server

For the applet version of this example, see QuoteClientApplet.java (page 728).

QuoteServer.java

SOURCE CODE: *http://java.sun.com/docs/books/tutorial/networking/datagrams/example-1dot1/QuoteServer.java*

1.0 SOURCE CODE: *http://java.sun.com/docs/books/tutorial/networking/datagrams/example/QuoteServer.java*

```
import java.io.*;
public class QuoteServer {
    public static void main(String[] args) throws IOException{
        new QuoteServerThread().start();
    }
}
```

QuoteServerThread.java

SOURCE CODE: *http://java.sun.com/docs/books/tutorial/networking/datagrams/example-1dot1/QuoteServerThread.java*

1.0 SOURCE CODE: *http://java.sun.com/docs/books/tutorial/networking/datagrams/example/QuoteServerThread.java*

```
import java.io.*;
import java.net.*;
import java.util.*;

public class QuoteServerThread extends Thread {
    protected DatagramSocket socket = null;
    protected BufferedReader in = null;
    protected boolean moreQuotes = true;

    public QuoteServerThread() throws IOException {
        this("QuoteServerThread");
    }

    public QuoteServerThread(String name) throws IOException {
        super(name);
        socket = new DatagramSocket(4445);
        try {
            in = new BufferedReader(
                    new FileReader("one-liners.txt") );
        } catch (java.net.SocketException e) {
            System.err.println("Could not open input file." +
                               "Serving time instead.");
        }
    }

    public void run() {
        while (moreQuotes) {
            try {
                byte[] buf = new byte[256];

                // receive request
                DatagramPacket packet = new DatagramPacket(buf,
                                                  buf.length);
                socket.receive(packet);
```

```
                // figure out response
                String dString = null;
                if (qfs == null)
                   dString = new Date().toString();
                else
                   dString = getNextQuote();
                buf = dString.getBytes();

                // send the response to the client
                InetAddress address = packet.getAddress();
                int port = packet.getPort();
                packet = new DatagramPacket(buf, buf.length,
                                            address, port);
                socket.send(packet);
            } catch (IOException e) {
                e.printStackTrace();
                moreQuotes = false;
            }
        }
        socket.close();
    }
    protected String getNextQuote() {
        String returnValue = null;
        try {
            if ((returnValue = in.readLine()) == null) {
                in.close();
                moreQuotes = false;
                returnValue = "No more quotes. Goodbye.";
            }
        } catch (IOException e) {
            returnValue = "IOException occurred in server.";
        }
        return returnValue;
    }
}
```

QuoteClient.java

SOURCE CODE: *http://java.sun.com/docs/books/tutorial/networking/datagrams/example-1dot1/QuoteClient.java*

1.0 SOURCE CODE: *http://java.sun.com/docs/books/tutorial/networking/datagrams/example/QuoteClient.java*

```
import java.io.*;
import java.net.*;
import java.util.*;

public class QuoteClient {
```

```
        public static void main(String[] args) throws IOException {

            if (args.length != 1) {
                 System.out.println("Usage: java QuoteClient " +
                                         "<hostname>");
                 return;
            }
            // get a socket
            DatagramSocket socket = new DatagramSocket();

            // send request
            byte[] buf = new byte[256];
            InetAddress address = InetAddress.getByName(args[0]);
            DatagramPacket packet = new DatagramPacket(buf,
                                     buf.length, address, 4445);
            socket.send(packet);

            // get response
            packet = new DatagramPacket(buf, buf.length);
            socket.receive(packet);

            // display response
            String received = new String(packet.getData());
            System.out.println("Quote of the Moment: " +
                                 received);

            socket.close();
        }
    }
```

one-liners.txt

SOURCE CODE: *http://java.sun.com/docs/books/tutorial/networking/datagrams/example-1dot1/one-liners.txt*

1.0 SOURCE CODE: *http://java.sun.com/docs/books/tutorial/networking/datagrams/example/one-liners.txt*

```
Life is wonderful. Without it we'd all be dead.
Daddy, why doesn't this magnet pick up this floppy disk?
Give me ambiguity or give me something else.
I.R.S.: We've got what it takes to take what you've got!
We are born naked, wet and hungry. Then things get worse.
Make it idiot proof and someone will make a better idiot.
He who laughs last thinks slowest!
Always remember you're unique, just like everyone else.
"More hay, Trigger?" "No thanks, Roy, I'm stuffed!"
A flashlight is a case for holding dead batteries.
Lottery: A tax on people who are bad at math.
```

```
Error, no keyboard - press F1 to continue.
There's too much blood in my caffeine system.
Artificial Intelligence usually beats real stupidity.
Hard work has a future payoff. Laziness pays off now.
"Very funny, Scotty. Now beam down my clothes."
Puritanism: The haunting fear that someone, somewhere may be
happy.
Consciousness: that annoying time between naps.
Don't take life too seriously, you won't get out alive.
I don't suffer from insanity. I enjoy every minute of it.
Better to understand a little than to misunderstand a lot.
The gene pool could use a little chlorine.
When there's a will, I want to be in it.
Okay, who put a "stop payment" on my reality check?
We have enough youth, how about a fountain of SMART?
Programming is an art form that fights back.
"Daddy, what does FORMATTING DRIVE C mean?"
All wiyht. Rho sritched mg kegtops awound?
My mail reader can beat up your mail reader.
Never forget: 2 + 2 = 5 for extremely large values of 2.
Nobody has ever, ever, EVER learned all of WordPerfect.
To define recursion, we must first define recursion.
Good programming is 99% sweat and 1% coffee.
```

EXAMPLE: The Multicasting Version of the Quote-of-the-Moment Example

MulticastServer.java

Where Explained: *Broadcasting to Multiple Recipients* (page 625)

SOURCE CODE: *http://java.sun.com/docs/books/tutorial/networking/datagrams/example-1dot1/MulticastServer.java*

1.0 SOURCE CODE: *http://java.sun.com/docs/books/tutorial/networking/datagrams/example/MulticastServer.java*

```
import java.io.*;
public class MulticastServer {
    public static void main(String[] args) throws IOException {
        new MulticastServerThread().start();
    }
}
```

MulticastServerThread.java

1.0 SOURCE CODE: *http://java.sun.com/docs/books/tutorial/networking/datagrams/example/MulticastServerThread.java*

```
import java.io.*;
import java.net.*;
import java.util.*;

public class MulticastServerThread extends QuoteServerThread {
    private long FIVE_SECONDS = 5000;
    public MulticastServerThread() throws IOException {
        super("MulticastServerThread");
    }

    pubic void run() {
        while (moreQuotes) {
            try {
                byte[] buf new byte[256];

                String dString = null;
                if (in == null)
                    dString = new Date().toString();
                else
                    dString = getNextQuote();
                buf = dString.getBytes();

                InetAddress group = InetAddress.getByName(
                                            "230.0.0.1");
                DatagramPacket packet;
                packet = new DatagramPacket(buf, buf.length,
                                            group, 4446);
                socket.send(packet);

                try {
                    sleep((long)Math.random() * FIVE_SECONDS);
                } catch (InterruptedException e) { }
            } catch (IOException e) {
                e.printStackTrace();
                moreQuotes = false;
            }
        }
        socket.close();
    }
}
```

MulticastClient.java

SOURCE CODE: *http://java.sun.com/docs/books/tutorial/networking/datagrams/example-1dot1/MulticastClient.java*

1.0 SOURCE CODE: *http://java.sun.com/docs/books/tutorial/networking/datagrams/example/MulticastClient.java*

```
import java.io.*;
import java.net.*;
import java.util.*;

public class MulticastClient {

    public static void main(String[] args) throws IOException {

        MulticastSocket socket = new MulticastSocket(4446);
        InetAddress group = InetAddress.getByName("230.0.0.1");
        socket.joinGroup(group);

        DatagramPacket packet;

        for (int i = 0; i < 5; i ++) {
            byte[] buf = new byte[256];
            packet = new DatagramPacket(buf, buf.length);
            socket.receive(packet);

            String received = new String(packet.getData());
            System.out.println("Quote of the Moment: " +
                               received);
        }
        socket.leaveGroup(group);
        socket.close();
    }
}
```

APPENDIX B

Reference

THIS appendix contains the following reference information:

Java Language Keywords

Table 41 lists Java's keywords in alphabetical order. These words are reserved; that is, you cannot use any of them as names in your Java programs. `true`, `false`, and `null` are not keywords but reserved words, so you cannot use them as names in your programs either.

Table 41: Reserved Java Keywords

abstract	double	int	strictfp **
boolean	else	interface	super
break	extends	long	switch
byte	final	native	synchronized
case	finally	new	this
catch	float	package	throw
char	for	private	throws

Table 41: Reserved Java Keywords

`class`	`goto *`	`protected`	`transient`
`const *`	`if`	`public`	`try`
`continue`	`implements`	`return`	`void`
`default`	`import`	`short`	`volatile`
`do`	`instanceof`	`static`	`while`

* indicates a keyword that is not currently used.

** indicates a keyword that was added for the Java 2 Platform.

Operator Precedence in Java

Table 42 lists the Java operators. Operators higher in the table have higher precedence than those lower in the table. Operators on the same line have the same precedence.

Table 42: Operator Precedence

Operator Category	**Operators**
postfix operators	`[]  .  (`*`params`*`)  `*`expr`*`++  `*`expr`*`--`
unary operators	`++`*`expr`*`  --`*`expr`*`  +`*`expr`*`  -`*`expr`*`  ~  !`
creation or cast	`new  (`*`type`*`)`*`expr`*
multiplicative	`*  /  %`
additive	`+  -`
shift	`<<  >>  >>>`
relational	`<  >  <=  >=  instanceof`
equality	`==  !=`
bitwise AND	`&`
bitwise exclusive OR	`^`
bitwise inclusive OR	`|`
logical AND	`&&`
logical OR	`||`
conditional	`?  :`
assignment	`=  +=  -=  *=  /=  %=  ^=  &=  |=  <<=  >>=  >>>=`

When operators of equal precedence appear in the same expression, some rule must govern which is evaluated first. In Java, all binary operators except for the assignment operators are evaluated in left-to-right order. Assignment operators are evaluated right-to-left.

The <APPLET> Tag

This section gives the complete syntax for the <APPLET> tag. A gentler introduction to the <APPLET> tag is in Displaying Documents in the Browser (page 192).

When you build <APPLET> tags, keep in mind that words such as `APPLET` and `CODEBASE` can be entered either as shown or in any mixture of uppercase and lowercase letters. In the following, entries in bold indicate something you should type in exactly as shown, except that letters don't need to be uppercase. Entries in *italic font* indicate that you must substitute a value for the word in italics. Square brackets ([and]) indicate that the contents within the brackets are optional. Parentheses ((and)) indicate that you must choose exactly one of the separated contents.

```
< APPLET
[CODEBASE = codebaseURL]
(CODE = appletFile | OBJECT = serializedApplet)
[ARCHIVE = archivesList]
[ALT = alternateText]
[NAME = appletInstanceName]
WIDTH = pixels HEIGHT = pixels
[ALIGN = alignment]
[VSPACE = pixels] [HSPACE = pixels]
>
[< PARAM NAME = appletParameter1 VALUE = value >]
[< PARAM NAME = appletParameter2 VALUE = value >]
. . .
[alternateHTML]
</APPLET>
```

`CODEBASE = codebaseURL`
This optional attribute specifies the base URL of the applet—the directory or folder that contains the applet's code. If this attribute is not specified, then the document's URL is used.

`CODE = appletFile`
This attribute gives the name of the file that contains the applet's compiled `Applet` subclass. This file is relative to the base URL of the applet. It cannot be absolute. Either `CODE` or `OBJECT` must be present.

OBJECT = serializedApplet

This attribute gives the name of the file that contains a serialized representation of an applet. The applet will be deserialized. The `init` method will *not* be invoked, but its `start` method will. Attributes that are valid when the original object was serialized are *not* restored. Any attributes passed to this `Applet` instance will be available to the applet. We advise you to exercise very strong restraint in using this feature. An applet should be stopped before it is serialized. One of `CODE` or `OBJECT` must be present.

ARCHIVE = archivesList

This optional attribute describes one or more archives containing classes and other resources that will be preloaded. The classes are loaded using an instance of an `AppletClassLoader` with the given `CODEBASE`.

ALT = alternateText

This optional attribute specifies any text that should be displayed if the browser understands the `<APPLET>` tag, but it can't run Java applets.

NAME = appletInstanceName

This optional attribute specifies a name for the `Applet` instance. Naming applets makes it possible for applets on the same page to find and communicate with each other.

WIDTH = pixels HEIGHT = pixels

These required attributes give the initial width and height in pixels of the applet display area, not counting any windows or dialogs that the applet brings up.

ALIGN = alignment

This required attribute specifies the alignment of the applet. Its possible values are the same (and have the same effects) as those for the `<IMG>` tag and are the following: `LEFT`, `RIGHT`, `TOP`, `TEXTTOP`, `MIDDLE`, `ABSMIDDLE`, `BASELINE`, `BOTTOM`, and `ABSBOTTOM`.

VSPACE = pixels HSPACE = pixels

These optional attributes specify the number of pixels above and below the applet (`VSPACE`) and on each side of the applet (`HSPACE`). They're treated in the same way as the `<IMG>` tag's `VSPACE` and `HSPACE` attributes.

< PARAM NAME = appletParameter1 VALUE = value >

Use of a `<PARAM>` tag is the only way to specify an applet-specific parameter. Applets read user-specified values for parameters by using the `getParameter` method. See Defining and Using Applet Parameters (page 200) for information about `getParameter`.

alternateHTML

If the HTML page containing this `<APPLET>` tag is viewed by a browser that doesn't understand the `<APPLET>` tag, then the browser will ignore the

`<APPLET>` and `<PARAM>` tags. It instead will interpret any other HTML code between the `<APPLET>` and `</APPLET>` tags. Java-compatible browsers ignore this extra HTML code.

In the online version of this tutorial, we use alternate HTML to show a snapshot of the applet running, with text explaining what the applet does. Other possibilities for this area are a link to a page that is more useful for the Java-ignorant browser or text that taunts the user for not having a Java-compatible browser.

POSIX Conventions for Command-Line Arguments

Command-Line Arguments (page 264) warns that the use of command-line arguments in a Java program may cause that program to be unportable (that is, it will not be 100% Pure Java). If a program requires command-line arguments, then it should follow the POSIX conventions for them. The POSIX conventions are summarized here:

- An *option* is a hyphen followed by a single alphanumeric character, like this: `-o`.
- An option may require an argument (which must appear immediately after the option); for example, `-o` *`argument`* or `-o`*`argument`*.
- Options that do not require arguments can be grouped after a hyphen, so, for example, `-lst` is equivalent to `-t -l -s`.
- Options can appear in any order; thus `-lst` is equivalent to `-tls`.
- Options can appear multiple times.
- Options precede other nonoption arguments: `-lst nonoption`.
- The `--` argument terminates options.
- The `-` option is typically used to represent one of the standard input streams.

JDK 1.1 Compatibility

In this section, you will find out how 1.1 is compatible with previous releases and the general compatibility policy governing the JDK's binary and source code, both upward and downward.

Binary Compatibility

JDK 1.1.x is upwards binary-compatible with 1.0.x except for the incompatibilities listed below. This means that class files built with a 1.0.x compiler (such as 1.0.2) will run correctly in 1.1.x.

Downward binary compatibility is generally supported, though not guaranteed. That is, class files built with a 1.1.x compiler, but relying only on APIs defined in 1.0.x, will generally run on 1.0.x versions of the Java Virtual Machine, but this "downwards" compatibility has not been extensively tested and cannot be guaranteed. Of course, if the class files depend on any new 1.1.x APIs, those files will not work on 1.0.x systems.

In general:

- Bug-fix releases (e.g. 1.1.1, 1.1.2) within a family (1.1.x) will maintain both upward and downward binary-compatibility with each other.
- Functionality releases (e.g. 1.1, 1.2) within a family (1.x) will maintain upward but not necessarily downward binary-compatibility with each other.
- Major releases (e.g. 2.0, 3.0) will not necessarily maintain any binary compatibility.

Source Compatibility

JDK 1.1.x is upwards source-compatible with 1.0.x, except for the incompatibilities listed below in Incompatibilities in JDK 1.1.x (page 935). This means that source files written to use the language features and APIs defined for 1.0.x can be compiled in 1.1.x and will run in 1.1.x.

Downward source compatibility is not supported. If source files use new language features or APIs in JDK 1.1.x, they will not be usable with an earlier version of Java.

In general:

- Bug-fix releases do not introduce any new language features or APIs, so they maintain source-compatibility in both directions.
- Functionality releases and major releases maintain upwards but not downwards source-compatibility.

JDK 1.1 introduces the concept of deprecated API. These are methods and classes that are supported **only** for backwards compatibility, and the compiler will generate a warning message whenever one of these is used. It is recommended that programs be modified to eliminate the use of deprecated methods and classes, but it has not been determined whether the deprecated elements will ever be removed entirely from the system. See Lists and Tables (page 664) for the methods and classes that have been deprecated and their appropriate replacements.

Incompatibilities in JDK 1.1.x

There are rare cases where upward incompatibility from 1.0.x to 1.1.x cannot be avoided. For example, occasionally an API has to be eliminated because of some potential security breach that it exposes. This affects both binary and source compatibility.

The following list describes all known cases where a program that works under 1.0.x would fail to work under 1.1.x:

1. Some APIs in the `sun.*` packages have changed. These APIs are not intended to be used directly by developers. They are there to support the `java.*` packages. Developers importing from `sun.*` do so entirely at their own risk.
2. The compiler, `javac`, now writes its error messages to standard error instead of standard output. This would only affect programs that execute the compiler.
3. The following methods have been changed to conform to the *Java Language Specification, section 20.10.15*. Previously these methods returned machine-specific results.

```
in java.io.Printstream
   print(double)
   println(double)

in java.lang.Double
   toString

in java.lang.String
   valueOf(double)
```

4. The following methods have been changed to conform to the *Java Language Specification, section 20.9.16*. Previously these methods returned machine-specific results.

```
in java.io.Printstream
   print(float)
   println(float)

in java.lang.Float
   toString

in java.lang.String
   valueOf(float)
```

5. The standard input, output, and error streams `System.in`, `System.out`, and `System.err` are now `final`. Applets cannot change their values. The following methods have been added to class `System` so that applications, but not applets, can reassign standard in, standard out, and standard err.

```
public static void setIn(InputStream in)
public static void setOut(PrintStream out)
public static void setErr(PrintStream err)
```

6. Several bug fixes in the AWT might result in incompatible behavior in programs that have a graphical user interface (GUI). See Incompatible Changes in the 1.1 AWT API (page 938) for details.
7. The method `checkPropertyAccess(String prop, String defval)` in `java.lang.SecurityManager` has been removed in this release. It is a useless method that was inadvertently included in JDK 1.0.2; it should never have been included.
8. Invalid code (code that relies on 1.0.x implementation bugs that are important to fix) that used to run in 1.0.x might not run in 1.1.x.
   - The 1.1.2 VM contains a security bugfix to the verifier that checks that the maximum number of locals specified for a byte-compiled method is large enough to accommodate the parameters to the method. However, code generated by compilers prior to 1.0prebeta1 would not always set the maximum number of locals correctly. Such erroneous code will be rejected by the 1.1.2 VM with the error `java.lang.ClassFormatError: Arguments can't fit into locals`.
   - The 1.0.2 VM did not check that a class implementing an interface in fact implements all the interface's methods. The 1.1.x VM correctly checks that, and causes certain classes to fail, even though these classes

can be loaded in 1.0.2. This fix is put in so that the VM now gives better error messages.

- In JDK 1.0.2, `Integer.parseInt("80000000", 16)` throws a NumberFormatException. Someone used this to generate a bit mask for IP address verification. In this case, `80000000` is out of the range of integer representation. In 1.1.x, the program should use `Integer.parseInt("-80000000", 16)` instead.

9. The 1.0.x Java compiler used incorrect linkage semantics for invocations of `super` methods. In particular, the 1.0.x compiler produced code for `super` invocations that instructed a Java Virtual Machine to invoke exactly the specified method of the specified class, as determined by the compiler's understanding of the class hierarchy at compile time.

   Unfortunately, this meaning of `super` invocation does not account for binary-compatible changes to classes, such as inserting new classes into the type hierarchy, or overriding the specified method in a class between the source class and target class of the `super` invocation. (This bug is described in *The Java Language Specification, section 13.4.5.*)

   Some Java APIs in JDK 1.1 contain exactly such binary-compatible changes. As a result, 1.0.x code compiled with the incorrect `super` semantics can behave unpredictably on 1.1 Java Virtual Machine, if they use these APIs via `super` invocation. This is because the new overriding methods may be necessary for correct operation of the updated class (for example, taking a lock before invoking the next method).

   The 1.1 (non-optimizing) Java compiler uses the correct semantics for `super` invocations. It records the fact that it uses the correct semantics by setting a flag in a generated class file; older compilers do not set this flag. A 1.0.2 or later Java Virtual Machine uses the correct `super` semantics for code in a class file when it finds this flag set. In all other cases, an old or new Virtual Machine will use the old, incorrect semantics for `super` invocation. (The possibility that some intermediate `super` methods were inlined means that a Java Virtual Machine cannot attempt to "correct" the semantics of `super` invocation in unflagged binaries at run time.)

10. Class name resolution changed in JDK 1.1 such that classes within packages of the same name can no longer be referenced if their names aren't fully qualified in a way that make them unique.

Incompatible Changes in the 1.1 AWT API

As a rule, 1.0 AWT code can be compiled without change in the 1.1 release (although you might see some warnings about "deprecated" API). Also, code compiled under a 1.0 release generally works (without recompilation) at least as well in a 1.1 runtime system as it did before. This document lists the AWT exceptions to these rules—the changes that might cause incompatible compilation or runtime behavior.

Here are the incompatible AWT changes:

1. On Windows 95/NT systems, menus no longer allow keyboard alternatives, known as mnemonics. Due to an implementation flaw, you used to be able to specify mnemonics in Windows 95/NT by putting an ampersand ("&") in the menu label. For example, a menu item with the label "Save &As..." defined "a" as the mnemonic and would result in "A" being underlined in the displayed menu item—but only on Windows 95/NT. Now, menus with "&" in the label simply display the "&" on Windows 95/NT, as they always have on other platforms. The reason the "&" hack no longer works is that it depended on the AWT using the native menu system, which it no longer does due to the need to support modifiable fonts and the display of non-Latin1 text. Support for menu mnemonics is planned for a future release.

   Note that 1.1 adds support for a similar feature, shortcuts, with the `MenuShortcut` class. See How to Use Menus (page 448) for more information on shortcuts.

2. On Windows 95/NT systems, canvases and panels might seem unable to get keyboard events. The reason is that they no longer automatically get the focus, which is required for receiving keyboard events. To give a canvas or panel the focus, use the `requestFocus` method. For example, your implementation of the `mouseClicked` method in the `MouseListener` for a custom component should invoke the `requestFocus` method on the component.

3. The following 1.0 methods in the `java.awt.peer` package have been removed in 1.1:

   - `java.awt.peer.ComponentPeer:`
     ```
     public abstract boolean handleEvent(java.awt.Event);
     public abstract void nextFocus();
     ```
   - `java.awt.peer.ScrollbarPeer:`
     ```
     public abstract void setValue(int);
     ```
   - `java.awt.peer.FramePeer:`
     ```
     public abstract void setCursor(int);
     ```

> **Note**: API in the `java.awt.peer` package is always subject to change because the peer classes aren't intended to be called directly by developers.

4. Attempting to add a window to a container now results in an `IllegalArgumentException`.
5. The `Graphics` `drawPolygon` method used to draw unclosed polygons if the end point wasn't the same as the start point. In 1.1, `drawPolygon` automatically closes the polygon. If you want to draw an unclosed polygon, you can use the new `drawPolyline` method instead.
6. Constructors for the `Color` class now check the range of the parameters passed in, and throw an `IllegalArgumentException` if out-of-range values are encountered.
7. Passing a null frame to a `Dialog` constructor now results in an `IllegalArgumentException`.
8. The public abstract method `nextFocus` has been removed from the `java.awt.peer.ComponentPeer` interface. This does not affect applications or applets, since the peer interfaces are private interfaces between the AWT and its implementations.
9. Bug fixes in Win32 event handling might mean that your components get more events than they used to. Details are in Improvements in Win32 Event Handling (page 939) below.
10. The synchronization model of the AWT has been revised to reduce the potential of deadlock. This might result in different behavior of existing programs. See Details of the New Synchronization Model (page 940) below.

Improvements in Win32 Event Handling

Many bugs were fixed in the event handling of the win32 implementation of the AWT. In particular, focus events were previously not delivered to certain components (buttons, etc.) in 1.0, but are now properly delivered on win32 in 1.1. If you have a `handleEvent` method which is not coded properly to handle these new events, you may see changes in the way your program runs. For example, if you had the following fragment in the `handleEvent` method of a Frame:

```
if (event.id == Event.GOT_FOCUS) {
    // do something...
}
```

This block will now be called when components within the `Frame` (such as buttons) get the focus. If the block isn't designed to handle this case, then your program may not run as it did in 1.0.

Details of the New Synchronization Model

The synchronization model of the AWT has been revised to significantly reduce (but not eliminate) the potential of deadlock that existed in the 1.0 JDK. This is not, strictly speaking, an incompatibility with previous releases, but it does have the potential to change the behavior of existing programs. The AWT never was, and still isn't, guaranteed to be free of race conditions or deadlocks, given all the ways it can be invoked from and subclassed by client code.

In the new synchronization model, the structure and layout of components inside containers is guarded by a single AWT-wide lock, using an object called `Component.LOCK`, declared as follows in the Component class:

```
public static final Object LOCK = new Object();
```

For example, `Container.validate`, `Container.add`, and `Container.remove` all contain synchronized blocks that use `Component.LOCK`.

Setter methods for individual component state, such as `Component.setEnabled` or `Button.setLabel`, are synchronized on the instance itself. Getter methods are generally not synchronized, but they are semi-guarded by the copy-to-stack strategy: a thread-local copy of shared data is made and then used in the method.

Code that uses the AWT should be carefully scrutinized for uniform locking order if it acquires locks of its own while overriding an AWT method invoked in a synchronized context. For example, if you acquire your own locks in your layout code, you have to be aware that this code is being called with the `Component.LOCK` lock already held. If your code in another thread holds your lock and then tries to invoke `validate`, your program can deadlock. When you identify cases like this, you should rewrite your code wherever possible to ensure a uniform locking order. This order is usually client lock first, then `Component.LOCK`.

Index

Note: An italic *e* after a page number indicates an entry in Appendix A, Code Examples.

Symbols

A

B

C

D

G

N

O

P

T

U

V

W

Y

Z

The Addison-Wesley Java™ Series

ISBN 0-201-31006-6

ISBN 0-201-31007-4

ISBN 0-201-48558-3

ISBN 0-201-43298-6

ISBN 0-201-31003-1

ISBN 0-201-31002-3

ISBN 0-201-48552-4

ISBN 0-201-63451-1

ISBN 0-201-63453-8

ISBN 0-201-63459-7

ISBN 0-201-31000-7

ISBN 0-201-63456-2

ISBN 0-201-69581-2

ISBN 0-201-32577-2

ISBN 0-201-43294-3

ISBN 0-201-32576-4

ISBN 0-201-43321-4

ISBN 0-201-43328-1

Please see our web site (http://www.awl.com/cseng/javaseries)
for more information on these titles.

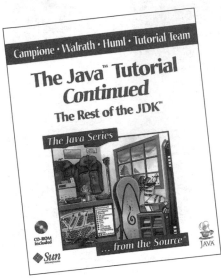

The Java Tutorial CD-ROM

The *Java Tutorial* CD-ROM that accompanies this book is loaded with development kits and documentation, including the content and code of all three books: *The Java Tutorial*, *The Java Tutorial Continued*, and *The JFC Swing Tutorial*. Where the release version is not noted, the most recent release at the time of printing is included.

Table 192 Development Kits on *The Java Tutorial* CD-ROM

Development Kits	Version(s)
Java 2 Platform (formerly JDK 1.2) Java Development Kit (JDK)	Standard, v 1.2 1.1.8, 1.02
Java Runtime Environment (JRE)	Java 2
Java Foundation Classes (JFC) *includes Swing 1.1*	1.1
Beans Development Kit (BDK)	1.0
JavaBeans Activation Framework (JAF)	1.0
Java Servlet Development Kit (JSDK)	2.0
Java Naming and Directory Interface (JNDI)	1.1

Table 193 Documentation on *The Java Tutorial* CD-ROM

Documentation	Version(s)
The Java Tutorial	
Java Programming Language API Documentation	Java 2, 1.1, 1.02
JFC 1.1 API Documentation	1.1
The Swing Connection	
The Java Platform White Paper	

Table 194 Products on *The Java Tutorial* CD-ROM

Products	Version(s)
HotJava Browser	3.0
Java Plug-In	1.2
`idltojava` Compiler	

Table 195 Specifications on *The Java Tutorial* CD-ROM

Specifications
Java 2D Specification
JavaBeans Specification
Servlet Specification
JDBC 1.2 and 2.0 Specifications
Security 1.2 Specification
Java Cryptography Architecture API Specification
Drag & Drop Specification

Table 196 Miscellaneous on *The Java Tutorial* CD-ROM

And more...
Java Code Conventions
Java Programming Language Glossary
100% Pure Java CookBook

The `README.html` file on the CD-ROM is the central HTML page that links you to all of its contents. To view this page, use the `Open Page` command or its equivalent in your Internet browser. On some platforms, you can simply double click on the HTML file to launch it in your browser.

You can check out the latest Sun Microsystems Java™ programming language product releases at: `http://java.sun.com/products/index.html`. If you sign up for the Java Developer Connection,[1] you will receive free, early access to such products, including the latest Java platform.

See this book's Web page at: `http://java.sun.com/docs/books/tutorial/uiswing/index.html` for pointers to the latest versions of this content.

1 http://developer.javasoft.com/index.html